*Model Codes for Post-Conflict Criminal Justice* provides excellent guidance for the implementation of new criminal laws in post-conflict states. The statutory offenses as well as the general rules for criminal liability and the proposed catalogue of penalties, including alternative sanctions and measures such as asset confiscation and victim compensation, reflect the state of the art in international standards and best practices.

—**Dmitry A. Shestakov,** Professor, Doctor of Law, and President of St. Petersburg Criminology Club, Russia

It is axiomatic that conflict destroys: it destroys people, their institutions, and the law in whole or in part. But conflict also breeds new companions who evolve, thrive, and finally outlive the hostilities: welcome to the world of the war-profiteer. Organized and wealthy, these individuals, and their illicit networks, often emerge from conflict with political and social power, which they use to accumulate enormous fortunes, siphoning off the money pouring into the country and basking in the absence of regulatory and enforcement mechanisms that could check their rampant corruption and criminality.

Any attempt by the international community to rebuild a shattered society will lie in peril without the presence, early on, of institutions that promote and safeguard the rule of law. And central to the maintenance of the rule of law is the existence of a criminal code. In societies emerging from conflict, the local authorities may well deem part or all of the old code unworkable, resulting in a need to refashion some provisions of the existing code or identify a stop-gap measure to adopt until a new code can be established. After all, even from the earliest days of recovery, police, prosecutors, judges, peacekeepers, and most importantly the citizenry need both the assurance that there is a law and clarity as to what that law is.

*Model Codes for Post-Conflict Criminal Justice* provides a crucial resource to address this need. It reflects clearly the input of hundreds of experts and practitioners drawn from across the globe. The codes and their commentaries will be invaluable to local governments and peacekeeping missions involved in law reform, providing a clear legal framework that meets with international standards and is cognizant of the challenges that come with post-conflict environments.

—**H.R.H. Prince Zeid Ra'ad Zeid al-Hussein,** Ambassador of the Hashemite Kingdom of Jordan to the United States, former Permanent Representative of the Hashemite Kingdom of Jordan to the United Nations, and former President, Assembly of States Parties, International Criminal Court

# Prepublication praise for Model Codes for Post-Conflict Criminal Justice

The publication of volume I of *Model Codes for Post-Conflict Criminal Justice* marks an advance of great international significance for post-conflict societies—the arrival of a criminal code drafted in admirably clear and uncomplicated language, supported by detailed commentaries, and designed explicitly for such societies. This code, with its measured approach, will enable jurisdictions emerging from conflict to move quickly toward reestablishing the rule of law and a fair criminal justice system, without the need to start the reform process afresh. It is an outstanding piece of work, and the publication of volume II later this year is eagerly awaited.

—**Andrew Ashworth,** Vinerian Professor of English Law, University of Oxford

Countries in transition from conflict routinely face seemingly irreconcilable challenges: extremely limited capacity of the criminal justice system, the need to establish law and order in the midst of rising crime, and the need to comport with international human rights standards—all of which have to be tackled while respecting local culture and traditions. These challenges have vexed local governments and those in peacekeeping missions alike. *Model Codes for Post-Conflict Criminal Justice* provides, for the first time, an invaluable guide to addressing these multiple demands—and should help shorten the path to consolidated peace, functioning state institutions, stability, and the rule of law.

—**Ambassador Lakhdar Brahimi,** former Special Representative of the Secretary-General for Afghanistan, Haiti, and South Africa; and former Chairman, Panel on United Nations Peace Operations

Many post-conflict states, including Liberia, find it necessary to reform their judicial systems so that their laws deal effectively with crimes, address gender and human rights issues, and conform to international norms and standards. I am, therefore, grateful for the opportunity to have participated in this admirable project, which, after years of arduous legal research and drafting, has culminated in the publication of *Model Codes for Post-Conflict Criminal Justice.*

*Model Codes for Post-Conflict Criminal Justice* will be an immensely useful resource for reformers in Liberia and elsewhere as they engage in the development and reform of their criminal justice system. Its provisions, drawn from the laws of different states and drafted in plain English, may be used in drafting new criminal laws or amending existing provisions. The accompanying commentaries, as well as the references and other resources contained in this volume, provide invaluable background information and guidance.

—**Felicia V. Coleman,** Counselor-at-Law, former Associate Justice of the Supreme Court of Liberia, and a Member of the Task Force for the Establishment of the Law Reform Commission of Liberia

In post-conflict countries, the challenges involved in rebuilding the judicial system are great. A model penal code seems particularly necessary to ensure compatibility between national criminal laws and international norms and standards. More than merely reflecting cultural diversity, such an instrument would enable the harmonization of national and international norms around common values.

—**Mireille Delmas-Marty,** Professor and Chair of Comparative Legal Studies and the Internationalization of Law, Collège de France

The importance of this work for societies in transition from conflict and oppression to freedom and democracy cannot be overemphasized. It is a model of clarity, and the commentaries on each section are a valuable resource not only for practitioners concerned with societies in transition but also for students. I also commend it to journalists who work in the field of law enforcement.

—**Richard Goldstone,** former Judge, Constitutional Court of South Africa; and former Prosecutor, International Criminal Tribunals for the former Yugoslavia and for Rwanda

*Model Codes for Post-Conflict Criminal Justice* is a valuable resource for criminal law reform in post-conflict states. Its contents reflect recent advances in international criminal law instruments and draw on the accumulated knowledge and experience of the international criminal law community. Moreover, *Model Codes* takes into account the particular challenges presented by post-conflict countries, making it both a targeted and a practical tool.

—**Ma Kechang,** Professor of Law, Wuhan University, People's Republic of China

This first volume in the *Model Codes* series displays not only a remarkable depth of thought but also a commendable breadth of perspective. In this time of sharp cultural clashes, publics in the Middle East and elsewhere may regard *Model Codes* skeptically, as yet another Western export intended to supplant Muslim traditions. To its credit, however, the Model Codes Project has gone beyond the borders of Western legal expertise and sought substantive contributions from legal experts in the Muslim world. Such teamwork between scholars and practitioners from both Western countries and Muslim-majority countries is all too rare, and I hope that publication of *Model Codes* will help pave the way for an open, inclusive discussion on the dilemmas facing post-conflict societies, particularly those in the Middle East. And in Muslim-majority countries emerging from conflict, we now need to approach the lawyers working in the Islamic seminaries and further integrate them and the language of Islamic law into the dialogue. By doing so, we will help facilitate the process by which such states can transition from violence to an enduring peace rooted in the rule of law.

—**Mohsen Rahami,** Professor of Criminal Law and Criminal Policy, Faculty of Law and Political Science, University of Tehran

# Model Codes
# for Post-Conflict Criminal Justice

## Volume I
## Model Criminal Code

# Model Codes for Post-Conflict Criminal Justice

## Volume I
## Model Criminal Code

Edited by Vivienne O'Connor and Colette Rausch

with Hans-Joerg Albrecht and Goran Klemencic

UNITED STATES INSTITUTE OF PEACE PRESS
Washington, D.C.

United States Institute of Peace
1200 17th Street NW, Suite 200
Washington, DC 20036-3011



First published 2007

Printed in the United States of America

The paper used in this publication meets the minimum requirements of American National Standards for Information Science—Permanence of Paper for Printed Library Materials, ANSI Z39.48-1984.

**Library of Congress Cataloging-in-Publication Data**
Model codes for post-conflict criminal justice / edited by Vivienne O'Connor and Colette Rausch, with Hans-Joerg Albrecht and Goran Klemencic.
p. cm.
Includes bibliographical references and index.
ISBN-13: 978-1-60127-011-5 (pbk. : alk. paper)
ISBN-10: 1-60127-011-9 (pbk. : alk. paper)
ISBN-13: 978-1-60127-012-2 (hardcover : alk. paper)
ISBN-10: 1-0127-012-7 (hardcover : alk. paper)
1. Criminal justice, Administration of—International cooperation. 2. Criminal law—International cooperation. 3. Reparation (Criminal justice). 4. Restorative justice. I. O'Connor, Vivienne M. 1977– II. Rausch, Colette. III. Albrecht, Hans-Joerg, 1950– IV. Klemencic, Goran V. Title.

K5001.M63 2007
345–dc22

2007008930

# Contents


**Foreword,** *by Louise Arbour and Antonio Maria Costa* xv

**Preface,** *by Neil J. Kritz and William Schabas* xvii

**Acknowledgments** xxi

**Editors** xxiii

**Contributors** xxv

## USER'S GUIDE

Introduction 1

1. The Model Codes Project: A Response to Post-Conflict Criminal Law Needs 3
2. Potential Uses of the Model Codes in a Criminal Law Reform Process 9
3. A Synopsis of the Model Criminal Code 17
4. Guiding Principles for the Criminal Law Reform Process 23

## PART I GENERAL PART

### Section 1 Definitions 31

Article 1 Definitions 31

### Section 2 Fundamental Principles 36

Article 2 Purpose and Limits of Criminal Legislation 36

Article 3 Principle of Legality 37

### Section 3 Jurisdiction 42

Article 4 Territorial Jurisdiction 42

Article 5 Extraterritorial Jurisdiction 43

Article 6 Universal Jurisdiction 46

Article 7 Personal Jurisdiction 47

### Section 4 *Ne Bis in Idem* 51

Article 8 *Ne Bis in Idem* (Double Jeopardy) 51

| | | |
|---|---|---|
| **Section 5** | **Statutory Limitations** | 56 |
| Article 9 | Statutory Limitations for Criminal Prosecution | 56 |
| Article 10 | Statutory Limitations Applicable to an Adult for Criminal Offenses Committed as a Juvenile | 57 |
| Article 11 | Nonapplicability of Statutory Limitations to Genocide, Crimes against Humanity, and War Crimes | 58 |
| Article 12 | Running and Suspension of Statutory Limitations | 59 |
| **Section 6** | **Time and Place of Commission of a Criminal Offense** | 61 |
| Article 13 | Time of Commission of a Criminal Offense | 61 |
| Article 14 | Place of Commission of a Criminal Offense | 61 |
| **Section 7** | **Criminal Offense, Criminal Responsibility, and Commission of a Criminal Offense** | 63 |
| Article 15 | Criminal Offense | 63 |
| Article 16 | Criminal Responsibility | 63 |
| Article 17 | Commission of a Criminal Offense | 65 |
| Article 18 | Intention, Recklessness, and Negligence | 66 |
| **Section 8** | **Criminal Responsibility of Legal Persons** | 72 |
| Article 19 | Criminal Responsibility of Legal Persons | 72 |
| **Section 9** | **Justification and Exclusion of Criminal Responsibility** | 76 |
| **Subsection 1** | **Justification** | 78 |
| Article 20 | Self-Defense | 78 |
| Article 21 | Necessity | 79 |
| Article 22 | Superior Orders | 80 |
| **Subsection 2** | **Exclusion of Criminal Responsibility** | 82 |
| Article 23 | Mental Incompetence | 82 |
| Article 24 | Intoxication | 83 |
| Article 25 | Duress | 84 |
| Article 26 | Mistake of Fact and Mistake of Law | 85 |
| **Section 10** | **Criminal Attempt** | 87 |
| Article 27 | Attempt | 87 |

| | | |
|---|---|---|
| **Section 11** | **Participation in a Criminal Offense** | 89 |
| Article 28 | Participation in a Common Purpose | 90 |
| Article 29 | Ordering, Soliciting, or Inducing | 93 |
| Article 30 | Incitement | 94 |
| Article 31 | Facilitation | 94 |
| Article 32 | Responsibility of Commanders and Other Superiors for the Criminal Offenses of Genocide, Crimes against Humanity, and War Crimes | 95 |
| Article 33 | Punishment as a Perpetrator | 97 |
| **Section 12** | **Penalties** | 98 |
| **Subsection 1** | **Purpose of Penalties, Fundamental Principle, and Other Principles Relating to Penalties** | 101 |
| Article 34 | Purposes of Penalties | 101 |
| Article 35 | Fundamental Principle | 104 |
| Article 36 | Other Principles Relevant to the Determination of Penalties | 105 |
| **Subsection 2** | **Penalty Structure** | 108 |
| Article 37 | General Penalty Structure | 108 |
| Article 38 | Principal Penalties | 110 |
| Article 39 | Alternative Penalties | 113 |
| Article 40 | Additional Penalties | 114 |
| **Subsection 3** | **Procedure for Determination of Penalties** | 116 |
| Article 41 | General Procedure for Determination of an Appropriate Penalty | 117 |
| Article 42 | Appraisal of the Applicable Minimum and Maximum Penalty | 121 |
| Article 43 | Augmentation of the Maximum Period of Imprisonment Based on Individual Aggravating Factors Set Out in the Special Part of the MCC | 122 |
| Article 44 | Augmentation of the Maximum Period of Imprisonment When a Criminal Offense Is Committed as Part of Organized Criminal Activity | 123 |
| Article 45 | Augmentation of the Maximum Period of Imprisonment When a Criminal Offense Is Motivated by Hatred | 124 |
| Article 46 | Augmentation of the Maximum Period of Imprisonment for a Criminal Offense Committed by a Public Official | 125 |
| Article 47 | Reduction of the Minimum Period of Imprisonment Due to Particularly Mitigating Circumstances | 126 |

Article 48 Reduction of the Minimum Period of Imprisonment for Attempted Offenses 127
Article 49 Determination of the Appropriateness of Life Imprisonment as a Principal Penalty 127
Article 50 Determination of the Appropriateness of a Fine as a Principal Penalty 129
Article 51 Determination of the Appropriate Term of Imprisonment in Light of General Mitigating and Aggravating Circumstances 130
Article 52 Determination of a Joint Penalty for Convictions on Two or More Criminal Offenses 136
Article 53 Subsequent Imposition of a Penalty on a Convicted Person 138
Article 54 Replacement of a Principal Penalty with an Alternative Penalty 138
Article 55 Suspended Sentence as an Alternative Penalty 140
Article 56 Community Service as an Alternative Penalty 142
Article 57 Semiliberty as an Alternative Penalty 144
Article 58 Supplementation of a Principal Penalty with Additional Penalties 145
Article 59 Supplementation of an Alternative Penalty with Additional Penalties 146
Article 60 A Fine as an Additional Penalty 146
Article 61 Confiscation of Property, Equipment, or Other Instrumentalities Used in or Destined for Use in a Criminal Offense as an Additional Penalty 147
Article 62 Payment of Compensation to a Victim as an Additional Penalty 149
Article 63 Deprivation of the Right to Be Elected as an Additional Penalty 151
Article 64 Deprivation of the Right to Possess or Carry Firearms as an Additional Penalty 152
Article 65 Prohibition on Holding a Post as a Public Official as an Additional Penalty 154
Article 66 Prohibition on the Exercise of Managerial or Supervisory Positions in Private Legal Entities as an Additional Penalty 155
Article 67 Expulsion of a Non-national as an Additional Penalty 156

**Subsection 4 Penalties for Legal Persons** 158

Article 68 Types of Penalties for Legal Persons 158
Article 69 Determination of Penalties for a Legal Person 159

| | | |
|---|---|---|
| **Section 13** | **Confiscation of the Proceeds of Crime and Property** | 162 |
| Article 70 | Definitions | 165 |
| Article 71 | Prohibition on Retention of Proceeds of Crime | 166 |
| Article 72 | Confiscation of Proceeds of Crime or Property of Corresponding Value from the Convicted Person | 166 |
| Article 73 | Confiscation of Proceeds of Crime or Property of Corresponding Value from a Third Party | 168 |
| **Section 14** | **Dispositions Applicable to Juveniles and Adults on Trial for Criminal Offenses Committed as Juveniles** | 170 |
| **Subsection 1** | **Scope of Application of Section 14 and General Principles** | 172 |
| Article 74 | Scope of Application of Section 14 | 172 |
| **Subsection 2** | **Purposes of Juvenile Dispositions and Principles Applicable to Juvenile Dispositions** | 173 |
| Article 75 | Purposes of Juvenile Dispositions | 173 |
| Article 76 | Fundamental Principle | 174 |
| Article 77 | Principles Applicable to Juvenile Dispositions | 175 |
| **Subsection 3** | **Structure of Juvenile Dispositions** | 178 |
| Article 78 | Principal Juvenile Dispositions | 178 |
| Article 79 | Additional Juvenile Dispositions | 181 |
| **Subsection 4** | **Procedure for Determining Juvenile Dispositions** | 183 |
| Article 80 | Procedure for Determining Juvenile Dispositions | 183 |
| **Subsection 5** | **Principal Juvenile Dispositions** | 185 |
| Article 81 | Judicial Admonition | 185 |
| Article 82 | Intensive Supervision of a Juvenile | 186 |
| Article 83 | Disciplinary Measures | 188 |
| Article 84 | Institutional Measures | 189 |
| Article 85 | Juvenile Imprisonment | 190 |

## PART II SPECIAL PART

Section 1 Genocide, Crimes against Humanity, and War Crimes 195

Article 86 Genocide 196

Article 87 Crimes against Humanity 201

Article 88 War Crimes 211

Section 2 Offenses against Life and Limb 219

Article 89 Unlawful Killing 219

Article 90 Assault 222

Article 91 Assault Causing Harm 223

Article 92 Assault Causing Serious Harm 223

Article 93 Threats to Kill or Cause Serious Harm 224

Section 3 Sexual Offenses 226

Article 94 Rape 227

Article 95 Sexual Intercourse and Acts of a Sexual Nature with a Child below the Age of Consent to Sexual Relations 229

Article 96 Violation of the Sexual Autonomy of a Defenseless Person 231

Article 97 Violation of Sexual Autonomy by Abuse of Authority 231

Article 98 Sexual Slavery 232

Article 99 Enforced Prostitution 233

Article 100 Sexual Violence 234

Section 4 Offenses against the Rights of Persons 236

Article 101 Torture 236

Article 102 Trafficking in Persons 238

Article 103 Establishing Slavery, Slavery-like Conditions, and Forced Labor 243

Article 104 Enforced Disappearance 244

Article 105 Domestic Violence 246

Article 106 Kidnapping 251

Article 107 Unlawful Deprivation of Liberty 252

Article 108 Criminal Coercion 253

Article 109 Unauthorized Search of a Person and His or Her Belongings 253

Article 110 Unauthorized Search of a Dwelling or Premises 254

Article 111 Unauthorized Visual Recording 255
Article 112 Violation of the Privacy and Confidentiality of Communications 257
Article 113 Abuse of Personal Data 258
Article 114 Abuse of Personal Secrets 259

Section 5 Offenses against Children 261

Article 115 Sale of Children 262
Article 116 Child Prostitution 263
Article 117 Child Pornography 264
Article 118 Possession of Child Pornography 266

Section 6 Property Offenses 268

Article 119 Theft 268
Article 120 Robbery and Aggravated Robbery 270
Article 121 Extortion 272
Article 122 Burglary 273
Article 123 Aggravated Burglary 274
Article 124 Receiving and Concealing Stolen Goods 274
Article 125 Bringing into the State Property Obtained through Crime 275
Article 126 Fraud 276
Article 127 Embezzlement of Property 277
Article 128 Forgery 279
Article 129 Using False Instruments 280
Article 130 Possessing False Instruments 281
Article 131 Arson 282
Article 132 Reckless Burning or Exploding 283
Article 133 Criminal Damage 284

Section 7 Economic Offenses 286

Article 134 Counterfeiting Money 286
Article 135 Money Laundering 288

Section 8 Organized Crime Offenses 293

Article 136 Participation in an Organized Criminal Group 293
Article 137 Offenses Related to the Smuggling of Migrants 297

| | | |
|---|---|---|
| **Section 9** | **Corruption Offenses** | 304 |
| Article 138 | Corruption Involving a Public Official | 307 |
| Article 139 | Corruption Involving a Foreign Public Official or an Official of a Public International Organization | 309 |
| Article 140 | Corruption in the Private Sector | 311 |
| **Section 10** | **Corruption-Related Offenses and Other Offenses Involving a Public Official** | 314 |
| Article 141 | Trading in Influence | 314 |
| Article 142 | Embezzlement, Misappropriation, or Other Diversion of Property by a Public Official | 316 |
| Article 143 | Abuse of Functions | 317 |
| Article 144 | Illicit Enrichment | 318 |
| Article 145 | Concealment | 319 |
| Article 146 | Threat and Improper Influence | 320 |
| **Section 11** | **Offenses against the State, Public Safety, and Security** | 321 |
| Article 147 | Financing Terrorism | 323 |
| Article 148 | Terrorist Bombing | 325 |
| Article 149 | Unlawful Seizure of Aircraft | 330 |
| Article 150 | Unlawful Acts against the Safety of Civil Aviation | 331 |
| Article 151 | Unlawful Acts of Violence at an Airport Serving International Civil Aviation | 333 |
| Article 152 | Offenses against Internationally Protected Persons | 334 |
| Article 153 | Taking of Hostages | 336 |
| Article 154 | Offenses Related to Nuclear Material | 338 |
| Article 155 | Unlawful Acts against the Safety of Maritime Navigation | 340 |
| Article 156 | Unlawful Acts against the Safety of Fixed Platforms | 342 |
| Article 157 | Piracy | 344 |
| Article 158 | Bombing | 345 |
| Article 159 | Disruption of Supply of Public Installations | 346 |
| Article 160 | Destruction or Unauthorized Removal of Cultural Property | 347 |
| Article 161 | Incitement to Crime on Account of Hatred | 350 |
| Article 162 | Unauthorized Border and Boundary Crossing | 352 |

Section 12 Offenses against United Nations and Associated Personnel 353

Article 163 Endangering United Nations and Associated Personnel 353

Section 13 Offenses Involving Firearms, Ammunition, Explosives, and Weapons 357

Article 164 Illicit Manufacturing or Trafficking in Firearms or Ammunition 359

Article 165 Illicit Obliteration, Removal, or Altering of Markings on Firearms 361

Article 166 Illicit Manufacturing or Trafficking in Explosives 363

Article 167 Unlawful Purchase of Firearms, Ammunition, Explosives, or Weapons 364

Article 168 Unlawful Possession, Control, or Ownership of Firearms, Ammunition, Explosives, or Weapons 366

Article 169 Unlawful Use of Firearms 368

Section 14 Drug Offenses 370

Article 170 Trafficking in Narcotic Drugs and Psychotropic Substances 373

Article 171 Possession or Purchase of Narcotic Drugs or Psychotropic Substances for the Purpose of Trafficking 376

Article 172 Organizing, Managing, or Financing Trafficking in Narcotic Drugs or Psychotropic Substances 377

Article 173 Cultivation of Opium Poppy, Coca Bush, or Cannabis Plant 378

Article 174 Manufacture, Transport, or Distribution of Precursors 381

Article 175 Manufacture, Transport, or Distribution of Equipment or Materials for Use in the Illicit Cultivation, Production, or Manufacture of Narcotic Drugs or Psychotropic Substances 382

Article 176 Possession or Purchase of Narcotic Drugs or Psychotropic Substances for Personal Use 383

Section 15 Election Offenses 386

Article 177 Preventing the Exercise of the Right to Vote 386

Article 178 Violating the Free Decision of Voters 387

Article 179 Abuse of the Right to Vote 388

Article 180 Violating Confidentiality in Voting 389

Article 181 Buying and Selling Votes 389

Article 182 Election Fraud 390

Article 183 Threat to an Election Candidate 391

Section 16 Cybercrime Offenses 392
Article 184 Illegal Access to a Computer System 393
Article 185 Illegal Interception of Computer Data 394
Article 186 Interference with Computer Data 395
Article 187 Interference with a Computer System 396
Article 188 Misuse of Devices 397

Section 17 Offenses against the Administration of Justice 399
Article 189 Alteration or Destruction of Evidence 399
Article 190 Fabrication of Evidence 400
Article 191 Presentation of False or Forged Evidence 401
Article 192 False Testimony 401
Article 193 Obstruction of Justice of a Witness 402
Article 194 Obstruction of Justice of a Justice or Policing Official 404
Article 195 Retaliation against a Witness 405
Article 196 Retaliation against a Justice or Policing Official 405
Article 197 Failure to Respect an Order of the Court 406
Article 198 Providing Assistance to Perpetrator after the Commission of a Criminal Offense 407
Article 199 False Statements of a Cooperative Witness 408
Article 200 Revealing the Sealed Order for Protective Measures or Anonymity 409

Annex 1 411

Annex 2 415

Annex 3 417

Further Reading and Resources
Legal Instruments 421
Further Reading Relevant to the General Part of the Model Criminal Code 426
Further Reading Relevant to the Special Part of the Model Criminal Code 430
Criminal Law Reform Resources 441
Useful Web Sites 447

Index 453

# Foreword

**Louise Arbour, United Nations High Commissioner for Human Rights**

**Antonio Maria Costa, Executive Director of the United Nations Office on Drugs and Crime**

Conflicts do not end suddenly. Even when violence stops, peace often remains fragile and will not become durable unless there is justice and a readiness to address not only the aftermath of a conflict but also its root causes. Many conflicts erupt because of perceptions of discrimination and injustice. Restoring the rule of law is, therefore, an important dimension of peacebuilding, one that requires sustained and patient engagement until the rule of law is strong. Where the rule of law is weak, public security is threatened and criminals feel empowered. Such a situation undermines efforts to restore respect for human rights and build democracy and civil society, it fuels crime and corruption, and it risks triggering a return to conflict. Criminal justice that is based on human rights is thus indispensable for making and sustaining peace.

The classic peacekeeping model brings to mind blue-helmeted soldiers working under the United Nations flag to restore order and maintain security. That kind of peacekeeping, while essential, will not by itself build durable peace. Long-term security depends first and foremost on the creation or restoration of the rule of law. The rule of law requires not just rule by law, but rule by laws that reflect fundamental principles of criminal responsibility and due process, including guarantees of transparency and clarity of the criminal justice process, nonretroactivity, fair and independent adjudication, and proportional punishment.

The United Nations Office on Drugs and Crime and the Office of the High Commissioner for Human Rights have therefore welcomed the initiative launched by the United States Institute of Peace and the Irish Centre for Human Rights to strengthen criminal justice in post-conflict societies, and have supported the project in several ways, including facilitating a number of experts' meetings to review the draft Model Codes.

Publication of *Model Codes for Post-Conflict Criminal Justice,* the product of five years of work involving hundreds of experts from across the world, is a significant contribution to the United Nations' efforts to strengthen peacebuilding. Based on United Nations standards, the Model Codes provide practical guidance on how to translate international human rights and criminal law standards into everyday practice.

There is no single recipe for effective criminal justice. The Model Codes are not a one-size-fits-all solution. On the contrary, they have been devised to be adaptable to a variety of post-conflict societies and situations in ways that are flexible yet consistent with international norms and standards. The Model Codes are a resource that should be used by all those engaged in building peaceful societies based on the rule of law. ■

# Preface

**Neil Kritz, Director, Rule of Law Program, United States Institute of Peace**

**William Schabas, Director, Irish Centre for Human Rights**

According to the *Oxford English Dictionary,* a code is a systematic collection or digest of laws, a body of laws so arranged as to avoid inconsistency and overlapping. The first extant code, the Code of Hammurabi, was composed nearly four millennia ago. Justinian created a code with which to rule the Roman Empire. Many countries still operate with the legacy of these early efforts at legal codification. Historically, codes were an instrument of law reform, often intended to make the law more accessible and coherent. Over time, it has become universally recognized that an effective framework of criminal law and procedure is essential to the development of a stable society.

Although the codes presented in *Model Codes for Post-Conflict Criminal Justice* share many of the same objectives as other codifications, they also have some unique and original purposes. Essentially, they are designed as a tool for what is today often referred to as "post-conflict justice." It is only recently that this has become a priority of the international community. Interest in the subject seems to have begun during the late 1970s and early 1980s, when human rights bodies began to focus on the duties of the state in terms of criminal justice. Soon, reports were circulating within the United Nations about the rights of victims, the need for accountability, and the fight against impunity. International standards and treaties were adopted to elaborate the human rights protections that had to be reflected in the administration of criminal justice.

In parallel, peacekeeping operations began to be increasingly robust, assuming responsibilities in a range of areas beyond the peacekeepers' traditional role of policing cease-fire lines. Human rights divisions began to figure in peace support operations, as did a growing agenda for various measures to promote peace, stability, and political and economic recovery. One important item on this agenda was ensuring some degree of accountability for the crimes of the past while promoting a sense of security and law and order in the present. Stabilization efforts had to maintain social order as conflict was winding down, deal with the general breakdown of authority, and confront the criminal vultures who routinely descend upon the disorganization of the post-conflict environment, while still promoting values of tolerance, fairness, and transparency and adherence to international human rights standards so as to help nurture the beginnings of democracy.

The idea of creating model codes for post-conflict justice was much discussed at the end of the 1990s by rule of law practitioners working with United Nations peace operations in places such as Cambodia, East Timor, and Kosovo. In each of these environments, professional jurists found the criminal justice system in disarray and a need not only for infrastructural renewal but also for substantive law reform. The confusion as to what constituted the applicable law in these and other post-conflict settings and how that law would be applied resulted in the loss of many crucial months in the stabilization effort. Public confidence in a peace process will be weak as long as that public faces rampant crime and an unfair justice system. Clearly, new tools were needed.

The model code concept received official recognition in the *Report of the Panel on United Nations Peace Operations,* often called the "Brahimi Report" after its distinguished chair, veteran diplomat Lakhdar Brahimi. The report saw model codes as an off-the-shelf legal system that could, if necessary, be applied as part of a peace support mission. Ambassador Brahimi's proposal did not sit well with everyone, however, apparently because of concern that model codes would be a creeping form of judicial imperialism. At the very least, the proponents of the model codes concept needed to refine its focus, emphasizing the flexibility of what was intended as a palette of options rather than a prescriptive, one-size-fits-all package.

Inspired by the Brahimi Report recommendation, in 2001 the United States Institute of Peace and the Irish Centre for Human Rights, in cooperation with the United Nations Office of the High Commissioner for Human Rights and the United Nations Office on Drugs and Crime, launched what soon became widely known as the "Model Codes Project."

Initially, a small group of experts was convened to create a draft of the Model Codes. In recognition of the critical importance of widespread consultation and participation, the expert group soon mushroomed into a network of three hundred experts from all regions of the world, encompassing both academic and practitioner communities. The experts included comparative and international law experts, judges, prosecutors, defense counsel, police, human rights advocates, and military officers. The meetings were a stimulating venue for debates and exchanges about comparative criminal law, involving the differing perspectives of the prosecution, the police, the defense, and the judiciary.

What began as a single code soon morphed into four separate but complementary instruments. Published in three volumes collectively known as *Model Codes for Post-Conflict Criminal Justice,* these instruments include a Model Criminal Code, a Model Code of Criminal Procedure, a Model Detention Act, and a Model Police Powers Act. The first volume to be published features the Model Criminal Code.

The Model Codes reflect elements drawn from all of the major criminal justice systems in the world. They are strongly influenced by the comparative law discourse of the international criminal tribunals, as well as the practice of post-conflict justice in countries around the world. The vision of no single criminal justice system is allowed to predominate. Indeed, it was deemed essential that jurists from a variety of traditions would, so to speak, recognize themselves in the finished product, finding familiar concepts and terminology—which means, of course, that there is also much that is unfamiliar for practically everyone.

The Model Codes are a tool of assistance and not imposition. They expand the range of options available to drafters of post-conflict criminal laws. Of singular importance, the Model Codes are especially useful because they are tailored to the exigencies of the challenging post-conflict environment.

With apologies to Winston Churchill, this is not the end of the Model Codes Project, but rather the end of the beginning. Tools to be used in building post-conflict justice, the Model Codes are very much a work in progress, to be refined and amended, more or less like all other codes. They will grow with our experience in this important endeavor of promoting justice, democracy, and peace.

We would like to express our appreciation to the editors, our partner organizations, and all those who have contributed to Model Codes Project. ■

# Acknowledgments

The Model Codes for Post-Conflict Criminal Justice Project was launched in 2001 by the United States Institute of Peace and the Irish Centre for Human Rights, in cooperation with the United Nations Office of the High Commissioner for Human Rights (OHCHR) and the United Nations Office on Drugs and Crime (UNODC). For their unwavering commitment to such an ambitious project, from its initial conception to the publication of this volume, we are deeply grateful to the president of the United States Institute of Peace, Ambassador Richard Solomon; to the Institute's associate vice president and director of its Rule of Law Program, Neil J. Kritz; and to the director of the Irish Centre for Human Rights, Professor William Schabas. Neil Kritz and William Schabas are due particular thanks for the wise advice and constant encouragement they provided throughout the project's development.

We would like to thank our project partners, OHCHR and UNODC, for sharing the vision of creating a set of model codes to assist in the reform of the criminal justice systems in post-conflict societies. We are particularly grateful to David Marshall and Tiyanjana Maluwa of OHCHR and to Jo Dedeyne, Mark Shaw, Slawomir Redo, Eduardo Vetere, Dimitri Vlassis, and Catherine Volz of UNODC, all of whom worked directly with us and shared their time and expertise.

The work of translating the project's ambitious goals into reality brought together a large community of experts in a truly collaborative effort. Each of these experts lent his or her skills and expertise freely, seeking no other reward than assisting national and international actors in rebuilding the rule of law in post-conflict societies. We often talk fondly of the "Model Codes family" that grew from a small group to encompass some three hundred people. The consultations and regional meetings that helped to clarify and amplify the text of the codes provided a unique opportunity for us to meet and become friends with a remarkable group of people dedicated to building peace. Every comment made, every question raised, and every suggestion put forward contributed to the breadth and depth of the final product. For this, we are grateful to everyone involved.

Our heartfelt thanks go also to those who acted as partners in regional consultation meetings, provided forums in which drafts of the codes were reviewed, gave presentations on the project, chaired consultation meetings, provided research assistance, reviewed the text of provisions, drafted commentaries, or facilitated our field research and consultations. This list of these generous and gifted people includes Ebba Abdon, Stuart Alford, Diane Amann, Kelly Askin, Louis Aucoin, Mohamed Abdel Aziz, Clive Baldwin, Elaine Banar, Cherif Bassiouni, Karen Belgiovine, Krisna Bovornratanaraks, Roger Clark, Tonya Cook-Pedersen, John Cubbon, Lynn Cuddington (who sadly passed away last year), Sylvia De Bertodano, Knut Doermann, William Durch, Rania

El Gamal, Ken Gallant, David Guinn, Fiana Gantheret, Jonas Grimheden, Michael Hartmann, Christiana Hoffman, Reyko Huang, Agnes Hurwitz, Pernille Ironside, Mark Kroeker, Istvan Lipniczki, Manuel Mazuelos, Daniel Nsereko, Jennifer Oades, Clementine Olivier, April O'Neill, Bruce Oswald, Giovanni Pasqua, Phillip Rapoza, David Reddin, Annamyriam Roccatello, Ali Saleem, Stephanie Smith, Adelina Sokoli, Charles Steenson, Janez Stusek, Christie Warren, Abla Williams, Gerard Winter, Renate Winter, and Lawrence Woocher.

We are thankful to the United Nations departments, agencies, and missions that allowed their representatives to work with us, to attend meetings, and to contribute in various other ways to the development of the Model Codes. In particular, we would like to thank Rob Pulver and Isabel Hight of the United Nations Department of Peacekeeping Operations for their wisdom and guidance.

We are grateful to our coeditors, Hans-Joerg Albrecht and Goran Klemencic. It has been a great pleasure to work with them and share ideas during the many long hours spent in meetings and conference calls over the past five years. They have become colleagues, friends, and wonderful comparative law teachers. Nigel Quinney, our developmental editor–extraordinaire, deserves particular mention for his patience, guidance, and support throughout the publication process.

Finally, we are forever thankful to our friends and family who have endured our seemingly never-ending immersion in the Model Codes Project. In particular, we want to thank Patrick and Calvin, and Declan and Bernadette—you are the best.

**Vivienne O'Connor, Irish Centre for Human Rights**

**Colette Rausch, United States Institute of Peace**

# Editors

Vivienne O'Connor is the rule of law project officer at the Irish Centre for Human Rights, National University of Ireland, Galway, and codirector of the Model Codes for Post-Conflict Criminal Justice Project. She is also a senior fellow of the University of Melbourne, where she lectures on criminal law and development. Her areas of expertise include international human rights law, international and comparative criminal law and procedure, police law, security-sector reform, and post-conflict rule of law. She has taught international human rights law as a guest lecturer at the National University of Ireland, Galway, and has lectured on the rule of law and criminal law reform at a variety of professional training courses. She has also been involved in criminal law reform efforts in a number of post-conflict states and has published several works on the subject.

Colette Rausch is deputy director of the United States Institute of Peace's Rule of Law program. Her work focuses on criminal justice and police reform initiatives, especially in Africa and Southeast Asia. Before joining the Institute, she worked at the Organization for Security and Co-operation in Europe's Mission in Kosovo, serving first as head of the Rule of Law Division and then as director of the Department of Human Rights and Rule of Law. Rausch also served as the U.S. Department of Justice's resident legal adviser, first in Hungary, where she worked on the development of a crime task force, and later in Bosnia in 1998–99. In 1999–2000, she was the Department of Justice's program manager for Central and East Europe, establishing criminal justice development and training projects in Albania, Bosnia, Croatia, Kosovo, and Macedonia. She has worked as a federal prosecutor with the U.S. Attorney's Office in Las Vegas, Nevada. She has published a number of articles and book chapters that examine reform of the criminal justice sector in post-conflict societies; she is also editor of *Combating Serious Crimes in Postconflict Societies: A Handbook for Policymakers and Practitioners.*

Hans-Joerg Albrecht is director of the Max Planck Institute for Foreign and International Criminal Law in Freiburg, Germany. He is professor of criminal law, criminal justice, and criminology at the University of Freiburg. Currently a guest professor at the Law Faculty of Beijing Normal University, he has also served as a guest professor at the Center for Criminal Law and Criminal Justice of the China University of Political Science and Law and the Law Faculty of Wuhan University in China. He has been awarded life membership at Clare Hall College, Cambridge University, and holds a permanent faculty membership at the Faculty of Law at

Qom High Education Center, Tehran. His numerous publications address comparative criminal law, sentencing theory, juvenile crime, drug policies, environmental crime, organized crime, terrorism, and trafficking in persons.

Goran Klemencic is a senior lecturer at the Faculty of Criminal Justice and Security Studies of the University of Maribor, Solvenia. His teaching, writing, and research focus on international comparative criminal law and procedure, law enforcement powers and human rights, and specialized criminal justice mechanisms to tackle corruption and organized crime. He is involved in various criminal justice reform efforts, particularly those involving legislative reform of criminal law and procedure, as well as reform of police and security services in transitional and post-conflict environments in Eastern and Southeastern Europe, Central Asia, China, and Latin America. He has previously worked for the Slovenian Ministry of Interior/Police, the Slovenian Independent Commission for the Prevention of Corruption, the Organisation for Economic Co-operation and Development, and the Council of Europe.

# Contributors

As the following lists of organizations and individuals who contributed to the Model Codes Project make clear, great efforts were made to obtain the input of a diverse community of experts with knowledge and experience relevant to the post-conflict criminal law reform process. In all, some three hundred people from more than one hundred organizations and over fifty countries contributed to the Model Codes Project. Some helped to create the broad framework for the project, others drafted specific provisions and commentaries, still others critiqued and refined those drafts; all of them gave generously of their time and considerable expertise.

## International and Regional Organizations

- African Commission on Human and Peoples' Rights
- Council of Europe
- European Commission and European Council
- Organization for Security and Co-operation in Europe (OSCE)
- United Nations
    - Children's Fund (UNICEF)
    - Department of Peacekeeping Operations (DPKO)
    - Department of Political Affairs (DPA)
    - Development Fund for Women (UNIFEM)
    - Development Programme (UNDP)
    - International Criminal Tribunal for Rwanda (ICTR)
    - International Criminal Tribunal for the former Yugoslavia (ICTY)
    - Office of Legal Affairs (OLA)
    - Office of the High Commissioner for Human Rights (OHCHR)
    - Office on Drugs and Crime (UNODC)

## Civil Society and Non-Governmental Organizations

- AIRE Centre
- Amnesty International
- Asian Human Rights Commission
- Cambodian Defenders Project

- Criminal Defence Resource Centre, Kosovo
- Foundation for Law, Human Rights and Justice, East Timor
- Informal Sector Service Centre, Nepal
- International Center for Transitional Justice
- International Committee of the Red Cross
- International Development Law Organization
- Minority Rights Group
- National Forum for Human Rights, Sierra Leone
- Open Society Justice Initiative
- Penal Reform International

## Professional Associations, Training Institutions, and National Commissions

- African Bar Association
- American Corrections Association
- Association of Female Lawyers, Liberia
- Commission for Reception, Truth and Reconciliation, East Timor
- International Association of Prosecutors
- International Corrections and Prisons Association
- International Criminal Defence Attorneys Association
- Joint Advisory Committee on Legislative Matters, Kosovo
- Justice Council, Institute of Training and Law Reform, Sudan
- Law Reform Commission Task Force, Liberia
- Liberian National Law Enforcement Association
- Kosovo Chamber of Advocates
- Magistrates School, Cambodia
- Nepal Bar Association
- National Human Rights Commission, Nepal
- Southeast Asia Regional Centre for Counter-Terrorism, Malaysia
- West African Bar Association

## Research and Academic Institutions

- Academy of Military Science, China
- Asia-Pacific Centre for Military Law, Australia
- Charles University, Czech Republic
- College of William and Mary, United States

- Defense Institute of International Legal Studies, United States
- Eins Shams University, Egypt
- Georgetown University, United States
- International Human Rights Law Institute, United States
- International Institute of Higher Studies in Criminal Sciences (ISISC), Italy
- International Peace Academy, United States
- Irish Centre for Human Rights
- John Jay College of Criminal Justice, United States
- Kathmandu School of Law, Nepal
- Max Planck Institute for Foreign and International Criminal Law, Germany
- National University of Rwanda
- National War College, Nigeria
- Örebro University, Sweden
- Rabat University, Morocco
- Raoul Wallenberg Institute, Sweden
- Rutgers University, United States
- The Henry L. Stimson Center, United States
- Umea University, Sweden
- United Nations Association of the United States
- United States of Institute of Peace
- University of Arkansas at Little Rock, United States
- University of Botswana
- University of Cairo, Egypt
- University of California at Davis, United States
- University of Catania, Italy
- University of Damascus, Syria
- University of Garyounis, Libya
- University of Maribor, Slovenia
- University of Melbourne, Australia
- University of Sarajevo, Bosnia and Herzegovina

## Personnel from the Following Peace Operations

- Office of the High Representative in Bosnia and Herzegovina (OHR)
- United Nations Advance Mission in the Sudan (UNAMIS)
- United Nations Border Relief Operation, Thailand (UNBRO)
- United Nations Mission in Kosovo (UNMIK)

- United Nations Mission in Liberia (UNMIL)
- United Nations Mission in Sierra Leone (UNAMSIL)
- United Nations Mission of Support in East Timor (UNMISET)
- United Nations Operation in Mozambique (ONUMOZ)
- United Nations Stabilization Mission in Haiti (MINUSTAH)
- United Nations Transitional Administration in East Timor (UNTAET)
- United Nations Transitional Authority in Cambodia (UNTAC)

## Judicial, Prosecutorial, Defense, Legal Advisory, Police, and Military Personnel Who Worked in or Originated from the Following Countries

- Afghanistan
- Australia
- Bangladesh
- Belgium
- Bosnia and Herzegovina
- Cambodia
- Canada
- Croatia
- Democratic Republic of the Congo
- East Timor
- Egypt
- Fiji
- Germany
- Ghana
- Haiti
- Hungary
- India
- Iraq
- Ireland
- Jordan
- Kosovo
- Liberia
- Malawi
- Malaysia
- Mauritius
- Mozambique
- Nepal
- The Netherlands
- New Zealand
- Nigeria
- Pakistan
- Philippines
- Poland
- Romania
- Rwanda
- Sierra Leone
- Singapore
- Slovenia
- South Africa
- Spain
- Sri Lanka
- Sudan
- Sweden
- Thailand
- Uganda
- Ukraine
- United Arab Emirates
- United Kingdom
- United States
- Zimbabwe

## Individuals

*The affiliations listed are those at the time the individual first contributed to the Model Codes Project.*

- Hugh Adsett — Legal Affairs Counselor, Permanent Mission of Canada to the United Nations
- Mohammed Akida — Department of Criminal Law, Eins Shams University, Egypt
- Abdel Rahim Al-Awadi — Islamic Affairs, Attorney General's Office, Ministry of the Justice, United Arab Emirates
- Hans-Joerg Albrecht — Director, Max Planck Institute for Foreign and International Criminal Law, Germany
- Stuart Alford — Barrister, United Kingdom, and former Prosecutor, Special Panels for Serious Crimes, East Timor
- Zeid Ra'ad Zeid Al-Hussein — Permanent Representative of Jordan to the United Nations
- Abboud Al-Sarraj — Faculty of Law, University of Damascus, Syria
- Diane Amann — School of Law, University of California at Davis, United States
- Ricarda Amberg — Rule of Law Section, Human Security Branch, UNODC
- Upendra Aryal — Senior Superintendent of Nepal Police, and former UN Civilian Police, East Timor
- William Aseltine — Defense Institute of International Legal Studies, United States
- Kelly Askin — Open Society Justice Initiative
- Louis Aucoin — United States Institute of Peace, and former Head, UNTAET Department of Justice
- Alfonso Avelar — Human Rights Unit, UNMISET
- Mohammed Ayat — Legal Advisor, ICTR, and Faculty of Law, Rabat University, Morocco
- Mohamed Abdel Aziz — President, International Human Rights Institute, College of Law, DePaul University, United States
- Mohamed Elewa Badar — Judge, Ministry of Justice, Egypt
- Clive Baldwin — Minority Rights Group, and former Legal Advisor to OSCE Mission in Kosovo
- Elaine Banar — U.S. Attorney's Office, New York, United States, and former Legal Advisor, UNMIK Police

- Pat Barron — Ireland's National Police Service
- Peira Barzano — Terrorism Prevention, Treaty Affairs Division, UNODC
- Cherif Bassiouni — International Human Rights Institute, College of Law, DePaul University, United States
- Kurt Bassuener — Political Department, OHR, Bosnia and Herzegovina
- Jeff Batha — Civilian Police Assistance Training Team, Iraq, and former Corrections Officer, United States
- Ahmad Belal — Faculty of Law, University of Cairo, Egypt
- Hudson Benzu — Police Commissioner, UNAMSIL
- Per Berling — Department of Law, Umea University, and former Rule of Law Advisor, OHR, Bosnia and Herzegovina
- Zulkifli bin Haji Alias — Training Program, Southeast Asia Regional Centre for Counter-Terrorism, Malaysia
- Kjell Bjornberg — Judge, Court of Appeals, Sweden, and former Head, Judicial System Assessment Programme, UN, Bosnia and Herzegovina
- Catarina Bolognese — Department of Crime Problems, Council of Europe
- Frits Bontekoe — Legal Advisor, UNAMIS
- Vinod Boolell — International Judge, UNMIK, and former Judge, Supreme Court, Mauritius
- Krisna Bovornratanaraks — Military Legislation/Foreign Affairs, Judge Advocate General's Department, Defense Ministry, Thailand
- Lakhdar Brahimi — Under-Secretary General, Special Advisor to the Secretary-General, United Nations
- Lois Lewis Bruthus — President, Association of Female Lawyers of Liberia
- Richard Buellesbach — Legal Advisor, Federal Ministry of Defense, Germany, and former Deputy Legal Advisor, KFOR
- Patrick Burgess — Legal Counsel, Commission for Reception, Truth and Reconciliation, East Timor
- Dammann Burkhard — Anti-Trafficking Unit, UNODC
- Jean Christian Cady — Deputy Special Representative of the Secretary-General, UNMIK

| | |
|---|---|
| • Susan Carroll | International Criminal Investigative Training Program, U.S. Department of Justice, Bosnia and Herzegovina |
| • Attaporn Charoenpanich | Judge Advocate General, Defense Ministry, Thailand |
| • Tom Chaseman | Rule of Law Advisor, OSCE, Bosnia and Herzegovina |
| • Paul Chia | Criminal Justice Division, Attorney General's Chambers, Singapore |
| • Demostenes Chryssikos | Crime Conventions Section, Treaty Affairs Division, UNODC |
| • Roger Clark | Faculty of Law, Rutgers University, United States |
| • Felicia Coleman | Law Reform Commission Task Force, Liberia and former Judge, Supreme Court, Liberia |
| • Michael Coleman | External and Politico-Military Affairs/Police Unit, Council of the European Union |
| • Tonya Cook-Pedersen | DPK Consulting, and former Advisor to the United Nations Police Commissioner, Bosnia and Herzegovina |
| • Nicholas Cowdery | President, International Association of Prosecutors |
| • David Crane | Chief Prosecutor, Special Court for Sierra Leone |
| • Jim Crane | U.S. Attorney's Office, Georgia, United States, and former Legal Advisor, U.S. Department of Justice, Bosnia and Herzegovina |
| • John Cubbon | Legal Advisor's Office, UNMIK |
| • Lynn Cuddington | Corrections Policy, Solicitor General's Office, Canada |
| • Anthony Cullen | Irish Centre for Human Rights |
| • Elisabeth Dallas | The Henry L. Stimson Center, United States |
| • Sylvia De Bertodano | Barrister, United Kingdom, and former Defense Counsel, ICTY |
| • Jo Dedeyne | Treaty Affairs Division, UNODC |
| • Rob Deere | Security Sector Advisor, UNMIL |
| • Michael de Feo | Terrorism Prevention Branch, UNODC |
| • Felipe De La Torre-Corral | Anti-Organized Crime and Terrorism Unit, UNODC |
| • Andrea de Maio | International Development Law Organization |

| | |
|---|---|
| • Anne Marie Devereaux | Legal Advisor, UNMISET |
| • Knut Doermann | Legal Division, International Committee of the Red Cross |
| • Martha Doggett | UN Department of Political Affairs |
| • Andrew Dunn | Military Justice, Defence Legal Services, Australia |
| • Michelle Dunn | Australian Federal Police, International Deployment Group |
| • William Durch | The Henry L. Stimson Center, United States |
| • Frederick Egonda-Ntende | International Judge, UNMIK, and Judge, Uganda |
| • Ahmad El-Gehani | Faculty of Law, University of Garyounis, Libya |
| • Awad Hassan el-Nour | Justice Council, Institute of Training and Law Reform, Sudan |
| • Paul English | Executive Director, Penal Reform International |
| • Charles Erdmann | Judge, United States Military Court of Appeals, and former Legal Advisor, OHR, Bosnia and Herzegovina |
| • Essa Faal | Serious Crimes Unit, UNTAET |
| • Megan Fairlie | Irish Centre for Human Rights, and former Legislative Counsel, New York, United States |
| • Alexander Faite | Legal Division, International Committee of the Red Cross |
| • Femi Falana | Secretary General, African Bar Association, President, West African Bar Association, and Lawyer, Nigeria |
| • Ravan Farhadi | Permanent Representative of Afghanistan to the United Nations |
| • Chandra Fernando | Inspector General of Police, Sri Lanka |
| • Peter Fitzgerald | Ireland's National Police Service, and former Commissioner, International Police Task Force, Bosnia and Herzegovina |
| • Dieter Fleck | International Agreements and Policy, Federal Ministry of Defense, Germany |
| • Joseph Flomo | Criminal Investigation Division and Interpol Affairs, Liberia National Police |
| • Alfred Fofie | Director, Legal and Judiciary System Support Division, UNMIL |

| | |
|---|---|
| • Joaquim Fonseca | Foundation for Law, Human Rights and Justice, East Timor |
| • Dara Francis | The Henry L. Stimson Center, United States |
| • Wilfredo Franco | UN Police Division, UNMIL |
| • Hakan Freeman | Judge of Appeals, Sweden, and Legal Expert, Swedish Ministry of Justice |
| • Gerald Gahima | Attorney General, Rwanda |
| • Kenneth Gallant | School of Law, University of Arkansas at Little Rock, United States |
| • Fiana Gantheret | Irish Centre for Human Rights |
| • Paddington Garwe | Judge, High Court, Zimbabwe |
| • Alan Gibbens | Legal Affairs, Permanent Mission of Ireland to the United Nations |
| • Martin Gillvray | British National Crime Squad, and former UNMIK Civilian Police |
| • Sheryl Goldstein | Lawyer, United States, and former Legal Advisor, OSCE, Criminal Defense Resource Centre, Kosovo |
| • James Gondles | Executive Director, American Corrections Association |
| • Andrea Goodman | UNDP, and former Legal Advisor, Department of Justice, UNMIK |
| • Giovanni Grasso | European Commission Representative and Law Faculty, University of Catania, Italy |
| • Cecil Griffiths | Liberia National Law Enforcement Association |
| • Jonas Grimheden | Raoul Wallenberg Institute, Lund University, Sweden |
| • Adalbert Gross | Police Force North Rhine-Westfalia, Germany, and former UNMIK Civilian Police |
| • Elise Groulx | International Criminal Defence Attorneys Association |
| • Jean-Marie Guehenno | Under-Secretary General, UNDPKO |
| • David Guinn | International Human Rights Law Institute, College of Law, DePaul University, United States |
| • Amod Gurung | Civilian Police Division, UNDPKO |
| • Alan Gutman | Defense Attorney, Special Panels for Serious Crimes, East Timor |

| | |
|---|---|
| • Michael Hanrahan | Military Advisor, Permanent Mission of Canada to the United Nations |
| • Michael Hartmann | International Prosecutor, UNMIK |
| • Enver Hasani | Faculty of Law, University of Pristina, Kosovo |
| • Kamran Hashemi | Irish Centre for Human Rights |
| • Shamin Hasnain | Judge, High Court Division, Supreme Court, Bangladesh |
| • Ahmet Hasolli | Criminal Defence Resource Centre, Kosovo |
| • Jill Heine | Legal Advisor, Amnesty International |
| • Isabel Hight | Corrections Policy Advisor, UNDPKO |
| • Gary Hill | International Scientific and Professional Advisory Council, Crime Prevention and Criminal Justice Programme, United Nations |
| • Lynn Holland | Law Enforcement Technical Advisor, Dyncorp International, and former Police Recruitment, Kosovo Police Service School |
| • Adrian Horn | Horn, Ltd., and former Head, Community Safety and Security Project for Sierra Leone Police, United Kingdom, Department for International Development |
| • Reyko Huang | Security-Development Nexus Program, International Peace Academy, United States |
| • Susan Hulton | Department of Political Affairs, United Nations |
| • Agnes Hurwitz | Security-Development Nexus Program, International Peace Academy, United States |
| • David Hutchinson | Office of Legal Affairs, United Nations |
| • Phyllis Hwang | Legal Advisor's Office, UNMIK |
| • Shelley Inglis | Criminal Law and Judicial Advisory Unit, Best Practices Section, UNDPKO |
| • Pernille Ironside | Rule of Law/Transitional Justice, UNICEF |
| • Mark Jalandoni | Department of Justice, Secretary of the Office of the President, Philippines |
| • Eva Jansen | Crime Prevention, UNODC |
| • Piyachart Jaroenpol | International Law Section, Judge Advocate General's Department, Defence Ministry, Thailand |
| • Michael Jarrett | Australian Federal Police, International Deployment Group |

- Stephane Jean — Civilian Police Division, UNDPKO
- Emry Jones Perry — Permanent Representative of the United Kingdom to the United Nations
- Michael Jorsback — Swedish Ministry of Justice, and former Civilian Police Division, UNDPKO
- Michael Karnavas — Defense Counsel, ICTY, and former Head, Law Revision Commission, Brcko, Bosnia and Herzegovina
- Bart Katureebe — Lawyer and former Attorney General, Uganda
- Nekibe Kelmendi — Head, Department of Judicial Affairs, Kosovo
- Shyam Khadka — Deputy Senior Superintendent of Nepal Police, and former UN Civilian Police, Mozambique and Kosovo
- Bill Kirk — Australian Federal Police (Ret.), and former civilian police, UN Border Relief Operations, Thailand
- Goran Klemencic — Faculty of Criminal Justice and Security Studies, University of Maribor, Slovenia
- Agnieszka Klonowiecka-Milart — International Judge, UNMIK, and Judge, Poland
- Alexander Knoops — Criminal Lawyer, The Netherlands, Defense Counsel, ICTY
- Neil Kritz — Director, Rule of Law Program, United States Institute of Peace
- Mark Kroeker — Civilian Police Division, UNDPKO, and former police commissioner, UNMIL
- Elizabeth Kuteesa — Director, Criminal Investigation Division, Uganda Police
- Richard Kuuire — Director-General of Prisons, Ghana
- Zaheer Laher — Legal Affairs, Permanent Mission of South Africa to the United Nations
- Nina Lahoud — Special Advisor to the Executive Director of UNIFEM
- Birgit Lange-Klepsch — International Judge, UNMIK, and former Judge, Germany
- Gilbert Laurin — Permanent Representative of Canada to the United Nations
- Paddy Leahy — Ireland's National Police Service

- Mark Lee — Australian Federal Police, and former Police Trainer, East Timor
- Anders Liden — Permanent Representative of Sweden to the United Nations
- Suzannah Linton — Solicitor, United Kingdom, and formerly with the Serious Crimes Unit, UNTAET
- Istvan Lipniczki — Human Rights and Protection Section, UNMIL, and former Inspector, Hungarian Police
- Terseli Loial — Office of Legal Affairs, United Nations
- Antero Lopes — Civilian Police Division, UNDPKO
- Christopher Lord — Institute of International Relations and Charles University, Prague
- Patrick Pierre Louis — UNDP
- Joyce Low — Supreme Court, Singapore
- Wiley McAfee — International Criminal Investigative Training Program, U.S. Department of Justice
- Sean McDonald — Deputy Permanent Representative of Ireland to the United Nations
- John McManus — War Crimes Division, Canadian Ministry of Justice
- Stephanie McPhail — Legal and Judicial System Support Division, UNMIL
- Jerzy Makarowski — First Secretary, Legal Affairs, Permanent Mission of Sweden to the United Nations
- Sunil Kumar Malik — Legal Advisor, Indian Air Force
- Tiyanjana Maluwa — OHCHR
- Sabelo Sivuyile Maqungo — Legal Advisor, Permanent Mission of South Africa to the United Nations
- David Marshall — OHCHR
- Ian Martin — International Center for Transitional Justice
- Manuel Mazuelos Fernandez-Figueroa — Judge, Spanish Judicial Network of Experts in International Judicial Cooperation
- Grace Mensah — Legal Advisory and Monitoring Unit, UNMIL
- Anthony Miller — Office of Legal Affairs, United Nations
- Khaled Ahmed Mohey — International Human Rights Law Institute, College of Law, DePaul University, United States
- Craig Mokhiber — OHCHR

| | |
|---|---|
| • Nuala Mole | The AIRE Centre (Advice on Individual Rights in Europe) |
| • Richard Monk | Senior Police Advisor, OSCE, and former Police Commissioner, IPTF, Bosnia and Herzegovina |
| • Longuinhos Monteiro | Prosecutor General, East Timor |
| • Jonathan Morrow | Legal Advisor, UNTAET |
| • Josephine Moss | Legal Advisor, UNMISET |
| • Dieumerci Mutombo | Lawyer, Legislature, Democratic Republic of the Congo |
| • Francis Ng | State Counsel, Criminal Justice Division, Singapore |
| • Patrick Ng | Operations Control, Singapore Prison Service |
| • Louis Nkopipie | UNDP |
| • Daniel Nsereko | Faculty of Law, University of Botswana |
| • Sylver Ntukamazina | Judge, Special Panels for Serious Crimes, UNTAET |
| • Kamudoni Nyasulu | International Prosecutor, UNMIK, and former Prosecutor, Malawi |
| • Bahame Tom Nyanduga | African Commission on Human and Peoples' Rights |
| • Jennifer Oades | International Corrections and Prisons Association |
| • Nnamdi Obasi | Center for Peace and Conflict Resolution, National War College, Nigeria |
| • Vivienne O'Connor | Irish Centre for Human Rights |
| • Sok Sam Oeun | Cambodian Defenders Project |
| • John Ohiorhenuan | UNDP |
| • Kaoru Okuizumi | Legal Advisor to the Registrar, Special Court for Sierra Leone |
| • Clementine Olivier | Irish Centre for Human Rights |
| • William O'Neill | Rule of Law Consultant, and former Chair, Executive Committee for Peace and Security Task Force on Rule of Law, United Nations |
| • Bruce Oswald | Asia-Pacific Centre for Military Law, University of Melbourne, Australia |
| • Sushil Kumar Pant | Lawyer, and former Attorney General, Nepal |
| • Tudor Pantiru | International Judge, UNMIK, and former Judge, Romania |

| | |
|---|---|
| • Giovanni Pasqua | Director, International Institute of Higher Studies in Criminal Sciences (ICISC), Italy |
| • Kenneth Payumo | Faculty of Public Management, John Jay College of Criminal Justice, United States, and former Policy Advisor to the United Nations Police Commissioner, East Timor |
| • Gordon Peake | Security-Development Nexus Program, International Peace Academy, United States |
| • Michael Peckover | South Yorkshire Police Force, United Kingdom, and former UN Civilian Police, East Timor |
| • Carl Peersman | Legal Advisor, Permanent Mission of the Netherlands to the United Nations |
| • Joe Robert Pemagbi | Permanent Representative of the Republic of Sierra Leone to the United Nations |
| • Maria Natercia Gusmao Pereira | Judge, Special Panels for Serious Crimes, East Timor |
| • Nadine Perrault | Legislative Reform, UNICEF |
| • Jesse Pilgrim | International Legal Consultant |
| • Chalermchai Pimolsri | Border Patrol Police, Thailand |
| • Michael Platzer | Rule of Law Section, Human Security Branch, UNODC |
| • Ben Playle | Legal Advisor, Permanent Mission of Australia to the United Nations |
| • Mark Plunkett | Barrister, Australia, and former Special Prosecutor, UNTAC |
| • Robert Pulver | Criminal Law and Judicial Advisory Unit, Best Practices Section, UNDPKO |
| • Riika Puttonen | Anti–Human Trafficking Unit, UNODC |
| • Subodh Pyakurel | Chairperson, Informal Sector Service Centre, Nepal |
| • Sushil Pyakurel | Former Commissioner, National Human Rights Commission, Nepal |
| • William Quade | Australian Federal Police, International Deployment Group |
| • Joseph Rahall | National Forum for Human Rights, Sierra Leone |
| • Radzi Rahman | Alternate Permanent Representative of Malaysia to the United Nations |
| • Phillip Rapoza | Judge, Special Panels for Serious Crimes, East Timor |

- Colette Rausch — Rule of Law Program, United States Institute of Peace
- David Reddin — British Army (Ret.), and former Military Legal Advisor for Peace Operations
- Slawomir Redo — Rule of Law Section, Human Security Branch, OHCHR
- Blerim Reka — Joint Advisory Committee on Legislation Matters, Kosovo
- Brendan Reynolds — International Corrections and Prisons Association
- Annamyriam Roccatello — Department of Justice, UNMIK
- Jorge Romeau — Legal Counselor, Permanent Mission of Spain to the United Nations
- Sylvain Roy — Principal Defender, Special Court for Sierra Leone
- Lauren Rumble — Rule of Law/Transitional Justice, UNICEF
- Ejup Sahiti — Faculty of Law, University of Pristina, Kosovo
- Ali Saleem — Asia Legal Resource Centre, Asian Human Rights Commission
- Ismet Salihu — Faculty of Law, University of Pristina, Kosovo
- Sanaka Samarasinha — UNDP
- Geeta Sangroula — Kathmandu School of Law, Nepal
- Yubaraj Sangroula — Executive Director, Kathmandu School of Law, Nepal
- Richard Sannerholm — Örebro University, Sweden
- Domingos Sarmento — Minister for Justice, East Timor
- Kim Sathavy — Magistrates School Director, Cambodia
- William Schabas — Director, Irish Centre for Human Rights
- Delphine Schantz — Global Programme against Money Laundering, UNODC
- David Scheffer — Center for International Human Rights, Georgetown University
- Eric Scheye — UNDP
- Vanessa Sedletzki — Legislative Reform, UNICEF
- Bigyan Sharma — Senior Superintendent of Nepal Police, and former Commander, UN Special Police Unit, Haiti

| | |
|---|---|
| • Mark Shaw | Criminal Justice Reform Unit, UNODC |
| • Milbert Shin | Office of the Prosecutor, ICTY |
| • Hajrija Sijercic-Colic | Faculty of Law, University of Sarajevo, Bosnia and Herzegovina |
| • Elmo Siryon | Human Rights Division, Ministry of Justice, Liberia |
| • Stephanie Smith | Staff Judge Advocate's Office, United States Marine Corps, and former Military Advisor for Peace Operations |
| • Adelina Sokoli | Kosovo Law Centre |
| • Adam Stapleton | Penal Reform International |
| • Charles Steenson | State Investigation and Protection Service, Bosnia and Herzegovina |
| • Oliver Stolpe | Anti-Corruption Unit, UNODC |
| • Janez Stusek | Faculty of Criminal Justice and Security Studies, University of Maribor, Slovenia |
| • Jitsiri Sukomorn | Advisory Section, Judge Advocate General's Department, Defence Ministry, Thailand |
| • Visal Suon | Cambodia Defenders Project |
| • Rakel Surlien | Independent Judicial Commission, OHR, Bosnia and Herzegovina |
| • Govind Thapa | Additional Inspector General of Police (Ret.), Nepal |
| • Shambhu Thapa | President, Nepal Bar Association |
| • Brenda Sue Thornton | Trial Attorney, U.S. Department of Justice |
| • James Tillman | International Criminal Investigative Training Program, U.S. Department of Justice, Bosnia and Herzegovina |
| • John Tobin | Faculty of Law, University of Melbourne, Australia |
| • Gabriel Tuan | Civilian Training Section, UNDPKO |
| • Aphophia Twiine | Faculty of Law, National University of Rwanda |
| • Sandra Valle | Treaty Affairs Division, UNODC |
| • Guy van Craen | International Judge, Bosnia and Herzegovina, and Judge, Court of Appeals, Belgium |
| • Johan van Lamoen | International Legal Consultant |
| • Eduardo Vetere | Director, Treaty Affairs Division, UNODC |
| • Robin Vincent | Registrar, Special Court for Sierra Leone |

| | |
|---|---|
| • Dimitri Vlassis | Crime Conventions Section, UNODC |
| • Adem Vokshi | Kosovo Chamber of Advocates |
| • Catherine Volz | Treaty Affairs Division, UNODC |
| • Christie Warren | Marshall-Wythe School of Law, College of William and Mary, United States |
| • Andrew Wells | Senior Legal Advisor, UNODC |
| • Erik Wennerstrom | Ministry of Justice, Sweden |
| • Deborah Wilkinson | International Prosecutor, UNMIK |
| • Abla Williams | Legal Affairs, Ministry of Justice, Liberia |
| • Gerard Winter | Judge, High Court, Fiji |
| • Renate Winter | International Judge, Special Court for Sierra Leone |
| • Lawrence Woocher | Global Policy Programs, United Nations Association of the United States |
| • He Xiadong | Department of Foreign Military Studies of the Academy of Military Science, China |
| • Juan Antonio Yanez-Barneuvo | Permanent Representative of Spain to the United Nations |
| • Alexandra Yuster | Juvenile Justice, UNICEF |
| • Hilmi Zhitja | Chief Public Prosecutor, Kosovo |

## Research and Program Assistants

*The following individuals provided research or program assistance at various times during the development of the Model Codes Project.*

| | |
|---|---|
| • Elisabeth Ahlquist | Irish Centre for Human Rights |
| • Marisa Bassett | United States Institute of Peace |
| • Karen Belgiovine | United Nations Association of the USA |
| • Christian De Vos | United States Institute of Peace |
| • Toluwanimi Fadeyi | United States Institute of Peace |
| • Karen Heymann | United States Institute of Peace |
| • Christiana Hoffman | United States Institute of Peace |
| • Delia Hau | Irish Centre for Human Rights |
| • Erin Hespe | United States Institute of Peace |
| • Erica Johnston | United States Institute of Peace |
| • Dmitri Karpash | Irish Centre for Human Rights |

| | |
|---|---|
| • Danielle Keenan | Irish Centre for Human Rights |
| • Yoonie Kim | United States Institute of Peace |
| • Vidal Martin-Hernando | Irish Centre for Human Rights |
| • Patrice Mattingly | United States Institute of Peace |
| • April O'Neill | United States Institute of Peace |
| • Ann-Marie Quinn | Irish Centre for Human Rights |
| • Kate Riggs | Irish Centre for Human Rights |
| • Emily Wann | United States Institute of Peace |
| • Nadia Zed | Irish Centre for Human Rights |

## Abbreviations

| | |
|---|---|
| ICTR | International Criminal Tribunal for Rwanda |
| ICTY | International Criminal Tribunal for the former Yugoslavia |
| IPTF | International Police Task Force |
| KFOR | Kosovo Force (NATO-led international military force) |
| OHCHR | Office of the United Nations High Commissioner for Human Rights |
| OHR | Office of the High Representative |
| OSCE | Organization for Security and Co-operation in Europe |
| UNAMIS | United Nations Advance Mission in the Sudan |
| UNAMSIL | United Nations Mission in Sierra Leone |
| UNDP | United Nations Development Programme |
| UNDPKO | United Nations Department of Peacekeeping Operations |
| UNICEF | United Nations Children's Fund |
| UNIFEM | United Nations Development Fund for Women |
| UMMIK | United Nations Mission in Kosovo |
| UNMIL | United Nations Mission in Liberia |
| UNMISET | United Nations Mission of Support in East Timor |
| UNODC | United Nations Office on Drugs and Crime |
| UNTAC | United Nations Transitional Authority in Cambodia |
| UNTAET | United Nations Transitional Administration in East Timor |

# User's Guide

# Introduction

This User's Guide introduces *Model Codes for Post-Conflict Criminal Justice,* a three-volume series designed to assist those working in criminal law reform in post-conflict states. The series is the product of a five-year project spearheaded by the United States Institute of Peace and the Irish Centre for Human Rights, in co-operation with the United Nations Office of the High Commissioner for Human Rights and the United Nations Office on Drugs and Crime.

This volume, volume I, contains the first of the Model Codes—the Model Criminal Code. Volume II contains the Model Code of Criminal Procedure, while volume III contains the Model Detention Act and the Model Police Powers Act.

This User's Guide is divided into four chapters. Chapter 1 outlines the need for criminal law reform in post-conflict states, the evolution of interest in the topic among the international community, and the drafting and consultation process used to create the Model Codes. Chapter 2 discusses the many potential uses of the Model Codes in post-conflict criminal law reform efforts. Chapter 3 provides a synopsis of the Model Criminal Code. Chapter 4 sets out guiding principles for those involved in the process of criminal law reform.

# Chapter 1
# The Model Codes Project
## A Response to Post-Conflict Criminal Law Needs

For national and international actors involved in post-conflict peacebuilding, the reestablishment of the rule of law is vital. Criminal justice systems are often shattered or severely debilitated in the aftermath of conflict. Prisons, police stations, and courthouses may be destroyed. Lawyers and judges may have fled the country. The police force may be nonexistent. In some cases, as United Nations peace operations have discovered to their dismay, the criminal justice system has ceased to function completely.

Such an environment can be a breeding ground for serious criminality, with criminals and criminal gangs operating freely in a climate of impunity. While war crimes and crimes against humanity may come to a halt as a cease-fire or peace agreement takes effect, crimes such as rape, extortion, murder, and kidnapping often continue unabated. Ethnic tensions may reemerge in the post-conflict period and manifest themselves as revenge attacks, hate speech, and attacks on personal and cultural property. Sexual violence is also prevalent in post-conflict states. In addition, organized criminal groups are often involved in a wide variety of serious crimes, including trafficking in persons, drugs, and weapons; smuggling; and money laundering.

Violent conflict and subsequent criminality in the post-conflict environment create a climate of fear, mistrust, and insecurity. Humans suffer both from direct exposure to violence and from extreme feelings of insecurity, and crave an environment in which others can be trusted again. Trust is a major ingredient of the social capital of a post-conflict society. It is vital to fostering public compliance with both social and legal norms, to ensuring that post-conflict states do not revert back to conflict, and to building peace.

Reestablishing or reforming a fractured criminal justice system is also critical to the success of peacebuilding efforts, but it is typically a Herculean task demanding the commitment and expertise of many different national and international actors. It can involve a host of interrelated activities, from providing basic resources such as pens and paper and police uniforms to rebuilding courthouses and prisons, from recruiting and vetting new criminal justice personnel to restructuring the entire police force or court system.

It is also critical to look beyond resources and infrastructure, staffing and restructuring, to the laws to be applied in the pursuit of justice. Even a system that is well resourced, well staffed, and institutionally robust will fail to serve the needs of the community unless its laws are adequate.

What constitutes an "adequate" legal framework? In practical terms, as discussed in the United Nations secretary-general's 2004 report *The Rule of Law and Transitional Justice in Conflict and Post-Conflict Societies* (UN doc. S/2004/616, paragraphs 6 and 7), all domestic laws must be "consistent with international human rights norms and standards"; be "legally certain" (i.e., clearly defined, accessible, foreseeable, and neither contradictory nor overlapping); and comply with the principle of justice (i.e., protect and vindicate rights, punish wrongs, and protect the rights of the accused while taking into account the interests of victims and the well-being of society at large).

Unfortunately, criminal laws in post-conflict societies rarely meet these criteria. "Legislative frameworks" in post-conflict states, comments *The Rule of Law and Transitional Justice,* "often show the accumulated signs of neglect and political distortion, contain discriminatory elements and rarely reflect the requirements of international human rights and criminal law standards." For instance, legal certainty was conspicuously absent from Afghanistan after the fall of the Taliban, with the country subject to some twenty-four hundred overlapping and often contradictory bodies of law that had been allowed to accumulate over the preceding four decades and changing administrations.

Furthermore, criminal justice legislation in post-conflict states is often outdated. To take just a few examples: In post-conflict Angola, the penal code dated to 1886. In Liberia, human trafficking was widespread but not adequately addressed in the penal code, which had not been amended since the 1970s. In Kosovo, human trafficking, terrorism, organized crime, and the possession and use of illegal firearms were all prevalent but were poorly covered in the applicable criminal law. To make matters worse, while many post-conflict states are plagued with complex crimes such as trafficking and money laundering, those states' legal frameworks typically do not contain provisions for covert surveillance, witness protection, and other measures that are vital to the investigation and prosecution of such crimes.

## Previous Post-Conflict Criminal Law Reform Efforts

The pronounced inadequacies of some post-conflict criminal laws have inspired several efforts to reform existing laws. In Cambodia, for instance, the dysfunctional criminal justice system bequeathed by the Khmer Rouge prompted significant legal reform both during the mandate (1992–93) of the United Nations Transitional Authority in Cambodia (UNTAC) and subsequently. Among other areas targeted by this legislation were criminal law and procedure, police powers, the prisons system, and the court system.

In Kosovo, the United Nations Mission (UNMIK) established in 1999 passed numerous regulations to fill gaps in the existing criminal law. Some regulations have been designed to ensure that the law complies with international human rights norms and standards; others have added new offenses, such as human trafficking; still others have sought to give police and prosecutors the tools they need to investigate and prosecute serious crimes.

The United Nations Transitional Administration in East Timor (UNTAET), whose mandate ran from October 1999 to May 2002, deemed the Indonesian criminal procedure code to be overly complicated and unsuitable for application in post-conflict East Timor, and so promulgated new regulations on criminal procedure and the courts. It also promulgated regulations on firearms and election-related criminal offenses.

Such attempts to reform the criminal law have not met with universal praise, however, underlining the complexity of the task and the heavy demands it places on time, resources, and expertise. In Cambodia, for instance, the UNTAC code, the first piece of law reform introduced during the country's transition, has been widely criticized for lacking clarity, contradicting other laws, and being inconsistent with basic human rights provisions.

In Kosovo, during UNMIK's first years, the special representative of the United Nations secretary-general issued executive orders for detention of individuals, even after the courts—including in some cases courts composed entirely of international judges—had ordered individuals released for lack of evidence, and even when the releases had been proposed by international prosecutors. Criticism of the executive orders came from many directions, including from the Organization for Security and Cooperation in Europe, international human rights organizations, and the UNMIK ombudsman, who argued that the orders for detention violated the principle of judicial independence and failed to provide for judicial review.

In East Timor, individuals in the justice system noted several fundamental gaps in UNTAET regulations that served as the transitional criminal procedure code until 2006. The regulations did not include issues such as the requisite burden of proof and standards relating to the competency of witnesses. Criminal justice actors effectively had to make up their own rules and fill the gaps in the applicable legislation, which enhanced the legal uncertainty in East Timor.

## Criminal Law Reform in the International Spotlight

The cases of Cambodia, Kosovo, and East Timor focused international attention on the importance of the rule of law in post-conflict states, and in particular on the importance of criminal law reform. Many actors involved in the law reform process in these three places spotlighted the deficiencies in both the substance of some of the laws that were drafted and the process by which they were drafted. In the late 1990s and early 2000, the subject of criminal law reform was widely debated, with practitioners and policymakers looking to learn lessons from past mistakes and move forward confidently and effectively.

Recognizing the need to reconfigure the international community's approach to post-conflict peacebuilding in peace operations, including criminal law reform, in 2000 the United Nations issued the *Report of the Panel on United Nations Peace Operations,* otherwise known as the Brahimi Report. One segment of the report focused primarily on reform efforts in Kosovo and East Timor, where the United Nations had executive authority to pass new laws. In light of the United Nations' immense difficulties in designating and speedily reforming the applicable laws in both territories, the report recommended the drafting of an interim criminal code to be used in future executive missions where confusion surrounded the applicable law. International personnel, such as United Nations Civilian Police and international judges and prosecutors, could familiarize themselves with the interim code before being deployed and could quickly apply its provisions pending reforms of the domestic legal framework.

The Brahimi Report elicited mixed reactions. While there was support from some quarters, many disagreed with the imposition of an interim code in a post-conflict state, even where the United Nations had law-making powers and where many international actors were working within the post-conflict criminal justice system. Others felt that the recommendation to create an interim code was not relevant, given that another executive mission was unlikely to be mandated in the near future.

In the years that followed the Brahimi Report, although no new executive mission was anticipated, post-conflict criminal law reform remained high on the international rule-of-law agenda. The discussion of the creation of an interim code morphed into a debate on the use of Model Codes as a law reform tool. This idea, which had been broached even before the Brahimi Report appeared, earned the support of the authors of the *Rule of Law and Transitional Justice,* who urged the international community "to eschew one-size-fits-all formulas and the importation of foreign models" and supported the creation of Model Codes as tools to inform a locally led reform process.

## The Evolution of the Model Codes Project

Within a year of publication of the Brahimi Report, the United States Institute of Peace and the Irish Centre for Human Rights launched the Model Codes for Post-Conflict Justice Project (hereafter, the Model Codes Project) to explore the issues the report had raised. The United Nations Office of the High Commissioner for Human Rights and the United Nations Office on Drugs and Crime subsequently joined the project, lending their technical expertise in the development of criminal law provisions designed for post-conflict situations.

The original purpose of the Model Codes Project was to draft a set of interim criminal codes that could be used either in the manner suggested in the Brahimi Report or as a resource in the process of post-conflict law reform generally. In the early days of the project, the main focus was on the former use; over time, however, the project began to concentrate on creating model laws to act as tools in domestic criminal law reform.

Over the next five years, the project brought together some three hundred experts from around the world to develop a set of codes. There were three phases in the process of drafting and consultation. The first phase commenced in late 2001, when a core team of experts—practitioners, lawyers, police officials, military personnel, and academics from different regions and different legal backgrounds—convened to exchange ideas and write early drafts of the codes. Eighteen months later, the group had completed their drafts of the four Model Codes: a criminal code, a code of criminal procedure, a detention act, and a police powers act.

The second phase was a broad consultative process during which the draft codes were vetted by a diverse group of experts from around the world. These experts hailed from the academic and the practitioner communities and included scholars of criminal law, comparative criminal law, international law, international human rights laws, and police law; international and national judges; prosecutors; defense lawyers; police officials; prison officials; human rights advocates; and military lawyers.

The second phase involved individual consultations with experts and fieldwork consultations in places ranging from East Timor, to Kosovo, Liberia, Nepal, and southern Sudan. In addition, consultations were held and presentations were made at various forums in Geneva, New York, Ireland, Vienna, Beijing, Washington D.C., Madrid, Canada, Berlin, and Sweden. Furthermore, a series of regional meetings were held to assess the potential utility of the codes in a regional context and test their compatibility with a variety of different legal systems. An Africa roundtable was held in Abuja, Nigeria, and a follow-on meeting was conducted in London. Asia roundtable meetings were held in Bangkok, Thailand, and Melbourne, Australia. A meeting of Islamic legal experts was convened in Siracusa, Italy. These meetings allowed a very broad range of opinions to be canvassed. (For a full list of individuals and organizations who contributed to the Model Codes Project, see the section "Contributors" near the beginning of this volume.)

In the third phase, a core group of experts collated and considered all the comments and suggestions made on the substantive provisions of the Model Codes. Some recommendations received during the consultation process required substantial changes to the text or the drafting of entirely new provisions. The group also expanded the commentaries based on suggestions received. Thereafter, a final round of expert review was conducted.

The value of the Model Codes as law reform tools derives in large part from the breadth and intensity of the consultation and review process conducted throughout the codes' development. The codes were developed through a rigorous, academically grounded process of research and drafting coupled with a vibrant and open discourse among a broad and diverse community of experts. Considerable comparative analysis, research, and debate went into the drafting of both the provisions and the commentaries.

The result of this process of collaborative drafting, extensive consultation, and thorough review was a set of four integrated Model Codes: the Model Criminal Code, the Model Code of Criminal Procedure, the Model Detention Act, and the Model Police Powers Act. None of these codes is the product of any one legal system or legal culture; to the contrary, each represents a blending of different legal elements, some drawn from international conventions or best-practice principles, others drafted specifically for this project.

# Publication of *Model Codes for Post-Conflict Criminal Justice*

The completed drafts were readied for publication by the United States Institute of Peace Press. It was decided to publish the four codes in three volumes, collectively known as *Model Codes for Post-Conflict Criminal Justice.*

Volume I (published in spring 2007) contains the Model Criminal Code (MCC). The MCC is a criminal code, or penal code, that focuses on substantive criminal law. Substantive criminal law regulates what conduct is deemed to be criminal, general principles of criminal law, the conditions under which a person may be held criminally responsible, and the relevant penalties that apply to a person convicted of a criminal offense. A synopsis of the substantive content of the MCC is presented in chapter 3 of this User's Guide.

Volume II (fall 2007) contains the Model Code of Criminal Procedure, which focuses on procedural criminal law, a body of rules and procedures that govern how a criminal case will be investigated and adjudicated.

Volume III (spring 2008) features both the Model Detention Act and the Model Police Powers Act. The Model Detention Act governs the laws and procedures to be applied by the criminal justice system to persons detained prior to and during a criminal trial, and also those who are convicted of a criminal offense. The Model Police Powers Act sets out relevant powers and duties of the police in the sphere of criminal investigations, in addition to relevant procedures to be followed in investigating criminal offenses. Moreover, the Model Police Powers Act contains additional police powers and duties and the relevant procedures to be followed by police in the maintenance of public order.

# Chapter 2

# Potential Uses of the Model Codes in a Criminal Law Reform Process

## A Tool Tailored to the Specific Needs of Post-Conflict States

A common practice in the process of post-conflict criminal law reform is to look for inspiration in bodies of laws from different states. This approach can significantly expedite the process of law reform and circumvent the need to draft new legal provisions from scratch. That said, a blind transplant of a legal provision from one state to another—without an assessment of whether the foreign legal provision is workable in another context and without consideration of whether the provision fits with the receiving state's culture and legal system—is unwise. But where it is considered appropriate and useful, the laws of other states may be used as the basis of new criminal provisions either by modifying them to fit the local context or by including them wholesale in newly drafted laws. Where an external legal provision is considered inappropriate for inclusion, it might still be useful as a source of inspiration or as a starting point in the drafting of entirely new legal provisions.

A yet more useful tool, however, is a source of law tailored specifically to the particular context of post-conflict criminal law reform. The four codes contained in *Model Codes for Post-Conflict Criminal Justice* are designed to be just such a tool. The term *model* is not meant to imply that a model law is the best or the only option in the criminal law reform process, or indeed that it should be used in whole. Instead, the term *model* is used in the sense of providing a sample law or a useful example. The Model Codes can be used along with any number of other sources in drafting new provisions of criminal law in post-conflict states.

The Model Codes as a potential tool of law reform are not meant to be imposed upon a post-conflict state; they are a tool of assistance and not a tool of imposition. Furthermore, if law reformers do opt to use the Model Codes, they can use them in any number of ways, from a means of sparking debate on one aspect of criminal law reform to the basis for drafting a new provision in a criminal law code.

Throughout the development of *Model Codes for Post-Conflict Criminal Justice,* the drafters asked themselves how the Model Codes could best assist actors working in post-conflict situations. For example, when they chose the sorts of criminal offenses to include in the Special Part of the MCC, the drafters focused not on the full range of criminal offenses found in many countries' criminal codes but instead on serious crimes, including those criminal offenses that occur most commonly in a post-conflict state and those that are often absent from existing criminal laws. Consultations and in-depth research resulted in the creation of a catalog of criminal offenses that reflects the specific needs of actors involved in post-conflict criminal law reform.

Filling the gaps in post-conflict criminal laws requires providing not only broad principles of law and specific legal provisions but also sufficient guidance on how to apply these principles and provisions. A common complaint about the criminal law framework in many post-conflict states, and indeed about newly drafted criminal legislation in post-conflict states, relates to the dearth of such guidance. Such shortcomings lead to confusion in the application of the law and sometimes result in the application of different standards by different actors, each interpreting the provisions in a different way. The need for specific guidance in criminal legislation is especially accentuated in post-conflict states, where criminal justice actors may have fled and criminal justice is often doled out by inexperienced or newly retrained police officers, judges, lawyers, and prison officials.

These oft-heard concerns about the need for clarity and guidance led to a specific style of drafting the Model Codes. First, the codes are drafted in a "plain-English style" that seeks to convey information in as simple and accessible a manner as possible. Obscure legal terms are replaced by more straightforward language without sacrificing the integrity of the text. Not only does this approach make laws more understandable to those applying them, but it also makes the laws more accessible to those to whom they are applied.

Second, the Model Codes are more detailed and prescriptive than most criminal laws. Often, criminal laws and procedures are supplemented by a "statutory instrument," "ancillary legislation," "implementing regulations," or "standard operating procedures" that fill the gaps in the more general text. To provide maximum guidance to criminal justice actors and to help close potential gaps that could lead to confusion or misapplication, the Model Codes contain both legal provisions and commentaries that contain guidance on the practical implementation of those provisions. The commentary to each provision elaborates on the purpose and content of the provision and explains how it should be applied.

These commentaries assist the reader in a number of other ways, too. For example, they explain wording choices. They also highlight other reforms or initiatives that may be necessary if a particular provision is introduced into law. These may include institutional reforms, other criminal law reforms, or reforms of bodies of law outside criminal law. They also provide comparative lessons drawn from other post-conflict cases.

In tailoring the Model Codes for use in post-conflict situations, the drafters were attentive to the fact that the existing criminal law framework in a post-conflict state does not always comply with international human rights norms and standards. In the aftermath of conflict, law reform efforts often focus on replacing old laws with laws that comply with human rights norms and standards. Many experts have cited the difficulty of translating abstract norms of international human rights law into concrete provisions of criminal law. To assist in this translation, the Model Codes have been drafted so as to transform international standards into concrete provisions of law that are compliant with these standards while still taking into account the exigencies of a post-conflict state, such as a lack of resources.

The Model Codes were also drafted to take into account potential cross-cultural application in a variety of settings around the world. As discussed above, a series of regional meetings tested the thesis that the Model Codes could potentially be used universally as a law reform tool. The experts who took part in the meetings supported this thesis, while of course acknowledging that criminal laws should fit the environment in which they are applied. The substantive provisions of the Model Codes were inspired by a variety of international legal systems and legislation. The Model Codes do not follow one particular legal tradition but instead blend legal systems to create a hybrid body of laws—an increasingly common occurrence in many criminal law reform processes.

## A Flexible Tool: Six Scenarios for the Use of the Model Codes

The practical uses of the Model Codes in post-conflict law reform are many and varied. The codes can be helpful to actors engaged in small-scale and ad hoc reforms of discrete sections of the existing criminal law, as well as to actors working on large-scale restructuring of an entire domestic criminal law framework.

In the rest of this chapter, we highlight six scenarios in which the Model Codes could prove a valuable resource:

- A post-conflict state is revising its existing criminal law framework (potentially including its criminal code, criminal procedure code, prisons legislation, and police legislation) to define new criminal offenses and include new tools with which to investigate those crimes and to update its existing criminal laws to replace provisions that do not comply with international human rights norms and standards.
- A post-conflict state is conducting long-term reforms of its entire criminal law framework (including its criminal code, criminal procedure code, prisons legislation, and police legislation) with a view to overhauling and modernizing it and wants to ensure that that legislation complies with international human rights norms and standards.
- Because of deficiencies in a certain segment of its criminal laws, a post-conflict state is drafting a transitional law (for example, a transitional code of criminal procedure) pending more long-term and substantial reforms.
- A post-conflict state has decided to update its criminal laws to adequately protect the rights of women and children, who have been deemed to be vulnerable groups in their society. The existing laws do not adequately address trafficking in persons and sexual offenses, which are being widely perpetrated.

- A post-conflict state that has decided to ratify the Rome Statute of the International Criminal Court is amending its existing legislation and procedures to comply with the various obligations arising from the statute (the introduction of the criminal offenses of genocide, crimes against humanity, and war crimes, for instance).
- A post-conflict state wishes to establish a new special chamber, tribunal, or court to deal with a specific crime problem (for instance, economic crimes, drug crimes, or organized crime) and needs to draft enabling legislation and the substantive and procedural provisions of law that the tribunal will apply.

## Updating Existing Criminal Laws to Include New Criminal Offenses and Investigative Tools

With its justice system shattered after years of conflict, State A is experiencing unprecedented crime problems. Organized crime is rampant. Criminal gangs are involved in everything from money laundering to the trafficking of women from neighboring states to the smuggling of weapons, cars, and drugs over the state's porous borders. The police are well aware of these activities but are unable to effectively combat them because organized crime, money laundering, and trafficking are not offenses set out in the existing penal code, or because existing provisions are inadequate. Even if domestic law contained adequate criminal offenses to cover the conduct of organized criminal gangs, the police and the prosecutorial service would have difficulties investigating these offenses. For example, prosecuting a member of an organized criminal gang involves heavy reliance on witness testimony, but witnesses in trafficking or organized crime cases are often afraid to testify, fearing retribution from criminal gangs. The laws of State A do not have a mechanism for petitioning the courts for protective measures for witnesses. It is also difficult to gather evidence without sufficient means of surveillance—a common tool in investigating organized criminal activities—which are also not provided for in the law.

The scenario outlined above is commonplace in many post-conflict states. The Model Codes help in a number of respects. First, State A needs to enact new laws that make organized crime, trafficking in persons, money laundering, and smuggling criminal offenses; all these offenses are defined in the MCC. The commentaries to the provisions on these offenses contain discussions on other amendments to the law or other institutional arrangements required to effectively combat these crimes. For example, in the case of money laundering, it is essential to make amendments to other bodies of law, such as domestic banking law. Furthermore, the commentaries discuss other practical issues of implementation, such as the setting up of special task forces or special police units to tackle specific serious crimes. The commentaries further highlight the resource implications inherent in enacting such provisions.

State A also needs to modify its criminal procedure law to provide police with adequate investigative powers and tools and to provide adequate witness protection and confidentiality. Such measures hold the potential for impinging on the rights of a suspect or an accused, however, and require a delicate balancing act between these two imperatives. Many experts from dozens of countries were consulted to ensure that the

Model Codes strike this balance and provide sufficient guidance to criminal justice actors who may apply these provisions of the MCC.

## Amending Laws to Comply with International Human Rights Norms and Standards

State B is emerging from a long conflict. Its laws date back to the nineteenth century, preceding the promulgation of international and regional human rights treaties and standards. The transitional legislative assembly wishes to amend its penal code, criminal procedure code, police laws, and prisons laws to comply with human rights standards.

The Model Codes can potentially save the drafters of new laws in State B from having to start from scratch in this process—a process that is both lengthy and research intensive. Drafting the Model Codes involved extensive research to ascertain applicable international human rights norms and standards in the sphere of criminal justice and to translate these standards into concrete provisions of law. In addition, accompanying commentaries discuss relevant human rights norms and standards in greater detail.

Suppose State B wishes to incorporate provisions on the right to challenge the lawfulness of detention (as enshrined in major international and regional human rights treaties). It must implement legal provisions to make the realization of this right practical and effective. In this scenario, it is not enough to include a broad and general principle on this right; a concrete mechanism must be created. In most states, this right is realized through the mechanism of habeas corpus or *amparo*, whereby a person challenges the legality of an arrest or detention. The Model Code of Criminal Procedure contains a number of provisions establishing a habeas corpus procedure to enable a person to challenge the lawfulness of his or her detention. These provisions may prove useful to those involved in reform of State B's laws.

## Creating New Transitional Laws

Laws in State C are sparse. Rather than addressing the needs of the local population and the protection of their rights, the few laws that exist are geared solely toward the criminalization of behavior that was deemed subversive and threatening to the power of the former ruling regime. Prior to the conflict, the military acted as the police force, without reference to any laws. In the aftermath of the conflict, the authorities plan to reform and resize the military and develop a newly trained civilian police force. The authorities face a huge problem: the laws that exist are completely inappropriate for continued application. These laws provide no guidance on what standards and procedures should be followed in the investigation of offenses and the maintenance of public order. The laws contain a few provisions on criminal offenses but do not cover all the criminal conduct currently being perpetrated in State C. The legislative authority has decided to convene a judicial reform commission to enact a provisional criminal code, procedure code, laws on police, and laws on prisons.

The criminal legislation of State D is so closely associated with the prior dictatorial regime that it is politically and popularly discredited. Under public pressure, the legislative assembly in State D has decided to create a provisional penal code and criminal procedure code that will apply until the state possesses the resources to completely overhaul the criminal justice system. The decision is made to create a rudimentary yet viable system of justice that protects the rights of accused persons while dealing with current crime problems. New offenses such as trafficking and smuggling will need to be added to the catalog of offenses contained in the new provisional penal code. Moreover, there is pressure in State D to get the provisional codes drafted and promulgated quickly.

Creating a body of law from scratch is a huge task: definitions of offenses need to be included, general principles of criminal law need to be drafted, and jurisdictional issues need to be addressed, as do issues related to penalties. Detailed procedures on basic investigative functions such as arrest, search of persons, and search of property need to be introduced. Provisions on detention of persons, both before trial and after conviction, need to be addressed, and relevant international standards must be incorporated into legislation. Public order powers may also need particular attention—for example, What procedures should the police follow in the use of force? When can police set up a roadblock? How should officers police public gatherings? Even if only rudimentary procedures and laws are introduced, there are still huge issues to be addressed.

Given that the Model Codes address all aspects of the justice system—criminal law and procedure, police and public order powers, and prisons standards—they may be a useful tool from which to borrow extensively in drafting provisional laws.

## Amending Laws to Adequately Protect Vulnerable Groups

State E is currently experiencing an unprecedented rise in crimes committed against children. The criminal justice system has been greatly weakened by conflict. A legal vacuum, in which criminal elements operate freely, has emerged. Many criminal elements have targeted orphaned children for exploitation. Some of these children have been trafficked out of State E and sold into slavery in other states. Inside State E, many children are being forced into prostitution and used in a child pornography ring. The laws of State E do not contain any offense of child pornography. Nor do they contain the criminal offenses of trafficking in persons or sale of children. State E has laws on prostitution, but they criminalize the person being prostituted rather than the person forcing someone to engage in prostitution. The transitional government in State E is determined to tackle these crime problems.

In addition to removing the domestic provision of law that penalizes children for being prostitutes, State E needs to significantly augment its penal law to include activities such as child pornography, trafficking in children, sale of children, and child prostitution. The MCC contains a chapter on offenses against children that draws upon definitions of offenses contained in pertinent UN conventions.

The law of State F, a state just emerging from conflict, has never adequately addressed criminal offenses against women. Rape was widespread during the conflict and is still widely perpetrated. Sexual slavery is also common. Levels of domestic violence have risen dramatically since the cessation of the conflict. In consultation with local women's groups, the transitional government is seeking to implement a more expansive definition of crimes against women.

Many post-conflict states are deficient in their laws on offenses against women. Often, laws are outdated; definitions have never been introduced or have not been updated to keep pace with modern criminal law standards. Crimes against women, particularly crimes of sexual violence, are a common feature of conflict and often do not stop once a conflict stops. In fact, some post-conflict states have registered an increase in crimes against women in the aftermath of conflict. Many post-conflict states have moved to reform their laws to criminalize acts of violence against women.

The Model Codes may be useful in this sort of law reform process. First, they provide definitions of the criminal offenses of rape, sexual slavery, and domestic violence. In addition, the Model Code of Criminal Procedure contains specific evidentiary rules that protect the victims of sexual violence, in addition to other protection measures for victims testifying at trial. The commentaries to the codes are a key tool in that they provide broader policy recommendations on dealing with criminal offenses such as domestic violence and point to other initiatives, legal and otherwise (such as protection orders), that need to be brought into effect to adequately address the problem.

## Amending Laws to Comply with the Rome Statute of the International Criminal Court

In State G, massive violations of international humanitarian law and international criminal law occurred during the course of a long-running conflict. Both crimes against humanity and war crimes were perpetrated on a large scale. State G is a party to the Rome Statute of the International Criminal Court and, after consultation with its civil society, has decided to prosecute these offenses through its domestic criminal justice system. State G's penal code, however, contains no provisions on crimes against humanity or war crimes. State G knows that, in accordance with Article 17(2) of the Rome Statute, it must ensure that the relevant substantive and procedural laws under which these crimes will be prosecuted comport with "general principles of due process recognized by international law."

The Model Codes may be a source of inspiration for State G. The integration of the substantive offenses of crimes against humanity and war crimes is not a huge task. The Rome Statute, combined with the document entitled *Elements of Crimes* that accompanies the statute, will be sufficient to provide provisions that the state's legislative authority can enact. But cleaning up State G's laws to comply with the "general principles of due process recognized by international law" will be more complicated. The Rome Statute of the International Criminal Court does not set out sufficiently clear guidelines on what is meant by this clause, although it has been interpreted to mean both binding and nonbinding international and regional instruments relating to international human rights standards.

In addition, other requirements of the Rome Statute need to be included in domestic legislation (for example, "command responsibility" as a ground of criminal liability). The Model Codes fully comply with the obligations on states parties to the Rome Statute. The relevant legal provisions have been included in the codes. The accompanying commentaries offer explanatory notes on the provisions and Rome Statute requirements.

## Creating a Special Tribunal to Address Specific Crime Problems

State H has experienced significant organized crime problems, including human and drug trafficking. Instead of prosecuting the crimes through its ordinary criminal justice system, it has decided to set up a special tribunal to prosecute these crimes. It has decided to draft a new set of laws that will apply solely to the special tribunal.

In creating the laws and procedures that will apply to the special tribunal, and to persons detained or imprisoned by the tribunal, State H may look to the Model Codes to ensure that the laws of the special tribunal comply with international human rights norms and standards. The MCC may prove a useful source for the drafting of a statute of the special tribunal, which would need to include provisions on issues such as jurisdiction, statutes of limitation, *ne bis in idem* (double jeopardy), criminal participation, grounds of criminal liability, defenses, and penalties. The Model Detention Act may provide a useful framework for developing a law relating to persons detained and imprisoned by the special tribunal.

* * *

The scenarios presented above illustrate some of the ways in which the Model Codes can be used as a tool for post-conflict criminal law reform. There are, of course, many other ways in which the codes could be useful to a state, whether it wishes to replace or add one provision of law or to overhaul its complete criminal law framework. Many of the examples sketched above are not mutually exclusive; a state usually has more than one purpose in reforming its criminal laws. For example, a state may wish both to combat serious crimes problems and to ensure that its laws comply with international human rights standards and protect the rights of vulnerable groups.

While the Model Codes have been drafted specifically for use in a post-conflict environment, they may be equally usefully employed in the context of a developing state or state in transition that is reforming its criminal law framework. Indeed, the potential use of the Model Codes in these contexts was frequently suggested by the experts who reviewed the codes, particularly those from developing or transitional states who saw how the codes could be employed in criminal law reform efforts in their home states.

# Chapter 3
# A Synopsis of the Model Criminal Code

Substantive criminal law regulates what conduct is deemed to be criminal in a particular state, the conditions under which a person may be held criminally responsible, and the relevant penalties that apply to a person convicted of a criminal offense. In some legal systems, substantive criminal law is a mixture of judge-made law and individual pieces of legislation. However, in a large number of states, it is fully codified and contained in a penal code or criminal code (which may be supplemented by other pieces of legislation).

Substantive criminal law is usually subdivided into a General Part and a Special Part. The General Part of a criminal code contains the general principles and rules of criminal law that apply to the determination of criminal responsibility for a criminal offense and to the determination of any consequential penalties. In some states, and in the MCC, the General Part also deals with the court's jurisdiction over a particular person or course of conduct. Supplementary to the General Part, the Special Part of a criminal code contains a catalog of criminal offenses, divided into different categories or families. The MCC also follows this structure.

## The Model Criminal Code: General Part

### Sections 1 and 2: Definitions and Fundamental Principles

Section 1 of the General Part of the MCC contains a preliminary list of definitions that are applicable throughout the MCC. Section 2 contains two fundamental principles that are applicable not only to the individual but also to the legislature: the scope and purposes of criminal legislation, and the principle of legality.

### Section 3: Jurisdiction

Section 3 addresses jurisdiction of domestic courts, dealing with the issues of territorial, extraterritorial, and universal jurisdiction and of personal jurisdiction. Section 3 defines the scope of jurisdiction over persons by setting a minimum age of criminal responsibility below which a person cannot be brought before a court for the commission of a criminal offense. It further provides that domestic courts have jurisdiction not only over human persons but also over legal persons.

## Section 4: *Ne Bis in Idem*

Section 4 addresses the principle of *ne bis in idem*, or double jeopardy. The principle of double jeopardy, like the principle of legality discussed above, is an international human right. It requires that no person be tried for a criminal offense of which he or she has previously been acquitted or convicted.

## Section 5: Statutory Limitations

Section 5 contains the provisions governing statute of limitations. A statute of limitations acts as a procedural bar to the prosecution of the alleged perpetrator of a crime by setting out specific time limits within which charges must be brought before a court. Section 5 also provides an exemption to the application of the statute of limitations, consistent with international standards, when a person is accused of the criminal offenses of genocide, crimes against humanity, or war crimes.

## Section 6: Time and Place of Commission of a Criminal Offense

To ascertain when a statute of limitations begins to run, it is essential to determine the time at which a criminal offense was committed. In some cases, this is a straightforward question. In other cases (such as a "continuing crime"), it becomes more complex. Section 6 sets out the general principles for determining the time of commission of a criminal offense.

## Section 7: Criminal Offense, Criminal Responsibility, and Commission of a Criminal Offense

Section 7 deals with the core issues of what a criminal offense is and the circumstances under which a person can be found to be criminally responsible for a criminal offense. The MCC provides that a person may be held criminally responsible for a particular criminal offense only where (a) he or she voluntarily committed a course of conduct, by act or omission, that is defined as a criminal offense in the Special Part; (b) did so with the requisite mental state (either intention, recklessness, or negligence as defined in the MCC); and (c) there is no excuse, justification, or other lawful ground excluding criminal responsibility.

## Section 8: Criminal Responsibility of Legal Persons

Section 8 addresses the circumstances under which a legal person may be held criminally responsible. The scope of liability for the commission of criminal offenses is broadened to include legal persons where a criminal offense is committed by any natural person with a management or supervisory role in the company. Such corporate criminal responsibility was once excluded from the ambit of criminal law, but it is increasingly being recognized and introduced into legislation around the world. Where corporate criminal responsibility comes into play under the MCC, both the corporate actor who commits the criminal offense and the legal person as a separate body may simultaneously be held liable for the offense.

## Section 9: Justification and Exclusion of Criminal Responsibility

Where a person is found to have voluntarily committed a certain course of conduct, either through an act or omission, with the requisite mental state, the person will be held criminally responsible only where there was no excuse, justification, or other lawful ground excluding criminal responsibility.

Section 9 contains three generally recognized and agreed-upon grounds of justification: self-defense, necessity, and superior orders (superior orders applying only to the criminal offenses of genocide, crimes against humanity, and war crimes). Section 9 also contains a number of well-recognized excuse defenses, namely, mental incompetence, intoxication, duress, and mistake of fact. Where a person falls under any category of excuse or under any justification defense, he or she may not be held liable for the commission of a criminal offense.

## Sections 10 and 11: Criminal Attempt and Participation in a Criminal Offense

Sections 10 and 11 of the MCC set out the relevant grounds by which a person is taken as having committed a criminal offense through his or her conduct, even though he or she was not necessarily the primary perpetrator of that offense. Section 10 contains provisions on criminal attempt, while Section 11 sets out a number of grounds of participation (additional to a person having committed the offense directly), including participation in a common purpose, ordering, soliciting, inducing, incitement, facilitation, and command responsibility.

## Sections 12 and 13: Penalties and Confiscation of the Proceeds of Crime

Once a person has been declared criminally responsible for his or her conduct, it is for the court to determine the applicable penalty that should be imposed. Section 12 sets forth the range of applicable penalties under the MCC (prison, community service, semiliberty, and so forth) and the process by which a court determines the penalty.

In addition to any penalties that may be imposed upon a person, a person convicted of a criminal offense may be subject to confiscation of the proceeds of criminality, which may include property acquired from the proceeds of crime or income derived from the proceeds of crime. Asset confiscation is an important legal tool that aims to deprive criminals of the fruits of their criminality. The principles underlying the confiscation of the proceeds of crime and property are set out in Section 13, while the accompanying confiscation procedure is dealt with in the Model Code of Criminal Procedure.

### Section 14: Dispositions Applicable to Juveniles and Adults on Trial for Criminal Offenses Committed as Juveniles

Given the vulnerable status of children, international human rights law provides that children who come into contact with the criminal justice system are entitled to special protection and consideration. This provision applies along the entire criminal procedure continuum, and it also applies to the determination of penalties against juveniles. Section 14 gives effect to the international standards on the treatment of juveniles, setting forth the adjudication of disposition applicable to juveniles or to persons who were juveniles at the time they committed criminal offenses.

## The Model Criminal Code: Special Part

The Special Part of the Model Criminal Code is a catalog of 114 separate criminal offenses grouped into 17 specific categories. While comprehensive, the MCC Special Part does not contain every offense usually found in a domestic criminal code. For example, notably absent are the petty offenses, minor crimes, and misdemeanors usually found in domestic legislation or, in some states, in a misdemeanor code. Instead of covering minor offenses, the MCC focuses on serious crimes, especially those that are prevalent in post-conflict states; pose a significant threat, if unchecked, to the process of stabilization and peaceful transition; and are often missing from or inadequately covered in existing penal legislation.

The drafters of the MCC conducted a comparative survey of serious crime problems in post-conflict states and the inadequacies of domestic criminal laws to see which offenses should be included in the code as a matter of priority. Consequently, the MCC addresses such serious crimes as organized crime, money laundering, terrorism, bombing, corruption, drug trafficking, cybercrime, and trafficking in persons. It also covers sexual offenses and gender-based violence, which often plague post-conflict states.

The MCC also covers criminal offenses that international law requires be included in domestic criminal legislation, either as part of the international human rights framework or as part of the international criminal law framework. These offenses include torture, enforced disappearances, child prostitution, child pornography, sale of children, genocide, crimes against humanity, war crimes, terrorist bombing, and financing of terrorism.

The categorization of the criminal offenses in the MCC is determined by "protected interest." For example, criminalizing the offense of unlawful killing is an attempt to protect a person's life and is included under offenses against life and limb. Criminalizing robbery and theft is an attempt to protect a person's property interest, and these crimes are included under offenses against property. There are seventeen categories of offenses in the Special Part of the MCC:

- Genocide, crimes against humanity, and war crimes
- Offenses against life and limb
- Sexual offenses

- Offenses against the rights of persons
- Offenses against children
- Property offenses
- Economic offenses
- Organized crime offenses
- Corruption offenses
- Corruption-related offenses and other offenses involving public officials
- Offenses against the state, public safety, and security
- Offenses against UN and associated personnel
- Offenses involving firearms, ammunition, explosives, and weapons
- Drug offenses
- Election offenses
- Cybercrime offenses
- Offenses against the administration of justice

Each of the offenses contained in the Special Part of the MCC is accompanied by a minimum and a maximum applicable penalty. As in the General Part, each provision is also accompanied by commentary. The commentary explains the origin, meaning, and scope of each criminal offense. It also discusses the offense's prevalence in post-conflict states and its potential destabilizing influence. Where the wording of a criminal offense is derived from an international or regional treaty, this information is highlighted. If the introduction of a specific criminal offense requires additional procedural provisions, institutional reforms (e.g., setting up a special police or investigation unit), or reforms outside the realm of criminal law (e.g., introduction of the criminal offense of money laundering may require significant changes to domestic banking law), the commentary highlights this as well. The commentary also highlights, where appropriate, the resource implications of introducing a particular new criminal offense into domestic criminal law.

# Chapter 4
# Guiding Principles for the Criminal Law Reform Process

Reforming criminal laws in any state is a time-consuming, intensive, and laborious process, requiring institutions and individuals with the requisite skills, expertise, and resources, as well as political will. Often, law reform efforts focus more on the final products than on the process by which laws are drafted. It is a mistake, however, to disregard the modalities of the law reform process as irrelevant. The process is integral to determining whether new laws are viable, practicable, and acceptable both to the general population and to the criminal justice community in the post-conflict state that is expected to apply the laws.

During the preparation of the Model Codes, in-depth research was conducted on the law reform process in post-conflict states, including extensive interviews with both national and international actors involved in past reform efforts. What follows is a summary of key recommendations for future processes, distilled into eight guiding principles.

## 1. Assess the existing laws and criminal justice system

The first step in law reform should be to assess both the applicable legal framework and the criminal justice system. This point may seem self-evident, but it is not unknown in post-conflict states for law reform actors to draft a new law without even checking to see if a law on the same subject already exists.

Assessment of the legal framework involves gathering all applicable laws, which may include the state's constitution, legal codes, legislation, regulations, bylaws, standard operating procedures, relevant and binding precedents, and even executive or presidential edicts or decrees. (For a discussion of exactly what constitutes a state's legal framework, see chapter 3 of Colette Rausch, ed., *Combating Serious Crimes in Postconflict Societies: A Handbook for Policymakers and Practitioners,* published by the United States Institute of Peace.) This task can be far more challenging than one might expect, either because some post-conflict states possess a multitude of contradictory bodies of applicable law or because copies of the existing laws are simply very hard to find (in some instances, researchers have had to look abroad to find a copy of a country's laws). The assessment of the criminal justice system should focus not on the law on paper but on the law in action. Investigators should determine how the criminal justice system is, or is not, functioning in the implementation and application of domestic criminal laws. As part of this effort, it is important to ascertain the types of crimes prevalent in the post-conflict state, so that the legal framework and the criminal justice system can be assessed in light of their respective abilities to tackle current crime problems; this assessment will help to identify which provisions need to be repealed, amended, or replaced and which new provisions need to be added. New provisions are often needed to ensure compliance with international human rights or criminal law treaties to which the state is a signatory. (See the section "Further Reading and Resources" in this volume, pages 421–25, for a list of those treaties.)

The Criminal Justice Reform Unit of the United Nations Office on Drugs and Crime has created a standardized and cross-referenced set of assessment tools for conducting a criminal justice assessment. The Criminal Justice Assessment Toolkit is designed for use both by UN agencies and by outside organizations and governments. Grouped by criminal justice system sectors (police, justice, and prisons), each tool provides a practical and detailed guide to the key issues to be examined and the relevant standards and norms. The toolkit is designed to be used around the world and with a variety of legal traditions and is particularly useful for countries undergoing transition or post-conflict reconstruction. (For details, see "Further Reading and Resources," page 442.)

All relevant actors—for instance, government institutions, national bar associations, faculty members of national law schools, non-governmental and international organizations that have been monitoring human rights abuses, and international legal experts—should be invited to contribute their perspectives on gaps and deficiencies in the legal framework and other impediments to enforcing criminal justice. It is also important to find out attitudes among the local public. Such sociological investigations can be conducted through a variety of means, including holding public meetings or organizing a campaign to solicit written opinions. (See also Principle 6, below.)

In evaluating the effectiveness of the existing legal framework and criminal justice system, it is important to be aware of any customary, nonstate, or traditional systems of justice that may exist in the country and to assess their role in the post-conflict state and their relationship to the state-run criminal justice system.

## 2. Criminal law reform is a holistic enterprise; a change to one part of the law may have side-effects in other parts of the law

Law reform actors must decide whether to work with the law as it is and postpone reform until a comprehensive program of reform can be conducted or engage in a small-scale reform process by pressing ahead immediately with ad hoc and minor reforms to specific elements of the law or reform of discrete segments of the legal framework (in hopes, perhaps, of a more holistic reform being conducted subsequently). Such small-scale, or targeted, reforms are often essential in post-conflict states (for instance, they may be necessary to deal with a particular crime problem that is plaguing the state and is not adequately addressed by existing laws) and, indeed, are conducted on an ongoing basis in many states around the world. However, in a post-conflict context, where the entire criminal law framework is often grossly inadequate, a more holistic reform process may be required in order to be effective. This process should address all criminal law in the state, including the criminal code, the criminal procedure code, prisons laws, and provisions governing police activities.

Where actors choose the small-scale, or targeted, option, they should recognize that making a change in one area of the law usually has side-effects in other areas of the law. In amending existing provisions of law or adding new provisions, reform actors should assess the relationship between new, amended, and existing provisions across the criminal justice continuum and the broader legal framework. For example, changes to criminal procedure laws may have implications for laws on police powers or laws on detention; changes in the criminal code, such as the addition of new criminal offenses, may require changes in criminal procedure laws. The commentary to many provisions in the Model Codes points out the linkage to other provisions elsewhere in the codes that would require a coordinated approach of this sort.

## 3. Coordination of reform efforts is often best entrusted to a single, independent body

Many states have a dedicated, permanent, and independent law reform commission or body tasked with studying existing domestic laws with a view to their systematic development and reform. Law reform commissions have worked effectively and dynamically in many states, providing policy advice to governments or legislatures on areas of law in need of reform or drafting legal provisions or larger pieces of legislation. Where they are independent, impartial, and have the ability to undertake an open, transparent, and inclusive process, law reform commissions are often considered good vehicles to drive fair and effective reform efforts.

If the decision is made to establish a permanent law reform commission in a post-conflict state, a variety of factors need to be considered. For example, new legislation needs to be drafted to establish the commission; budgetary, staffing, and operational plans have to be developed; and provision must be made for the full financing, housing, and outfitting of the commission. Strategic plans should set out the fundamental principles underpinning reform efforts (e.g., openness, inclusiveness, responsiveness, and multidisciplinary approaches) and determine the process by which the law reform commission will undertake its work. A secretariat and a research component of the law reform commission need to be established and staffed, and commissioners need to be appointed.

Where small-scale, rather than large-scale, reform efforts are undertaken in a post-conflict state, the task of coordination may be performed by an ad hoc, non-permanent working group focused on priority law reform in the immediate term. Such an arrangement requires adequate financial support, often including provision for a dedicated secretariat and a research component. Such a working group should be independent, impartial, and adhere to the same fundamental principles as a full-time law reform commission.

## 4. Set realistic time frames for large-scale reform efforts; expect the process to take years, not months

Given the inadequacies of domestic legislation in some post-conflict states, the urge to push ahead quickly with large-scale reform is perfectly understandable. But such urgency can lead to laws being drafted so hastily that, when put into practice, they prove to be unworkable.

Large-scale law reform is an intensive and complex endeavor that requires time—often, five to ten years in the case of a functioning, peacetime legal system to conduct effectively. Post-conflict states that set deadlines of a few months or, at most, a few years for the completion of the entire reform process ignore this fact and, typically, pay the consequences. Given the length of time required, it is essential to prioritize the areas in need of reform and work on the most important first.

## 5. Examine other legal models but take care if engaging in transplantation of laws from one state to another

The transplantation of legal provisions from one legal system to another is not uncommon. Legal drafting frequently involves reference to other models, which can save the drafter from having to reinvent the wheel. The key to whether or not a transplant will be successful, however, is process. Among other factors, careful consideration must be given to local conditions and culture and recourse should be had to a range of different legal models that could potentially be used. Foreign sources of law used in drafting new laws will likely require adaptation for use in the new context.

## 6. The process should be as broad and inclusive as possible

It is important to seek input from a wide range of criminal justice actors: police officers, judges, lawyers, paralegals, prosecutors, prison officials, court administrators, the staff of civil society organizations and victims' groups that focus on criminal justice issues, law professors, and so forth. Some of these actors should have a general knowledge of criminal laws and procedures, police laws, and prison laws, while others should be experts in specific areas such as organized crime or human rights. Many law reform bodies or commissions also engage the services of experts from different disciplines, including sociologists, anthropologists, political scientists, and psychologists.

## 7. Calculate the resource and financial implications of law reforms

Some new criminal laws have significant resource implications. For example, new laws on witness protection may require evidence to be given remotely or videotaped in advance; implementation of new provisions on covert surveillance measures may require the purchase of sophisticated electronic equipment; new laws on prisons may require substantial changes to prisoner registration systems and even infrastructural changes to prisons (such as the creation of separate facilities for juveniles). In some post-conflict states, new laws have not been implemented because of a lack of resources.

The resource implications of new laws should be considered both before and during the drafting process. Among other things, a financial analysis of the projected costs of proposed reforms must be undertaken to enable drafters to weigh the theoretical merits of a new law against its practical viability.

## 8. The law reform process does not end once laws have been enacted

Putting new laws on the books does not necessarily mean that those laws will be implemented. During and after the drafting and adoption of a new law, attention should be focused on its application. Perhaps the most important key to effective implementation is to ensure that criminal justice actors are aware of the new law and to train them in its provisions before they come into effect. Training institutes and universities will also need to adopt their curricula. It is also important to cultivate awareness of their new legal obligations and rights among the general population; public education campaigns are vital in this regard.

Some states have established oversight mechanisms for the implementation of new laws. In some states, a body originally tasked with reforming laws was transformed into implementation/oversight bodies to assess and oversee the application of new laws.

# Model Criminal Code

# Part I
# General Part

# Section 1: Definitions

## Article 1: Definitions

1. *Accused* means a person against whom one or more counts in an indictment have been confirmed in accordance with the Model Code of Criminal Procedure.
2. *Child* means any person under the age of eighteen years.
3. *Convicted person* means a person who has been tried and found criminally responsible in a final court decision.
4. *Evidence* includes all the means by which any alleged matter of fact, the truth of which is submitted to investigation, is established or disproved.
5. *Juvenile* means a child between the ages of twelve and eighteen years.
6. *MCC* means the Model Criminal Code.
7. *MCCP* means the Model Code of Criminal Procedure.
8. *Property* includes property of any description, whether corporeal or incorporeal, movable or immovable, and legal documents or instruments evidencing title to, or interest in, such property.
9. *Public official* means:
   (a) a person who holds a legislative, executive, administrative, or judicial office, whether appointed or elected, whether temporary or permanent, whether paid or unpaid, irrespective of the person's seniority;
   (b) a person who performs a public function, including one for a public agency or public enterprise, or provides a public service as defined under the applicable law; or
   (c) any other person defined as a public official under the applicable law.

10. *State* includes an organized area or entity, such as an autonomous territory or a separate customs territory.
11. *Suspect* means a person against whom there exists a reasonable suspicion of his or her having committed a criminal offense.
12. *Territory* means the land, coastal seas, and water surfaces within the territory of [insert name of state], as well as the air space over these areas.
13. *Victim* means a person against whom a criminal offense has been committed. When a criminal offense is committed against a child, his or her parents or legal guardians are also classified as victims. When the person against whom a criminal offense is committed is killed or incapacitated, his or her spouse, parent, child, brother, sister, grandparent, grandchild, adopted parent, adopted child, adopted brother, adopted sister, adopted grandparent, adopted grandchild, or foster parent is classified as a victim, except if that person is accused of the criminal offense.
14. *Witness* means a person who is summonsed or has relevant knowledge and may be summonsed to testify before a court in the course of criminal proceedings.

## Commentary

Paragraph 1: The terms *accused* and *suspect* are both used throughout *Model Codes for Post-Conflict Criminal Justice* (hereafter, the Model Codes). A suspect is a person against whom there is a reasonable suspicion of him or her having committed a criminal offense, as defined in Paragraph 11. A *suspect* becomes an *accused* when an indictment against him or her is prepared, submitted to the court, and confirmed by it. After the confirmation of the indictment, the accused must stand trial before the court. Reference should be made to Chapter 9, Part 1, and Chapter 10, Part 2, of the MCCP.

Paragraph 2: The definition of the term *child* as contained in Paragraph 2 is taken from Article 1 of the United Nations Convention on the Rights of the Child. It is important to stress the distinction between the terms *child* and *juvenile,* both of which are used throughout the Model Codes. A juvenile falls within the definition of a child (that is, he or she is under the age of eighteen years). However, the term *juvenile* has a distinct meaning for the purposes of asserting jurisdiction over the person. Under the MCC, a court may assert criminal jurisdiction over a juvenile, meaning a child over the age of twelve, but not over a child. Reference should be made to Article 7 of the MCC and its accompanying commentary, which deals with personal jurisdiction over juveniles.

International human rights norms and standards provide that a child (and by necessary implication a juvenile) who is involved in criminal proceedings not only should be afforded the same guarantees and protections as an adult but also is entitled to additional protections on account of his or her vulnerable status. Rule 2(2)(a) of the United Nations Standard Minimum Rules for the Administration of Juvenile Justice specifically provides that a juvenile is a person who is tried "in a manner which is different from an adult." The protective legal framework aimed at safeguarding the rights of children consists of international conventions (e.g., the United Nations Convention on the Rights of the Child and the African Charter on the Rights and Welfare of the Child) and a number of nonbinding instruments (e.g., the United Nations Standard Minimum Rules for the Administration of Juvenile Justice [the Beijing Rules], the United Nations Guidelines for the Protection of Juveniles Deprived of Their Liberty, and the United Nations Guidelines for the Prevention of Juvenile Delinquency [the Riyadh Guidelines]). The drafters of the Model Codes have sought to integrate these international norms and standards applicable to children into the codes' substantive provisions. Reference should be made to Section 14 of the MCC, on juvenile penalties, and Chapter 15 of the MCCP, which specifically deals with the procedural rights of juveniles involved in criminal proceedings.

Paragraph 5: Reference should be made to the commentary to Paragraph 2.

Paragraphs 6 and 7: The Model Codes are a set of four model codes published in three volumes under the title *Model Codes for Post-Conflict Criminal Justice.* The Model Criminal Code and the Model Code of Criminal Procedure make up volumes I and II, respectively; volume III contains a Model Detention Act and a Model Police Powers Act. For a discussion of the origins, aims, and content of the Model Codes, see the User's Guide at the beginning of this volume.

Paragraph 8: The definition of *property* in Paragraph 8 is taken from Article 1(b) of the Council of Europe Convention on Laundering, Search, Seizure and Confiscation of the Proceeds from Crime and on the Financing of Terrorism. The definition is similar to that contained in the United Nations Convention against Transnational Organized Crime, Article 1(d), and the United Nations Convention against Corruption, Article 2(d). The only distinction is the omission of the terms *tangible* and *intangible.* The reason for this exclusion is that *tangible* (meaning property that is detectable with the senses, such as a painting or jewelry) and *intangible* (meaning property that cannot be detected with the senses, such as a claim to a bank account, a stock, or a bond) are already subsumed within the terms *corporeal* and *incorporeal,* which are found in the Council of Europe's definition of property.

Paragraph 9: The definition of *public official* has been taken from Article 2(a) of the United Nations Convention against Corruption, currently the most comprehensive definition of public official in international and regional instruments. This definition is relevant to criminal offenses involving public officials, such as corruption involving a public official (Article 138), and trading in influence (Article 141), to name but a few, and to offenses that may be perpetrated against public officials, such as threat and improper influence (Article 146). Furthermore, the definition of public official is relevant to the prohibition on holding a post as a public official, an additional penalty that may be imposed upon a public official under Article 65.

Paragraph 10: The precise legal definition of the term *state* is a subject of debate among scholars of public international law and is beyond the scope of this work. Paragraph 10 is intended not to provide a definitive statement of what a state is but instead to provide an inclusive definition of the term *state.* The purpose of doing so is to ensure that when the MCC refers to a state, other entities are included. The reform of post-conflict laws may take place outside the context of a recognized state—for example, in Kosovo and in the early stages of the peace operation in East Timor (before East Timor was recognized as an independent state at an international level). In some articles of the Model Codes, it will be obvious to the reader where the term could refer only to a state proper, such as with the signing of extradition treaties mentioned in Chapter 14, Part 2, of the MCCP, a function that may be conducted only by a recognized state. The inclusive definition contained in the MCC is inspired by the commentaries to the Organization for Economic Cooperation and Development's Convention on Combating Bribery of Foreign Public Officials in International Business Transactions, which discuss the scope of the term *foreign country* as defined in Article 1(4)(b) of the convention.

Paragraph 11: Reference should be made to the commentary to Paragraph 1.

Paragraph 12: The definition of *territory* is important in determining whether a state possesses territorial jurisdiction over a criminal offense under Article 4. It is also relevant to the determination of extraterritorial jurisdiction under Article 5. The question of territoriality of coastal seas and air space is one that is regulated by public international law and should be determined on a case-by-case basis. With regard to coastal seas, the generally recognized rule is that the waters 12 nautical miles from the coast of a state are considered part of its territory. A state may have certain rights regarding seas up to 200 nautical miles from its coast as part of an "exclusive economic zone" designated for the purpose of exploitation of resources; the state, however, does not have criminal jurisdiction over these waters.

Paragraph 13: The drafters of the Model Codes originally considered using the definition of *victim* contained in the United Nations Declaration of Basic Principles of Justice for Victims of Crime and Abuse of Power (Principle 1). The declaration defines victims as "persons who, individually or collectively have suffered damage, including physical or mental injury, emotional suffering, economic loss or substantial impairment of their fundamental rights, through acts or omissions that are in violation of criminal law operative within Member States." While this definition is both comprehensive and accurate in terms of defining victimhood in a general sense, it was decided to narrow this definition slightly for the purposes of drafting a legal definition of victim for use in the Model Codes. The intent of the drafters was to create a definition that is practical and workable. The interests of victims are protected throughout the Model Codes (see, for example, Chapter 5 of the MCCP), and the drafters were concerned that such rights should be enforceable in a practical sense. If the definition of victim from the United Nations Declaration of Basic Principles of Justice for Victims of Crime and Abuse of Power were used in the MCC, a broad reading of it would require—for example, in Chapter 8, Part 1, of the MCCP ("Notification of Victims")—that the police make efforts to inform every person in the state who has been personally or collectively affected by a criminal offense of the progress of the criminal proceedings. In theory, this requirement may impose an obligation upon the police to inform large numbers of individual "victims," an impracticable task that may have the adverse result of depriving victims who are more closely related to the criminal offense of their rights. The definition of victim contained in Paragraph 13 was based on a comparative survey of national legislation and the legal definition of the term *victim* contained in that legislation. The definition that was constructed gives both the person against whom the criminal offense was committed and close family members of that person enforceable rights under the MCCP. A partner (meaning a person in a nonmarital committed relationship with the person against whom the criminal offense was committed) has not been included in the definition of victim. A state may wish to consider adding partner to the list of victims. Reference should be made to Chapter 5 and Chapter 8, Part 1, of the MCCP and their accompanying commentaries, which address the rights of victims.

In Articles 12(2), 51(1)(b), 51(2)(f), 51(2)(g), 51(2)(h), 51(2)(i), 97.1, 102.1(3), and 153.1(2) of the MCC, for example, the term *victim* refers only to the person against whom the criminal offense is directly committed.

Paragraph 13 refers to an adopted parent and an adopted child. In some legal systems, it is not possible to "adopt" a child in the sense that the child will take the name of the adoptive parents. Different terminology is used to describe a relationship that is akin to adoption but in which the child maintains his or her family name. In a state that does not recognize adoption, the definition of victim used in domestic legislation should include any relationships that operate similarly to adoption.

Paragraph 14: The definition of the term *witness* in Paragraph 14 is intentionally wide. This is because the drafters did not want to limit the definition of *witness* to persons who will testify during a trial. Persons who provide information on a criminal offense during the investigation of a criminal offense should also be included in the definition of witness.

# Section 2: Fundamental Principles

## Article 2: Purpose and Limits of Criminal Legislation

1. Criminal offenses and penalties must be prescribed only for acts threatening or violating human rights and fundamental freedoms, as well as other rights and social values guaranteed and protected by the constitution of [insert name of state] or international law.
2. Criminal offenses and penalties must be prescribed only where the protection of human rights and fundamental freedoms, as well as other rights and social values guaranteed and protected by the constitution of [insert name of state] or international law, could not be realized without criminal justice compulsion.
3. Criminal offenses, as well as the types and the range of penalties attached to them, must be based upon:
   (a) the necessity for criminal justice compulsion; and
   (b) its proportionality with the degree and nature of the danger against human rights and fundamental freedoms, as well as other rights and social values guaranteed and protected by the constitution of [insert name of state] or international law.

### Commentary

In a post-conflict setting, the general public's view of what the criminal law represents is often shaped by unhappy past experiences, such as the law being used to oppress or discriminate against the local population or to violate the fundamental rights and freedoms of individuals or certain groups. The drafters thus considered it appropriate to commence the MCC with a general affirmative statement of what the purpose of criminal legislation is to be. This statement is a common feature of many criminal codes around the world, and its inclusion is meant to signal a paradigm shift and an affirmative statement of the manner in which the criminal law is to operate in the future. Criminal law should no longer be able to be created at the whim of a government, president, or legislature. It should serve a different and legally defined purpose. The future promulgation of laws by the competent legislative body must be done within the parameters of this article.

The rationale behind the criminal law is a complex philosophical question that has been debated for centuries and is far beyond the scope of the present discussion. Article 2 highlights a number of fundamental aspects of the criminal law that are particularly important to emphasize in the context of a state emerging from conflict or in states that have been ruled by oppressive regimes. First, the criminal law's rationale is to provide a framework to uphold the rights and maintain the security of society at large through the criminalization and penalization of behavior that violates human rights and fundamental freedoms—rights and values that are constitutionally guaranteed and rights that derive from international law.

Second, criminal offenses and penalties must not be prescribed where these rights and values can be realized and protected through other means. The principle of proportionality underlies this provision, meaning that use of the criminal justice system is a measure of last resort and must be based upon necessity. This idea is sometimes known as the principle of minimum criminalization. The requirement that the range of penalties be provided for by law is taken up later in the MCC. Reference should be made to Section 12 of the General Part of the MCC and its accompanying commentary.

Another point of note is that inherent in Article 2 is the notion that criminal law is reflective of the particular society it governs and its mores or social values. Thus the criminal law of each state, while it may be markedly similar to the law of other states, will also have elements that are unique to its particular context.

# Article 3: Principle of Legality

1. Criminal offenses and penalties must be prescribed only by law.
2. No penalty may be imposed upon any person for committing a criminal offense that did not constitute a criminal offense prior to it being committed and for which a penalty was not prescribed by law.
3. Paragraphs 1 and 2 do not prejudice the trial and punishment of any person for any act or omission that, at the time when it was committed, was criminal according to the general principles of law recognized by the community of nations.

4. The definition of *criminal offense* must be strictly construed, and the use of analogy in the interpretation of a criminal offense is prohibited.
5. If the law was amended on one or more occasions after a criminal offense was perpetrated, the law that most favors the accused must be applied.
6. A penalty that is heavier than the one that was applicable at the time a criminal offense was committed may not be imposed upon a person convicted of that offense.

## Commentary

The principle of legality is common to all legal systems and is based on the requirement of certainty of the law. Legal certainty is an inherent element of the general definition of the rule of law. While it is recognized by all legal systems, it is articulated in a different manner in different systems, depending on the legal traditions to which they adhere.

It is relevant to note that in applying the law, there cannot be a total absence of judicial discretion. The MCC, for example, sets down the applicable defenses available to a person who has committed a criminal offense, as required by the legality principle. Article 21, on necessity, sets out the interests that a person can protect by his or her act of necessity, including "other protected interests." This phrase requires judicial interpretation to give it a legal meaning. The distinction between this discretion and the sort of discretion found in systems that have a generally flexible attitude toward judicial discretion, though, is that the discretion is limited and is defined by law, as opposed to being a broad, open, and general one.

Article 3 articulates four elements that constitute the principle of legality: (1) the law must not operate retroactively to prosecute and penalize a person for behavior that was not classed as a criminal offense at the time the behavior was undertaken or where no penalty was prescribed by law; (2) the law must be derived from a legislative act and must be written; (3) the law must be specific and clear; (4) the use of analogy is prohibited (this element includes the principle that where interpretations of the law conflict, they must be read in favor of the accused).

**Paragraphs 1 and 2:** These paragraphs are relatively self-explanatory and proclaim the general principle of legality that criminal offenses and penalties must be prescribed by law that is promulgated by the legislature. These principles are sometimes called *nullum crimen sine lege* (no crime without law) and *nulla poena sine lege* (no punishment without law). They are contained in the constitutions and criminal legislation of many states and are included in international instruments such as the Universal Declaration of Human Rights (Article 11), the International Covenant on Civil and Political Rights (Article 15), the European Convention for the Protection of Human Rights and Fundamental Freedoms (Article 7), the African Charter of Human and Peoples' Rights (Article 7), and the American Convention on Human Rights (Article 9). The principles contained in Paragraphs 1 and 2 provide a guarantee of protection from retroactive or ex post facto laws, meaning that if a certain course of conduct was not contrary to domestic criminal law at the time it was undertaken, then a person who engaged in this conduct cannot subsequently be punished for it. The idea behind this right is that individuals should have adequate notice of what the law is, what their legal rights and obligations are, and what the consequences of their actions are. It also prevents arbitrary use of power by the legislature and is a core component of the rule of law principle.

Criminal offenses must exist either in the criminal code or in another written piece of legislation. This legislation must also set down specific penalties for each criminal offense. Some states declare only maximum penalties for criminal offenses, while other states declare both a minimum and a maximum penalty. Both approaches comply with the principle of legality set out in the MCC. In some states that adopt a more flexible approach to the principle of legality, penalties are often not set out in legislation. This approach was not followed in the MCC. The drafters of the MCC chose to follow a minimum-maximum penalty structure. Reference should be made to Article 38 and its accompanying commentary.

Implicit in the principles set out in Paragraphs 1 and 2 lies the principle of specificity, which holds that legislation on criminal offenses must be drafted clearly and in such a way that a person may ascertain the legality of a particular course of conduct. Legal provisions may not be overexpansive or imprecise. The International Covenant on Civil and Political Rights (Article 15) states that "no one shall be held guilty of any criminal offense on account of any act or omission which did not constitute a criminal offense . . . at the time when it was committed." The same wording is used in the European Convention for the Protection of Human Rights and Fundamental Freedoms (Article 7), the African Charter on Human and Peoples' Rights (Article 7), and the American Convention on Human Rights (Article 9). In interpreting this provision, the European Court of Human Rights held that implicit in this provision was the principle that the law must be clear and certain (*Baskaya and Okcuoglu v. Turkey*, paragraph 39). The court has also declared that a qualitative requirement of this provision is that the law should be accessible and foreseeable. This requirement has implications for a post-conflict environment, where new laws that are promulgated are often not published in local languages or distributed to those who are to apply the law, such as judges, lawyers, prosecutors, and police. During the course of the vetting process for the Model Codes, many experts recounted instances in which laws drafted in the post-conflict period were not even distributed to the judges who were to apply them. To comply with the present article and international standards, efforts should be made to publish the laws, in either an official journal or a collection, in print or electronically. Public notices or awareness campaigns may also be required to inform the local population of any changes in the law.

As regards the point discussed above about the degree of precision required for criminal offenses, while the law must be sufficiently clear and precise, an element of judicial interpretation will always remain. As stated by the European Court of Human Rights, "However clearly drafted a legal provision may be, there is an inevitable element of judicial interpretation. There will always be a need for elucidation of doubtful points or for adaptation to changing circumstances" (*Baskaya and Okcuoglu v. Turkey*, paragraph 39). This need for judicial discretion in interpreting the law is discussed above, in the general commentary to Article 3.

Paragraph 3: There is one exception to the general principle of nonretroactivity set out in Paragraphs 1 and 2. It is contained in Article 15(2) of the International Covenant on Civil and Political Rights, which provides that "[n]othing in this Article shall prejudice the trial and punishment of any person for any act or omission which, at the time when it was committed, was criminal according to the general principles of law recognized by the community of nations." Many commentators have interpreted this provision to mean that the criminal offenses of genocide, crimes against humanity, and war crimes may be prosecuted even if they were not spelled out in national law at the time of their commission because these acts have been recognized as criminal offenses in international criminal law for many years. The definition of *genocide* was recognized in international criminal law with adoption of the 1948 Genocide Convention. The definitions of crimes against humanity and war crimes used in the MCC are based on provisions in the Rome Statute of the International Criminal Court, adopted by general agreement in July 1998. But the definition derived from the Rome Statute of the International Criminal Court itself largely reflects customary international law and "the general principles of law recognized by the community of nations."

When these criminal offenses are prosecuted without recourse to a provision of domestic law, consistent with Paragraph 3, instead of relying on domestic legal provisions, recourse must be made to customary international law as the basis for the prosecution. Just like international conventions, customary international law is recognized as a source of international law (see Article 38 of the Rome Statute of the International Court of Justice). In essence, a norm of customary international law is one that is recognized as general practice by states and that consequently creates obligations among states. To mount a prosecution against a person in the absence of domestic criminal provisions applicable at the time of commission of the criminal offense, the definitions of the criminal offenses of genocide, crimes against humanity, and war crimes must therefore be sourced from customary international law. The definition that should be applied is the one that was recognized under customary international law at the time the criminal offense was committed. Because the definitions of crimes against humanity have evolved considerably since they were first set out in the 1945 London Charter, some care may be necessary in prosecuting cases that occurred before the Statute of the International Criminal Court was adopted to ensure that texts are consistent with customary international law in force at the time. If problems arise, reference for guidance should be made to judgments of the ad hoc tribunals for Rwanda and the former Yugoslavia, to national prosecutions and legislation, to work of authoritative bodies such as the International Law Commission, and to academic commentators.

The prosecution of genocide, crimes against humanity, and war crimes may be undertaken in a post-conflict environment where justice is sought for such criminal offenses through the mechanism of the criminal justice system, even if these categories of crimes were not previously defined in national legislation. In the course of consultation on the MCC, many experts highlighted the fact that the criminal codes of many post-conflict states, such as Liberia and the Democratic Republic of the Congo (DRC), often lacked any provisions defining these criminal offenses. Thus, if prosecutions are to be brought against those accused of committing genocide, crimes against humanity, or war crimes, those prosecutions must be based on customary international law, as discussed above. This rule makes prosecutions much more complicated than those based on provisions of domestic criminal law. In the alternative, a state could introduce legislation criminalizing genocide, crimes against humanity, and war crimes and prosecute these offenses retrospectively under this legislation without violating the principle of legality.

**Paragraph 4:** This paragraph sets forth the "strict construction" principle, a common feature of the principles of interpretation of criminal law in many states. Related to this principle is the ban on the use of analogy, an aspect of the principle of legality. The ban on analogy applies to the interpretation of substantive provisions of law. It also governs the manner in which evidence is assessed through the principle of *in dubeo pro reo*, meaning that where there are doubts relating to evidence, the court should adopt the interpretation most favorable to the accused person.

**Paragraphs 5 and 6:** Related to the ban on the use of analogy is the principle that where interpretations of the law conflict, the one that most favors the accused should be applied. Paragraph 5 sets out this general principle, while Paragraph 6 applies it to the interpretation of penalties.

# Section 3: Jurisdiction

## Article 4: Territorial Jurisdiction

The criminal legislation of [insert name of state] applies to any person who commits a criminal offense within its territory.

### Commentary

Article 4 expresses a principle that is common to all legal systems: criminal laws apply to persons who commit criminal offenses in the territory of a state. This is an undisputable and universally recognized ground of jurisdiction based on the premise that territorial jurisdiction over criminal offenses is an aspect of a state's sovereign powers. Reference should be made to Article 1(12), on the meaning of *territory*, and its accompanying commentary.

The application of this ground of jurisdiction is generally straightforward. However, an issue may arise with regard to the application of territorial jurisdiction in cases in which one element of the criminal offense was committed in one state and another element was committed in another state. In such a case, and according to Article 14 of the MCC ("a criminal offense is committed where one of its elements was committed"), two states may have territorial jurisdiction over a criminal offense. Reference should be made to Article 14 and its accompanying commentary. The *Report on Extraterritorial Criminal Jurisdiction,* drafted by the Council of Europe Select Committee of Experts on Extraterritorial Jurisdiction (page 11), observes that when faced with a scenario like the one just described, "the question is approached from the pragmatic point of view that the actions associated with the principle act form an indivisible whole with that act and that the unity of the offense leads to a unity of jurisdiction and procedure." The report notes that many states resort to such a construction even where both states have a considerable claim to jurisdiction. In addition, the principle of external *ne bis in idem,* or double jeopardy, set out in Article 8 of the MCC, may also act as a control mechanism for such clashes. Reference should be made to Article 8 and its accompanying commentary.

# Article 5: Extraterritorial Jurisdiction

1. The criminal legislation of [insert name of state] also applies:
   (a) to a ship flying the flag of [insert name of state] at the time the criminal offense is committed;
   (b) to an aircraft registered in [insert name of state] while in flight, regardless of its location at the time of commission of a criminal offense;
   (c) with regard to unlawful seizure of aircraft, under Article 149, and unlawful acts against the safety of civil aviation, under Article 150, to an aircraft leased without crew to a lessee who has his or her principal place of business or his or her permanent residence in [insert name of state]; or
   (d) with regard to unlawful seizure of aircraft, under Article 149, and unlawful acts against the safety of civil aviation, under Article 150, to any aircraft on board which the criminal offense of unlawful seizure of aircraft or unlawful acts against civil aviation is committed when the aircraft lands in the territory of [insert name of state] with the alleged perpetrator still on board.
2. The criminal legislation of [insert name of state] applies to any national or any stateless person who has his or her habitual residence in [insert name of state] and commits a criminal offense outside the territory of [insert name of state], where the offense is also criminalized in the second state.
3. The criminal legislation of [insert name of state] applies to any person who commits a criminal offense against a national of [insert name of state] outside the territory, where the offense is also criminalized in the second state.
4. In relation to offenses against internationally protected persons, under Article 152, the criminal legislation of [insert name of state] applies to any person who commits a criminal offense against an internationally protected person, as defined by Article 152(2), who enjoys his or her status by virtue of functions that he or she exercises on behalf of [insert name of state].

## Commentary

Extraterritorial jurisdiction is a much more controversial area of criminal jurisdiction than is territorial jurisdiction. Although many states have introduced criminal legislation providing for extraterritorial criminal jurisdiction, many other states have not. Recent law reforms show a movement toward the inclusion of extraterritorial jurisdiction in domestic criminal legislation, particularly where states are battling transnational criminal offenses such as organized crime, drug trafficking, terrorist acts, and trafficking in persons.

A state asserts extraterritorial criminal jurisdiction over a person when the criminal offense occurs outside of its "territory." Reference should be made to Article 1(12), on the meaning of *territory,* and its accompanying commentary.

For a state to assert extraterritorial jurisdiction, there must be some link between the state and the person who committed the criminal offense, the state and victim, the state and the criminal offense, or, in the case of Paragraph 1, the state and a vessel (an aircraft or ship). As mentioned in the commentary to Article 4, territorial jurisdiction is based on the fact that a state has a sovereign right to prosecute criminal offenses committed in its territory. To justify extraterritorial jurisdiction as a valid ground of jurisdiction, it is vital to demonstrate a link to the state's sovereignty that consequently gives the state a valid interest in prosecuting the criminal offense. In the case of criminal offenses committed by a national of the state (Paragraph 2), the national is considered to be an aspect of the state's sovereignty, and therefore there is enough of a nexus to assert jurisdiction. The same reasoning applies to a situation where a criminal offense is committed against a national of the state (Paragraph 3). Under Paragraph 2 of Article 5, a person who is habitually resident in a state is deemed to have "functional" nationality and is covered in the same manner as a national. The nexus between the vessels discussed in Paragraph 1 and the state's sovereignty is based on the "flag principle," discussed below, under which the vessels flying the flag of a state are considered to be part of that state's sovereignty, although they are technically outside its territory as defined in Article 1(12) of the MCC.

The assertion of extraterritorial jurisdiction will often occur in a situation where two states have jurisdiction over the same criminal offense. This clash may be dealt with in the manner discussed in the commentary to Article 4. The principle of external *ne bis in idem,* set out in Article 8, may also act as a control mechanism for such clashes. Reference should be made to Article 8 and its accompanying commentary.

Articles 5(2) and 5(3) require that the criminal offense for which extraterritorial jurisdiction is asserted is also a criminal offense in the state in which the criminal offense occurred. According to the *Report on Extraterritorial Criminal Jurisdiction* (paragraph 14) drafted by the Council of Europe Select Committee of Experts on Extraterritorial Jurisdiction, this provision is a common feature of legal systems that assert extraterritorial jurisdiction over all criminal offenses.

In the course of drafting the MCC, the drafters considered whether to introduce another ground of extraterritorial jurisdiction, one based on the "security principle." This provides a court with jurisdiction over acts that threaten the security of the state or the population of that state even if they occur outside its territory. The drafters did not include this principle because of reservations as to its validity as a ground of jurisdiction under public international law. Additionally, this ground is somewhat ill defined in terms of meaning and how it would be interpreted and applied in practice. The drafters also considered the "effects principle" as a possible ground of extraterritorial jurisdiction. Under this form of jurisdiction, a state may prosecute a criminal offense based on the injurious effects the offense had on the state. This form of jurisdiction was not included in the MCC for the same reasons that prompted the exclusion of the security principle of jurisdiction.

Paragraph 1: This paragraph sets out the "flag principle" under Paragraphs (a) and (b) and an extended form of the principle under Paragraphs (c) and (d). The flag principle is recognized in numerous international conventions as a ground of extraterritorial jurisdiction that states must assert over the criminal offenses covered in the relevant conventions. The extended form of flag principle jurisdiction found in Paragraphs (c) and (d) is unique to the Convention for the Suppression of Unlawful Seizure of Aircraft, Article 4(1)(c), and the Convention for the Suppression of Unlawful Acts against the Safety of Civil Aviation, Article 5(1)(d), as mandatory grounds of extraterritorial jurisdiction that states parties to both conventions should assert over the criminal offenses of unlawful seizure of aircraft (Article 149) and unlawful acts against the safety of civil aviation (Article 150).

Under the flag principle, criminal jurisdiction may be asserted over offenses committed on board ships or aircraft flying the flag of the state. All states claim jurisdiction over their domestic vessels or aircraft. The only issue that may arise is competing claims of jurisdiction—for example, when a ship flying the flag of one state is sailing in the territorial waters of another state. According to the *Report on Extraterritorial Criminal Jurisdiction* (paragraph 11), drafted by the Council of Europe Select Committee of Experts on Extraterritorial Jurisdiction, "There is no evidence of general international law rules for allocating competence among states, one of whom claims flag jurisdiction." Jurisdiction on the basis of the flag principle is commonly found in many international conventions.

Paragraph 2: Jurisdiction based on the nationality of an offender is commonly called jurisdiction based on the active personality principle. As mentioned above, it is based on the fact that a national is considered an aspect of a state's sovereignty. It is found in a number of domestic criminal codes and also in numerous international conventions. The principle of jurisdiction based on nationality is also found in the Statute of the International Criminal Court, Article 12(2)(b). When a state wishes to comply with its obligation under the statute, it must ensure its domestic legislation asserts jurisdiction based on the nationality of a person, although only with respect to the criminal offenses of genocide, crimes against humanity, and war crimes.

Under the MCC, jurisdiction based on the nationality of the offender applies to both a national and a stateless person who has habitual residence in the state. As mentioned above, persons with habitual residence in a state are deemed to have "functional" nationality and are covered in the same manner as nationals. Specific reference is made in numerous international conventions to the need for states to assert jurisdiction over stateless persons with habitual residence in a state.

Paragraph 3: The ground of jurisdiction provided for in Paragraph 3 is known as passive personality jurisdiction. This means that a state may assert jurisdiction over aliens for acts committed abroad against its nationals. Like the flag principle and jurisdiction based on active personality, this ground of jurisdiction is commonly found in many international conventions.

Paragraph 4: The jurisdiction asserted in Paragraph 4 comes from Article 3 of the Convention for the Protection of Internationally Protected Persons.

# Article 6: Universal Jurisdiction

The criminal legislation of [insert name of state] applies to any person who commits any of the following criminal offenses, regardless of the place of commission:

(a) genocide as defined in Article 86;

(b) crimes against humanity as defined in Article 87;

(c) war crimes as defined in Article 88;

(d) torture as defined in Article 101;

(e) establishing slavery, slavery-like conditions, and forced labor as defined in Article 103; and

(f) piracy as defined in Article 157.

## Commentary

When a state asserts universal jurisdiction over particular criminal offenses, it can prosecute a person for these offenses irrespective of where they took place, who committed them, or whom they were committed against. Universal jurisdiction is a ground of jurisdiction that does not require linkages to the sovereignty of the state in the way that territorial and extraterritorial jurisdiction do (see the commentaries to Articles 4 and 5). In fact, when a state asserts universal jurisdiction over a criminal offense, that offense will not have taken place on the territory of the state. Nor will it have been committed by or against a national of the state or on board a vessel flying the flag of the state. The criminal offenses contained in Article 6 of the MCC are those that are recognized under international criminal law as offenses subject to universal jurisdiction. Their status as criminal offenses subject to universal jurisdiction derives from either conventional (treaty) law or customary international law. For a fuller discussion on universal jurisdiction, reference can be made to the *Princeton Principles on Universal Jurisdiction* and Amnesty International's *14 Principles for the Effective Exercise of Universal Jurisdiction*. Amnesty International has also produced an extensive and detailed briefing paper titled *Legal Memorandum on Universal Jurisdiction*.

# Article 7: Personal Jurisdiction

1. Subject to Paragraph 3, the criminal legislation of [insert name of state] applies to any natural person who commits a criminal offense.
2. Under the conditions set out in Article 19, the criminal legislation of [insert name of state] applies also to any legal person who commits a criminal offense.
3. The criminal legislation of [insert name of state] does not apply to a child who was under the age of twelve at the time of committing a criminal offense.
4. The criminal legislation of [insert name of state] applies to juveniles.

## Commentary

Paragraph 2: In addition to asserting jurisdiction over natural persons, the MCC also applies to legal persons, such as companies and corporations. For a fuller discussion of scope and meaning and of the reasons the drafters included jurisdiction over legal persons in the MCC, reference should be made to Section 8, "Criminal Responsibility of Legal Persons," and its accompanying commentaries.

Paragraph 3: Paragraph 3 provides that a court cannot exercise jurisdiction over a child—a person under the age of eighteen years as defined in Article 1(2) of the MCC—who was under the age of twelve years at the time he or she perpetrated a criminal offense.

Originally, the drafters considered whether or not persons under the age of eighteen years should fall within the jurisdiction of the MCC at all. Some thought they should not and that a system of juvenile justice should be drafted, separately from the Model Codes, to address criminal offenses committed by persons under the age of eighteen years. However, in the course of the consultation process on the Model Codes, many people noted that in post-conflict states that do not have operational juvenile justice systems, and that do not subject juveniles to criminal jurisdiction in "adult" courts, juveniles perpetrate serious criminal offenses for the benefit of organized criminal gangs with impunity. This was the case in post-conflict states such as Afghanistan, Kosovo, and Bosnia and Herzegovina. Moreover, this phenomenon is not restricted to post-conflict countries. UNICEF has reported that in many states children are involved in a wide variety of criminal offenses, including drug distribution and trafficking and firearms offenses (see UNICEF, *Innocenti Digest: Juvenile Justice*). In light of these facts, the drafters decided that it was imperative to include jurisdiction over children in the MCC. This is not to say that children who commit criminal offenses will necessarily end up in prison. The MCCP requires that diversion measures be set up to ensure that, where possible, children do not have to enter the criminal justice system in the first place. If the juvenile enters the criminal justice system, the MCC provides for a range of noncustodial dispositions that can be applied to convicted juveniles. In addition, under the MCC, children under the age of sixteen years cannot be sentenced to imprisonment. Reference should be made to Chapter 15 of the MCCP and Article 85 of the MCC and their accompanying commentaries.

The age of criminal responsibility in the MCC is set at twelve years. International standards on the rights of the child do not define an appropriate age of criminal responsibility that should be followed by states. What is provided, however, according to the Convention on the Rights of the Child, Article 40(3)(a), is that an age of criminal responsibility must be set in the penal law of a state. The United Nations Standard Minimum Rules for the Administration of Juvenile Justice, Article 4(1), qualifies this provision by stating that the age "shall not be fixed at too low an age level, bearing in mind the facts of emotional, mental and intellectual maturity." The official commentary on this provision states:

> The minimum age of criminal responsibility differs widely owing to history and culture. The modern approach would be to consider whether a child can live up to the moral and psychological components of criminal responsibility; that is, whether a child, by virtue of her or his individual discernment and understanding, can be held responsible for essentially anti-social behavior. If the age of criminal responsibility is fixed too low or if there is no lower age limit at all, the notion of criminal responsibility would become meaningless.

The Committee on the Rights of the Child (a body set up under the Convention on the Rights of the Child to monitor state compliance with obligations under the convention) consistently urges states to set the age of criminal responsibility at the highest level possible and has declared that setting the age of criminal responsibility below the age of ten years is unacceptable. This position has been supported by Penal Reform International, which in its *Ten Point Plan for Juvenile Justice* urges states to follow a similar course. The age of criminal responsibility varies from state to state. In some states it is set as low as seven years, while in others it is as high as eighteen years.

After surveying of the age of criminal responsibility set in different states around the world, it was decided to set twelve years as the age at which criminal jurisdiction may be exercised over children. In some legal systems, the law contains rebuttable presumptions regarding criminal responsibility—for example, children below the age of fifteen are deemed not to have the requisite mental element, or mens rea, to commit an offense, but if this presumption can be rebutted by the prosecution where it can prove that the child had the requisite mental element, then a child between the ages of seven and fourteen years will be held criminally responsible. For the sake of certainty and to avoid unnecessary legal proceedings, rebuttable presumptions have not been included in the MCC. While the age of twelve years has been provided for in the MCC, a state should set the age of criminal responsibility in light of the state's specific legal tradition and culture, bearing in mind that the age cannot be set too low. The current trend among states is to raise the age of criminal responsibility in domestic criminal law.

The issue of how to determine the age of a person is dealt with in Chapter 15 of the MCCP. The United Nations Guidelines for Action on Children in the Criminal Justice System, paragraph 12, urges states to ensure the effectiveness of birth registration programs and, where the age of a child involved in the justice system is unknown, to take measures to ensure an "independent and objective" assessment of the true age of the child. In a post-conflict state, it may be the case that adequate birth records are not available, especially in places like Kosovo and East Timor, where the conflict resulted in the destruction of many records. This situation may require significant efforts to draft legislation on birth registration and to fund and establish a system to implement the legislation. It should be borne in mind that in many states children are not registered on their actual birthdates. For example, if the birth registration center is far from a family's home, the parents may wait and then register a number of children at one time—resulting in children having "real" and "official" birthdays. In the absence of documentation and a reliable birth registration system, another method is required to determine age. Where there is no reliable documentation and where police or prosecutors suspect that a person is under the age of twelve years, a qualified medical expert should determine the age, taking into account the child's emotional, mental, and intellectual maturity.

Paragraph 4: Once a child reaches the age of criminal responsibility, he or she is termed a juvenile and is subject to prosecution for any criminal offense he or she is alleged to have committed. A child is a person under the age of eighteen years. A juvenile is a person from age twelve to eighteen years. Reference should be made to the commentary to Article 1(2) for a discussion of the meaning of the term *juvenile* and of international standards regarding the treatment of juveniles in criminal proceedings.

General Note: Where all other grounds of jurisdiction exist to prosecute a person, personal jurisdiction may be excluded by any other legislation on immunity from prosecution that exists in the post-conflict state. The issues of domestic immunity, immunity for foreign officials, and immunity of United Nations and other international personnel, including members of militaries, in relation to criminal offenses committed in a post-conflict state is very relevant to whether the state can assert personal jurisdiction over a person. Prosecutors should be aware of the existence of domestic legislation or agreements that would preclude them from taking a case before the domestic courts. Also, prosecutors may need to look to any relevant status of force agreements (SOFAs) made by a post-conflict state and an international military force serving in the state, any memoranda of understanding (MOUs) between the post-conflict state and an international organization, or even any Security Council resolutions that exempt civilian staff of the organization from the jurisdiction of domestic courts. The MCC does not address the issue of immunity from prosecution. Immunities may exist at a domestic level, where the constitution of a state or another piece of legislation prohibits the criminal prosecution of a monarch, president, ministers, or members of the government or parliament. Diplomatic or consular immunity—that is, immunity for officials of foreign states—may also preclude criminal prosecution in some cases.

In post-conflict states where international personnel are immune from prosecution, for example through immunity granted to United Nations officials, immunity is not always absolute. In the case of the United Nations, for example, under certain conditions, the secretary-general can waive immunity. When immunity is lifted, a person who commits a criminal offense in the host state may be prosecuted for the offense. This has occurred in Kosovo, for example, where immunity for international staff members accused of committing criminal offenses was lifted on the understanding that the cases would be prosecuted and tried by an international prosecutor and an international judge in Kosovo.

The lifting of immunity is less common in relation to criminal offenses committed by a member of the military of a troop-contributing country. This does not mean that military personnel who commit criminal offenses in post-conflict states are never held to account. Many states have legislation that allows them, under military laws or military codes, to prosecute offenses by members of their militaries for crimes committed abroad. The issue of immunity of international personnel for criminal offenses committed in peace operations is a controversial one, especially when the offenses involve sexual exploitation of women and children. The issue is currently being addressed within the United Nations and is the topic of a report by Jordan's permanent representative to the United Nations, Prince Zeid Ra'ad Zeid Al-Hussein, entitled *A Comprehensive Strategy to Eliminate Future Sexual Exploitation and Abuse in United Nations Peacekeeping Operations.*

The area of immunities is a complex one and in-depth research should be conducted when a post-conflict state is considering this issue. One of the most contentious issues is that of immunity from prosecution relating to offenses committed in the context of a conflict by persons who were protected from prosecution by reason of their official capacity. The situation might arise, for example, when a member of a government or parliament is prosecuted in the domestic legal system for offenses committed while he or she was a member of the government or parliament.

The question of whether or not domestic or international immunities apply when prosecuting the offenses of genocide, crimes against humanity, and war crimes is much debated and has been litigated in domestic and international courts. It is especially complicated when the issue is the prosecution of current heads of state or government officials, as was evidenced in case of *Arrest Warrant of 11 April 2000 (Democratic Republic of the Congo v. Belgium)* before the International Court of Justice. A full analysis of the debate is beyond the scope of this work. Reference should be made to the extensive literature and case law on this subject. In the creation of specialized domestic tribunals in the post-conflict states in East Timor and Sierra Leone, the issue has been dealt with by simply declaring no immunities, past or present. In East Timor, for example, where a special panel was established to deal with the criminal offenses of genocide, crimes against humanity, and war crimes, along with other serious offenses, Section 15(2) of UNTAET Regulation 2000/15 on the Establishment of Panels with Exclusive Jurisdiction over Serious Criminal Offenses declared that "immunities or special procedural rules which may attach to the official capacity of a person, whether under national or international law, shall not bar the panels from exercising its jurisdiction over such a person."

# Section 4: *Ne Bis in Idem*

## Article 8: *Ne Bis in Idem* (Double Jeopardy)

A person may not be tried for a criminal offense for which he or she has previously been finally convicted or acquitted, unless the proceedings:

(a) were for the purpose of shielding the person concerned from criminal responsibility; or

(b) were not conducted independently and impartially in accordance with the norms of due process recognized by international law, and were conducted in a manner that, under the circumstances, was inconsistent with an intent to bring the person concerned to justice.

### Commentary

The principle of *ne bis in idem*, also known as double jeopardy, is deemed a constitutional right and a procedural right in the constitutions or the domestic legislation of many states. It is also an internationally protected human right under the International Covenant on Civil and Political Rights, Article 14(7); the American Convention on Human Rights, Article 8(4); and Protocol 7 to the 1950 European Convention for the Protection of Human Rights and Fundamental Freedoms, Article 4(1). The purpose of a provision on *ne bis in idem* is to protect the individual against the arbitrary power of a state and to prevent a state from prosecuting someone for the same offense twice. In addition to being held as a constitutional right and a human right, *ne bis in idem* is sometimes viewed as a procedural defense to a criminal charge (as opposed to the substantive defenses contained in Section 9 of the General Part of the MCC) that bars its prosecution. In other jurisdictions, it is seen as a substantive defense to a criminal charge.

Four issues will be discussed before turning to a discussion of how the *ne bis in idem* principle operates internally (i.e., in a domestic context) versus how it operates externally (i.e., in an international context). They are: (1) What does *ne bis in idem* apply to? (2) To whom does it apply? (3) When does *ne bis in idem* begin to apply? (4) What is the scope of the exceptions to the *ne bis in idem* principle?

As regards question 1, there are variations in state practice. In some states, *ne bis in idem* applies to the historical facts, or a particular set of events. Once a person has been prosecuted for a criminal offense arising from a set of historical facts, he or she cannot be further prosecuted for other criminal offenses arising from the same set of historical facts. This practice accords with the literal meaning of *ne bis in idem*, where *idem* means "circumstances." Of course, a person may be prosecuted for a number of offenses arising from the same historical facts, but this must all be done together and at the same trial and under the same indictment. In systems that look to the historical facts as the determinant of the *ne bis in idem* principle, a distinction is often made between internal and external operation of *ne bis in idem*. While historical facts may govern the application of this principle with regard to domestic trials, externally the criminal offenses are looked at. In this case, when a person has been prosecuted for a particular criminal offense in another state, the first state can prosecute him or her again for a different criminal offense that occurred as part of the same historical episode and still not violate the external *ne bis in idem* principle. In a domestic context, the state could prosecute the person for the criminal offenses only where they were part of a different historical episode.

In other legal systems, and under the MCC, double jeopardy applies, both externally and internally, to a particular criminal offense, not to a historical episode. In this way, if a person is convicted or acquitted of the offense of assault causing serious harm, he or she cannot subsequently be tried for the same offense, whether the first prosecution took place in the state or outside the state, but could be prosecuted for another offense that took place as part of the historical episode at which the offense of assault causing serious harm was allegedly committed. In another example, where a person robs a shop and in doing so shoots the owner, it would not be a breach of Article 8 if he or she were convicted or acquitted of robbery and then later tried for unlawful killing. One issue of note relates to "lesser included offenses," meaning an offense that can give rise to a number of offenses, one of them being the "less serious" of the two. In relation to the "assault causing serious harm" example mentioned above, the person cannot subsequently be tried for the lesser criminal offense of assault as this is the lesser included offense of assault causing serious harm. By the same token, if a person is convicted or acquitted of assault, he or she cannot subsequently be tried for the more serious offense of assault causing serious harm. The legislation in states that apply the *ne bis in idem* principle to criminal offenses, as opposed to a historical set of facts, often contains provisions that limit a prosecutor from instigating separate prosecutions or indictments against the same person for criminal offenses arising from the same historical set of facts when the prosecutor knew of the offenses at the trial of the first offense. A post-conflict state introducing a provision on *ne bis in idem* may choose to include a similar provision in domestic criminal legislation.

Where a person is accused of two criminal offenses arising from the same criminal episode, there is still the possibility of the court ordering that the offenses be tried separately. This order has no effect on the application of *ne bis in idem*. Reference should be made to Chapter 10, Part 1, of the MCCP and its accompanying commentary.

Question 2 relates to whom the *ne bis in idem* applies—namely, does it apply to a legal person where a natural person has already been convicted or acquitted of the same criminal offense, and vice versa? The answer is "no." Under the generally accepted interpretation of the *ne bis in idem* principle, the trial of a natural person for a particular criminal offense does not apply to the subsequent trial of a legal person for the same offense. Equally, the trial of a legal person for a particular criminal offense does not apply to the subsequent trial of a natural person for the same offense. Reference should be made to Article 19(3), which sets out this principle.

The third question of when *ne bis in idem* begins to apply is an important one. The answer depends very much on the criminal procedure law in place in the state, particularly whether the law provides for prosecutorial appeals of final judgments or whether it allows retrials. Reference should be made to the general commentary to Chapter 12 of the MCCP, which discusses different approaches to appeals in different legal systems. The third question relates to the term *finally convicted or acquitted*, a term that has been widely interpreted to mean that all modes of review and appeal have been exhausted and all waiting limits have expired. Appeals, either by the convicted person or by a prosecutor, are not considered a breach of *ne bis in idem*, as they are merely a continuation of the same case. It is the use of the term *finally* that is determinative to when double jeopardy applies. The relevant question is: When are the proceedings considered final and complete? In some jurisdictions, where the prosecutor has no right to appeal after the accused is acquitted or convicted (and he or she has exhausted his or her appeal options), *ne bis in idem* starts to apply. In other jurisdictions, where the prosecution may appeal an acquittal on an error of law or fact and where a retrial can be ordered, just like in the system developed under the MCCP, *ne bis in idem* will apply either when all appeals have been exhausted or when the time limit for appeals has expired. Reference should be made to Chapter 12, Part 1, of the MCCP, which set out the procedures and time limits for filing appeals, and their accompanying commentaries.

Finally, question 4, and the scope of exceptions to *ne bis in idem*, should be considered. In some states, in relation to internal *ne bis in idem*, there is a blanket prohibition on the trial of a person once he or she has been finally convicted or acquitted. This prohibition often leads to discontent among the population, as, for example, when it is clear that the proceedings were not carried out fairly or when they were seen as a sham designed to exonerate a person who clearly committed an offense. Some states allow exceptions to the principle of *ne bis in idem* when the proceedings were a fraud or a sham, such as when the accused bribed the judge. This exception allows the court to look into the substance of the previous case to determine whether another trial for the same criminal offense can go ahead. The MCC allows for an exception to the principle of *ne bis in idem* to preempt a situation involving the unfair application of the principle. The wording of Article 8 is taken from Articles 20(3)(a) and 20 (3)(b) of the Statute of the International Criminal Court.

The provisions of Articles 20(3)(a) and 20(3)(b) of the Statute of the International Criminal Court allow the International Criminal Court to exercise jurisdiction where a person has been previously tried, if the trial was conducted to shield a person from prosecution or was not conducted in an "independent and impartial manner" and was "inconsistent with an intent to bring the person concerned to justice." If a state is party to the statute, this provision will form part of the International Criminal Court's determination of whether to exercise jurisdiction with respect to the criminal offenses within its jurisdiction (genocide, crimes against humanity, and war crimes). In the context of the MCC, this provision governs a domestic court's determination of whether it can legally retry a person for the same criminal offense, notwithstanding the fact that he or she has been "finally acquitted or convicted" of the offense. The notion of shielding contained in Article 8(a) seems to suggest an element of bad faith on the part of the prosecuting state or court (e.g., a state wants to appear to other states to be holding a person accountable for the commission of serious criminal offenses, but in reality the state shields the person by conducting a sham trial designed to exonerate the person). In assessing whether the proceedings were for the purpose of shielding the person concerned from criminal responsibility, the court must look at the totality of the proceedings. When looking at the second qualification to the *ne bis in idem* principle under Article 8(b), the court will have to look to relevant international standards on the independence and impartiality of criminal proceedings contained in conventional law and in nonbinding norms of international law. Reference should be made to Chapter 2, Part 4, of the MCCP, which discuss these norms in greater detail. In addition to finding a lack of independence and impartiality, the court must also find that the proceedings were "inconsistent with an intent to bring the person concerned to justice." As with Article 8(b), the court will be looking for an element of bad faith on the part of the court. It should also assess the totality of the proceedings to make its determination.

Article 8 may not only apply a qualified *ne bis in idem* principle internally but may also apply it externally, meaning in instances in which a person has been finally convicted or acquitted by a court in another state. Many states do not apply the principle of *ne bis in idem* to proceedings conducted outside of their jurisdictions. Additionally, some federal states do not apply this principle to states within the federation. This means that the state, or a state within a federation, will not see the trial of a person for a particular criminal offense in another state as a bar on it prosecuting the person for the same offense. The practice of not applying the principle of *ne bis in idem* is sometimes justified on the basis of "dual sovereignty." In federal states that do not recognize the external application of the *ne bis in idem* principle, a person can be tried at the state level for a criminal offense and also at the federal level. In the context of an issue arising between two states, it would mean that a person could be tried for a criminal offense irrespective of any foreign trial. The lack of total unanimity as to the application of external *ne bis in idem* is evidenced in the Schengen Agreement, which operates between European states. Article 54 recognizes that external *ne bis in idem* applies between states. However, Article 55 allows states to opt out of it. In the realm of international human rights law, under which *ne bis in idem* is protected (as discussed above), the Human Rights Committee (the United Nations body established under Article 28 of the International Covenant on Civil and Political Rights to interpret states parties' adherence to the covenant) has stated that the prohibition of double jeopardy does not apply externally (see *A. P. v. Italy,* case no. 204/1986 of the United Nations Human Rights Committee). In contrast, external *ne bis in idem* is recognized without qualification in the Charter of Fundamental Rights of the European Union (Article 50). Some states have included this unqualified approach in domestic legislation or it has been approved of by their constitutional courts.

The drafters of the MCC are of the view that external *ne bis in idem* should be recognized. Three determinative factors persuaded the drafters to include the external *ne bis in idem* rule in the MCC. First, under the MCC, there are wide grounds for the assertion of territorial, extraterritorial, and universal jurisdiction. Where there is a jurisdictional overlap, it would cause undue hardship to an accused person if the principle of *ne bis in idem* were not recognized as an externally applicable principle. This response to jurisdictional overlap is recognized and supported in the *Princeton Principles on Universal Jurisdiction,* Principle 9, as is the need to qualify this principle. Second, given the breadth of jurisdiction under the MCC, and the inevitable potential for conflicts of jurisdiction, the recognition of *ne bis in idem* at an international level is an important mechanism to control conflicts of jurisdiction. Third, in the context of a post-conflict criminal justice system, which is likely to have severely limited capacity and resources, it would generally be inadvisable to focus those scarce resources on the retrial of a case that had already been credibly prosecuted elsewhere. However as mentioned above, the MCC does not contain a blanket prohibition on the retrial of a person for the same criminal offense where a person has been tried abroad for it but instead qualifies this prohibition on the basis of Paragraphs (a) and (b). Thus the domestic court can look into the substance of the proceedings conducted in the other state to determine whether they fall within the exceptions to *ne bis in idem.* This process is consistent with the provisions of the Statute of the International Criminal Court. It also accords with the position adopted by the United Nations International Law Commission. The International Law Commission has stated that "international law [does] not make it an obligation for States to recognize a criminal judgment handed down in a foreign State" where the proceedings were not conducted impartially, independently, or in a manner designed to shield the accused from international criminal responsibility (UN document A/51/10 1996).

# Section 5: Statutory Limitations

## Article 9: Statutory Limitations for Criminal Prosecution

Except as otherwise provided for in Articles 10–12, the prosecution of a criminal offense is barred after the following periods have elapsed:

(a) thirty years in the case of a criminal offense for which a maximum penalty of thirty years or life imprisonment is prescribed;

(b) twenty-five years in the case of a criminal offense for which a maximum penalty of twenty years or life imprisonment is prescribed;

(c) twenty years in the case of a criminal offense for which a maximum penalty of fifteen years is prescribed;

(d) fifteen years in the case of a criminal offense for which a maximum penalty of ten years is prescribed; and

(e) ten years in the case of a criminal offense for which a maximum penalty of five years is prescribed.

### Commentary

Statutory limitations act as a time constraint upon the court hearing a case concerning a particular criminal offense. After a certain period of time has elapsed, the prosecutor may no longer prosecute the alleged perpetrator of a criminal offense. The primary rationale behind a statute of limitations is to safeguard the suspect against the possibility of prejudice from excessive delays in prosecution. As time progresses, it becomes increasingly difficult for the defense to gather evidence to mount a defense to the criminal charges. The passage of time also makes it equally difficult for the prosecution to gather the evidence necessary to prove a criminal offense. For example, material evidence may have been destroyed or lost and witnesses may no longer be available, especially in post-conflict environments, where residents may have fled the jurisdiction due to the conflict and where records may have been destroyed in the course of the conflict. Another rationale in support of limitation periods stems from the theory that the passage of time lessens the justification for prosecution, since the victim, relatives, and society may have moved on and reconciled themselves with the wrongs of the past. Therefore, opening things up may do more harm than good.

Under the MCC, and generally under the domestic criminal legislation in many states, the more serious the criminal offense, the more time is granted to prosecute a person for it. The need for a state to ensure long statutory limitation periods for more serious offenses is also recognized in a number of international conventions, such as the United Nations Convention against Transnational Organized Crime, Article 11(5); the United Nations Convention against Illicit Traffic in Narcotic Drugs and Psychotropic Substances, Article 3(8); and the United Nations Convention against Corruption, Article 29. The particular limitation periods set out in Article 9 were arrived at following a comparative study of the statutory limitations in various states and taking into account international obligations relating to statutory limitations contained in the international conventions mentioned above.

Although not provided for in the MCC, some legal systems also provide for statutory limitations on the enforcement of punishments, whereby the imposed punishment cannot be carried out after a designated period has elapsed.

It should be noted that in some legal systems there are no statutory limitations. A number of Islamic legal experts consulted while the Model Codes were being vetted pointed out that in some states domestic legislation does not provide for statutory limitations.

The limitation periods in Article 9 are fixed. The periods can be extended only where the statutory limitations can be lawfully suspended for a certain period of time under Article 12. In practice, therefore, the period between completion of a criminal offense and prosecution for the offense may be longer than the applicable period set out in Article 9. Reference should be made to Article 12 and its accompanying commentary.

# Article 10: Statutory Limitations Applicable to an Adult for Criminal Offenses Committed as a Juvenile

1. Article 9 does not apply to a person over the age of twenty-one years who allegedly committed a criminal offense when he or she was under the age of sixteen years.

2. Article 9 does not apply to a person between the ages of eighteen years and twenty-one years who has allegedly committed a criminal offense, except for:
   (a) a criminal offense committed when he or she was over the age of sixteen years and under the age of eighteen years; or
   (b) a criminal offense with a minimum penalty of two years' imprisonment that was committed when he or she was under the age of sixteen years.

## Commentary

Article 10 operates to exclude the operation of Article 9 in certain circumstances outlined in Paragraphs 1 and 2, barring the prosecution of persons for criminal offenses committed as juveniles in some cases. A comparative survey of criminal codes and criminal legislation from different states found that this provision was a feature of domestic criminal laws in many jurisdictions where statutory limitation of criminal offenses is recognized.

# Article 11: Nonapplicability of Statutory Limitations to Genocide, Crimes against Humanity, and War Crimes

Genocide, crimes against humanity, and war crimes are not subject to any statutory limitations.

## Commentary

In contrast to other criminal offenses in the Special Part of the MCC, the offenses of genocide, crimes against humanity, and war crimes are not subject to statutory limitation periods. This means that a person can be prosecuted at any time after the alleged commission of the criminal offense. The approach taken in the MCC follows that of the Rome Statute of the International Criminal Court (Article 29) and many criminal codes, all of which exclude limitation periods for these particular criminal offenses. This approach is also consistent with the Convention on the Non-Applicability of Statutory Limitations to War Crimes and Crimes against Humanity (1970) and the European Convention on the Non-Applicability of Statutory Limitations to Crimes against Humanity and War Crimes (1974). The rationale behind the prohibition on statutory limitations for crimes against humanity and war crimes, as set out in the preamble to the Convention on the Non-Applicability of Statutory Limitations to War Crimes and

Crimes against Humanity, is that providing limitation periods for "the gravest crimes under international law" prevents their prosecution, which is an important element in preventing their future perpetration and in protecting human rights and fundamental freedoms.

# Article 12: Running and Suspension of Statutory Limitations

1. The statutory limitation period begins to run from the day on which the criminal offense is completed.
2. Where a criminal offense was committed against a person when the victim was a child, the statute of limitations does not begin to run until the person reaches the age of eighteen years.
3. The statutory limitation period may be suspended when:
   (a) the prosecutor has formally suspended the investigation under the MCCP;
   (b) the suspect or the accused has evaded the administration of justice;
   (c) a request to obtain evidence located in a foreign jurisdiction is pending before a foreign court or authority, under Chapter 14, Part 1, of the MCCP; or
   (d) other valid grounds bar the prosecution of the criminal offense.
4. The statutory limitation period recommences from the beginning if the perpetrator commits an equally grave or graver criminal offense before the statutory limitation period has expired.

## Commentary

Paragraph 1: This paragraph presents no difficulty when a criminal offense is perpetrated through an act or a series of acts that culminate at a certain period in time. The difficulty may arise when an offense is a "continuing offense." The question of when the offense was committed then arises. In many jurisdictions, the statute of limitations does not begin to run until the criminal conduct in its totality has ceased. This is the approach most favored by the drafters of the MCC.

Paragraph 2: The "freezing" of the statute of limitations with respect to a criminal offense committed against a person under the age of eighteen years is a common feature of domestic criminal law in many states.

**Paragraph 3:** It is a universal feature of states that possess statutory limitation periods that there are statutorily defined circumstances in which the period can be suspended temporarily. In some systems, this process is called tolling. The MCC defines four instances in which the statute of limitations should be suspended: when the prosecutor has suspended the investigation; when the perpetrator has evaded the administration of justice; when a request for evidence abroad is pending; and when "other valid grounds bar the prosecution of the criminal offense." Evading the administration of justice means that a person has left his or her home and has concealed himself or herself to avoid punishment. The person does not have to leave the jurisdiction or the territory in order to evade justice. The fourth ground upon which the statutory limitations can be suspended, under Paragraph 3(d), is more open-ended and is subject to judicial interpretation. Such a provision could include, for example, an instance in which prosecution of a person is impossible for a period of time because he or she possess certain immunities or other privileges that preclude it.

# Section 6: Time and Place of Commission of a Criminal Offense

## Article 13: Time of Commission of a Criminal Offense

A criminal offense is committed at the time the perpetrator acts or ought to have acted, irrespective of when the consequences of his or her action or omission to act occurred.

### Commentary

The time at which a criminal offense was committed is relevant to the running of the statutory limitations that relates to that offense. Reference should be made to Article 9 on the applicable statutory limitations for different criminal offenses and to the remainder of Section 5 (Articles 10–12). It is clear from Article 13 that it is the action or inaction of the perpetrator of the criminal offense that is determinative of the time of the commission of a criminal offense, rather than the time when the consequences of the action or inaction occurred.

## Article 14: Place of Commission of a Criminal Offense

1. A criminal offense is committed where one of its elements was committed. The place of commission may be both:

(a) the place where the perpetrator acts or ought to have acted; and

(b) the place where the consequences of the perpetrator's action or omission to act, fully or partially, occurs.

2. In the case of an attempted criminal offense, the offense is committed both:

   (a) at the place where the perpetrator acts or ought to have acted; and

   (b) at the place where the consequences of the perpetrator's action or omission to act, fully or partially, ought to have occurred according to his or her expectations.

## Commentary

Article 14 is relevant to the question of territorial or extraterritorial jurisdiction, as the place where a criminal offense occurred will, by necessity, determine which state has jurisdiction to prosecute the perpetrator. Reference should be made to Article 4 ("Territorial Jurisdiction") and Article 5 ("Extraterritorial Jurisdiction") and their accompanying commentaries.

# Section 7: Criminal Offense, Criminal Responsibility, and Commission of a Criminal Offense

## Article 15: Criminal Offense

A criminal offense is an unlawful act:

(a) that is prescribed as a criminal offense by law;

(b) whose characteristics are specified by law; and

(c) for which a penalty is prescribed by law.

### Commentary

This provision reiterates some of the aspects of the principle of legality and others relating to the purposes and limits of criminal legislation. Reference should be made to Article 2 ("Purpose and Limits of Criminal Legislation") and Article 3 ("Principle of Legality") and their accompanying commentaries.

## Article 16: Criminal Responsibility

A person who commits a criminal offense is criminally responsible if:

(a) he or she commits a criminal offense, as defined under Article 15, with intention, recklessness, or negligence as defined in Article 18;

(b) no lawful justification exists under Articles 20–22 of the MCC for the commission of the criminal offense;

(c) there are no grounds excluding criminal responsibility for the commission of the criminal offense under Articles 23–26 of the MCC; and

(d) there are no other statutorily defined grounds excluding criminal responsibility.

## Commentary

When a person is found criminally responsible for the commission of a criminal offense, he or she can be convicted of this offense, and a penalty or penalties may be imposed upon him or her as provided for in the MCC.

Article 16 lays down the elements required for a finding of criminal responsibility against a person. A court that is assessing the criminal responsibility of a person must address the following issues:

- Whether the criminal offense was "committed," referring to physical elements that will be set out in its definition in the Special Part of the MCC and also referring to the voluntariness of the physical acts as set out in Article 17. Reference should be made to Article 17 and its accompanying commentary.
- Whether the accused has the requisite mental element for the commission of the criminal offense, meaning: Did he or she intend to commit it? In cases where the MCC specifies that the offense can be committed through recklessness or negligence, the issue is whether the accused acted either recklessly or negligently as defined by the MCC. Reference should be made to Article 18 and its accompanying commentary. At this stage, any "specific" or "special" intention requirements or knowledge requirements that may form part of the elements of the criminal offense should be assessed. This issue is discussed in greater detail in the commentary to Article 18.
- Whether there were any justifications for the conduct of the accused person, meaning that he or she may satisfy the two criteria laid out above but still may escape criminal responsibility because he or she has a valid defense to the commission of the criminal offense. Justification defenses are those where what was clearly criminal conduct is deemed not to be so because the circumstances make the conduct socially acceptable in some way. For a detailed discussion of justification defenses, reference should be made to Articles 20–22 and their accompanying commentaries, in addition to the general commentary to Section 9 of the General Part of the MCC.
- As with lawful justifications, if a person's conduct falls within any of the grounds for excluding criminal responsibility set out in the MCC, he or she may escape criminal responsibility. Defenses based on exclusion of criminal responsibility excuse a person from moral blame even when his or her conduct was criminal, such as when his or her conduct was not voluntary or when he or she did not

have the capacity to commit the criminal offense. For a detailed discussion of grounds of exclusion of criminal responsibility, reference should be made to Articles 23–26 and their accompanying commentaries, in addition to the general commentary to Section 9 of the General Part of the MCC.

- Whether there are other lawful grounds that make the particular act a noncriminal one. To ascertain this situation, the court may have to look to other pieces of legislation. For instance, legislation such as a police act may provide the police with the authority to use force under certain circumstances and not be held criminally responsible.

Reference should be made to annex 1, which sets out the process of evaluating criminal responsibility in a diagrammatic format.

# Article 17: Commission of a Criminal Offense

1. A criminal offense may be committed by either an omission to act or a voluntary act.
2. A criminal offense is committed by an omission to act only where the perpetrator has an obligation to act but fails to do so.
3. A criminal offense may be committed by an individual, jointly with or through another person, regardless of whether that other person is criminally responsible.

## Commentary

**Paragraph 1:** Common to all legal systems is the principle that a criminal offense can be committed either through a positive act or alternatively through a failure to act—that is, an omission. Another integral element of a criminal offense is that it must be committed voluntarily. The term *voluntary* is difficult to define and thus will be subject to judicial interpretation on a case-by-case basis to determine its scope. Examples excluded from the ambit of voluntary action include involuntary body movement (i.e., a reflex or convulsion) and acts committed while unconscious, asleep or sleepwalking, or in a hypnotic trance.

**Paragraph 2:** The instances in which a person can be held liable for a failure to act differ from state to state. In some states, the inclusion of a criminal offense of "failure to assist a person in danger" creates a positive legal obligation. In other states, there is no such obligation to assist. Ultimately, liability for omissions to act is really a question of policy. In many legal systems, and under the MCC, liability for omissions will be found in the positive criminal law as part of the elements of the substantive criminal offense.

Paragraph 3: Paragraph 3 broadly articulates the grounds of participation in a criminal offense as set out in Section 11 of the MCC. The wording is derived from Article 25(2) of the Rome Statute of the International Criminal Court. Reference should be made to Section 11 and its accompanying commentaries, where the grounds of participation are dealt with in greater detail. This paragraph also states clearly that criminal liability of persons who participated in the criminal offense is not dependent on the criminal liability of the primary perpetrator.

# Article 18: Intention, Recklessness, and Negligence

1. A person acts intentionally when he or she acts purposely or knowingly.
2. A person acts recklessly when he or she takes a risk that is objectively unjustifiable having regard to the circumstances known to the person.
3. A person acts negligently when he or she, unaware of any risk, takes a risk that is objectively unjustifiable having regard to the circumstances known to the person.
4. A person must not be held criminally responsible for a criminal offense on the basis of recklessness and negligence, unless specifically provided for in the MCC.
5. When the commission of a criminal offense resulted in a consequence that exceeded the intent of the perpetrator, he or she is criminally responsible for that consequence only when he or she acted recklessly or negligently in relation to the consequence.

## Commentary

Article 18 deals with the mental element required for the commission of a criminal offense, sometimes referred to as the mens rea ("guilty mind"). The principle of mens rea is recognized as one of the prerequisites to ascribing criminal responsibility to a person for the commission of a criminal offense. This means that criminal responsibility may be established only if a person is sufficiently aware of acts and the consequences of acts. The basis for requiring that the mental element of a criminal offense be proven is the principle of autonomy and the assumption of a capacity to make choices between various options to act. The basis of criminal responsibility therefore lies in conscious decision making. To establish criminal responsibility, the act (and its consequences) must be the result of a (voluntary or free and conscious) decision. Mens rea also encompasses the "belief principle." According to this principle, persons should be judged only on the basis of what they believed they were doing, not on the consequences of their acts.

There is considerable divergence among states in how the mental element required for a criminal offense is expressed in domestic legislation. In essence, the laws of most states are similar in scope, meaning they criminalize the same forms of mental elements, but the nomenclature—or how the different aspects of the mental element are categorized—differs. This is true even among states that share a common legal tradition. In essence, there are four main concepts of the mental element of a criminal offense: purposefulness, intention, recklessness (or willful blindness), and negligence. The differences and similarities between states in terms of specific aspects of the mental element of a criminal offense will be discussed in more detail below. The wording of Article 18 was arrived at after an extensive comparative survey of the criminal legislation of many states around the world. A study was also made of the legal doctrine and case law that has built up around these concepts. At one stage, Article 30 from the Rome Statute of the International Criminal Court was considered for use in the MCC. However, this provision seemed confusing and unclear to the drafters and to the many experts who reviewed it. The categorization that was finally decided upon was chosen for its simplicity, brevity, and potential ease of application and understanding. To understand the meaning of the terms *intention, recklessness,* and *negligence* in the context of the MCC, a reader must suspend any preexisting conceptions and look beyond the definitions of those terms that he or she is familiar with in his or her own system and examine the precise meaning ascribed to them under the MCC.

The two main approaches taken in different legal systems will be discussed separately below. This discussion is important as it forms the background for the discussion on the substance of Article 18. It is worth noting that this is a general discussion based on legal systems that were reviewed during the drafting of the MCC; it does not presume to be an exhaustive analysis.

*Legal Systems That Categorize the Mental Element of a Criminal Offense as Intention (Including Purposefulness), Recklessness, or Negligence.* In systems wherein the concepts of intention, recklessness, and negligence are employed, intention can be *direct* or *indirect* (sometimes called *oblique* intention). Direct intention means that a person desires to bring about a particular consequence and that he or she does his or her best to do so. In this case, the person has volition, or will, to bring about this consequence.

Indirect or oblique intention means that a person sees that a consequence is virtually certain, although he or she does not desire it, but nonetheless goes ahead with the course of conduct. The person takes a deliberate action but a consequence that he or she does not desire occurs. While direct intention is premised on the basis of volition with regard to the particular consequence, indirect intention is premised on the basis of cognition, or awareness, of the consequence. In relation to this consequence of indirect intention, it is important that the person sees it as virtually certain. It is not enough that it is highly probable. Where there is a high probability of a particular consequence happening, the discussion moves out of the realm of intention and into that of recklessness. In some jurisdictions, legislation makes specific reference to the fact that the court must not make inferences or presume that the person intended the natural and probable consequences of his or her actions. The legislation emphasizes that even if the consequences of a person's action may be objectively deemed to be the natural and probable consequences of his or her action, a person cannot be deemed to intend these consequences unless he or she possessed the cognition that the consequences were virtually certain.

In the case of recklessness, a person does not have the volition to bring about a particular result; he or she has cognition, just as with indirect intention. However, the level of cognition required for recklessness differs from that of intention. Recklessness does not require virtual certainty; "high probability" is enough. The essence of recklessness is that a person takes an unjustified risk. The question that has been answered differently in legal systems is this: By what standard is recklessness judged? In some systems, a subjective standard has been used, meaning the court will look at the accused person's state of mind vis-à-vis the particular consequence. In other systems, an objective standard is employed. In employing this objective standard in some jurisdictions, the test requires that the accused person did not consider the consequences of his or her actions and took an objectively unjustifiable risk. This objective approach has been criticized for leaving a significant loophole, so that where the accused did in fact consider the consequences of his or her action but carried on nonetheless, he or she cannot be held liable under the definition of recklessness. In some other systems, a mixture of the objective and subjective is employed. Thus recklessness will be found where the accused person knew about an objectively unjustifiable risk, which he or she took anyway. In short, in systems with the same categorization of intention, recklessness, and negligence, there is no commonly held view as to the precise parameters of recklessness.

The scope of negligence is easier to define. While recklessness requires an awareness of a risk, negligence does not. Negligence requires that a person, unaware of any consequences, take a course of action that falls below the objective standard that would be expected of a "reasonable person" or a "law-abiding citizen." This form of liability is completely objective and based upon objective standards that are independent of any subjective desires or beliefs of the accused person. A person is penalized because he or she *should* have been aware of the risks involved in his or her conduct. Relatively few criminal offenses are defined in terms of negligence. The most common are traffic offenses and environmental offenses.

*Legal Systems That Categorize the Mental Element of a Criminal Offense as Intention and Negligence.* Some legal systems use the term *intention* to define the mental element of both intention and recklessness, as defined above. The term *negligence* as used in these systems can also have a broader definition than *negligence* as discussed above. Intention can be classified as *direct intention (dolus directus)* or *indirect intention (dolus indirectus)*, or, alternatively, as *direct intention in the first degree* (equivalent to direct intention) or *direct intention in the second degree* (equivalent to indirect intention). In addition to these grounds of intention, there is an additional one called *eventual intent (dolus eventualis)*. Direct intention, or direct intention in the first degree, requires volition, or will. In such cases, indirect intention, or direct intention in the second degree, requires cognition or knowledge, rather than volition, or will. The degree of cognition held by the perpetrator under indirect intention must be such that he or she knows or foresees with absolute certainty that his or her act will have a particular consequence.

Eventual intent requires an element of cognition, albeit a much lesser degree of cognition than required under the principle of indirect intention. The concept of eventual intent is similar in many ways to the concept of recklessness used in the systems mentioned above. Just as in these systems, wherein there is dispute about the meaning of recklessness, so too is there dispute in relation to the precise meaning of eventual intent. It is clear that some element of cognition is required; the debate centers on what level of cognition will suffice. Some would say the accused needs to be aware of the consequences and accept the possibility of them occurring, while others would say indifference to the consequences or an appraisal of the possibility of those consequences occurring would suffice. The latter classification of eventual intent overlaps considerably with the concept of negligence as defined in these systems. Negligence is often classified as "conscious" or "unconscious" negligence. Conscious negligence, similar to eventual intent, requires that the accused considered the possibility of certain consequences but thought they would not occur. Unconscious negligence is identical to the sort of negligence discussed above in relation to the other legal systems, requiring that a person fall below an objective standard of behavior.

The discussion will now move to Article 18 of the MCC and its substance, in light of the background provided in the comparative appraisal of the mental element in different systems. But first, two issues of note should be mentioned. First, many legal systems also provide for "strict liability" offenses, where a person may be found criminally responsible irrespective of intention, recklessness, or negligence. This form of mental element is not contained in the MCC. Second, some offenses contained in the MCC have additional intention requirements, sometimes referred to as special intention, specific intention, or *dolus specialis.* A good example is the criminal offense of genocide under Article 86, which requires the intention to destroy, in whole or in part, a member of a national, ethnic, religious, or racial group. This specific intention must be proven, in addition to general intention, before a person can be held criminally liable. Some other offenses, such as crimes against humanity, also contain additional knowledge requirements under Article 87. Under this offense, it is necessary to prove that the perpetrator had knowledge of a widespread or systematic attack directed against a civilian population. These added intention or knowledge requirements should be looked at in the process of assessing criminal responsibility and should be considered at the stage of assessing the mental element required for the offense.

Paragraph 1: The concept of intention used in the MCC covers the concepts of both direct intention and indirect intention, as discussed above. The term *purposely* relates to the volition of a person in carrying out a course of conduct, meaning the person desires to bring about a particular consequence, and he or she does his or her best to do so. The term *knowingly* refers to a person's cognition, meaning a person sees that a consequence is virtually certain, although he or she does not desire it, but nonetheless goes ahead with the course of conduct. As mentioned earlier, there should be a practical or virtual certainty that the consequence will occur. The determination of whether a person acts "purposely" or "knowingly" is based on a subjective test of the person's mental state and not on any objective standards of expected behavior.

Paragraph 2: The MCC has adopted an approach that includes recklessness as a ground for criminal liability rather than a categorization based on direct intention, indirect intention, and eventual intention. Direct and indirect intention are covered in Paragraph 1. Paragraph 2 covers what is known as recklessness or, in other systems, eventual intention or *dolus eventualis*. Recklessness involves cognition of a risk by a person, who nonetheless goes ahead and takes the unjustifiable risk. The cognitive element required for recklessness is less than that required for indirect intention; the probability or the possibility that the consequences will occur could suffice for a finding of recklessness by a court. Under Paragraph 2, indifference to the consequences would also suffice to fulfill the criteria for recklessness. As mentioned earlier, in many legal systems there is considerable disagreement and uncertainty as to the scope of recklessness or its equivalent, *dolus eventualis*. The MCC takes a mixed subjective-objective approach to recklessness. The intention of the drafters was to create a compromise position between a strictly objective test and a strictly subjective one, relating to all levels of knowledge of the person who carried out the criminal offense. Thus it covers the concept of conscious negligence, discussed above.

Paragraph 3: The definition of negligence employed in Paragraph 3 relates solely to a situation in which the person who commits a criminal offense is unaware of the potential consequences of his or her conduct in a situation where he or she should have been aware (i.e., he or she took an objective, unjustifiable risk). The person has neither cognition nor volition, as required in Paragraphs 1 and 2. Despite the test for negligence being objective, account will be taken of the subjective circumstances known to the person at the time. Thus the court is appraising whether the risk was objectively unjustifiable for a person in the subjective position of the alleged perpetrator at the time the criminal offense was committed.

Paragraph 4: There is a presumption in criminal law that offenses are committed intentionally. If a person is liable for the reckless or negligent commission of a criminal offense, this must be specified in legislation. In relation to specific criminal offenses, reference should be made to the individual provisions of the Special Part of the MCC. Reference should also be made to Article 19(2) and its accompanying commentary, which provide that a legal person is liable for the negligent commission of criminal offenses in certain circumstances. Another form of liability for negligent conduct is found in Article 32, "Responsibility of Commanders and Other Superiors for the Criminal Offenses of Genocide, Crimes against Humanity, and War Crimes." Reference should be made to Article 32 and its accompanying commentary.

Paragraph 5: Paragraph 5 articulates the principle that when a person acts intentionally (through either direct or indirect intention), he or she is liable for unforeseen consequences when he or she was reckless or negligent as to these consequences. This is a form of "constructive liability," wherein the consequences of the conduct of a person who intends to commit a criminal offense exceed his or her intention. In this case, given the fact that the person had the intention to commit a criminal offense in the first place, the law deems it correct to hold the person liable for consequences that he or she could have foreseen (i.e., he or she acted recklessly as to the consequences) or that could have been foreseen by an objective person (i.e., he or she acted negligently as to the consequences). For example, if A intends to hit B with a bat until B is seriously injured but not dead, and B dies as a result of the attack, A is liable for the death of B, as A was reckless as to the consequences of seriously attacking B. Strictly speaking, applying the "unforeseen mode" principle abrogates from the "causation principle" or can break what is known in criminal law as the chain of causation. The causation principle requires that there be a proximate and causal link between the conduct of the perpetrator and the harm that is set out in the definition of the criminal offense. Public policy reasons dictate that this abrogation is defensible given that the person intended to commit a criminal offense in the first place. There are also limits placed on this abrogation. In the above example, A will be liable for consequences that occurred to B only if A was reckless or negligent with regard to the consequences. Thus, if something completely unforeseen by A happens to B, or something that, objectively speaking, was completely unforeseeable (an *actus novus interviens*) happens, A will not be liable for what happens to B. An *actus novus interviens* could be anything from a natural force to something the victim did. In the above example, if B was hit repeatedly by the bat but was not dead, and then jumped from a cliff and died as a result of the fall, then A would not be liable for B's death. Although many states allow the operation of *actus novus interviens* in relation to the victim's conduct, the condition of the victim prior to the commission of the crime will not count to exclude the operation of Paragraph 5. In some states, this provision is called the eggshell skull rule. It means, essentially, that the perpetrator must take the victim as he or she finds him or her, and if the victim has some health condition that exacerbates the injury caused by the perpetrator, then this will not exclude criminal responsibility. If, in the above example, B had a weak heart that caused him or her to die as a result of the trauma of being beaten, then A would be liable for B's death.

Under Paragraph 5, a person may also be held criminally liable where, for example, he or she intended to kill one person but ended up killing another person instead. This situation is sometimes known as transferred intention, while the example outlined in the preceding paragraph is known as unforeseen mode. Applying transferred intention means that the perpetrator did not have the requisite mental element vis-à-vis the subsequent victim of his or her criminal conduct (which was intended for a different victim). However, public policy reasons dictate that a person should in fact be held liable for his or her conduct where he or she had the intention in the first place to commit the criminal offense, just not against the same person.

# Section 8: Criminal Responsibility of Legal Persons

## Article 19: Criminal Responsibility of Legal Persons

1. A legal person is criminally responsible for a criminal offense:
   (a) committed in the name of, on behalf of, or for the benefit of a legal person; or
   (b) committed by any natural person, acting either individually or as part of an organ of the legal person, who has a management or supervisory position within the legal person based on:
      (i) a power of representation of the legal person;
      (ii) an authority to take decisions on behalf of the legal person; or
      (iii) an authority to exercise control within the legal person.
2. A legal person is also responsible for a criminal offense where the lack of due supervision or control by a natural person, referred to in Paragraph 1(b), has made possible the commission of the criminal offense for the benefit of the legal person.
3. The responsibility of a legal person under Paragraphs 1 and 2 does not exclude criminal proceedings against a natural person who is responsible as the perpetrator of a criminal offense or who has participated in the criminal offense.

## Commentary

The old maxim that a corporation cannot commit a criminal offense is no longer entirely valid based on practice at the domestic and international levels. Originally, because criminal law focused on assigning moral culpability for the commission of certain acts, it was considered inappropriate that a legal person (such as a business or corporation), incapable of moral culpability, could be subjected to it. This idea has changed greatly, particularly in response to current crime trends in which serious criminal offenses such as organized crime, corruption, money laundering, and the financing of terrorism are perpetrated through corporate entities as well as through individuals. Given the complex structures of corporate entities, it is sometimes difficult to identify a natural person who is the perpetrator of the criminal offense. The introduction of legal provisions in domestic law that provide for liability of legal persons serves to address the difficulty of identifying the natural person who is the perpetrator, to tackle serious criminal offenses perpetrated by those who try to shield their criminal conduct through the use of corporations, and to target the assets of a corporation used as a front for criminal conduct.

At a domestic level, an increasing number of states are implementing legislation that provides for corporate criminal liability or criminal liability of legal persons. This trend is evidenced particularly in newly drafted criminal codes from post-conflict states such as Kosovo and Bosnia and Herzegovina. At an international level, an increased number of international and regional conventions have included obligations upon states parties to implement or to consider implementing provisions in domestic legislation providing for liability of legal persons. These conventions include the United Nations Convention against Transnational Organized Crime (Article 10); the United Nations Convention against Corruption (Article 26); the Organization for Economic Cooperation and Development's Convention on Combating Bribery of Foreign Public Officials (Article 2); the Council of Europe Criminal Law Convention on Corruption (Article 18); and the Council of Europe Convention on Laundering, Search, Seizure and Confiscation of Proceeds from Crime and on the Financing of Terrorism (Article 10). A similar recommendation is made in *The Forty Recommendations* of the Financial Action Task Force (Recommendation 2).

In some domestic jurisdictions, corporate criminal responsibility is ascribed through civil or administrative laws and not through criminal laws. Recognizing this fact, most international conventions do not specifically require that criminal liability over legal persons be asserted by states parties to the convention; civil or administrative liability will suffice to fulfill the criteria of the convention. The drafters of the MCC chose to introduce criminal liability based on the fact that, of late, many commentators have argued against the effectiveness of civil or administrative liability of legal persons. Instead, they have supported moves to bring liability into the criminal realm. Criminal law is seen as a better deterrent than civil law or administrative law alone. As stated in the *Legislative Guide to the United Nations Convention against Transnational Organized Crime and the Protocols Thereto* (page 116, paragraph 240), "Criminal liability of a legal entity may also have a deterrent effect, partly because reputational damage can be very costly and partly because it may act as a catalyst for more effective management and supervisory structures to ensure compliance." In addition, the capacity to impose and enforce administration sanctions against criminal organizations will often be far more limited in a post-conflict environment than the potential to confront their activities through criminal prosecution.

The wording of Article 19 is taken from Article 10 of the Council of Europe Convention on Laundering, Search, Seizure and Confiscation of Proceeds from Crime and on the Financing of Terrorism. Reference should be made to paragraphs 103–109 of the explanatory report to the convention for a discussion of the meaning of this provision. Useful reference can be made to the *Legislative Guide to the United Nations Convention against Transnational Organized Crime and the Protocols Thereto,* pages 115–130, which discusses the issue of liability of legal persons and includes samples of domestic and international legislation on this topic.

The crux of Article 19, as is the crux of the doctrine of corporate criminal responsibility, is that a legal person can be held liable for the acts of its officers in certain cases. There are a number of theories under this form of criminal liability, such as the "directing mind principle," vicarious liability, and a holistic theory of liability. Under the latter, a company and its procedures and culture can create a dangerous environment in which offenses can occur, and therefore the company is held directly responsible for the criminal act. Under vicarious liability, another form of liability used in a domestic context, the company is responsible for the actions of all of its actors. This is generally a concept used within the context of civil law that has been adopted by criminal law in the context of corporate criminal responsibility. The theoretical underpinning of Article 19 is that of the directing mind principle. It holds that a certain limited number of officers of a legal person act with a requisite degree of authority and control in the legal person so as to make it appropriate to attribute their actions to that of the company. In the context of the directing mind principle, Article 19 sets out a definition of persons whose actions are attributable to the legal person under Paragraph 1(b). It is a matter for judicial interpretation how far down the chain of command in a company the doctrine of criminal responsibility for a company will stretch.

When a court determines that a legal person is criminally responsible for a criminal offense, the legal person is subject to certain penalties, many of which are specific to legal persons. Reference should be made to Section 12, Subsection 4, for a discussion of the particular penalties applicable to a legal person and the rationale for including them in the MCC.

The term *legal person* is not defined in the MCC. The definition will be a matter for judicial interpretation and will also very much depend on the company/corporations/business enterprise law in place in the state. Drafters in post-conflict states may consider including a definition in their criminal legislation that is consistent with other bodies of domestic law. The definition may include corporations, companies, associations, firms, partnerships, and other business enterprises in the state.

It is worth noting that Article 19 applies to all criminal offenses, including genocide, crimes against humanity, and war crimes. There was some discussion of and support for including criminal responsibility of legal persons in the Statute of the International Criminal Court. However, it proved too difficult to reach agreement on the modalities of corporate liability within the limited time available for discussion, and the concept was dropped in the final stages of the negotiations on the statute in order to ensure consensus.

Reference should be made to Chapter 6 of the MCCP, which deals with procedural issues relating to the prosecution of a legal person, including the designation of a representative for the legal person, service of documents on a legal person, and other provisions relating to the indictment and trial of a legal person.

In addition to including the provisions of Article 19 of the MCC and Chapter 6 of the MCCP in its domestic legislation, a state should consider legal reforms outside of criminal law vis-à-vis legal persons. It is important that an adequate body of company law/corporate law/laws on business enterprises is developed in a post-conflict state so that all the actors know of their obligations and the consequences of failure to comply. Such a body of law is also extremely important for a state wishing to attract international businesses to its territory.

Paragraph 2: This paragraph introduces negligence to the issue of criminal responsibility of legal persons. Article 18(4) of the MCC provides that a person, meaning a "natural person" or a "legal person," may be held liable on account of negligence only when it is provided for in the MCC. With regard to a legal person, Article 19 sets out the principle that a legal person is liable for the negligent commission of any criminal offense contained in the MCC when one of the actors described in Paragraph 1(b) is negligent with regard to his or her supervision or control.

Paragraph 3: The prosecution of a person for his or her participation in a criminal offense does not preclude the prosecution of the legal person for the same offense. The reverse is also true; a person may be prosecuted subsequently even where a legal person has been held criminally liable for the same offense, or even been acquitted. As mentioned in the commentary to Article 8 on *ne bis in idem* (double jeopardy), no issues relating to double jeopardy arise, as the legal person and the natural person are different, and double jeopardy applies only to one particular person being prosecuted twice for the same criminal offense. Reference should be made to the commentary on Article 8.

# Section 9: Justification and Exclusion of Criminal Responsibility

## General Commentary

As articulated in Article 16, a person can be held criminally responsible only if he or she commits a criminal offense with intention, recklessness, or negligence. Even if a person has committed the physical element of a criminal offense with the requisite intention, recklessness, or negligence, he or she may still evade criminal responsibility if there is either a lawful justification for the commission of the criminal offense or a ground excluding criminal responsibility. Reference should be made to Article 16 and its accompanying commentary.

Both "lawful justification" and "exclusion of criminal responsibility" fall under the broad rubric of what are commonly known as defenses. However, there is a philosophical and practical distinction between these terms. Justification defenses are those where what was clearly criminal conduct is deemed not to be so because the circumstances make the conduct socially acceptable in some way. Exactly what is classified as a "lawful justification" is a policy decision for a state, although most states, irrespective of their particular legal traditions, seem to adopt similar classifications.

Defenses that fall under the category of "excuse" or "exclusion of criminal responsibility" excuse a person from moral blame even where his or her conduct was criminal. Criminal responsibility may be excluded where the person's behavior is not voluntary (e.g., under duress) or where the person lacked capacity (e.g., in the case of insanity). As with justification defenses, deciphering what is included under "exclusion of criminal responsibility" is a matter of public policy for a state. For example, states that allow criminal responsibility to be excluded on the basis of intoxication commonly preclude the use of this defense where a person has become voluntarily intoxicated, as it is well known that intoxication can impede a person's judgment.

In some legal systems, "partial defenses" may operate with respect to certain criminal offenses. A partial defense will not completely exonerate a person from criminal responsibility but it may serve to reduce the offense and any applicable penalty. For example, in the case of murder, the presence of provocation may reduce the charge to that of manslaughter or voluntary homicide. The defense of diminished responsibility is also relevant in some systems in the same way. There are no partial defenses contained in the MCC. Where provocation or diminished responsibility is present, it is listed as a mitigating factor that should be taken into account in determining the applicable penalty to impose upon a convicted person under Article 51(1)(a). Some systems also categorize "automatism" as a defense that excludes criminal responsibility, as the person's behavior is not voluntary. *Automatism* means that a person who has perpetrated a criminal offense may have done so while subject to the total absence of voluntary control over his or her actions (where the person is in a hypnotic trance, for example) and where he or she did not voluntarily induce this state. In the MCC, automatism is not covered under "defenses" but instead is treated as an aspect of volition, going to the voluntariness of the perpetrator's conduct. Article 17(1) provides that a criminal offense can be committed only by a "voluntary" act. Reference should be made to Article 17 and its accompanying commentary.

In many systems, infancy is also treated as an excuse defense to a criminal offense. In the MCC, the issue of infancy is dealt with under Article 7(3). Reference should be made to Article 7, "Personal Jurisdiction," and its accompanying commentary. Finally, in yet other systems, alibi is also conceived of as a defense. Alibi is not treated as such in the MCC. The accused person is not asserting that he or she committed the criminal offense and seeking a justification or to be excused from his or her conduct. Instead, he or she is asserting that he or she did not commit the conduct alleged in the first place. The alibi should be considered when the court is examining whether the person committed the criminal offense, either directly or through a form of participation. Reference should be made to the commentary to Article 17.

All the defenses contained in the Rome Statute of the International Criminal Court are contained in the provisions of the MCC. The statute also contains a provision, Article 31(3), that provides for the introduction of additional defenses relevant to the crimes within the International Criminal Court's jurisdiction. These defenses (e.g., military necessity, consent, and reprisal) mostly exist under international humanitarian law and would be relevant to war crimes prosecutions. A post-conflict state that is trying a war crimes case should be aware of this fact.

The provisions of the Rome Statute of the International Criminal Court were used as the basis of the MCC defenses, but they were not used in their totality. Any deviation in wording and substance will be discussed under the relevant provision.

When a post-conflict state is considering the reform of its criminal law as it relates to defenses, it not only may consider adding specific defenses but may also need to consider removing some defenses. For example, it is common to find the defense of honor killings in some systems. There has been widespread opposition to such a defense and states have been urged not to apply this defense in domestic criminal law.

# Section 9

## Subsection 1: Justification

### Article 20: Self-Defense

1. An act committed in self-defense is not a criminal act.
2. Self-defense is an act that is necessary to avert an imminent and unlawful attack against a person or his or her property or against another person or the property of that other person.
3. The harm caused by the act of self-defense must not be grossly disproportionate to the interest it sought to protect.
4. Justification on account of self-defense based on defense of property does not apply with the criminal offenses of genocide (Article 86) and crimes against humanity (Article 87).
5. Self-defense based on defense of property may be raised only in relation to war crimes (Article 88) when the property is essential for the survival of the person or another person, or is essential for the survival of a military mission. The fact that the person was involved in a defensive operation conducted by forces may not in itself constitute a ground for excluding criminal responsibility under this article.

#### Commentary

Notwithstanding the fact that a person has perpetrated a criminal offense, he or she may rely on the justification of self-defense to exempt himself or herself from criminal responsibility. In the case of an imminent attack, a person is given wide powers to respond to this attack. Self-defense is expressed in different ways in different states. For example, in some states, it is permissible to use lethal force to protect property, while in others this is impermissible. It is up to each individual state to define the exact parameters of this defense.

Integral to the particular articulation of self-defense in the MCC is the requirement that the attack to be defended against is both "imminent" and "unlawful." There cannot be a substantial break of time between the act defended against and the act of self-defense. As for the term *unlawful,* if a police officer is conducting a lawful arrest, for example, a person cannot use force to resist and then claim self-defense to the charge of assault. The act of self-defense must also be "necessary," meaning that a person possessed no alternative means with which to defend himself or herself.

The interests a person can protect by means of self-defense are his or her person and property and the person and property of another. In some states, it is impermissible to use self-defense in defense of property (see also the discussion on defense of property with regard to international offenses, below). In the context of a post-conflict state, where there may be no fully functioning police force to protect a person's property, the drafters thought it was important to include this ground of liability, tempered by the "proportionality" restriction articulated in Paragraph 3. Paragraph 3 sets out the principle that the harm or force used by the person acting in self-defense must be proportionate to this interest. This means it would be disproportionate to use a great degree of force against someone for stealing a chicken when you have a chicken farm. However, if a person sought to protect a chicken that was the sole source of food for his or her family, a greater degree of force might be permissible.

**Paragraphs 4 and 5:** These paragraphs follow the wording of Article 31(1)(c) of the Statute of the International Criminal Court, which deals with self-defense vis-à-vis the criminal offenses of genocide, crimes against humanity, and war crimes. The provision declares that a person cannot act in defense of property, except with regard to war crimes and where the property is "essential for the survival of the person, or another person or property which is essential for the accomplishment of a military mission." It also states that "the fact that the person was involved in a defensive operation conducted by forces shall not in itself constitute a ground for excluding criminal responsibility under this Article." It should be noted that many legal commentators have objected to the inclusion of a defense of property with regard to war crimes, and one state, Belgium, has formulated a declaration objecting to it. The drafters of the MCC decided to follow the position adopted in the Statute of the International Criminal Court; however, a state may wish to deviate from this position and to exclude completely defense of property as a defense to war crimes.

# Article 21: Necessity

1. An act committed by necessity is not a criminal act.
2. Necessity is an act that is necessary to avert an imminent danger to life, property, or other protected interests.
3. The harm caused by averting the danger must not be disproportionate to the interest it sought to protect.

## Commentary

Justification on account of necessity is relevant where a person commits a criminal offense to prevent a greater evil. In some states, the defense of necessity is seen as closely related to the defense of duress, set out in Article 25 more specifically as "duress by circumstances" (as opposed to the second category of duress, "duress by threats"). Under the MCC, necessity is categorized as a justification defense, and duress is categorized as an "exclusion of criminal responsibility" defense, because the designation of necessity is a matter of public policy, while duress is deemed an involuntary action on the part of the perpetrator.

For a person to qualify under the defense of necessity in relation to his or her criminal conduct, the following must be present: (1) a danger to life, property, or other interests; (2) the danger is imminent; (3) an act was undertaken to avert the danger; and (4) the harm caused by averting the danger was not disproportionate to the protected interest. In the case of necessity, the protected interests are life, property, and "other protected interests." The meaning of *other protected interests* is one for judicial interpretation. It is again really a matter of state policy. Any "other protected interests" that are deemed allowable by the court should be important enough to merit inclusion under the justification defense of necessity.

Article 31 of the Rome Statute of the International Criminal Court merges both the defense of necessity and the defense of duress under Paragraph 1(d), treating necessity like a category of duress—duress by circumstances. As mentioned above, the MCC has not followed this position. Despite the distinction in how necessity is categorized, the substance of the defense of necessity contained in the statute is covered in Article 21 of the MCC.

# Article 22: Superior Orders

1. An act committed under an order of a government or of a superior, whether military, security service, law enforcement, or civilian, is not a criminal act, where:
   (a) the person was under a legal obligation to obey orders of the government or the superior in question;
   (b) the person did not know that the order was unlawful; and
   (c) the order was not manifestly unlawful.
2. Orders to commit genocide, crimes against humanity, torture, and enforced disappearances are manifestly unlawful.

## Commentary

The wording of Article 22 is taken from Article 33 of the Rome Statute of the International Criminal Court. Article 33 applies only to genocide, crimes against humanity, and war crimes, as these are the offenses currently within the jurisdictional reach of the International Criminal Court.

The defense of superior orders takes into account the fact that persons in a superior-subordinate relationship may be ordered to undertake certain actions, which they are expected to obey. The duty to obey, however, cannot be held to absolve a person of all liability when he or she commits a criminal offense. In some states—and under the statutes of the International Criminal Tribunal for the former Yugoslavia, the International Criminal Tribunal for Rwanda, and the Special Court for Sierra Leone—superior orders are viewed as a mitigating factor in the determination of penalties only, rather than as a defense. In contrast, when the requirements of Article 22 are met, superior orders operate as a full defense to the commission of a criminal offense.

To comply with Article 22, it must first be established that a superior-subordinate relationship exists, whether it is military or civilian in nature. Second, it must be proved that the person did not know that the order was unlawful. This requirement may be relevant in only a small number of cases and is probably most pertinent in relation to the area of war crimes, where parts of international humanitarian law, upon which many of the war crimes provisions are based, can be either unclear or controversial. Third, in the case of certain defined "manifestly unlawful orders," a person may not invoke the defense and claim he or she did not know the order. Orders to commit genocide and crimes against humanity are defined as such in Article 33(2) of the Statute of the International Criminal Court. It is noteworthy that war crimes were excluded from the scope of Article 33(2) for the reasons mentioned previously. Paragraph 2, above, broadens the scope of the provision in the convention, adding torture and enforced disappearances to the list. The addition of torture is required by Article 2(3) of the Convention against Torture and Other Cruel, Inhuman or Degrading Treatment or Punishment. The addition of enforced disappearance is in accordance with Article 6 of the United Nations Principles on the Protection of All Persons from Enforced Disappearances and in the United Nations Convention on Enforced Disappearances.

# Section 9

## Subsection 2: Exclusion of Criminal Responsibility

### Article 23: Mental Incompetence

1. Criminal responsibility is excluded when a mentally incompetent person commits a criminal offense.
2. A person is mentally incompetent when, at the time of committing the criminal offense, he or she suffers from a mental disease or defect that destroys his or her capacity to appreciate the unlawfulness or nature of his or her conduct, or destroys his or her capacity to control his or her conduct to conform with the requirements of the law.

#### Commentary

The presence of mental incompetence in the perpetrator of a criminal offense means that he or she is not considered morally blameworthy due to a lack of capacity. Therefore the person can benefit from the defense set out in Article 23. The MCC uses the term *mental incompetence* in describing a defense that is often referred to as an insanity defense in domestic criminal legislation. The precise wording of Paragraph 2 is taken from Article 31(1)(a) of the Rome Statute of the International Criminal Court, which is consistent with the principles on the defense of mental incompetence in most legal systems. In essence, Article 31 replicates what have been commonly called the M'Naughton Rules in many legal systems (after the original case that elaborated the principles applicable to the defense of insanity in English common law).

To avail of the defense of mental incompetence, the following must exist: (1) that the person had a "mental disease or defect"; and (2) this defect destroyed his or her capacity to (a) appreciate the unlawfulness of his or her conduct; or (b) appreciate the nature of his or her conduct (i.e., not understand the physical nature and quality of his or her act); or (c) control his or her conduct to conform with the law. The latter ground should not be confused with "diminished responsibility," which is a partial defense to the charge of murder in some states (see the general commentary to Section 9, above). Diminished responsibility involves not the "destruction" of a person's capacity but rather the diminution of it through an abnormality of mind that substantially impairs his or her mental responsibility for his or her acts. Diminished responsibility may be a mitigating factor in determining a penalty under the MCC, but it cannot be a defense. Reference should be made to Article 51(1)(a) and its accompanying commentary.

For the defense to succeed, the person must be mentally incompetent at the time the criminal offense is committed. The fact that the person suffers from mental incompetence at the time of the trial does not establish that he or she was in that state when the offense was committed, although it definitely has a bearing on the person's fitness to stand trial. Reference should be made to Chapter 7, Part 3, of the MCCP, which also sets out the applicable procedure to be followed when a person claims mental incompetence.

In some systems, when a person is found eligible to benefit from the defense of mental incompetence, a verdict of "not guilty by reason of insanity" is declared, and rather than being set free, the person may, if appropriate, be detained for psychiatric care. This is a matter for a state to determine and is, of course, contingent on adequate facilities, which are often lacking in post-conflict states. Also often lacking in post-conflict states are medical experts who can interview and ascertain whether a person is mentally incompetent and later testify in court on this issue. Many experts who had worked in the criminal justice system in post-conflict states pointed out the need to ensure that arrangements are made to access medical experts in trials where a person's mental competency to commit a criminal offense is at issue. This factor should be taken into account for the effective implementation and application of Article 23.

# Article 24: Intoxication

1. Criminal responsibility is excluded when a person commits a criminal offense while intoxicated and where the intoxication destroys his or her capacity to appreciate the unlawfulness or nature of his or her conduct or destroys his or her capacity to control his or her conduct to conform to the requirements of law.

2. Criminal responsibility is not excluded on account of intoxication when a person has become voluntarily intoxicated under such circumstances that he or she knew or disregarded the risk that as a result of the intoxication, he or she was likely to engage in such conduct.

## Commentary

Intoxication of the perpetrator of a criminal offense means that he or she is not considered morally blameworthy due to a lack of capacity, and therefore the person can benefit from the defense set out in Article 24. The wording of Paragraph 1 is taken from Article 31(1)(a) of the Rome Statute of the International Criminal Court. Intoxication refers to intoxication from alcohol, drugs, or other intoxicants. Where it is proven that the intoxicant destroyed a person's capacity to (1) appreciate the unlawfulness of his or her conduct; (2) appreciate the nature of his or her conduct (i.e., not understand the physical nature and quality of his or her act); or (3) control his or her conduct to conform to the requirements of law, the person may avail of the defense of intoxication. The defense is directed primarily at the phenomenon of involuntary intoxication. In the case of voluntary intoxication, a person cannot avail of the defense of intoxication where he or she knew or disregarded a risk that, by reason of taking the intoxicant, he or she was likely to engage in criminal behavior. The typical case would be a person drinking alcohol to gain the courage to subsequently perpetrate a criminal offense.

# Article 25: Duress

1. Criminal responsibility is excluded when a person commits a criminal offense under duress.
2. A person is deemed to act under duress when the person, faced with an imminent danger to life, limb, or freedom that cannot otherwise be averted, commits an unlawful act to avert the danger away from himself or herself, a relative, or a person close to himself or herself.

## Commentary

As mentioned in the commentary to Article 21, duress and necessity are similar defenses. For the reasons mentioned under Article 21, necessity is classified as a justification defense, and duress as an exclusion of criminal responsibility defense. Duress involves a situation where the threat of imminent danger to life, limb, and freedom is so great as to overbear the will of a person, who then commits a criminal offense to avert the danger away from himself or herself, a relative, or a person close to himself or herself. This defense has been described as a concession to human frailty, allowing the excusal of criminal responsibility based on the fact that the perpetrator of the criminal act under duress does not have the capacity to form a "guilty mind" and fulfill the mens rea element of the offense. It is important in assessing whether duress was present to look at whether the person who committed the criminal offense had any other means to counteract the "imminent danger," the question being, Was his or her response reasonable and proportionate?

Article 31 of the Rome Statute of the International Criminal Court merges both the defense of necessity and the defense of duress under Paragraph 1(d). The substance of the defense of duress contained in the statute is covered in Articles 21 and 25 of the MCC.

# Article 26: Mistake of Fact and Mistake of Law

1. Criminal responsibility is excluded when a person commits a criminal offense under a mistake of fact.
2. A person acts under a mistake of fact when he or she mistakenly and honestly believes that circumstances exist that, if they are true, justify his or her conduct.
3. A person who was in error as to his or her mistake of fact due to negligence will be held liable for a criminal offense where the offense may be committed by negligence.
4. A mistake of law does not exclude criminal responsibility.

## Commentary

**Paragraphs 1 and 2:** Mistake of fact is recognized as an excuse to the commission of a criminal offense in most jurisdictions. A mistake of fact negates a person's intention to commit a criminal offense, and therefore it is deemed an excuse. This idea is expressly recognized in the formulation of "mistake of fact" under the Rome Statute of the International Criminal Court, Article 32(1). Even though the MCC contains different wording than the statute, the crux of Article 32(1) is contained in Article 26, above. In most systems, the law holds that the mistake of fact must be an "honest" mistake as to circumstances that justify the conduct, were they to exist. Domestic courts generally judge the validity of the mistaken belief on objective grounds.

**Paragraph 3:** As discussed above, mistake of fact negates the intention to commit a criminal offense. Mistake of fact therefore cannot apply to offenses that may be committed negligently, as negligent conduct does not involve any element of cognition or awareness on the part of the perpetrator: the perpetrator cannot be mistaken about a fact, as he or she never considered it in the first place. As articulated in Article 18(3), a person may not be held liable for a criminal offense through negligence unless it is specified in the MCC. Only certain offenses fall into this category, but when they do, the defense of mistake of fact cannot be invoked. Consequently, as stated in Paragraph 3, a person may be held criminally liable for this negligent offense irrespective of a mistake of fact.

**Paragraph 4:** Mistake of fact, as mentioned above, negates the intent of the perpetrator. Distinct from mistake of fact, mistake of law excludes culpability and not intent. When a person acts under a mistake of law, he or she is aware of all the circumstances surrounding his or her conduct but is operating under the mistaken belief that his or her conduct is legal. Legal systems differ about whether a mistake of law constitutes a defense to the commission of a criminal offense. Some systems, based on public policy grounds, abide by the maxim "ignorance of the law is no defense." In other systems, a mistake of law is a permissible defense in certain circumstances, for example, where the mistake was unavoidable, or where the person who committed the criminal offense can prove that he or she had a justification for the mistake of law. In systems that allow for a mistake of law, there is a very high threshold to prove the defense, and it is rarely invoked in practice. The defense of mistake of law is not included in the MCC.

# Section 10: Criminal Attempt

## Article 27: Attempt

1. It is a criminal offense to attempt to commit a criminal offense by taking action that commences its execution by means of a substantial step, but where the offense does not occur because of circumstances independent of the intentions of the person.
2. A person who abandons his or her effort to commit a criminal offense or who otherwise prevents the completion of the offense is not criminally responsible under the MCC for the attempt to commit that offense, if that person completely and voluntarily gave up his or her criminal purpose.

## Commentary

Paragraph 1: Commonly, attempt is treated as an inchoate or incomplete offense. This position has been adopted in the MCC. Attempt, as an incomplete offense, is distinct from the modes of liability contained in Section 11 on participation, where a participant in a criminal offense is treated as having committed—or, in other words, completed—an offense. Consequently, attempted criminal offenses are subject to modified penalty ranges under Article 48, given the fact that the criminal offense was not actually completed. Reference should be made to Article 48 and its accompanying commentary. To be found liable for an attempted criminal offense, the perpetrator must have the intention to commit the criminal offense (mental element), coupled with an act that progresses sufficiently toward completion of the offense—a "substantial step." In the case of attempt, the frustrated efforts of the perpetrator resulted in the noncommission of the offense. But for this, he or she would have committed the criminal offense. It is not enough to think about committing a criminal offense or to prepare for it. In some jurisdictions, where it is legally or physically impossible for a person to attempt a particular criminal offense, this legal or physical impossibility is deemed a defense to attempt.

The wording of Article 27 is taken from Article 25(3)(f) of the Statute of the International Criminal Court. A state wishing to implement its obligations under the statute should ensure that attempt is contained in its domestic legislation.

Paragraph 2: In some systems, the abandonment of attempt does not result in the exclusion of criminal responsibility for an attempted criminal offense. This is a matter of policy. In the MCC, the approach of the drafters was to exclude criminal responsibility for the abandonment of attempt where the person "completely and voluntarily gives up his or her criminal purpose." It also excludes criminal responsibility where a person prevents the completion of the offense, if that person "completely and voluntarily gives up his or her criminal purpose."

# Section 11: Participation in a Criminal Offense

## General Commentary

It is not only the principal perpetrator of a criminal offense or the principal perpetrator of its attempted commission who may be criminally liable. Persons who participated in the criminal offense in a wider sense may also be liable. The MCC sets out five grounds upon which a person may be held to have participated in a criminal offense: (1) participation in a common purpose; (2) ordering, soliciting, or inducing the commission of a criminal offense; (3) inciting the commission of a criminal offense; (4) facilitating the commission of a criminal offense (through aiding, abetting, or otherwise assisting the perpetrator of the criminal offense); and (5) in accordance with the doctrine of "command responsibility" in relation to the criminal offenses of genocide, crimes against humanity, and war crimes. The commentaries to each individual article below discuss each ground of participation.

In some states, a person who participates in a criminal offense under any of these five grounds of liability is considered to be an *accessory* to a criminal offense. The implication of being designated as an accessory to a criminal offense is that the person is viewed by the court as having assisted in the criminal offense but not as having directly participated. An accessory is regarded in a different light by the court than the principal perpetrator and, when convicted of a criminal offense, is punished in a different manner.

In contrast, Article 33 of the MCC, like the criminal codes of many states, treats an aider or an abettor as an *accomplice* to the criminal offense. An accomplice is liable for a criminal offense in the same way as the principal perpetrator of the offense. The implication of accomplice liability as provided for under Article 33 of the MCC is that an aider or an abettor will be subject to the same penalty range that applies to a principal perpetrator of the criminal offense. Given that some of the grounds listed in Articles 28–31 may involve a lesser degree of participation than that of the person who actually perpetrates the criminal offense, a court determining the appropriate penalty for an accomplice may consider this lesser degree of participation as a mitigating factor. Reference should be made to Article 51(1)(e) and its accompanying commentary.

In this sense, the person can be charged with a criminal offense (albeit on the grounds of aiding, abetting, ordering, and so forth) and is liable to the same penalties as the principal perpetrator if convicted of the offense. So, for example, if A orders B to kill C, then A will be liable if B murders C and will face a penalty of ten to thirty years' imprisonment or life imprisonment.

The grounds of participation contained in the MCC include those contained in Article 25 of the Rome Statute of the International Criminal Court. A state that is party to the statute should ensure that all of these grounds of participation are covered in domestic legislation, or that equivalent grounds exist. Commonly, grounds of participation such as aiding and abetting are already covered in existing domestic legislation. What might not be covered is command responsibility, a ground specific to the crimes of genocide, crimes against humanity, and war crimes. The precise articulation of this ground of participation is contained in Article 28 of the Rome Statute of the International Criminal Court. Article 32, below, integrates the precise language used in Article 28 into the MCC.

# Article 28: Participation in a Common Purpose

It is a criminal offense to contribute to the commission or attempted commission of a criminal offense by a group of persons acting with a common purpose. Such contribution must be intentional and must:

(a) be made with the aim of furthering the criminal activity or criminal purpose of the group, where such activity or purpose involves the commission of a criminal offense under the MCC; or

(b) be made in the knowledge of the intention of the group to commit the criminal offense.

## Commentary

The form of liability contained in Article 28 is taken from Article 25(3)(d) of the Rome Statute of the International Criminal Court. A state seeking to comply with its obligations under the statute must ensure that domestic legislation contains this ground of criminal liability. This form of liability is also contained in Article 2(5)(g) of the United Nations Convention for the Suppression of the Financing of Terrorism.

"Common purpose liability" has frequently been used as a ground of participation before the International Criminal Tribunal for the former Yugoslavia. The terminology used at the International Criminal Tribunal for the former Yugoslavia is that of "joint criminal enterprise," or criminal enterprise encompassing a "common criminal plan" or a "common criminal purpose" (for the multiplicity of terms, see the summary in *Prosecutor v. Radoslav Brdjanin, Momir Talic*, case no. IT-99-36-PT, Decision on Form of Further Amended Indictment and Prosecution Application to Amend,

June 26, 2001, paragraph 24). Much jurisprudence exists on the precise meaning of *joint criminal enterprise.* It is instructive to look to this jurisprudence for guidance as to the meaning of Article 25(3)(d) of the Rome Statute of the International Criminal Court (replicated here in this article of the MCC).

This form of liability is not explicitly provided for by the statutes of the international tribunals. The Appeals Chamber of the International Criminal Tribunal for the former Yugoslavia considered that it was implied by the statute, however, and found support for the concept of joint criminal enterprise (JCE) in several domestic sources of law as well as in post–World War II prosecutions by military tribunals. Among these are the concepts of "criminal association," which exists in some systems, and "common design," which exists in other systems. JCE may be distinguished from grounds of liability such as conspiracy, penalizing membership in certain groups, and complicity, concepts frequently used at a domestic level in different systems. The distinctiveness of JCE is that co-perpetration in a joint criminal enterprise is a form of commission of the criminal offense. As opposed to merely knowing about the commission of the criminal offense, the co-perpetrator in a JCE shares the intent of the principal perpetrator. The defendant Ojdanic in the *Mulitinovic* decision unsuccessfully argued that JCE does not constitute a mode of liability within the tribunal's jurisdiction because "it is equivalent to a collective responsibility based upon membership in a criminal organization." To demonstrate that JCE is not a "vehicle for organisational liability," the Appeals Chamber stated that "[c]riminal liability pursuant to a joint criminal enterprise is not liability for mere membership or for conspiring to commit crimes, but a form of liability concerned with the participation in the commission of a crime as part of a joint criminal enterprise, a different matter" (*Prosecutor v. Mulitinovic et al.*, Decision on Dragoljub Ojdanic's Motion Challenging Jurisdiction—Joint Criminal Enterprise, case no. IT-99-37-AR72, May 21, 2003, paragraph 26).

JCE is a mode of participation in a criminal offense that consists of "an understanding or arrangement amounting to an agreement between two or more persons that they will commit a crime" (*Prosecutor v. Krnojelac*, case no. IT-97-25-T, Judgment, March 15, 2002, paragraph 80). As mentioned previously, the participants in the venture may be individually liable for the acts of the other members.

Three categories of this mode of liability have been established by the international tribunals. The first category refers to cases where all co-accused possess the same criminal intention to act pursuant to the common design. This type of JCE constitutes the basis of the doctrine, as the participants in the enterprise may be held criminally liable for acts they did not commit but that they agreed to commit in a collective sense. Comparison between this form of participation and the law of conspiracy used in some legal systems stops when one considers the finding of the Appeals Chamber in the *Mulitinovic* case. It stated that where proving the existence of a mere agreement suffices in the case of conspiracy, liability for participation in a JCE is incurred when the parties to the agreement take action in furtherance of that agreement (*Prosecutor v. Mulitinovic et al.*, case no. IT-99-37-AR72, Decision on Dragoljub Ojdanic's Motion Challenging Jurisdiction—Joint Criminal Enterprise, May 21, 2003, paragraph 23).

The second category of JCE is known as the systemic form (*Prosecutor v. Vasiljević*, Appeal Judgment, February 25, 2004, case no. IT-98-32-A, paragraph 98) and refers to an organized system of ill treatment. It is a variation of the first category, created to refer specifically to the cases of concentration camps, where JCE is performed through an institutional structure. In this case, the prisoners of the camp are ill treated in pursuance of the JCE by "members of military and administrative units such as those running concentration camps; i.e. by groups of persons acting pursuant to a concerted plan" (*Prosecutor v. Tadić*, case no. IT-94-1-A, Appeal Judgment, July 15, 1999, paragraph 202). This category of JCE may not only apply to international crimes such as genocide, crimes against humanity, and war crimes but may also extend to other criminal offenses perpetrated through any institutional structure.

The third category of JCE supported by the international tribunals concerns "cases involving a common design to pursue one course of conduct where one of the perpetrators commits an act which, while outside the common design, was nevertheless a natural and foreseeable consequence of the effecting of that common purpose" (*Tadić* appeal judgment, paragraph 204). This type of JCE refers especially to cases of mob violence. It will be a matter for a court interpreting Article 28 to consider whether it wishes to go so far as to include this third category of JCE in its interpretation of JCE. It must be borne in mind when deciding this issue that the International Criminal Tribunal for the former Yugoslavia adjudicated only on the criminal offenses of genocide, crimes against humanity, and war crimes and not on other offenses commonly found in the domestic legislation or in the MCC. Many scholars and practitioners believe that this category stretches the definition and meaning of JCE too far, going beyond the definition of JCE elucidated in many domestic courts. Certainly, in the case of a domestic court implementing Article 28, the court should assess very carefully exactly how far it wishes to extend this concept in relation to "ordinary" criminal offenses. In such a case, a person may be more properly charged under Article 31 of the MCC, rather than Article 28, for facilitating the criminal offense.

The subjective element required for proof of participation in a JCE differs according to the category of the doctrine under consideration. With regard to the first category, the intent to perpetrate a certain criminal offense must be shared by all participants in the JCE. Within the frame of the second category, the participant must have had personal knowledge of the system of ill treatment, as well as the intent to further it. The intention to further the criminal purpose and to contribute to the joint criminal enterprise is required to establish the existence of the third category of JCE. Moreover, criminal liability for a crime falling outside the common purpose may arise if (1) it was foreseeable that such a crime might be perpetrated by one or other members of the group, and (2) the accused willingly took that risk.

In relation to the material element, or the *actus reus*, the following must be proven: (1) a group of persons; (2) the existence of a common plan, design, or purpose that amounts to or involves the commission of a crime; and (3) the participation of the accused in the common design involving the perpetration of one of the crimes provided for in the statute (*Tadić* appeal judgment, paragraphs 227–228).

# Article 29: Ordering, Soliciting, or Inducing

1. It is a criminal offense to order, solicit, or induce the commission of a criminal offense that in fact occurs.
2. It is a criminal offense to attempt to order, solicit, or induce a criminal offense that carries with it a penalty of more than five years, where no criminal offense was in fact committed.

## Commentary

The terms *ordering, soliciting,* and *inducing* are all found in Article 25(3)(b) of the Rome Statute of the International Criminal Court. A state wishing to implement its obligations under the convention should ensure that these grounds of liability are contained in domestic legislation. Various other international conventions require that these grounds of liability be included in domestic legislation.

The term *order* implies that a person in a position of authority, through the use of a superior-subordinate relationship, compels another person to commit a criminal offense. *Order* is synonymous with *direct,* a ground of participation found in many systems and also referred to in a number of international conventions, such as the Protocol against the Illicit Manufacturing of and Trafficking in Firearms, Their Parts and Components and Ammunition, supplementing the United Nations Convention against Transnational Organized Crime, Article 5(2)(b). The use of solicitation to bring about a criminal offense is a more oblique form of participation under which a person seeks to instigate or bring about the offense, for example through prompting the perpetrator. There are some overlaps between the terms *solicit* and *induce.* The latter ground of participation also involves a person seeking to instigate the commission of a criminal offense. Inducement involves some asserting of persuasion or influence.

In relation to criminal offenses carrying with them a penalty of one to five years, a person who ordered, solicited, or induced their commission cannot be prosecuted unless the criminal offense actually occurred. This means that a person who ordered, solicited, or induced the commission of such an attempted criminal offense cannot be prosecuted for it. For criminal offenses that carry a penalty of more than five years, there is no need to prove that the criminal offense in fact occurred.

# Article 30: Incitement

1. It is a criminal offense for one person to incite another person to commit a criminal offense if the incited criminal offense was committed under the inciter's influence.
2. Attempt under Article 27 applies to Article 30 only where the incited criminal offense carries with it a penalty of more than five years.

## Commentary

The term *incitement* is classified very differently in different legal systems. In some systems, incitement of another person to commit a criminal offense is termed an inchoate offense or an incomplete offense. This means the perpetrator is punished for the act of incitement, irrespective of whether the act prompted the incitee to commit the criminal offense. Incitement is in itself a substantive criminal offense. In other legal systems, incitement is treated as a participatory offense. This means the inciter is punished in the same manner as the principal perpetrator of the offense (reference should be made to Article 33). In such cases, the inciter is punished only when the incitee commits the criminal offense that he or she was incited to commit. In other systems, incitement as a participatory offense is punished irrespective of whether the offense occurred (although the law usually requires that the offense that is incited be a serious criminal offense). Under the MCC, a person will be punished as a principal perpetrator where the criminal offense is subsequently committed by the incitee under the influence of the inciter. In the case of more serious criminal offenses (i.e., those carrying a penalty of more than five years), the inciter can be charged with attempt under Article 27.

In addition to incitement as a ground of participation, there is also a specific "incitement to crime on account of hatred" offense. Under Article 161, for a person to be convicted, the incitement must be both "public" and "direct." In addition, the motivating factor for committing the criminal offense must be hatred. Reference should be made to Article 161, "Incitement to Crime on Account of Hatred," and its accompanying commentary.

# Article 31: Facilitation

It is a criminal offense, for the purpose of facilitating the commission of a criminal offense, to aid, abet, or otherwise assist in its commission or its attempted commission, including providing the means for its commission.

## Commentary

The terms *aid, abet,* and *otherwise assist* are all found in Article 25(3)(f) of the Statute of the International Criminal Court. Various other international conventions also require that these grounds of liability be included in domestic legislation.

Often the terms *aid* and *abet* are merged and taken to mean the same thing. Their meaning is distinct, however. To aid means to give assistance to someone, while to abet means to facilitate the commission of a criminal offense. The term *otherwise assist* could include other means of facilitating or supporting the commission of a criminal offense, such as counseling (giving help or advice prior to the commission of the offense), instructing the perpetrator on how to carry out the offense, or providing the perpetrator with the instrumentalities of crime. There is an overlap between aiding, abetting, and otherwise assisting, the latter being a residual ground of liability for facilitation of a criminal offense.

The mental element, or mens rea, of aiding and abetting is the intention on the part of the aider or the abettor that his or her conduct facilitate the commission of the criminal offense, denoted by the words "for the purpose of facilitating the commission of a criminal offense," contained in Article 31. While the aider or abettor may know of the mens rea of the principal perpetrator, he or she does not have to share it. Instead, a separate intention element is considered. For a discussion of the meaning of *intention,* reference should be made to Article 18, "Intention, Recklessness, and Negligence," and its accompanying commentary. In the context of the MCC, intention can involve either the volition on the part of the perpetrator to facilitate a criminal offense or cognition that the act of aiding, abetting, or otherwise assisting will facilitate the commission of a criminal offense.

If the principal perpetrator of a criminal offense does not fully complete the offense and merely attempts it (thereby being liable for attempted commission of the offense), a person may still be held liable for aiding, abetting, or otherwise assisting the attempted commission of a criminal offense, unless the principal perpetrator abandons his or her efforts to commit a criminal offense or otherwise prevents its completion as discussed in Article 27.

# Article 32: Responsibility of Commanders and Other Superiors for the Criminal Offenses of Genocide, Crimes against Humanity, and War Crimes

1. In the case of genocide, crimes against humanity, and war crimes, a criminal offense is committed by a military commander or a person effectively acting

as a military commander when genocide, crimes against humanity, or war crimes are committed by forces under his or her effective command and control, or effective authority and control as the case may be, as a result of his or her failure to exercise control properly over such forces, in a situation where:

(a) that military commander or person either knew or, owing to the circumstances at the time, should have known that the forces were committing or about to commit such criminal offenses; and

(b) that military commander or person failed to take all necessary and reasonable measures within his or her power to prevent or repress their commission or to submit the matter to the competent authorities for investigation and prosecution.

2. With respect to superior and subordinate relationships not described in Paragraph 1, a criminal offense is committed by a superior when genocide, crimes against humanity, or war crimes are committed by subordinates under his or her effective authority and control, as a result of his or her failure to exercise control properly over such subordinates, where:

(a) the superior either knew or consciously disregarded information that clearly indicated that the subordinates were committing or about to commit such criminal offenses;

(b) the criminal offenses concerned activities that were within the effective responsibility and control of the superior; and

(c) the superior failed to take all necessary and reasonable measures within his or her power to prevent or repress their commission or to submit the matter to the competent authorities for investigation and prosecution.

## Commentary

Command responsibility is a form of participation that is unique to the international offenses of genocide, crimes against humanity, and war crimes. Two sorts of persons may be held liable under the doctrine of command responsibility: military commanders under Article 32(1) and nonmilitary commanders who are in a superior-subordinate relationship with the perpetrators of genocide, crimes against humanity, and war crimes under Article 32(2). This ground of liability is used to convict commanders who may hold a great deal of responsibility for the commission of genocide, crimes against humanity, and war crimes but who may have never "gotten their hands dirty" in that they did not actually commit the physical acts of the criminal offense. There may have been a direct order to commit an act of genocide, crimes against humanity, or war crimes but there may be difficulty proving there was such an order. Alternatively, the commander may not have issued direct orders or taken any positive steps to induce his or her subordinates to commit the offense. In the latter case, under the doctrine of command responsibility, a commander may be held liable for his or her negligence in not preventing, repressing, or retrospectively dealing with the commission of the offense. It is not a form of vicarious liability where the commander is actually held liable for the actions or his or her forces or subordinates but rather a direct form of liability grounded in negligence. Negligence is a ground of liability when a person falls below a standard of behavior expected of a reasonable person.

Military commanders and nonmilitary commanders are held to different standards of expected behavior under Article 32, as is evidenced by the differences in wording of the two provisions. Once it is established that a person is a commander, the court will move to look at the actions or inactions of the commander in light of the requirements of Article 32. In the case of command responsibility, the commander is liable when forces under his or her "effective command and control"—"effective authority or control" in the case of military commanders and "effective authority and control" in the case of nonmilitary commanders—commit the criminal offenses of genocide, crimes against humanity, and war crimes. A military commander is responsible when he or she knew the forces were going to commit these offenses, or ought to have known, and where he or she did not take reasonable measures to repress or prevent the offenses, or submit the matter to competent authorities for investigation or prosecution. A nonmilitary commander is responsible only when he or she knew or consciously disregarded information that clearly indicated that subordinates were committing or were about to commit an offense. It must also be proven that the criminal offense concerned activities within the "effective responsibility and control" of the nonmilitary superior.

When these three elements are proven, a person may be convicted upon this ground of participation. The International Criminal Tribunal for the former Yugoslavia and the International Criminal Tribunal for Rwanda, both of which have examined the doctrine of command responsibility, have held that a conviction for command responsibility does not preclude conviction upon other grounds of participation. But as a general rule, where an offender is convicted as a principal perpetrator or accomplice, no conviction is entered under the heading of command or superior responsibility.

In considering the precise meaning and scope of the provision, reference should be made to the jurisprudence of the International Criminal Tribunal for the former Yugoslavia, the International Criminal Tribunal for Rwanda, and the International Criminal Court. When reading the jurisprudence of the former tribunals, it is worth bearing in mind that their governing statutes—Article 7(3) of the Statute of the International Criminal Tribunal for the former Yugoslavia and Article 6(3) of the Statute of the International Criminal Tribunal for Rwanda—use different wording than the Statute of the International Criminal Court, which is the basis of Article 32 of the MCC.

# Article 33: Punishment as a Perpetrator

The same penalties that apply to a perpetrator apply to a person who has participated in a criminal offense under Articles 28–32.

# Section 12: Penalties

## General Commentary

The manner in which criminal penalties are determined varies greatly among different legal traditions. Even states that share the same legal tradition often have different means for determining criminal penalties. Indeed, even states that are part of the same federal system sometimes vary in how they determine penalties. Given such disparities, it was impossible for the drafters of the MCC to determine what is generally agreed-upon practice, or even best practice, in the determination of penalties. Thus the MCC provides its own penalties framework, one that is influenced by the practices in many different states and legal traditions but that is unique.

Many legal systems allow for a great deal of discretion in the determination of penalties. Some of these systems articulate the purposes of penalties in criminal legislation as a judicial starting point. In some but not all cases, maximum penalties (but not minimum penalties) are set for individual criminal offenses. In these systems, legislation may also provide for the development of sentencing guidelines by certain bodies established by law for this purpose. Often a sentencing commission is formed to create sentencing guidelines and then to collect and distribute empirical data on penalties to assist judges in the determination of penalties. Sentencing guidelines can be either binding or nonbinding. A typical sentencing guidelines system works in the following way: Sentencing guidelines create a presumptive sentence that is calculated by recourse to a matrix. On one axis of the matrix is the particular offense, graded according to its severity. On the other axis of the matrix is the "criminal history score" of the convicted person. Various aggravating factors, such as whether the convicted person has a criminal record, whether he or she used a firearm in commission of the offense, and whether the victim was seriously injured, are added together to create an overall score. Once the aggravating factors have been added up, the point where the criminal history score meets the particular offense of which the person has been convicted is plotted on a graph. This point is called the presumptive sentence and can be departed from only under "substantial and compelling circumstances." Some commentators argue that the merits of this system are that it is specific but not too rigid. Other commentators, however, argue that sentencing guidelines infringe upon judicial discretion and interfere with the judge's role as arbiter of penalties.

Some legal systems, in contrast, neither articulate the purposes of penalties nor set maximum penalties for all offenses. In addition, sentencing guidelines are not used to guide the process of determining penalties. Judges are afforded complete discretion.

They may use compendiums of cases for guidance, looking to particular penalties assigned by other judges in similar cases. A somewhat related method of determining penalties works on the premise of "starting points," "pathfinders," or "informed judicial discretion." This method requires the creation of a database of past sentencing practice that identifies the most important elements in sentencing. This database is a starting point for judges to work from in determining appropriate penalties.

In some systems, the legislature sets down a maximum penalty for the particular criminal offense. Less commonly, the legislature may set down mandatory penalties for certain criminal offenses—murder and treason, for example. Some systems are moving to abolish or limit their mandatory penalties, with opponents of mandatory penalties arguing that such penalties are arbitrary and do not allow for the judicial consideration of individual circumstances relevant to the particular convicted person or the particular criminal offense.

In sharp contrast to the aforementioned systems, some legal systems are quite rigid in their approach to the determination of penalties, allowing little if any room for judicial discretion. Under these sorts of systems, there is very little individualization of the penalty according to the particular convicted person and the particular criminal offense he or she committed.

A midpoint between these approaches discussed above is an approach that has been termed *structured discretion* (see Council of Europe, *Recommendation No. R[92] 17 of the Committee of Ministers to Member States Concerning Consistency in Sentencing*, and *Recommendations of Professor Ashworth*, document PC-R-SN [90]11 [paragraph 1], which was submitted to the committee during the drafting of the recommendation). This approach blends consistency and flexibility, rejecting the rigid approach that might create inconsistency through treating different cases as if they were alike. Under structured discretion, clear aims of penalties are provided for in domestic legislation, as are principles on aggravating and mitigating circumstances, in addition to the requirement that a court give reasons for the particular penalty or penalties it decides to impose.

The drafters of the MCC were reticent to adopt a wholly discretionary approach to penalties for three reasons. First, post-conflict states often suffer from a dearth of legal personnel, including judges. New practitioners may be inexperienced and unfamiliar with the determination of penalties. It is therefore preferable to provide as comprehensive and prescriptive a framework as possible in the MCC. (This is not to say that the MCC contains no element of judicial discretion. This issue will be discussed in greater detail below.) Second, the public in a post-conflict society may mistrust the criminal justice system because its officials may have been involved in violations of human rights. In addition, judges may not have been independent and impartial and may have succumbed to corruption. Reinstilling the local population's trust in the justice system requires provisions that limit judicial discretion. Third, the principle of legality comes into play in determining how penalties are dealt with. Many of the experts consulted in the course of drafting the codes were concerned that the MCC should lay down all the rules, principles, and procedures applicable to the determination of penalties, consistent with the strict principle of legality articulated in Article 3 of the MCC. There was also a concern that individual minimum and maximum penalties should be set out for the offenses contained in the Special Part of the MCC.

But the drafters were reluctant to develop an entirely inflexible system that allowed no room for judicial discretion when determining penalties. Judicial discretion is essential to individualize a penalty and provide for equality of treatment between convicted persons. Some would argue that a strict procedure applied to all persons ensures equality for all. However, the drafters took *equality* to mean that convicted persons are treated equally, meaning persons with similar aggravating and mitigating circumstances who have committed similarly serious criminal offenses should be treated similarly.

The drafters decided to adopt a form of structured discretion in which judges are guided by the following: (a) the purposes of penalties, the fundamental principle, and other principles relating to penalties; (b) a set penalty structure; and (c) a procedure for the determination of penalties. For a more detailed discussion of each of these aspects of the MCC penalty provisions, reference should be made to the provisions below and their accompanying commentaries, which give room for judicial discretion in the determination of penalties within the confines of the structured approach that has been designed.

In considering the available options for incorporating structured discretion into the MCC, the drafters decided not to adopt the quasi-discretionary sentencing guidelines because of growing criticism of these sorts of guidelines in some jurisdictions. Another reason for not using sentencing guidelines in the MCC is that many sentencing guidelines focus on imprisonment exclusively, a position that the drafters of the codes do not support for reasons that are discussed below in the commentary to Article 39. Finally, sentencing guidelines can be complicated, so the drafters of the codes opted for a more simple and straightforward approach. The idea of creating starting points or pathfinders was also rejected, given the probable lack of statistical data in a post-conflict state, as well as resource issues related to establishing a mechanism of data compilation and analysis.

Instead, specific legal provisions, rather than nonstatutory guidelines or pathfinders, have been set out in the MCC. Subsection 1 provides for the broad purposes of penalties and applicable principles that should be taken into account throughout the penalty process. Subsection 2 then sets out the penalty structure in articulating the applicable penalties under the MCC, including the fact that the MCC adopts an approach that sets out a minimum-maximum penalty for each individual criminal offense. Subsection 3 then sets out a step-by-step procedure for ascertaining the appropriate penalty. This procedure has been transferred into a diagrammatic format. Reference should be made to annex 3. Reference should also be made to Chapter 11, Part 7, of the MCCP on the determination of penalties. Penalties will be determined at a separate hearing after the trial.

# Section 12

## Subsection 1: Purposes of Penalties, Fundamental Principle, and Other Principles Relating to Penalties

### Article 34: Purposes of Penalties

The fundamental purpose of penalties is to contribute, along with crime prevention initiatives, to respect for the law and the maintenance of a just, peaceful, and safe society by imposing just penalties that have one or more of the following objectives:

(a) to denounce unlawful conduct;

(b) to deter the convicted person and other persons from committing criminal offenses;

(c) to separate convicted persons from society, where necessary;

(d) to assist in rehabilitating convicted persons;

(e) to provide reparations for harm done to victims or the community; and

(f) to promote a sense of responsibility in convicted persons and acknowledgement of the harm done to victims and to the community.

### Commentary

It is essential that each state consider the purposes of criminal penalties. The essential question is: Why does the criminal justice system provide for penalties? This question is important from both a broad philosophical perspective and a practical perspective. With regard to the former, it is important that criminal penalties seek to achieve defined philosophical objectives. The imposition of penalties should be the means to a defined end, which must be specified by law. The creation of a cohesive and coherent criminal policy should be considered, openly debated among both the legal community and the general community, and then set out in criminal legislation. This criminal policy should reflect both its specific environment of operation and application and the views of the population. It is also vital that this policy is well researched and considers progressive research and findings on criminal policy and penology from around the world. From a practical perspective, having a defined criminal policy means that judges can refer to this policy when they are considering the appropriate penalties in a particular case. This policy promotes greater equality and uniformity in judicial decision making, as judges cannot merely take into account any purposes that they themselves consider important. All judges should make reference to a uniform set of principles that are on notice to the public through their inclusion in domestic criminal legislation. While some states have not included these aims in their domestic criminal legislation, the majority of states have.

For the reasons mentioned above, it was considered appropriate to include the purposes of penalties in the MCC. The question of the appropriate purposes of penalties is a hotly debated one. The aims may be divided into two broad categories: moral grounds and utilitarian grounds. The former ground, which is retrospective in nature, aims to punish the convicted person for his or her criminal acts and to seek retribution. The latter ground, which is prospective in nature, instead looks at broad utilitarian aims such as rehabilitation, deterrence, and incapacitation (or separation of the convicted person from society to prevent him or her from committing any more criminal offenses against society). These grounds have been widely recognized in different legal systems for centuries. Another ground that dates back centuries and is not so widely recognized as a stated aim of penalties is compensation of the victim. This ground was originally recognized as integral to the redress for harm committed against a person, and as a primary purpose of dispute resolution and prevention of acts of revenge. But later, when states adopted a monopoly over redress for wrongs against individuals, it was not as widely enforced. That said, it remained a vital component of the determination of penalties in many states around the world.

A comparative survey of criminal legislation from around the world reveals many different articulations of the purposes and principles of criminal legislation, with some states focusing more on deterrence and others focusing more on retribution. Article 34 of the MCC articulates both a general purpose and specific purposes of penalties. The general purpose is to maintain "a just, peaceful, and safe society." This provision was considered particularly apt with regard to a post-conflict state that may be emerging from years of conflict and lawlessness. Also integral to the general aim of penalty determination is the notion of just penalties. In the post-conflict era, and in the return to the rule of law, it is imperative that the concept of justice become an integral aspect of the assignment of criminal penalties. It is noteworthy that the provision refers also to other crime prevention initiatives, signaling the fact that criminal penalties alone cannot bring about the general and specific aims articulated in Article 34.

The specific objectives laid out in Article 34 contain a mixture of both moral and utilitarian purposes of penalties. The moral aim set out in Paragraph (f) is the promotion of a sense of responsibility in the convicted person for the harm done to the victim and the community. This is a slight deviation from the strong retributive language of other criminal codes, as it focuses more on accountability than retribution. Paragraph (a) also speaks to the denouncement of unlawful conduct, which relates specifically to the convicted person (i.e., the denouncement of his or her particular conduct) and also generally to the community (i.e., a general denouncement of that particular criminal conduct). Utilitarian aims include deterrence, Paragraph (b); incapacitation, Paragraph (c); and rehabilitation, Paragraph (d). Paragraph (f) also speaks to the acknowledgment of harm done to the community. Also contained in Article 34 is another purpose aimed at victim rehabilitation, discussed above.

As mentioned above, the chief consideration in creating a policy on penalties is that it is coherent and therefore less susceptible to abuse. States, however, often do not take into account that the prescribed purposes in domestic legislation may represent competing values, particularly with regard to moral versus utilitarian grounds of punishment. If a state is to ensure that the purposes are translated into practice coherently, it needs to prioritize among those values, or at least to declare one value as paramount. For this reason, the MCC has added another layer to the purposes of penalties: the applicable principles set out in Articles 35 and 36. Article 35 prioritizes one particular purpose of penalties that is to be held paramount in the determination of penalties, namely, the just deserts principle. The just deserts principle is discussed in greater detail in the commentary to Article 35.

As mentioned above, Article 34 refers to "crime prevention initiatives" to contribute to the overall purposes set out in it. The particular penalties set out in the MCC will certainly not achieve these aims without supplementation by other crime prevention initiatives. For example, a post-conflict state requires a strong, well-staffed, and well-trained police force to protect the public and to act as the first line of defense in crime prevention. In addition to adopting crime prevention initiatives, a post-conflict state may wish to consider other means of addressing criminal behavior and consequently preventing it. A prime example, not included in the MCC but widely recommended, is restorative justice.

Restorative justice, as a means to supplement the criminal justice system or as an alternative to criminal justice prosecution, is common around the world. Some restorative justice initiatives are localized, whereas others form part of the national criminal policy and are contained in domestic criminal legislation. In some cases, restorative justice programs may run in conjunction with criminal proceedings, and their outcomes will be considered at the stage of determination of penalties. Restorative justice can be defined either in terms of the process or in terms of its outcome. The United Nations' definition of a restorative justice program as "any programme that uses restorative processes and seeks to achieve restorative outcomes" encapsulates both these concepts (see paragraph 2, *United Nations Basic Principles on the Use of Restorative Justice Programmes in Criminal Matters,* UN document E/2002/INF/2/Add.2). A restorative process is any process in which the victim and the offender, and where appropriate other individuals or community members affected by a criminal offense, participate together actively in the resolution of matters arising from the crime, generally with the help of a facilitator. Restorative processes may include mediation, conciliation, conferencing, and sentencing circles (see paragraph 3, *United Nations Basic Principles on the Use of Restorative Justice Programmes in Criminal Matters*). A restorative outcome, as mentioned in the definition of a restorative justice program, is "an agreement reached as a result of a restorative justice process. Restorative outcomes include responses and programmes such as reparation, restitution and community service, aimed at meeting the individual and collective needs and responsibilities of the parties and achieving the reintegration of the victim and the offender." It is apparent from these definitions that restorative justice is a more utilitarian-focused endeavor that seeks to rehabilitate and reintegrate the convicted person. Importantly, restorative justice focuses on reparation of harm to the victim and the community, one of the specific purposes set out in Article 34.

For a more detailed discussion of the use, operation, and development of restorative justice programs, reference should be made to the *United Nations Basic Principles on the Use of Restorative Justice Programmes in Criminal Matters*. Reference should also be made to the *Report of the Secretary-General on Restorative Justice* (UN document E/CN.15/2002/5/Add.1). A lot of work is currently being undertaken both outside and inside the United Nations system on restorative justice. Within the United Nations system, work has involved the Group of Experts on Restorative Justice, which should be looked at by any state considering implementing restorative justice mechanisms. Outside of the United Nations system, the work of the Working Party on Restorative Justice may be very useful (see www.cpcalliance.org).

# Article 35: Fundamental Principle

**A penalty must be proportionate to the gravity of the criminal offense and the degree of responsibility of the convicted person.**

## Commentary

As mentioned above, notwithstanding the articulation of the purposes of the penalties above, the fundamental principle under Article 35 trumps or supersedes the others in the determination of an appropriate penalty. Without having one primary principle of penalties, judges will be left to decipher penalties based on often-competing principles of penalties, which can result in unequal treatment for convicted persons. The Council of Europe's *Recommendation No. R(92) 17 of the Committee of Ministers to Member States Concerning Consistency in Sentencing* (paragraph A3), and *Recommendations of Professor Ashworth,* document PC-R-SN (90)11 (paragraph A1), which was submitted to the committee during the drafting of the recommendation, recommend that a primary aim of sentencing should be declared. That principle is articulated in Article 35 and is commonly known as the just deserts principle, wherein the appropriate penalty is determined in proportion to the seriousness of the criminal offense (or the harm caused) and the convicted person's degree of responsibility or culpability. The just deserts principle is being integrated into domestic legislation in many states that have undertaken reforms of their domestic laws on penalties. Some proponents of the just deserts principle hold that other utilitarian factors should not be considered in conjunction with it. However, the drafters of the MCC did not entirely agree with this, and felt that other secondary considerations may be taken into account, albeit to a lesser extent. The gravity of the criminal offense and the degree of responsibility must also be read in conjunction with other principles relating to penalties, set out in Article 36. One of those other principles, as set forth in Article 36(a), requires that the court look at aggravating or mitigating circumstances in determining a penalty. This requirement adds an extra dimension to the court's reasoning and provides for a greater individualization of the penalty based on the individual circumstances of the convicted person. The aggravating and mitigating circumstances set out in Article 51 also relate to the seriousness of the criminal offense and the gravity of the convicted person's criminal responsibility.

The just deserts principle not only requires that the court consider the gravity of the criminal offense, the degree of responsibility of the convicted person, and individual aggravating and mitigating factors but also requires that the applicable penalty range is proportionate to the level of seriousness of the criminal offense. This means that criminal offenses should be graded according to their seriousness. This issue is dealt with in Article 38 and discussed at length in its accompanying commentary. The just deserts principle also requires that a convicted person's individual penalty be proportionate to other criminal offenses of a similarly serious nature. This second issue is discussed in Article 36(b).

One final issue that arises in relation to the just deserts principle is whether any prior convictions can be taken into account when the court is determining the penalty. One view of the just deserts principle is that prior convictions cannot be considered in any respect, as the person has already been convicted of the other offense, and the court must begin afresh to configure a new penalty based only on the factors set out in Article 35. That said, many states whose legislation provides for the just deserts principle of penalties allow for a consideration of prior penalties as aggravating factors, thus departing somewhat from the "pure" principle of just deserts. The issue of whether or not to consider prior penalties as aggravating factors represents a fundamental tension between the principle of just deserts and that of crime control, which requires that individuals who commit multiple offenses (recidivists) be subjected to more severe penalties than first-time offenders. The MCC follows the position taken in many states and allows a consideration of recidivism as an aggravating factor under Article 51(2)(m). Reference should be made to Article 51 and its accompanying commentary.

# Article 36: Other Principles Relevant to the Determination of Penalties

In addition to the principles set out in Articles 34 and 35, a court imposing a penalty upon a person must also take into consideration the following principles:

(a) a penalty should be increased or reduced to account for any relevant aggravating or mitigating circumstances;

(b) a penalty should be similar to penalties imposed on similar convicted persons for similar criminal offenses committed in similar circumstances;

(c) all available sanctions under the MCC, other than imprisonment, that are reasonable in the circumstances should be considered for all convicted persons;

(d) a convicted person must not be deprived of liberty if less restrictive sanctions may be appropriate in the circumstances; and

(e) when a joint penalty for a person convicted of two or more criminal offenses is being imposed under Article 52 or Article 53, the combined penalty should not be unduly long or harsh.

## Commentary

Article 36 provides a number of secondary considerations that should be taken into account along with the fundamental principle under Article 35.

Paragraph (a): As mentioned in the commentary to Article 35, in addition to the fundamental principle, it is imperative that the court consider the individual circumstances of the convicted person. This process may work in the favor of the convicted person (i.e., reducing the severity of his or her penalty) or against the convicted person (i.e., increasing the severity of his or her penalty). Reference should be made to Article 35 and its accompanying commentary for a more detailed discussion on aggravating and mitigating factors.

Paragraph (b): Also mentioned in the commentary to Article 35 is the fact that the just deserts principle requires the court to consider the seriousness of the convicted person's criminal act in relation to acts of a similarly serious nature. This principle is articulated in Paragraph (b). How exactly is this done? Some states have set up special sentencing bodies or commissions that conduct empirical research on penalties handed down in different cases. Essentially, those bodies group cases according to their similarities, analyze them, and distribute the results to the judges in the state. In other instances, a case compendium is created. Some jurisdictions also draft judges' bench books to give the judge guidance in determining penalties. Commonly, statistical figures on penalties are also provided to judges. Some jurisdictions use training sessions to ensure consistency in the determination of penalties.

Paragraph (c): This paragraph introduces the principle of judicial restraint, a principle that is common in newly reformed laws on penalties in many states. It requires that a penalty of imprisonment be used only as a matter of last resort, having regard to the purposes and principles of penalties and any mitigating and aggravating factors. Judicial restraint is closely linked to the principle of proportionality. It requires that judges look to alternatives to imprisonment. In the MCC, these would include the alternative penalties set out in Articles 55–57. A particular post-conflict state may also rely on restorative justice mechanisms instead of imprisonment. The use of judicial restraint as set out in Paragraph (c) not only introduces an element of proportionality but also softens the blow of the just deserts principle.

In this paragraph, use of the term *sanctions* instead of *penalties*, meaning penalties provided for in the MCC, is deliberate in that it conceives of other measures and sanctions outside the MCC. These measures could include restorative justice outcomes. Reference should be made to the general commentary to Section 12 of the General Part of the MCC, which discusses restorative justice outcomes in more detail.

Some practical issues regarding imprisonment as a potential penalty must also be taken into consideration. In a post-conflict state, prisons have typically either been destroyed or are overcrowded and in a state of disrepair. The result is that there is usually not enough prison space to hold convicted persons. Systems that rely heavily on imprisonment as a penalty for criminal offenses, as has been evidenced in many post-conflict states, encounter great problems in terms of trying to find the resources with which to build or modernize prisons and to ensure that convicted persons are treated humanely and in compliance with international human rights standards. For further elaboration on these issues, reference should be made to the Model Detention Act and its accompanying commentaries. Many states are now turning to alternatives to imprisonment.

Paragraph (d): Like Paragraph (c), Paragraph (d) introduces a proportionality and restraint requirement on the court in determining a penalty. Paragraph (d) requires that deprivation of liberty be imposed only when less restrictive measures are not appropriate. Unlike Paragraph (c), Paragraph (d) applies to all deprivations of liberty and thus can apply not only to imprisonment but also to alternative penalties such as semiliberty. The use of the term *sanctions* instead of *penalties* in this paragraph is deliberate in that it conceives of other measures and sanctions outside of the MCC. Thus, for example, Paragraph (d) could include not only noncustodial penalties under the MCC but also restorative justice outcomes. Reference should be made to the general commentary to Section 12 of the General Part of the MCC, which discusses restorative justice outcomes in more detail.

Paragraph (e): This paragraph is relevant only where a person is being tried for multiple offenses or where he or she is found criminally responsible for an offense during the execution of a penalty. This paragraph should be read in light of Articles 52 and 53. For a further discussion of this issue, reference should be made to these articles and their accompanying commentaries.

# Section 12

## Subsection 2: Penalty Structure

### Article 37: General Penalty Structure

1. The following penalties are provided for in the MCC:
   (a) principal penalties;
   (b) alternative penalties; and
   (c) additional penalties.
2. Penalties for legal persons are dealt with in Section 12.
3. Penalties for juvenile persons are dealt with in Section 14 and are considered separately from penalties under Section 12.

### Commentary

Paragraph 1: As discussed in the general commentary to this section, state practices differ greatly with regard to applicable penalties. Given that the MCC has adopted the structured discretion approach (discussed in the general commentary to Section 12 of the General Part of the MCC), it is imperative to lay down a set of applicable penalties. Later on, the MCC sets out a structured approach to determining the appropriate penalty. In addition, the MCC contains provisions on the relationship between principal penalties, alternative penalties, and additional penalties.

The terms *principal penalty, alternative penalty,* and *additional penalty* may not be familiar to some people, although their equivalents (e.g., *primary, additional,* and *ancillary penalties*) are used in their legal systems. While the nomenclature—and the procedure for determining the penalties—may be different, the particular penalties contained in the MCC are common around the world. Article 38, below, defines principal penalty. Article 39 defines alternative penalties, and Article 40 defines additional penalties.

Security measures, or "safety measures" as they are termed in some states, are a common feature in domestic criminal law. These measures may include compulsory treatment in a psychiatric institution and compulsory treatment of persons addicted to alcohol or drugs. The former is usually ordered after a person is found to have been mentally incompetent at the time of the commission of the criminal offense (reference should be made to Article 23, "Mental Incompetence") or where a person is found to have diminished capacity at the time of commission of the criminal offense; this is not a defense per se but is taken into account as a mitigating factor in the determination of penalties under Article 51(1)(a). In a number of post-conflict environments such as Kosovo persons with serious mental defects were sent to prison rather than to separate treatment facilities due to lack of such facilities. Security measures involving compulsory drug or alcohol addiction treatment are also commonly found in domestic criminal legislation. They are also contained as an international obligation for states parties to the Convention on Psychotropic Substances (1971), Article 22(1)(b), and the United Nations Convention against Illicit Traffic in Narcotic Drugs and Psychotropic Substances (1988), Article 3(4)(b). Compulsory psychiatric treatment and mandatory treatment for drug and alcohol addiction are not considered as separate measures of the MCC. Instead, both can be ordered in conjunction with a suspended sentence under Article 55 or with an order for semiliberty under Article 57.

The other feature of many legal systems not found in the MCC is the penalty of judicial admonition, as it is termed in some systems. In these systems, a judicial admonition exists as a statutory penalty. In systems that have a wide degree of judicial discretion, and consequently where there is no need for legislation to empower a judge to impose a judicial admonition, judicial admonitions or warnings are also commonly used as penalties. A judicial admonition or warning essentially means that the judge warns a person that his or her behavior is serious but does not merit a more severe penalty, and that he or she is free, but that if another offense is subsequently committed, the person may be subject to a more severe penalty. Its most common usage is with minor offenses, such as those carrying a maximum penalty of less than six months' imprisonment. Given the fact that the MCC does not contain minor offenses—the lowest maximum penalty being one year's imprisonment—it was considered inappropriate to include judicial admonition as an applicable penalty. For states implementing new criminal law with less severe penalties that could be addressed through the use of judicial admonition, consideration should be given to including a provision in domestic law as part of the alternative penalties available to the court.

The use of parole, or conditional release, which is not a penalty so much as it is a postpenalty noncustodial disposition, is dealt with in Chapter 11, Part 9, of the MCCP. Reference should be made to the relevant provisions and their accompanying commentaries.

When a state is reforming its domestic laws on penalties, it examines the preexisting penalties that apply under its laws. In addition to adding new penalties, it may wish to consider removing others. For example, many states, in amending their domestic legislation, have chosen to abolish the death penalty as an applicable criminal penalty. Other states have also systematically abolished penalties such as corporal punishment. Corporal punishment, as set out in Amnesty International's *Fair Trials Manual* (section 25.4), is physical punishment involving blows to the body or mutilation, imposed by judicial order. Corporal punishment is considered a violation of international human rights standards, specifically the right to freedom from cruel, inhuman, and degrading punishment. For further discussion of this issue, reference should be made to section 25.4 of the *Fair Trials Manual.*

Paragraph 2: Reference should be made to Articles 68–69 and their accompanying commentaries.

Paragraph 3: While there is some interaction between the provisions of Section 12, on the applicable penalties for legal persons, and Section 14, Section 14 must be read completely separately from Section 12 on the basis that the penalties applicable to persons over the age of eighteen years are not relevant to the unique structure that has been created to apply to juveniles. Reference should be made to Section 14 and its accompanying commentaries.

# Article 38: Principal Penalties

1. The following principal penalties are provided for in the MCC:
   (a) imprisonment;
   (b) life imprisonment; and
   (c) a fine as an alternative principal penalty.
2. A minimum and maximum term of imprisonment for each criminal offense is set out in the Special Part of the MCC.
3. The following minimum and maximum terms of imprisonment are provided for in the MCC:
   (a) one to five years;
   (b) two to ten years;
   (c) three to fifteen years;
   (d) five to twenty years; and
   (e) ten to thirty years.

## Commentary

As is common in many systems, the principal penalties under the MCC are imprisonment or a fine. All the criminal offenses in the Special Part of the MCC have been assigned a specific penalty range, as discussed below. Only a small number of the most serious offenses carry with them a potential penalty of life imprisonment. Conversely, only those considered the least serious of serious offenses carry with them the potential for a principal penalty of a fine instead of imprisonment. A fine may exist either as a principal penalty or as an additional penalty to supplement a principal or alternative penalty. Reference should be made to Articles 50 and 60, below, and their accompanying commentaries.

**Paragraph 1:** For a full discussion on imprisonment, life imprisonment, and fines, reference should be made to Articles 49–51 and their accompanying commentaries.

**Paragraph 2:** There was considerable discussion during the drafting of the Model Codes about whether or not to assign maximum terms of imprisonment or minimum-maximum terms of imprisonment for offenses contained in the MCC. As has been previously discussed, some states allow judges complete discretion in determining the penalty of imprisonment for some criminal offenses. In other states, only the maximum penalty is contained in criminal legislation. Sometimes this is a mandatory maximum penalty, as discussed above in the commentary to Article 38. In other states, both a minimum and a maximum penalty are provided for. The mandatory penalty approach was rejected by the drafters of the MCC because of its lack of flexibility and inability to account for individual circumstances. While some of the experts consulted during the process of vetting the MCC favored the use of maximum penalties only, the approach most favored was assignment of a maximum and minimum term of imprisonment to each criminal offense. Many of the experts consulted felt that this better respected the principle *nulla poena sine lege*, or no penalty without a law.

**Paragraph 3:** One of the greatest criticisms of maximum penalties or minimum-maximum penalties that are set down in legislation is that they are arbitrary and inconsistent with one another. For example, in a particular state (where only maximum penalties are laid down), the maximum penalty of imprisonment for blackmail is the same as the maximum penalty for murder. This situation is common in many states and derives from the fact that penalties for different offenses were not all assigned at the same time. Instead, many penalties in modern criminal codes were decided upon many years ago. Newer criminal offenses are commonly accorded penalties that are often more severe than penalties assigned in the past. The assignment of penalties to new criminal offenses is also often done without reference to preexisting penalties. The law reform commissions of many states have called for a complete overhaul of applicable penalties and a classification and gradation system that accords with the seriousness of the offense. The Council of Europe's *Recommendation No. R(92) 17 of the Committee of Ministers to Member States Concerning Consistency in Sentencing* (paragraph B1) and *Recommendations of Professor Ashworth*, document PC-R-SN (90)11 (paragraph 1), which was submitted to the committee during the drafting of the recommendation (paragraph B1), recommend that "maximum penalties for offenses, and where applicable, minimum penalties should be reviewed so that they form a coherent structure which reflects the relative seriousness of different types of offenses." In some cases, the legislature has followed this advice. In considering law reforms in a post-conflict state, account should be taken of the fact that new penalties should fit with preexisting ones. A post-conflict state may also wish to give consideration to the total reclassification and reassignment of penalty ranges for all offenses under its domestic criminal law.

With regard to the MCC, because all the offenses were drafted at the same time, it was possible to look at the Special Part of the MCC and its offenses holistically and produce coherent and consistent penalties that accord with the seriousness of the criminal offenses. First, offenses were listed and ranked in order of seriousness from one to five. The purpose of this step was to create a hierarchy of criminal offenses and to group similarly serious criminal offenses together within one minimum-maximum penalty range. A group of experts from a variety of legal systems and backgrounds was assigned the task of ranking the seriousness of different criminal offenses. As might be expected, there were differences of opinion as to which offenses were the most serious. Indeed, throughout the consultation and vetting process, there were differences of opinion as to the seriousness of particular criminal offenses and, consequently, the appropriateness of the penalty range assigned to them. Some experts looked at particular provisions and were surprised at how lenient the penalties were, while other experts looked at the same provisions and observed that the penalties were too harsh. This situation demonstrates the subjective nature of penalties and the need for the legal community and the community at large in a post-conflict state to consider how their society views different criminal offenses.

Once the criminal offenses contained in the MCC were ranked according to their seriousness, the next task was to designate appropriate penalty ranges. The drafters were aware that the Council of Europe's *Recommendation No. R(92) 17 of the Committee of Ministers to Member States Concerning Consistency in Sentencing* (paragraph B2) and the *Recommendations of Professor Ashworth* (paragraph B2) recommended that the range of penalties provided for an offense should not be so wide as to afford little guidance to courts on the relative seriousness of the offense. Five penalty ranges, set out in Paragraph 3, were decided upon, mirroring the five-tier ranking of the seriousness of the criminal offenses.

As mentioned previously, the issue of the sorts of penalties that should be contained in domestic legislation, the relative seriousness of particular criminal offenses, and the appropriate penalty ranges that should be assigned to criminal offenses are all sensitive issues. They are also very subjective issues. The penalty provisions of the MCC are an expression of the opinions of the drafters and the many experts from around the world and from many different legal systems who were consulted during the process of vetting the MCC. A post-conflict state may choose to adopt the MCC's provisions, but, of course, it may instead determine for itself the seriousness of particular criminal offenses and the relevant penalty ranges. The most important thing is that a sound and reasoned process and methodology for deciding upon these issues is followed, so that the determinations made are coherent and logical.

# Article 39: Alternative Penalties

The following alternative penalties are provided for in the MCC:

(a) suspended sentences;

(b) community service; and

(c) semiliberty.

## Commentary

Article 36(c), above, provides for the principle that all available sanctions other than imprisonment that are reasonable in the circumstances should be considered by the judge prior to imprisoning a convicted person. Article 39 provides a range of alternatives to imprisonment. There are good reasons for considering alternatives to imprisonment. One reason is that public safety and security can in some cases be protected without recourse to imprisonment as a penalty. Another reason is that the principle of just deserts in some cases can be served through alternatives to imprisonment; indeed, alternative penalties can serve other principles, too, such as rehabilitation, reparations to the community, promotion of a sense of responsibility in the convicted person, and acknowledgement of harm done to the community, all of which are set out in Article 34. Additionally, post-conflict states may face a lack of prisons or prison space, as well as a lack of personnel and resources to run a prison service in accordance with basic standards of humanity and international human rights. In Rwanda, to cite an extreme example, as many as 125,000 persons accused of participation in the 1994 genocide were crowded into the state's prisons, creating a situation that became not only politically problematic but also financially untenable.

Many states, both post-conflict and non–post-conflict, are currently reconsidering their approaches to penalties, most especially the excessive use of imprisonment, in favor of the use of alternative penalties. The United Nations has also introduced a body of principles known as the United Nations Standard Minimum Rules for Non-Custodial Measures (the Tokyo Rules). The Tokyo Rules say that a state should "provide a wide range of non-custodial measures from pre-trial to post-sentencing dispositions" (paragraph 2.3). They also state that alternative penalties should be provided for by law (paragraph 3.1). Reference should be made to the rules, which offer a longer list of alternative penalties (see paragraph 8.2) than is contained in the MCC and also provide many guidelines on the implementation of alternative penalties. Reference should also be made to Penal Reform International's *A Draft 10-Point Plan: To Reduce Imprisonment*, which also advocates the use of alternative penalties (Point 6).

A post-conflict state that is revising its criminal laws should seriously consider the integration of alternative penalties, which are proving successful in societies across the world. Research indicates that alternative penalties such as community service programs are cheaper than imprisonment over the long term. That is not to say that such programs do not pose demands on the meager resources available to post-conflict states. For example, establishing a community service program also requires establishing a body to oversee the program's implementation. A post-conflict state introducing alternative penalties needs to provide sufficient financial, staffing, and other resources to facilitate the execution of the particular penalty prior to its introduction into force through legislation. Otherwise, a judge may have no option other than imprisonment, thus augmenting preexisting problems of prison overcrowding. Fortunately, civil society organizations and non-governmental organizations, both domestic and international, often offer funding and assistance in the establishment of alternative penalties programs.

In light of the principle of judicial restraint articulated in Article 36, courts must give due consideration and priority to the use of alternatives to imprisonment. In some post-conflict states, such as Kosovo, research has found that despite the introduction of alternative penalties, judges are still relying on the use of imprisonment simply because they have long been accustomed to imposing prison sentences and, like most people, are slow to embrace new practices. Accordingly, judicial education and awareness training on the use of alternatives to imprisonment might be required when alternative penalties are introduced.

Reference should be made to Articles 55–57 and their accompanying commentaries, below, for a full discussion on suspended sentences, community service, and semi-liberty. The provisions of the relevant articles regulate matters such as the supervision, duration, conditions, and consequences for breach of conditions of a court order.

# Article 40: Additional Penalties

The following additional penalties are provided for in the MCC:

(a) a fine;

(b) confiscation of the instruments and objects of a criminal offense;

(c) payment of compensation to a victim;

(d) deprivation of the right to be elected to public office;

(e) deprivation of the right to possess or carry firearms;

(f) prohibition on holding a post as a public official;

(g) prohibition on the exercise of managerial or supervisory positions in private legal entities; or

(h) expulsion of a non-national.

## Commentary

Articles 58 and 59 of the MCC provide that an additional penalty may supplement either a principal penalty or an alternative penalty. Additional penalties are useful in that they provide the judge with a wider range of options to pursue the secondary purposes of penalties set out in Article 34. By imposing an additional penalty upon a convicted person, a judge can fulfill the purpose of penalties such as the provision of reparations for harm done to the victim through the payment of compensation to the victim under Paragraph (c). Additional penalties also have a role in safeguarding the public from future criminal conduct, related to some degree to the "incapacitation" principle of penalties, through the expulsion of a non-national under Paragraph (h); the prohibition on a convicted person holding a managerial or supervisory position in a private legal entity under Paragraph (g) (appropriate where a person has been convicted of a criminal offense such as embezzlement); the prohibition on holding a post as a public official under Paragraph (f) (appropriate where a public official has committed a criminal offense); the deprivation of the right to be elected to public office under Paragraph (d); and the prohibition on the right to possess or carry firearms under Paragraph (e). Finally, additional penalties may be used in conjunction with principal penalties and alternative penalties to further promote a sense of responsibility in the convicted person, for example, through imposition of fines under Paragraph (a) and the confiscation of the instruments and objects of a criminal offense under Paragraph (e).

Paragraph (h) should be applied bearing in mind fundamental human rights principles, notably the prohibition of expulsion to a state where an individual would be subjected to a violation of the right to life; to torture or other cruel, inhuman, or degrading treatment or punishment; or to other violations of human rights with irreparable consequences.

Reference should be made to Articles 60–67 and their accompanying commentaries for a full discussion of the additional penalties set out in Article 40.

# Section 12

## Subsection 3: Procedure for Determination of Penalties

### General Commentary

The purposes and principles applicable to the determination of penalties, as well as the range and nature of the penalties provided for in the MCC, have been set out and discussed above. This section explains the procedure by which the penalties are determined in light of the purposes and principles of penalties, and in light of those penalties that are available under the MCC.

This subsection lays out, step by step, the method of reasoning to be followed in deciding what penalty to impose upon a convicted person. It has been drafted in a way that brings a judge sequentially through the various factors and considerations that need to be taken into account before arriving at a final penalty. At first glance, the procedure may appear to be a little unconventional, but it does in fact offer the most straightforward way of applying the relevant provisions of the MCC. The procedure lays out all possible steps that the court may take in cases concerning criminal offenses under the MCC. Only some of these steps will have to be taken in any individual case.

The provisions and the procedure have been reproduced in diagrammatic format. The diagram also illustrates when a court may skip a particular step. Reference should be made to annex 3.

# Article 41: General Procedure for Determination of an Appropriate Penalty

1. The court must decide upon the appropriateness of a particular penalty in light of the fundamental principle set out in Article 35 and the general principles set out in Article 36.
2. The court must adhere to the following procedure:
   (a) in all cases, the court must first look to the minimum and maximum penalty set out in the MCC for the particular offense for which the convicted person has been found criminally responsible;
   (b) in all cases, the court must assess whether there are grounds to adjust the appropriate penalty range, either by augmenting the applicable maximum penalty or by reducing the applicable minimum penalty as set out in Articles 43–47;
   (c) in a relevant case where a person is convicted of the attempted commission of a criminal offense, the court must adjust the penalty range in accordance with Article 48;
   (d) in a relevant case where life imprisonment is an optional penalty, the court must assess the appropriateness of life imprisonment in light of Article 49;
   (e) in a relevant case where a fine is an optional principal penalty for the criminal offense for which the convicted person was found criminally responsible, the court must assess the appropriateness of imposing a fine as set out in Article 50;
   (f) in all cases, the court must then assess the appropriate term of imprisonment to impose, within the applicable penalty range. In doing so, it must take into account the aggravating and mitigating factors set out in Article 51;
   (g) where a person has been convicted of two or more offenses or where a person is convicted of a criminal offense while under the execution of another penalty, the court must determine a joint penalty under Articles 52 and 53;
   (h) in relevant cases, once a specific term of imprisonment has been imposed under Paragraph (g), the court must assess under Article 54 whether an alternative penalty is appropriate, instead of a penalty of imprisonment under Articles 54–57; and

(i) in all cases, once the court has determined an appropriate principal penalty of life imprisonment, imprisonment, or an alternative penalty, the court must assess whether any additional penalties are appropriate under Articles 58–67.

## Commentary

The crux of the procedure established under Article 41 is that the judge first consider the appropriate penalty range provided for in the MCC, then consider any adjustments that can be made to that range. Once the appropriate range has been determined, the judge will consider the appropriate penalty within that range in light of aggravating and mitigating circumstances. It is very important to note that under the MCC a principal penalty (generally one of imprisonment) is imposed upon a person before it is transformed into an alternative penalty. An alternative penalty can be utilized only if a penalty of less than three years' imprisonment is imposed upon the person. So, for example, if X commits a simple robbery and gets one year's imprisonment as a principal penalty, he or she is eligible for an alternative penalty. Where appropriate, the judge will designate an alternative penalty as provided for in the MCC. The importance of designating the original principal penalty becomes relevant if the person does not comply with the conditions of the alternative penalty. In this case, he or she may have to serve the original principal penalty from its beginning. Once an alternative penalty has been assigned, or a principal penalty has been assigned because there was no option to assign an alternative penalty (i.e., where a principal penalty of more than three years' imprisonment was imposed upon the person), the court may then consider whether an additional penalty is also merited.

As mentioned above under the general commentary to Section 12 of the General Part of the MCC, the MCC does not provide for restorative justice programs. Where restorative justice programs are in effect in a state, they must be considered during the determination of the penalty. In some cases, they may act as a mitigating factor only, having no binding legal effect. However, in other domestic jurisdictions, the completion of successful restorative justice programs may preclude the imposition of imprisonment and/or alternative penalties.

**Paragraph 1:** At all times during the penalty determination process, the fundamental principle articulated in Article 35 and the principles set out in Article 36 should be considered. As mentioned throughout the commentaries to this section, the purposes of penalties may also be considered, but only in alignment with Article 35.

**Paragraph 2(a):** At this stage, the judge should look to the specific criminal offense for which the person has been convicted. Reference should be made to the Special Part of the MCC. This minimum-maximum range represents the starting point for the judicial determination of the appropriate penalty.

**Paragraph 2(b):** Articles 44–46 of the MCC set out a number of general aggravating factors that serve to augment the applicable penalty range of a criminal offense, namely, where the criminal offense is committed as part of an organized criminal gang (Article 44); where the convicted person's actions were motivated by hatred (Article 45); or where the convicted person committed the criminal offense as a public official (Article 46). In each of these cases, when the criteria of the particular article are met, the judge may augment the maximum applicable penalty by up to one-half the maximum penalty. Reference should be made to Articles 44–46 and their accompanying commentaries.

Under the Special Part of the MCC, a number of individual aggravating factors may have the same effect as general factors in augmenting the applicable penalty range for a particular criminal offense. Reference should be made to Article 43 and its accompanying commentary.

The aggravating factors under both the General Part and the Special Part of the MCC that have just been discussed are considered separately from those aggravating circumstances set out in Article 51(1), although there may be some overlap in terms of what qualifies. The aggravating factors mentioned in Article 51(1) serve to augment the penalty *range*, as opposed to the individual *term* of the penalty within the defined range. Aggravating factors that augment the term of the penalty to be imposed are considered during a later stage of the determination process. They are set out in Article 51 and considered in more detail in its accompanying commentary.

In the case of mitigation of penalties, Article 47 provides that in "the presence of particularly mitigating circumstances," the court may reduce the minimum period of imprisonment. Unlike the situation regarding augmentation of penalty ranges, there is an overlap between mitigating factors that are considered vis-à-vis the reduction of the penalty *range* and the reduction of the specific *term* of the penalty within a defined range. In deciding whether to adjust the minimum range of the penalty, the court must regard the factors set out in Article 51(1). At this stage, the court may declare, for example, that a penalty range of one to five years should be amended and the new minimum penalty should be three months. The court will then move on in its determination of the appropriate penalty within that range as provided for under the proceedings paragraphs. The rationale and procedure for reducing the penalty range in this fashion are discussed in more detail in the commentary that accompanies Article 51.

**Paragraph 2(c):** Under Article 48, when a person is convicted of the attempted commission of a criminal offense, the penalty range may be reduced by half. So, for example, if a person is held criminally responsible for the attempted commission of an offense carrying a minimum penalty of one year and a maximum penalty of five years, the penalty range may be adjusted to six months minimum, two and one-half years maximum. Reference should be made to Article 48 and its accompanying commentary.

**Paragraph 2(d):** Paragraph 2(d) applies only to the limited number of criminal offenses for which life imprisonment is optional, namely, genocide (Article 86), crimes against humanity (Article 87), war crimes (Article 88), and unlawful killing (Article 89), or where a person is convicted of three or more offenses that carry a potential penalty of five to twenty years' imprisonment (Article 52).

The court should consider the appropriateness of life imprisonment as the principal penalty in accordance with the limitations imposed on this penalty in Article 49. Reference should be made to Article 49 and its accompanying commentary.

**Paragraph 2(e):** Paragraph 2(e) applies only to the limited number of criminal offenses that carry a penalty of one to five years' imprisonment, such as assault (Article 90); threats to kill or cause serious harm (Article 93); unauthorized search of a person and his or her belongings (Article 109); unauthorized search of a dwelling or premises (Article 110); unauthorized visual recording (Article 111); possession of child pornography (Article 118); theft (Article 119); fraud (Article 126); possessing false instruments (Article 130); criminal damage (Article 133); counterfeiting money (Article 134); threat and improper influence (Article 146); unauthorized border and boundary crossing (Article 162); unlawful purchase of firearms, ammunition, explosives, or weapons (Article 167); unlawful possession, control, or ownership of firearms, ammunition, explosives, or weapons (Article 168); unlawful use of firearms (Article 169); cultivation of opium poppy, coca bush, or cannabis plant (Article 173); possession or purchase of narcotic drugs or psychotropic substances (Article 176); preventing the exercise of the right to vote (Article 177); violating the free decision of voters (Article 178); abuse of the right to vote (Article 179); violating confidentiality in voting (Article 180); buying and selling votes (Article 181); alteration or destruction of evidence (Article 189); fabrication of evidence (Article 190); presentation of false or forged evidence (Article 191); false testimony (Article 192); obstruction of justice of a witness (Article 193); obstruction of justice of a justice or policing official (Article 194); failure to respect an order of the court (Article 197); providing assistance to a perpetrator after the commission of a criminal offense (Article 198); false statements of a cooperative witness (Article 199); and revealing a sealed order for protective measures or anonymity (Article 200). With regard to these offenses, the court should consider the appropriateness of a fine as the principal penalty in accordance with the limitations imposed in Article 50. Reference should be made to Article 50 and its accompanying commentary.

**Paragraph 2(f):** Once the procedure set out in Paragraphs 2(a) through 2(e) is carried out or, with regard to offenses other than those that fall into Paragraphs 2(b) through 2(e), once the penalty range has been established following the procedure in Paragraph 2(a), the court must consider the term of the penalty to be imposed upon the convicted person within the penalty range. In doing so, the court must take into account the fundamental principle of just deserts (encapsulating the seriousness of the criminal offense and the convicted person's culpability) and the other principles of penalties in the MCC, as provided for in Paragraph 1 of this article, in addition to the aggravating and mitigating factors set out in Article 51. Implicit in the principle of just deserts and also explicit in Paragraph (b) of Article 36, covering other applicable principles, is the fact that similar penalties should be imposed on similar convicted persons for similar criminal offenses committed in similar circumstances—in other words, the principle of like treatment of like convicted persons should be respected. The commentary to Paragraph (b) of Article 36 discusses how this is achieved. Reference should be made to this commentary. During the determination of penalties phase, provision should be made to implement the aforementioned principle in a practical way.

Paragraph 2(g): This paragraph relates only to a situation where a person has been tried and convicted for two or more criminal offenses at the same time, or where the person is convicted separately of another criminal offense during the execution of the original penalty. Reference should be made to Articles 52 and 53 and their accompanying commentaries.

Paragraph 2(h): Once the precise term of the imprisonment has been calculated based on Paragraph 2(f), and where applicable Paragraph 2(g), the court must consider the appropriateness of alternative penalties. This step will apply only where the penalty for a single offense, or the aggregate penalty for two or more offenses under Paragraph 2(g), totals three years' imprisonment or less. In this case, the court can then move to determine, based on Articles 55, 56, and 57, whether a suspended sentence, community service, or semiliberty would be an appropriate penalty. Reference should be made to these articles and their accompanying commentaries. In cases where the single or aggregate penalty is greater than three years, the court must consider the appropriateness of additional penalties under Paragraph 2(i), without considering alternative penalties.

Paragraph 2(i): Where a principal penalty or an alternative penalty has been decided upon by the court, it may also supplement the penalty with an additional penalty. Reference should be made to Articles 58 and 59 and Articles 60–67 and their accompanying commentaries.

# Article 42: Appraisal of the Applicable Minimum and Maximum Penalty

The court must look to the relevant provision of the Special Part of the MCC for the minimum and maximum penalty applicable to the criminal offense for which a person has been convicted.

# Article 43: Augmentation of the Maximum Period of Imprisonment Based on Individual Aggravating Factors Set Out in the Special Part of the MCC

The court must look to the relevant provision of the Special Part of the MCC to ascertain whether there are any individual aggravating factors applicable to the criminal offense for which a person has been convicted.

## Commentary

The MCC contains two types of aggravating factors whose application may result in the augmentation of the applicable penalty range for a particular criminal offense. The first type of aggravating factor, an individual aggravating factor, is dealt with in Article 43 and in the Special Part of the MCC. Individual aggravating factors include factors such as those contained under Article 137, "Offenses Related to the Smuggling of Migrants," which augments the applicable penalty range where the commission of the offense endangered, or was likely to endanger, the lives or safety of the migrants concerned, or where it entailed inhuman or degrading treatment. Reference should be made to the commentary to Article 137. In relation to property offenses such as theft, fraud, criminal damage, and embezzlement, the applicable penalty range is augmented where the property that was stolen or was subject to fraud or criminal damage was of "high value." For both drug offenses and offenses relating to firearms, ammunition, weapons, or explosives, individual aggravating factors were included in provisions augmenting the applicable penalty range where a person has been convicted of dealing with "large quantities" or "trafficable quantities" of either drugs, firearms, ammunition, weapons, or explosives. Reference should be made to Article 167, "Unlawful Purchase of Firearms, Ammunition, Explosives, or Weapons"; Article 168, "Unlawful Possession, Control, or Ownership of Firearms, Ammunition, Explosives, or Weapons"; Article 170, "Trafficking in Narcotic Drugs and Psychotropic Substances"; Article 171, "Possession or Purchase of Narcotic Drugs or Psychotropic Substances for the Purpose of Trafficking"; Article 172, "Organizing, Managing, or Financing Trafficking in Narcotic Drugs and Psychotropic Substances"; Article 173, "Cultivation of Opium Poppy, Coca Bush, or Cannabis Plant"; and Article 174, "Manufacture, Transport, or Distribution of Precursors."

The individual aggravating factors discussed above and contained in the MCC are in contrast to the general aggravating factors contained in Articles 44–46. Both general and individual aggravating factors should be considered in the course of determining an appropriate penalty.

# Article 44: Augmentation of the Maximum Period of Imprisonment When a Criminal Offense Is Committed as Part of Organized Criminal Activity

1. The court may augment the maximum penalty prescribed for a particular criminal offense, for a period up to one-half of the maximum penalty prescribed for that criminal offense, when this course is justified by the presence of aggravating circumstances and when the convicted person committed the criminal offense as part of the organized criminal activity.
2. Article 44 does not apply to the criminal offense of participation in an organized criminal group, discussed in Article 136.
3. When the maximum period of imprisonment is augmented by the court, it may not impose a period of imprisonment longer than thirty years.

## Commentary

Article 44 lays out a general aggravating factor that may be applied to any criminal offense with the exception of the offense of participation in an organized criminal group, discussed in Article 136, as this offense already involves the sort of activity covered in this article. Article 44, in contrast to Article 136, looks at participation in an organized criminal *activity*, as opposed to an organized criminal *group*, as the applicable aggravating factor. When a convicted person is found to have committed the applicable criminal offense as part of an organized criminal activity, and where there are aggravating circumstances, the maximum penalty may be augmented. In a post-conflict state where organized criminal activities pose a significant threat to stability, such a provision may be an important tool.

Where the court chooses not to augment the applicable penalty range, it may still consider the commission of the criminal offense as part of an organized criminal group to be an aggravating factor in determining an appropriate penalty, as provided for in Article 51(2)(l).

Paragraph 3: This paragraph sets out the principle that in augmenting the maximum period of imprisonment, the court may not impose a period of imprisonment of more than thirty years. Thirty years' imprisonment is the highest applicable penalty, bar that of life imprisonment. Because life imprisonment under the MCC is imposed only in a small number of the most serious offenses, it was considered inappropriate to extend its scope to other individual offenses. Thus Paragraph 3 precludes the use of life imprisonment when the maximum penalty is augmented based on participation in an organized criminal activity.

# Article 45: Augmentation of the Maximum Period of Imprisonment When a Criminal Offense Is Motivated by Hatred

1. Except in relation to the criminal offense of "Incitement to Crime on Account of Hatred," under Article 161, the court may augment the maximum penalty prescribed for a particular criminal offense, for a period of up to one-half of the maximum penalty prescribed for that criminal offense, when this course is justified by the presence of aggravating circumstances and when the criminal offense was motivated by hatred based on race; color; religion or belief; gender; age; political or other opinion; national, ethnic, or social origin; disability; sexual orientation; or birth status.
2. When the maximum period of imprisonment is augmented by the court, the court may not impose a period of imprisonment longer than thirty years.

## Commentary

Article 161 of the MCC criminalizes a person for incitement to crime on account of hatred. Reference should be made to Article 161 and it accompanying commentary. The MCC does not criminalize the commission of a criminal offense with a specific hate motive, as is the case in some jurisdictions. The criminalization of incitement to crime on account of hatred is an international obligation, as discussed in the commentary to Article 161. However, there is considerable disagreement among different states, and a considerable divergence in practice, in relation to the penalization of the perpetrator of a criminal offense motivated by hate. Some states have criminalized this form of aggravated commission of a criminal offense and provide for steep penalties. The drafters of the MCC were cognizant of the importance, particularly in a post-conflict state, of addressing hate crimes. However, they were also aware that the power to punish hate crimes is a very powerful tool that can be abused. A compromise position was thus reached that allows the applicable penalty range for a criminal offense motivated by hatred to be augmented when the court considers it appropriate.

Where the court chooses not to augment the applicable penalty range, the court may still consider the presence of hatred to be an aggravating factor in sentencing, as provided for in Article 51(2)(e).

The criminal offense of incitement to crime on account of hatred is excluded from the ambit of this article, as there is already an aggravating hate factor contained in the elements of the criminal offense.

Paragraph 2: Reference should be made to the commentary to Article 44(3).

# Article 46: Augmentation of the Maximum Period of Imprisonment for a Criminal Offense Committed by a Public Official

1. The court may augment the maximum penalty prescribed for a particular criminal offense, for a period of up to one-half the maximum penalty prescribed for that criminal offense, when the criminal offense was committed by a public official while he or she was acting in his or her role as a public official.
2. This provision does not apply to the commission of the criminal offenses:
   (a) of corruption involving a public official as defined in Article 138;
   (b) of corruption involving a foreign public official or an official of a public international organization as defined in Article 139; and
   (c) contained in Section 10 of the Special Part of the MCC.
3. When the maximum period of imprisonment is augmented by the court, the court may not impose a period of imprisonment longer than thirty years.

## Commentary

The elements of some criminal offenses, such as those listed in Paragraph 2, require that they be committed by a public official. Reference should be made to the relevant articles. These offenses are excluded from the scope of Article 46 because the penalties attached to them already take into consideration the fact that they were perpetrated by a public official who abused his or her position of trust. For all other criminal offenses, the court may augment its applicable maximum penalty when the criminal offense was committed by a person while he or she was acting in his or her role as a public official. Reference should also be made to Article 1(9) on the definition of *public official.*

The underlying rationale for Article 46 is to encourage public officials to perform their duties with integrity and honesty. A similar rationale underlies the prohibition on holding a post as a public official set out in Article 65 as an additional penalty. The drafters of the MCC considered it important to take strong measures against the abuse of a position of trust by a public official. Post-conflict states may well have a history of abuse of public office and corruption, a history that must be addressed to build a society that is governed by the rule of law.

Paragraph 2: Reference should be made to the commentary to Article 44(3).

# Article 47: Reduction of the Minimum Period of Imprisonment Due to Particularly Mitigating Circumstances

The court may reduce the minimum penalty prescribed for a particular criminal offense by one-half the minimum penalty prescribed for that criminal offense when the presence of particularly mitigating circumstances justifies the reduction.

## Commentary

During the course of drafting the penalties provisions in the MCC, there was much debate among experts about whether to use the minimum-maximum penalty system or simply to provide for a maximum penalty for each individual criminal offense. The drafters eventually decided to adopt the minimum-maximum penalty system, but they also decided to put that system within the framework of structured discretion. As a consequence, while the penalty structure and penalty procedure exist, they are not totally rigid. For example, mitigating and aggravating circumstances have a substantial effect on the particular term of imprisonment that is decided upon within the applicable minimum and maximum penalty range.

Despite this flexibility, the drafters of the MCC and many of the experts consulted in the course of vetting the MCC were concerned about a rigid minimum penalty. Many argued that this system could provide for unjust results, where a person is convicted of a criminal offense but where significant mitigating circumstances merit a penalty below the minimum provided for the particular offense. They argued that there should be a mechanism that allows a court to impose a penalty of less than one year's imprisonment in the case of a criminal offense carrying a potential penalty of one to five years' imprisonment or, in relation to the other penalty ranges, to depart from the minimum periods of imprisonment. This is why Article 47 has been included in the MCC. Its effect is on the minimum-maximum penalty range rather than on the term of imprisonment within that range. Some experts expressed concern that allowing for a reduction in the minimum period of imprisonment runs counter to the principle of legality set out in Article 3. The structured-discretion approach adopted in the

MCC is, however, consistent with the principle of legality. As discussed in the commentary to Article 3, the principle of legality does not require that judges have no discretion but rather that this discretion be appropriately guided by legislation, which is the case in Article 47.

# Article 48: Reduction of the Minimum Period of Imprisonment for Attempted Offenses

The court may reduce the minimum penalty prescribed for a particular criminal offense by one-half the minimum penalty prescribed for that criminal offense when the convicted person is convicted of attempt to commit a criminal offense.

## Commentary

Reference should be made to Article 27, "Attempt," and its accompanying commentary. As mentioned in that commentary, despite the intention of the perpetrator, an attempt does not become a completed offense if he or she has been frustrated in one way or another. The fact that the criminal offense was not fully completed merits some consideration by the court in determining an appropriate penalty. Where the court sees fit, it may reduce the minimum applicable penalty range for an attempted offense.

# Article 49: Determination of the Appropriateness of Life Imprisonment as a Principal Penalty

1. Life imprisonment is provided for as a principal penalty in the MCC.
2. Life imprisonment may be imposed as a principal penalty only where it is specified in the Special Part of the MCC and only where:
   (a) the criminal offense was committed intentionally; and

(b) life imprisonment is justified by the presence of particularly aggravating circumstances.

3. Life imprisonment may also be imposed in accordance with Article 52.

4. Life imprisonment may not be imposed upon a convicted person who was under eighteen years of age at the time of the commission of a criminal offense.

## Commentary

States differ greatly in principle and in practice in their approaches to the issue of life imprisonment. In some states, life imprisonment is constitutionally prohibited as cruel, inhuman, or degrading punishment and therefore is not an applicable penalty. In other states, despite a lack of constitutional prohibition, there exists a legal prohibition on life imprisonment through setting the maximum allowable period of imprisonment at a particular level, for example, thirty years. In yet other states, life imprisonment is provided as a mandatory sentence with respect to some serious criminal offenses. The MCC allows for the possibility of life imprisonment for a small number of criminal offenses, namely, genocide (Article 86), crimes against humanity (Article 87), war crimes (Article 88), and unlawful killing (Article 89). The court is restrained in the imposition of life imprisonment by two limitations specified in Article 49(2). First, the criminal offense must be committed intentionally. Second, there must be "particularly aggravating circumstances." In considering whether to impose a penalty of life imprisonment upon a person, the court must have regard to the fundamental principle in Article 35 and the other principles in Article 36 (including aggravating and mitigating circumstances), in particular Paragraph (b) on judicial restraint in imposing a sentence of imprisonment.

Paragraph 3: Reference should be made to Article 52 and its accompanying commentary.

Paragraph 4: It is prohibited to impose a penalty of life imprisonment upon a convicted person who was under eighteen years old at the time of commission of the criminal offense. This provision is based on the fact that there are different purposes applicable to juvenile dispositions that are not met by providing for a term of life imprisonment for a juvenile, as discussed in Section 14 of the General Part and its accompanying commentaries. Article 37(a) of the United Nations Convention on the Rights of the Child prohibits life imprisonment without the possibility of release for persons who were under the age of eighteen years when the offense was committed. Paragraph 4 seeks to implement this international standard. All the experts consulted during the process of vetting the MCC supported the prohibition on life imprisonment for juveniles and for adults who committed a criminal offense while still a juvenile.

# Article 50: Determination of the Appropriateness of a Fine as a Principal Penalty

1. A fine as an alternative principal penalty applies to criminal offenses that carry a potential penalty of one to five years' imprisonment, as set out in the Special Part of the MCC.
2. A fine may be no less than [insert monetary amount] and may not exceed [insert monetary amount].
3. The court must consider the convicted person's ability to pay the fine in assigning a particular fine.
4. In imposing a fine, the court must allow the convicted person a reasonable period of time in which to pay the fine.
5. The court may provide for payment of a lump sum or payment by way of installments paid at designated dates during a designated time frame.
6. In the case of willful nonpayment of a fine, the court, where it is satisfied that all available enforcement measures have been exhausted, may impose upon the convicted person:
   (a) a term of imprisonment for a period not exceeding one year; or
   (b) an alternative penalty under Subsection 4 of Section 12.

## Commentary

The use of a fine as a principal penalty is applicable only to certain less serious offenses. Article 50 sets out principles and procedures relevant to the imposition of fines.

In considering whether to impose a penalty of a fine upon a person, the court must have regard to the fundamental principle in Article 35 and the other principles in Article 36 (including aggravating and mitigating factors), in particular Paragraph (c) on judicial restraint in imposing a sentence of imprisonment and the principle that requires that the less restrictive penalty be imposed if appropriate.

Paragraph 1: The method of determining an appropriate fine differs from state to state. Some states have a complex system of fine calculation in which the convicted person is fined in proportion to his or her daily income. This is called the day fine system. The daily income of a convicted person is assessed and a set number of days are designated as the penalty to be imposed upon the person. For example, he or she may be required to pay the equivalent of thirty days of income. This mode of calculation is considered superior in some respects because it takes the individual earning capacity of the convicted person into account. Critics of the day fine system charge that it works to the prejudice of poor convicted persons while allowing rich convicted persons to escape imprisonment. Some consideration was given to the use of the daily fine system, although it was eventually decided not to include it into the MCC in spite of its apparent merits. One reason it was not included is because systems using this mode of calculation have experienced difficulties in determining and calculating the actual income of convicted persons. Another reason for not using this process in the MCC is that it is quite complicated and requires systems and structures that might not be available in a post-conflict state. Further, in many post-conflict states, accurate and official earning records may simply not exist. Instead, minimum and maximum fines have been introduced into the MCC. The proviso to this process, set out in Paragraph 3, is that the court must look at the convicted person's ability to pay the fine in this regard.

Paragraph 6: The issue of what to do when a convicted person defaults on the payment of a fine is hotly debated in states considering the reform of penalty provisions, including systems for the payment of fines. In some states, default on a fine leads to automatic imprisonment. Were this system to be adopted in the MCC, the problem of lack of prison space and resources would come into play. Instead of a system of automatic imprisonment for fine default, the MCC allows the court to consider either an alternative penalty or a term of imprisonment, not in excess of one year.

# Article 51: Determination of the Appropriate Term of Imprisonment in Light of General Mitigating and Aggravating Circumstances

1. In determining an appropriate penalty to impose upon a convicted person, the court must take into account any mitigating factors based on the individual circumstances of the convicted person, including but not limited to:
   (a) circumstances falling short of grounds for exclusion of criminal responsibility, for example, diminished mental capacity;
   (b) evidence of provocation by the victim;
   (c) the personal circumstances and character of the convicted person;

(d) evidence that the convicted person played a relatively minor role in the criminal offense;

(e) the fact that the convicted person participated in the criminal offense not as the principal perpetrator but through aiding, abetting, or otherwise assisting him or her;

(f) the age of the convicted person, whether young or elderly;

(g) evidence that restitution or compensation was made to the victim by the convicted person;

(h) general cooperation with the court, including voluntary surrender of the convicted person;

(i) the voluntary cooperation of the perpetrator in a criminal investigation or prosecution;

(j) the entering of a plea of criminal responsibility (a guilty plea);

(k) any remorse shown by the convicted person;

(l) post-conflict conduct of the convicted person; and

(m) in the case of a person convicted of the criminal offense of enforced disappearance, under Article 104, effectively contributing to bringing the disappeared person forward alive or voluntarily providing information that contributes to solving cases of enforced disappearance or identifying those responsible for the criminal offense of enforced disappearances.

2. In determining an appropriate penalty to impose upon a convicted person, the court must take into account any aggravating factors based on the individual circumstances of the convicted person, including but not limited to:

(a) a high degree of participation of the convicted person in the criminal offense;

(b) a high degree of intention on the part of the convicted person, including any evidence of premeditation;

(c) the presence of actual or threatened violence in the commission of the criminal offense;

(d) whether the criminal offense was committed with particular cruelty;

(e) whether the criminal offense was committed for any motive involving discrimination on account of hatred for a national, ethnic, racial, religious, or similarly identifiable group;

(f) whether the criminal offense involved multiple victims;

(g) whether the victim of the criminal offense was particularly defenseless or vulnerable;

(h) the age of the victim, whether young or elderly;

(i) the extent of the damage caused by the convicted person, including death, permanent injury, the transmission of a disease to the victim, and any other harm caused to the victim and his or her family;

(j) any abuse of power or official capacity by the convicted person in the perpetration of the criminal offense;

(k) evidence of a breach of trust by the convicted person;

(l) whether the criminal offense was committed as part of the activities of an organized criminal group; or

(m) any relevant prior criminal convictions of the convicted person.

3. The court must designate a period of imprisonment within the minimum and maximum terms of imprisonment provided for the particular criminal offense based on any aggravating or mitigating circumstances.

4. Once the court has designated a term of imprisonment, it must then deduct the time, if any, previously spent in detention under court order or in an institute for the care of mentally ill persons, prior to or during the trial. The court may deduct any time otherwise spent in detention in connection with conduct underlying the criminal offense.

5. The period of imprisonment imposed by the court under Paragraph 3, and the period of imprisonment that the convicted person must serve, if different (based on any time that has been deducted under Paragraph 4), must be pronounced in years, months, and days.

## Commentary

Once the court has determined the applicable penalty range, it must then decide what term of imprisonment to impose upon a convicted person within that particular range. Whether that term is high or low will depend on the presence or absence of aggravating and mitigating factors, the former augmenting the potential term and the latter reducing the potential term. In this phase of the determination of the penalty, the court takes into account individual factors relating to the convicted person and to the particular offense he or she has committed. The mitigating and aggravating factors provided for in this article are elaborative but not exhaustive; the court may take into account any other relevant factors in addition to the ones mentioned in Article 51. In line with the Council of Europe's *Recommendation No. R(92) 17 of the Committee of Ministers to Member States Concerning Consistency in Sentencing* and *Recommendations of Professor Ashworth* (document PC-R-SN [90]11, paragraph C2), major aggravating and mitigating factors must be clarified in law.

Paragraph 1: The mitigating factors set out in Paragraph 1 have been arrived at after a comparative survey of sentencing/penalties legislation from different legal systems around the world. The list has also been lengthened by incorporating the suggestions of individual experts consulted during the process of vetting the MCC. Considerable attention was also given to international conventions that specify, in relation to certain criminal offenses, particular mitigating factors that should be taken into account in the determination of a penalty (see the discussion under Paragraph 1[m]). Also included in the comparative survey was a detailed study of mitigating factors that have been taken into account by the International Criminal Tribunal for the former Yugoslavia and the International Criminal Tribunal for Rwanda. The purpose of this study was to elucidate factors that were common in both domestic and international practice and to ensure that factors relevant to the penalization of persons convicted of the criminal offenses of genocide, crimes against humanity, and war crimes were included in Article 51 (given that these criminal offenses are contained in the Special Part of the MCC). Most of the mitigating factors considered in international forums are common to domestic systems, bar factors such as those in Paragraph 1(l).

The MCC imposes a mandatory obligation upon the court to consider these mitigating factors, in addition to any other relevant factors. In its judgment, the court must articulate which factors it took into account and how they affected the term of imprisonment to be imposed.

Paragraph 1(a): The MCC sets out various grounds for excluding criminal responsibility in Section 9, Articles 23–26. When a person falls under any of these grounds, he or she is not held to be criminally responsible for the criminal offense he or she committed. In some cases, a person may not qualify for a defense based on one of these grounds, as the evidence of the defense is not strong enough to fully absolve the person from criminal responsibility. That said, the evidence taken into account may be applied to mitigate a penalty rather than to absolve a person from this penalty. Mental incompetence, under Article 23, is a prime example. A person may not qualify under this ground, as Article 23 provides for a very strict test. Reference should be made to Article 23 and its accompanying commentary. A person may not be "mentally incompetent," but he or she may be suffering from "diminished responsibility," meaning his or her mental competence is not "destroyed" (as required in Article 23) but is "diminished" through an abnormality of mind that substantially impairs his or her mental responsibility for his or her acts. In some states, diminished responsibility is known as a "partial defense," under which a person found criminally responsible for murder may be liable only for manslaughter if diminished responsibility is proven. Under the MCC, diminished responsibility is a mitigating factor rather than a partial defense.

Paragraph 1(b): In some legal systems, the existence of provocation, like diminished responsibility discussed above, is a partial defense to criminal offenses such as murder. Provocation means that the offender, by reason of things that were done or said to him or her, was provoked by the victim to lose his or her self-control.

Paragraph 1(c): This is a general provision that allows for the introduction of character evidence about the convicted person and evidence as to his or her personal circumstances that would act in mitigation of the penalty. It might show, for example, that the exhibition of violence during the commission of a criminal offense was totally out of character for the convicted person.

Paragraph 1(e): Under Article 31, a person who aids, abets, or otherwise assists in the commission of a criminal offense is held to be liable for the perpetration of the criminal offense. The position adopted by the drafters of the MCC is that the person is an accomplice to the commission of the criminal offense rather than an accessory (in which case the person could not be held liable as the principal perpetrator). In states that have adopted a line of reasoning similar to that adopted by the drafters of the MCC, domestic legislation contains specific reference to the mitigation of the applicable penalty on the basis that the person's level of participation was not as serious as that of the principal perpetrator of the criminal offense. The court may wish to take this into account in assigning an appropriate penalty to a convicted person. The exact mitigating effect this will have on the penalty to be imposed will depend on the level of aiding, abetting, or otherwise assisting. Obviously, the less the degree of assistance, aid, or abetment provided to the perpetrator, the more leniently a court may look upon a convicted person.

Paragraph 1(g): Restorative justice programs may be considered under this mitigating ground. Reference should be made to the general commentary to Section 12 and Article 34 of the General Part of the MCC.

Paragraph 1(i): Under the MCCP, a person may qualify as a cooperative witness where the criteria laid down in Chapter 8, Part 4, Section 3, are met. Reference should be made to the relevant articles and their accompanying commentaries. Where a person does not satisfy the criteria, or where he or she is ineligible to apply to be a cooperative witness (e.g., where he or she is accused of genocide, crimes against humanity, or war crimes and is thus precluded from applying for cooperative witness status), under Paragraph 1(i) any cooperation with the court may still be considered a factor that will act in favor of the convicted person when the penalty is being determined.

Paragraph 1(j): The MCCP provides a mechanism called proceedings upon admission of criminal responsibility, under which a person can claim criminal responsibility for a criminal offense, often in the hope of receiving a mitigation of his or her penalty. An agreement may even be entered into with the prosecutor. The agreement with the prosecutor is not binding upon the court. However, it can play a considerable role in the mitigation of a penalty under this paragraph. The court may wish to take any plea agreement between the prosecutor and the convicted person, although it is not bound by it.

Paragraph 1(l): As mentioned above, a survey of mitigating factors taken into account by the two international ad hoc criminal tribunals was undertaken in the course of drafting the MCC provisions. One finding that is unique to the tribunals and not contained in domestic legislation is that of the post-conflict conduct of the convicted person. This could include, for example, any efforts of the convicted person to bring about national reconciliation after the conflict.

Paragraph 1(m): This mitigating factor is specified in the United Nations Declaration on the Protection of All Persons from Enforced Disappearances, Article 4(2), and the United Nations International Convention on the Protection of All Persons from Forced Disappearances, Article 5(2).

Paragraph 2: The aggravating factors set out in Paragraph 2 were arrived at after a comparative survey of sentencing/penalties legislation from different legal systems around the world.

The MCC imposes a mandatory obligation upon the court to consider these aggravating factors, in addition to any other relevant factors. In its judgment, the court must articulate which factors it took into account and how they affected the term of imprisonment to be imposed.

Paragraphs 2(e), 2(j) (in the context of the person being a public official), and 2(l) are also factors that the court may use to augment the penalty *range*, as opposed to the *term* of the penalty. Where the court decides not to augment the penalty term, it may still consider these factors as aggravating factors in determining the term of the penalty within the original penalty range.

Paragraphs 2(a) through 2(e) of Paragraph 2 deal with the conduct and intention of the convicted person during the criminal offense; Paragraphs 2(f) through 2(i) deal with issues relating to the victim; Paragraphs 2(j) and 2(k) address abuses of position in the commission of the criminal offense; Paragraph 2(l) discusses the commission of the criminal offense in the context of organized criminal activities; and, finally, Paragraph 2(m) relates to recidivism, an issue aside from that of the criminal offense in question.

Paragraph 2(a): Whether the convicted person directly perpetrated the criminal offense or had a lesser degree of participation, such as aiding or abetting, should be taken into account in the determination of a penalty. Obviously, the greater the degree of participation in the criminal offense, the greater the importance of this aggravating factor. Reference should be made to Section 11 of the General Part, “Participation in a Criminal Offense,” and its accompanying commentaries.

Paragraph 2(b): Where there is a high degree of intention on the part of the convicted person, such as where the criminal offense was premeditated or planned, this will constitute an aggravating factor.

Paragraph 2(m): As mentioned in the commentary to Article 35, a fundamental tension exists between the just deserts principle followed in the MCC and the augmentation of penalties on account of recidivism. *Recidivism* means a relapse in criminal behavior. Paragraph 2(m) thus applies to repeat offenders or persons who exhibit a pattern of criminal behavior. The Council of Europe’s *Draft Recommendations on Consistency in Sentencing of the Committee of Ministers of the Council of Europe* (paragraph D1) provides that recidivism should not be used mechanically at any stage of the proceedings against the defendant; while recidivism can be taken into account as an aggravating factor, the focus should be on the seriousness of the offense and not on prior tendencies toward criminality. The *Recommendations of Professor Ashworth* (document PC-R-SN [90]11) states that "the imposition of substantial penalties on recidivists convicted of minor crimes goes against the policy of judicial restraint in the use of imprisonment, as well as fostering inconsistency." Ultimately, the court will need to look at the criminal history of the convicted person and consider the seriousness of any prior offenses in addition to the pattern of criminal conduct and their proximity in time and type to the current offense.

Paragraph 3: If a penalty of less than three years' imprisonment is imposed upon the convicted person at this stage in the determination of a penalty, the court may move to consider the possibility of alternative penalties. If a penalty of more than three years' imprisonment is imposed upon the person, the court must move to Paragraph 4 and deduct any prior periods of detention from the term of imprisonment imposed.

Paragraph 4: Any time spent in detention prior to the trial or during the trial must be deducted from the final term of imprisonment imposed upon a convicted person. This is standard practice throughout the world. Therefore, if a person were sentenced to five years' imprisonment, but he or she had already served one year in pretrial detention and detention during trial, the judgment should state that the term of imprisonment is five years but the convicted person will serve four years' imprisonment. In addition to time spent in detention pretrial or during the trial, any time spent in an institute for the care of mentally ill persons should be deducted from the final term of imprisonment. A person may spend time in an institute for the care of mentally ill persons when he or she has been declared temporarily mentally incompetent.

# Article 52: Determination of a Joint Penalty for Convictions on Two or More Criminal Offenses

1. When a person has been convicted of two or more criminal offenses in the same proceedings, the court must pronounce a penalty for each individual criminal offense and then impose a joint penalty.
2. The joint penalty must exceed the highest individual penalty pronounced and must be less than the sum of all the individual penalties pronounced. In the case of a penalty of imprisonment, the joint penalty must not exceed thirty years.

3. In the case of a penalty of imprisonment, the joint penalty must not exceed ten years when each of the individual penalties imposed by the court is less than three years.
4. Exceptionally, a joint penalty of life imprisonment may be imposed when the court has pronounced individual penalties each exceeding fifteen years' imprisonment for at last three criminal offenses and where life imprisonment is justified by particularly aggravating circumstances.

## Commentary

Paragraph 1: When a person is convicted of two or more offenses, the applicable term of imprisonment for each offense should be considered separately. The procedure set out in Article 41 should be undertaken for each criminal offense, and individual applicable terms should be determined.

Paragraph 2: Under the MCC, where a person has been found criminally responsible for two or more criminal offenses, the court must decide upon a joint penalty for all the criminal offenses. This joint penalty must be greater than the highest individual penalty pronounced by the court but must also not exceed thirty years. Thirty years was determined by the drafters of the MCC as the maximum joint penalty that should be imposed upon a convicted person, except as provided for in Paragraph 4 (or where a particular criminal offense provides for life imprisonment as the maximum potential penalty). The restrictions on the maximum length of the joint penalty apply to imprisonment but also to alternative penalties, such as semiliberty and community service, and also to additional penalties, such as expulsion of a non-national.

Paragraph 3: The purpose of this paragraph is to ensure that, where a person is convicted of a number of criminal offenses for which the court pronounces a relatively low penalty, the person is not sentenced to a joint penalty that is disproportionate to the gravity of the individual offenses.

Paragraph 4: Under this paragraph, where the court pronounces individual penalties each of fifteen or more years' imprisonment, the court has the option to impose a joint penalty of imprisonment. Thus, for instance, where a person is convicted on three separate counts of rape (all of which are committed in a particularly heinous manner) and in each case a penalty of sixteen years' imprisonment is pronounced by the court, the court may impose a joint penalty of life imprisonment rather than be limited by the thirty-year maximum limitation set out in Paragraph 2. By its nature, this provision is limited to those situations concerning criminal offenses in the higher penalty ranges. In addition, life imprisonment may only be imposed as a joint penalty where the court finds particularly aggravating circumstances.

# Article 53: Subsequent Imposition of a Penalty on a Convicted Person

1. When a person who is currently serving a penalty for an offense is convicted of another offense that was committed prior to the conviction for the first offense, the court must impose a joint penalty under Article 52 for the first and the second offenses.
2. When a person who is currently serving a penalty for an offense commits another offense, the court must impose a separate penalty for the new criminal offense, which will come into effect only when the previous penalty has expired.

## Commentary

This article applies to criminal offenses committed during the execution of a penalty or prior to the imposition of the initial penalty. Paragraph 1 deals with a scenario where a person who has been convicted of a criminal offense (offense 1) and is serving this sentence is then convicted of another criminal offense (offense 2) that was committed prior to conviction on offense 1. In this scenario, the penalties pronounced for offense 1 and offense 2 are taken into account together to create a joint penalty under Article 52.

Under Paragraph 2, a person is serving a penalty for a criminal offense and commits a criminal offense while he or she is serving that penalty (i.e., after the person has been convicted by the court). In this scenario, in contrast to Paragraph 1, the offenses and their accompanying penalties are dealt with separately rather than by way of joint penalty.

# Article 54: Replacement of a Principal Penalty with an Alternative Penalty

1. When the court pronounces a penalty of imprisonment not exceeding three years, either for a single offense or for multiple offenses, prior to any deductions spent in detention under Article 51(4), it may then replace this principal penalty of imprisonment with an alternative penalty.

2. In determining whether an alternative penalty is more appropriate than the principal penalty of imprisonment, the court must have regard to:
   (a) the gravity of the criminal offense committed;
   (b) the gravity of the consequences of the criminal offense;
   (c) the degree of criminal responsibility of the convicted person;
   (d) any aggravating and mitigating factors set out in Article 51; and
   (e) the character and personal circumstances of the convicted person.

## Commentary

Reference should be made to the commentary to Article 39, discussing alternative penalties. Reference should also be made to the commentary to the principles applicable to penalties, particularly Articles 36(c) and 36(d), which also discuss the need and benefits of imposing alternative penalties.

Paragraph 1: After the court has imposed a term of imprisonment upon a person, and that term for either a single offense or multiple offenses is less than three years, the court moves to a new stage in the determination of the penalty: determination of the appropriateness of an alternative penalty. If this step is considered appropriate, the court must choose which alternative penalty to impose, and then it must follow the guidelines set out in Article 55 (on suspended sentences), Article 56 (on community service), or Article 57 (on semiliberty). Obviously, alternative penalties will not be appropriate in all cases. Nor are they appropriate in the case of very serious criminal offenses, which is why a three-year term of imprisonment was chosen as a cut-off point. The MCC contains only relatively serious offenses. In post-conflict states where legislation regulates less serious offenses, alternative penalties are a valuable tool in dealing with this level of criminality. According to the Council of Europe's Recommendation (92)17 Concerning Consistency in Sentencing, paragraph B5(2), "custodial sentences should be regarded as a sanction of last resort, and should therefore be imposed only in cases where, taking due account of other relevant circumstances, the seriousness of the offense would make any other sentence clearly inadequate."

Paragraph 2: Many factors that the court must take into account in considering whether to impose an alternative penalty are considered under Article 51 on aggravating and mitigating factors and in Articles 35 and 36 on the fundamental principle and other principles relevant to penalties, respectively. The crux of Paragraph 2 is to direct the court to consider the appropriateness of an alternative penalty in light of the seriousness of the offense, the level of culpability of the convicted person (both required under the fundamental principle), aggravating and mitigating factors (required under Article 36[a]), and the character and individual circumstances of the convicted person. The last issue is important from the perspective of not only whether an alternative penalty is appropriate but also which one would be appropriate in light of the character and circumstances of the convicted person. For example, a convicted person may be the sole money provider in a family, and he or she may be working more than full-time to earn money and is not deemed a safety risk to the community. In this case, a suspended sentence or semiliberty may be appropriate. It might not be appropriate to impose community service upon him or her, given that he or she may already work a large number of hours per week.

## Article 55: Suspended Sentence as an Alternative Penalty

1. A suspended sentence is an alternative penalty.
2. When the court pronounces a penalty of imprisonment not exceeding three years, either for a single offense or for multiple offenses, it may then replace this principal penalty of imprisonment with a suspended sentence.
3. A suspended sentence means that a sentence of imprisonment has been imposed upon a convicted person; however, the court orders that the sentence of imprisonment will not be enforced, subject only to its potential revocation under Paragraphs 5, 6, and 11(b).
4. When the court decides to impose a suspended sentence instead of the principal penalty of imprisonment, the court must set a probation period for the convicted person. The probation period determined by the court must not be less than one year and must not be greater than five years.
5. If the convicted person commits a criminal offense and is convicted of this offense within the probation period or five years afterward, the court must revoke the suspended sentence. When the suspended sentence is revoked, the convicted person must be imprisoned and must serve the original penalty of imprisonment that was imposed upon him or her.
6. The court may revoke a suspended sentence and order execution of the penalty of imprisonment if, after the suspended sentence is imposed:
   (a) the court learns that the convicted person perpetrated another criminal offense prior to the imposition of the suspended sentence and was convicted for this criminal offense within the probation period or five years afterward; and
   (b) in the court's view, had the existence of the previously committed offense been known to the court, a suspended sentence would not have been merited.

7. In the event of revocation of the suspended sentence for prior or new criminal offenses under Paragraphs 5 and 6, the court must impose a joint penalty for both criminal offenses in accordance with Article 52.
8. In imposing the suspended sentence, the court may impose additional penalties under Article 59 and it may also require that the convicted person:
   (a) undergo counseling or treatment for alcohol and other substance abuse or addiction;
   (b) undergo mental health, including psychiatric or psychological, counseling or treatment;
   (c) be prohibited from staying at designated places or areas;
   (d) stay away from and refrain from contacting certain persons; or
   (e) comply with any other obligations prescribed by law.
9. In imposing additional obligations under Paragraph 8, the court must determine the time limit for the performance of these obligations. The same time limits set out for the probation period in Paragraph 4 apply to these additional obligations.
10. The court may appoint a supervisory organ to monitor the convicted person's compliance with the additional obligations.
11. When the court has imposed one of the obligations listed in Paragraph 8, and the convicted person fails to perform that obligation within the time limit determined by the court, the court may:
    (a) extend the time limit for the performance of the obligation; or
    (b) revoke the suspended sentence and order execution of the penalty of imprisonment.

## Commentary

Pursuant to Article 55, it is possible for a person to be convicted and sentenced to imprisonment but never spend any time in detention, where the conditions in Article 55 are met. Article 55 contains a basic framework regulating issues surrounding suspended sentences, such as the setting of a probation period (Paragraph 4), revocation and breach of an order for a suspended sentence (Paragraphs 5–7 and 11[b]), additional orders to a suspended sentence (Paragraphs 8 and 9), and supervision of a suspended sentence (Paragraph 10).

# Article 56: Community Service as an Alternative Penalty

1. Community service is an alternative penalty.
2. When the court pronounces a penalty of imprisonment not exceeding three years, either for a single offense or for multiple offenses, it may then replace this principal penalty of imprisonment with community service.
3. Community service means that a sentence of imprisonment has been imposed upon a convicted person, but the court orders that the sentence of imprisonment will not be enforced if the convicted person works, without monetary compensation, for a specific organization or institution for the purpose of benefiting the community.
4. The consent of the convicted person is required when the court wishes to impose the penalty of community service work upon him or her.
5. When the court decides to impose a community service order instead of the principal penalty of imprisonment, the court must set a specified number of hours of community service.
6. The specified number of hours of community service must not be less than 40 or greater than 340 hours.
7. The length of time in which community service should be completed must not exceed six months.
8. In imposing the penalty of community service work, the court must:
   (a) determine the type of community service to be performed by the convicted person;
   (b) designate a specific organization or institution for which the convicted person will perform the community service;
   (c) decide what days of the week and hours community service will be performed, in consultation with the designated organization or institution; and
   (d) appoint a supervisor to report back to the court on the performance of community service by the convicted person.
9. The court must revoke the order of community service and order the execution of the penalty of imprisonment if, during the duration of the community service term:
   (a) the convicted person commits a criminal offense; or

(b) the court learns that the convicted person had perpetrated another criminal offense prior to the imposition of the penalty of community service.

10. In the event of revocation of the penalty of community service for prior or new criminal offenses, the court must impose a joint penalty for both criminal offenses, in accordance with Article 52.

11. If the convicted person fails to perform the community service work as determined by the court, the court may:

    (a) extend the length of community service in accordance with the limits set out in Paragraphs 6 and 7; or

    (b) revoke the penalty of community service and order the execution of the penalty of imprisonment.

## Commentary

More and more states around the world—both post-conflict and non–post-conflict states—are introducing community service as a form of penalty. In addition to making a convicted person take responsibility for his or her actions, community service provides compensation to society for harm done, as set out in Article 34, "Purposes of Penalties." Community service may have a strong rehabilitative effect on a convicted person, a factor that is articulated as another purpose of penalties in Article 34. Council of Europe Resolution (76)10 states that community service is a way "for the community to contribute actively to the rehabilitation of the offender by accepting his cooperation in voluntary work."

Community service programs have been introduced particularly in states with chronic problems of prison overcrowding and other prison resource issues. Their effectiveness has been reported widely, as has the satisfaction of local communities with this form of penalty for a convicted person. The work that a person may undertake in the community is wide and varied and depends on the particular state in question. Community service is supported as an alternative penalty under the United Nations Standard Minimum Rules for Non-Custodial Measures (the Tokyo Rules), paragraph 8.2(i), and by the United Nations Economic and Social Council in its Resolution 1998/23, paragraph 3(c). Annexed to the resolution is the Kadoma Declaration on Community Service, which came about as a result of the International Conference on Community Service Orders in Africa (1997). A plan of action and a network of national committees on community service were also implemented subsequently to the declaration.

Article 56 sets out the basic principles and procedures to be followed in imposing a penalty of community service. The most important thing to note about community service as a penalty is that it requires the consent of the convicted person. It is also important that the court assess the suitability of the person for community service based on the seriousness of the offense, his or her degree of culpability, community safety issues, and his or her character and personal circumstances. Once the court considers the person suitable for community service and the person has consented to it, the court will then designate a certain number of hours that the convicted person will have to work (not exceeding 340 hours over six months), in addition to deciding what work he or she will undertake, for whom, and when (Paragraph 8). As stated in Paragraph 8(d), the community service program will be supervised. In general, a body is established to oversee and run the community service program once the penalty has been handed down. For a post-conflict state, this system has obvious resource implications, which should be considered prior to implementing legislation on community service measures. Adequate staff, premises, and funding should be provided to the body responsible for supervising the community service program.

As stated in Paragraph 9(a), a community service order will be revoked if the convicted person commits another criminal offense while undertaking the program. According to Paragraph 9(b), the order will be revoked if the convicted person has perpetrated another criminal offense prior to the imposition of the order for community service. When a community service order is revoked, the penalty of imprisonment that was originally imposed by the court is reactivated, and the person must serve the original penalty of imprisonment.

A community service order may also be breached when a person does not fulfill his or her duties under it. In such a case, the court may ask for either the extension of the community service order or execution of the original penalty of imprisonment, similar to revocation of the order (Paragraph 11).

# Article 57: Semiliberty as an Alternative Penalty

1. Semiliberty is an alternative penalty.
2. When the court pronounces a penalty of imprisonment not exceeding three years, either for a single offense or for multiple offenses, it may then replace this principal penalty of imprisonment with semiliberty.
3. Semiliberty means that a sentence of imprisonment has been imposed upon a convicted person; however, the court orders that due to his or her obligations related to work, education, vocational training, or family, the convicted person may leave the detention center at defined times during the day. The convicted person must return immediately to the detention center after any obligations have been fulfilled.
4. The court may also order semiliberty to allow a person to attend medical or rehabilitative treatment.
5. If the convicted person does not perform his or her obligations related to work, education, vocational training, family, or medical or rehabilitative

treatment, the court must revoke the order for semiliberty and order execution of the remainder of the penalty of imprisonment.

## Commentary

Semiliberty as an alternative penalty is found in many states around the world. In some states it is called periodic detention. In essence, it means that a penalty of imprisonment is imposed upon a person but that he or she may leave the detention center at certain designated times to perform work-related activities, educational or vocational training, family responsibilities, or medical or rehabilitative treatment. In some states, a person may leave the detention center for the entire work week and will serve his or her penalty of imprisonment only on weekends. Under the MCC, a person may leave only during the hours of work and must return immediately upon completion of work.

The penalty of semiliberty may be used, for example, where the court believes a period of imprisonment is merited, but the person does not pose a safety threat to the community, the person is the sole earner in a family, and it would compromise the family as a whole if the person were held in prison, unable to work. It may also be used where the court wishes to support the person's efforts at education or his or her pursuit of a vocation, a factor that may assist in preventing him or her from committing future criminal offenses. The *Green Paper on the Approximation, Mutual Recognition and Enforcement of Criminal Sanctions in the European Union* (page 71) states another benefit of a penalty of semiliberty, in that it "seeks to offset one of the major disadvantages of prison, namely the desocialization of the prisoner. Compared with suspended sentence, detention with day release seems more successfully to reconcile the needs of rehabilitation and public protection."

Paragraph 4: The MCC does not have a specific provision for rehabilitative programs, such as drug rehabilitation, except as part of an order for a suspended sentence under Article 55 and in the current article. Article 55 allows the court to impose a suspended sentence upon a person and then order the person to attend a drug or alcohol rehabilitation program. Article 57 allows the court to ensure enhanced supervision of the convicted person by placing him or her in prison, while at the same time focusing on the rehabilitation of the person through mandatory rehabilitative treatment.

# Article 58: Supplementation of a Principal Penalty with Additional Penalties

The court may impose one or more additional penalties in addition to a principal penalty.

## Commentary

Where the court has set a principal penalty of imprisonment and has considered the imposition of additional penalties, where applicable, it must turn to the question of whether to impose an additional penalty. The question for the court's consideration is whether the provision of additional penalties will fulfill the purposes of penalties set out in Article 34. While the court is required to give precedence to the fundamental principle over other purposes of penalties set out in Article 35, when it comes to additional penalties, the court is free to impose penalties that fulfill the other purposes of penalties. For example, a person may be imprisoned based on the seriousness of the criminal offense and his or her degree of culpability. However, if this penalty will not serve other purposes, such as the provision of reparations to the victim, the court may decide to impose an additional penalty of compensation to a victim under Article 62.

# Article 59: Supplementation of an Alternative Penalty with Additional Penalties

The court may impose one or more additional penalties in addition to an alternative penalty.

## Commentary

The same issues arise regarding the imposition of additional penalties with alternative penalties as with their imposition with principal penalties. Reference should be made to Article 58 and its accompanying commentary.

# Article 60: A Fine as an Additional Penalty

1. A fine is an additional penalty.
2. The court may impose a fine as an additional penalty for any criminal offense for which a fine is not expressly prescribed as an alternative principal punishment when the convicted person committed the offense for the purpose of obtaining undue material benefit.

3. In imposing a fine, the court must allow the convicted person a reasonable period of time in which to pay the fine.
4. The court may provide for payment of a lump sum or payment by way of installments paid at designated dates during a designated time frame.
5. In the case of willful nonpayment of a fine, where no penalty of imprisonment has been imposed, the court may order the convicted person to appear before it to explain the reasons for the nonpayment of the fine.
6. Where the convicted person, having been called before the court under Paragraph 5, continues to withhold the payment of the fine, the court may impose a term of imprisonment upon the person, not exceeding three months. Where a person is already serving a penalty of imprisonment, the court may extend the term of imprisonment by up to three months.

## Commentary

A fine may be imposed upon a person as a principal penalty under Article 50. Under Article 60, a fine may be imposed upon a convicted person where he or she is not subject to the principal penalty of a fine and where he or she has committed a criminal offense for the purpose of obtaining material benefit. The purpose of a fine as an additional penalty is to make the convicted person responsible for his or her criminal behavior, similar to the punitive effect of a fine as a principal penalty. For a more detailed discussion on fines and the method of calculating a fine, reference should be made to the commentary to Article 50. A default on the payment of a fine may result in an extension of the prison term for a person serving a term of imprisonment. For persons not serving terms of imprisonment, it is within the court's discretion to impose a penalty of less than three months' imprisonment (Paragraph 6).

# Article 61: Confiscation of Property, Equipment, or Other Instrumentalities Used in or Destined for Use in a Criminal Offense as an Additional Penalty

1. Confiscation of property, equipment, or other instrumentalities used in or destined for use in a criminal offense is an additional penalty.

2. The court may, without prejudice to the rights of bona fide third parties, order the confiscation of property, equipment, or other instrumentalities used in or destined for use in a criminal offense.

## Commentary

Article 61 involves the permanent deprivation of property, equipment, or other instrumentalities used in or destined for used in a criminal offense. The United Nations Convention against Transnational Organized Crime, Article 12(1)(b), and the United Nations Convention against Corruption, Article 31(1)(b), require states parties to introduce legislation allowing for this provision in relation to organized crime, corruption, and corruption-related offenses. The Protocol against the Illicit Manufacturing of and Trafficking in Firearms, Their Parts and Components and Ammunition, supplementing the United Nations Convention against Organized Crime (Article 6), specifically requires that firearms, their parts and components, and ammunition that have been illicitly manufactured or trafficked be confiscated. Similarly, the United Nations Convention against Illicit Traffic in Narcotic Drugs and Psychotropic Substances, Article 5(1)(b), requires that narcotic drugs and psychotropic substances, materials and equipment, or other instrumentalities used in relation to drug offenses be confiscated.

The sort of confiscation envisaged in Article 61 is distinct from that of Articles 70–73, below, which provide for the confiscation of proceeds of crime and property to the value of the proceeds of crime. Articles 70–73 are not regarded as a "penalty" under the MCC but rather a mechanism that prevents a convicted person from enjoying the fruits of criminality or, worse still, reinvesting proceeds of crime into further criminal activity. Under Articles 70–73, the proceeds of crime or property of corresponding value may be confiscated. Under Article 61, property that was "used in or destined for use in" the criminal offense is the subject of the order. Confiscation under Article 61 is more of a penalty than the measure provided for under Articles 70–73. The practical ramification of this penalty, for example, is that a car usually used for personal use and used only once in the commission of a criminal offense could be confiscated as a penalty. Premises where drugs were illicitly manufactured could be confiscated even if the premises were also used for legitimate purposes. Computers belonging to and used by persons convicted of cybercrime offenses may also be confiscated under Article 61; restrictions may also be imposed on a convicted person's use and possession of computers and access to the Internet. In addition to this sort of confiscation, Article 61 includes confiscation of more obvious objects used solely and directly in a criminal offense, such as narcotic drugs or a firearm used in a robbery.

The *Legislative Guide to the United Nations Convention against Transnational Organized Crime and the Protocols Thereto* (page 146) states that the term *destined for use in* is "meant to signify an intention of such a nature that it may be viewed as tantamount to an attempt to commit a criminal offense." Reference should be made to Article 27, "Attempt," and its accompanying commentary.

For the definition of *property*, reference should be made to Article 1(8). Reference should also be made to the MCCP's provisions regarding procedural issues related to confiscation of property, equipment, or other instrumentalities used in or destined for used in a criminal offense.

One very relevant issue in relation to seizure of property is that of third-party claims to the property. Usually, third-party claims are determined in separate proceedings after the court has made an order for confiscation. The procedural provisions dealing with claims by bona fide third parties to property that is subject to an order for confiscation are dealt with under the MCCP.

Although confiscation provisions can be very useful, caution must be exercised in their implementation to prevent abuse. The court should exercise some restraint in what it confiscates. There is also a need to ensure that rules and procedures govern what happens to confiscated property, in case public officials with access to this property are tempted to sell it privately or use it personally. Reference should be made to the general commentary to Section 13 of the General Part of the MCC, which discusses this issue in greater detail.

# Article 62: Payment of Compensation to a Victim as an Additional Penalty

1. Payment of compensation to a victim is an additional penalty.
2. In imposing the payment of compensation to the victim, the court must allow the convicted person a reasonable period of time in which to make the payment.
3. The court may provide for payment of a lump sum or payment by way of installments made at designated dates during a designated time frame.
4. In the case of willful nonpayment of compensation where a penalty of imprisonment has also been imposed by the court, and where all available enforcement measures have been exhausted, the court may extend the term of imprisonment for a period not exceeding three months.
5. In the case of willful nonpayment of compensation by the convicted person where no penalty of imprisonment has been imposed, the court may order the convicted person to appear before it to explain the reasons for the nonpayment of compensation.
6. Where the convicted person, having being called before the court pursuant to Paragraph 5, continues to withhold the payment of compensation, the court

may impose a term of imprisonment upon the person not exceeding three months.

## Commentary

The principles set out in Article 34 reference the compensation of victims as a purpose of penalties. Penalties that accrue to the state, such as imprisonment or fines, do not serve this aim. As the court must consider the just deserts principle in preference to the other purposes of penalties, the principal or alternative penalty must be geared toward fulfilling that aim. In deciding upon the appropriateness of an additional penalty, such as compensation to the victim, the court is entitled to look to this secondary aim of penalties set out in Article 34. The provisions of Article 62, in addition to compensating victims, also serve a deterrent effect and, according to some, a rehabilitative effect. Some of the experts consulted during the process of vetting the MCC emphasized the importance of victim compensation in their states and the consequential need to include a provision such as Article 62 in the MCC. The United Nations Declaration of Basic Principles of Justice for Victims of Crime and Abuse of Power requires that convicted persons, where appropriate, make fair restitution to victims, including payment for the harm or loss suffered (paragraph 8). The declaration urges states to review their practices, regulations, and laws to consider restitution as a sentencing option (paragraph 9). The MCC provides only for the payment of compensation to a victim. A post-conflict state may also wish to consider making provisions for the restitution, or return, of property that has been stolen or embezzled from the victim. To ensure that the penalty is effective and enforced, it is advisable that prior to ordering compensation, a court consider the ability of the convicted person to pay that compensation.

Despite the symbolic value of awarding compensation to the victim, the nonpayment of compensation may disappoint a victim greatly. If the convicted person does not have the means to pay the compensation, this may result in his or her imprisonment or the extension of a preexisting prison term. It is a matter for the court's discretion as to whether or not to impose a penalty of imprisonment in the case of willful nonpayment of compensation. Many domestic courts, after calling the convicted person before the court to explain the reasons for nonpayment and after reordering the payment of the compensation, often make the pragmatic choice not to impose a penalty of imprisonment on the convicted person. This decision is based on reticence to impose a penalty of imprisonment for the nonpayment of a monetary sum where it is infeasible to obtain the compensation.

# Article 63: Deprivation of the Right to Be Elected as an Additional Penalty

1. The deprivation of the right to be elected is an additional penalty.
2. The court may deprive a convicted person of the right to be elected in national, regional, or local elections if:
   (a) the convicted person was convicted of any criminal offense in connection with the elections, and a penalty of imprisonment was imposed on him or her; or
   (b) a penalty of imprisonment for more than five years was imposed upon the convicted person.
3. When the court decides to impose the additional penalty of deprivation of the right to be elected, it must determine the time limit of the penalty. The length of the penalty must not be less than one year and not greater than five years from the day the judgment becomes final.
4. When the court imposes the additional penalty of deprivation of the right to be elected, in addition to the penalty of imprisonment or semiliberty, the time limit for the deprivation of the right to be elected starts when the person is released from imprisonment or semiliberty.

## Commentary

In certain cases, a court may decide that a convicted person should not stand for election for a set period of years after being convicted of a criminal offense. This provision applies to situations in which the person is found criminally responsible for any of the election offenses under Section 15 of the Special Part of the MCC or where a penalty of imprisonment of more than five years is imposed upon him or her. The rationale for this practice is to ensure that persons who have acted illegally with respect to elections in the past are separated from the object of their criminal offenses. The second class of persons to which this additional penalty applies, those sentenced to more than five years' imprisonment, consists of those who have committed a serious criminal offense or offenses and thus should not be eligible to take public office after an election.

# Article 64: Deprivation of the Right to Possess or Carry Firearms as an Additional Penalty

1. The deprivation of the right to possess or carry firearms is an additional penalty.
2. The court may deprive a convicted person of the right to possess or carry firearms if the person:
   (a) was convicted of any criminal offense committed by the use of firearms or any criminal offense related to firearms, such as the offenses listed in Section 13 of the Special Part of the MCC; or
   (b) has committed a criminal offense involving violence for which the court imposed a penalty of more than three years' imprisonment.
3. When the court decides to impose the additional penalty of deprivation of the right to possess or carry firearms, it must determine the time limit of the penalty. The length of the penalty must not be less than one year or greater than ten years from the day the judgment becomes final.
4. When the court imposes the additional penalty of deprivation of the right to possess or carry firearms, in addition to the penalty of imprisonment or semiliberty, the time limit for the deprivation of the right to possess or carry firearms starts at the end of the term of imprisonment or semiliberty.
5. Where a convicted person who has served a term of imprisonment and is subject to an order under Article 64 violates the order not to possess or carry weapons during the time limit designated by the court under Paragraph 3, the convicted person may be prosecuted for the criminal offense of unlawful possession, control, or ownership of firearms, under Article 168, or for the criminal offense of failure to respect an order of the court, under Article 197.
6. Where a convicted person who is serving an alternative penalty violates the order not to possess or carry weapons during the time limit designated by the court under Paragraph 3, in addition to potential prosecution as set out in Paragraph 5, the court may also order that the alternative penalty be revoked and that the person must serve the original term of imprisonment imposed upon him or her. The court may also lengthen the duration of the order for deprivation of the right to carry firearms.

## Commentary

As discussed in the general commentary to Section 13 of the Special Part of the MCC, the right to possess and carry a firearm in a post-conflict state should be governed by laws or regulations on who is eligible to carry firearms, what firearms or weapons are subject to restrictions, and the procedure for obtaining a license to carry firearms. Reference should be made to the general commentary to Section 13 of the Special Part of the MCC. Irrespective of any restrictions under the legislation on firearms (or irrespective of whether any legislation exists), Article 64 allows the court to impose a prohibition on convicted persons carrying or possessing firearms for a designated period of time. The prohibition applies to persons who have perpetrated criminal offenses through the use of firearms or who have perpetrated violent criminal offenses and who, therefore, are manifestly unsuitable to carry or possess firearms.

# Article 65: Prohibition on Holding a Post as a Public Official as an Additional Penalty

1. The prohibition on holding a post as a public official is an additional penalty.
2. The court may prohibit a convicted person from holding a post as a public official if the person:
   (a) has abused his or her functions as a public official in connection with the commission of a criminal offense; or
   (b) has committed a criminal offense for which the court imposed a sentence of more than five years' imprisonment.
3. When the court decides to impose the additional penalty of prohibition on holding a post as a public official, it must determine the time limit of the penalty. The length of the penalty must not be less than one year or greater than five years from the day the judgment becomes final.
4. When the court imposes the penalty of prohibition on holding a post as a public official in addition to the penalty of imprisonment or semiliberty, the time limit for the deprivation of the right to hold a post as a public official starts when the person is released from imprisonment or semiliberty.

## Commentary

Article 65 sets out a procedure and principles for prohibiting a convicted person from holding a post as a public official for a designated period of time. Reference should be made to Article 1(9) for the definition of *public official.* This sort of prohibition is particularly relevant for corruption and corruption-related offenses. In fact, Article 30(6) of the United Nations Convention against Corruption urges states parties to introduce penalties such as those in Article 65 into domestic legislation "to the extent consistent with the fundamental principles of [their] legal system[s]." Article 65 applies to a public official who has abused his or her position to perpetrate a criminal offense or has been sentenced to more than five years' imprisonment, meaning the offense was a relatively serious one. The court may consider the inappropriateness of these two classes of persons serving in the future as public officials, and it may then prevent this service for a designated period of time.

# Article 66: Prohibition on the Exercise of Managerial or Supervisory Positions in Private Legal Entities as an Additional Penalty

1. A prohibition on the exercise of managerial or supervisory positions in private legal entities is an additional penalty.
2. The court may prohibit a convicted person from exercising managerial or supervisory positions if the person:
   (a) has abused his or her functions as a manager or supervisor in connection with the commission of a criminal offense, and a penalty of imprisonment was imposed on him or her; or
   (b) has committed a criminal offense for which the court imposed a sentence of more than five years' imprisonment.
3. When the court decides to impose the additional penalty of prohibition on the exercise of managerial or supervisory positions in private legal entities, it must determine the time limit of the penalty. The length of the penalty must not be less than one year or greater than five years from the day the judgment becomes final.
4. When the court imposes the penalty of prohibition on the exercise of managerial or supervisory positions in private legal entities in addition to the penalty of imprisonment or semiliberty, the time limit for the deprivation of the right to exercise managerial or supervisory positions in private legal entities starts when the person is released from imprisonment or semiliberty.

## Commentary

Article 66 sets out a procedure and principles for prohibiting a convicted person from exercising managerial or supervisory functions in a private legal entity. This additional penalty may be relevant, for example, to a person who has been convicted of embezzlement in a private entity, under Article 142. In fact, Article 30(6) of the United Nations Convention against Corruption urges states parties to introduce penalties like that in Article 66 into domestic legislation "to the extent consistent with the fundamental principles of [their] legal system[s]." Article 66 also applies more widely to persons who abused their functions in connection with a criminal offense and persons who have been sentenced to more than five years' imprisonment, meaning the offense was a relatively serious one. The court may consider the inappropriateness of these two classes of persons serving in the future in managerial or supervisory positions in private legal entities, and it may then prevent this service for a designated period of time.

# Article 67: Expulsion of a Non-national as an Additional Penalty

1. Expulsion of a non-national is provided for as an additional penalty in the MCC.
2. The court may order the expulsion of a non-national from [insert name of state] when the non-national has committed a criminal offense for which the court has imposed a penalty of imprisonment.
3. When the court decides to impose the additional penalty of expulsion of a non-national, it must determine the time limit of the penalty. The length of the penalty must not be less than one year or greater than ten years from the day the judgment becomes final.
4. When the court is determining whether to impose the additional penalty of expulsion of a non-national and the time limit of this penalty, it must take into account the following:
   (a) the type and gravity of the criminal offense;
   (b) the convicted person's motives for committing the criminal offense; and
   (c) the convicted person's personal, family, economic, and social ties to [insert name of state].
5. The additional penalty of expulsion of a non-national must not be imposed if the execution of the expulsion would be contrary to international human rights standards regarding the expulsion of non-nationals.
6. The time limit for the order of expulsion commences from the day of the final judgment.
7. When the court imposes the penalty of expulsion of a non-national in addition to the penalty of imprisonment or semiliberty, the time limit for the expulsion starts when the person is released from imprisonment or semiliberty.

## Commentary

Article 67 allows the court to expel a person who is not a national of the state from the state for a designated period of time on account of his or her criminal behavior. This sort of additional penalty is contained in the criminal legislation of a number of states around the world.

Paragraph 5: The applicable domestic and international law on refugees should be taken into account when determining whether to expel a non-national from a state. International human rights law absolutely prohibits the expulsion (or *refoulement*) of a person where there is a threat of a violation of the right to life; of torture or cruel, inhuman, or degrading treatment or punishment; or other violation of that person's human rights that could cause irreparable harm.

# Section 12

## Subsection 4: Penalties for Legal Persons

### Article 68: Types of Penalties for Legal Persons

The court may apply any combination of the following penalties upon a legal person:

(a) confiscation of property, equipment, or other instrumentalities used in or destined for use in a criminal offense;

(b) payment of compensation to a victim;

(c) a fine;

(d) confiscation of assets of the legal person;

(e) termination of the legal person;

(f) public announcement and publication of the judgment; and

(g) prohibition of a specific commercial activity or activities, indefinitely or for a specified period of time.

#### Commentary

Reference should be made to Article 19 and its accompanying commentary, which discuss the criminal liability of legal persons in more detail. The penalties provided for under Article 68 will all be carried out against a legal person rather than a natural person. Obviously, a legal person cannot be imprisoned. Therefore, a range of other penalties appropriate to legal persons have been included in Article 68. Some of these penalties under Article 68 (a fine; confiscation of assets; payment of compensation to victims; confiscation of property, equipment, or other instrumentalities used in or destined for use in a criminal offense) are also provided for as applicable penalties for natural persons. The remainder (confiscation of assets, public announcement and publication of the judgment, prohibition of a specific commercial activity, or termination of the legal person) are specific to legal persons.

As mentioned in the commentary to Article 19, not every state has domestic legislation on the criminal liability of legal persons. Very often, legal persons are sanctioned through administrative or civil law. To compile the applicable penalties for legal persons in the MCC, comparative research was carried out on the sorts of penalties that exist in states that possess legislation on the criminal liability of legal persons. Reference was also made to the suggested list of sanctions for legal persons in the Council of Europe's *Recommendation R (88) 18 Concerning Liability of Enterprises Having Legal Personality for Offenses Committed in the Exercise of Their Activities.* The most commonly used penalty is a fine. However, the rest of the penalties outlined in Article 68 are also contained in domestic criminal legislation.

The penalties for a legal person are not divided into principal, alternative, and additional penalties. The court may impose any combination of these penalties, guided by the purposes of penalties set out in Article 34, the fundamental principle in Article 35, and the other principles applicable to penalties under Article 36.

In addition to the penalties set out in Section 12, the proceeds of crime, or property of equivalent value, may be confiscated from a legal person under Articles 70–73. Reference should be made to Articles 70–73 and their accompanying commentaries.

# Article 69: Determination of Penalties for a Legal Person

1. When the court is determining an appropriate penalty or penalties for a legal person, the court must follow the principles set out in Articles 34–36.
2. When the court determines that the confiscation of property, equipment, or other instrumentalities used in or destined for use in a criminal offense is an appropriate penalty, it must apply Article 61.
3. When the court determines that payment of compensation to the victim is an appropriate penalty for a legal person, it must apply Articles 62(2) and 62(3).
4. When the court determines that a fine is an appropriate penalty for a convicted person, it must impose a fine that is no less than [insert monetary amount] and no more than [insert monetary amount].
5. The court may order the confiscation of a legal person's assets or the termination of the legal person only when:

(a) the activity of the legal person was entirely or predominantly used for the execution of criminal offenses; and

(b) the penalty is justified by the presence of particularly aggravated circumstances.

6. The confiscation of the legal person's assets must not exceed one-half of the legal person's assets.

7. The lawful interests of creditors and bona fide third parties must be taken into consideration when imposing the penalties of confiscation of assets and termination of the legal person.

8. In the case of willful nonpayment of compensation to a victim under Article 62, the willful nonpayment of a fine under Article 68(c), or the prohibition on carrying out certain commercial activities, the court may subsequently impose another penalty upon the convicted legal person under Article 68.

## Commentary

Article 69 sets out some broad principles for the imposition of penalties upon a legal person. Where possible, reference has been made to the procedures for the imposition of similar penalties on natural persons under the MCC.

Paragraph 5: Given the fact that the termination of a legal person and the confiscation of its assets are very serious penalties, the MCC provides certain limitations on their imposition, namely that activities of the legal person were used either entirely or predominantly for the execution of criminal offenses (very common in relation to organized criminal activity) and that "particularly aggravated circumstances" be present. When the court orders the termination or winding up of the operation or functions of the legal person, the court must either designate a receiver to terminate the legal person or follow the legal mechanism for the termination of legal persons under the applicable domestic law.

Paragraph 6: As is the case with confiscation of property from natural persons, there must be a procedure for the storage and disposal of confiscated assets of the legal person. Reference should be made to the general commentary to Section 13 of the General Part of the MCC, which discusses this issue in greater detail.

Paragraph 7: The legal interests of bona fide third parties with potential interests in the assets and creditors to a legal person that is to be terminated must be dealt with under legislation. Ordinarily, their interests would be dealt with in proceedings separate to criminal proceedings. This situation is beyond the scope of the MCC. If not already in existence, legislative provisions should be introduced to address the grounds upon which a claim to the assets of a legal person may be made, as well as the procedures by which they are made and by which their validity is determined.

Paragraph 8: When a natural person defaults on a fine or the payment of compensation, he or she may be liable to imprisonment or an alternative penalty under the MCC. As imprisonment is not an option for legal persons, the court may subsequently revisit its original determination of the appropriate penalties and add to it.

# Section 13: Confiscation of the Proceeds of Crime and Property

## General Commentary

Section 13 deals with confiscation, or forfeiture as it is also commonly known. Confiscation means the permanent deprivation of the proceeds of crime or of property of corresponding value. Confiscation is based upon the principle that proceeds of crime should be forfeited, as a convicted person should not benefit from his or her criminal activity. Confiscation is consequently not termed a penalty and has been placed apart from the penalties section in the MCC. According to the *Legislative Guide to the United Nations Convention against Transnational Organized Crime and the Protocols Thereto,* "[C]riminalizing the conduct from which substantial illicit profits are made does not adequately punish or deter organized criminal groups. Even if arrested and convicted, some of these offenders will be able to enjoy their illegal gains for their personal use and for maintaining the operations of their criminal enterprises. Despite some sanctions, the perception would still remain that crime pays. . . . Practical measures to keep offenders from profiting from their crimes are necessary. One of the most important ways to do this is to ensure that States have strong confiscation regimes" (pages 140–141).

Many states have recently introduced legislation to allow for the confiscation of proceeds of crime, while many others are in the process of amending their domestic criminal laws to do so. A number of international conventions place a positive duty on states parties to introduce legislation on confiscation of the proceeds of crime. The first such convention was the United Nations Convention against Illicit Traffic in Narcotic Drugs and Psychotropic Substances (1988), Article 5. More recently the United Nations Convention against Transnational Organized Crime, Article 12; the United Nations Convention against Corruption, Article 31 and Chapter 5; and the International Convention for the Suppression of the Financing of Terrorism, Article 8, have included similar duties. Domestic measures on the confiscation of the proceeds of crime are particularly important when it comes to serious criminal offenses such as drug offenses, organized crime, corruption, and the financing of terrorism, as referenced in the relevant conventions. The international conventions just mentioned apply to only a short list of criminal offenses. Rather than apply confiscation to those offenses only, the MCC provisions apply to all criminal offenses contained in the Special Part of the MCC, as is urged by the *Legislative Guide to the United Nations Convention against Transnational Organized Crime and the Protocols Thereto* (page 145).

It is important to point out that confiscation of assets is extraordinarily complicated and requires a lot of time, money, and specialized personnel to investigate and determine the value of proceeds of crime and what property of equivalent value may be seized. Many states struggle to implement domestic confiscation regimes. The Council of Europe's *Combating Organized Crime: Best Practice Surveys of the Council of Europe* highlights the fact that "proceeds of crime only rarely fall into the lap of the courts or government like ripe fruit from the tree or vine. What is not investigated by financial intelligence or other personnel may never be learned about at all, for it is very difficult to reconstruct financial flows from crimes long after they have occurred, and harder still to get the money back. . . . Merely to pass laws . . . will not *ipso facto* lead to a substantial increase in recoveries from offenders or third parties. This extra recovery can happen only if unspent assets can be found, and can be attributed to the possession or control of someone against whom an order can be made" (page 46). In addition to resources, intensive training programs will be required for those involved in the investigation of proceeds of crime. It may be necessary to establish special units or teams to undertake the investigations. The teams may be composed of actors from different sectors of the justice system and beyond, including prosecutors, police, and experts in forensic accounting. This process is discussed in more detail in *Combating Serious Crimes in Post-conflict Societies* (pages 74–79), edited by Colette Rausch and published by the United States Institute of Peace. It may also be necessary to establish a financial intelligence unit. Article 58 of the United Nations Convention against Corruption urges states parties to consider the establishment of a financial intelligence unit "to be responsible for receiving, analyzing and disseminating to the competent authorities reports of suspicious financial transactions."

Implementation of a confiscation regime will likely require yet more measures to be taken. First, criminal procedure laws will have to be amended to allow police and prosecutors to gain information on the banking transactions of a convicted person and any money held in accounts with a bank. Article 12(6) of the United Nations Convention against Transnational Organized Crime requires a state party to "empower its courts or other competent authorities to order that bank, financial or commercial records be made available or be seized. States Parties shall not decline to act . . . on the ground of bank secrecy." Article 31(7) of the United Nations Convention against Corruption imposes an identical obligation upon states parties. The *Legislative Guide to the United Nations Convention against Transnational Organized Crime and the Protocols Thereto* (page 123) states that "financial records" include those of other financial service companies and that "commercial records" include real estate transactions and records of shipping lines, freight forwarders, and insurers. Second, other changes to domestic banking laws may be required. The most elaborate and extensive provisions on the sorts of amendments required are contained in Article 52 of the United Nations Convention against Corruption and include a requirement that financial institutions verify the identity of customers, take reasonable steps to determine the identity of beneficial owners of funds deposited in high-value accounts, conduct enhanced scrutiny of certain accounts, and maintain adequate records of transactions.

Third, it will also be necessary to regulate procedures for the handling of confiscated proceeds and property. Regulations should specify who is responsible for taking the confiscated property and holding it, where it should be held, and what will be done with the property. The United Nations Convention against Corruption, Article 31(3), and the United Nations Convention against Transnational Organized Crime, Article 14, actually specify that states parties should make provisions to regulate the administration and disposal of confiscated property. Inherent in this provision is the question of what use will be made of the confiscated proceeds or property. In some states, proceeds and property go to a victims' fund, or directly to the victim of the criminal offense in question when the victim lost property or money as a result of it. Article 14(2) of the United Nations Convention against Transnational Organized Crime urges states parties to consider doing this. The *Legislative Guide to the United Nations Convention against Transnational Organized Crime and the Protocols Thereto* states that "for most confiscation systems, a key objective is to restore to victims property taken from them by criminals and it is extremely useful to provide for a procedure under domestic law to enable sharing of confiscated assets with domestic and foreign victims" (page 152). Article 57 of the United Nations Convention against Corruption provides that confiscated property be returned to its prior legitimate owner.

According to the Council of Europe report, *Combating Organized Crime: Best Practice Surveys of the Council of Europe,* in some states the proceeds of confiscation do not go to the state but instead go to activities such as law enforcement police training or prevention activities (page 71). The Council of Europe report stresses the importance of transparency of expenditure, so the public knows where the funds end up. In the case of transborder criminal offenses, as set out in Article 14 of the United Nations Convention against Transnational Organized Crime, the state that has confiscated the proceeds or property may consider sharing it with the other state or using it to cover costs of mutual legal assistance provided by the other state.

Confiscation can be distinguished from seizure or freezing, wherein a person is temporarily prohibited from transferring, converting, disposing of, or moving his or her property or other "economic advantages" as set out in Article 70(b), below. A person whose assets have been confiscated has probably already had his or her assets seized. Seizure usually occurs during the investigation of a criminal offense and after an application to the court by a prosecutor. The MCCP contains provisions on seizure. Reference should be made to Chapter 8, Part 3, Section 3, of the MCCP and the accompanying commentaries, which discuss the issue in greater detail.

# Article 70: Definitions

For the purpose of Section 13:

(a) *confiscation* means a measure ordered by a court following proceedings in relation to a criminal offense or criminal offenses resulting in the final deprivation of property;

(b) *proceeds of crime* means any economic advantage derived from or obtained directly or indirectly from a criminal offense or criminal offenses. It may consist of any property as defined in Article 1(8); and

(c) *property* has the same meaning as in Article 1(8).

## Commentary

Paragraph (a): The definition of *confiscation* has been taken from Article 1(c) of the Council of Europe Convention on Laundering, Search, Seizure and Confiscation of the Proceeds from Crime and on the Financing of Terrorism (2005). It is similar to the definition contained in Article 2(g) of the United Nations Convention against Transnational Organized Crime, except that the former is more illustrative. The explanatory report to the Council of Europe Convention on Laundering, Search, Seizure and Confiscation of the Proceeds from Crime and on the Financing of Terrorism states that the definition of *confiscation* implicitly includes forfeiture, a fact that is made explicit in the United Nations conventions.

Paragraph (b): This definition was taken from Article 1(a) of the Council of Europe Convention on Laundering, Search, Seizure and Confiscation of the Proceeds from Crime and on the Financing of Terrorism. The United Nations Convention against Transnational Organized Crime, Article 1(e), and the United Nations Convention against Corruption, Article 2(e), also define proceeds of crime, although more narrowly. The definition in both United Nations conventions refers only to property derived from crime, rather than to any economic advantage derived from crime, which is contained in the Council of Europe convention. The Council of Europe definition and the MCC definition both include property but go much further. The explanatory report to the Council of Europe Convention on Laundering, Search, Seizure and Confiscation of the Proceeds from Crime and on the Financing of Terrorism states, at paragraph 21, that "the definition of 'proceeds' was intended to be as broad as possible."

Paragraph (c): For the definition of *property,* reference should be made to Article 1(8).

# Article 71: Prohibition on Retention of Proceeds of Crime

1. No person may retain the proceeds of crime.
2. Proceeds of crime must be confiscated by the court after a person has been convicted of a criminal offense.

## Commentary

Paragraph 2: In some states, given problems related to organized crime, legislation has been introduced to allow for the confiscation of the proceeds of crime through civil actions in the civil courts (as opposed to the criminal courts), irrespective of a criminal conviction. This model of confiscation was not considered for inclusion in the MCC as it focuses only on criminal law and not civil law remedies.

In most states, and in the MCC, confiscation occurs after the final decision in a criminal case and where a person is convicted of a criminal offense or offenses. Confiscation after a conviction can be undertaken in two ways. One method is to decide upon confiscation at the end of the criminal proceedings, upon conviction, at the same time that penalties are being imposed. Another method is to decide upon confiscation after a trial is done, in proceedings in a civil court, separate and apart from criminal proceedings (but always after they have concluded). In such cases, it is common for the procedure to use the civil burden of proof relating to the source of assets. This means that instead of the prosecutor having to prove "beyond a reasonable doubt" (in legal systems using that burden of proof in criminal cases) that certain property, including any economic advantages, derived from crime, he or she would have to prove "on the balance of probabilities" or "the preponderance of the evidence" that the economic advantage was derived from crime. In the MCC, confiscation occurs at the end of the criminal trial, when the court is deciding on other penalties.

# Article 72: Confiscation of Proceeds of Crime or Property of Corresponding Value from the Convicted Person

1. Proceeds of crime, or property that corresponds in value to such proceeds, must be confiscated from the convicted person.

2. Confiscation encompasses the proceeds of crime, or property that corresponds in value to such proceeds, such as:
   (a) property into which the proceeds of crime have been transformed or converted;
   (b) property acquired from legitimate sources, if proceeds of crime have been intermingled, in whole or in part, with such property, up to the assessed value of the intermingled proceeds; and
   (c) income or other benefits derived from proceeds of crime, property into which proceeds of crime have been transformed or converted, or property with which proceeds of crime have been intermingled, up to the assessed value of the intermingled proceeds, in the same manner and to the same extent as the proceeds.
3. Where the confiscation of proceeds of crime or property of corresponding value is not feasible, the court may oblige the convicted person to pay an amount of money that corresponds to the proceeds of crime.

## Commentary

Paragraph 1: There are many models for confiscation in different states, as mentioned above. There are also many different approaches to what should be confiscated by the courts. As stated in the *Legislative Guide to the United Nations Convention against Transnational Organized Crime and the Protocols Thereto* (page 289), some states opt for a property-based system of confiscation, others opt for a value-based system, while others combine both approaches. Under the first model, property that represents the proceeds of crime is confiscated. Under the second model, the value of the proceeds of crime is assessed and money of equivalent value is confiscated. This approach is often called a value confiscation order. The model adopted in the MCC combines both approaches. It targets the proceeds of crime first and then property of corresponding value. It also allows, at the court's discretion, the payment of money instead of the confiscation of property.

Paragraph 2(a): This paragraph is inspired by Article 12(3) of the United Nations Convention against Transnational Organized Crime and Article 31(4) of the United Nations Convention against Corruption, both of which provide that "if proceeds of crime [have] been transformed or converted, in part or in full, into other property, such property" will be liable to confiscation.

Paragraph 2(b): This paragraph is inspired by Article 12(4) of the United Nations Convention against Transnational Organized Crime and Article 31(5) of the United Nations Convention against Corruption.

Paragraph 2(c): This paragraph is inspired by Article 12(5) of the United Nations Convention against Transnational Organized Crime and Article 31(6) of the United Nations Convention against Corruption. The *Legislative Guide to the United Nations Convention against Transnational Organized Crime and the Protocols Thereto* (page 308) states that "an interpretive note [to the convention] indicates that the words 'other benefits' are intended to encompass material benefits as well as legal rights and interests of an enforceable nature that are subject to confiscation."

Paragraph 3: Under this paragraph, where it is not feasible for a convicted person, for whatever reason, to hand over property, such as when it has been damaged or no longer exists, the court may, at its discretion, allow the convicted person to pay the equivalent amount to the court. This matter will be negotiated between the court and the convicted person, usually at the request of the convicted person.

# Article 73: Confiscation of Proceeds of Crime or Property of Corresponding Value from a Third Party

1. Proceeds of crime or property of corresponding value must be confiscated from a third party where:
   (a) the proceeds of crime or the property was transferred to the third party by the convicted person or another person without compensation, or the proceeds of crime or the property was transferred to the third party by the convicted person or another person for compensation that did not correspond to the real value of the proceeds or the property; and
   (b) the third party knew or should have known that the property was acquired through the perpetration of a criminal offense.
2. Where a legal person acquires the proceeds of crime or property of corresponding value, the proceeds or the property must be confiscated where:
   (a) the proceeds of crime or the property was transferred to the legal person by the convicted person or another person without compensation; or
   (b) the proceeds of crime or the property was transferred to the legal person by the convicted person or another person for compensation that did not correspond to the real value of the proceeds or the property.
3. Where a close relative of the convicted person acquires the proceeds of crime or property of corresponding value, the proceeds or the property must be confiscated, unless the person can prove that he or she gave the convicted

person compensation that corresponds to the real value of the proceeds or the property.

## Commentary

Paragraph 1: Often, a convicted person will have transferred the proceeds of crime or property to a third party prior to his or her trial in order to conceal it from domestic authorities and in an attempt to exempt it from the confiscation regime. Where a transfer has been made for no consideration, or for consideration that did not amount to its real value, and where the recipient either knew, or should have known, that the proceeds or property derived from a criminal offense, the property or proceeds will also be subject to confiscation.

Paragraph 2: It is common that in an effort to conceal the proceeds of crime, a convicted person may transfer the proceeds of crime to a legal person for no consideration or for consideration that does not equate to the real value of the property or proceeds. When this sort of transaction has occurred, the court must confiscate the property. Unlike in Paragraph 1, there is no need to prove any knowledge that the proceeds or property derived from a criminal offense.

Paragraph 3: The transfer of property or proceeds of crime to a close relative is often more common than the transfer to a third-party nonfamily member or legal person. The court will not accept the excuse that the property was a gift, nor will its transfer for nominal consideration be accepted by the court as a reason for allowing the family member to retain the property. Where a close relative has received property or the proceeds of crime, the MCC requires that the close family member gave the convicted person consideration that was equivalent to real value of the property or proceeds. In contrast to Paragraph 1 which relates to third-party recipients of property or proceeds of crime, Paragraph 3 allows confiscation even absent proof that the close relative knew or ought to have known that the proceeds or property derived from a criminal offense.

# Section 14: Dispositions Applicable to Juveniles and Adults on Trial for Criminal Offenses Committed as Juveniles

## General Commentary

Section 14 of the General Part of the MCC should be read in light of Chapter 15 of the MCCP on juvenile justice, which contains additional provisions on procedural aspects of the determination of a juvenile disposition. The Model Detention Act also contains provisions on the detention and imprisonment of juveniles.

Preferably, a state should create a wholly separate juvenile justice system, because juveniles who commit criminal offenses should be treated differently than adults by the criminal justice system. While they benefit from the same rights and protections applicable to adults under international human rights law, they are also entitled to additional rights contained in international human rights norms and standards, and these rights should be reflected in domestic criminal law. In a post-conflict state, the creation of a separate juvenile justice system may not always be a viable option for a variety of reasons, mostly relating to resources. Many of the experts consulted during the vetting process for the Model Codes were strongly in favor of a separate juvenile justice system. However, they were willing to concede the potential impossibility of establishing this system in some post-conflict situations, where resources are already overstretched. That said, everyone agreed that a post-conflict state should work toward the creation of a separate juvenile justice system. For the interim period, the Model Codes address the issue of juveniles within the regular criminal justice system, an option that a post-conflict state could initially follow. It would be inappropriate to treat adults and juveniles in the same way. Therefore, the MCC sets out separate provisions on penalties. Separate provisions on procedural protections for juveniles are contained in the MCCP, and separate provisions on the detention and imprisonment of juveniles are integrated into the Model Detention Act.

The purpose of Section 14 of the MCC is to incorporate the international standards relating to dispositions for juveniles contained in the International Covenant on Civil and Political Rights, the Convention on the Rights of the Child, and the United Nations Standard Minimum Rules for the Administration of Juvenile Justice (the Beijing Rules). Reference should be made to these instruments, in particular the commentary that accompanies the Beijing Rules, which may be instructive for drafters of legal provisions on juvenile dispositions. The International Covenant on Civil and Political Rights, Article 14(4), emphasizes the desirability of promoting the rehabilitation of juveniles in conflict with the law. Article 37(b) of the Convention on the Rights of the Child states that imprisonment of a child shall be used as a measure of last resort and for the shortest appropriate period of time. Part 3 of the United Nations Standard Minimum Rules for the Administration of Juvenile Justice sets out relevant standards on the disposition of criminal cases involving juveniles. The focus of juvenile dispositions is more on rehabilitation and less on retribution. The rationale for dealing with juveniles under a separate section relates not only to the differences in the purposes of penalties for adults and for juveniles but also to the suitability, or unsuitability, for children of penalties applicable to adults.

The term *disposition* instead of *penalty* has been used throughout Section 14 to underscore the predominantly nonpunitive nature of measures applied to juvenile convicted persons.

# Section 14

## Subsection 1: Scope of Application of Section 14 and General Principles

### Article 74: Scope of Application of Section 14

1. Section 14 is applicable to a juvenile who is convicted of a criminal offense or a person over the age of eighteen years who is being tried for a criminal offense committed when he or she was a juvenile.
2. Section 12 of the MCC does not apply to juveniles.

#### Commentary

For the reasons discussed previously and also below, the penalty provisions applicable to adult convicted persons do not apply to juveniles. Nor do they apply to adults who have been convicted for criminal offenses committed while they were juveniles. This provision underscores the fact that a court must not apply Section 12 of the MCC in either of these cases.

# Section 14

## Subsection 2: Purposes of Juvenile Dispositions and Principles Applicable to Juvenile Dispositions

## Article 75: Purposes of Juvenile Dispositions

The following are the purposes of juvenile dispositions:

(a) the promotion of the rehabilitation and reintegration of the juvenile and his or her resumption of a constructive role in society;

(b) the promotion of a sense of responsibility in the juvenile convicted person and acknowledgement of harm done to the community;

(c) the deterrence of the convicted juvenile person and other juvenile persons from committing criminal offenses;

(d) the separation of the convicted person from society, where necessary; and

(e) the provision of reparations for harm done to victims or the community.

### Commentary

As discussed in the commentary to Article 34, "Purposes of Penalties," relating to the purposes of adult penalties, it is imperative that a state articulate a particular criminal policy on the purposes of penalties to guide the judicial determination of penalties. Reference should be made to this discussion in the commentary to Article 34. It is equally important to do this for dispositions applicable to juveniles. The purposes of juvenile dispositions set out in Article 75 are very similar to those in Article 34 relating to adults, with the addition of Paragraph (a). The placement of this purpose at the top of the list of purposes of dispositions, and as the fundamental principle in Article 76, below, highlights the fact that the rehabilitation and reintegration of a juvenile and his or her resumption of a constructive role in society are key to juvenile dispositions. Reference should be made to Article 76 and its accompanying commentary, which discuss this issue in greater detail. The other principles of penalties can be taken into consideration as secondary factors to be considered by a court in assigning an appropriate juvenile disposition.

# Article 76: Fundamental Principle

The court must consider the rehabilitation and the reintegration into society of the juvenile person and his or her resumption of a constructive role in society as the fundamental principle in determining a juvenile disposition.

## Commentary

The applicable fundamental principle that guides the determination of adult penalties emphasizes the notion of just deserts—a principle that trumps all other purposes of penalties. For a more detailed discussion of the just deserts principle, reference should be made to Article 35 and its accompanying commentary. In short, this principle dictates that the type of penalty, and the term of imprisonment, if one is imposed, will be determined primarily by reference to the seriousness of the criminal offense and the culpability of the convicted person, although other principles set out in Article 34 can also be taken into consideration. The principle of just deserts is not appropriate as a guiding principle for juvenile dispositions, for reasons discussed below.

The need to prioritize the rehabilitation and reintegration of a juvenile convicted person is highlighted in Article 40(1) of the Convention on the Rights of the Child. Article 17(3) of the African Charter on the Rights and Welfare of the Child states that "the essential aim of treatment of every child during the trial and also if found guilty of infringing the penal law shall be his or her reformation, re-integration into his or her family and social rehabilitation." As mentioned above, the International Covenant on Civil and Political Rights, Article 14(4), also emphasizes the desirability of promoting the rehabilitation of juveniles in conflict with the law, as does the United Nations Standard Minimum Rules for the Administration of Juvenile Justice (the Beijing Rules). The Beijing Rules discuss this issue in the commentary to Principle 17, "Guiding Principles in Adjudication and Disposition." The rules do not set out a particular purpose of juvenile dispositions, given the difficulties inherent in this task, but the commentary specifies that "strictly punitive approaches are not appropriate." It also states that "whereas in adult cases, and possibly also in cases of severe offenses by juveniles, just desert and retributive sanctions might be considered to have some merit, in juvenile cases such considerations should be outweighed by the interest of safeguarding the well-being and the future of the young person." It is certainly true that making a juvenile responsible for his or her conduct is also of paramount importance. However, these considerations will apply not in preference to the rehabilitative aim but in conjunction with it. Rehabilitation is considered for adults, but only as a secondary consideration under Article 34, above. Much has been written on the ineffectiveness of criminal penalties in the rehabilitation of adult convicted persons. In contrast, there has been more success in rehabilitating juveniles. In the course of the consultation and vetting process of the MCC, many of the experts strongly supported the emphasis on rehabilitation and reintegration of juveniles as the primary purposes of juvenile dispositions.

# Article 77: Principles Applicable to Juvenile Dispositions

1. The following guiding principles must be taken into account by the court in determining the disposition applicable to the juvenile convicted person:
   (a) in determining the appropriate disposition for a juvenile, the court must consider the best interests of the juvenile as a primary consideration;
   (b) the disposition must be in proportion not only to the circumstances and gravity of the criminal offense but also to the circumstances and age of the juvenile and the needs of the juvenile as well as the needs of society;
   (c) restrictions on the personal liberty of the juvenile must be imposed only after careful consideration and must be limited to the possible minimum; and
   (d) deprivation of the personal liberty of the juvenile must be a measure of last resort, and the deprivation must be for the shortest period possible.
2. When the court is determining the appropriate juvenile disposition, it must look at individual factors relating to the juvenile convicted person, including but not limited to:
   (a) the age of the juvenile;
   (b) the type and gravity of the criminal offense;
   (c) the degree of his or her psychological development;
   (d) his or her psychological state at the time the criminal offense was committed;

(e) his or her motives in perpetrating the criminal offense;

(f) his or her education and upbringing;

(g) his or her environment and living conditions;

(h) whether he or she has previously been convicted of a criminal offense and what penalties were previously ordered against the juvenile; and

(i) for adults who are convicted of a criminal offense committed as a juvenile, the time elapsed since the commission of the criminal offense.

## Commentary

The principles set out in Article 77 are meant to guide a court in determining juvenile dispositions, in conjunction with the purposes of juvenile dispositions set out in Article 75 and the fundamental principle in Article 76. These principles are derived mainly from Principle 17 of the Beijing Rules, "Guiding Principles in Adjudication and Disposition."

Paragraph 1(a): This paragraph expresses the "best interests of the child principle," which lies at the core of international standards on the rights of the child. It is contained in Article 3(1) of the United Nations Convention on the Rights of the Child and Article 4(1) of the African Charter on the Rights and Welfare of the Child and is applicable to all the rights of the child, not just those relating to criminal justice. This principle should be considered at every stage of the judicial proceedings, not just at the penalty determination stage.

Paragraph 1(b): This paragraph is based on Principle 17.1(a) of the Beijing Rules. It introduces a proportionality requirement that requires a judge to consider not only the objective seriousness of a criminal offense but also subjective features of the juvenile convicted person, such as his or her age, circumstances, and needs. In addition, and as implied in Article 75(e), it is permissible for a court to consider the needs of society in conjunction with the needs of the juvenile convicted person. Of course, this purpose should be read in light of the fundamental principle contained in Article 77.

Paragraph 1(c): Paragraph 1(c) duplicates the language contained in Principle 17.1(b) of the Beijing Rules. This principle of minimal interference with the personal liberty of a juvenile implicitly encourages the use of alternative dispositions for juveniles. Reference should be made to the commentary to Article 78, which discusses this issue in greater detail.

Paragraph 1(d): The principle expressed in Paragraph 1(d) is also expressed in the MCC in relation to adult convicted persons. This paragraph closely mirrors the language of Principle 17.1(c) of the Beijing Rules. It also echoes the provisions of the United Nations Convention on the Rights of the Child, Article 37(b). The commentary to Principle 17.1 of the Beijing Rules states that this provision "aims at avoiding incarceration in the case of juveniles unless there is no other appropriate response that will protect the public safety." As will be seen below, the MCC provides for noncustodial and custodial dispositions and, in exceptional circumstances, juvenile imprisonment. The avoidance of the deprivation of personal liberty is facilitated through the use of alternative noncustodial dispositions. Reference should be made to the commentary to Article 78, which discusses these issues in greater detail.

Paragraph 2: It is essential that the court look at the individual circumstances of the convicted juvenile person to assist in determining an appropriate juvenile disposition. The court must create an individualized disposition based on the individual characteristics of the convicted juvenile person and the circumstances surrounding the particular criminal offense that he or she committed. Paragraph 2 enumerates an illustrative but not exhaustive list of individual factors that a court must take into account when determining a juvenile disposition.

# Section 14

## Subsection 3: Structure of Juvenile Dispositions

### Article 78: Principal Juvenile Dispositions

The applicable juvenile dispositions are:

(a) judicial admonition;

(b) intensive supervision of a juvenile;

(c) a disciplinary measure, either on its own or coupled with subsequent intensive supervision;

(d) an institutional measure, either on its own or coupled with intensive supervision; and

(e) juvenile imprisonment or juvenile imprisonment with a suspended sentence.

#### Commentary

Principle 18 of the Beijing Rules provides that a large variety of dispositions be available to courts when dealing with juvenile convicted persons. It gives a variety of examples, many of which have been integrated into the MCC. The rules focus on avoiding institutional measures, which in Principle 19 are said to be "a disposition of last resort." Institutional measures encompass facilities such as juvenile correctional facilities, juvenile prisons, and prisons where adult convicted persons are held. The MCC and international standards on the rights of juveniles aim to keep juveniles as far away from any kind of institutionalization as possible. Some states, however, tend to use imprisonment as an automatic punishment for juveniles and to place the juveniles not in juvenile facilities or centers but in adult prisons, where they are exposed to the negative influences and to physical or sexual abuse at the hands of adults.

Many studies have shown the limited positive impact of prison on the rehabilitation of juveniles. The commentary to Principle 19 of the Beijing Rules states that "progressive criminology advocates the use of non-institutional over institutional treatment. Little or no difference has been found in terms of the success of institutionalization as compared to non-institutionalization. The many adverse influences on an individual that seem unavoidable within any institutional setting evidently cannot be outbalanced by treatment efforts. This is especially the case for juveniles, who are vulnerable to negative influences." When institutionalization is used as a measure of last resort, international standards are clear that its focus must be on providing care, protection, education, and vocational skills to juveniles, with a view to assisting them to assume socially constructive and productive roles in society (see Principle 26 of the Beijing Rules).

Article 78 provides a range of dispositions—some noninstitutional, one semi-institutional, and others institutional. Supplementing these, the seven dispositions contained under Article 79 on additional dispositions form part of the range of dispositions a court may impose upon a juvenile convicted person. A court can be creative in how it combines these dispositions. For example, the court may admonish a juvenile person under Article 78(a). It may combine this admonition with an order that a juvenile attend school on a regular basis, as described in Article 79(a). As described in Article 79(c), it may order the juvenile to refrain from contacting certain persons or going to certain areas, both of which may tempt the juvenile to commit a criminal offense.

The main focus of the dispositions contained in the MCC, in line with the purpose of juvenile penalties in Article 75, is the rehabilitation of the convicted juvenile person, his or her reintegration into society, and the resumption of a constructive role in society. Where a juvenile convicted person is separated from society through semi-institutional or institutional measures, the focus of these dispositions should also be rehabilitation. For example, during the term of a disciplinary measure under Article 83, the juvenile will be engaged in useful activities that aid in the development of a sense of responsibility. Institutional measures involve staying at an educational, rehabilitation, or treatment center. Juvenile imprisonment involves a period of time served in a detention center. Juvenile imprisonment is a measure of last resort and may be imposed only in exceptional circumstances. When a juvenile is imprisoned, the institution should offer a variety of programs aimed at rehabilitating the juvenile. For a more detailed discussion, cross-reference should be made to the commentary to Article 85.

The Beijing Rules provide that "volunteers, volunteer organizations, local institutions and other community resources shall be called upon to contribute effectively to the rehabilitation of juveniles in a community setting" (Rule 25.1) and consequently to the execution of juvenile dispositions. The commentary to Rule 25 states that "co-operation with the community is indispensable if the directives of the competent authority are to be carried out effectively. Volunteers and voluntary services, in particular, have proved to be valuable resources but are at present underutilized." There are many examples of cooperative ventures between state and voluntary organizations in the realm of juvenile dispositions. The authorities in a post-conflict state should consider seeking out reputable organizations to work with in this venture.

Before a state implements semi-institutional and institutional measures into its domestic legislation, it should ensure that sufficient resources are provided to build and maintain the institutions (or, where they already exist, to modernize and repair them), staff the institutions, and fund their work and activities. Semi-institutional and institutional measures are often under-resourced, being underprioritized in the budgets of the governments of post-conflict states and underfunded by international donors. In Kosovo, for example, according to the Organization for Security and Cooperation in Europe report entitled *Kosovo, Review of the Criminal Justice System (April 2003–October 2004): Crime, Detention and Punishment*, the execution of juvenile dispositions is hampered by a lack of adequate institutions for convicted juveniles (page 57). The institutions contained in the Kosovo Code of Criminal Procedure—namely, disciplinary centers, educational institutions, special-care facilities, and foster-care facilities—were not budgeted or established by the time the law came into force. The Probation Service established in Kosovo also lacks the capacity to undertake its role envisaged vis-à-vis juvenile dispositions.

Additionally, training programs for judges should be undertaken to educate them about juvenile penalties. In Kosovo, according to the OSCE report, judges made almost immediate recourse to custodial dispositions rather than considering alternatives. This judicial reflex is common in many other post-conflict states. It must be addressed through training and education for judges; public awareness campaigns targeting the local population, who share the judges' views, may also be valuable.

**Paragraph (a):** Reference should be made to Article 81 and its accompanying commentary.

**Paragraph (b):** Reference should be made to Article 82 and its accompanying commentary.

**Paragraph (c):** Reference should be made to Article 83 and its accompanying commentary.

**Paragraph (d):** Reference should be made to Article 84 and its accompanying commentary.

**Paragraph (e):** Reference should be made to Article 85 and its accompanying commentary.

# Article 79: Additional Juvenile Dispositions

In addition to a principal disposition, the court may order the convicted juvenile person to:

(a) attend school on a regular basis;

(b) accept employment or training for a profession, appropriate to his or her abilities or skills;

(c) refrain from contacting certain individuals who are likely to have a negative influence on the juvenile;

(d) refrain from visiting certain places or locations that are likely to have a negative influence on the juvenile;

(e) refrain from the use of drugs or alcohol;

(f) undergo counseling or treatment for alcohol and other substance abuse or addiction; or

(g) undergo mental health, including psychiatric or psychological, counseling or treatment.

## Commentary

The additional dispositions in Article 79 may be used to supplement the principal dispositions provided for in Article 78, where their use is in the best interests of the juvenile convicted person. The primary dispositions stress the central purpose of juvenile penalties: rehabilitation. The additional dispositions may further assist in rehabilitation, for example, through prohibiting a juvenile convicted person from contacting certain individuals who have, in the past, been engaged in criminal activities with the juvenile, or through providing counseling or treatment to a juvenile who has a drug or alcohol addiction or mental illness. The use of a personal apology to a victim may not only have a rehabilitative effect but may also provide some satisfaction to the victim of a criminal offense and to society, thus serving one of the other purposes of juvenile dispositions.

Obviously, most of the additional dispositions cannot be imposed upon a person who is subject to a custodial disposition such as institutionalization. The additional dispositions can be ordered to apply, however, once the juvenile convicted person is no longer serving a custodial disposition.

Just as with principal dispositions, the authorities in a post-conflict state should consider joining forces with reputable volunteers, volunteer organizations, local institutions, and other community resources to implement the additional juvenile dispositions.

One issue not dealt with in the substance of the MCC is the consequence of not complying with an additional juvenile disposition. The drafters of the MCC struggled with this issue. Ordinarily, this is an issue that might be dealt with by a state probationary body rather than the court. Otherwise, bringing a juvenile convicted person before the court every time an order for additional dispositions is breached would unnecessarily burden the court. A state implementing legislation on juvenile dispositions should make provision for the consequences of a breach of an additional juvenile disposition. This provision may be contained in the relevant legislation on the body established by law to oversee the execution of penalties and juvenile dispositions (i.e., the probation service).

Paragraph (f): As with many of the principal dispositions discussed in Article 78, sufficient resources and personnel are necessary to implement this disposition. As just discussed, the authorities may wish to consider cooperating with a reputable voluntary organization in providing this disposition.

# Section 14

## Subsection 4: Procedure for Determining Juvenile Dispositions

### Article 80: Procedure for Determining Juvenile Dispositions

1. The court must decide upon the appropriateness of a particular juvenile disposition in light of the purposes of juvenile dispositions under Article 75, the fundamental principle under Article 76, and the principles applicable to juvenile dispositions under Article 77, including the individual circumstances of the convicted juvenile person under Article 77(2).
2. When a juvenile, or an adult who committed a criminal offense as a juvenile, has been found criminally responsible for two or more criminal offenses, the court must impose a joint disposition.
3. The court must first determine which principal disposition to impose upon a convicted juvenile person. In doing so, the court must take into consideration the suitability of each disposition in relation to its potential rehabilitative effect upon the juvenile convicted person.
4. The court must then follow the procedure and principles set out in the relevant article on the particular principal disposition that has been selected.
5. After imposing a principal disposition on the convicted juvenile person, the court may also impose an additional disposition.

#### Commentary

Paragraph 1: This paragraph articulates the overarching principles that should be considered during each step of determining the appropriate juvenile penalty.

Paragraph 2: When an adult is convicted of two or more criminal offenses, either resulting from the same criminal episode or prior to or after a conviction, a court must assign a penalty for each offense and then move to consider a joint penalty. Reference should be made to Articles 52 and 53 and their accompanying commentaries. This procedure does not apply to juveniles. Where a juvenile commits more than one offense, only one principal juvenile disposition can be imposed upon the juvenile. Of course, the principal disposition can be supplemented by additional dispositions where necessary. The fact that the juvenile has committed more than one criminal offense will certainly be an important factor in the court's decision on which particular principal disposition it imposes.

Paragraph 3: Each disposition under the MCC has the same general purpose and potential effect—that is, to rehabilitate the juvenile convicted person. In some cases, rehabilitation might require only a judicial admonition. In other cases, temporary custodial measures or institutional measures may be necessary to rehabilitate the juvenile. The approach will depend on the individual circumstances of the juvenile convicted person. A court should assess each disposition in light of these circumstances.

Paragraph 5: Reference should also be made to Article 79, on additional dispositions, and its accompanying commentary.

# Section 14

## Subsection 5: Principal Juvenile Dispositions

## Article 81: Judicial Admonition

1. A judicial admonition is a measure by which the court informs the juvenile that he or she has committed a harmful and dangerous act that constitutes a criminal offense and that if he or she commits such an act again, the court will impose a more severe disposition upon him or her.
2. The court may impose a judicial admonition upon a juvenile where such a measure is deemed sufficient and in the best interests of the child in order to rehabilitate the juvenile convicted person and to positively influence his or her behavior.

### Commentary

A judicial admonition is called a warning in some systems. It is the least severe of the applicable juvenile dispositions and can be used when a court considers it sufficient to rehabilitate and positively influence a juvenile's behavior and when it is appropriate based on the best interests of the child principle. In some instances, going through the criminal process, being found criminally responsible, and being warned that any future criminal conduct will result in a more severe disposition is enough to rehabilitate the juvenile convicted person without the need to deprive him or her of personal liberty. A judicial admonition can be supplemented by an additional disposition, such as an apology, as set out in Article 79.

# Article 82: Intensive Supervision of a Juvenile

1. Intensive supervision is a measure under which a juvenile is placed under the intensive supervision of his or her parents, adoptive parents, legal guardians, foster parents, or [insert name of social care body].
2. The court may impose a measure of intensive supervision upon a juvenile where he or she would benefit from an extended measure of education, rehabilitation, or treatment under adequate supervision but where it is not necessary to totally isolate the juvenile from his or her home environment.
3. The court may order that the parents, adoptive parents, or legal guardians of the juvenile intensively supervise the child, where it deems the parents, adoptive parents, or legal guardians to be capable of exercising such supervision.
4. The court may also order that the [insert name of social care body] monitor the enforcement of the supervision order or render assistance to the parents, adoptive parents, or legal guardians in supervising the juvenile.
5. Where the court determines that the parents, adoptive parents, or legal guardians cannot reasonably be expected to intensively supervise the juvenile, and where it is in the best interest of the juvenile, the court may order the juvenile to be placed in a foster home for intensive supervision.
6. The court may also order that the [insert name of social care body] monitor the enforcement of the supervision order or render assistance to the foster parents in supervising the juvenile.
7. The court may discontinue intensive supervision in a foster home where it subsequently becomes possible for the parents, adoptive parents, or legal guardians to exercise this role.
8. Where the parents, adoptive parents, or legal guardians cannot reasonably be expected to intensively supervise the juvenile on their own, and where no foster home is available for the juvenile to undergo intensive supervision, the court may order the [insert name of social care body] to be responsible for the supervision of the juvenile.
9. Where the court orders the [insert name of social care body] to be responsible for supervising the juvenile, the juvenile will stay with his or her parents, adoptive parents, or legal guardians, and the intensive supervision over him or her will be exercised by an authorized person of the [insert name of social care body].

10. When the court orders intensive supervision by a parent, adoptive parent, legal guardian, foster parent, or the [insert name of social care body], it must include in its order the parties' duties in intensively supervising the juvenile.
11. The court may at any time terminate or modify the special obligations it has ordered the juvenile to fulfill or the duties it has imposed upon parents, adoptive parents, legal guardians, foster parents, or the [insert name of social care body].
12. The court may order intensive supervision for a minimum period of three months and a maximum period of three years.
13. In the event that the orders are not fulfilled, the court may substitute the order for intensive supervision with another disposition. At the time the obligation is imposed, the court must warn the juvenile convicted person of the consequences of not fulfilling an obligation imposed upon him or her.
14. The court may also terminate the order for intensive supervision or substitute another juvenile disposition for it where:
    (a) circumstances that had not existed or were unknown at the time the court made its order arise; and
    (b) such circumstances might have affected the outcome of the court's order.

## Commentary

Intensive supervision is a noncustodial, noninstitutional disposition that involves the juvenile convicted person remaining at home or being placed in a foster home and being supervised by parents, adopted parents, legal guardians, foster parents, or the relevant social care body in the state. Intensive supervision can last anywhere from three months to three years. It is a good alternative to institutionalization, as the juvenile is adequately supervised but at the same time does not have to leave his or her home environment. It might be usual to supplement intensive supervision with an additional disposition, particularly one relating to education, rehabilitation, or treatment, given the aim of intensive supervision. A court will assign another body—the social care body—to assist in overseeing the execution of the juvenile disposition. Of course, in a post-conflict state, social care bodies may not exist or may be underfunded. A post-conflict state should strive to ensure that sufficient resources are directed to the establishment and/or running of a social care body tasked with, among other things, overseeing court-ordered intensive supervision of juvenile convicted persons. Legislation may be required to establish the social care body and define its relevant powers and purposes. Another issue that should be addressed by the post-conflict state relates to foster care. Many states have developed systems for foster care under the ambit of family law. A post-conflict state should look at its laws on foster care prior to implementing this provision. If there are no laws on foster care, the state should consider addressing this issue, where appropriate, and inserting provisions relating to court-ordered intensive supervision of juvenile convicted persons within the laws on the domestic foster care system. These issues become particularly important to juvenile justice in the post-conflict context, in which supervision by the juvenile's natural parents may not be an option if the parents have been killed or incapacitated or have fled the country during the conflict.

In the case of a breach of an intensive supervision order, the court may have to have recourse to another juvenile disposition, which may involve imposing an institutional measure on the juvenile convicted person. The same goes for a situation in which certain circumstances that would have influenced how the court determined the disposition are uncovered, as set out in Paragraph 14.

# Article 83: Disciplinary Measures

1. A disciplinary measure is a short-term institutional measure under which a juvenile convicted person is committed to a juvenile disciplinary center.
2. In the juvenile disciplinary center, the juvenile will be engaged in useful activities, as appropriate for his or her age, skills, and interests. The aim of these activities is to develop a sense of responsibility in the juvenile convicted person.
3. The court may impose a disciplinary measure upon a juvenile where:
   (a) a juvenile perpetrated a criminal offense out of thoughtlessness or carelessness; and
   (b) the disciplinary measure is deemed sufficient to positively influence his or her behavior and is in his or her best interest.
4. The court may impose a disciplinary measure:
   (a) for a maximum of four days of a school or public holiday for up to eight hours per day;
   (b) for a specified number of hours during a day but for not more than one month; or
   (c) for a continuous stay over a specified number of days totaling not more than twenty days.
5. When the court orders a disciplinary measure against a juvenile, it must ensure that the order does not hinder his or her regular employment or school activities.
6. After the juvenile has completed the disciplinary measure, additional intensive supervision may be imposed.

## Commentary

A disciplinary measure can involve either semi-institutionalization or full institutionalization for a short period of time (not exceeding twenty days). A disciplinary measure is an appropriate disposition in a situation where a juvenile committed a criminal offense out of thoughtlessness or carelessness and where it is sufficient, to rehabilitate the juvenile convicted person, that he or she undergo a short period in an institution. The period of institutionalization can be either served all at once or spread out over a longer time, during which the juvenile might attend the institution only on weekends and holidays, for example. Where this option is chosen, a court may have concluded that judicial admonition would be insufficient in the particular case. Intensive supervision at home or in a foster home may also have been deemed insufficient to meet the purpose of rehabilitation. An additional degree of supervision may be required in the juvenile disciplinary center. In this institution, the juvenile must undertake useful activities intended to help him or her develop a sense of responsibility. To implement this measure, funding, resources, and personnel will be required. Reference should be made to the commentary to Article 78, which discusses this issue in greater detail.

A disciplinary measure may be coupled with intensive supervision that applies after the period of the disciplinary measure has expired. In imposing intensive supervision on the juvenile convicted person, a court is also at liberty to impose additional dispositions.

# Article 84: Institutional Measures

1. An institutional measure is an extended custodial measure under which a juvenile convicted person is committed to a juvenile institution.
2. In the juvenile institution, the juvenile will be engaged in useful activities appropriate for his or her age, skills, and interests. The aim of these activities is to rehabilitate and educate the juvenile convicted person.
3. The court may impose an institutional measure upon a juvenile where he or she would benefit from an extended measure of education, rehabilitation, or treatment under adequate supervision, and where his or her best interests would be served by isolation from his or her previous environment.
4. The court may order an institutional measure up to a maximum period of three years.
5. The court may terminate an institutional measure or substitute another juvenile penalty for it where:
   (a) circumstances that had not existed or were unknown at the time the court made its order arise; and

(b) such circumstances might have affected the outcome of the court's order.

6. Intensive supervision may be imposed in addition to a disciplinary measure after the juvenile has completed the institutional measure.

## Commentary

When the court concludes that a judicial admonition would not serve the rehabilitative needs of a juvenile convicted person, and where supervision at home or in a foster home or short-term institutional facility would not result in the rehabilitation of the juvenile convicted person, the court may consider more long-term institutional measures. In the institution, which may be an educational, rehabilitation, or treatment center, the juvenile should be engaged in educational or rehabilitative activities that will assist in his or her future reintegration into society. The term *juvenile institution* has been used generically to describe a place where the juvenile will spend his or her time while an institutional measure is in effect. Potentially, an institutional measure could be served in the same institution as a disciplinary measure. In other cases, where the state has treatment centers—for example, for drug or alcohol addiction—the juvenile may spend the term of the institutional measure there. The same considerations relating to funding, staffing, and resources apply, as with all institutional measures. Reference should be made to the commentary to Article 78, which discusses this issue in greater detail.

# Article 85: Juvenile Imprisonment

1. Juvenile imprisonment may be imposed only where:

   (a) the juvenile was between the ages of sixteen years and eighteen years at the time of the commission of the criminal offense;

   (b) the juvenile has committed a serious criminal offense;

   (c) the juvenile possesses a high degree of culpability; and

   (d) the court concludes that other juvenile dispositions will not aid sufficiently in the fundamental principle of rehabilitation of the juvenile.

2. The imprisonment of a juvenile must be used as a measure of last resort and for the shortest appropriate period of time.

3. When the court orders the imprisonment of a juvenile, the court must not impose a period of imprisonment in excess of half the maximum penalty provided for the relevant criminal offense.

4. The court may order the imprisonment of a juvenile for a period of time less than the minimum penalty provided for the relevant criminal offense.
5. In determining the length of the period of imprisonment, the court must consider the aggravating and mitigating circumstances, set out in Article 77(2).
6. When the court orders the imprisonment of a juvenile, it may suspend the sentence of imprisonment.
7. The provisions of Article 55 apply, with the necessary modifications, to a suspended sentence to be imposed upon a juvenile convicted person.

## Commentary

The imprisonment of a juvenile is permissible only in certain circumstances. The person must be between the ages of sixteen and eighteen years when he or she commits the criminal offense. In addition, the criminal offense must be serious and the juvenile convicted person must have a high degree of culpability. Finally, the court must determine that none of the other juvenile dispositions in the MCC would serve to rehabilitate the juvenile. Imprisonment, as it is envisaged in the MCC, is a measure of last resort. This idea echoes the provisions of the Convention on the Rights of the Child, Article 37(b); the Beijing Rules (Rule 17); and paragraph 1 of the United Nations Rules for the Protection of Juveniles Deprived of Their Liberty. If possible, juveniles should be placed in a separate juvenile prison, rather than being imprisoned with adults in the same facility. If this is not an option, arrangements should be made for the segregation of juveniles and adults within the prison facility and for the elimination of contact or interaction between adults and juveniles, consistent with international human rights standards. In Kosovo, for example, in the early days of the peace operation, when the international military force in Kosovo, KFOR, was responsible for ensuring law and order, it worked with UNICEF and United Nations civilian staff on the issue of juvenile detention. Because of the devastation to the criminal justice infrastructure during the conflict, there were no separate juvenile prisons or institutions, so KFOR worked with UNICEF and the United Nations to ensure that juveniles were housed separately within a prison that also housed adults. Juveniles had their own, separate quarters and ate and exercised at separate times so that adults and juveniles did not come into contact. Eventually, a separate juvenile facility was built.

Reference should be made to the discussion in the Model Detention Act of international standards relating to the detention and imprisonment of juveniles and practical ways to implement these standards.

As set out in Article 76, the primary focus of juvenile imprisonment should be rehabilitation and not retribution. Juveniles should be engaged in educational and rehabilitative activities in the prison. The United Nations Rules for the Protection of Juveniles Deprived of Their Liberty emphasizes this idea in section E (paragraphs 38–46) on education, vocational training, and work. Penal Reform International's *Ten*

*Point Plan for Juvenile Justice* stresses that juveniles should be held at "small open facilities with minimal security measures" and that "education and rehabilitation should be the main priorities." These issues are discussed in greater detail in the commentary to the Model Detention Act.

# Model Criminal Code

# PART II
# SPECIAL PART

# Section 1: Genocide, Crimes against Humanity, and War Crimes

## General Commentary

The criminal offenses of genocide, crimes against humanity, and war crimes are requisite parts of domestic legislation where a state wishes to prosecute persons for atrocities committed in the course of a conflict. These offenses have long been recognized as crimes under international law but have often not been incorporated into national legislation. Fortunately, states—including, of course, post-conflict states—are free to adopt legislation providing for prosecution of these crimes committed in the past, despite the general prohibition of retroactive prosecutions. This is because Article 11(2) of the Universal Declaration of Human Rights, and equivalent provisions in all of the major human rights treaties (replicated in Article 3[3] of the MCC), declares that the rule against retroactive prosecution is not infringed if a crime was recognized previously under international law, and this is clearly the case for genocide, crimes against humanity, and war crimes.

Where no legislation on genocide, crimes against humanity, and war crimes is passed, a state will almost invariably be able to prosecute a person for the crimes against the person that underlie the international offenses of genocide, crimes against humanity, or war crimes—offenses such as unlawful killing, rape, and assault. However, even if a post-conflict state takes this latter option, the state should nonetheless include the international offenses in its new criminal legislation. In this way, the offenses apply prospectively from the date of implementation of the legislation. Where a state is a party to the Rome Statute of the International Criminal Court, the state is also expected to implement these offenses into domestic law. The easiest way to implement a state's obligations under the Rome Statute is to take definitions from the statute, as has been done in the MCC.

Because of the highly specialized requirements of the body of law surrounding genocide, crimes against humanity, and war crimes, a state may consider creating a separate court or specialized panel of the regular court system to try these offenses. Reference should be made to Article 3 of the MCCP, which discusses the creation of separate court structures in greater detail. Whether these cases are tried by a separate court, chamber, or panel or within the regular criminal justice system itself, it is essential that persons involved in the prosecution and defense of such cases are well trained in what is a very complicated area of law. Judges will also need adequate training to adjudicate the case.

Judges, prosecutors, and defense counsel involved in domestic cases involving these criminal offenses in post-conflict Kosovo and East Timor, and consulted in the course of the process of vetting the Model Codes, complained that they had not received such training. Many had little or no previous experience in criminal law, let alone in the complicated areas of international criminal law, international humanitarian law, or international human rights law.

Comprehensive training programs should be adequately resourced and established prior to, or at the time of, the introduction of domestic legislation. It may also be necessary to establish structures to offer research and logistical support to those involved in trying, adjudicating, or defending these cases—defense counsel are particularly likely to be under-resourced. In a post-conflict state, support structures may be established and resourced by the state, an international organization, or a nongovernmental organization. In some states, experts from academic institutions in other states have provided research assistance free of charge to prosecutors, defense counsel, and judges involved in these sorts of cases.

# Article 86: Genocide

## *Article 86.1: Definition of Offense*

A person commits the criminal offense of genocide when he or she commits any of the following acts with intent to destroy, in whole or in part, a national, ethnical, racial, or religious group as such:

(a) killing members of the group;

(b) causing serious bodily or mental harm to members of the group;

(c) deliberately inflicting on the group conditions of life calculated to bring about its physical destruction in whole or in part;

(d) imposing measures intended to prevent births within the group;

(e) forcibly transferring children of the group to another group.

### Commentary

The definition in Article 86 copies the one contained within Article II of the 1948 Convention for the Prevention and Punishment of the Crime of Genocide, which has subsequently been incorporated unchanged into a number of international instruments, including the Rome Statute of the International Criminal Court, the Statute of the International Criminal Tribunal for Rwanda (ICTR), the Statute of the International Criminal Tribunal for the former Yugoslavia (ICTY), and, in East Timor, UNTAET Regulation 2000/15 on the Establishment of Panels with Exclusive Jurisdiction over Serious Criminal Offenses. The jurisprudence of the ICTY and the ICTR has been instrumental in deconstructing the definition of genocide and is referred to at length in the commentary below. The prosecution of the criminal offense of genocide, in addition to articulation of a precise meaning of this criminal offense, is complicated. The following commentary provides an introductory discussion on the definition of genocide. For those involved in the prosecution, defense, or adjudication of persons accused of genocide, further research will be necessary. For a fuller discussion of the meaning and scope of the definition of genocide, including relevant case law, reference should be made to William A. Schabas, *Genocide in International Law.* Human Rights Watch has compiled a basic compendium of case law on genocide entitled *Genocide, War Crimes and Crimes against Humanity: Topical Digests of the Case Law of the International Criminal Tribunal for Rwanda and the International Criminal Tribunal for the former Yugoslavia.*

The main feature that distinguishes the criminal offense of genocide from those of crimes against humanity, war crimes, or other offenses such as unlawful killing is the requirement to prove that the perpetrator possessed "the intent to destroy, in whole or in part, a national, ethnical, racial, or religious group." The ICTY and the ICTR have called this requirement genocide's special intent, or *dolus specialis.* According to one ICTY trial chamber, the terms *special intent* and *dolus specialis* can be used interchangeably. In its commentary on the 1996 Draft Code of Crimes against the Peace and Security of Mankind (page 144), the International Law Commission qualified genocide's specific intent as "the distinguishing characteristic of this particular crime under international law." Proof of this intent may be inferred from the facts, the concrete circumstances, or a pattern of purposeful action. But "[w]here an inference needs to be drawn, it has to be *the only reasonable inference available on the evidence*" (italics in original) (*Prosecutor v. Brđanin,* case no. IT-99-36-T, Judgment, September 1, 2004, paragraph 970; see also *Prosecutor v. Krstić,* case no. IT-98-33-A, Judgment, April 19, 2004, paragraph 41).

The intent of the perpetrator of genocide must be to "destroy" the group. In the *Krstić* case before the ICTY, a trial chamber said that "customary international law limits the definition of genocide to those acts seeking the physical or biological destruction of all or part of the group. Hence, an enterprise attacking only the cultural or sociological characteristics of a human group in order to annihilate these elements which give to that group its own identity distinct from the rest of the community would not fall under the definition of genocide" (*Prosecutor v. Krstić,* case no. IT-98-33-T, Judgment, August 2, 2001, paragraphs 576, 580).

As to what the perpetrator of genocide must seek to destroy, the definition of genocide contains an exhaustive list, requiring that he or she must intend to destroy "a national, ethnical, racial, or religious group." The ICTY and the ICTR, in interpreting the meaning of the criminal offense of genocide, have moved toward a subjective approach in determining the existence and identity of the group. If the perpetrator or the victim considers the group to exist, this is a compelling indicator for the application of the criminal offense of genocide. The tribunals, however, combine this subjective test with an analysis of case-specific objective factors in determining what constitutes a "group." "This is so," wrote an ICTY trial chamber, "because subjective criteria alone may not be sufficient to determine the group targeted for destruction and protected by the *Genocide Convention*, for the reason that the acts identified in subparagraphs (a) to (e) of Article 4(2) must be in fact directed against 'members of the group'" (*Prosecutor v. Brđanin*, case no. IT-99-36-T, Judgment, September 1, 2004, paragraph 684).

It is necessary to prove only that the perpetrator of genocide intended to destroy the group "in part." The ICTY and the ICTR have interpreted this requirement by adding the adjective *substantial*, which indicates a quantitative dimension, or *significant*, which suggests a qualitative dimension. The ICTR has said "that 'in part' requires the intention to destroy a considerable number of individuals" (*Prosecutor v. Kayishema et al.*, case no. ICTR-95-1-T, Judgment and Sentence, May 21, 1999, paragraph 97). An ICTY and ICTR trial chamber said that genocide must involve the intent to destroy a "substantial" part, although not necessarily a "very important part" (*Prosecutor v. Jelisić*, case no. IT-95-10-T, Judgment, October 19, 1999; *Prosecutor v. Bagilishema*, case no. ICTR-95-1A-T, Judgment, June 7, 2001, paragraphs 56–59). In another judgment, the ICTY referred to a "reasonably substantial" number relative to the group as a whole (*Prosecutor v. Jelisić*, case no. IT-95-10-T, Judgment, October 19, 1999; *Prosecutor v. Bagilishema*, case no. ICTR-95-1A-T, Judgment, June 7, 2001, paragraphs 56–59). The intent requirement that the destruction contemplate the group "in whole or in part" should not be confused with the scale of the participation by an individual perpetrator. The perpetrator may be involved in only one or a few killings or other punishable acts. No single perpetrator, as the principal perpetrator of the physical acts, could plausibly be responsible for destroying a group in whole or in part. Some judgments have held that it is enough to target a "significant" part of the group, such as its religious or political elite. This approach was endorsed by an ICTY trial chamber in the *Jelisić* case, which held that it might be possible to infer the requisite genocidal intent from the "desired destruction of a more limited number of persons selected for the impact that their disappearance would have upon the survival of the group as such" (*Prosecutor v. Jelisić*, case no. IT-95-10-T, Judgment, December 14, 1999, paragraph 82).

The ICTY and ICTR appeals chambers have held that there is no need to establish a "plan" to commit genocide. This means it is possible to prove the commission of genocide without any evidence of involvement by a state or an organized statelike entity. According to the Appeals Chamber of the ICTY, "the existence of a plan or policy is not a legal ingredient of the crime. However, in the context of proving specific intent, the existence of a plan or policy may become an important factor in most cases. The evidence may be consistent with the existence of a plan or policy, or may even show such existence, and the existence of a plan or policy may facilitate proof of the crime" (*Prosecutor v. Jelisić*, case no. IT-95-10-A, Judgment, July 5, 2001, paragraph 48). In another case, the appeals chamber referred to this paragraph in support of its conclusion not to require proof of a "plan or policy" with respect to genocide (*Prosecutor v. Kunarac et al.*, case no. IT-96-23/1-A, Judgment, June 12, 2002, paragraph 98, fn. 114).

According to the ICTR Appeals Chamber, "as such" was included in Article II of the 1948 Genocide Convention to resolve an impasse among the negotiators as to whether or not proof of genocidal *motive* should be added to the requirement of a specific or special intent. The chamber said the expression has the "*effet utile* of drawing a clear distinction between mass murder and crimes in which the perpetrator targets a specific group because of its nationality, race, ethnicity or religion." But "as such" does not prohibit a conviction for genocide "in a case in which the perpetrator was also driven by other motivations that are legally irrelevant in this context" (*Prosecutor v. Niyitegeka*, case no. ICTR-96-14-A, Judgment, July 9, 2004, paragraph 53; see also *Prosecutor v. Ntakirutimana*, case nos. ICTR-96-10-A and ICTR-96-17-A, Judgment, December 13, 2004, paragraph 363).

Article 86 lists five punishable acts of genocide. Each of these acts has its own mental and physical elements, which must be proven in addition to the elements in the chapeau, or introductory paragraph, for there to be a conviction. The list is an exhaustive one and does not permit other acts that might result in the destruction of a protected group.

Paragraph (a): Intentional killing can be prosecuted under the MCC as a war crime (willful killing), a crime against humanity (murder), and genocide (killing). Under Article 86, intentional killing as genocide must be committed with the specific intent to destroy in whole or in part a national, ethnical, racial, or religious group as such.

The act of killing, under genocide, consists of three material elements: the victim is dead, the death resulted from an unlawful act or omission of the perpetrator or a subordinate, and, at the time of the killing, the accused or a subordinate had the intention to kill or inflict grievous bodily harm on the deceased knowing that such bodily harm is likely to cause the victim's death or is reckless about whether the death ensues or not (*Prosecutor v. Akayesu*, case no. ICTR-96-4-T, Judgment, September 2, 1998, paragraph 589). The perpetrator must intend this result or recklessly disregard the likelihood that death will result from such acts or omissions. There is no requirement that the killing be premeditated (*Prosecutor v. Kayishema et al.*, case no. ICTR-95-1-A, Judgment [Reasons], June 1, 2001, paragraph 151), but it must be proven that the death of a person resulted from the actions or omissions of the perpetrator. The actions or omissions need not be the sole cause of death, but they must be "a substantial cause" (*Prosecutor v. Kordić et al.*, case no. IT-95-14/2-T, Judgment, February 26, 2001, paragraphs 236, 229; see also *Prosecutor v. Krnojelac*, case no. IT-97-25-T, Judgment, March 15, 2002, paragraphs 323–324). To establish the mens rea, or mental element, of the offense, there must be evidence that the perpetrator had the intent to kill. Alternatively, the ICTY has held that it is sufficient to demonstrate that the perpetrator intended to inflict serious bodily injury in reckless disregard of human life (*Prosecutor v. Kordić et al.*, case no. IT-95-14/2-A, Judgment, December 17, 2004, paragraph 36; *Prosecutor v. Delalić et al.*, case no. IT-96-21-A, Judgment, February 20, 2001, paragraph 422). While there must be proof that a person is dead, this fact can be inferred, and it is not necessary to show that the body was recovered. It has been held that causing the suicide of a person may amount to killing where the accused's acts or omissions "induced the victim to take action which resulted in his death, and that his suicide was either intended, or was an action of a type which a reasonable person could have foreseen as a consequence" (*Prosecutor v. Krnojelac*, case no. IT-97-25-T, Judgment, March 15, 2002, paragraph 329).

Paragraph (b): The ICTR has held "serious bodily or mental harm, without limiting itself thereto, to mean acts of torture, be they bodily or mental, inhumane or degrading treatment or persecution" (*Prosecutor v. Akayesu*, case no. ICTR-96-4-T, Judgment, September 2, 1998, paragraph 504). Another trial chamber of the ICTR defined serious bodily or mental harm as "harm that seriously injures the health, causes disfigurement or causes any serious injury to the external, internal organs or senses" (*Prosecutor v. Kayishema et al.*, case no. ICTR-95-1-T, Judgment and Sentence, May 21, 1999, paragraph 109). A trial chamber of the ICTY has likewise considered torture and inhuman or degrading treatment to fall within the provision's scope (*Prosecutor v. Karadžić et al.*, case nos. IT-95-5-R61 and IT-95-18-R6 and Review of the Indictment Pursuant to Rule 61 of the Rules of Procedure and Evidence, July 11, 1996, paragraph 93). It has been held that "inhuman treatment ... and deportation are among the acts which may cause serious bodily or mental injury" (*Prosecutor v. Krstić*, case no. IT-98-33-T, Judgment, August 2, 2001, paragraph 513). Rape and sexual violence may constitute "serious bodily or mental harm" on both a physical and a mental level (*Prosecutor v. Akayesu*, case no. ICTR-96-4-T, Judgment, September 2, 1998, paragraphs 731–733). Causing serious bodily or mental harm to members of the group does not necessarily mean the harm is permanent and irremediable, but it needs to be serious (*Prosecutor v. Kayishema et al.*, case no. ICTR-95-1-T, Judgment and Sentence, May 21, 1999, paragraph 108; *Prosecutor v. Rutaganda*, case no. ICTR-96-3-T, Judgment and Sentence, December 6, 1999, paragraph 51).

Paragraph (c): This act of genocide refers to methods of destruction apart from direct killings, such as subjecting the group to a subsistence diet, systematic expulsion from homes, and denial of the right to medical services (*Prosecutor v. Stakić*, case no. IT-97-24-PT, Second Amended Indictment, October 5, 2001, paragraph 20; *Prosecutor v. Akayesu*, case no. ICTR-96-4-T, Judgment, September 2, 1998, paragraphs 505–506). It also includes circumstances that would lead to a slow death, such as lack of proper housing, clothing, and hygiene or excessive work or physical exertion (*Prosecutor v. Stakić*, case no. IT-97-24-T, Judgment, July 31, 2003, paragraph 517; *Prosecutor v. Kayishema et al.*, case no. ICTR-95-1-T, Judgment and Sentence, May 21, 1999, paragraphs 115–116).

Paragraphs (d) and (e): The last two punishable acts, set out in Paragraphs (d) and (e), are rarely encountered in practice.

## *Article 86.2: Penalty*

1. The applicable penalty range for the criminal offense of genocide is ten to thirty years' imprisonment.
2. In exceptional circumstances, and in accordance with Article 49, the court may impose a penalty of life imprisonment for the criminal offense of genocide.

# Article 87: Crimes against Humanity

## *Article 87.1: Definition of Offense*

1. A person commits the criminal offense of crimes against humanity when he or she commits any of the following acts when committed as part of a widespread or systematic attack directed against any civilian population, with knowledge of the attack:
   (a) murder;
   (b) extermination;
   (c) enslavement;
   (d) deportation or forcible transfer of population;
   (e) imprisonment or other severe deprivation of physical liberty in violation of fundamental rules of international law;
   (f) torture;
   (g) rape, sexual slavery, enforced prostitution, forced pregnancy, enforced sterilization, or any other form of sexual violence of comparable gravity;
   (h) persecution against any identifiable group or collectivity on political, racial, national, ethnic, cultural, religious, gender, or other grounds that are universally recognized as impermissible under international law, in connection with any act referred to in this article or in Section 1 of the Special Part of the MCC;
   (i) enforced disappearance of persons;
   (j) the crime of apartheid; or
   (k) other inhumane acts of a similar character intentionally causing great suffering or serious injury to body or to mental or physical health.
2. For the purposes of Article 87:
   (a) *attack directed against any civilian population* means a course of conduct involving the multiple commission of acts referred to in Paragraph 1 of Article 87 against any civilian population, pursuant to or in furtherance of a state or organizational policy to commit such attack;
   (b) *extermination* includes the intentional infliction of conditions of life, inter alia the deprivation of access to food and medicine, calculated to bring about the destruction of part of a population;

(c) *enslavement* means the exercise of any or all of the powers attaching to the right of ownership over a person and includes the exercise of such power in the course of trafficking in persons, in particular women and children;

(d) *deportation or forcible transfer of population* means forced displacement of the persons concerned by expulsion or other coercive acts from the area in which they are lawfully present, without grounds permitted under international law;

(e) *torture* means the intentional infliction of severe pain or suffering, whether physical or mental, upon a person in the custody and under the control of the accused; except that torture does not include pain or suffering arising from, inherent in, or incidental to, lawful sanctions;

(f) *forced pregnancy* means the unlawful confinement of a woman forcibly made pregnant, with the intent of affecting the ethnic composition of any population or carrying out other grave violations of international law;

(g) *persecution* means the intentional and severe deprivation of fundamental rights contrary to international law by reason of the identity of the group or collectivity;

(h) *the crime of apartheid* means inhumane acts of a character similar to those referred to in Paragraph 1 of Article 87, committed in the context of an institutionalized regime of systematic oppression and domination by one racial group over any other racial group or groups and committed with the intention of maintaining that regime; and

(i) *enforced disappearance of persons* means the arrest, detention, or abduction of persons by, or with the authorization, support, or acquiescence of, a state or a political organization, followed by a refusal to acknowledge that deprivation of freedom or to give information on the fate or whereabouts of those persons with the intention of removing them from the protection of the law for a prolonged period of time.

## Commentary

Paragraph 1: The definition of crimes against humanity in the MCC is taken verbatim from Article 7 of the Rome Statute of the International Criminal Court. The concept of crimes against humanity was first developed in the Trial of the Major War Criminals, held in Nuremberg in 1945–46. The definition has evolved over the years, adding specific punishable acts that were not in the original provisions and eliminating the so-called nexus requirement, which meant that crimes against humanity could be committed only in the context of international armed conflict. It is now generally recognized that crimes against humanity may also be committed in peacetime, a fact that is acknowledged through the omission of the nexus requirement in the definition of crimes against humanity in Article 7 of the Rome Statute of the International Criminal Court and in the above provision.

The precise meaning and scope of crimes against humanity have been the subject of much jurisprudence at the ICTY and the ICTR. Much of the following commentary discusses specific cases of the international tribunals to provide a general description of the meaning and scope of crimes against humanity. The following commentary provides an introductory discussion to the definition of crimes against humanity. For those involved in the prosecution, defense, or adjudication of an accused person, further research will be necessary. For a complete discussion of the meaning and scope of the definition of crimes against humanity, including relevant case law, reference should be made to M. Cherif Bassiouni, *Crimes against Humanity in International Criminal Law.* Reference may also be made of Human Rights Watch's *Genocide, War Crimes and Crimes against Humanity: Topical Digests of the Case Law of the International Criminal Tribunal for Rwanda and the International Criminal Tribunal for the former Yugoslavia*, a compendium of relevant case law from the international tribunals.

For a crime against humanity to be committed, a civilian population must be the object of a "widespread or systematic attack." The words are disjunctive rather than conjunctive. Thus, to prove a crime against humanity, it is sufficient to prove the existence of either a "widespread" *or* a "systematic" attack. The "widespread characteristic refers to the scale of the acts perpetrated and the number of victims" (*Prosecutor v. Blaškić*, case no. IT-95-14-T, Judgment, March 3, 2000, paragraph 206; see also *Prosecutor v. Kordić et al.*, case no. IT-95-14/2-A, Judgment, December 17, 2004, paragraph 94). In *Akayesu*, an ICTR trial chamber said that "[t]he concept of 'widespread' may be defined as massive, frequent, large scale action, carried out collectively with considerable seriousness and directed against a multiplicity of victims" (*Prosecutor v. Akayesu*, case no. ICTR-96-4-T, Judgment, September 2, 1998, paragraph 580). A "widespread" criminal offense may involve the "cumulative effect of a series of inhumane acts or the singular effect of an inhumane act of extraordinary magnitude" (*Prosecutor v. Kordić et al.*, case no. IT-95-14/2-T, Judgment, 26 February 2001, paragraph 179. See also *Prosecutor v. Kordić et al.*, case no. IT-95-14/2-A, Judgment, December 17, 2004, paragraph 94). The "systematic" character of a crime against humanity refers to the organized nature of the pattern—that is, the nonaccidental repetition of similar criminal conduct and the improbability of its random occurrence (*Prosecutor v. Kunarac et al.*, case no. IT-96-23/1-A, Judgment, June 12, 2002, paragraph 94). A court will obviously consider the number of victims and the nature of the acts (*Prosecutor v. Kunarac et al.*, case no. IT-96-23/1-A, Judgment, June 12, 2002, paragraph 95; *Prosecutor v. Jelisić*, case no. IT-95-10-T, Judgment, December 14, 1999, paragraph 53). It will also take into account the existence of a political objective and an acknowledged policy or plan pursuant to which the attack is perpetrated, or an ideology, in the broad sense of the word, that contemplates the destruction, persecution, or weakening of a community; the preparation and use of significant public or private resources; and the participation of high-level political or military authorities (*Prosecutor v. Blaškić*, case no. IT-95-14-T, Judgment, March 3, 2000, paragraph 203; *Prosecutor v. Kunarac et al.*, case no. IT-96-23/1-A, Judgment, June 12, 2002, paragraph 95; *Prosecutor v. Jelisić*, case no. IT-95-10-T,

Judgment, December 14, 1999, paragraph 53). It is the attack itself that must be "widespread or systematic" and not the specific acts with which the accused is charged (*Prosecutor v. Kordić et al.*, case no. IT-95-14/2-A, Judgment, December 17, 2004, paragraph 94; *Prosecutor v. Blaškić*, case no. IT-95-14-A, Judgment, July 29, 2004, paragraph 101, referring to *Prosecutor v. Kunarac et al.*, case no. IT-96-23/1-A, Judgment, June 12, 2002, paragraph 96).

Although the term *attack* may appear to connote the existence of an armed conflict, as mentioned above, the existence of armed conflict is not a requirement, and the two concepts are distinct and independent: "The attack has been defined as a course of conduct involving the commission of acts of violence. The attack can precede, outlast, or continue during the armed conflict, but need not be a part of the conflict under customary international law" (*Prosecutor v Naletilic and Martinovic*, case no. IT-98-34 Judgment, March 31, 2003, paragraph 233). It is not limited to an armed attack and may involve any mistreatment of the civilian population and even nonviolent attacks, such as establishment of a system of apartheid (*Prosecutor v. Vasiljević*, case no. IT-98-32-T, Judgment, November 29, 2002, paragraphs 29, 30; *Prosecutor v. Kunarac et al.*, case no. IT-96-23/1-A, Judgment, June 12, 2002, paragraph 86).

There must be some connection or nexus between the acts of the perpetrator and the attack itself, but the specific acts with which the accused is charged need not be shown to be widespread and systematic (*Prosecutor v. Kunarac et al.*, case nos. IT-96-23-T and IT-96-23/1-T, Judgment, February 22, 2001, paragraph 431). Under certain circumstances, even a single act can constitute a crime against humanity when committed within the appropriate context, but an isolated act cannot (*Prosecutor v. Kupreškić et al.*, case no. IT-95-16-T, Judgment, January 14, 2000, paragraph 550).

In addition to the nexus between the act of the perpetrator and the attack itself, the perpetrator must have some knowledge that the attack is widespread or systematic (*Prosecutor v. Kunarac et al.*, case no. IT-96-23/1-A, Judgment, June 12, 2002, paragraph 102; *Prosecutor v. Krnojelac*, case no. IT-97-25-T, Judgment, March 15, 2002, paragraph 59; *Prosecutor v. Tadić*, case no. IT-94-1-A, Judgment, July 15, 1999, paragraph 271). A perpetrator who lacks such knowledge cannot be found criminally responsible for crimes against humanity, although he or she may still be liable for prosecution by national courts for underlying criminal behavior, such as murder (*Prosecutor v. Tadić*, case no. IT-94-1-A, Judgment, July 15, 1999, paragraph 271).

The ICTY has held that the civilian population must be the "primary object of the attack" (*Prosecutor v. Naletilić et al.*, case no. IT-98-34-T, Judgment, March 31, 2003, paragraph 235). There is no need to show that the entire population of a geographic entity was targeted by the attack, as long as the attack was not directed against "a limited and randomly selected number of individuals" (*Prosecutor v. Kunarac et al.*, case no. IT-96-23/1-A, Judgment, June 12, 2002, paragraph 90). Another judgment says the "civilian population" requirement is "intended to imply crimes of a collective nature and thus excludes single or isolated acts" (*Prosecutor v. Bagilishema*, case no. ICTR-95-1A-T, Judgment, June 7, 2001, paragraph 80). The population must be "predominantly civilian in nature," although noncivilians may be present (*Prosecutor v. Kordić et al.*, case no. IT-95-14/2-T, Judgment, February 26, 2001, paragraph 180). Crimes against humanity can also be perpetrated against members of a resistance movement and former combatants, regardless of whether they have worn uniforms, to the extent that they were no longer taking part in hostilities when the crimes were perpetrated because they had either left the army or were no longer bearing arms, or ultimately had been placed hors de combat (out of combat), in particular due to wounds or being detained (*Prosecutor v. Blaškić*, case no. IT-95-14-T, Judgment, March 3, 2000, paragraph 214). This wide definition "includes all persons *except* those who have the duty to maintain public order and have the legitimate means to exercise force" (*Prosecutor v. Kayishema et al.*, case no. ICTR-95-1-T, Judgment and Sentence, May 21, 1999, paragraphs 127–129). Generally, the concept of a civilian population should be construed liberally, in order to promote the principles underlying the prohibition of crimes against humanity, which are to safeguard human values and protect human dignity (*Prosecutor v. Kupreškić et al.*, case no. IT-95-16-T, Judgment, January 14, 2000, paragraphs 547–549; *Prosecutor v. Jelisić*, case no. IT-95-10-T, Judgment, December 14, 1999, paragraph 54).

The definition of crimes against humanity consists of a chapeau, or introductory paragraph, followed by a list of punishable acts. The list is exhaustive and does not explicitly invite courts to add new categories, although the final act of crimes against humanity, "other inhumane acts," gives a court some scope to consider acts beyond those defined in the list of punishable acts.

Paragraph 1(a): The ICTY and the ICTR have held that the term *murder* has an identical meaning to the act of genocide of killing, the war crime of willful killing under the grave breaches provision of Article 88, and the war crime of murder (*Prosecutor v. Krstić*, case no. IT-98-33-T, Judgment, August 2, 2001, paragraph 499; *Prosecutor v. Rutaganda*, case no. ICTR-96-3-T, Judgment and Sentence, December 6, 1999, paragraphs 83–84; *Prosecutor v. Musema*, case no. ICTR-96-13-T, Judgment and Sentence, January 27, 2000, paragraph 218; *Prosecutor v. Ntakirutimana et al.*, case nos. ICTR-96-10 and ICTR-96-17-T, Judgment, February 21, 2003, paragraph 813). In the context of the MCC, murder is equated with unlawful killing. Reference should be made to Article 89 on unlawful killing and its accompanying commentary.

Paragraph 1(b) and Paragraph 2(b): Extermination, the second punishable act of crimes against humanity, refers to "acts committed with the intention of bringing about the death of a large number of victims either directly, such as by killing the victim with a firearm, or less directly, by creating conditions provoking the victim's death" (*Prosecutor v. Krstić*, case no. IT-98-33-T, Judgment, August 2, 2001, paragraph 499). The ICTR Appeals Chamber has said: "Murder as a crime against humanity does not contain a materially distinct element from extermination as a crime against humanity; each involves killing within the context of a widespread or systematic attack against the civilian population, and the only element that distinguishes these offenses is the requirement of the offense of extermination that the killings occur on a mass scale" (*Prosecutor v. Ntakirutimana et al.*, case nos. ICTR-96-10-A and ICTR-96-17-A, Judgment, December 13, 2004).

"There must be evidence that a particular population was targeted and that its members were killed or otherwise subjected to conditions of life calculated to bring about the destruction of a numerically significant part of the population" (*Prosecutor v. Krstić*, case no. IT-98-33-T, Judgment, August 2, 2001, paragraph 503). An ICTR trial chamber said that extermination could be distinguished from murder in that it was directed against a population rather than individuals (*Prosecutor v. Semanza*, case no. ICTR-97-20-T, Judgment and Sentence, May 15, 2003, paragraph 340). However, "[t]he scale of the killing required for extermination must be substantial. Responsibility for a single or a limited number of killings is insufficient" (*Prosecutor v. Semanza*, case no. ICTR-97-20-T, Judgment and Sentence, May 15, 2003, paragraph 340). There is no requirement that a precise list of victims be furnished to the court to establish commission of the criminal offense (*Prosecutor v. Ntakirutimana et al.*, case nos. ICTR-96-10-A and ICTR-96-17-A, Judgment, December 13, 2004, paragraphs 518, 521). Moreover, "any attempt to set a minimum number of victims in the abstract will ultimately prove unhelpful; the element of massive scale must be assessed on a case-by-case basis in light of the proven criminal conduct and all relevant factors" (*Prosecutor v. Blagojević*, case no. IT-02-60-T, Judgment, January 17, 2005, paragraph 573).

Paragraph 1(c) and Paragraph 2(c): Slavery has been defined as "the exercise of any or all of the powers attaching to the right of ownership over a person" (*Prosecutor v. Kunarac et al.*, case nos. IT-96-23-T and IT-96-23/1-T, Judgment, February 22, 2001, paragraph 539). The traditional concept of slavery, as defined in the 1926 Slavery Convention and often referred to as chattel slavery (or slavery over "things"), has evolved to encompass various contemporary forms of slavery that are also based on the exercise of any or all of the powers attaching to the right of ownership. According to the ICTY Appeals Chamber, "[i]n the case of these various contemporary forms of slavery, the victim is not subject to the exercise of the more extreme rights of ownership associated with 'chattel slavery,' but in all cases, as a result of the exercise of any or all of the powers attaching to the right of ownership, there is some destruction of the juridical personality; the destruction is greater in the case of 'chattel slavery' but the difference is one of degree. The Appeals Chamber considers that at the time relevant to the alleged crimes, these contemporary forms of slavery formed part of enslavement as a crime against humanity under customary international law" (*Prosecutor v. Kunarac et al.*, case no. IT-96-23/1-A, Judgment, June 12, 2002, paragraph 117).

International humanitarian law does not prohibit all labor by protected persons in armed conflicts. For example, Article 51 of the fourth Geneva Convention seeks to regulate the practice of forced labor, declaring that an occupying power may not compel protected persons to work unless they are over eighteen years of age, and then they may perform only work that is necessary for the needs of the army of occupation; for public utility services; or for the feeding, sheltering, clothing, transportation, or health of the population of the occupied country. Article 5 of Additional Protocol II to the four Geneva Conventions also contemplates forms of forced labor: "In addition to the provisions of Article 4 the following provisions shall be respected as a minimum with regard to persons deprived of their liberty for reasons related to the armed conflict, whether they are interned or detained. … [T]hey shall, if made to work, have the benefit of working conditions and safeguards similar to those enjoyed by the local civilian population." In peacetime, however, the prohibition of slavery or enslavement would appear to be an absolute one, consistent with nonderogable norms in international human rights treaties. The case law of the ICTY has established that "the exaction of forced or compulsory labour or service" is an "indication of enslavement" and a factor "to be taken into consideration in determining whether enslavement was committed" (*Prosecutor v. Kunarac et al.*, case nos. IT-96-23-T and IT-96-23/1-T, Judgment, February 22, 2001, paragraphs 542–543). Often forced or compulsory labor or service is without remuneration, and frequently, though not necessarily, it involves physical hardship, sex, prostitution, and human trafficking, and these too are factors to be assessed (*Prosecutor v. Kunarac et al.*, case no. IT-96-23/1-A, Judgment, June 12, 2002, paragraph 542). Evidence that a person was kept in captivity in the absence of other indications would not be enough to establish the crime of enslavement. Duration is a factor in determining enslavement, but it is not an element. Lack of consent or resistance is not an element of the crime of enslavement (*Prosecutor v. Kunarac et al.*, case no. IT-96-23/1-A, Judgment, June 12, 2002, paragraph 120).

In addition to the crime against humanity of slavery, the MCC also contains the criminal offense of "establishing slavery, slavery-like conditions, and forced labor." Reference should be made to Article 103 and its accompanying commentary.

Paragraph 1(d) and Paragraph 2(d): Deportation implies forcible transfer beyond a state's borders, whereas forcible transfer refers to internal displacement. The terms *forcible transfer* and *forcible displacement* are treated as synonyms (*Prosecutor v. Blagojević*, case no. IT-02-60-T, Judgment, January 17, 2005, paragraph 595, fn. 1962). According to an ICTY trial chamber, evacuation is distinct from forcible transfer or forcible displacement: "Evacuation is by definition a temporary and provisional measure and the law requires that individuals who have been evacuated shall be transferred back to their homes as soon as hostilities in the area in question have ceased" (*Prosecutor v. Blagojević*, case no. IT-02-60-T, Judgment, January 17, 2005, paragraph 597). The trial chamber further noted that international humanitarian law had long recognized not only the right but also the duty of military commanders to evacuate civilians when they are in danger as a result of military operations. It concluded that humanitarian reasons are also a justification for evacuation of a civilian population (paragraphs 597–600).

Paragraph 1(e): The crime against humanity of imprisonment consists of an act or omission that results in arbitrary deprivation of physical liberty or that is reasonably likely to effect that result. Arbitrary deprivation of liberty occurs when there is no legal justification for the detention (*Prosecutor v. Krnojelac*, case no. IT-97-25-T, Judgment, March 15, 2002, paragraph 115; *Prosecutor v. Kordić et al.*, case no. IT-95-14/2-T, Judgment, February 26, 2001, paragraphs 302–303). According to the ICTY Appeals Chamber, imprisonment "should be understood as contemplating arbitrary imprisonment, that is to say, the deprivation of liberty of the individual without due process of law, as part of a widespread or systematic attack directed against a civilian population" (*Prosecutor v. Kordić et al.*, case no. IT-95-14/2-T, Judgment, February 26, 2001, paragraph 302).

Paragraph 1(f) and Paragraph 2(e): The international criminal offense of torture has been defined as involving "the infliction, by act or omission, of severe pain or suffering, whether physical or mental," for the purpose of "obtaining information or a confession, or . . . punishing, intimidating or coercing the victim or a third person, or . . .

discriminating, on any ground, against the victim or a third person" (*Prosecutor v. Kunarac et al.*, case no. IT-96-23/1-A, Judgment, June 12, 2002, paragraph 142). To qualify as the crime against humanity of torture, the act or omission must be carried out with a prohibited purpose or goal: "The act or omission must aim at obtaining information or a confession, or at punishing, intimidating or coercing the victim or a third person, or at discriminating, on any ground, against the victim or a third person" (*Prosecutor v. Kunarac et al.*, case no. IT-96-23/1-A, Judgment, June 12, 2002, paragraphs 142, 155). The list of prohibited purposes is drawn from Article 1 of the Convention against Torture or Other Cruel, Inhuman or Degrading Treatment or Punishment, but it has been taken as a representative and not an exhaustive enumeration (*Prosecutor v. Delalić et al.*, case no. IT-96-21-T, Judgment, November 16, 1998, paragraph 470; *Prosecutor v. Kvočka et al.*, case no. IT-98-30/1-T, Judgment, November 2, 2001, paragraph 140). For example, "humiliating the victim or a third person constitutes a prohibited purpose for torture under international humanitarian law" (*Prosecutor v. Kvočka et al.*, case no. IT-98-30/1-T, Judgment, November 2, 2001, paragraph 140). It has been noted that torture is not a gratuitous act of violence but seeks to attain a certain result or purpose. In the absence of such purpose or goal, even infliction of very severe pain would not qualify as torture (*Prosecutor v. Krnojelac*, case no. IT-97-25-T, Judgment, March 15, 2002, paragraph 180). But while there must be evidence of the prohibited purpose, it need not be the sole or even the predominant purpose for inflicting the severe pain or suffering (*Prosecutor v. Kvočka et al.*, case no. IT-98-30/1-T, Judgment, November 2, 2001, paragraph 153; *Prosecutor v. Kunarac et al.*, case nos. IT-96-23-T and IT-96-23/1-T, Judgment, February 22, 2001, paragraph 486). The list of prohibited purposes in the definition of torture has been held not to be exhaustive but merely representative. Torture for purely private purposes, however, falls outside the scope of the definition.

There is no requirement that one of the perpetrators of torture be a public official or someone not acting in a private capacity. An ICTY trial chamber explained that "the state actor requirement imposed by international human rights law is inconsistent with the application of individual criminal responsibility for international crimes found in international humanitarian law and international criminal law" (*Prosecutor v. Kvočka et al.*, case no. IT-98-30/1-T, Judgment, November 2, 2001, paragraph 139).

It is the severity of the pain or suffering inflicted in the case of torture that sets it apart from similar offenses. In assessing the seriousness of such mistreatment, it has been held that the objective severity of the harm inflicted must first be assessed. Then a court should consider subjective criteria, such as the physical or mental effect of the treatment upon the particular victim and, in some cases, factors such as the victim's age, sex, or state of health (*Prosecutor v. Kvočka et al.*, case no. IT-98-30/1-T, Judgment, November 2, 2001, paragraphs 142–143). According to one ICTY trial chamber, "When assessing the seriousness of the acts charged as torture, the Trial Chamber must take into account all the circumstances of the case, including the nature and context of the infliction of pain, the premeditation and institutionalisation of the ill-treatment, the physical condition of the victim, the manner and method used, and the position of inferiority of the victim. The extent that an individual has been mistreated over a prolonged period of time will also be relevant" (*Prosecutor v. Krnojelac*, case no. IT-97-25-T, Judgment, March 15, 2002, paragraph 182). Although torture often causes permanent damage to the health of its victims, permanent injury is not a requirement (*Prosecutor v. Kvočka et al.*, case no. IT-98-30/1-T, Judgment, November 2, 2001, paragraph 148). The mental suffering of an individual forced to watch severe mistreatment of a relative could reach the level of gravity required for the crime of torture. An ICTY trial chamber wrote: "[B]eing forced to watch serious sexual attacks inflicted on a female acquaintance was torture for the forced observer. The presence of onlookers, particularly family members, also inflicts severe mental harm amounting to torture on the person being raped" (*Prosecutor v. Kvočka et al.*, case no. IT-98-30/1-T, Judgment, November 2, 2001, paragraph 149). The tribunal has noted that "[t]he psychological suffering of persons upon whom rape is inflicted may be exacerbated by social and cultural conditions and can be particularly acute and long lasting" (*Prosecutor v. Delalić et al.*, case no. IT-96-21-T, Judgment, November 16, 1998, paragraph 495).

In addition to the crime against humanity of torture, under Article 101, the MCC also contains the offense of torture committed outside the context of crimes against humanity. Reference should be made to Article 101 and its accompanying commentary.

Paragraph 1(g) and Paragraph 2(f): The term *rape* is widely used in national justice systems, but its definition varies considerably. The definition has also evolved considerably over the years, reflecting changing attitudes toward the nature and gravity of sexual violence. Article 7 of the Rome Statute of the International Criminal Court does not define *rape*. It is, however, defined in Article 7(1)(g)-1 of the Elements of Crimes of the Rome Statute of the International Criminal Court. This same definition is used in Article 94 of the MCC. Reference should be made to Article 94 on "rape" and its accompanying commentary. The Elements of Crimes of the Rome Statute of the International Criminal Court also provide definitions of *sexual slavery, enforced prostitution, enforced sterilization*, and *other forms of sexual violence of comparable gravity.* Reference should be made to Article 7(1)(g)-2 (on the crime against humanity of sexual slavery), Article 7(1)(g)-3 (on the crime against humanity of enforced prostitution), Article 7(1)(g)-5 (on the crime against humanity of enforced sterilization), and Article 7(1)(g)-6 (on the crime against humanity of other forms of sexual violence). The term *forced pregnancy* is defined in Paragraph 2(f).

Paragraph 1(h) and Paragraph 2(g): An ICTY trial chamber has said that persecution refers to "a discriminatory act or omission" that "denies or infringes upon a fundamental right laid down in international customary or treaty law" and that is perpetrated with "an intent to discriminate on racial, religious, or political grounds" (*Prosecutor v. Naletilić et al.*, case no. IT-98-34-T, Judgment, March 31, 2003, paragraph 634). The ICTY Appeals Chamber has defined persecution as "an act or omission which: 1. discriminates in fact and which denies or infringes upon a fundamental right laid down in international customary or treaty law (the *actus reus*); and 2. was carried out deliberately with the intention to discriminate on one of the listed grounds, specifically race, religion or politics (the *mens rea*)" (*Prosecutor v. Kordić et al.*, case no. IT-95-14/2-A, Judgment, December 17, 2004, paragraph 101).

Like the criminal offense of genocide, with which it has important similarities, the crime against humanity of persecution is a crime of "specific intent" (*Prosecutor v.*

*Kvočka et al.*, case no. IT-98-30/1-A, Judgment, February 28, 2005, paragraph 460). The discriminatory intent can be demonstrated by omission as well as by act. Discriminatory intent can be inferred from knowingly participating in a system or enterprise that discriminates on political, racial, or religious grounds. But "[t]he requirement that an accused consciously intends to discriminate does not require the existence of a discriminatory policy or, where such a policy is shown to exist, participation by the accused in the formulation of that discriminatory policy or practice by an authority" (*Prosecutor v. Vasiljević*, case no. IT-98-32-T, Judgment, November 29, 2002, paragraph 248). The law does not require that a discriminatory policy exist or that there be proof that the accused took part in formulating a discriminatory policy or practice by an authority (*Prosecutor v. Krnojelac*, case no. IT-97-25-T, Judgment, March 15, 2002, paragraph 435). "The accused must consciously intend to discriminate" (*Prosecutor v. Vasiljević*, case no. IT-98-32-T, Judgment, November 29, 2002, paragraph 248), and "[w]hile the intent to discriminate need not be the primary intent with respect to the act, it must be a significant one" (*Prosecutor v. Krnojelac*, case no. IT-97-25-T, Judgment, March 15, 2002, paragraph 435). This discriminatory intent must be established with respect to the specific act that is charged rather than the attack in general. But in addition to the intent itself, it must be established that there were discriminatory consequences; in other words, it is not enough to show that the perpetrator conducted an act with the intent to discriminate. It must be shown that a victim was actually persecuted (*Prosecutor v. Vasiljević*, case no. IT-98-32-T, Judgment, November 29, 2002, paragraph 245).

In considering whether or not acts fall under the heading of persecution, the ICTY has stated that they should not be evaluated in isolation but rather in their contexts, taking particular account of their cumulative effects. Individual acts might not amount to persecution, but their combined effect would (*Prosecutor v. Kupreškić et al.*, case no. IT-95-16-T, Judgment, January 14, 2000, paragraph 622; *Prosecutor v. Vasiljević*, case no. IT-98-32-T, Judgment, November 29, 2002, paragraph 247), although this does not mean that a single act might not also constitute a crime of persecution (*Prosecutor v. Kupreškić et al.*, case no. IT-95-16-T, Judgment, January 14, 2000, paragraph 624).

Persecutions may involve the infliction of physical or mental harm, or infringements upon individual freedom, such as the unlawful detention, deportation, or forcible transfer of civilians (*Prosecutor v. Vasiljević*, case no. IT-98-32-T, Judgment, November 29, 2002, paragraph 246; *Prosecutor v. Blaškić*, case no. IT-95-14-T, Judgment, March 3, 2000, paragraph 220). Persecutions can even involve attacks on political, social, and economic rights. An ICTY trial chamber has referred in particular to "acts rendered serious not by their apparent cruelty but by the discrimination they seek to instil within humankind" (*Prosecutor v. Blaškić*, case no. IT-95-14-T, Judgment, March 3, 2000, paragraph 227). Acts of "harassment, humiliation and psychological abuse" may also amount to persecution (*Prosecutor v. Kvočka et al.*, case no. IT-98-30/1-A, Judgment, February 28, 2005, paragraphs 324–325). Persecution can include crimes that target property, which appear on the surface to be less serious, but where the victimization involves discrimination (*Prosecutor v. Blaškić*, case no. IT-95-14-T, Judgment, March 3, 2000, paragraph 233).

Paragraph 1(i) and Paragraph 2(i): The MCC contains the criminal offense of enforced disappearance in Article 104. The wording of Article 104 differs slightly from that of Article 87(2)(i). Reference should be made to Article 104 and its accompanying commentary.

Paragraph 1(k): "The phrase 'Other inhumane acts' was deliberately designed as a residual category, as it was felt undesirable for this category to be exhaustively enumerated. An exhaustive categorization would merely create opportunities for evasion of the letter of the prohibition" (*Prosecutor v. Kupreškić et al.*, case no. IT-95-16-T, Judgment, January 14, 2000, paragraph 563).

Serious physical and mental injury, falling short of murder, can be prosecuted as "other inhumane acts" (*Prosecutor v. Blaškić*, case no. IT-95-14-T, Judgment, March 3, 2000, paragraph 239). Criminal behavior deemed in judgments of the ICTY and the ICTR to fall within "other inhumane acts" has included mutilation and other types of severe bodily harm, beatings and other acts of violence, serious physical and mental injury, inhumane and degrading treatment, forced prostitution, and forced disappearance (*Prosecutor v. Kvočka et al.*, case no. IT-98-30/1-T, Judgment, November 2, 2001, paragraph 208). An ICTR trial chamber found that acts of sexual violence that were not subsumed within other paragraphs of the crimes against humanity provision, such as forced nudity, could be prosecuted as other inhumane acts (*Prosecutor v. Akayesu*, case no. ICTR-96-4-T, Judgment, September 2, 1998, paragraphs 688, 697).

## *Article 87.2: Penalty*

1. The applicable penalty range for the criminal offense of crimes against humanity is ten to thirty years' imprisonment.
2. In exceptional circumstances, and in accordance with Article 49, the court may impose a penalty of life imprisonment for the criminal offense of crimes against humanity.

# Article 88: War Crimes

## *Article 88.1: Definition of Offense*

1. A person commits the criminal offense of war crimes when he or she commits:
   (a) grave breaches of the Geneva Conventions of August 12, 1949, namely, any of the following acts against persons or property protected under the provisions of the relevant Geneva Convention:

(i) willful killing;

(ii) torture or inhuman treatment, including biological experiments;

(iii) willfully causing great suffering or serious injury to body or health;

(iv) extensive destruction and appropriation of property, not justified by military necessity and carried out unlawfully and wantonly;

(v) compelling a prisoner of war or other protected person to serve in the forces of a hostile power;

(vi) willfully depriving a prisoner of war or other protected person of the rights of fair and regular trial;

(vii) unlawful deportation or transfer or unlawful confinement;

(viii) taking of hostages.

(b) other serious violations of the laws and customs applicable in international armed conflict, within the established framework of international law, namely, any of the following acts:

(i) intentionally directing attacks against the civilian population as such or against individual civilians not taking direct part in hostilities;

(ii) intentionally directing attacks against civilian objects, that is, objects that are not military objectives;

(iii) intentionally directing attacks against personnel, installations, material, units, or vehicles involved in a humanitarian assistance or peacekeeping mission in accordance with the Charter of the United Nations, as long as they are entitled to the protection given to civilians or civilian objects under the international law of armed conflict;

(iv) intentionally launching an attack in the knowledge that such attack will cause incidental loss of life or injury to civilians or damage to civilian objects, or widespread, long-term, and severe damage to the natural environment that would be clearly excessive in relation to the concrete and direct overall military advantage anticipated;

(v) attacking or bombarding, by whatever means, towns, villages, dwellings, or buildings that are undefended and are not military objectives;

(vi) killing or wounding a combatant who, having laid down his or her arms or having no longer means of defense, has surrendered at discretion;

(vii) making improper use of a flag of truce or of the flag or the military insignia and uniform of the enemy or of the United Nations, as well as the distinctive emblems of the Geneva Conventions, resulting in death or serious personal injury;

(viii) the transfer, directly or indirectly, by the occupying power of parts of its own civilian population into the territory it occupies, or the deportation or transfer of all or parts of the population of the occupied territory within or outside this territory;

(ix) intentionally directing attacks against buildings dedicated to religion, education, art, science, or charitable purposes, historic monuments, hospitals, and places where the sick and wounded are collected, provided they are not military objectives;

(x) subjecting persons who are in the power of an adverse party to physical mutilation or to medical or scientific experiments of any kind that are neither justified by the medical, dental, or hospital treatment of the person concerned nor carried out in his or her interest, and that cause death to or seriously endanger the health of such person or persons;

(xi) killing or wounding treacherously individuals belonging to the hostile nation or army;

(xii) declaring that no quarter will be given;

(xiii) destroying or seizing the enemy's property unless such destruction or seizure be imperatively demanded by the necessities of war;

(xiv) declaring abolished, suspended, or inadmissible in a court of law the rights and actions of the nationals of the hostile party;

(xv) compelling the nationals of the hostile party to take part in the operations of war directed against their own country, even if they were in the belligerent's service before the commencement of the war;

(xvi) pillaging a town or place, even when taken by assault;

(xvii) employing poison or poisoned weapons;

(xviii) employing asphyxiating, poisonous, or other gases and all analogous liquids, materials, or devices;

(xix) employing bullets that expand or flatten easily in the human body, such as a bullet with a hard envelope that does not entirely cover the core or is pierced with incisions;

(xx) employing weapons, projectiles, and material and methods of warfare that are of a nature to cause superfluous injury or unnecessary suffering or that are inherently indiscriminate in violation of the international law of armed conflict, provided that such weapons, projectiles, and material and methods of warfare are the subject of a comprehensive prohibition;

(xxi) committing outrages upon personal dignity, in particular humiliating and degrading treatment;

(xxii) committing rape, sexual slavery, enforced prostitution, forced pregnancy, enforced sterilization, or any other form of sexual violence also constituting a grave breach of the Geneva Conventions;

(xxiii) utilizing the presence of a civilian or other protected person to render certain points, areas, or military forces immune from military operations;

(xxiv) intentionally directing attacks against buildings, material, medical units and transport, and personnel using the distinctive emblems of the Geneva Conventions in conformity with international law;

(xxv) intentionally using starvation of civilians as a method of warfare by depriving them of objects indispensable to their survival, including willfully impeding relief supplies as provided for under the Geneva Conventions;

(xxvi) conscripting or enlisting children under the age of fifteen years into the national armed forces or using them to participate actively in hostilities.

(c) in the case of an armed conflict not of an international character, serious violations of Article 3 common to the four Geneva Conventions of August 12, 1949, namely, any of the following acts committed against persons taking no active part in the hostilities, including members of armed forces who have laid down their arms and those placed hors de combat by sickness, wounds, detention, or any other cause:

(i) violence to life and person, in particular, murder of all kinds, mutilation, cruel treatment, and torture;

(ii) committing outrages upon personal dignity, in particular, humiliating and degrading treatment;

(iii) taking of hostages;

(iv) the passing of sentences and the carrying out of executions without previous judgment pronounced by a regularly constituted court affording all judicial guarantees that are generally recognized as indispensable.

(d) other serious violations of the laws and customs applicable in armed conflicts not of an international character, within the established framework of international law, namely, any of the following acts:

(i) intentionally directing attacks against the civilian population as such or against individual civilians not taking direct part in hostilities;

(ii) intentionally directing attacks against buildings, material, medical units and transport, and personnel using the distinctive emblems of the Geneva Conventions in conformity with international law;

(iii) intentionally directing attacks against personnel, installations, material, units, or vehicles involved in a humanitarian assistance or peacekeeping mission in accordance with the Charter of the United Nations, as long as they are entitled to the protection given to civilians or civilian objects under the international law of armed conflict;

(iv) intentionally directing attacks against buildings dedicated to religion, education, art, science or charitable purposes, historic monuments, hospitals and places where the sick and wounded are collected, provided they are not military objectives;

(v) pillaging a town or place, even when taken by assault;

(vi) committing rape, sexual slavery, enforced prostitution, forced pregnancy, enforced sterilization, and any other form of sexual violence also constituting a serious violation of Article 3 common to the four Geneva Conventions;

(vii) conscripting or enlisting children under the age of fifteen years into armed forces or groups or using them to participate actively in hostilities;

(viii) ordering the displacement of the civilian population for reasons related to the conflict, unless the security of the civilians involved or imperative military reasons so demand;

(ix) killing or wounding treacherously a combatant adversary;

(x) declaring that no quarter will be given;

(xi) subjecting persons who are in the power of another party to the conflict to physical mutilation or to medical or scientific experiments of any kind that are neither justified by the medical, dental, or hospital treatment of the person or persons concerned nor carried out in his or her or their interest, and that cause death to or seriously endanger the health of such person or persons;

(xii) destroying or seizing the property of an adversary unless such destruction or seizure be imperatively demanded by the necessities of the conflict.

2. Paragraph 1(c) applies to armed conflicts not of an international character and does not apply to situations of internal disturbances and tensions, such as riots, isolated and sporadic acts of violence, or other acts of a similar nature.
3. Paragraph 1(d) applies to armed conflicts not of an international character and does not apply to situations of internal disturbances and tensions, such as riots, isolated and sporadic acts of violence, or other acts of a similar nature. It applies to armed conflicts that take place in the territory of a state when there is protracted armed conflict between governmental authorities and organized armed groups or between such groups.
4. Nothing in Paragraphs 1(c) and 1(d) shall affect the responsibility of a government to maintain or reestablish law and order in the state or to defend the unity and territorial integrity of the state by all legitimate means.

## Commentary

The text of Article 88 is taken almost verbatim from Article 8 of the Rome Statute of the International Criminal Court, dealing with war crimes. The requirement in Article 8(1) that war crimes can be prosecuted only "as part of a plan or policy or as part of a large-scale commission of such crimes" has not, however, been duplicated in the MCC. The purpose of this wording is to ensure that the International Criminal Court focuses on war crimes that are "the most serious crimes of concern to the international community" (Rome Statute of the International Criminal Court, preamble, paragraph 4), while all other war crimes not of this character will be prosecuted before national courts under what is known as the complementarity regime.

War crimes are violations of a body of law known as international humanitarian law or the law of armed conflict. International humanitarian law began its life as the "laws of war," customary rules that governed the conduct of warfare between states. Eventually, these rules became codified in international treaties. At the same time, certain rules that are not codified can be recognized under public international law if they are deemed to be norms of customary international law. Reference should be made to the commentary to Article 3(3), which discusses the meaning of *customary international law.* Not all violations of international humanitarian law, whether treaty-based or part of customary international law, incur individual criminal responsibility. A small number of international prosecutions of war crimes after World War I and also after World War II served as a preliminary clarification of the sorts of war crimes for which a person could be held criminally responsible and consequently could be forced to stand trial. However, it was the jurisprudence of the ICTY and the ICTR that paved the way for the drafting of Article 8 of the Rome Statute of the International Criminal Court, which sets out a full list of violations of international humanitarian law that should be subject to both international criminal law and domestic criminal law. In interpreting Articles 2 and 3 of the Statute of the International Criminal Tribunal for the former Yugoslavia and Article 4 of the Statute of the International Criminal Tribunal for Rwanda, respectively, the ICTY and the ICTR, with great judicial innovation, considerably expanded the preexisting corpus of war crimes subject to individual criminal responsibility.

Article 8 of the Statute of the International Criminal Court, from which Article 88 of the MCC is derived, is a long and complicated provision. It is divided into four parts. The first and second parts of the article are concerned with violations of international humanitarian law during international armed conflict, while the third and fourth parts are concerned with violations that occur during internal armed conflict. Article 88 of the MCC also contains these four elements. Article 88.1(1)(a) covers "grave breaches" of the four Geneva Conventions of 1949. The Geneva Conventions are part of treaty-law-based international humanitarian law. Under the provisions of the Geneva Conventions, states parties are required to ensure that grave breaches are subject to individual criminal responsibility at a domestic level. The second part of the article, Article 88.1(b), covers "other serious violations of the laws and customs applicable in international armed conflict." This provision consists of a detailed and exhaustive list of twenty-six such violations. These violations are sourced from treaties dealing with international humanitarian law (including the Geneva Conventions, Additional Protocol I to the four Geneva Conventions, and the Hague Conventions) and from customary international law. The third part of the provision, Article 88.1(1)(c), reproduces Common Article 3 of the Geneva Conventions. Common Article 3, as the name suggests, is contained in all four Geneva Conventions. Common Article 3 was included to cover situations "of armed conflict not of an international character," in contrast to the rest of the conventions, which focus only on matters relating to the conduct of international armed conflict. The final category of war crimes, Article 88.1(1)(d), relates to "other serious violations of the laws and customs applicable in armed conflict not of an international character." Many of these provisions are taken from Additional Protocol II to the four Geneva Conventions, which governs the conduct of noninternational armed conflict and expands upon the laconic text of Common Article 3 to the Convention. In addition to the provisions of Article 8 of the Statute of the International Criminal Court, the *Elements of Crimes* provides a further elaboration on the legal elements of war crimes. To interpret Article 88 of the MCC, reference should be made to this document.

A detailed discussion of the nature and origins of international humanitarian law, the criminalization of aspects of international humanitarian law, and the precise meaning of each individual war crime covered in Article 88 of the MCC is beyond the scope of this commentary. For a fuller discussion on the meaning of war crimes in the Statute of the International Criminal Court, reference should be made to Knut Dörmann, *Elements of War Crimes under the Rome Statute of the International Criminal Court: Sources and Commentary.* Reference may also be made of Human Rights Watch, *Genocide, War Crimes and Crimes against Humanity: Topical Digests of the Case Law of the International Criminal Tribunal for Rwanda and the International Criminal Tribunal for the former Yugoslavia*, which is a compendium of relevant case law from the international criminal tribunals. As mentioned in the general commentary to Section 1 of the Special Part, those involved in prosecuting, defending, or adjudicating on persons accused of war crimes will need extensive training to do so. This will include training on international humanitarian law and international criminal law.

Paragraph 1: The wording of this paragraph comes from Articles 8(2)(a), 8(2)(b), 8(2)(c), and 8(2)(e) of the Rome Statute of the International Criminal Court.

Paragraph 1(b)(xx): The wording of Paragraph 1(b)(xx) comes from Article 8(2)(b)(xx) of the Rome Statute of the International Criminal Court. Article 8(2)(b)(xx) further provides, after the words "are the subject of a comprehensive prohibition" (contained in the MCC provision also) that the weapons, projectiles, materials, and methods of warfare subject to the comprehensive prohibition should also be "included in an annex to this Statute [the Rome Statute of the International Criminal Court] by an amendment in accordance with the relevant provisions set forth in articles 121 and 123." This wording is particular to the Rome Statute of the International Criminal Court and therefore has not been replicated in the MCC. In interpreting the meaning of Paragraph 1(b)(xx) of the MCC, and what weapons, projectiles, and material and methods of warfare are "inherently indiscriminate in violation of the international law of armed conflict" and that are also "the subject of a comprehensive prohibition," reference may be made to Protocol II to the Convention on Prohibitions or Restrictions on the Use of Certain Conventional Weapons Which May Be Deemed to Be Excessively Injurious or to Have Indiscriminate Effects, October 10, 1980, which contains a prohibition on chemical weapons, biological weapons, nondetectable fragments, blinding laser weapons, and booby traps. There is also a strong case to be made that antipersonnel landmines and nuclear weapons would also fall within the ambit of Paragraph 1(b)(xx).

Paragraph 2: The wording of this paragraph comes from Article 8(2)(d) of the Rome Statute of the International Criminal Court.

Paragraph 3: The wording of this paragraph comes from Article 8(2)(f) of the Rome Statute of the International Criminal Court.

Paragraph 4: The wording of this paragraph comes from Article 8(3) of the Rome Statute of the International Criminal Court.

## *Article 88.2: Penalty*

The applicable penalty range for the criminal offense of war crimes is ten to thirty years' imprisonment.

# Section 2: Offenses against Life and Limb

## Article 89: Unlawful Killing

### *Article 89.1: Definition of Offense*

A person commits the criminal offense of unlawful killing when he or she:

(a) kills another person in a planned and deliberate manner;

(b) kills another person with the intention to kill; or

(c) kills another person recklessly or negligently.

#### Commentary

Reaching agreement upon a common definition of unlawful killing was one of the most difficult tasks to accomplish during the drafting of the MCC. Different legal systems diverge to such an extent on the precise scope and meaning of the terms *unlawful killing*, *murder*, *manslaughter*, and *homicide* that it was hard to find a definition that satisfied the experts consulted on this provision. It was even difficult to agree upon the title for this provision. Some advocated use of the terms *murder* and *manslaughter*, while others favored the use of *homicide*. Finding a suitable definition for use in the MCC was consequently not just a matter of taking a definition from another legal system. Instead, the drafters decided to create a new definition of *unlawful killing* (the agreed-upon term) that would incorporate elements from a variety of different states and legal systems.

The definition contained in Article 89 is a compromise between various definitions in domestic laws. Different states create various categories or scales of the criminal offense of killing another person, according to the seriousness of the basic offense adjudged in light of the mental element of the perpetrator. Thus the killing of another person is categorized according to whether it was planned, premeditated, desired, intended, or committed recklessly or with gross negligence. By creating different categories of the criminal offense of killing another, it is then possible to assign different penalty ranges to them, depending on the level, heinousness, or seriousness of the killing. Obviously, the killing of a person with premeditation, for example, would merit a more severe penalty than the killing of a person through gross negligence.

Threats to kill are also deemed to be a criminal offense under the MCC. Reference should be made to Article 93 and its accompanying commentary.

Paragraph (a): Paragraph (a) sets out the most serious form of unlawful killing. There are various approaches to identifying the most serious forms of unlawful killing in domestic legal systems. In some systems, planning or premeditation is the defining feature of "murder in the first degree" or "premeditated murder." Another commonly used approach establishes motives or special circumstances that have to accompany a killing to make such a killing "murder," or "murder in the first degree," as it is often known.

In some systems, such motives or circumstances are specifically defined. The legislation of different states makes specific references to sexual motives, motives related to greed, the facilitation of other criminal offenses, the evasion of criminal investigation and prosecution, escape from custody, and killing for profit. Other criminal codes refer to circumstances that make a particular killing the most serious of its kind, such as where the killing was carried out with particular cruelty or torture; multiple killings; where the circumstances of the killing endangered public safety; or the killing of specific types of persons, such as children, police officers, judges, government officials, and witnesses to criminal offenses. In quite a number of states, the most serious unlawful killings involve some element of premeditation or planning. Other states use less specific language, wherein a killing that is intentional and accompanied by heinous circumstances related to the act or motives will result in the killing being designated, for the purpose of penalties, as the most serious form of killing under domestic law. It is worth noting that in one state where the language was so open as to allow a broad interpretation by the domestic courts as to the assignment of the maximum penalty, the provision was held to be unconstitutional by the constitutional court. Imprecision in the definition of the most serious form of murder may also breach the principle of legality contained in Article 3 of the MCC.

While some states thus spell out aggravating factors that make a particular killing rise to the most serious form of killing, other states include no such factors. In their legal systems, all killings perpetrated with intention to kill or to cause serious or grievous bodily harm, or with "callous recklessness," "extreme disregard for human life," or "malice aforethought," are defined as the most serious forms of unlawful killing. The term *murder* is commonly used to describe this form of killing. The experts consulted in the drafting of Article 89 considered whether or not to adopt this approach, and ultimately decided that it was in fact necessary to include another level above murder. After considering all the aggravating factors set out above that serve to define the most serious level of unlawful killing, the experts and the drafters agreed to define the most serious form of unlawful killing in terms of the planning, premeditation, and advance preparation that go into it.

Paragraph (b): Paragraph (b) defines a second, less serious category of unlawful killing, one that encompasses all other intentional killings (i.e., all unlawful killings committed without premeditation, planning, and/or other aggravating motives and circumstances). The definition of intention (see Article 18) provides that when a person kills another purposely or knowingly, then he or she may be found criminally responsible for the criminal offense of unlawful killing under Paragraph (b). Whereas some legal systems provide that either the intention to kill or the intention to cause serious bodily injury or harm will suffice for this level of unlawful killing, in Paragraph (b) only the intention to kill will suffice.

It is worth noting that some domestic legal systems have another category of unlawful killing below the level defined in Paragraph (b). This category of unlawful killing involves particularly mitigating circumstances. For example, a person would qualify under this lesser form of unlawful killing if he or she killed another following a serious demand to be killed by the victim or under extreme conditions such as stress or provocation. In other legal systems, when a person commits an intentional killing in such circumstances, he or she may avail of so-called partial defenses such as "provocation" and "diminished responsibility." Where these partial defenses are found to exist, the person is liable for a lesser degree of unlawful killing, similar to the sort of unlawful killing set out in Paragraph (c). The MCC does not create the lesser form of unlawful killing under mitigating circumstances, nor does it contain provisions on partial defenses, as discussed in the commentary to Article 51(1)(a). Instead, provocation or diminished responsibility will be recognized as a mitigating factor at the stage of the determination of penalties. Reference should be made to Article 51(1)(a) and its accompanying commentary.

Paragraph (c): The third category of unlawful killing contained in the MCC equates to the offense known as manslaughter in many legal systems. It also includes the criminal offense of negligent homicide, contained in some legal systems. This category involves a person causing the death of another, although the person did not have the intention to kill but instead was reckless or negligent in doing so. Reference should be made to Article 18 and it accompanying commentary, which discuss the meaning and scope of the terms *recklessness* and *negligence.*

## *Article 89.2: Penalty*

1. The applicable penalty range for the criminal offense of unlawful killing is:
   (a) ten to thirty years' imprisonment for a planned and deliberate killing;
   (b) five to twenty years' imprisonment for killing with intention to kill;
   (c) three to fifteen years' imprisonment for killing recklessly or negligently.
2. In exceptional circumstances, and in accordance with Article 49, the court may impose a penalty of life imprisonment for the criminal offense of planned and deliberate killing.

# Article 90: Assault

## *Article 90.1: Definition of Offense*

A person commits the criminal offense of assault when he or she, unlawfully:

(a) threatens, by an act or gesture, to apply force to another person, if he or she causes that other person to believe on reasonable grounds that he or she has the present ability to effect his or her purpose; or

(b) without the consent of another person, applies force intentionally to the other person, whether directly or indirectly.

### Commentary

Some legal systems draw a distinction between assault (where a person is put in fear of the use of force against him or her) and battery (where force is used against a person). Article 90 covers the offenses of assault and battery (or criminal force, as it is known in some legal systems). Assault is contained in Paragraph (a), and battery is contained in Paragraph (b). The term *unlawfully* is used in this article to exclude cases of lawful use of force, for example, by a police officer lawfully using force in the course of his or her duties.

Force has been held in some states to include the application of heat, light, electric current, noise, or another other form of energy and the application of matter in solid, liquid, or gaseous form. Most courts in interpreting *force* have deemed that words alone cannot amount to an assault; an act or a gesture is required. Some commentators have argued that words alone should be allowable under the definition of assault. However, this argument is not universally accepted and has not been included in the definition of assault under Article 90. Paragraph (a) uses the term *present ability* to underscore the fact that the threatened use of force must be immediate. It further introduces an objective test (through the use of *reasonable grounds*) as to the apprehended use of force.

## *Article 90.2: Penalty*

1. The applicable penalty range for the criminal offense of assault is one to five years' imprisonment.
2. The court may impose a fine, as a principal penalty, upon a person convicted of assault.

# Article 91: Assault Causing Harm

## *Article 91.1: Definition of Offense*

1. A person commits the criminal offense of assault causing harm when he or she assaults a person, causing him or her harm.
2. For the purposes of Article 91, *harm* means harm to the body or mind that includes pain and unconsciousness.

### Commentary

Some legal systems define assault causing harm as "aggravated assault," "grievous bodily harm," "aggravated bodily harm," or "assault occasioning actual bodily harm." The aggravating factor that transforms assault into the criminal offense of assault causing harm differs from state to state. Some systems define the offense in relation to the means by which the assault was undertaken, whereas others define it in terms of its effects on the victim or in terms of both means and effects. The definition of assault causing harm under the MCC focuses on effects.

To prove that assault causing harm occurred, it is necessary to prove the elements of assault under Article 90, plus the infliction of harm as defined in Paragraph 2. Reference should be made to Article 90, "Assault," and its accompanying commentary.

## *Article 91.2: Penalty*

1. The applicable penalty range for the criminal offense of assault causing harm is two to ten years' imprisonment.
2. The court may impose a fine, as a principal penalty, upon a person convicted of assault causing harm.

# Article 92: Assault Causing Serious Harm

## *Article 92.1: Definition of Offense*

1. A person commits the criminal offense of assault causing serious harm when he or she assaults another person, causing him or her serious harm.

2. For the purposes of Article 92, *serious harm* means the wounding, maiming, or disfiguring of a person or endangering his or her life.

## Commentary

Some legal systems define assault causing serious harm as "aggravated assault," "grievous bodily harm," "aggravated bodily harm," or "assault occasioning actual bodily harm." The aggravating factor that transforms assault into the offense of assault causing serious harm differs from state to state. Some systems define the offense in relation to the means by which the assault was undertaken, whereas others define it in terms of its effects on the victim or in terms of both means and effects. The definition of assault causing serious harm under the MCC focuses on effects.

Proof of assault causing serious harm requires establishing the elements of assault under Article 90, plus the infliction of serious harm. Reference should be made to Article 90, "Assault," and its accompanying commentary.

## *Article 92.2: Penalty*

The applicable penalty range for the criminal offense of assault causing serious harm is three to fifteen years' imprisonment.

# Article 93: Threats to Kill or Cause Serious Harm

## *Article 93.1: Definition of Offense*

1. A person commits the criminal offense of threatening to kill or cause serious harm when he or she:

   (a) threatens to kill or cause serious harm to another person; and

   (b) intending the other person to receive the threat, communicates it by any means to the person.

2. For the purposes of Article 93, *serious harm* has the same meaning as it does in Article 92.1(2).

## Commentary

In addition to criminalizing the actual application of force under Article 90.1(b), harm under Article 91, and serious harm under Article 92, the MCC criminalizes threats to kill or cause serious harm, which are covered in Article 93. It is an essential element of the criminal offense that the perpetrator, with the intention that the other person receive the threat, communicates the threat by any means. It is not imperative that the person against whom the threat was directed actually received the threat, although this is normally the case.

Reference should be made to Article 92.1(2) for the meaning of *serious harm*.

## *Article 93.2: Penalty*

1. The applicable penalty range for the criminal offense of threat to kill or cause serious harm is one to five years' imprisonment.
2. The court may impose a fine, as a principal penalty, upon a person convicted of threat to kill or cause serious harm.

# Section 3: Sexual Offenses

## General Commentary

Sexual offenses are often committed during wartime, occupation, and in post-conflict states. Sexual offenses are regularly perpetrated against civilians in the context of acts of genocide, crimes against humanity, and war crimes. Reference should be made to Article 86 ("Genocide"), Article 87 ("Crimes against Humanity"), and Article 88 ("War Crimes"), and in particular Articles 87.1(1)(g), 88.1(1)(b)(xxii), and 88.1(1)(d)(vi), which explicitly refer to the sexual offenses of rape, sexual slavery, enforced prostitution, forced pregnancy, enforced sterilization, and other forms of sexual violence. Sexual offenses may also be prosecuted under other provisions, even where not specifically mentioned in the text of the article, for example, under Article 86.1(b) (as has been determined by the ICTR in the case of *Prosecutor v. Akayesu*, case no. ICTR-96-4-T, Decision, September 2, 1998), Article 87.1(1)(f) (as has been determined at the ICTY in the cases of *Prosecutor v. Delalić et al.*, case no. IT-96-21-T, Decision, November 16, 1998, and *Prosecutor v. Furundzija*, case no. IT-95-17/1-T, Decision, December 10, 1998), and Article 87.1(1)(h) (as has been determined at the ICTY in the case of *Prosecutor v. Kvočka*, case no. IT-98-30/1-T, Decision, December 15, 2000). Thus sexualized torture (or torture by means of rape) and gender-based persecution are also prosecutable. Rape and other forms of sexual violence have been successfully prosecuted as instruments of genocide, crimes against humanity, and war crimes before the ICTY and the ICTR.

Section 3 of the Special Part of the MCC deals with sexual offenses outside of the context of the criminal offenses of genocide, crimes against humanity, and war crimes. Often, the legislation in post-conflict states either is outdated, in which case so are the definitions of sexual offenses, or is purposely discriminatory against women in the articulation of sexual offenses. Given that instances of sexual offenses have often risen in the aftermath of a conflict, it is crucial that a post-conflict state examine the adequacy of its existing legislation to combat and punish such criminal offenses.

Coupled with the introduction of new legislation dealing with sexual offenses, a state may need to address other issues to adequately combat this crime problem. One of the primary challenges in post-conflict states in bringing prosecutions for sexual offenses (after new legislation has been introduced) is the stigma attached to the victim of a sexual offense. For example, as is evidenced in post-conflict societies such as Kosovo, East Timor, Liberia, Afghanistan, Rwanda, and Cambodia, victims are reluctant to come forward and report criminal offenses due to social, religious, or cultural stigmas or other obstacles attached to sexual offenses. Some cases are settled by compensating the victim's family, marrying the victim to the perpetrator, or sending the victim away. In some locales, victims of sexual offenses are even forced to prove the sexual offense themselves or else they may be at risk of trial for criminal offenses such as adultery or fornication outside of marriage. Public awareness and education campaigns are often necessary in a post-conflict state to address the issues just mentioned.

In states in which police or prosecutors are unwilling to investigate and prosecute sexual offenses, education and training may be necessary to ensure that police and prosecutors apply the law, deal with victims in a sensitive and competent manner, and treat sexual offenses as crimes of violence. It is important to ensure that trained female members of the police force or the prosecution service are available to handle these cases. To properly investigate sexual offenses, medical and forensic expertise may also be required. Although post-conflict states have limited resources, every effort should be made to make "rape kits" available to medical professionals to assist them in the examination of a rape victim. (A rape kit consists of boxes, microscope slides, and plastic bags for collecting and storing evidence, such as bodily fluids or skin cells, that may later be used in the prosecution of this offense.) Similarly, despite resource constraints, every effort should be made to provide forensic laboratories. Additionally, a state or a nongovernmental organization or civil society organization with the requisite capabilities, competence, and skills should provide medical assistance, counseling, and rehabilitation to the victims of sexual offenses.

# Article 94: Rape

## *Article 94.1: Definition of Offense*

A person commits the criminal offense of rape when:

(a) he or she invades the body of another person by conduct resulting in penetration, however slight, of any part of the body of that person or of the perpetrator with a sexual organ, or of the anal or genital opening of the other person with any object or any other part of the body; and

(b) the invasion was committed by force, or by threat of force or coercion, such as that caused by fear of violence, duress, detention, psychological oppression, or abuse of power, against such person or another person, or by taking advantage of a coercive environment; or the invasion was committed against a person incapable of giving genuine consent.

## Commentary

The wording of Article 94 is taken from the *Elements of Crimes*, accompanying the Rome Statute of the International Criminal Court, Articles 7(1)(g)-1, 8(2)(b)(xxii)-1, and 8(2)(e)(vi)-1). The definition of rape in the *Elements of Crimes* applies only to rape in the context of crimes against humanity and war crimes. Nonetheless, the drafters of the MCC viewed it as suitable for use as a stand-alone definition of rape. The definition of rape in the *Elements of Crimes* was arrived at after extensive negotiations between representatives from states around the world. The fact that the definition is generally accepted by numerous states rather than derived from one particular legal system made it the most obvious choice for the definition of rape in the MCC. The delegates who drafted the *Elements of Crimes* grappled with the many different definitions of rape that existed at the time, both in international law (under the jurisprudence of the ICTY and the ICTR) and in domestic law, before coming up with this novel definition.

This definition, now widely commended, does not have many of the deficiencies contained in outdated definitions of rape found in some legal systems. Significantly, the definition of rape in Article 94 does not include lack of consent as an element that needs to be proven to convict a person accused of rape. In many domestic jurisdictions, the inclusion of the nonconsent of the victim to the sexual act really means there is an effective presumption that a victim consented. Thus the only way to convict a person of rape is for the prosecutor to rebut this presumption by bringing forward evidence that the victim did not consent. In such cases, the court may look to the fact that a person consented verbally or implicitly to the sexual act. However, the court may not always look at whether this consent was genuine. If a person verbally said yes to sexual relations but did so only because the person feared for his or her life, this is not genuine consent and should not be allowed to preclude a conviction. Chapter 11, Part 3, of the MCCP addresses the issue of consent in relation to cases of sexual violence. It sets out "Principles of Evidence in Cases Involving Sexual Violence." Reference should be made to the relevant article and its accompanying commentary. Also of relevance in Chapter 11, Part 3, is the provision on "Exclusion of Evidence of Sexual Conduct," which governs the introduction of evidence relating to the prior sexual conduct of the victim. For a full discussion, reference should be made to Chapter 11, Part 3, of the MCCP.

Another merit of the definition of rape taken from the *Elements of Crimes* is that rape is categorized as a violation of the bodily integrity and sexual autonomy of a person, rather than as a crime relating to the honor of a person, which is how it is classified in the criminal laws of some states. Furthermore, the definition of rape in the *Elements of Crimes* and in Article 94 applies the criminal offense of rape to all persons. This means that rape can be perpetrated against a man or a woman, not just a woman. The application of rape to all persons also extends to a perpetrator who is married to the alleged victim. The definition of rape in the legislation of many post-conflict states provides that a man cannot be held criminally responsible for the rape of his wife. This exclusionary clause has been gradually removed from the legislation of post-conflict and non–post-conflict states that have reformed their laws on rape, and it is not found in the MCC definition of rape.

Other strengths of the definition of rape contained in the MCC include the following:

- The recognition that rape can be committed either through penetration of a bodily orifice by a sexual organ or through the invasion of the anus or the genital opening of a person by any object. This aspect moves away from definitions of rape that focus only on the invasion of one sexual organ with another sexual organ.
- Use of the term *invasion* rather than the term *penetration*, which is used in some jurisdictions. The use of *invasion* was welcomed by the delegates at the drafting of the *Elements of Crimes* as it more accurately portrays the criminal offense of rape from the perspective of the victim rather than that of the perpetrator. It is also a more gender-neutral term. Footnote 15 to the *Elements of Crimes* states that "the concept of invasion is intended to be broad enough to be gender-neutral."
- Broadening the definition of force used in some domestic definitions of rape. Under Article 94, the criminal offense of rape can be committed through force, threat of force, or coercion against a person incapable of giving genuine consent. It is worth noting that in the context of armed conflict (which would relate to the prosecution of rape as a war crime), the ICTR found that coercion may be "inherent" when military personnel are present (*Prosecutor v. Akayesu*, case no. ICTR-96-4-T, Judgment, September 2, 1998, paragraph 688).

## *Article 94.2: Penalty*

The applicable penalty range for the criminal offense of rape is five to twenty years' imprisonment.

# Article 95: Sexual Intercourse and Acts of a Sexual Nature with a Child below the Age of Consent to Sexual Relations

## *Article 95.1: Definition of Offense*

1. A person commits the criminal offense of sexual intercourse or acts of a sexual nature with a child below the age of consent to sexual relations when he or she:
   (a) has sexual intercourse with a person of the same or opposite sex under the age of [insert age of consent to sexual relations]; or

(b) performs an act of a sexual nature with a person of the same or opposite sex under the age of [insert age of consent to sexual relations] or forces a person to submit to an act of a sexual nature.

2. A person under the age of eighteen who commits the criminal offense set out in Paragraph 1 will be held criminally responsible only if he or she committed the acts by exploiting the lack of capacity of sexual self-determination of the person under the age of consent to sexual relations.

## Commentary

Article 95 contains two elements: sexual intercourse with a person below the age of consent to sexual relations, and acts of a sexual nature with a person below the age of consent to sexual relations. The former offense is often known as statutory rape. The age of consent to sexual relations has been left blank in the above article and should be inserted by a state. The age at which a person can consent to sexual relations varies from state to state. The average age of consent to sexual relations based on a world survey is around fifteen or sixteen years. The age of consent determined by a state should not be set too low.

Paragraph 2: The purpose of Paragraph 2 is to create an exception to Article 95 to cover cases in which a person under the age of eighteen has sexual intercourse with a person below the age of consent and where the sexual intercourse or other act of a sexual nature did not involve any exploitation of the lack of capacity of sexual self-determination of a person under the age of consent to sexual relations. This exemption envisages a situation where, for example, teenagers who are very close in age voluntarily and consensually have sexual intercourse or are involved in acts of a sexual nature with each other. It would not apply where an adult and a young child or teenager engage in sexual intercourse or other acts of a sexual nature.

## *Article 95.2: Penalty*

The applicable penalty range for the criminal offense of sexual intercourse or acts of a sexual nature with a child below the age of consent to sexual relations is three to fifteen years' imprisonment.

# Article 96: Violation of the Sexual Autonomy of a Defenseless Person

## *Article 96.1: Definition of Offense*

1. A person commits the criminal offense of violation of the sexual autonomy of a defenseless person when he or she has sexual intercourse with a defenseless person or performs or forces a defenseless person to perform or submit to any act of a sexual nature.
2. A defenseless person is a person who is suffering from a mental disease, temporary or permanent mental disorder or sickness, or any other state owing to which that person is not capable of giving genuine consent.

### Commentary

This provision aims to protect vulnerable persons who are incapable of giving genuine consent to sexual intercourse or other sexual acts.

## *Article 96.2: Penalty*

The applicable penalty range for the criminal offense of violation of the sexual autonomy of a defenseless person is three to fifteen years' imprisonment.

# Article 97: Violation of Sexual Autonomy by Abuse of Authority

## *Article 97.1: Definition of Offense*

A person commits the criminal offense of violation of sexual autonomy by abuse of authority when he or she induces his or her subordinate, a person who depends on him or her, or a person over whom he or she has authority, to have sexual intercourse with him or her or to perform or submit to any act of a sexual nature. The victim may be of the same or opposite sex.

## Commentary

This provision aims to protect persons who are in an unequal position to a person who induces them to have sexual intercourse with him or her or to submit to any sexual act. In this case, the act of sexual intercourse or other sexual act occurred by reason of the perpetrator's power over the victim. The perpetrator may be a person who has authority in a work setting or in an educational institution, a family member on whom the victim depends, or another person on whom the victim depends (e.g., a provider of medical care).

### *Article 97.2: Penalty*

The applicable penalty range for the criminal offense of violation of sexual autonomy by abuse of authority is three to fifteen years' imprisonment.

# Article 98: Sexual Slavery

### *Article 98.1: Definition of Offense*

A person commits the criminal offense of sexual slavery when he or she exercising any or all of the powers attaching to the right of ownership over one or more persons, such as by purchasing, selling, lending, or bartering such a person or persons, or by imposing on them a similar deprivation of liberty causes such person or persons to engage in one or more acts of a sexual nature.

## Commentary

The wording of Article 98 is taken from the *Elements of Crimes*, Articles 7(1)(g)-2, 8(2)(b)(xxii)-2, and 8(2)(e)(vi)-2. The definition in the *Elements of Crimes* applies only to sexual slavery in the context of genocide, crimes against humanity, and war crimes. However, the drafters of the MCC viewed the definition as suitable for use as a stand-alone definition of sexual slavery. The definition of sexual slavery in the Statute of the International Criminal Court, just like that of rape, was arrived at after extensive negotiations between representatives from states around the world. The fact that the definition is generally accepted by numerous states, rather than derived from one particular legal system, made it the most obvious choice for the MCC definition of sexual slavery.

The definition of slavery in Article 98 is the same as the definition of the crime against humanity of enslavement found in Article 7(1)(c) of the *Elements of Crimes.* Footnote 11 to the provision in the *Elements of Crimes* states that "it is understood that such deprivation of liberty may, in some circumstances include exacting forced labor or otherwise reducing a person to a servile status, as defined in the Supplementary Convention to the Abolition of Slavery, the Slave Trade, and Institutions and Practices Similar to Slavery of 1956. It is also understood that the conduct described in this element includes trafficking in persons, in particular women and children." The ICTY has stated that

> indications of enslavement include elements of control and ownership; the restriction or control of an individual's autonomy, freedom of choice or freedom of movement; and, often, the accruing of some gain to the perpetrator. The consent or free will of the victim is absent. It is often rendered impossible or irrelevant by, for example, the threat or use of force or other forms of coercion; the fear of violence, deception or false promises; the abuse of power; the victim's position of vulnerability; detention or captivity, psychological oppression or socio-economic conditions. Further indications of enslavement include exploitation; the exaction of forced or compulsory labor or service, often without remuneration and often, though not necessarily, involving physical hardship; sex; prostitution; and human trafficking ... and control of sexuality.

(See *Prosecutor v. Kunarac et al.*, case nos. IT-96-23 and IT-96-23/1, Judgment, February 22, 2001.)

## *Article 98.2: Penalty*

The applicable penalty range for the criminal offense of sexual slavery is five to twenty years' imprisonment.

# Article 99: Enforced Prostitution

## *Article 99.1: Definition of Offense*

A person commits the criminal offense of enforced prostitution when he or she:

(a) forces one or more persons to engage in one or more acts of a sexual nature by force, or by threat of force or coercion, such as that caused by fear of violence, duress, detention, psychological oppression, or abuse of power, against such person or persons or another person, or by taking advantage of a coercive environment or such a person's or persons' incapacity to give genuine consent;

(b) where the perpetrator or another person obtained or expected to obtain pecuniary or other advantage in exchange for or in connection with the acts of a sexual nature.

## Commentary

The wording of Article 99 is taken from the *Elements of Crimes*, Articles 7(1)(g)-3, 8(2)(b)(xxii)-3, and 8(2)(e)(vi)-3. The definition in the *Elements of Crimes* applies only to enforced prostitution in the context of genocide, crimes against humanity, and war crimes. However, the drafters of the MCC viewed it as suitable for use as a standalone definition of enforced prostitution. The definition of enforced prostitution in the *Elements of Crimes*, just like the definitions of rape and sexual slavery, was arrived at after extensive negotiations between representatives from states around the world. The fact that the definition is generally accepted by numerous states, rather than derived from one particular legal system, made it the most obvious choice for the definition of enforced prostitution in the MCC. There are some overlaps between Article 99 and Article 98, dealing with sexual slavery. In some cases, prosecution may be possible under both articles. Experts in the laws relating to sexual offenses pointed out that victims generally favor the term *sexual slavery* as an accurate depiction of the criminal offense committed against them rather than a term that suggests a linkage to prostitution.

### *Article 99.2: Penalty*

The applicable penalty range for the criminal offense of enforced prostitution is five to twenty years' imprisonment.

## Article 100: Sexual Violence

### *Article 100.1: Definition of Offense*

A person commits the criminal offense of sexual violence when he or she:

(a) commits an act of a sexual nature against one or more persons or causes such person or persons to engage in an act of a sexual nature;

(b) by force, or by threat of force or coercion, such as that caused by fear of violence, duress, detention, psychological oppression, or abuse of power, against such person or persons or another person, or by taking advantage of a coercive environment or such a person's or persons' incapacity to give genuine consent.

## Commentary

The wording of Article 100 is taken from the *Elements of Crimes*, Articles 7(1)(g)-6, 8(2)(b)(xxii)-6, and 8(2)(e)(vi)-6). The definition in the *Elements of Crimes* applies only to sexual violence in the context of genocide, crimes against humanity, and war crimes. However, the drafters of the MCC viewed it as suitable for use as a stand-alone definition of sexual violence. The definition of sexual violence in the *Elements of Crimes*, just like the definitions of rape, enforced prostitution, and sexual slavery, was arrived at after extensive negotiations between representatives from states around the world. The fact that the definition is generally accepted by numerous states, rather than derived from one particular legal system, made it the most obvious choice for the definition of sexual violence in the MCC. Article 100 is a residual provision that catches acts of sexual violence that cannot be classified as rape, sexual slavery, or any of the other offenses contained in Section 3.

## *Article 100.2: Penalty*

The applicable penalty range for the criminal offense of sexual violence is three to fifteen years' imprisonment.

# Section 4: Offenses against the Rights of Persons

## Article 101: Torture

### *Article 101.1: Definition of Offense*

A person commits the criminal offense of torture when he or she:

(a) intentionally inflicts severe pain or suffering, whether physical or mental, upon a person in his or her custody or under his or her control;

(b) for such purposes as to obtain from him or her, or a third person, information or a confession, or to punish him or her for a criminal offense that he or she, or a third person, has perpetrated or is suspected of having perpetrated, or to intimidate or coerce him or her, or a third person, for any other reason based on discrimination of any kind.

## Commentary

The right of a person to be free from torture is one that is protected by many international instruments, including the Universal Declaration of Human Rights (Article 5), the International Covenant on Civil and Political Rights (Article 7), the American Convention on Human Rights (Article 5), the African Charter on Human and People's Rights (Article 5), and the Convention on the Rights of the Child (Article 37). The United Nations Convention against Torture and Other Cruel, Inhuman or Degrading Treatment or Punishment was drafted and adopted in 1984. Article 4 of the convention requires that a state party "ensure that all acts of torture are offenses under its criminal law."

In Article 1, the convention contains a definition of torture that is used as the basis for the wording of Article 101.1 of the MCC. Under the definition of torture in the United Nations convention, there are three requisite elements of the offense: (1) the infliction of "severe pain or suffering" (discussed below); (2) for a number of purposes listed in the convention (discussed below); and (3) at the instigation of or with the consent or acquiescence of a public official or other person acting in an official capacity. The first two elements of the United Nations convention definition of torture are contained in Article 101. In contrast to the United Nations definition, Article 101 does not require that the act of torture be committed by a public official or an associated person. Thus the definition broadens the scope of the criminal offense of torture. In a state marred by conflict, and often in post-conflict states, torture can be perpetrated by public officials but also by indirect state actors, guerrilla movements, paramilitary groups, and organized criminal groups. It is often difficult to find substantial proof that a person acted at the instigation or with the consent or acquiescence of a public official. To ensure the full protection of a person from torture, the offense applies to a state or a nonstate actor where the victim is "in his or her custody or under his or her control."

It is important to note that torture may be either physical or mental. A common misconception is that torture involves merely physical acts. Article 2 of the Inter-American Convention to Prevent and Punish Torture elaborates on this point, stating that "torture shall also be understood to be the use of methods upon a person intended to obliterate the personality of the victim or to diminish his physical or mental capacities, even if they do not cause physical pain or mental anguish." The definition of torture does not contain a definitive list of acts that constitute torture because the perpetrators of torture continuously devise new methods of torture. Therefore it is impossible to define the full range of acts of torture. Many of the new techniques are more subtle, performed with the hope of their escaping definition as acts of torture. It is also important to note that the list of purposes set out in Paragraph (b) is not exhaustive, illustrated by use of the phrase *for such purposes as*.

The Convention against Torture and Other Cruel, Inhuman or Degrading Treatment or Punishment requires that, in addition to penalizing the principal perpetrator of an act of torture, domestic criminal legislation also penalize persons who are complicit or who participate in torture. This issue is covered in Section 11 of the General Part of the MCC. Reference should be made to Articles 27–31 and their accompanying commentaries. The convention also requires that criminal jurisdiction be asserted, if the state considers it appropriate, when the criminal offense of torture is committed on the territory of a state or on board a ship or aircraft registered in the state, when the alleged offender is a national of the state, or when the victim is a national of that state (Article 5). It also provides that a state may assert universal jurisdiction over acts of torture. The grounds of jurisdiction, both mandatory and discretionary, contained in the convention are covered in the MCC under Article 4 ("Territorial Jurisdiction"), Article 5 ("Extraterritorial Jurisdiction"), and Article 6 ("Universal Jurisdiction").

Furthermore, the Convention against Torture and Other Cruel, Inhuman or Degrading Treatment or Punishment declares, under Article 2(3), that orders to commit torture may not be invoked as justification for acts of torture. Reference should be made to Article 22 ("Superior Orders"), where orders to commit torture are declared manifestly unlawful. Finally, the convention contains numerous other procedural provisions, in addition to substantive provisions, on issues such as investigation and prosecution of torture (Articles 6, 7, and 12), extradition (Article 8), mutual legal assistance (Article 9), training of law enforcement and criminal justice personnel (Article

10), the right to complain and seek redress for acts of torture (Articles 13 and 14), the prevention of cruel, inhuman, and degrading treatment (Article 16), and the exclusion of evidence obtained through torture (Article 15). Many of these obligations are dealt with in the MCCP. Reference should be made to Chapter 14, Part 2, on extradition, Chapter 14, Part 1, on mutual legal assistance, and Chapter 11, Part 3, which addresses exclusion of evidence obtained through torture.

For the investigation of acts of torture, reference can be made to the *Manual on the Effective Investigation and Documentation of Torture and Other Cruel, Inhuman or Degrading Treatment or Punishment* (the Istanbul Protocol) and *Combating Torture: A Manual for Judges and Prosecutors*, produced by the Human Rights Centre, University of Essex. Reference should also be made, more generally, to the work of the United Nations Special Rapporteur on Torture and the United Nations Committee against Torture. Also of relevance is the work of the European Committee for the Prevention of Torture and Inhuman or Degrading Treatment or Punishment (CPT), set up under the European Convention for the Prevention of Torture and Inhuman or Degrading Treatment or Punishment. The CPT has published a report entitled *The CPT Standards: "Substantive" Sections of the CPT's General Reports*, which provides helpful guidance on the prevention of torture.

Acts of torture may be committed as part of the criminal offenses of genocide, crimes against humanity, and war crimes. Reference should be made to Articles 86–88 of the MCC and their accompanying commentaries.

### *Article 101.2: Penalty*

The applicable penalty range for the criminal offense of torture is five to twenty years' imprisonment.

## Article 102: Trafficking in Persons

### *Article 102.1: Definition of Offense*

1. A person commits the criminal offense of trafficking in persons when he or she, for the purpose of exploitation:
   (a) recruits, transports, transfers, harbors, or receives persons;
   (b) by means of:
      (i) the threat or use of force or other forms of coercion;
      (ii) abduction;
      (iii) fraud;

(iv) deception;

(v) the abuse of power or a position of vulnerability; or

(vi) the giving or receiving of payments or benefits to achieve the consent of a person having control over another person;

2. Exploitation includes, at a minimum, the exploitation or the prostitution of others or other forms of sexual exploitation, forced labor or services, slavery or practices similar to slavery, servitude, or the removal of organs.
3. The consent of a victim of trafficking in persons to the intended exploitation is irrelevant where any of the means set forth in Paragraph 1(b) have been used.
4. The recruitment, transportation, transfer, harboring, or receipt of a child for the purpose of exploitation is considered trafficking in persons, even if the act does not involve any of the means set forth in Paragraph 1(b).

## Commentary

Given the usual absence of a strong criminal justice system in a post-conflict state, organized criminal elements often operate with impunity. One of the fastest-growing criminal activities in post-conflict states is trafficking in persons. From Sierra Leone to Kosovo to Bosnia and Herzegovina to Liberia, domestic and international authorities have been faced with massive problems of trafficking in persons. According to *Human Trafficking and United Nations Peacekeeping: DPKO Policy Paper* (March 2004), "[H]uman trafficking is a destructive phenomenon afflicting many post-conflict environments and which can seriously impede UN peacekeeping and other UN objectives in host countries" (paragraph 3). It also violates many fundamental human rights of victims, including freedom from slavery; freedom from torture; freedom from cruel, inhuman, or degrading treatment; and freedom of liberty, to name a few.

Often, a primary difficulty in dealing with this widespread crime problem in post-conflict states is the fact that domestic legislation is outdated and does not contain the criminal offense of trafficking in persons. Many acts committed while persons are being trafficked (e.g., kidnapping or assault) may fall under different criminal offenses already contained in domestic law. However, the criminal act of trafficking has generally not been criminalized. In addition to the inclusion of the substantive offense of trafficking in domestic law, other provisions are required to combat and investigate trafficking and to deal with the victims of trafficking, as is discussed below. In many post-conflict states, much attention has been focused on the problem of trafficking, including the adoption of legislation implementing the substantive and procedural provisions required to investigate and prosecute this criminal offense.

In Kosovo, in the aftermath of the conflict, UNMIK Regulation 2001/4 on the Prohibition of Trafficking in Persons in Kosovo was promulgated. This regulation introduced both substantive and procedural provisions aimed at tackling the problem of trafficking in persons. The United Nations Mission in Kosovo also established five regional special police antitrafficking units, and a Victim Advocacy and Assistance Unit was established to coordinate an assistance policy for victims of trafficking. In Bosnia and Herzegovina, the United Nations Mission in Bosnia and the Office of the High Commissioner for Human Rights established the Special Trafficking Operations Programme (STOP). The details of STOP are discussed in great detail in *Women, Peace and Security*, a study submitted to the Security Council by the secretary-general in 2000.

There have been a number of regional conventions specifically on trafficking, including the Inter-American Convention on International Traffic in Minors and the South Asian Association for Regional Cooperation Convention on Preventing and Combating Trafficking in Women and Children for Prostitution. In addition, the Protocol to the African Charter on Human and People's Rights on the Rights of Women in Africa, Article 4(2)(g), provides that trafficking in women be prevented, condemned, and prosecuted. Many other instruments have dealt with aspects of trafficking in persons, such as slavery, forced labor, or slavery for the purpose of sexual exploitation. A full list is contained on page 262 of the *Legislative Guide to the United Nations Convention against Transnational Organized Crime and the Protocols Thereto.*

The first internationally agreed upon definition of trafficking is contained in the Protocol to Prevent, Suppress and Punish Trafficking in Persons, Especially Women and Children, supplementing the United Nations Convention against Transnational Organized Crime. The purpose of the protocol is to prevent and combat trafficking, protect and support the victims of trafficking, and promote cooperation between states parties to the convention (Article 2). The convention contains not only provisions on the criminalization of trafficking (Article 5) and the procedural measures necessary to investigate and prosecute trafficking but also provisions on the protection of victims of trafficking in persons (chapter 2), the prevention of trafficking, cooperation between states, and other measures (chapter 3). In addition to these obligations, according to Article 1 of the protocol, the obligations contained in the Convention against Transnational Organized Crime apply unless otherwise provided for in the protocol. Reference should therefore be made to the commentary to Article 136, which discusses the relevant obligations under the convention.

It is worth noting that two additions to the domestic criminal law, outlined in the United Nations Convention against Transnational Organized Crime, are particularly important for the investigation and prosecution of trafficking in persons. First, witness protection measures as contained in Chapter 8, Part 4, Section 1, of the MCCP (and referenced in Article 24 of the United Nations Convention against Transnational Organized Crime) are vitally important to ensure the safety of trafficking victims who testify at trial. Often, it is impossible to persuade a victim of trafficking to testify without an assurance of safety and protection. Reference should be made to the relevant sections of the MCCP and their accompanying commentaries. Second, covert surveillance measures (dealt with under Article 20 of the convention) are important for investigating trafficking in persons, as with other organized criminal activities.

A full discussion of all the obligations under the convention and the protocol is outside the scope of this commentary. Reference should be made to the *Legislative Guide to the United Nations Convention against Transnational Organized Crime and the Protocols Thereto.* Reference should also be made to the *Interpretative Notes for the*

*Official Records of the Negotiation of the United Nations Convention against Transnational Organized Crime and the Protocols Thereto* (UN document A/55/383/Add.1) and *Recommended Principles and Guidelines on Human Rights and Human Trafficking: Report of the United Nations High Commissioner for Human Rights to the Economic and Social Council* (UN document E/2002/68/Add.1). The Central European and Eurasian Law Initiative (CEELI) has published *Human Trafficking Assessment Tool and An Introduction to the Human Rights Assessment Tool: An Assessment Tool Based on the Protocol to Prevent, Suppress and Punish Trafficking in Persons, Especially Women and Children, Supplementing the United Nations Convention against Transnational Organized Crime,* and the International Human Rights Law Group has published *The Annotated Guide to the Complete UN Trafficking Protocol.* For a discussion of trafficking in the context of peace operations and current United Nations policy, reference should be made to *Human Trafficking and United Nations Peacekeeping: DPKO Policy Paper* (March 2004).

Paragraph 1: The wording of Paragraph 1 comes from Article 3(a) of the Protocol to Prevent, Suppress and Punish Trafficking in Persons, Especially Women and Children, supplementing the United Nations Convention against Transnational Organized Crime. The *Legislative Guide to the United Nations Convention against Transnational Organized Crime and the Protocols Thereto* (page 268) breaks the criminal offense down into three constituent elements: (1) the action (recruitment, transportation, transfer, harboring, or receipt of persons); (2) the means (threat, use of force or other forms of coercion, abduction, fraud, deception, abuse of power or of a position of vulnerability, or the giving or receiving of payments or benefits to achieve the consent of a person having control over another person); and (3) the purpose (exploitation). The legislative guide states, on page 268, that the obligation upon states parties to the convention is "to criminalize trafficking as a combination of constituent elements and not the elements themselves." This means that a state must implement the definition of trafficking contained in Article 3(a) of the protocol.

CEELI's *An Introduction to the Human Rights Assessment Tool* contains an extremely detailed discussion on the precise meaning of the action, means, and purposes of trafficking, having recourse to domestic legislation of different states to see how they have interpreted the provisions of the protocol (see pages 31–44). A full discussion of this issue is beyond the scope of this commentary, and reference should be made to the valuable resource just mentioned, in addition to the *Legislative Guide to the United Nations Convention against Transnational Organized Crime and the Protocols Thereto.*

Article 5 of the protocol requires that an attempt to commit the criminal offenses of trafficking or participation as an accomplice and of organizing or directing trafficking be criminalized. In the MCC, these obligations are covered under Articles 27, 29, and 31. Reference should be made to the relevant articles and their accompanying commentaries.

Paragraph 2: The wording of Paragraph 2 comes from Article 3(a) of the Protocol to Prevent, Suppress and Punish Trafficking in Persons, Especially Women and Children, supplementing the United Nations Convention against Transnational Organized Crime. It is worth noting that this list is illustrative and not exhaustive. Other exploitation purposes, such as the use of victims in armed conflicts or in the pornography industry—examples given in CEELI's *Human Trafficking Assessment Tool* (page 39)—may also fulfill the requisite element of exploitation in the offense of trafficking in persons. The CEELI trafficking tool provides useful descriptions and definitions of the forms of exploitation mentioned in Paragraph 2 (see pages 38–44).

Paragraph 3: Ordinarily, consent can be used by the alleged perpetrator of a criminal offense as a defense to the criminal offense of trafficking. In such cases, the court will assess whether or not the consent is true and informed. For example, if a person aware of all the factual circumstances at hand fully consented to be recruited, transported, transferred, or harbored (the means set out in Paragraph 1) for an apparently exploitative purpose such as prostitution, this would not constitute trafficking in persons. Instead, the person or persons who transported the person from one state to another could be liable for migrant smuggling under Article 137. Where any of the means mentioned in Paragraph 1(b) are used, however, the consent of the victim cannot be described as true consent. Through the inclusion of Paragraph 3, the potential for the alleged perpetrator to raise consent as a defense is cut off when any exploitative means have been employed. It is vital that this paragraph be included as an accompaniment to the substantive offense of trafficking in persons.

Paragraph 4: In a case of trafficking involving a child, meaning a person below the age of eighteen years, the issue of consent is completely irrelevant. Therefore, it does not matter whether the means set out in Paragraph 1 were used or not; there are no circumstances in which a child can consent to be recruited, transported, transferred, or harbored for an apparently exploitative purpose such as prostitution. Consequently, the prosecutor will need only to prove that the recruitment, transportation, transfer, harboring, or receipt was for the purpose of exploitation. The CEELI trafficking tool has criticized the protocol for not adequately dealing with the rights of trafficked child victims (see pages 45–46). The *Recommended Principles and Guidelines on Human Rights and Human Trafficking: Report of the United Nations High Commissioner for Human Rights to the Economic and Social Council* (UN document E/2002/68/Add.1) provides a number of valuable suggestions on how to do so and should be referred to by a state implementing legislation on trafficking in persons.

## *Article 102.2: Penalty*

The applicable penalty range for the criminal offense of trafficking in persons is three to fifteen years' imprisonment.

# Article 103: Establishing Slavery, Slavery-like Conditions, and Forced Labor

## *Article 103.1: Definition of Offense*

A person commits the criminal offense of establishing slavery, slavery-like conditions, and forced labor when he or she, and with the intention of establishing slavery, slavery-like conditions, or forced labor:

(a) places, holds, maintains, purchases, sells, hands over, or delivers a person into slavery, slavery-like conditions, or forced labor;

(b) mediates the purchase, sale, or handing over of another person into slavery, slavery-like conditions, or forced labor; or

(c) induces someone to sell his or her freedom into slavery, slavery-like conditions, or forced labor.

## Commentary

The criminal offense of establishing slavery, slavery-like conditions, and forced labor under Article 103 is in some respects related to the offense of trafficking in persons under Article 102, as trafficking may involve the exploitation of a person through slavery, practices similar to slavery, and forced labor. Slavery was the first human rights issue to arouse international concern. The first international convention concerning slavery drawn up under the League of Nations (the predecessor to the United Nations) was the Slavery Convention of 1926, followed by the Convention for the Suppression of the Traffic in Persons and of the Exploitation of the Prostitution of Others in 1949. (A supplementary convention to the 1926 convention was drafted in 1956.) Slavery still remains a problem in contemporary society. Slavery is defined under Article 1(1) of the 1926 convention as "the status or condition of a person over whom any or all of the powers attaching to the right of ownership are exercised." There are numerous examples of slavery-like conditions, including debt bondage, serfdom, forced marriage, and sale of children, some of which are dealt with in Article 1 of the 1956 supplementary convention to the 1926 convention. The United Nations Working Group on Contemporary Forms of Slavery has discussed other slavery-like conditions, including child labor (also falling under the definition of forced labor) and forced recruitment of children in armed conflict. Forced labor is defined by the International Labor Organization's Forced Labor Convention No. 29, Article 2(1), as "all work or service which is exacted from any person under the menace of any penalty for which the said person has not offered himself voluntarily."

Under Article 103, a variety of different acts and actors involved in putting a person into slavery, slavery-like practices, or forced labor, or keeping the person in this condition are penalized. Unlike under Article 102, above, there is no need to prove that illegitimate means were used in placing or inducing a person into slavery, slavery-like practices, or forced labor.

For further discussion on issues relating to slavery, including its prevention and other methods of addressing the problem, reference should be made to the work of the United Nations Working Group on Contemporary Forms of Slavery.

It is important to note that to convict a person of slavery, the intention to establish slavery, slavery-like conditions, or forced labor will have to be established. For example, if a taxi driver unknowingly delivers a person into slavery, he or she cannot be convicted of the criminal offense unless he or she had the requisite intention to establish slavery, slavery-like conditions, or forced labor.

## *Article 103.2: Penalty*

The applicable penalty range for the criminal offense of establishing slavery, slavery-like conditions, or forced labor is three to fifteen years' imprisonment.

# Article 104: Enforced Disappearance

## *Article 104.1: Definition of Offense*

A person commits the criminal offense of enforced disappearance when he or she deprives another person of his or her liberty, in whatever form or for whatever reason, brought about by agents of the state or by persons or groups of persons acting with the authorization, support, or acquiescence of the state, followed by an absence of information, or refusal to acknowledge the deprivation of liberty or information, or concealment of the fate or whereabouts of the disappeared person.

### Commentary

Typically, an enforced disappearance involves a person being removed by an official of the state (e.g., a police officer or member of the military) from his or her home or other location without any arrest warrant and without any notification of where he or she will be held, after which the person is never seen again by his or her family. In many cases, the victim of an enforced disappearance is tortured and then killed, and his or her body is disposed of without the knowledge of the family.

Enforced disappearances breach a variety of individual rights of the victim—such as the right to life; freedom from torture or cruel, inhuman, and degrading treatment or punishment; the right to liberty and security; and the right to recognition as a person before the law—and rights of the person's family in the sphere of economic rights (e.g., depriving a family not only of a member but also of its main earner). As stated in the *Report Submitted by Mr. Manfred Nowak, Independent Expert Charged with Examining the Existing International Criminal and Human Rights Framework for the Protection of Persons from Enforced or Involuntary Disappearances, Pursuant to Paragraph 11 of the Commission Resolution 2001/46* (UN document E/CN.4/2002/71, January 8, 2001, paragraph 70): "[E]nforced disappearance is a very complex and cumulative violation of human rights and humanitarian law." Disappearances are now a global phenomenon and often occur in states suffering from internal armed conflicts. Many individuals in post-conflict states are victims of enforced disappearances, their relatives having been "disappeared" by officials of a prior regime. In other states, enforced disappearance continues to be used as a tool of political repression.

A number of international instruments address the phenomenon of enforced disappearance, including the Inter-American Convention on Forced Disappearance of Persons, the United Nations Declaration on the Protection of All Persons from Enforced Disappearances, and the United Nations International Convention on the Protection of All Persons from Forced Disappearances. The wording of Article 104 is taken from Article 1 of the United Nations International Convention on the Protection of All Persons from Forced Disappearances, which is very similar to the wording contained in the Inter-American Convention on Forced Disappearance of Persons. According to Article 7 of the United Nations convention, a state must adopt the necessary legislative measures to define an enforced disappearance as an independent offense. In order to comply with the obligation contained in the convention, it is not enough that the state rely on preexisting provisions of law on deprivation of liberty, torture, intimidation, excessive violence, and so on; enforced disappearances must constitute a separate offense.

In addition to the substantive requirement to introduce a criminal offense of enforced disappearance, the United Nations International Convention on the Protection of All Persons from Forced Disappearances contains several procedural requirements that a state should look at in order to create a full protective framework against enforced disappearance. One of the most useful mechanisms in protecting persons against the possibility of enforced disappearance is a habeas corpus mechanism, whereby any person can petition the court where another person has been detained illegally. Reference should be made to Chapter 15 of the MCCP. Also of great importance in combating enforced disappearance are the procedural provisions relating to detention. In this regard, reference should be made to the Model Detention Act.

The criminal offense of enforced disappearance is also recognized as an international crime, specifically a crime against humanity—see Article 7(1)(i) of the *Statute of the International Criminal Court* and Article 3 of the *International Convention on the*

*Protection of All Persons from Forced Disappearance*. Reference should be made to Article 87 of the MCC and its accompanying commentary.

## *Article 104.2: Penalty*

The applicable penalty range for the criminal offense of enforced disappearance is three to fifteen years' imprisonment.

# Article 105: Domestic Violence

## *Article 105.1: Definition of Offense*

1. A person commits the criminal offense of domestic violence when he or she commits any of the following criminal offenses against a person with whom he or she has a domestic relationship:
   (a) rape as defined in Article 94;
   (b) sexual intercourse or acts of a sexual nature with a child below the age of consent to sexual relations as defined in Article 95;
   (c) violation of the sexual autonomy of a defenseless person as defined in Article 96;
   (d) violation of sexual autonomy by abuse of authority as defined in Article 97;
   (e) sexual slavery as defined in Article 98;
   (f) enforced prostitution as defined in Article 99;
   (g) sexual violence as defined in Article 100;
   (h) assault as defined in Article 90;
   (i) assault causing harm as defined in Article 91;
   (j) assault causing serious harm as defined in Article 92;
   (k) threat to kill or cause serious harm as defined in Article 93;
   (l) kidnapping as defined in Article 106;
   (m) unlawful deprivation of liberty as defined in Article 107;
   (n) establishing slavery, slavery-like conditions, or forced labor as defined in Article 103;

(o) arson as defined in Article 131; and

(p) criminal damage as defined in Article 133.

2. For the purposes of Article 105, *domestic relationship* means a relationship between:

(a) a husband and wife or former husband and wife;

(b) a women and a man who are cohabiting without marriage;

(c) a boyfriend and girlfriend;

(d) two people who are related by marriage, blood, or adoption or by a guardian relationship;

(e) a person and a household worker.

## Commentary

Paragraph 1: In earlier drafts of the MCC, domestic violence was addressed much as it was in many domestic criminal codes—as an aggravating factor relevant to the penalties of certain offenses. Consequently, if the particular criminal offenses set out in Paragraph 1(a) were committed in the context of a domestic relationship as defined in Paragraph 2, the applicable penalty range of the relevant offense could be augmented. While there was agreement among the drafters and experts consulted during the process of vetting the MCC that the commission of a criminal offense against a victim with whom the perpetrator had a domestic relationship merited special attention, and also merited augmentation of the applicable penalty for the underlying offense committed, there was much debate about whether the MCC should treat domestic violence as an aggravating factor or should include a separate definition of domestic violence. As a compromise, it was agreed that domestic violence should be contained in a separate provision, while the applicable penalty ranges should be determined by reference to the applicable penalty ranges of the predicate, or underlying, offenses of domestic violence—that is, those offenses set out in Paragraph 1 of this article.

There are a number of reasons for recognizing domestic violence as a separate criminal offense in the MCC. First, by giving the criminal offense of domestic violence its own autonomous provision, the drafters sought to highlight the necessity of adequately addressing this issue in a post-conflict state. Many post-conflict states have experienced a considerable upsurge in domestic violence in the aftermath of conflict. In East Timor, for example, domestic violence was reportedly the most widely perpetrated criminal offense in 2000, one year after the cessation of conflict. This elevated level of domestic violence was probably driven by several different factors, including the high incidence of post-traumatic stress disorder among former combatants, increased unemployment, and a widespread sense of the acceptability of violence after years of conflict. *Women, Peace and Security* discusses the urgent need to address domestic violence (see paragraphs 278–286) and recommends that post-conflict states undertake legal reforms to address the issue (see paragraph 392).

The second reason for the inclusion of domestic violence as a separate criminal offense of domestic violence goes beyond the specific needs of a post-conflict state and relates also to non-post-conflict states. This reason goes to the need to set domestic violence apart from other criminal offenses on account of its distinguishing feature: acts of physical, psychological, or sexual violence that occur within the private sphere and violate the rights of an individual in a domestic relationship with the perpetrator as defined in Paragraph 2. Historically, and in some states even today, there has been a reticence to acknowledge the interest of a state in criminalizing acts of violence that occur in the private sphere, for example, between a husband and a wife. Recently, however, there has been a growing movement worldwide to recognize the state's interest in acts of violence that occur in the private sphere and to introduce specific legislation regarding them.

The United Nations Special Rapporteur on Violence against Women, Its Causes and Consequences has stated that where domestic violence is not recognized as a separate criminal offense, and where prosecutions are brought under other general laws, such as those dealing with assault or battery, "cases are rarely prosecuted and women continue ... to suffer in silence" (see *Integration of the Human Rights of Women and the Gender Perspective: Violence against Women*, UN document E/CN.4/2003/75, paragraph 26). The United Nations Committee on the Convention for the Elimination of Discrimination against Women (established under the convention), in General Recommendation No. 19, requires states parties to the convention to introduce specific legislation on violence against women, as does the Inter-American Convention on the Prevention, Punishment and Eradication of Violence against Women, Article 7, and the Protocol to the African Charter on Human and People's Rights on the Rights of Women in Africa, Article 4(2).

Some experts consulted during the drafting of the MCC argued that the provision should refer only to violence perpetrated against women, since statistically domestic violence against men is not very common, and international efforts to combat domestic violence tend to focus on the need to protect women, not men. The *Framework for Model Legislation on Domestic Violence*, drafted by the Special Rapporteur on Violence against Women, Its Causes and Consequences and adopted by the United Nations Commission on Human Rights (see UN document E/CN.4/1996/53/Add.2), states in paragraph 2(b) that domestic violence is "gender-specific violence directed against women." That said, at a domestic level, legislation has been introduced that protects both men and women from abuse within a domestic relationship. While acknowledging that domestic violence predominantly affects women and stems from historical and traditional power imbalances between the two genders, the drafters of the MCC chose to follow an approach that covered domestic violence against both men and women.

After dealing with the question of whom should be covered by the offense of domestic violence, the drafters considered a further issue: Which offenses should be contained in the provision? The particular criminal offenses included in Article 105 as the predicate offenses for domestic violence are those offenses contained in the MCC that involve physical, psychological, and sexual violence. The most common forms of domestic violence include battering of women, marital rape, incest, forced prostitution, violence against domestic workers, violence against female children, and traditional practices affecting the health of women and children. Domestic violence also includes acts of psychological violence such as intimidation, coercion, stalking, and verbal abuse. Furthermore, property offenses such as arson and criminal damage have been included in domestic violence legislation, an approach that has been followed in the MCC.

The introduction of a substantive criminal offense is not, however, sufficient to effectively combat domestic violence in a post-conflict state. At the level of legislative reform, other modifications of the legal framework have to be made; in particular, criminal procedure reforms must be introduced to enable domestic violence to be successfully investigated and prosecuted. A collection of suggested procedural reforms relating to domestic violence investigation and prosecution is set out in the *Framework for Model Legislation on Domestic Violence*, mentioned above. It includes procedural provisions addressing issues such as the duty of police officers to respond to requests for assistance in cases of domestic violence; the requirement that police officers complete a domestic violence report after responding to a domestic violence complaint; the rights of victims of domestic violence; and the duties of criminal justice actors in investigating, prosecuting, and trying domestic violence cases. Reference should also be made to the annex to Crime Prevention and Criminal Justice Measures to Eliminate Violence against Women (United Nations General Assembly Resolution 1998/86), which discusses procedural requirements relating to criminal procedure, police, and sentencing and corrections. The *Framework for Model Legislation on Domestic Violence* also refers to complementary reforms in the civil law sphere required to supplement criminal legislation on domestic violence. It is essential for a state wishing to tackle the problem of domestic violence to implement laws that provide for temporary restraining orders or more long-term protective measures, such as protection orders in favor of victims of domestic violence.

In addition to criminal and civil law reforms, a post-conflict state tackling the problem of domestic violence must also look to other measures, such as the training and sensitization of police officers or other criminal justice actors involved in the investigation, prosecution, or adjudication of domestic violence cases. Some states have also undertaken institutional reforms, such as establishing special police units (often staffed by female police officers), or even special police stations, to deal solely with domestic violence. Rehabilitative measures aimed at treating the victims of domestic violence may also be required. Victims may need counseling, health care, and social services. Often, such services are provided by nongovernmental organizations working in conjunction with the state. Services such as the establishment and running of hotlines for reporting incidents of domestic violence, and the provision of shelters to house the victims of domestic violence who cannot return home, may also be required. Reference may be made to the International Centre for Criminal Law Reform and Criminal Justice Policy manual entitled *Model Strategies and Practical Measures on the Elimination of Violence against Women in the Field of Crime Prevention and Criminal Justice*, which discusses the substantive and procedural reforms required to address domestic violence, as well as training, sensitization, service delivery for victims of domestic violence, and institutional reforms.

Given that many post-conflict states exhibit a cultural acceptance of domestic violence, other measures have focused on public awareness, public dialogue, and public education campaigns. In East Timor, for example, when the laws on domestic violence were being drafted, a sixteen-day campaign against domestic violence was implemented. The United Nations Mission in East Timor also worked with specific sectors of society; for example, it provided journalists with training on gender-sensitive reporting of domestic violence.

Paragraph 2: The definition of domestic relationship is taken from paragraph 7 of the *Framework for Model Legislation on Domestic Violence*, drafted by the Special Rapporteur on Violence against Women, Its Causes and Consequences. This definition is relatively wide in order to include all the sorts of domestic relationships within which domestic violence commonly occurs, including those involving female household workers, who are commonly the subject of domestic violence in the homes in which they work and live.

## *Article 105.2: Penalty*

The applicable penalty range for the criminal offense of domestic violence must be calculated by augmenting the maximum applicable penalty for the relevant predicate criminal offense set out in Article 105.1(1) by one-half.

### Commentary

As mentioned in the commentary to Article 105, the drafters of the MCC decided to create a separate criminal offense of domestic violence. But instead of determining separate penalties for domestic violence, they decided that the applicable penalties should be determined by reference to the penalties for the predicate offenses of domestic violence. For example, if an act of assault is perpetrated against a victim who is in a domestic relationship with the perpetrator, then the appropriate penalty range is that for assault, plus augmentation to the maximum penalty set out in Article 105.2. In this case, the applicable penalty range will be one to seven and one-half years (the original penalty range for assault is one to five years). Adopting this sort of approach to the penalties for domestic violence seemed the most straightforward solution, as all the different predicate offenses of domestic violence carry varying penalty ranges, based on the seriousness of the predicate offense. The drafters originally struggled to find an appropriate one-size-fits-all penalty range for the vast array of predicate offenses covered in Article 105.1(1) and eventually resolved to adopt an approach to the designation of an appropriate penalty range that is unique in the MCC.

# Article 106: Kidnapping

## *Article 106.1: Definition of Offense*

A person commits the criminal offense of kidnapping when he or she takes or detains another person, without the other person's consent, with the intention of:

(a) holding that other person to ransom or as a hostage;

(b) taking or sending that other person out of the jurisdiction; or

(c) committing a criminal offense against that person or a third person.

### Commentary

Kidnapping—particularly the kidnapping of international personnel—has become a widespread occurrence in post-conflict states such as Cambodia, Iraq, and Nepal. In some post-conflict environments, kidnapping has been perpetrated by terrorist groups to inflame tensions and stoke insecurity; in others states, organized criminal groups have used kidnapping to make money. The phenomenon of kidnapping has become so serious that the Economic and Social Council of the United Nations has twice asked the secretary-general to produce a report on the subject. Reference should be made to two reports, one published in 2003 and the other in 2004 but both having the same title, *International Cooperation in the Prevention, Combating and Elimination of Kidnapping and in Providing Assistance to Victims* (UN document E/CN.15/2003/7 and UN document E/CN.15/2004/7, respectively). Both reports contain information on how to combat kidnapping, and they posit a variety of legal responses, operational practices required to deal with kidnapping, and preventive strategies.

The criminal offense of kidnapping is a form of aggravated unlawful deprivation of liberty (under Article 107). Both offenses involve the taking or detaining of another person without his or her consent. Unlawful deprivation of liberty rises to the level of kidnapping, and therefore enters a higher penalty range, when any of the three aggravating factors above are present. The wording of Article 106 is taken from Section 5.1.30 of the Australian Model Penal Code. For more detail on kidnapping's precise scope and meaning, reference should be made to the code and its commentaries.

Article 35 of the Convention on the Rights of the Child instructs states to take all appropriate measures to prevent the abduction of children out of the jurisdiction. These measures include criminalizing this offense. Some states recognize a separate offense of child abduction, in addition to kidnapping. Under the MCC, the offense of kidnapping encapsulates the kidnapping or abduction of children.

The Australian code states that "a person who takes or detains a child is to be treated as acting without the consent of the child." The Committee on the Rights of the Child (a body set up under the Convention on the Rights of the Child to monitor compliance with state obligations under the convention) has debated whether the offense of child abduction should include a situation in which a child consents to leave one guardian in favor of another. According to the commentary to the Australian Model Criminal Code (page 89), the committee believes it should not. For example, a teenage girl who leaves the custody of a parent in favor of living with an aunt would not open the aunt to criminal prosecution. A state implementing a new provision on kidnapping should consider which of these positions it wishes to take. Where the consent of a child is permissible, the court will have to assess whether the consent was genuine.

### *Article 106.2: Penalty*

The applicable penalty range for the criminal offense of kidnapping is three to fifteen years' imprisonment.

## Article 107: Unlawful Deprivation of Liberty

### *Article 107.1: Definition of Offense*

A person commits the criminal offense of unlawful deprivation of liberty when he or she takes or detains another person, or otherwise restricts the personal liberty of another person, without lawful authority and without the consent of that person.

#### Commentary

The criminal offense of unlawful deprivation of liberty is known as false imprisonment in many states. To negate this offense, consent of the victim may be proven. In this case, consent must be genuine.

### *Article 107.2: Penalty*

The applicable penalty range for the criminal offense of deprivation of liberty is two to ten years' imprisonment.

# Article 108: Criminal Coercion

## *Article 108.1: Definition of Offense*

A person commits the criminal offense of criminal coercion when he or she:

(a) by use of force, or threat of serious harm;

(b) compels a person to do or refrain from doing an act.

## *Article 108.2: Penalty*

1. The applicable penalty range for the criminal offense of criminal coercion is one to five years' imprisonment.
2. The court may impose a fine, as an alternative principal penalty, upon a person convicted of criminal coercion.

# Article 109: Unauthorized Search of a Person and His or Her Belongings

## *Article 109.1: Definition of Offense*

A person commits the criminal offense of unauthorized search of a person or of items in his or her possession when he or she, without lawful authorization or without the consent of that person:

(a) conducts a search of another person; or

(b) conducts a search of his or her belongings or items in his or her possession.

### Commentary

Unauthorized search of a person or his or her belongings is criminalized because it represents a substantial and unjustified intrusion into the privacy of an individual. The right to privacy is protected under the constitutions or domestic legislation of many states and also protected under international and regional human rights instruments, such as the International Covenant on Civil and Political Rights, Article 17; the Convention on the Rights of the Child, Article 40(2)(b)(vii); the European Convention on Human Rights and Fundamental Freedoms, Article 8; the American Convention on Human Rights, Article 11; and the African Charter on the Rights and Welfare of the Child, Article 10. The right to privacy is a "limited" as opposed to an "absolute" right, and therefore intrusions can sometimes be justified on grounds such as public safety, the protection of the rights and freedoms of others, and the prevention of disorder or crime—all of which are articulated in Article 8(2) of the European Convention on Human Rights and Fundamental Freedoms.

Article 109 applies to all persons, including public officials and policing officials. With regard to policing officials, Chapter 8, Part 3, Section 4, of the MCCP contains detailed provisions on the search of persons, as does the Model Police Powers Act. Where a policing official conducting a search of a person acts outside the scope of the powers bestowed upon him or her by the MCCP or the Model Police Powers Act, and therefore acts unlawfully, he or she may be liable to criminal prosecution under Article 109. Reference should be made to the relevant section of the MCCP and the Model Police Powers Act and their accompanying commentaries.

### *Article 109.2: Penalty*

1. The applicable penalty range for the criminal offense of unauthorized search of a person or his or her belongings is one to five years' imprisonment.
2. The court may impose a fine, as a principal penalty, upon a person convicted of unauthorized search of a person or his or her belongings.

## Article 110: Unauthorized Search of a Dwelling or Premises

### *Article 110.1: Definition of Offense*

A person commits the criminal offense of unauthorized search of a dwelling or premises when he or she:

(a) conducts a search of a dwelling or private premises;

(b) without lawful authorization or without the consent of that person.

## Commentary

This provision applies to both public officials and nonpublic officials.

With regard to policing officials, Chapter 8, Part 3, Section 4, of the MCCP contains detailed provisions on the search of a dwelling or premises. A similar provision on search (outside the context of criminal investigation) is contained in the Model Police Powers Act. Reference should be made to the MCCP and the Model Police Powers Act and their accompanying commentaries. The search of dwellings or premises represents an intrusion on the right to privacy—a right protected under the constitutions or domestic legislation of many states, as discussed in greater detail above under Article 109. Under the MCCP and the Model Police Powers Act, the right to privacy of an individual has been carefully balanced against these grounds. If a policing official follows these provisions, there will be no violation of the right to privacy; the policing official will possess "lawful authorization." Without lawful authorization to conduct a search of a dwelling or premises, a policing official may be liable for a criminal offense under Article 110.

## *Article 110.2: Penalty*

1. The applicable penalty range for the criminal offense of unauthorized search of a dwelling or premises is one to five years' imprisonment.
2. The court may impose a fine, as a principal penalty, upon a person convicted of unauthorized search of a dwelling or premises.

# Article 111: Unauthorized Visual Recording

## *Article 111.1: Definition of Offense*

1. A person commits the criminal offense of unauthorized visual recording when he or she:
   (a) takes one or more photographs or other visual recordings by technical means of a person or his or her dwelling or private premises;
   (b) without lawful authorization or the consent of the person concerned; and
   (c) by taking a photograph or photographs or other visual recordings unjustifiably interferes with that person's reasonable expectation of privacy.

2. A person also commits a criminal offense of unauthorized visual recording when he or she:
   (a) transmits or presents one or more photographs or other visual recordings by technical means of a person or his or her dwelling or private premises to a third person or otherwise intentionally enables a third person to see such photographs or recordings;
   (b) without lawful authorization or the consent of the person concerned; and
   (c) by transmitting or presenting the photograph or photographs or other visual recordings unjustifiably interferes with that person's reasonable expectation of privacy.

## Commentary

Unauthorized visual recording is criminalized because it represents a substantial and unjustified intrusion into the privacy of an individual, a right that is discussed in the commentary to Article 109. In Article 111, the act criminalized is unjustifiable interference with another person's privacy through the taking of photographs or other visual recordings of a person or his or her premises or at his or her dwelling. Article 111 also criminalizes the related offenses of transmitting or presenting unauthorized photographs or recordings, thereby allowing a third person to see them. The question of whether there has been unjustifiable interference with another person's privacy is one for judicial interpretation. For example, if a person has a particularly high public profile (e.g., a nationally known politician), he or she may have a lesser expectation of privacy than an "ordinary" person. Therefore, what may qualify as an unjustifiable interference in the case of an ordinary person might not qualify in the case of a public figure. Different considerations will also apply in public and private situations; a person obviously has a lesser expectation of privacy when he or she is in public.

Unauthorized visual recording is an offense that may be perpetrated by either a public official or an individual. The use of the term "a lawful authorization" is pertinent to the recording of persons or premises by police officers. Under the MCCP, which deals with covert and other measures of surveillance, visual recording of a person or premises is permissible in certain circumstances. If a police officer is following the provisions of the MCCP, he or she is not unlawfully interfering with a person's privacy.

## *Article 111.2: Penalty*

1. The applicable penalty range for the criminal offense of unauthorized visual recording is one to five years' imprisonment.
2. The court may impose a fine, as an alternative principal penalty, upon a person convicted of unauthorized visual recording.

# Article 112: Violation of the Privacy and Confidentiality of Communications

## *Article 112.1: Definition of Offense*

1. A person commits the criminal offense of violation of the privacy and confidentiality of communications when he or she, without lawful authorization, justification, or the consent of the persons party to the communication:
   (a) by the use of technical means intercepts, eavesdrops, accesses, records, opens, stores, destroys, or otherwise infringes privacy and confidentiality of communications;
   (b) opens a sealed communication or by the use of chemical agents or technical means obtains knowledge of the content of a sealed communication not addressed to him or her;
   (c) transmits or delivers the content of a private or confidential communication to a third person or otherwise intentionally enables a third person to obtain knowledge of the content of such communications.
2. For the purposes of Article 112, communications includes:
   (a) verbal communications;
   (b) letters;
   (c) telegrams;
   (d) facsimiles;
   (e) sealed packages;
   (f) telephone communications; and
   (g) other communications conducted by computer networks and other means of information technology.
3. For the purposes of Article 112, confidentiality and privacy of communications conducted over telephone, computer network, and other means of information technology encompasses:
   (a) the contents of communication; and
   (b) traffic data, including location data.

## Commentary

The violation of the privacy and confidentiality of communications is criminalized because it represents a substantial and unjustified intrusion into the privacy of an individual. The right to privacy is discussed in greater detail above under Article 109.

Chapter 8, Part 3, Section 5, of the MCCP, which deals with covert and other technical measures of surveillance or investigation, limits a person's right to privacy by allowing the interception of communications in certain circumstances. When a policing official follows the provision of the MCCP, this represents a lawful justification as discussed in Article 112. However, if the officer exceeds or does not follow the provisions laid out in the MCCP, this is an unauthorized and unlawful violation of the person's right to privacy and may be prosecuted a criminal offense under Article 112.

Article 112 also applies to individuals other than policing officials.

Paragraph 3: For a discussion of the meaning of traffic data, reference may be made to the Explanatory Report to the Convention on Cybercrime, paragraphs 28–31. Location data is included in the definition of traffic data.

### *Article 112.2: Penalty*

1. The applicable penalty range for the criminal offense of violations of the privacy and confidentiality of communications is one to five years' imprisonment.
2. The court may impose a fine, as an alternative principal penalty, upon a person convicted of violations of the privacy and confidentiality of communications.

## Article 113: Abuse of Personal Data

### *Article 113.1: Definition of Offense*

A person commits the criminal offense of abuse of personal data when he or she without authorization accesses stored personal data for himself or herself or another person, which was not intended for him or her and is protected against unauthorized access.

## Commentary

Abuse of personal data is criminalized because it represents a substantial and unjustified intrusion into the privacy of an individual. The right to privacy is discussed in greater detail above under Article 109. This offense applies to all persons, including public officials and policing officials. Article 113 should be read in light of domestic legislation that regulates the use and access of personal data.

### *Article 113.2: Penalty*

1. The applicable penalty range for the criminal offense of abuse of personal data is one to five years' imprisonment.
2. The court may impose a fine, as an alternative principal penalty, upon a person convicted of abuse of personal data.

# Article 114: Abuse of Personal Secrets

### *Article 114.1: Definition of Offense*

A person commits the criminal offense of abuse of personal secrets when he or she discloses a secret of another person, in particular, a secret that belongs to the realm of personal privacy or a business or trade secret, which was confided to or otherwise made known to him or her in his capacity as a:

(a) doctor, dentist, psychologist, psychiatrist, veterinarian, pharmacist, or member of another medical profession;

(b) lawyer;

(c) marriage or family counselor as well as counselor in matters of addiction;

(d) social worker; or

(e) public official.

### *Article 114.2: Penalty*

1. The applicable penalty range for the criminal offense of abuse of personal secrets is one to five years' imprisonment.

2. The court may impose a fine, as an alternative principal penalty, upon a person convicted of abuse of personal secrets.

# Section 5: Offenses against Children

## General Commentary

Two optional protocols to the Convention on the Rights of the Child have been drafted and have entered into force. They are the Optional Protocol to the Convention on the Rights of the Child on the Involvement of Children in Armed Conflict and the Optional Protocol to the Convention on the Rights of the Child on the Sale of Children, Child Prostitution and Child Pornography. This section of the MCC seeks to implement aspects of the latter protocol, specifically on the criminalization of three offenses: sale of children, child prostitution, and child pornography. The criminalization of these offenses is an international obligation for states parties to the protocol. The Convention on the Rights of the Child also contains an international obligation for states parties to "protect the child from all forms of sexual exploitation and sexual abuse" (Article 34), with specific reference to child prostitution and child pornography. Similar sentiments are expressed in Article 27 of the African Charter on the Rights and Welfare of the Child.

The Optional Protocol to the Convention on the Rights of the Child on the Sale of Children, Child Prostitution and Child Pornography goes into more detail than the Convention on the Rights of the Child or the African Charter on the Rights and Welfare of the Child, providing definitions of offenses and other provisions relating to the investigation and prosecution of these offenses. The definitions in the MCC are taken from the protocol. The protocol provides that the perpetrators, those who are complicit, or those who participate in any of the offenses be prosecuted. Reference should be made to Articles 28–33 of the MCC, which deal with participation in criminal offenses. Furthermore, Article 4 of the protocol provides that jurisdiction be asserted over these offenses when they are committed on the territory of a state, when the alleged offender is a national of the state, or when the victim is a national of the state. These grounds of jurisdiction are covered in Article 4 ("Territorial Jurisdiction") and Article 5 ("Extraterritorial Jurisdiction") of the MCC. Reference should be made to both articles and their accompanying commentaries. Finally, Article 3(4) of the protocol requires states to ensure that, where appropriate, liability over legal persons should be established for these offenses. This provision is covered in the MCC under Article 19 ("Criminal Responsibility of Legal Persons"). Reference should be made to Article 19 and its accompanying commentary.

A state should consider other elements of the protocol when domestically implementing its provisions, including provisions on extradition (Article 5), mutual legal assistance and international cooperation (Articles 6 and 10), seizure and confiscation of goods and proceeds derived from crime (Article 7), and procedural issues in the investigation of these offenses (Article 8). On these issues, reference should be made to the following: Chapter 14, Part 2, of the MCCP on extradition; Chapter 14, Part 1, of the MCCP on international cooperation; Chapter 8, Part 3, Section 4, of the MCCP; Articles 61 and 70–73 of the MCC on seizure of instruments and proceeds of crime; and Chapter 8, Part 4, Section 2, of the MCCP on protection of witnesses and victims. The problems of sale of children, child prostitution, and child pornography, of course, cannot be solved through criminalization measures alone. Strategies and plans beyond the criminal justice system are required. Article 9 of the protocol discusses potential measures of prevention and should be looked at closely by a state wishing to combat these serious offenses.

Reference should also be made to the work of the United Nations Special Rapporteur of the Commission on Human Rights on the Sale of Children, Child Prostitution and Child Pornography. The special rapporteur was appointed in 1990 by the Commission on Human Rights to consider matters relating to the sale of children, child prostitution, and child pornography. The special rapporteur has produced numerous reports and recommendations that should be taken into account by states considering the issue of offenses against children.

# Article 115: Sale of Children

## *Article 115.1: Definition of Offense*

A person commits the criminal offense of sale of children when he or she engages in any act or transaction whereby a child is transferred by any person or group of persons to another person or group of persons for remuneration or any other consideration. The criminal offense of sale of children includes:

(a) the offering, delivering, or accepting, by whatever means, a child for the purpose of sexual exploitation of the child, transfer of organs of the child for profit, or engagement of the child in forced labor; and

(b) improperly inducing consent, as an intermediary, for the adoption of a child in violation of applicable legal instruments on adoption.

## Commentary

The wording of Article 115 is derived from Articles 2(a) and 3(1)(a) of the Optional Protocol to the Convention on the Rights of the Child on the Sale of Children, Child Prostitution and Child Pornography. This provision sets out a number of specific aspects of the sale of children that are common around the world, including the sale of children for sexual exploitation, the sale of children's organs for profit, the sale of children into forced labor, and the improper inducement of consent to adoption of another person's child. This list is merely elaborative and is not exhaustive.

## *Article 115.2: Penalty*

The applicable penalty range for the criminal offense of sale of children is three to fifteen years' imprisonment.

# Article 116: Child Prostitution

## *Article 116.1: Definition of Offense*

1. A person commits the criminal offense of child prostitution when he or she offers, obtains, procures, or provides a child for child prostitution.
2. *Child prostitution* means the use of a child in sexual activities for remuneration or any other form of consideration.

## Commentary

In many states, the issue of child prostitution is dealt with under ordinary legislation relating to prostitution, which often criminalizes the child prostitute. The provision in the MCC on child prostitution does not criminalize the actions of the child, who is in fact an innocent victim. States should reconsider the classification of child prostitutes as criminals and focus more on adults who force children to commit such acts. The MCC penalizes adults who offer, obtain, procure, or provide a child prostitute. The wording of Article 116 is derived from Articles 2(b) and 3(1)(b) of the Optional Protocol to the Convention on the Rights of the Child on the Sale of Children, Child Prostitution and Child Pornography. The definition of child prostitution not only refers to the use of children for the purpose of sexual intercourse but is broader and may cover all sexual activities.

## *Article 116.2: Penalty*

The applicable penalty range for the criminal offense of child prostitution is five to twenty years' imprisonment.

# Article 117: Child Pornography

## *Article 117.1: Definition of Offense*

1. A person commits the criminal offense of child pornography when he or she produces, offers, makes available, distributes, disseminates, transmits, imports, exports, offers, or sells child pornography.
2. The criminal offense of child pornography includes:
   (a) the production of child pornography for the purpose of its distribution through a computer system;
   (b) offering, making available, distributing, disseminating, and transmitting child pornography through a computer system; and
   (c) procuring child pornography through a computer system for oneself or for another person.
3. For the purposes of Article 117:
   (a) *child pornography* means any representation, by whatever means, of a child engaged in real or simulated explicit sexual activities or any representation of the sexual parts of a child for primarily sexual purposes; child pornography includes a person appearing to be a minor engaged in sexually explicit conduct or realistic images representing a child engaged in sexually explicit conduct; and
   (b) *computer system* means any device or group of interconnected or related devices, one or more of which, pursuant to a program, performs automatic processing of data.

## Commentary

In many states, the issue of child pornography is dealt with under ordinary legislation relating to pornography. The issue of pornography is not dealt with under the MCC, except as it relates to child pornography. In a post-conflict state with a shattered criminal justice system, organized gangs are often quick to prey upon young children for the purposes of making child pornography. Child pornography operations have been found in a number of post-conflict states, all of which lack sufficient legislation on child pornography to prosecute the perpetrators of this offense.

Reference should be made to Chapter 8, Part 3, Section 4 of the MCCP, which provide police with the power to search and seize information from computer systems that may be relevant to the investigation of child pornography.

Paragraph 1: The wording of Article 117 is derived from Article 3(1)(c) of the Optional Protocol to the Convention on the Rights of the Child on the Sale of Children, Child Prostitution and Child Pornography.

Paragraph 2: The wording of Paragraph 2 comes from Article 9(1) of the Council of Europe Convention on Cybercrime, and it covers child pornography perpetrated through the medium of computers. For a detailed discussion of the substantive content of these provisions, reference should be made to paragraphs 91–106 of the explanatory report to the Convention on Cybercrime.

Paragraph 3(a): This paragraph comes from Article 2(c) of the Optional Protocol to the Convention on the Rights of the Child on the Sale of Children, Child Prostitution and Child Pornography and Article 9(2) of the Council of Europe Convention on Cybercrime.

Paragraph 3(b): This paragraph is derived from Article 1(a) of the Council of Europe Convention on Cybercrime. For a discussion on the meaning of *computer system*, reference should be made to paragraphs 23–24 of the explanatory report to the Convention on Cybercrime.

## *Article 117.2: Penalty*

The applicable penalty range for the criminal offense of child pornography is three to fifteen years' imprisonment.

# Article 118: Possession of Child Pornography

## *Article 118.1: Definition of Offense*

1. A person commits the criminal offense of possession of child pornography when he or she possesses child pornography.
2. The criminal offense of possession of child pornography includes possessing child pornography in a computer system or on a computer data-storage medium.
3. For the purposes of Article 118:
   (a) *child pornography* means any representation, by whatever means, of a child engaged in real or simulated explicit sexual activities or any representation of the sexual parts of a child for primarily sexual purposes; child pornography includes a person appearing to be a minor engaged in sexually explicit conduct or realistic images representing a child engaged in sexually explicit conduct; and
   (b) *computer system* means any device or group of interconnected or related devices, one or more of which, pursuant to a program, performs automatic processing of data.

## Commentary

The issue of possession of child pornography, in addition to the other child pornography offenses set out in Article 117, is dealt with in Article 3(1)(c) of the Optional Protocol to the Convention on the Rights of the Child on the Sale of Children, Child Prostitution and Child Pornography. Possession of child pornography has been placed in a separate provision because it is subject to a different penalty range than offenses that involve the making or distribution of child pornography—offenses that were considered more serious by the drafters of the MCC and consequently are subject to a higher penalty range.

Paragraph 2: The wording of Paragraph 2 comes from Article 9(1) of the Council of Europe Convention on Cybercrime, and it covers child pornography that is perpetrated through the medium of computers. For a detailed discussion of the substantive content of these provisions, reference should be made to paragraphs 91–106 of the explanatory report to the Convention on Cybercrime.

Paragraph 3(a): This paragraph comes from Article 2(c) of the Optional Protocol to the Convention on the Rights of the Child on the Sale of Children, Child Prostitution and Child Pornography and Article 9(2) of the Council of Europe Convention on Cybercrime.

Paragraph 3(b): This paragraph comes from Article 1(a) of the Council of Europe Convention on Cybercrime. For a discussion on the meaning of *computer system*, reference should be made to paragraphs 23–24 of the explanatory report to the Convention on Cybercrime.

## *Article 118.2: Penalty*

The applicable penalty range for the criminal offense of possession of child pornography is one to five years' imprisonment.

# Section 6: Property Offenses

## General Commentary

This section contains property offenses, the majority of which are contained in almost all states, although with varying classifications and some variety in the elements of the criminal offenses. The section was drafted after a comparative survey of penal codes from a variety of legal traditions.

## Article 119: Theft

### *Article 119.1: Definition of Offense*

1. A person commits the criminal offense of theft when he or she unlawfully appropriates property belonging to another, with the intention of depriving the other person of it.
2. For the purpose of Article 119, *property* means:
   (a) movable property, whether tangible or intangible; and
   (b) immovable, intangible property.

## Commentary

Paragraph 1: The offense of theft is often defined as larceny in many penal codes, but the two terms are synonymous. In some systems, primarily those using the old common law doctrine on larceny, the intention element required is the intention to *permanently* deprive a person of his or her property, meaning that something like taking a car for the purpose of joyriding is not considered theft. This intention element has not been followed in the MCC. Thus joyriding could fall within the scope of theft under Article 119. Otherwise, a separate offense of joyriding, theft of a motor vehicle, or taking a motor vehicle without consent would have to be included in the penal code.

Paragraph 2: The definition of property contained in Article 1(8) of the MCC does not apply to the criminal offense of theft under Article 119. This is because the definition in Article 1(8) is too broad for the purposes of theft and many of the other property-related offenses contained in Section 6. As is general practice in many states around the world, property offenses do not apply to certain types of property, for example, immovable property. A definition of property that is specific to the criminal offenses of theft, robbery, aggravated robbery, receiving and concealing stolen goods, extortion, bringing into the state property obtained through crime, fraud, and criminal damage has been drafted and integrated into these provisions. Reference should be made to the commentary to Paragraphs 2(a) and 2(b).

Paragraph 2(a): Movable property is property that is capable of being moved or displaced. Tangible property is property that is detectable with the senses, such as a painting or jewelry, as opposed to intangible property that cannot be detected with the senses. Paintings and jewelry are both tangible and movable and are capable of being objects of theft. Intangible objects that are movable also fall under the definition of property. Examples include light, heat, and electricity. Some definitions of theft in domestic laws do not cover intangible movable property but create a separate offense dealing with actions similar to theft of intangible movable property. Instead of drafting two separate offenses, the drafters of the MCC combined both such offenses into the offense of theft.

Paragraph 2(b): The general rule in most systems is that immovable property—for example, land and buildings—cannot be the subject of theft, except where something forming part of the land is severed from it and unlawfully appropriated, thereby being converted from immovable to movable property (for example, when an apple is plucked from a tree on a property, it becomes movable property, and thus the act of removal falls under the ambit of theft). An exception to this general rule is contained in Article 119.1(2)(b), where the immovable property is intangible. In this case, it is included under the definition of property for the purpose of the criminal offense of theft. An example of intangible, immovable property is credit in a bank account or claims to property, which can be the subject of theft under the MCC.

Another exception to the general rule that is often integrated into legislation on the noninclusion of tangible, immovable property in the offense of theft is where a trustee or personal representative with power to sell or transfer tangible, immovable property, such as land, appropriates the property in breach of trust or other duties. Drafters of the offense of theft may wish to consider including this exception in new legislation. It has not been included in the MCC. Alternatively, drafters could consider a separate criminal offense of abuse of authorization or breach of trust with the intent to acquire property for oneself or a third party. This offense would have to be drafted in light of the laws on trusts and personal representation in the state concerned.

## *Article 119.2: Penalty*

1. The applicable penalty range for the criminal offense of theft is one to five years' imprisonment.
2. The applicable penalty range for the criminal offense of theft is two to ten years' imprisonment when the theft is of property of high value.
3. The court may impose a fine, as an alternative principal penalty, upon a person convicted of theft where the applicable penalty range is one to five years' imprisonment.

### Commentary

Paragraph 2: When deciding upon an appropriate penalty range for the criminal offense of theft, the drafters thought it was preferable to provide two different ranges, depending on the value of the goods stolen. Ordinarily, domestic legislation would include a defined amount, above which a person would be liable for a higher penalty range. The drafters of the MCC did not include a defined amount of money to differentiate between the applicable penalty ranges for theft. Instead, the term *high value* was used to differentiate between the applicable penalty ranges. If a state incorporates this provision into its criminal legislation, it should define *high value* in terms of its domestic currency.

# Article 120: Robbery and Aggravated Robbery

## *Article 120.1: Definition of Offense*

1. A person commits the criminal offense of robbery when he or she commits theft by force or threat of force.
2. A person commits the criminal offense of aggravated robbery when he or she:
   (a) commits any robbery in company with one or more other persons; or
   (b) commits any robbery and at the time has a firearm, an imitation firearm, or an offensive weapon with him or her.

3. For the purposes of Article 120:

   (a) *firearm* means any portable barreled weapon that expels, is designed to expel, or may be readily converted to expel a shot, bullet, or projectile by the action of an explosive;

   (b) *imitation firearm* means any object that has the appearance of a firearm and that could reasonably be mistaken for a firearm; and

   (c) *offensive weapon* means:

      (i) any article that has a blade or sharp point; or

      (ii) any other article made or adapted for causing injury to or incapacitating a person, or intended by the person having it with him or her for such use or for threatening such use.

## Commentary

Paragraph 1 and Paragraph 2: Reference should be made to the elements of the criminal offense of theft in Article 119 and its accompanying commentary as the elements of theft will need to be proven for a person to be convicted of robbery or aggravated robbery.

Paragraph 3: The definition of firearm has been taken from Article 3(a) of the Protocol against the Illicit Manufacturing of and Trafficking in Firearms, Their Parts and Components and Ammunition, supplementing the United Nations Convention against Transnational Organized Crime (2001). The two definitions contained in Paragraphs (b) and (c) were sourced from domestic legislation on aggravated robbery.

## *Article 120.2: Penalty*

1. The applicable penalty range for the criminal offense of robbery is two to ten years' imprisonment.
2. The applicable penalty range for the criminal offense of aggravated robbery is three to fifteen years' imprisonment.

# Article 121: Extortion

## *Article 121.1: Definition of Offense*

A person commits the criminal offense of extortion when he or she:

(a) with the intention of making an unlawful material gain for himself or herself or another person;

(b) by use of force or threat of serious harm;

(c) compels a person to do or refrain from doing an act to the detriment of his or her property or the property of another person.

### Commentary

Extortion is a common crime problem in many post-conflict societies (e.g., Nepal and Kosovo). Extortion may be used during a conflict to fund conflict-related activities. It is also often used both during and after conflict by organized criminal gangs, who seek to extort money from business owners or other persons believed to be holding wealth.

## *Article 121.2: Penalty*

1. The applicable penalty range for the criminal offense of extortion is one to five years' imprisonment.
2. The applicable penalty range for the criminal offense of extortion is two to ten years' imprisonment when the extortion relates to property of high value.
3. The court may impose a fine, as an alternative principal penalty, upon a person convicted of extortion where the applicable penalty range is one to five years' of imprisonment.

### Commentary

Paragraph 2: When deciding upon an appropriate penalty range for the criminal offense of extortion, the drafters thought it was preferable to provide two different ranges, depending on the value of the goods subject to the act of extortion. Ordinarily, domestic legislation would include a defined amount, above which a person would be liable for a higher penalty range. The drafters of the MCC did not define a particular amount of money, opting instead to use the term *high value* to differentiate between the applicable penalty ranges If a state incorporates this provision into its criminal legislation, it should define *high value* in terms of its domestic currency.

# Article 122: Burglary

## *Article 122.1: Definition of Offense*

A person commits the criminal offense of burglary when he or she:

(a) enters any building, or part of a building, without consent of the owner or lawful justification and with intent to commit a criminal offense; or

(b) being present in any building, or part of a building, commits a criminal offense.

### Commentary

In some states, the offense of burglary is defined as grand larceny.

It is worth noting that, under Paragraph (b) it is not necessary that the perpetrator entered the building, or part of the building, unlawfully or nonconsensually, as is necessary under Paragraph (a). Instead, it is sufficient that the perpetrator committed a criminal offense while lawfully or unlawfully in any building or part of a building. In Paragraph (a), the required elements include the intention to commit a criminal offense and unlawful or nonconsensual entry into a building or part of a building. There is no need in this case to prove the commission of a criminal offense.

Vehicles that are inhabitable (e.g., caravans, vessels [e.g., boats]) or other inhabited temporary movable structures may fall under the definition of building.

## *Article 122.2: Penalty*

The applicable penalty range for the criminal offense of burglary is two to ten years' imprisonment.

# Article 123: Aggravated Burglary

## *Article 123.1: Definition of Offense*

1. A person commits the criminal offense of aggravated burglary when he or she commits burglary, in circumstances where the perpetrator has a firearm, an imitation firearm, or an offensive weapon with him or her at the time.
2. For the purposes of Article 123:
   (a) *firearm* has the same meaning as in Article 120.1(3)(a);
   (b) *imitation firearm* has the same meaning as in Article 120.1(3)(b); and
   (c) *offensive weapon* has the same meaning as in Article 120.1(3)(c).

### Commentary

Paragraph 1: Reference should be made to Article 122 on burglary and its accompanying commentary.

Paragraph 2: Reference should be made to Article 120.1(3) and its accompanying commentary.

## *Article 123.2: Penalty*

The applicable penalty range for the criminal offense of aggravated burglary is three to fifteen years' imprisonment.

# Article 124: Receiving and Concealing Stolen Goods

## *Article 124.1: Definition of Offense*

1. A person commits the criminal offense of receiving or concealing stolen goods when he or she receives or conceals stolen property or property

obtained through fraud, knowing or believing the property to be stolen or obtained by fraud.

2. For the purposes of Article 124:

   (a) *property* has the same meaning as in Article 119.1(2); and

   (b) *fraud* has the same meaning as in Article 126.1(1).

## Commentary

Reference should be made to Article 126 on fraud and Article 119.1(2) on the definition of property for the purpose of property offenses. Property is considered stolen when it was taken by way of theft, robbery, aggravated robbery, or extortion. Reference should be made to Articles 119 and 120.

### *Article 124.2: Penalty*

1. The applicable penalty range for the criminal offense of receiving and concealing stolen goods is two to ten years' imprisonment.
2. The court may impose a fine, as an alternative principal penalty, upon a person convicted of receiving and concealing stolen goods.

# Article 125: Bringing into the State Property Obtained through Crime

### *Article 125.1: Definition of Offense*

1. A person commits the criminal offense of bringing into the state property obtained through crime when he or she brings into or has in the state anything that he or she has obtained outside the state by an act that would have been a criminal offense if it had been committed in the state.
2. For the purposes of Article 125, *property* has the same meaning as in Article 119.1(2).

## Commentary

While this offense is oftentimes contained in the penal codes of states, the importance of including this criminal offense in the MCC, and the penal codes of post-conflict states, was insisted upon by practitioners who had experience in the peace operation in Kosovo, where there was an influx of stolen cars from surrounding states.

Reference should be made to Article 119.1(2) on the definition of property for the purpose of property offenses.

### *Article 125.2: Penalty*

1. The applicable penalty range for the criminal offense of bringing into the state property obtained through crime is two to ten years' imprisonment.
2. The court may impose a fine, as an alternative principal penalty, upon a person convicted of bringing into the state property obtained through crime.

# Article 126: Fraud

### *Article 126.1: Definition of Offense*

1. A person commits the criminal offense of fraud when he or she:
   (a) with the intention of making an unlawful material gain for himself or herself or another, or of causing loss to another;
   (b) induces another person by deception;
   (c) to do or refrain from doing an act to the detriment of his or her property or the property of another.
2. For the purposes of Article 126, *property* has the same meaning as in Article 119.1(2).

## Commentary

In some states, the criminal offense of fraud requires that the perpetrator obtain the property of the other person through deception, with the added element of intention to permanently deprive the person of his or her property. In other states, fraud requires the total relinquishment of the victim's property to the perpetrator. The approach taken in the MCC is somewhat wider in that it requires only that the victim act or refrain from doing an act to the detriment of property, whether belonging to him or her or someone else.

Reference should be made to Article 119.1(2) on the definition of property for the purpose of property offenses.

## *Article 126.2: Penalty*

1. The applicable penalty range for the criminal offense of fraud is one to five years' imprisonment.
2. The applicable penalty range for the criminal offense of fraud is two to ten years' imprisonment when the fraud relates to property of high value.
3. The court may impose a fine, as an alternative principal penalty, upon a person convicted of fraud where the applicable penalty range is one to five years.

### Commentary

Paragraph 2: When deciding upon an appropriate penalty range for the criminal offense of fraud, the drafters thought it was preferable to provide two different ranges, depending on the value of the goods subject to the act of fraud. Ordinarily, domestic legislation would include a defined amount, above which a person would be liable for a higher penalty range. The drafters of the MCC did not include a defined amount of money to differentiate between the applicable penalty ranges for fraud. Instead, the term *high value* was used to differentiate between the applicable penalty ranges. If a state incorporates this provision into its criminal legislation, it should define *high value* in terms of its domestic currency.

# Article 127: Embezzlement of Property

## *Article 127.1: Definition of Offense*

1. A person commits the criminal offense of embezzlement of property when he or she:
   (a) being a person who directs or works, in any capacity, in a private-sector entity;
   (b) in the course of economic, financial, or commercial activities;

(c) embezzles property, private funds, or securities or any other thing of value entrusted to him or her by virtue of his or her position.

2. For the purposes of Article 127, *property* has the same meaning as in Article 1(8).

## Commentary

Paragraph 1: The criminal offense of embezzlement involves the theft of property by a person who is entrusted to look after or manage this property. The wording of this section is taken from Article 22 of the United Nations Convention against Corruption. The offense of embezzlement by a public official is also contained in the MCC. Reference should be made to Article 142.

Paragraph 2: The definition of property for the purposes of embezzlement is different from the definition used for some of the other offenses in this section of the MCC because the sort of property that can be embezzled is historically much wider than the sort of property that is subject to other property offenses, such as theft. For a further discussion on the meaning of *property* for the purpose of the criminal offense of embezzlement, reference should be made to Article 1(8) and its accompanying commentary.

# *Article 127.2: Penalty*

1. The applicable penalty range for the criminal offense of embezzlement is one to five years' imprisonment.
2. The applicable penalty range for the criminal offense of embezzlement is two to ten years' imprisonment when the embezzlement relates to property of high value.

## Commentary

Paragraph 2: When deciding upon an appropriate penalty range for the criminal offense of embezzlement, the drafters thought it was preferable to provide two different ranges, depending on the value of the goods embezzled. Ordinarily, domestic legislation would include a defined amount, above which a person would be liable for a higher penalty range. The drafters of the MCC did not include a defined amount of money to differentiate between the applicable penalty ranges for embezzlement. Instead, the term *high value* was used to differentiate between the applicable penalty ranges. If a state incorporates this provision into its criminal legislation, it should define *high value* in terms of its domestic currency.

# Article 128: Forgery

## *Article 128.1: Definition of Offense*

1. A person commits the criminal offense of forgery when he or she:
   (a) makes a false instrument with the intention that he or she or another will use it to induce another to accept it as genuine; and
   (b) by reason of so accepting it, to obtain a gain or cause a loss.
2. For the purposes of Article 128, *instrument* means any document, of an informal or formal character, excluding counterfeit money as defined in Article 134.1(2), and includes but is not limited to any:
   (a) disc, tape, soundtrack, or other device on or in which information is recorded or stored by mechanical, electronic, or other means;
   (b) money orders;
   (c) postage stamps;
   (d) official licenses or stamps issued by [insert name of state];
   (e) checks, including traveler's checks and bank drafts;
   (f) credit cards, debit cards, or other charge cards;
   (g) share certificates; and
   (h) passports or other documents that can be used instead of a passport.

## Commentary

In interpreting the meaning of *false* under Article 128.1(1)(a), the following definition of false instrument may be helpful: An instrument may be considered false for the purpose of this provision if it purports: (a) to have been made in the form in which it is made by a person who did not in fact make it in that form; (b) to have been made in the form in which it is made on the authority of a person who did not in fact authorize its making in that form; (c) to have been made in the terms in which it is made by a person who did not in fact make it in those terms; (d) to have been made in the terms in which it is made on the authority of a person who did not in fact authorize its making in those terms; (e) to have been altered in any respect by a person who did not in fact alter it in that respect; (f) to have been altered in any respect on the authority of a person who did not in fact authorize the alteration in that respect; (g) to have been made or altered on a date on which, or at a place at which, or otherwise in circumstances in which, it was not in fact made or altered; or (h) to have been made or altered by an existing person where that person did not in fact exist. In relation to the making of a false instrument, a person should be treated as making a false instrument if he or she alters an instrument so as to make it false in any respect (whether or not it is false in some other respect apart from that alteration).

The making of money as a false instrument is excluded by the provisions of Article 128.1(2). This offense is covered in Article 134 ("Counterfeiting of Money"). Reference should be made to Article 134 and its accompanying commentary.

Where the making of false instruments is done as part of organized criminal activity, which is common in many post-conflict states, this factor may be taken into account in the determination of an appropriate penalty. See Article 44 ("Augmentation of the Maximum Period of Imprisonment When a Criminal Offense Is Committed as Part of Organized Criminal Activity"). The accused may also be charged with participation in an organized criminal gang under Article 136.

Paragraph 2: The list of instruments contained in Paragraph 2 is illustrative and not exhaustive.

### *Article 128.2: Penalty*

1. The applicable penalty range for the criminal offense of forgery is two to ten years' imprisonment.
2. The court may impose a fine, as an alternative principal penalty, upon a person convicted of forgery.

## Article 129: Using False Instruments

### *Article 129.1: Definition of Offense*

1. A person commits the criminal offense of using false instruments when he or she uses a false instrument, knowing that it is false:
   (a) with the intention to induce another to accept it as genuine; and
   (b) by reason of so accepting it, to obtain a gain or cause a loss.
2. For the purposes of Article 129, *instrument* has the same meaning as in Article 128.1(2).

## Commentary

Reference should be made to the commentary accompanying Article 128, above.

### *Article 129.2: Penalty*

1. The applicable penalty range for the criminal offense of using false instruments is two to ten years' imprisonment.
2. The court may impose a fine, as an alternative principal penalty, upon a person convicted of using false instruments.

# Article 130: Possessing False Instruments

### *Article 130.1: Definition of Offense*

1. A person commits the criminal offense of possession of false instruments when he or she has in his or her possession a false instrument, knowing that it is false:
   (a) with the intention that that person or another will use it to induce another to accept it as genuine; and
   (b) by reason of so accepting it, to obtain a gain or cause a loss.
2. For the purposes of Article 130, *instrument* has the same meaning as in Article 128.1(2).

## Commentary

Reference should be made to the commentary accompanying Article 128, above.

### *Article 130.2: Penalty*

1. The applicable penalty range for the criminal offense of possessing false instruments is one to five years' imprisonment.
2. The court may impose a fine, as an alternative principal penalty, upon a person convicted of possessing false instruments.

# Article 131: Arson

## *Article 131.1: Definition of Offense*

1. A person commits the criminal offense of arson when he or she starts a fire or causes an explosion with the purpose of destroying a building or occupied structure of another person.
2. For the purposes of Article 131, *occupied structure* means any structure, vehicle, or place adapted for overnight accommodation of persons, or for carrying on business, whether or not a person is actually present.

### Commentary

In some states the criminal offense of arson is treated as a form of aggravated criminal damage. A definition of criminal damage is provided in Article 133 of the MCC. Definitions of aggravated criminal damage involve damage to property through fire, coupled with the intention of the perpetrator to endanger life or to be reckless in endangering life. Some other states include the endangerment of bodily safety as well as endangerment to life as aggravating features in the definition of criminal damage. Under the legislation of these states, aggravated criminal damage can be committed against all types of tangible property. Another approach is to define arson as an offense that can be committed against all types of property and where the focus of the provision is on the endangerment of life.

Instead of following the above approaches, the drafters of the MCC decided to draft a criminal offense based on the traditional definition of arson and another accompanying provision on recklessly burning or exploding. In Article 131, on arson, the focus of the criminal offense is on the destruction of a building or occupied structure by a person wishing to destroy that building or structure. Traditionally, arson could be committed only on a building or occupied structure. In addition, the requisite intention for the criminal offense of arson was not to endanger life but instead to destroy the building or occupied structure. A further offense of recklessly burning or exploding is contained under Article 132. Article 132 focuses more on the danger to life, body, and property and does not require the intention to destroy the building or occupied structure. Reference should be made to Article 132 and its accompanying commentary.

The criminal offense of arson has been prevalent in post-conflict states, particularly after interethnic conflicts. After a conflict, certain ethnic groups have been punished, or retribution has been sought, through the commission of arson.

Paragraph 2: Instead of listing the different types of buildings and structures that may be the subject of arson, the drafters decided to include a broad definition that focuses on buildings or structures used for the purpose of either habitation or business.

## *Article 131.2: Penalty*

The applicable penalty range for the criminal offense of arson is three to fifteen years' imprisonment.

# Article 132: Reckless Burning or Exploding

## *Article 132.1: Definition of Offense*

1. A person commits the criminal offense of reckless burning or exploding when he or she intentionally starts a fire or causes an explosion, whether on his or her own property or on another's, and thereby recklessly:
   (a) places another person in danger of death or bodily injury; or
   (b) places a building or occupied structure of another person in danger of damage or destruction.
2. For the purposes of Article 132, *occupied structure* has the same meaning as in Article 131.1(2).

### Commentary

Unlike the criminal offense of arson under Article 131, the criminal offense of reckless burning or exploding does not require the intention to destroy the building or occupied structure. It focuses more on the danger to life, body, or property.

Damage to property is quite common in the aftermath of interethnic conflict. Members of one ethnic group may damage the homes of the members of a different group with the intention, not of destroying the homes, but of scaring their residents into leaving the area. Such conduct falls under the criminal offense not of arson but of reckless burning or exploding.

Paragraph 2: Reference should be made to the commentary to Article 131.1(2).

## *Article 132.2: Penalty*

The applicable penalty range for the criminal offense of reckless burning or exploding is two to ten years' imprisonment.

# Article 133: Criminal Damage

## *Article 133.1: Definition of Offense*

1. A person commits the criminal offense of criminal damage when he or she unlawfully destroys or damages any property belonging to another.
2. For the purposes of Article 133, *property* means tangible property, whether movable or immovable.

### Commentary

Paragraph 1: The level of damage or destruction required to prosecute a person for criminal damage is ordinarily more than nominal damage, but it does not have to be irreversible damage.

Paragraph 2: Reference should be made to the commentary to Article 119.1(2), which discusses movable, immovable, and tangible property. In contrast to the definition of property under Article 119 ("Theft"), which precludes the theft of immovable tangible property, the offense of criminal damage can be committed against tangible, immovable property (e.g., land and buildings), as well as tangible, movable property (e.g., personal items). Therefore, acts such as spraying graffiti on the walls of buildings or damaging the land of another (e.g., by dumping garbage that costs a lot to remove) would be included under the criminal offense of criminal damage.

## *Article 133.2: Penalty*

1. The applicable penalty range for the criminal offense of criminal damage is one to five years' imprisonment.
2. The applicable penalty range for the criminal offense of criminal damage is two to ten years' imprisonment when the criminal damage relates to property of high value.

3. The court may impose a fine, as a principal penalty, upon a person convicted of criminal damage where the applicable penalty range is one to five years' imprisonment.

## Commentary

Paragraph 2: When deciding upon an appropriate penalty range for the criminal offense of criminal damage, the drafters thought it was preferable to provide two different ranges, depending on the value of the goods damaged. Ordinarily, domestic legislation would include a defined amount, above which a person would be liable for a higher penalty range. The drafters of the MCC did not include a defined amount of money to differentiate between the applicable penalty ranges for criminal damage. Instead, the term *high value* was used to differentiate between the applicable penalty ranges. If a state incorporates this provision into its criminal legislation, it should define *high value* in terms of its domestic currency.

# Section 7:
# Economic Offenses

## Article 134: Counterfeiting Money

### *Article 134.1: Definition of Offense*

1. A person commits the criminal offense of counterfeiting money when he or she:
   (a) makes counterfeit money;
   (b) buys, receives, or offers to buy or receive counterfeit money;
   (c) has in his or her custody or possession counterfeit money;
   (d) introduces counterfeit money into the state;
   (e) uses or deals with counterfeit money;
   (f) sells counterfeit money; or
   (g) passes or circulates counterfeit money as legal tender or puts it forth upon the market.
2. For the purposes of Article 134, counterfeit money includes:
   (a) a false coin or false paper money that resembles or is apparently intended to resemble or pass for a current coin or current paper money;
   (b) a forged banknote or forged blank banknote, whether complete or incomplete;
   (c) a genuine coin or genuine paper money that is prepared or altered to resemble or pass for a current coin or current paper money of a higher denomination;

(d) a current coin from which the milling is removed by filing or cutting the edges and on which new milling is made to restore its appearance;

(e) a coin cased with gold, silver, nickel, or another metal that is intended to resemble or pass for a current gold, silver, nickel, or other metal coin; and

(f) a coin or a piece of metal or mixed metals that is washed or colored by any means with a wash or material capable of producing the appearance of gold, silver, or another metal and that is intended to resemble or pass for a current gold, silver, or other metal coin.

## Commentary

The counterfeiting of money in post-conflict states is often perpetrated. In some cases, this situation has necessitated a total change in the currency used in the state to prevent the use of large quantities of counterfeit money. Article 134 covers the making of both domestic and foreign counterfeit money.

# *Article 134.2: Penalty*

1. The applicable penalty range for the criminal offense of counterfeiting money is one to five years' imprisonment.
2. The applicable penalty range for the criminal offense of counterfeiting money is two to ten years' imprisonment when the counterfeiting is of an amount of high value.
3. The court may impose a fine, as an alternative principal penalty, upon a person convicted of counterfeiting money where the applicable penalty range is one to five years' imprisonment.

## Commentary

Paragraph 2: When deciding upon an appropriate penalty range for the criminal offense of counterfeiting money, the drafters thought it was preferable to provide two different ranges, depending on the value of the money counterfeited. Ordinarily, domestic legislation would include a defined amount, above which a person would be liable for a higher penalty range. The drafters of the MCC did not include a defined amount of money to differentiate between the applicable penalty ranges for the criminal offense of counterfeiting money. Instead, the term *high value* was used to differentiate between the applicable penalty ranges. If a state incorporates this provision into its criminal legislation, it should define *high value* in terms of its domestic currency.

# Article 135: Money Laundering

## *Article 135.1: Definition of Offense*

1. A person commits the criminal offense of money laundering when he or she:
   (a) converts or transfers property, knowing that such property is the proceeds of crime, for the purpose of concealing or disguising the illicit origin of the property;
   (b) conceals or disguises the true nature, source, location, disposition, movement, ownership of, or rights with respect to property, knowing that such property is the proceeds of crime; or
   (c) acquires, possesses, or uses property, knowing at the time of receipt that such property is the proceeds of crime.
2. An offense under Paragraph 1 is also established when a person was reckless or negligent to the origins of the proceeds of crime.
3. For the purposes of Article 135:
   (a) *proceeds of crime* means any economic advantage derived from or obtained, directly or indirectly, from predicate offenses. It may consist of any property defined in Article 135(2)(b);
   (b) *property* has the same meaning as in Article 1(8); and
   (c) *predicate offense* means any criminal offense committed under the MCC or the applicable law and includes offenses committed both inside and outside the jurisdiction of [insert name of state].

## Commentary

The criminal offense of money laundering seeks to penalize individuals who, having made gains from criminal activity, take measures—normally through a series of complex financial transactions—to make the money "clean" again and ready for use without raising the suspicion of the authorities. This is done through converting, transferring, concealing, or disguising the money. Money laundering is very closely linked to the activities of organized criminal groups. It is for this reason that the United Nations Convention against Transnational Organized Crime (Article 7) imposes an obligation on states parties to criminalize money laundering. A similar obligation is contained in the United Nations Convention against Illicit Traffic in Narcotic Drugs and Psychotropic Substances (1988), Article 3(b), and the Council of

Europe Convention on Laundering, Search, Seizure and Confiscation of the Proceeds of Crime and the Financing of Terrorism, Article 9.

The obligations contained in the United Nations Convention against Transnational Organized Crime go beyond criminalization and require states parties to take other measures to combat money laundering (Article 7), such as instituting comprehensive domestic regulatory and supervisory regimes for banks and nonbank financial institutions; ensuring that bodies tasked with combating money laundering can cooperate and exchange information at a domestic and international level; establishment of a financial intelligence unit to serve as a national center for the collection, analysis, and dissemination of information regarding potential money laundering; and the monitoring and detection of the movement of cash and appropriate negotiable instruments across borders. Similar obligations are contained in the Council of Europe Convention on Laundering, Search, Seizure and Confiscation of the Proceeds of Crime. A full discussion of these obligations is outside the scope of this commentary. Reference should be made to the *Legislative Guide to the United Nations Convention against Transnational Organized Crime and the Protocols Thereto* and the explanatory report to the Council of Europe Convention on Laundering, Search, Seizure and Confiscation of the Proceeds of Crime. The United Nations Office on Drugs and Crime runs the Global Program against Money Laundering. The program has produced several publications, including *An Overview of the UN Conventions and the International Standards Concerning Anti-Money Laundering Legislation*. It has also produced model money laundering legislation for common-law countries. The Commonwealth Organization has produced the Commonwealth Model Law for the Prohibition of Money Laundering and Supporting Documentation. In the fight against money laundering, leading international organizations have established the International Money Laundering Information Network. Government employees around the world can access the network, which includes an international database, reference documents, national legislation, and various model laws.

Reference should also be made to the Financial Action Task Force, an intergovernmental body whose purpose is to develop and promote national and international policies to combat money laundering and the financing of terrorism. The Asian Development Bank has produced an extensive publication entitled *Manual on Countering Money Laundering and the Financing of Terrorism*. The World Bank has a Web site devoted to combating money laundering and terrorism. Finally, the Egmont Group runs an informal network of international financial intelligence units that cooperate and share information, training, and expertise. This network would be useful for a state wishing to establish a financial intelligence unit to combat money laundering.

In addition to prevention measures and the criminalization of money laundering, many post-conflict states have established special anti–money laundering police units to work in a dedicated manner on money laundering, often in concert with a financial intelligence unit.

Paragraph 1(a): The wording of Paragraph 1(a) is based on Article 6(1)(a)(i) of the United Nations Convention against Transnational Organized Crime.

According to the *Legislative Guide to the United Nations Convention against Transnational Organized Crime and the Protocols Thereto* (page 44), states must take legislative and other measures to establish money laundering as a criminal offense. The guide further states that the term *conversion or transfer* includes instances in which financial assets are converted from one form or type to another, for example, by using illicitly generated cash to purchase real estate or by the sale of illicitly acquired real estate, as well as instances in which assets are moved from one place or jurisdiction to another or from one bank account to another (paragraph 100). The *Interpretative Notes for the Official Records of the Negotiation of the United Nations Convention against Transnational Organized Crime and the Protocols Thereto* (UN document A/55/383/Add.1) states in paragraph 11 that "concealing or disguising" should be understood to include preventing the discovery of the illicit origins of property. Under Paragraph 1(a), the person who does the actual conversion or transfer, with the intention of concealing property that represents the proceeds of crime, may be held criminally responsible, as may any other person who helps the perpetrator of a criminal offense evade the consequences of his or her action by converting, disguising, or transferring the property.

Article 6(b)(ii) of the convention requires that the following grounds of criminal liability be included in domestic criminal legislation: participation, association with or conspiracy to commit, attempt, aiding and abetting, facilitation, and counseling. All these grounds of liability are covered in Section 10 ("Criminal Attempt") and Section 11 ("Participation in a Criminal Offense") of the General Part of the MCC. The term *counseling* is not used in the MCC, although it is subsumed in Article 29. Reference should be made to the commentary accompanying Article 29. The term *association* is covered in Article 28, "Participation in a Common Purpose."

**Paragraph 1(b):** The wording of Paragraph 1(b) comes from Article 6(1)(a)(ii) of the United Nations Convention against Transnational Organized Crime. Similar language is used in Article 9(1)(b) of the Council of Europe Convention on Laundering, Search, Seizure and Confiscation of the Proceeds of Crime. The *Legislative Guide to the United Nations Convention against Transnational Organized Crime and the Protocols Thereto* (paragraph 105) points out that "the elements of this offense are quite broad, including the concealment and disguise of almost any aspect of or information about property." It further states that the mental element required for proving a criminal offense under Paragraph 1(b) is less stringent than that required under Paragraph 1(a), as the former requires no need to prove that the purpose of the concealment or disguise is to frustrate the tracing of an asset or conceal its true origin (paragraph 106). The *Interpretative Notes for the Official Records of the Negotiation of the United Nations Convention against Transnational Organized Crime and the Protocols Thereto* (UN document A/55/383/Add.1) states in paragraph 11 that "concealing or disguising" should be understood to include preventing the discovery of the illicit origins of property.

**Paragraph 1(c):** The wording of Paragraph 1(c) comes from Article 6(1)(a)(ii) of the United Nations Convention against Transnational Organized Crime. Similar language is used in Article 9(1)(b) of Council of Europe Convention on Laundering, Search, Seizure and Confiscation of the Proceeds of Crime. Article 6(1)(a)(ij) of the United Nations Convention against Transnational Organized Crime (which is mirrored in

Paragraph 1[c]) criminalizes the recipient of the laundered property who acquires, possesses, or uses it. It further states that the requisite mental element that needs to be proven is less than that required in Paragraph 1(b). All that needs to be proven is the acquisition, possession, and use of property where the recipient knew at the time that the property represented the proceeds of crime.

Paragraph 2: This paragraph expands the potential scope of liability under Article 135 to situations where a person converts, transfers, conceals, disguises, acquires, possesses, or uses property that is the proceeds of crime, where the person knew or should have known that the property was the proceeds of crime. This is a requirement of the Council of Europe Convention on Laundering, Search, Seizure and Confiscation of the Proceeds of Crime and the Financing of Terrorism (Article 9[3]). The wording used in Paragraph 2 is *reckless or negligent.* Reference should be made to Article 18, which discusses the scope and meaning of the terms *recklessness* and *negligence.*

Paragraph 3(a): This definition was taken from Article 1(a) of the Council of Europe Convention on Laundering, Search, Seizure and Confiscation of the Proceeds from Crime and on the Financing of Terrorism. The United Nations Convention against Transnational Organized Crime, Article 2(e), and the United Nations Convention against Corruption, Article 1(e), also define proceeds of crime, although more narrowly. The definition in both United Nations conventions refers only to property derived from crime, rather than "any economic advantage," wording contained in the Council of Europe convention. The Council of Europe definition and the MCC definition both include property but go much further. The explanatory report to the Council of Europe Convention on Laundering, Search, Seizure and Confiscation of the Proceeds from Crime and on the Financing of Terrorism states, at paragraph 31, that "the definition of 'proceeds' was intended to be as broad as possible."

Paragraph 3(b): Reference should be made to Article 1(8) of the MCC, which defines property, and its accompanying commentary.

Paragraph 3(c): The definition of predicate offense is an original definition. The term *predicate offense* means the underlying offense that generated the proceeds of crime that were then laundered. Article 6(2)(a) of the United Nations Convention against Transnational Organized Crime urges states parties to apply the criminal offense of money laundering to "the widest range of predicate offenses" and at a minimum to "include ... a comprehensive range of offenses associated with organized criminal groups." In some states there are a limited number of predicate offenses for money laundering. This means that only the laundering of proceeds for certain serious criminal offenses, such as drug trafficking, trafficking in persons, and migrant smuggling, could be prosecuted. Under the MCC, there is no limitation on the predicate offenses in connection with which money laundering can take place. Paragraph 3(c) covers all the offenses under the MCC and under domestic criminal law in an effort to cast a wide net around those persons involved in money laundering and to comply with the convention.

It is important to note that a person may be determined to have perpetrated the criminal offense of money laundering even if the predicate offense has not been previously proven with a final conviction or judgment.

## *Article 135.2: Penalty*

The applicable penalty range for the criminal offense of money laundering is three to fifteen years' imprisonment.

# Section 8: Organized Crime Offenses

## General Commentary

The offenses contained in Section 8 derive from the United Nations Convention against Transnational Organized Crime and its additional protocol, the Protocol against the Smuggling of Migrants by Land, Sea, and Air. There are two more protocols to the convention, one relating to firearms (Protocol against Illicit Manufacturing of and Trafficking in Firearms, Their Parts and Components and Ammunition) and the other on trafficking in persons (Protocol to Prevent, Suppress and Punish Trafficking in Persons, Especially Women and Children). The former is contained in Section 13 of the MCC Special Part, "Offenses Involving Firearms, Ammunition, Explosives, and Weapons." The latter is contained in Section 4, "Offenses against the Rights of Persons."

## Article 136: Participation in an Organized Criminal Group

### *Article 136.1: Definition of Offense*

1. A person commits the criminal offense of participation in an organized criminal group when he or she, with knowledge of either the aim and general criminal activity of an organized criminal group or its intention to commit the criminal offenses in question, takes an active part in:

   (a) criminal activities of the organized criminal group; or

   (b) other activities of the organized criminal group in the knowledge that his or her participation will contribute to the achievement of the above-described criminal aim.

2. The knowledge, intent, aim, purpose, or agreement referred to in Paragraph 1 may be inferred from objective factual circumstances.
3. For the purposes of Article 136:
   (a) *organized criminal group* means a structured group of three or more persons, existing for a period of time and acting in concert with the aim of committing one or more criminal offense under the MCC or the applicable law, in order to obtain, directly or indirectly, a financial or other material benefit;
   (b) *structured group* means a group that is not randomly formed for the immediate commission of a criminal offense and that does not need to have formally defined roles for its members, continuity of its membership, or a developed structure; and
   (c) *property* has the same meaning as in Article 1(8).

## Commentary

Paragraph 1: Organized crime, perpetrated through organized criminal groups, is often deeply entrenched in post-conflict societies. This is not surprising since much of the "war economy" during a conflict is based on organized crime activities, such as weapons and gasoline trafficking and trafficking in goods, diamonds, or other resources. Additionally, in the absence of a functioning government during the conflict, organized criminal groups or parties to the conflict often fill the vacuum of authority and perform traditional government services, such as "authorizing" the opening of businesses and providing funding mechanisms for public utilities and amenities. After a conflict, it is common for organized criminal groups and the former parties to the conflict to continue their organized criminal activities, sometimes changing the focus of their activities, for example, from weapons trafficking to trafficking in persons. Most post-conflict states have had to grapple with the problem of organized crime. In Kosovo organized crime was a huge problem right from the outset of the peace operation, exacerbated by the fact that the applicable law did not provide for organized crime offenses. In 2001 UNMIK promulgated UNMIK Regulation 2001/22 on Measures against Organized Crime. Many other peace operations around the world have faced or are facing similar problems. A good primer on organized crime in the context of peace operations, the reasons behind its existence, difficulties experienced in post-conflict environments, and potential solutions and strategies may be found in *Organized Crime as an Obstacle to Successful Peacebuilding*, a publication of Zentrum fur Internationale Friedenseinsatze (ZIF). Reference could also be made to *Combating Serious Crimes in Postconflict Environments: A Handbook for Policymakers and Practitioners*, edited by Colette Rausch and published by the United States Institute of Peace Press.

Organized crime does not exclusively affect post-conflict states. On the contrary, it is widespread in non–post-conflict states also. International efforts have been under way for several years to tackle organized crime in both a domestic context and a transnational context. In 2002 the United Nations Convention against Transnational Organized Crime was promulgated. It sought to "promote cooperation to prevent and combat transnational organized crime more effectively" (Article 1). The convention contains some provisions on the prevention of organized crime (Article 31); however, for the most part the focus is on the criminalization, prosecution, and adjudication of organized crime offenses. The convention deals with a wide range of issues, including which offenses should be implemented into domestic law (Article 5); which offenses related to corruption and closely tied to organized crime—namely, corruption, obstruction of justice, and money laundering (Articles 6, 7, 8, and 23)—should also be criminalized; confiscation and disposal of proceeds of crime (Articles 12–14); investigative techniques that should be employed in relation to organized crime (Article 20); witness-protection measures (Article 24); mutual legal assistance (Article 18); and extradition of alleged perpetrators of organized crime (Article 16). The latter three issues are dealt with in greater detail in the substance and commentaries to the MCCP, which deals with the procedural aspects of prosecuting organized crime as opposed to the substantive criminal aspects, which are dealt with in the MCC. Reference should be made to Chapter 14, Parts 1 and 2, and Chapter 8, Part 4, Section 1, of the MCCP. General reference should be made to the *Legislative Guide to the United Nations Convention against Transnational Organized Crime and the Protocols Thereto.* Reference should also be made to the Council of Europe Octopus Programme report, *Combating Organized Crime: Best Practice Surveys of the Council of Europe.*

It is worth noting that many post-conflict states have established specialized anti–organized crime units of the domestic police force to deal exclusively with organized crime.

The first step in tackling organized crime from a substantive criminal law perspective is to ensure that the sorts of offenses perpetrated by organized criminal groups are contained in domestic legislation. In post-conflict states in particular, many of these offenses, particularly newer offenses, are absent from legislation. In surveying the penal codes of post-conflict states in the course of drafting the MCC, it was apparent that offenses such as money laundering, trafficking in persons, trafficking in drugs, smuggling in persons, and corruption were not adequately provided for. Definitions of these offenses are contained in the MCC and can be drawn upon for inspiration when the authorities in a post-conflict state seek to criminalize these offenses.

As stated in the *Legislative Guide to the United Nations Convention against Transnational Organized Crime and the Protocols Thereto* (page 19), in relation to the perpetration of the offenses committed by organized criminals,

> frequently, people assist organized criminal groups in the planning and execution of serious offenses without direct participation in the commission of the criminal act. In response to this problem, many countries have adopted criminal laws proscribing lesser participation in criminal groups. The approaches countries have adopted so far vary depending on historical, political, and legal backgrounds. ... Common law countries have used the offense of conspiracy, while civil law jurisdictions have used offenses that proscribe an involvement in criminal organizations. ... The Convention does not deal with prohibition of membership in specific organizations.

Instead, it criminalizes participation in the activities of criminal groups, another criminal offense that must be added to domestic criminal law to effectively combat organized crime. Article 136 incorporates this offense into the MCC.

The wording of Article 136 is taken from Article 5(1)(a)(ii) of the United Nations Convention against Transnational Organized Crime. Article 5 of the convention sets out two offenses, either or both of which should be implemented into domestic law. The first offense is akin to a conspiracy offense and has not been included in the MCC, as conspiracy is not contained herein as a ground of criminal liability. The second offense has been included, however. It involves the offense of criminal association, where a person takes part in the criminal activities of an organized criminal group, or takes part in other activities of the group, in the knowledge that his or her participation will contribute to the achievement of the criminal aim. The *Legislative Guide to the United Nations Convention against Transnational Organized Crime* states, with regard to "other activities" as provided for in this article, that "[t]hese other activities may not constitute crimes, but they perform a supportive function for the group's criminal activities and goals" (page 24). Elaborating on the elements of the crime of participation in an organized criminal group, the guide further states that "the mental element of the activity in question would also apply. For instance, active participation in kidnapping or obstruction of justice would require the mental element for those offenses. In the case of taking part in non-criminal but supportive activities, an additional requirement is that of knowledge that such involvement will contribute to the achievement of a criminal aim of the group. . . . [In relation to the offense], the knowledge, intent, aim, purpose or agreement referred to above may be inferred from objective factual criteria" (paragraphs 62–65).

Article 5(1)(b) of the convention requires that a person who organizes, directs, aids, abets, facilitates, or counsels the commission of a serious crime involving an organized criminal group also be penalized. These grounds of criminal responsibility are covered in Section 11 of the General Part of the MCC. Reference should be made to Articles 29–32 and their accompanying commentaries. The convention requires that legal persons be liable for the offense set out in Article 136. This requirement is addressed in Article 19 of the General Part of the MCC. Reference should be made to this article and its accompanying commentary.

In Article 15, the convention sets out mandatory grounds of jurisdiction for the offense of participation in an organized criminal group. Jurisdiction must be asserted when the offense is committed in the territory of the state, on board an aircraft registered in that state, on board a vessel flying the flag of that state, or by a national of that state. These grounds are covered by Article 4 ("Territorial Jurisdiction") and Article 5 ("Extraterritorial Jurisdiction") of the General Part of the MCC. The discretionary grounds of jurisdiction in the convention require states to consider asserting jurisdiction where the offense is committed by or against a national of the state or by a stateless person who has his or her habitual residence in its territory; where the offense is committed outside the territory with a view to the commission of a serious crime within the territory (serious crime is defined in Article 1[b] of the convention as an offense that is punishable with at least four years of deprivation of liberty); or where a money laundering offense is committed outside the territory with a view to the commission of an organized crime offense. The first discretionary ground of jurisdiction is contained in the MCC under Article 5. Reference should be made to Article 5 ("Extraterritorial Jurisdiction") and its accompanying commentary.

Paragraph 2: The wording of this paragraph is taken from Article 5(2) of the United Nations Convention against Transnational Organized Crime.

Paragraph 3(a): The wording of this paragraph is taken from Article 1(a) of the United Nations Convention against Transnational Organized Crime.

Paragraph 3(b): The wording of this paragraph is taken from Article 1(c) of the United Nations Convention against Transnational Organized Crime.

Paragraph 3(c): Reference should be made to Article 1(8) of the MCC, which defines property, and its accompanying commentary.

## *Article 136.2: Penalty*

The applicable penalty range for the criminal offense of participation in an organized criminal group is three to fifteen years' imprisonment.

# Article 137: Offenses Related to the Smuggling of Migrants

## *Article 137.1: Definition of Offense*

1. A person commits the criminal offense of smuggling of migrants when he or she:
   (a) procures the illegal entry of a person into the state when the person is not a national or permanent resident of the state;
   (b) in order to obtain, directly or indirectly, a financial or other material benefit.
2. A person commits the criminal offense of producing a fraudulent travel or identity document for a smuggled person when he or she:
   (a) in order to obtain, directly or indirectly, a financial or other material benefit;
   (b) for the purpose of enabling the smuggling of migrants;

(c) produces a fraudulent travel or identity document for a smuggled person.

3. A person commits the criminal offense of procuring, providing, or possessing a fraudulent travel or identity document for a smuggled person when he or she:

   (a) in order to obtain, directly or indirectly, a financial or other material benefit;

   (b) for the purpose of enabling the smuggling of migrants;

   (c) procures, provides, or possesses a fraudulent travel or identity document for a smuggled person.

4. A person commits the criminal offense of enabling illegal residence when he or she:

   (a) in order to obtain, directly or indirectly, a financial or other material benefit;

   (b) enables a person who is not a national or a permanent resident to remain in the state without complying with the necessary requirements for legally remaining in the state by:

      (i) producing a fraudulent travel or identity document for a smuggled person;

      (ii) procuring, providing, or possessing a fraudulent travel or identity document for a smuggled person; or

      (iii) any other illegal means.

5. For the purposes of Article 137:

   (a) *illegal entry* means crossing borders without complying with the necessary requirements for legal entry into the receiving state;

   (b) *fraudulent travel or identity document* means any travel or identity document:

      (i) that has been falsely made or altered in some material way by anyone other than a person or agency lawfully authorized to make or issue the travel or identity document on behalf of a state;

      (ii) that has been improperly issued or obtained through misrepresentation, corruption, or duress or in any other unlawful manner; or

      (iii) that is being used by a person other than the rightful holder.

6. A person is not criminally responsible under Article 137 if he or she is a migrant who is the object of the criminal offense provided for in this article.

## Commentary

Migrant smuggling has become a global business, generating huge profits (estimated at between $3.5 billion and $10 billion annually) for the organized criminal gangs that typically perpetrate it (see the Eleventh United Nations Congress on Crime Prevention and Criminal Justice, *Effective Measures to Combat Transnational Organized Crime: Working Paper Prepared by the Secretariat*, UN document A/CONF.2003/4, paragraph 14). Post-conflict states are a prime market for organized criminals involved in migrant smuggling. In many of these states, smugglers have seized upon the fact that people are willing to pay to escape the violence and poor living conditions that characterize post-conflict societies.

The criminal offense of migrant smuggling targets those persons who run smuggling operations. It does not target the persons who are smuggled, although those persons may be liable to sanctions (e.g., for unlawful border crossing) under other provisions of the criminal law or under migration law. The definitions of the criminal offenses contained in Article 137 come from the Protocol against the Smuggling of Migrants by Land, Sea and Air, supplementing the United Nations Convention against Transnational Organized Crime (Article 6). The protocol requires states parties to introduce legislation criminalizing smuggling and other related offenses, all of which are contained in Article 137, above. Migrant smuggling is a relatively recent phenomenon. Consequently, a survey of the criminal legislation of post-conflict states, and indeed of non–post-conflict states, found that this offense was rarely if ever included in domestic law. A post-conflict state should consider including the offenses contained in the MCC and the protocol in order to combat organized criminal activity of this sort.

The protocol contains other provisions on cooperation between states (Article 7); measures against the smuggling of migrants by sea (Articles 8 and 9); and prevention, cooperation, and other measures against smuggling (Articles 10–18), including border measures (Article 11), security and control of documents (Article 12), and migrant protection and assistance (Article 16). For a detailed discussion on how to implement these noncriminal aspects of the protocol into domestic law, reference should be made to the *Legislative Guide to the United Nations Convention against Transnational Organized Crime and the Protocols Thereto.* Under Article 1 of the protocol, the provisions of the Convention against Transnational Organized Crime apply, unless otherwise provided for in the protocol. Reference should therefore be made to the commentary to Article 136, which discusses the obligations under the convention.

Prevention is the cornerstone of any antismuggling policy. The protocol includes many prevention measures, but at the core of the problem of smuggling are economic disparities between states, the reduction of which should be looked at as a core prevention method (see the Eleventh United Nations Congress on Crime Prevention and Criminal Justice, *Effective Measures to Combat Transnational Organized Crime: Working Paper Prepared by the Secretariat*, UN document A/CONF.2003/4, paragraph 18). In addition, public information or awareness campaigns are needed in a post-conflict state or any state wishing to combat smuggling in persons. Persons should be made aware both of the dangers of smuggling and of available legal mechanisms for migration (paragraph 18).

Before discussing the particular offenses contained in Article 137, it is worth discussing in brief the distinction between migrant smuggling and trafficking in persons (Article 102 of the MCC). Both acts are covered by protocols additional to the United Nations Convention against Transnational Organized Crime. Both acts also involve the transport of persons between states. However, this is where the similarities end. People who are smuggled are smuggled through their own free will. In fact, they usually pay the smuggler to smuggle them. Trafficking involves coercive, deceptive, or abusive means. Trafficked persons are treated as victims and consequently are afforded certain rights under the Protocol to Prevent, Suppress and Punish Trafficking in Persons, Especially Women and Children (reference should be made to the commentary accompanying Article 102). In addition, trafficked persons are transported "for the purpose of exploitation." This is not a constituent element of the criminal offense of migrant smuggling, although smuggled persons often end up being exploited once they reach their final destinations.

Paragraph 1: The wording of Paragraph 1 is taken from Article 3(a) of the Protocol against the Smuggling of Migrants by Land, Sea and Air, supplementing the United Nations Convention against Transnational Organized Crime. The *Interpretative Notes for the Official Records of the Negotiation of the United Nations Convention against Transnational Organized Crime and the Protocols Thereto* (paragraph 92) states that the offense "targets those who smuggle others for gain and is not directed at those who procure their own illegal entry or the entry of another where there is no gain made." In the latter case, the notes state in paragraph 92 that "the activities of those who provided support to migrants for humanitarian reasons or on the basis of close family ties" are excluded from the scope of the criminal offense of migrant smuggling.

Entry is usually procured by bringing migrants over the border in hiding and without a declaration to the border police or agents or through the use of forged or falsified travel or identity documents (an act that is itself an offense under Article 128 of the MCC). In cases where a migrant's documents are valid but are used improperly (e.g., where a tourist visa is obtained but the migrant stays in the state beyond its expiration), as the *Legislative Guide to the United Nations Convention against Transnational Organized Crime and the Protocols Thereto* points out (page 342), this is a separate offense—an offense laid out in Paragraph 4 of Article 137. The *Interpretative Notes for the Official Records of the Negotiation of the United Nations Convention against Transnational Organized Crime and the Protocols Thereto* also states, at paragraph 112, that a "permanent resident" is one who has "longer term but not necessarily indefinite residence." It states at paragraph 94 that "any other illegal means" refers to illegal means as defined under domestic law. Finally, the *Legislative Guide to the United Nations Convention against Transnational Organized Crime and the Protocols Thereto*, at page 342, states that to be found criminally responsible for migrant smuggling, "there must have been some primary intention to procure illegal entry and there must have been a second intention, that of obtaining a financial or other material benefit."

For this, and for the other smuggling-related offenses, Article 6(2) of the protocol provides that attempts to commit any of the offenses; participation as an accomplice, in relation only to the offenses contained in Articles 137.1(1), 137.1(2), and 137.1(4); and organizing or directing migrant smuggling or related offenses be criminalized in domestic legislation. In the MCC, these obligations are covered under Articles 27, 29, and 31. Reference should be made to the relevant articles and their accompanying commentaries.

Paragraph 2: The wording of Paragraph 2 is taken from Article 6(1)(b)(i) of the Protocol against the Smuggling of Migrants by Land, Sea and Air, supplementing the United Nations Convention against Transnational Organized Crime. The intention element in this criminal offense is to produce a fraudulent travel or identity document, with the added intention of obtaining a financial or other material benefit. Coupled with this situation, the perpetrator of the offense must produce the fraudulent travel or identity document for the purpose of enabling the smuggling of migrants (see the *Legislative Guide to the United Nations Convention against Transnational Organized Crime and the Protocols Thereto*, page 344). If this intention element cannot be proven, the person is not criminally liable under this paragraph. Instead, he or she may be liable for forgery under Article 128.

Paragraph 3: The wording of Paragraph 3 is taken from Article 6(1)(b)(ii) of the Protocol against the Smuggling of Migrants by Land, Sea and Air, supplementing the United Nations Convention against Transnational Organized Crime. The intention element is the same as in Paragraph 2. The *Interpretative Notes for the Official Records of the Negotiation of the United Nations Convention against Transnational Organized Crime and the Protocols Thereto* (paragraph 93) states that this offense "was adopted on the understanding that … [it] would only apply when the possession was for the purpose of smuggling migrants. … Thus, a migrant who possessed a fraudulent document to enable his or her own smuggling would not be included" (paragraph 93).

Paragraph 4: The wording of Paragraph 4 is taken from Article 6(1)(c) of the Protocol against the Smuggling of Migrants by Land, Sea and Air, supplementing the United Nations Convention against Transnational Organized Crime. The *Legislative Guide to the United Nations Convention against Transnational Organized Crime and the Protocols Thereto* provides that "the intention in establishing this offense was to include cases where the smuggling scheme itself consisted of procuring the entry of migrants using legal means, such as the issuance of visitors' permits or visas, but then resorting to illegal means to enable them to remain for reasons other than those used for entry or beyond the length of time covered by their permits or authorizations to enter" (page 343). The *Interpretative Notes for the Official Records of the Negotiation of the United Nations Convention against Transnational Organized Crime and the Protocols Thereto* states, at paragraph 94, that any other illegal means refers to illegal means as defined under domestic law. Finally, the *Legislative Guide to the United Nations Convention against Transnational Organized Crime and the Protocols Thereto*, at page 343, states that to be found criminally responsible for the kinds of offenses set out here under Article 137.1(4), "there must have been the intention to commit whatever act is alleged as having enabled illegal residence and the further intent or purpose of obtaining some financial or other material benefit."

Paragraph 5(a): The wording of Paragraph 5(a) is taken from Article 3(b) of the Protocol against the Smuggling of Migrants by Land, Sea and Air, supplementing the United Nations Convention against Transnational Organized Crime. The state will need other pieces of legislation (e.g., migration laws) to determine whether the entry was legal or illegal.

Paragraph 5(b): The wording of Paragraph 5(b) is taken from Article 3(c) of the Protocol against the Smuggling of Migrants by Land, Sea and Air, supplementing the United Nations Convention against Transnational Organized Crime. The *Interpretative Notes for the Official Records of the Negotiation of the United Nations Convention against Transnational Organized Crime and the Protocols Thereto* states, at paragraph 89, that travel documents include any type of document required for entering or leaving a state under its domestic law and that identity documents include any document commonly used to establish the identity of a person in a state under the laws or procedures of that state. It further states, at paragraph 90, that *falsely made or altered* should be interpreted as including not only the creation of false documents but also the alteration of legitimate documents and the filling in of stolen blank documents and should include both documents that have been forged and genuine documents that had been validly issued but were used by a person other than the lawful holder. Further reference should be made to paragraph 42 of the *Legislative Guide to the United Nations Convention against Transnational Organized Crime and the Protocols Thereto*, which discusses the definition of fraudulent travel or identity documents in greater detail.

Paragraph 6: The wording of Paragraph 6 is taken from Article 5 of the Protocol against the Smuggling of Migrants by Land, Sea and Air, supplementing the United Nations Convention against Transnational Organized Crime. This paragraph underscores a point made in the commentaries above: the offense of migrant smuggling targets smugglers and does not target smuggled persons. A smuggled person may be liable for other sanctions under domestic migration law or criminal law. For example, a smuggled person may be liable for possession of a false instrument under Article 130 of the MCC or for unauthorized border crossing under Article 162.

## *Article 137.2: Penalty*

1. The applicable penalty range for offenses related to the smuggling of migrants is two to ten years' imprisonment.
2. The applicable penalty range for offenses related to the smuggling of migrants is three to fifteen years' imprisonment where the offense related to the smuggling of migrants:
   (a) endangered or was likely to endanger the lives or safety of the migrants concerned; or
   (b) entailed inhuman or degrading treatment, including exploitation of such migrants.

## Commentary

Paragraph 2: Article 6(3) of the Protocol against the Smuggling of Migrants by Land, Sea and Air, supplementing the United Nations Convention against Transnational Organized Crime, requires that states include the circumstances set out in Paragraph 2 as aggravating circumstances in domestic legislation. The *Legislative Guide to the United Nations Convention against Transnational Organized Crime and the Protocols Thereto* (page 346) states that "the fundamental obligation [of states parties] is to ensure that, where the aggravating circumstances are present, offenders are subject to at least the risk of harsher punishments." Hence, in the MCC, the presence of these aggravating factors means the applicable penalty range is increased from two to ten years' to three to fifteen years' imprisonment. Reference should be made to the *Legislative Guide to the United Nations Convention against Transnational Organized Crime and the Protocols Thereto* (pages 346–347).

# Section 9: Corruption Offenses

## General Commentary

Corruption has proven a major challenge in many post-conflict states. In many such states, corruption was an endemic practice before and during the conflict and persists when hostilities have officially ended. It often has links with trafficking, smuggling in persons, and organized crime. Corruption frequently involves criminals seeking to ensure impunity from prosecution by bribing criminal justice actors. Other acts of corruption by government officials divert public funds or foreign aid intended to benefit the local population, and thus help to undermine public confidence in state institutions. Corruption in procurement of government contracts for post-conflict reconstruction is also a serious issue. In a statement to the General Assembly on the adoption of the United Nations Convention against Corruption (the statement was subsequently included as the foreword to the convention), the United Nations secretary-general highlighted the hugely destabilizing effects of corruption in a society: "Corruption hurts the poor disproportionately—by diverting funds intended for development, undermining a government's ability to provide basic services, feeding inequality and injustice and discouraging foreign investment and aid." The secretary-general added that "corruption is an insidious plague that has a wide range of corrosive effects on societies. It undermines democracy and the rule of law, leads to violations of human rights, distorts markets, erodes the quality of life and allows organized crime, terrorism and other threats to human security to flourish."

A significant number of international conventions deal with corruption. These include the following regional conventions: the European Union Convention on the Fight against Corruption Involving Officials of the European Communities or Officials of Member States of the European Union; the South African Development Community Protocol against Corruption; the African Union Convention on Preventing and Combating Corruption; the Council of Europe Criminal Law Convention on Corruption; the Council of Europe Civil Law Convention on Corruption; the Inter-American Convention against Corruption; and the Organization for Economic Cooperation and Development Convention on Combating Bribery of Foreign Public Officials in International Business Transactions. Two United Nations conventions, the United Nations Convention against Corruption and the United Nations Convention against Transnational Organized Crime, also deal with corruption.

A stand-alone criminal law provision is insufficient to tackle this mammoth problem, although it is a valuable starting point and one that is required by both the United Nations Convention against Corruption (chapter 3) and the United Nations Convention against Transnational Organized Crime (Article 8). Both conventions, the former in particular, contain a comprehensive range of measures and strategies aimed at preventing and criminalizing corruption. A full discussion of these prevention strategies is beyond the scope of the MCC, but such strategies are integral to the successful combating of corruption and should be addressed as a matter of urgency in a post-conflict state, simultaneously with criminal law reform. A short synopsis of these prevention strategies, in addition to some useful reference materials, is provided below.

Chapter 1 of the United Nations Convention against Corruption addresses measures to prevent corruption. It requires that states develop preventive anticorruption policies and practices (Article 5) and that preventive, independent anticorruption bodies be set up to implement and oversee anticorruption policies and to increase and disseminate knowledge about anticorruption measures (Article 6). Furthermore, states are urged to strengthen systems for recruitment, hiring, retention, promotion, and retirement of civil servants and other nonelected public officials (Article 7) and to introduce codes of conduct for public officials with reference to the United Nations International Code of Conduct for Public Officials (Article 8). States parties are also obliged to establish transparent and competitive public procurement systems (Article 9) and to take measures to enhance transparency in public administration (Article 10). In the judiciary and the prosecutorial sphere, states are obliged to take measures to strengthen judicial integrity and to prevent opportunities for corruption (Article 11). With regard to the private sector, Article 12 of the convention contains numerous other preventive measures. Chapter 4 of the convention concerns international cooperation. Reference should be made to Chapter 14, Part 1, of the MCCP and its accompanying commentaries. Chapter 4 also contains provisions on the need for special techniques to investigate corruption. Reference should be made to Chapter 8, Part 3, Section 5, of the MCCP and its accompanying commentaries. Meanwhile, Chapter 5 deals with asset recovery, an issue addressed previously in the MCC under Articles 70–73. Chapter 6 contains provisions on training (Article 60) and the collection of information on corruption (Article 61). Article 60 also deals with technical assistance and mentions the role of the United Nations Office on Drugs and Crime (UNODC) in this respect. Because of its obligations under the convention, UNODC operates numerous technical assistance projects in developing countries. It also has created a number of useful tools, including the *Anti-Corruption Toolkit*, the *Anti-Corruption Resource Guide*, the *Compendium of International Legal Instruments on Corruption*, and the *United Nations Guide for Anti-Corruption Policies. Legislative Guides for the Implementation of the United Nations Convention against Corruption* was published in 2006, and (as of April 2007) the *United Nations Handbook on Practical Anti-Corruption Measures for Prosecutors and Investigators* is forthcoming. Corruption, as it relates to organized crime, is also discussed in the *Legislative Guide to the United Nations Convention against Transnational Organized Crime and the Protocols Thereto* and its *Anti-Corruption Resource Guide.* Another useful resource is the World Bank Web site (www1.worldbank.org), which contains, for example, diagnostic tool kits on corruption and other valuable publications.

The Council of Europe Octopus Programme has published *Anti-corruption Services: Good Practice in Europe*, which provides a conceptual framework for setting up anticorruption services, an assessment of Council of Europe experience to date, and profiles of anticorruption services in Europe. Recourse may also be had to the Council of Europe's Resolution (97)24 on the Twenty Guiding Principles for the Fight against Corruption. General reference should also be made to the Web sites of the anticorruption division of the Organization for Economic Cooperation and Development (www.anticorruptionnet.org) and Transparency International (www.transparency.org). Transparency International, which produces annual global corruption reports, has produced a useful publication entitled *The Corruption Fighter's Toolkit* and has developed International Minimum Standards for Public Procurement.

The MCC deals exclusively with the criminalization of corruption, as opposed to the other measures discussed above. Chapter 3 of the United Nations Convention against Corruption requires states parties to implement a number of corruption offenses: bribery of national public officials (Article 15); bribery of foreign public officials and officials of public international organizations (Article 16); embezzlement, misappropriation, and other diversion of property by a public official (Article 17); trading in influence (Article 18); abuse of function (Article 19); illicit enrichment (Article 20); bribery in the private sector (Article 21); and embezzlement of property in the private sector (Article 22). The convention also contains a number of related offenses, namely, laundering of proceeds of crime (Article 23); concealment (Article 24); and obstruction of justice (Article 25). All the corruption offenses are contained in the Special Part of the MCC, although not all are in Section 9. The MCC or the MCCP deal with many other obligations in chapter 3, such as the need for witness protection measures, an issue dealt with under Chapter 8, Part 4, Section 1, of the MCCP, and the requirement that states parties assert liability of legal persons, addressed in Article 19 of the MCC.

It is noteworthy that the offenses contained in the United Nations Convention against Corruption all involve discrete acts of corruption. The *Draft United Nations Handbook on Practical Anti-Corruption Measures for Prosecutors and Investigators* states that "there is no comprehensive, universally accepted definition of corruption.... Attempts to develop a more precise definition invariably encounter legal, criminological and in many countries, political problems. When the negotiation of the United Nations Convention against Corruption began in 2002, one option under consideration was to avoid the problem of defining corruption by simply listing a whole series of specific types or acts of corruption. After much discussion, 'corruption' was not defined at all, but repeated examples of what is covered by the expression appear throughout the text [of the convention]" (page 23). The same approach has been adopted in the MCC.

# Article 138: Corruption Involving a Public Official

## *Article 138.1: Definition of Offense*

1. A person commits the criminal offense of corruption involving a public official when he or she:
   (a) promises, offers, or gives to a public official, directly or indirectly, an undue benefit, for the public official himself or herself or another person or entity, in order that the public official act or refrain from acting in the exercise of his or her official duties; or
   (b) being a public official, solicits or accepts, directly or indirectly, an undue advantage, for himself or herself or another person or entity, in order that the official act or refrain from acting in the exercise of his or her official duties.
2. It is no defense to prosecution under Article 138 that a person whom the perpetrator sought to influence was not qualified to act in the desired way, because he or she had not yet assumed office or lacked jurisdiction, or for any other reason.

## Commentary

Paragraph 1(a): The offense contained in Article 138.1(1)(a) covers acts that are ordinarily labeled corruption or bribery. The wording is taken from Article 15(a) of the United Nations Convention against Corruption, which requires states to implement the criminal offense of bribery of national public officials into domestic law. Article 15(a) replicates the wording contained in Article 8(1)(a) of the United Nations Convention against Transnational Organized Crime. Similar wording is found in Article 2 of the Council of Europe Criminal Law Convention on Corruption.

The offense covers "active corruption," meaning giving an undue advantage to public officials. The *Legislative Guide to the United Nations Convention against Transnational Organized Crime and the Protocols Thereto* states, at page 83, that

> the required elements of this offense are those of promising, offering or actually giving something to a public official. The offense must cover instances where it is not a gift of something tangible that is offered .... The undue advantage does not have to be given immediately or directly to a public official of the State. It may be promised, offered or given directly or indirectly. A gift, concession or other advantage may be given to some other

> person, such as a relative or political organization. The undue advantage or bribe must be linked to the official's duties. The required mental element for this offense is that the conduct must be intentional. In addition, some link must be established between the offer or advantage and inducing the official to act or refrain from acting in the course of his or her official duties.

As mentioned in the legislative guide, the undue advantage given to a public official can be many things, such as cash, shares, sexual favors, or employment. The explanatory report to the Council of Europe Criminal Law Convention on Corruption (paragraph 37) states that "the undue advantages given are usually of an economic nature but may also be of a non-material nature. What is important is that the perpetrator (or any other person, for instance a relative) is placed in a better position than he was before the commission of the offense and that he is not entitled to the benefit." The explanatory report (paragraph 36) also provides that "'promising' may, for example, cover situations where the briber commits himself to give an undue advantage later. ... 'Offering' may cover situations where the briber shows his readiness to give the undue advantage at any moment. ... Finally, 'giving' may cover situations where the briber transfers the undue advantage."

Reference should be made to Article 1(9) of the MCC, for the definition of public official, and its accompanying commentary.

Paragraph 1(b): This paragraph covers "passive corruption," meaning the acceptance of any undue advantage by a public official. The wording is taken from Article 15(b) of the United Nations Convention against Corruption, which replicates the wording contained in Article 8(1)(b) of the United Nations Convention against Transnational Organized Crime. Similar wording is found in Article 3 of the Council of Europe Criminal Law Convention on Corruption.

The *Legislative Guide to the United Nations Convention against Transnational Organized Crime and the Protocols Thereto*, at page 83, states that "the required elements are soliciting or accepting the bribe. The link with the influence of official conduct must also be established. As with [active corruption] the undue advantage may be for the official or some other person or entity. The solicitation or acceptance must be by the public official or through an intermediary, that is, directly or indirectly. The mental element is only that of intending to solicit or accept the undue advantage for the purpose of altering one's conduct in the course of official duties." Many issues discussed in the commentary to Paragraph 1(a) also relate to Paragraph 1(b). The explanatory report to the Council of Europe Criminal Law Convention on Corruption (paragraphs 41–42) states that "'requesting' may for example refer to a unilateral act whereby the public official lets another person know, explicitly or implicitly, that he will have to 'pay' to have some official act done or abstained from. . . . 'Receiving' may for example mean the actual taking the benefit, whether by the public official himself or by someone else ... for himself or for someone else." The explanatory report (paragraph 43) further highlights the fact that "if there is a unilateral request or a corrupt pact, it is essential that the act or omission of acting by the public official takes place after the request or the pact, whereas it is immaterial in such a case at what point in time the undue advantage is actually received. Thus, it is not a criminal offense ... to receive a benefit after the act has been performed by the public official, without prior offer, request or acceptance."

Paragraph 2: This paragraph is not contained in the United Nations Convention against Corruption but is included in the MCC to underscore that the important element of corruption is that the public official acted or refrained from acting in the manner that the person offering the undue advantage wished.

## *Article 138.2: Penalty*

The applicable penalty range for the criminal offense of corruption involving a public official is three to fifteen years' imprisonment.

# Article 139: Corruption Involving a Foreign Public Official or an Official of a Public International Organization

## *Article 139.1: Definition of Offense*

1. A person commits the criminal offense of corruption involving a foreign public official or an official of a public international organization when he or she:
   (a) promises, offers, or gives to a foreign public official or an official of a public international organization, directly or indirectly, an undue benefit, for the official himself or herself or another person or entity, in order that the official act or refrain from acting in the exercise of his or her official duties, in order to obtain or retain business or other undue advantage in relation to the conduct of international business; or
   (b) being a foreign public official or an official of a public international organization, solicits or accepts, directly or indirectly, an undue advantage, for himself or herself or another person or entity, in order that the official act or refrain from acting in the exercise of his or her official duties.
2. It is no defense to prosecution under Article 139 that a person whom the perpetrator sought to influence was not qualified to act in the desired way, because he or she had not yet assumed office or lacked jurisdiction, or for any other reason.

3. For the purposes of Article 139:

   (a) *foreign public official* means a person who holds a legislative, executive, administrative, or judicial office of a foreign state, whether appointed or elected, and any person exercising a public function for a foreign state, including for a public agency or public enterprise; and

   (b) *official of a public international organization* means an international civil servant or any other person who is authorized by such an organization to act on behalf of that organization.

## Commentary

The recent trend in international conventions on corruption is to apply laws on corruption not only to domestic officials but also to foreign public officials. On the offense of corruption involving foreign public officials, the explanatory report to the Council of Europe Criminal Law Convention on Corruption (paragraphs 47–48) states that

> corruption not only undermines good governance and destroys public trust in the fairness and impartiality of public administrations but it may also seriously distort competition and endanger economic development when foreign public officials are bribed, e.g., by corporations to obtain business. ... The protected legal interest is twofold in the case of this offense: transparency and fairness of the decision-making process of foreign public administrations—this was traditionally considered a domestic affair but the globalization has made this consideration obsolete—and the protection of fair competition in businesses. The criminalization of corrupt behavior occurring outside national territories finds its justification in the common interests of States to protect these interests.

In relation to bribery of officials of a public international organization, the explanatory report at paragraph 57 states that "the need to criminalize bribery is even greater in the case of officials of a public international organization than in the case of foreign public officials. ... The protected legal interest in general is the transparency and impartiality of the decision-making process of public international organizations, which, according to their specific mandate, carry out activities on behalf or in the interest of their member States. Some of these organizations do handle large quantities of goods and services."

Paragraph 1(a): The wording of Paragraph 1(a) is taken from Article 16(1) of the United Nations Convention against Corruption, which requires states to implement the criminal offense of bribery of foreign public officials and officials of public international organizations into domestic law. Similar wording is found in Article 5 of the Council of Europe Criminal Law Convention on Corruption and Article 1 of the OECD Convention on Combating Bribery of Foreign Public Officials in International Business Transactions. This paragraph involves active bribery or active corruption, meaning the promising, offering, or giving of undue advantage to a foreign public official. It is important to note that this offense applies only to the conduct of international business and would not, for example, apply to purely domestic business. Reference should be made to the commentary to Article 138, above, which discusses the meaning of *promise, offer,* and *give* in more detail, in addition to other elements of the criminal offense of active corruption.

Paragraph 1(b): The wording of Article 139.1(1)(b) is taken from Article 16(2) of the United Nations Convention against Corruption. Similar wording is found in Article 5 of the Council of Europe Criminal Law Convention on Corruption. In contrast to Paragraph 1(a), this paragraph involves passive bribery or passive corruption, meaning the solicitation of an undue advantage by a public official. As with active bribery, this article applies only to the conduct of international business and would not, for example, apply to purely domestic business. Reference should be made to the commentary to Article 138.1, above, which discusses the meaning of *solicit* and *accept* in more detail, in addition to other elements of the criminal offense of passive corruption.

Paragraph 3(a): The definition of foreign public official is taken from Article 2(b) of the United Nations Convention against Corruption.

Paragraph 3(b): The definition of official of a public international organization is taken from Article 2(c) of the United Nations Convention against Corruption.

## *Article 139.2: Penalty*

The applicable penalty range for the criminal offense of corruption involving a foreign public official or an official of a public international organization is three to fifteen years' imprisonment.

# Article 140: Corruption in the Private Sector

## *Article 140.1: Definition of Offense*

1. A person commits the criminal offense of corruption in the private sector when he or she, in the course of economic, financial, or commercial activities:

(a) promises, offers, or gives, directly or indirectly, an undue advantage to any person who directs or works, in any capacity, for a private-sector entity, for that person himself or herself or for another person, in order that he or she, in breach of his or her duties, act or refrain from acting; or

(b) being a person who directs or works, in any capacity, for a private-sector entity, solicits or accepts, directly or indirectly, an undue advantage, for the person himself or herself or for another person, in order that he or she, in breach of his or her duties, act or refrain from acting.

## Commentary

The wording of Article 140 is taken from Article 21 of the United Nations Convention against Corruption. Similar wording is found in Articles 7 and 8 of the Council of Europe Criminal Law Convention on Corruption. The United Nations Convention against Corruption covers acts of corruption not only in the public sector but also in the private sector. The explanatory report to the Council of Europe Criminal Law Convention on Corruption (paragraph 52) provides that

> corruption in the private sector has, over the last century, been dealt with by civil (e.g., competition) or labor laws or general criminal provisions. Criminalizing private corruption appeared as a pioneering but necessary effort to avoid gaps in a comprehensive strategy to combat corruption. The reasons for introducing criminal law sanctions for corruption in the private sphere are manifold. First of all, because corruption in the private sphere undermines values like trust, confidence or loyalty, which are necessary for the maintenance and development of social and economic relations.... Secondly, criminalization of private sector corruption was necessary to ensure respect for fair competition. Thirdly, it also has to do with the privatization process. Over the years important public functions have been privatized (education, health, transport, telecommunications, etc.). The transfer of such public functions to the private sector ... entails transfers of substantial budgetary allocations and of regulatory powers. It is therefore logical to protect the public from the damaging effects of corruption in businesses as well, particularly since the financial or other powers concentrated in the private sector, necessary for their new functions, are of great social importance.

It is worth noting that nonprofit activities are not included under private corruption, by use of the phrase "economic, financial, or commercial activities."

Paragraph 1(a): The wording of Article 140.1(1)(a) is taken from Article 21(a) of the United Nations Convention against Corruption. The convention requires states to consider implementing the criminal offense of bribery in the private sector. This paragraph involves active bribery or active corruption, meaning the promising, offering, or giving of undue advantage to a person who directs or works, in any capacity, for a private-sector entity. The explanatory report to the Council of Europe Criminal Law Convention on Corruption (paragraph 54) states that the phrase "person who 'directs or works in any capacity'" should be interpreted widely as "it covers the employer-employee relationship but also other types of relationships such as partners, lawyer and client and others in which there is no contract of employment. Within private enterprises it should cover not only employees but also the management from top to the bottom, including members of the board, but not the shareholders." The explanatory report also explains that "private-sector entities" refers to "companies, enterprises, trusts and other entities which are entirely or to a determining extent owned by private persons. ... They can be corporations but also entities with no legal personality." Finally, at paragraph 55, the report provides that "'in breach of his duties' does not aim only at ensuring respect for specific contractual obligations but rather to guarantee that there will be no breach of the general duty of loyalty in relation to the principal's affair or business. ... The notion of 'breach of duty' can also be linked to that of 'secrecy,' that is the acceptance of the gift to the detriment of the employer or principal and without obtaining his authorization or approval. It is the secrecy of the benefit rather than the benefit itself that is the essence of the offense. Such secret behavior threatens the interests of the private-sector entity and makes it dangerous." Reference should be made to the commentary to Article 138, above, which discusses the meaning of *promise*, *offer*, and *give* in more detail, in addition to other elements of the criminal offense of active corruption.

Paragraph 1(b): The wording of Article 140.1(1)(b) is taken from Article 21(b) of the United Nations Convention against Corruption. This paragraph involves passive bribery or passive corruption, meaning the solicitation or acceptance of an undue advantage by a person who directs or works, in any capacity, for a private-sector entity. Reference should be made to the commentary to Article 138, above, which discusses the meaning of *solicit* and *accept* in more detail, in addition to other elements of the criminal offense of passive corruption. Reference should also be made to the commentary to Paragraph 1(a), as it is relevant to the meaning of the terms *private-sector entity*, *breach of duty*, and *directs or works, in any capacity*, also used in Paragraph 1(b).

## *Article 140.2: Penalty*

The applicable penalty range for the criminal offense of corruption in the private sector is two to ten years' imprisonment.

# Section 10: Corruption-Related Offenses and Other Offenses Involving a Public Official

## Article 141: Trading in Influence

### *Article 141.1: Definition of Offense*

1. A person commits the criminal offense of trading in influence when he or she:

   (a) promises, offers, or gives to a public official, a foreign public official, an official of a public international organization, or any other person, directly or indirectly, an undue advantage, in order that the public official, foreign public official, official of a public international organization, or the person abuse his or her real or supposed influence and with a view to obtaining from an administration or public authority an undue advantage for the original instigator of the act or for any other person; or

   (b) being a public official, a foreign public official, an official of a public international organization, or any other person, solicits or accepts an undue advantage, directly or indirectly, for himself or herself or another person or entity, in order that the public official, foreign public official, official of a public international organization, or the person abuse his or her real or supposed influence with a view to obtaining from an administration or public authority an undue advantage.

2. For the purposes of Article 141:

   (a) *foreign public official* has the same meaning as in Article 139(3)(a);

(b) *official of a public international organization* has the same meaning as in Article 139(3)(b).

## Commentary

Trading in influence is a somewhat different corruption offense. As stated in the explanatory report to the Council of Europe Criminal Law Convention on Corruption (paragraph 64), the inclusion of this offense in domestic legislation serves to close the gap on those involved in corruption: "[C]riminalizing trading in influence seeks to reach the close circle of the official or the political party to which he belongs and to tackle the corrupt behavior of those persons who are in the neighborhood of power and try to obtain advantages from their situation, contributing to the atmosphere of corruption."

Paragraph 1(a): The wording of Article 141.1(a) is based on Article 18 of the United Nations Convention against Corruption. It also integrates the criminal offense of trading in influence of foreign public officials and officials of public international organizations that is contained in Article 12 of the Council of Europe Criminal Law Convention on Corruption and Article 1 of the OECD Convention on Combating Bribery of Foreign Public Officials in International Business Transactions. These conventions require states to consider implementing the criminal offense of trading in influence into domestic legislation. This paragraph criminalizes a corrupt trilateral relationship where a public official, foreign public official, or official of a public international organization, having real or supposed influence, trades this influence for an undue advantage from someone seeking this influence. In this paragraph, it is the person seeking the influence and promising, offering, or actually giving any undue advantage to a public official who is guilty of a criminal offense. This offense is termed *active trading in influence.* In contrast to Article 138, above, there is no requirement that the public official, foreign public official, or official of a public international organization "act or refrain from acting" in the course of his or her duties. Instead, it is enough that the public official exerts, or proposes to exert, improper influence. The link with the influence of official conduct must also be established. It is irrelevant whether or not the supposed influence is exerted or whether or not it leads to the intended result.

Reference should be made to Article 1(9), for the definition of public official, and its accompanying commentary. Reference should also be made to the commentary to Article 138, above, which discusses the meaning of *promise, offer,* and *give* in more detail.

Paragraph 1(b): The wording of Paragraph 1(b) is taken from Article 18(b) of the United Nations Convention against Corruption. Similar wording is found in Article 12 of the Council of Europe Criminal Law Convention on Corruption. This paragraph criminalizes a corrupt trilateral relationship where a public official, having real or supposed influence, trades this influence for an undue advantage from someone seeking this influence. In this paragraph, it is the person who has the influence and who solicits or accepts an undue advantage for himself or herself who is guilty of a criminal offense.

This offense is termed *passive trading in influence*. In contrast to Article 138, above, there is no requirement that the public official, foreign public official, or official of a public international organization "act or refrain from acting" in the course of his or her duties. Instead, it is enough that the public official, foreign public official, or official of a public international organization exerts, or proposes to exert, improper influence. The link with the influence of official conduct must also be established. It is irrelevant whether or not the supposed influence is exerted or whether or not it leads to the intended result.

Reference should be made to Article 1(9) of the MCC, for the definition of public official, and its accompanying commentary. Reference should also be made to the commentary to Article 138, above, which discusses the meaning of solicit and accept in more detail.

## *Article 141.2: Penalty*

The applicable penalty range for the criminal offense of trading in influence is three to fifteen years' imprisonment.

# Article 142: Embezzlement, Misappropriation, or Other Diversion of Property by a Public Official

## *Article 142.1: Definition of Offense*

A person commits the criminal offense of embezzlement, misappropriation, or other diversion of property by a public official when he or she:

(a) being a public official;

(b) embezzles, misappropriates, or diverts any property, public or private funds or securities, or any other thing of value entrusted to him or her by virtue of his or her position;

(c) for his or her benefit or for the benefit of another person or entity.

## Commentary

The MCC contains two embezzlement offenses—one relating to embezzlement in the private sector (Article 127) and the present article on embezzlement involving a public official. Essentially, embezzlement involves theft of property by a person who is entrusted to look after or manage it. The protected interest under Article 127 is another person's property, whereas in Article 142 the protected interest is public property, funds, or securities. The wording of Article 142 is taken from Article 17 of the United Nations Convention against Corruption, which requires states to implement the criminal offense of embezzlement, misappropriation, or other diversion of property by a public official into domestic law. This offense covers misappropriation and diversion of property, funds, securities, or any other thing of value entrusted to the public official by virtue of his or her position.

### *Article 142.2: Penalty*

1. The applicable penalty range for the criminal offense of embezzlement, misappropriation, or other diversion of property by a public official is two to ten years' imprisonment.
2. The applicable penalty range for the criminal offense of embezzlement, misappropriation, or other diversion of property by a public official is three to fifteen years' imprisonment when the embezzlement, misappropriation, or other diversion involves property of high value.

## Article 143: Abuse of Functions

### *Article 143.1: Definition of Offense*

A person commits the criminal offense of abuse of functions when he or she:

(a) being a public official;

(b) in the discharge of his or her functions;

(c) performs or fails to perform his or her duties, in violation of the applicable law;

(d) for the purpose of obtaining an undue advantage for himself or herself or for another person or entity.

## Commentary

The criminal offense contained in Article 143 is taken from Article 19 of the United Nations Convention against Corruption, which requires states to consider implementing the criminal offense of abuse of functions into domestic criminal law. Before such an offense is included in domestic legislation, it is essential that the domestic law set out the duties of a public official. This process may involve amendments to domestic administrative law. In many cases, the law will be amended to combat corruption by providing for less discretion for individual public officials, therefore providing fewer opportunities for corruption. The process may also require the promulgation of a code of conduct for policing officials (as required under Article 8 of the United Nations Convention against Corruption). Reference should be made to the International Code of Conduct for Public Officials (UN document A/51/59) and the Council of Europe's Model Code of Conduct for Public Officials (appendix to Council of Ministers Recommendation No. R [2000] 10).

### *Article 143.2: Penalty*

The applicable penalty range for the criminal offense of abuse of functions is two to ten years' imprisonment.

# Article 144: Illicit Enrichment

### *Article 144.1: Definition of Offense*

A person commits the criminal offense of illicit enrichment when the assets of the person, being a public official, significantly increase in a manner that cannot reasonably be explained in relation to his or her lawful income.

## Commentary

The wording of Article 144 is taken from Article 20 of the United Nations Convention against Corruption, which requires states to consider implementing the criminal offense of illicit enrichment into domestic criminal law. This offense has been added to the domestic legislation of many states to broaden the net to catch corrupt officials. There has been considerable controversy in many post-conflict states over public officials possessing assets that could not have been obtained by recourse to their incomes only. These assets have included houses, vehicles, and many other things. The term assets is extremely broad, although it includes only tangible assets rather than intangible things (e.g., legal rights) or nonmaterial benefits (e.g., sexual favors).

## *Article 144.2: Penalty*

The applicable penalty range for the criminal offense of illicit enrichment is two to ten years' imprisonment.

# Article 145: Concealment

## *Article 145.1: Definition of Offense*

Without prejudice to Article 135, a person commits the criminal offense of concealment when he or she:

(a) after the commission of a corruption-related criminal offense;

(b) without having participated in the offense;

(c) conceals or continues to retain any property when he or she knows that such property is the result of a corruption-related offense.

### Commentary

The wording of Article 145 is taken from Article 24 of the United Nations Convention against Corruption, which requires states to consider implementing the criminal offense of concealment into domestic criminal law. According to the convention, the implementation of this offense into domestic legislation is a matter for the discretion of a state. There is a certain overlap between this offense and that of money laundering under Article 135. Both offenses cover the concealment of property when the perpetrator knows it is the proceeds of crime or that it was acquired as a result of a corruption-related offense. What is not covered in Article 135 on money laundering is the continued retention of the property. Such retention is addressed and criminalized in Article 145. For the purpose of Article 145, corruption-related offenses include those corruption offenses contained in Sections 9 and 10 of the Special Part of the MCC.

### *Article 145.2: Penalty*

The applicable penalty range for the criminal offense of concealment is two to ten years' imprisonment.

## Article 146: Threat and Improper Influence

### *Article 146.1: Definition of Offense*

1. A person commits the criminal offense of threat and improper influence when he or she:
   (a) threatens unlawful harm to a public official;
   (b) with the purpose of influencing him or her to act or refrain from acting in the exercise of his or her duties.
2. It is no defense to prosecution under Article 146 that a person whom the actor sought to influence was not qualified to act in the desired way, because he or she had not yet assumed office or lacked jurisdiction, or for any other reason.

#### Commentary

The criminal offense of threat and improper influence involves the perpetrator seeking to achieve the same results as with corruption and corruption-related offense, but using the threat of harm rather than a bribe to achieve this purpose. Reference should be made to Article 1(9) and its accompanying commentary on the meaning of *public official.*

### *Article 146.2: Penalty*

1. The applicable penalty range for the criminal offense of threat and improper influence is one to five years' imprisonment.
2. The court may impose a fine, as an alternative principal penalty, upon a person convicted of threat and improper influence.

# Section 11: Offenses against the State, Public Safety, and Security

## General Commentary to Articles 147–157

In Security Council Resolution 1373 of 2001, paragraph 2(b), the Security Council declared that United Nations member states should take all necessary steps to prevent the commission of terrorist acts. Member states were called upon to become parties to the relevant international conventions and protocols relating to terrorism. These conventions and protocols are the Convention on Offenses and Certain Other Acts Committed on Board Aircraft; the Convention for the Suppression of Unlawful Seizure of Aircraft; the Convention for the Suppression of Unlawful Acts against the Safety of Civil Aviation; the Convention on the Prevention and Punishment of Offenses against Internationally Protected Persons, Including Diplomatic Agents; the International Convention on the Taking of Hostages; the Convention on the Physical Protection of Nuclear Material; the Protocol for the Suppression of Unlawful Acts of Violence at Airports Serving International Civil Aviation; the Convention for the Suppression of Unlawful Acts against the Safety of Maritime Navigation; the Protocol for the Suppression of Unlawful Acts against the Safety of Fixed Platforms Located on the Continental Shelf; the Convention on the Marking of Plastic Explosives for the Purpose of Detection; the International Convention for the Suppression of Terrorist Bombing; and the International Convention for the Suppression of the Financing of Terrorism.

As stated in the United Nations Office on Drugs and Crime's *Legislative Guide to the Universal Anti-Terrorism Conventions and Protocols*, at page 4, full implementation of the antiterrorism conventions "has many aspects, including national security doctrine, budgetary allocations and administrative and personnel measures. The development of legislation is, however, the initial practical obstacle to compliance by a State party with resolution 1373(2001) and to ratification of the global anti-terrorism conventions." Articles 147–157 seek to domestically implement the penal provisions of the antiterrorism conventions through the creation of criminal offenses. It must be noted that two of the twelve international conventions, namely, the Convention on the Marking of Plastic Explosives for the Purpose of Detection and the Convention on Offenses and Certain Other Acts Committed on Board Aircraft, do not contain requirements to domestically enact criminal offenses. Therefore, there are only ten offenses related to terrorist acts in the MCC. Reference is made in the relevant provisions of the MCC to other obligations, outside the scope of penal law, that each convention imposes upon states parties, including issues such as extradition, international cooperation, mutual legal assistance, and jurisdiction (to ensure that there is no safe haven for terrorists). It is also worth noting that conventions, being international in nature, require some international element to the offense before they will apply. An example would be Article 151, which applies only to airports serving international civil aviation. Of course, a state could go beyond the scope of the provision and apply the substantive criminal offense to airports serving domestic civil aviation. The international element of each offense is defined in its governing convention or protocol.

To ensure that a post-conflict state has fulfilled its international obligations on terrorism, reference should be made to Security Council Resolution 1373 (2001), the *Legislative Guide to the Universal Anti-Terrorism Conventions and Protocols*, and the United Nations Office on Drugs and Crime's *Checklists For the 12 Universal Anti-Terrorism Conventions and for Security Council Resolution 1373 (2001).* Reference should also be made to the Security Council's counterterrorism committee, whose mandate is to monitor states' compliance with Resolution 1373 (2001). The counterterrorism committee also facilitates the provision of technical assistance to states through various means, including maintaining a directory of technical-assistance providers. The International Monetary Fund has also developed the *Handbook on Legislation Drafting*, which deals with drafting legislation on antiterrorism offenses.

There was considerable debate during the drafting of the MCC about whether or not to include the offense of terrorism in the MCC in addition to the terrorist offenses already defined under internationally agreed-upon conventions and protocols. Given the occurrence of terrorism in many post-conflict environments, such as Iraq, Afghanistan, and Kosovo (where the United Nations Mission in Kosovo needed to promulgate Regulation No. 2001/12 on the Prohibition on Terrorism and Related Offenses), many argued that terrorism should be included in the MCC. At one stage in the consultation and vetting process for the MCC, the drafters considered a draft terrorism provision. But there was considerable disagreement, first about whether or not it should be in the codes in the first place, and second about its substantive content. A definition that was agreeable and satisfactory to the drafters and the experts consulted in the course of the codes, vetting and consultation period was elusive, and given the amount of opposition, the offense was omitted. International efforts are currently under way to draft a convention that deals specifically with terrorism. As yet, a definition has not been agreed upon. The Council of Europe has adopted the Council of Europe Convention on the Prevention of Terrorism (2005). However, the convention does not define terrorism except in relation to terrorist acts listed in preexisting international conventions. It contains a number of offenses related to terrorism, including public provocation to commit terrorism (Article 5), recruitment for terrorism (Article 6), and training for terrorism (Article 7), which a state may wish to consider implementing whether or not it is bound by the convention. Reference should be made to the explanatory report to the convention. The Inter-American Convention against Terrorism (2002) defines terrorism in a similar manner to the Council of Europe Convention on the Prevention of

Terrorism. The only international instrument with a self-standing definition of terrorism is the Arab Convention on the Suppression of Terrorism 1998, Article 2. Many states when referring to terrorism in domestic legislation refer to discrete acts of terrorism defined in international law rather than creating a self-standing definition of terrorism. It should be noted that just because there is no definition of terrorism per se in the MCC, a person will not go unpunished for acts that may be viewed as terrorism. The predicate, or underlying, offenses, such as bombing, are criminalized in the MCC (as well as aiding, abetting, and financing these underlying offenses), and a person who commits these offenses can be prosecuted accordingly.

# Article 147: Financing Terrorism

## *Article 147.1: Definition of Offense*

1. A person commits the criminal offense of financing terrorism when he or she:
   - (a) unlawfully;
   - (b) by any means, directly or indirectly;
   - (c) provides or collects funds;
   - (d) with the intention that they should be used, or in the knowledge that they are to be used, in full or in part, to carry out:
     - (i) the criminal offenses of terrorist bombing (Article 148), unlawful seizure of an aircraft (Article 149), unlawful acts against the safety of civil aviation (Article 150), unlawful acts of violence at airports serving international civil aviation (Article 151), offenses against internationally protected persons (Article 152), taking of hostages (Article 153), offenses relating to nuclear material (Article 154), unlawful acts against the safety of maritime navigation (Article 155), unlawful acts against the safety of fixed platforms (Article 156), piracy (Article 157), or
     - (ii) any other act intended to cause death or serious bodily injury to a civilian, or to any other person not taking an active part in the hostilities in a situation of armed conflict, when the purpose of such an act, by its nature or context, is to intimidate a population or to compel a government or an international organization to do or to abstain from doing an act.

2. For the purposes of Article 147, *funds* mean assets of every kind, whether tangible or intangible, movable or immovable, however acquired, and legal documents or instruments in any form, including electronic or digital, evidencing title to, or interest in, such assets, including but not limited to bank credits, traveler's checks, bank checks, money orders, shares, securities, bonds, drafts, and letters of credit.

## Commentary

Paragraph 1: The criminal offense of financing terrorism is derived from Article 2(1) of the International Convention for the Suppression of the Financing of Terrorism. This is also the definition used in the Council of Europe Convention on Laundering, Search, Seizure and Confiscation of the Proceeds from Crime and on the Financing of Terrorism, Article 1(h). For a discussion of the drafting of this convention and its substantive content, reference should be made to the *Legislative Guide to the Universal Anti-Terrorism Conventions and Protocols*, prepared by the United Nations Office on Drugs and Crime. The ratification and implementation of the convention is an international obligation under Security Council Resolution 1373 (2001), as discussed above.

Article 2(1)(a) of the International Convention for the Suppression of the Financing of Terrorism refers to the financing of "an act within the scope of and as defined in one of the treaties listed in the annex [to the convention]." Instead of retaining this reference, Paragraph 1(d)(i), above, makes specific reference to the offenses contained in these treaties as they are contained in the MCC. Also included in this reference is the offense of piracy, which is not referenced in Article 2(1)(a) of the International Convention for the Suppression of the Financing of Terrorism. Piracy is however included as a terrorist offense in the Council of Europe Convention on the Prevention of Terrorism.

Article 2(4) of the United Nations convention requires that any person who attempts the financing of terrorism or, under Article 2(5), any person who participates as an accomplice, organizes or directs another, or contributes to the commission of financing of terrorism through a common purpose also be liable to criminal prosecution. While these grounds of liability are not specifically ennumerated in Article 147, attempt is covered under Article 27 of the MCC, and accomplice liability is covered under Article 31. Organizing or directing a criminal offense is dealt with in Article 29, and common purpose liability is covered in Article 28.

Article 7 of the convention further requires that jurisdiction over the financing of terrorism be asserted where the act is committed in the territory of the state, on board an aircraft registered in that state, on board a vessel flying the flag of that state, or by a national of the state. The convention also provides for a number of discretionary grounds of jurisdiction: when the offense is directed toward or carried out in the territory of the state; when the offense is committed in an attempt to compel the state to do or abstain from doing any act; when the offense is committed on board an aircraft operated by the government of that state; when the offense is directed toward or carried out in a state or government facility of that state abroad (including an embassy or other diplomatic or consular premises of that state); when the offense is committed by a stateless person who has his or her habitual residence in the territory of that state; and when the offense is directed toward or carried out against a national of the state. The mandatory grounds of jurisdiction provided for in the convention are covered in Article 4 ("Territorial Jurisdiction") and Article 5 ("Extraterritorial Jurisdiction") of the MCC. The latter two discretionary grounds of jurisdiction are also provided for in Article 5 of the MCC. Furthermore, the convention requires that jurisdiction be asserted over legal persons (Article 5). This requirement is covered under Article 19 ("Criminal Responsibility of Legal Persons").

Finally, the convention contains provisions on seizure and forfeiture of funds (Article 8), investigation (Articles 9, 16, and 17), prosecution (Article 10), extradition (Articles 1, 13, 14, and 15), mutual assistance (Articles 12–15), and prevention of terrorism (Article 18). These provisions should also be examined when domestically implementing the provisions of the convention. Reference should be made to Chapter 14, Parts 1 and 2, of the MCCP, on extradition and mutual legal assistance, respectively. Reference should also be made to Articles 70–73 of the MCC on confiscation of the proceeds of crime (the equivalent of forfeiture) and Chapter 8, Part 3, Section 4, of the MCCP on seizure.

For a more in-depth discussion on the drafting of this convention and its substantive content, including the provisions just mentioned, reference should be made to the *Legislative Guide to the Universal Anti-Terrorism Conventions and Protocols*, prepared by the United Nations Office on Drugs and Crime.

Paragraph 2: This paragraph is taken from Article 1(1) of the International Convention for the Suppression of the Financing of Terrorism.

## *Article 147.2: Penalty*

The applicable penalty range for the criminal offense of financing of terrorism is three to fifteen years' imprisonment.

# Article 148: Terrorist Bombing

## *Article 148.1: Definition of Offense*

1. A person commits the criminal offense of terrorist bombing when he or she:
    (a) unlawfully;
    (b) delivers, places, discharges, or detonates an explosive or incendiary weapon or device;

(c) in, into, or against a place of public use, a state or governmental facility, a public transportation system, or an infrastructure facility;

(d) with the intent to cause death or serious bodily injury or extensive destruction of such a place, facility, or system, where such destruction results in or is likely to result in major economic loss.

2. For the purposes of Article 148:

(a) *explosive or incendiary weapon or device* means:

(i) dynamite and all other forms of explosives;

(ii) any explosive, incendiary, or poison gas:

(a) bomb;

(b) grenade;

(c) rocket;

(d) missile;

(e) mine; or

(f) similar device, including any device that can be carried or thrown by one individual acting alone and consisting of or including a breakable container containing flammable liquid or compound and a wick composed of any material that, when ignited, is capable of lighting the flammable liquid or compound;

(iii) any type of firearm, by whatever name known, that will, or that may be readily converted to, expel a projectile by the action of an explosive or other propellant; and

(iv) any combination of parts either designed or redesigned for use in converting any device into one of those described in subparagraphs (ii) and (iii) and from which such a device may be readily assembled;

(b) *place of public use* means those parts of any building, land, street, waterway, or other location that are accessible or open to members of the public, whether continuously, periodically, or occasionally, and encompasses any commercial, business, cultural, historical, educational, religious, governmental, entertainment, recreational, or similar places that are so accessible or open to the public;

(c) *state or governmental facility* means any permanent or temporary facility or conveyance used or occupied by representatives of a state; members of government, the legislature, or the judiciary; or by officials or employees of a state, any other public authority or entity, or by employees or officials of an intergovernmental organization in connection with their official duties;

(d) *public transportation system* means all facilities, conveyances, and instrumentalities, whether publicly or privately owned, that are used in or for publicly available services for the transportation of persons or cargo; and

(e) *infrastructure facility* means any publicly or privately owned facility providing or distributing services for the benefit of the public, such as water, sewerage, energy, fuel, or communications.

3. The criminal offense of terrorist bombing does not apply to activities of armed forces during an armed conflict, as those terms are understood under international humanitarian law, which are governed by that law, and the activities undertaken by military forces of a state in the exercise of their official duties, inasmuch as they are governed by other rules of international law.

## Commentary

The criminal offense of terrorist bombing is derived from the International Convention for the Suppression of Terrorist Bombing. For a discussion of the drafting of this convention and its substantive content, reference should be made to the *Legislative Guide to the Universal Anti-Terrorism Conventions and Protocols*, prepared by the United Nations Office on Drugs and Crime. The ratification and implementation of the convention is an international obligation under Security Council Resolution 1373 (2001), as discussed above.

The wording of Article 148 is taken from Article 2(1) of the convention. In addition to the criminal acts listed above in Article 148, Articles 2(2) and 2(3) of the convention require that attempts to commit any of the acts mentioned in Article 1, or being an accomplice to, organizing, directing, or "in any other way contributing ... by a group of persons acting with a common purpose" to any of these acts, should also be criminalized in domestic legislation. While these grounds of liability are not specifically ennumerated in Article 148, attempt is covered under Article 27 of the MCC and accomplice liability is covered under Article 31. Organizing or directing a criminal offense is dealt with in Article 29 and common purpose liability in Article 28.

Article 6 of the convention further requires that jurisdiction over terrorist bombing be asserted where the act is committed in the territory of the state; on board an aircraft registered in that state; on board a vessel flying the flag of that state; or by a national of the state. The convention also provides for a number of discretionary grounds of jurisdiction: when the offense is committed against a state or government facility of that state abroad (including an embassy or other diplomatic or consular premises of that state); when the offense is committed in an attempt to compel that state to do or abstain from doing any act; where the offense is commited on board an aircraft operated by the government of that state; when the offense is committed against a national of that state; or when the offense is committed by a stateless person who has his or her habitual residence in the territory of that state. The mandatory grounds of jurisdiction provided for in the convention are covered in Article 4 ("Territorial Jurisdiction") and Article 5 ("Extraterritorial Jurisdiction") of the MCC. The latter two discretionary grounds of jurisdiction are also provided for in Article 5 of the MCC. Finally, the convention contains provisions on investigation (Articles 7, 13, and 14), prosecution (Article 8), extradition (Articles 9, 11, and 12), and mutual assistance (Articles 10–12). These provisions should also be looked at when domestically implementing the provisions of the convention. Reference should be made to Chapter 14, Parts 1 and 2, of the MCCP, on extradition and mutual legal assistance.

Paragraph 2(a): Article 1(3) of the International Convention for the Suppression of Terrorist Bombing defines "explosive or other lethal device." The definition of explosive, incendiary, or other lethal device used in the MCC differs slightly from the definition used in the convention. The MCC definition was altered to make it more detailed and illustrative, thus specifying more individual explosive or incendiary weapons or devices rather than having them fall under broad wording such as "similar device" that is used in Article 1(3) of the convention. That said, it is impossible to ennumerate every explosive, incendiary, or other lethal device, so it was still necessary to retain "other similar device" in the definition to cover new or novel explosive, incendiary, or other lethal devices that may be used by the perpetrators of terrorist bombings.

With regard to Paragraph 2(a)(ii), it is important to note that it makes specific reference to any device that can be carried or thrown by one individual acting alone and consisting of or including a breakable container containing flammable liquid or compound and a wick composed of any material that, when ignited, is capable of lighting the flammable liquid or compound. This definition covers the Molotov cocktail. This homemade explosive is commonly used and consequently merits specific reference in the definition of explosive, incendiary, or other lethal device.

Paragraph 2(a)(iii) covers all manner of firearms that may be used in terrorist bombings. In some domestic jurisdictions, certain firearms, such as shotguns used for sporting purposes, are excluded from the definition of explosive, incendiary, or other lethal device. This is not the case in the MCC, but a post-conflict state introducing legislation on terrorist bombing or bombing may wish to make such exclusions.

Paragraph 2(a)(iv) covers combinations of parts that have been designed or redesigned for use as an explosive, incendiary, or other lethal device. It is important to cover this concept, as sometimes an explosive, incendiary, or other lethal device will be stored in parts rather than fully assembled. This provision is important, for example, when a person is being prosecuted for delivery or placing of an explosive, incendiary, or other lethal device into a place of public use, rather than for discharging or detonating it. It is also important when a person is prosecuted for an attempt to commit terrorist bombing. Paragraph 2(a)(iv) does not cover a situation where a person possesses only some of the parts necessary for use as an explosive, incendiary, or other lethal device, for example, where the person possesses only the firing circuits and the bomb containers. Thus, where different components are held in different places (one or more of which has not been discovered), a person cannot be prosecuted under this paragraph. A state wishing to address this scenario could create a separate criminal offense (that would carry a lesser penalty) penalizing a person who unlawfully possesses any substance, material, or combination of substances or materials with the intention to make a destructive device or explosive.

It is important to note that in some domestic jurisdictions and under international conventions such as the Protocol against Illicit Manufacturing of and Trafficking in Firearms, Their Parts and Components and Ammunition, supplementing the United Nations Convention against Transnational Organized Crime (Article 3[1]), certain items that could technically fall within the definition of explosive, incendiary, or other lethal device are excluded from the definition, including antique firearms or their replicas, devices used for signaling (signaling flares), and pyrotechnics. With regard to antique firearms or replicas, Article 3(1) of the Protocol against Illicit Manufacturing of and Trafficking in Firearms, Their Parts and Components and Ammunition provides that "in no case, however, shall antique firearms include firearms manufactured after 1899." A state should consider what items, if any, it wishes to exclude from the definition.

Paragraph 2(b): This paragraph is taken from Article 1(5) of the International Convention for the Suppression of Terrorist Bombing.

Paragraph 2(c): This paragraph is taken from Article 1(1) of the International Convention for the Suppression of Terrorist Bombing.

Paragraph 2(d): This paragraph is taken from Article 1(6) of the International Convention for the Suppression of Terrorist Bombing.

Paragraph 2(e): This paragraph is taken from Article 1(2) of the International Convention for the Suppression of Terrorist Bombing.

Paragraph 3: The wording of Paragraph 3 comes from Article 19(2) of the International Convention for the Suppression of Terrorist Bombing, The term *military force*, referred to in Article 19(2) of the convention, is defined in Article 1(4) of the convention as "the armed forces of a State which are organized, trained and equipped under its internal law for the primary purpose of national defense or security and persons acting in support of those armed forces who are under their formal command, control and responsibility."

## *Article 148.2: Penalty*

The applicable penalty range for the criminal offense of terrorist bombing is five to twenty years' imprisonment.

# Article 149: Unlawful Seizure of Aircraft

## *Article 149.1: Definition of Offense*

1. A person commits the criminal offense of unlawful seizure of aircraft when he or she:
   (a) being on board an aircraft in flight;
   (b) unlawfully;
   (c) by force or threat of force or any other form of intimidation;
   (d) seizes or exercises control of that aircraft.
2. An aircraft is considered to be in flight at any time from the moment all its external doors are closed following embarkation until the moment any door is opened for disembarkation. In the case of forced landing, the flight is deemed to continue until the competent authorities take over responsibility for the aircraft and for persons and property on board.

### Commentary

The criminal offense of unlawful seizure of aircraft is derived from the Convention for the Suppression of Unlawful Seizure of Aircraft. For a discussion of the drafting of this convention and its substantive content, reference should be made to the *Legislative Guide to the Universal Anti-Terrorism Conventions and Protocols*, prepared by the United Nations Office on Drugs and Crime. The ratification and implementation of the convention is an international obligation under Security Council Resolution 1373 (2001), discussed above.

The wording of Article 149 is taken from Article 1 of the convention. In addition to the criminal acts listed above in Article 149, Article 1(b) requires that attempts to commit any of the acts mentioned in Article 1, or being an accomplice to any of these acts, be criminalized in domestic legislation. While these grounds of liability are not specifically ennumerated in Article 149, attempt is covered under Article 27 of the MCC and accomplice liability is covered under Article 31. Article 4 of the convention further requires that jurisdiction over unlawful seizure of aircraft be asserted where the act is committed in the territory of the state; on board an aircraft registered in that state; or on board an aircraft leased, without crew, to a lessee who has his or her principal place of business or his or her permanent residence in that state. These grounds of jurisdiction are covered in Article 4 ("Territorial Jurisdiction") and Article 5 ("Extraterritorial Jurisdiction") of the MCC. The convention also contains provisions on the investigation of unlawful seizure of aircraft (Article 6), prosecution (Article 7), extradition (Article 8), and mutual assistance (Article 10). These provisions should be looked at when domestically implementing the provisions of the convention. Reference should be made to Chapter 14, Parts 1 and 2, of the MCCP, on mutual legal assistance and extradition.

Article 2(1) of the convention provides that the convention does not apply to aircraft used in military, customs, or police services.

Paragraph 2: This paragraph is taken from Article 3(1) of the Convention for the Suppression of Unlawful Seizure of Aircraft.

## *Article 149.2: Penalty*

The applicable penalty range for the criminal offense of unlawful seizure of aircraft is five to twenty years' imprisonment.

# Article 150: Unlawful Acts against the Safety of Civil Aviation

## *Article 150.1: Definition of Offense*

1. A person commits the criminal offense of unlawful acts against the safety of civil aviation when he or she:
   - (a) performs an act of violence against a person on board an aircraft in flight, if that act is likely to endanger the safety of that aircraft;
   - (b) destroys an aircraft in service or causes damage to such an aircraft that renders it incapable of flight or is likely to endanger its safety in flight;
   - (c) places or causes to be placed on an aircraft in service, by any means whatsoever, a device or substance that is likely to destroy that aircraft, cause damage that renders it incapable of flight, or cause damage that is likely to endanger its safety in flight;
   - (d) destroys or damages air navigation facilities or interferes with their operation, if any such act is likely to endanger the safety of aircraft in flight; or
   - (e) communicates information that the person knows to be false, thereby endangering the safety of an aircraft in flight.
2. An aircraft is considered to be in flight at any time from the moment when all its external doors are closed following embarkation until the moment when any door is opened for disembarkation. In the case of forced landing, the flight

is deemed to continue until the competent authorities take over responsibility for the aircraft and for persons and property on board.

3. An aircraft is considered to be in service from the beginning of the preflight preparation of the aircraft by ground personnel or by the crew for a specific flight until twenty-four hours after any landing. The period of service, in any event, extends for the entire period during which the aircraft is in flight as defined in Paragraph 2.

## Commentary

The criminal offense of unlawful acts against the safety of civil aviation is derived from the Convention for the Suppression of Unlawful Acts against the Safety of Civil Aviation. For a discussion of the drafting of this convention and its substantive content, reference should be made to the *Legislative Guide to the Universal Anti-Terrorism Conventions and Protocols*, prepared by the United Nations Office on Drugs and Crime. The ratification and implementation of the convention is an international obligation under Security Council Resolution 1373 (2001), discussed above.

The wording of Article 150 is taken from Article 1 of the convention. In addition to the criminal acts listed above in Article 150, Articles 1(2)(a) and 1(2)(b) of the convention require that attempts to commit any of the acts mentioned in Article 1, or being an accomplice to any of these acts, should also be criminalized in domestic legislation. While these grounds of liability are not specifically ennumerated in Article 150, attempt is covered under Article 27 of the MCC, and accomplice liability is covered under Article 31. Article 5 of the convention further requires that jurisdiction over unlawful acts against civil aviation be asserted where an act is committed in the territory of the state; where an act is committed on board an aircraft registered in that state; when an aircraft upon which unlawful acts against civil aviation have been committed lands in the territory of a state with the perpetrator still on board; and when the offense is committed on board an aircraft leased, without crew, to a lessee who has his or her principal place of business or his or her permanent residence in that state. These grounds of jurisdiction are covered in Article 4 ("Territorial Jurisdiction") and Article 5 ("Extraterritorial Jurisdiction") of the MCC. The convention also contains provisions on investigation of unlawful acts (Article 6), prosecution (Article 7), extradition (Article 8), and mutual assistance (Article 11). These provisions should be looked at when domestically implementing the provisions of the convention. Reference should be made to Chapter 14, Parts 1 and 2, of the MCCP, on extradition and mutual legal assistance.

Article 4(1) of the convention provides that the convention does not apply to aircraft used in military, customs, or police services. The MCC makes no statement on whether Article 150 should apply to the aircraft of military, customs, or police services; this decision should be made by the individual post-conflict state.

**Paragraph 2:** This paragraph is taken from Article 2(a) of Convention for the Suppression of Unlawful Acts against the Safety of Civil Aviation.

Paragraph 3: This paragraph is taken from Article 2(b) of Convention for the Suppression of Unlawful Acts against the Safety of Civil Aviation.

## *Article 150.2: Penalty*

The applicable penalty range for the criminal offense of unlawful acts against the safety of civil aviation is five to twenty years' imprisonment.

# Article 151: Unlawful Acts of Violence at an Airport Serving International Civil Aviation

## *Article 151.1: Definition of Offense*

A person commits the criminal offense of unlawful acts of violence at an airport serving international civil aviation when he or she, unlawfully, and using any device, substance, or weapon:

(a) performs an act of violence against a person at an airport serving international civil aviation that causes, or is likely to cause, serious injury or death; or

(b) destroys or seriously damages the facilities of an airport serving international civil aviation or aircraft not in service located there, or disrupts the services of the airport, if such an act endangers or is likely to endanger safety at the airport.

## Commentary

The criminal offense of unlawful acts of violence at airports serving international civil aviation is derived from the Protocol for the Suppression of Unlawful Acts of Violence at Airports Serving Civil Aviation, which supplements the Convention for the Suppression of Unlawful Acts against the Safety of Civil Aviation. For a discussion of the drafting of this protocol and its substantive content, reference should be made to the *Legislative Guide to the Universal Anti-Terrorism Conventions and Protocols*, prepared by the United Nations Office on Drugs and Crime. The ratification and implementation of the convention is an international obligation under Security Council Resolution 1373 (2001), discussed above.

The wording of Article 151 is taken from Article II(1) of the protocol. The provisions on jurisdiction that apply to the Convention for the Suppression of Unlawful Acts against Civil Aviation also apply to the protocol. The provisions of the convention on investigation, prosecution, extradition, and mutual assistance also apply to unlawful acts of violence at airports serving international civil aviation and should be looked at when domestically implementing the provisions of the protocol. Reference should be made to the commentary under Article 150. Reference should also be made to Chapter 14, Parts 1 and 2, of the MCCP, on mutual legal assistance and extradition.

## *Article 151.2: Penalty*

1. The applicable penalty range for the criminal offense of unlawful acts of violence at an airport serving international civil aviation is five to twenty years' imprisonment.
2. Where an unlawful act of violence at an airport serving civil aviation results in a loss of life, the applicable penalty range is ten to thirty years' imprisonment.

# Article 152: Offenses against Internationally Protected Persons

## *Article 152.1: Definition of Offense*

1. A person commits an offense against an internationally protected person when he or she:
   (a) commits the criminal offense of unlawful killing under Article 89, the criminal offense of kidnapping under Article 106, or another attack upon the person or liberty of an internationally protected person;
   (b) commits a violent attack upon the official premises, private accommodations, or means of transport of an internationally protected person such that the attack is likely to endanger his or her person or liberty; or
   (c) threatens to commit any such attack.
2. For the purposes of Article 152, *internationally protected person* means:

(a) a head of state, including any member of a collegial body performing the functions of a head of state under the constitution of the state concerned, a head of government, or a minister of foreign affairs, whenever any such person is in a foreign state, as well as family members who accompany him or her;

(b) any representative or official of a state or any official or other agent of an international organization of an intergovernmental character who, at the time when and in the place where a criminal offense against him or her, his or her official premises, his or her private accommodations, or his or her means of transport is committed, is entitled pursuant to international law to special protection from any attack on his or her person, freedom, or dignity, as well as on family members forming part of his or her household.

## Commentary

The criminal offense of offenses against internationally protected persons is derived from the Convention on the Prevention and Punishment of Crimes against Internationally Protected Persons. For a discussion of the drafting of this protocol and its substantive content, reference should be made to the *Legislative Guide to the Universal Anti-Terrorism Conventions and Protocols*, prepared by the United Nations Office on Drugs and Crime. The ratification and implementation of the convention is an international obligation under Security Council Resolution 1373 (2001), discussed above.

The wording of Article 152 is taken from Article 2(1) of the convention. In addition to the criminal acts listed above in Article 152, Articles 2(d) and 2(e) of the convention require that attempts to commit any of the acts mentioned in Article 1, or being an accomplice to any of these acts, should also be criminalized in domestic legislation. Attempt is covered under Article 27 of the MCC and accomplice liability is covered under Article 31. Article 3 of the convention further requires that jurisdiction over crimes against internationally protected be asserted where the act is committed in the territory of the state; on board an aircraft or ship registered in that state; by a national of the state; or against an internationally protected person who enjoys his or her status by virtue of functions he or she exercises on behalf of the state. These grounds of jurisdiction are covered in Article 4 ("Territorial Jurisdiction") and Article 5 ("Extraterritorial Jurisdiction") of the MCC. The convention also contains provisions on prosecution (Articles 3, 5, and 7), extradition (Article 8), and mutual assistance (Articles 4 and 10) in relation to this criminal offense. These provisions, should be looked at when domestically implementing the provisions of the convention. Reference should be made to Chapter 14, Parts 1 and 2, of the MCCP, on mutual legal assistance and extradition.

Paragraph 2: This paragraph is taken from Article 1(1)(a) and Article 1(1)(b) of the Convention on the Prevention and Punishment of Crimes against Internationally Protected Persons.

## *Article 152.2: Penalty*

1. The applicable penalty range for an offense against an internationally protected person is five to twenty years' imprisonment.
2. Where an offense against an internationally protected person involves unlawful killing, the applicable penalty range is ten to thirty years' imprisonment.

# Article 153: Taking of Hostages

## *Article 153.1: Definition of Offense*

1. A person commits the criminal offense of taking of hostages when he or she:
   (a) seizes or detains another person; and
   (b) threatens to kill, injure, or continue to detain the person;
   (c) in order to compel a third party, namely, a state, an international intergovernmental organization, a natural or juridical person, or a group of persons, to do or abstain from doing any act as an explicit or implicit condition for the release of the hostage.
2. Insofar as the Geneva Conventions of 1949 for the protection of war victims or the Additional Protocols to those conventions are applicable to a particular act of hostage-taking, and in so far as states parties to this convention are bound under those conventions to prosecute or hand over a hostage-taker, Article 153 does not apply to an act of hostage-taking committed in the course of armed conflicts as defined in the Geneva Conventions of 1949 and the protocols thereto, including armed conflicts mentioned in Article 1, paragraph 4, of Additional Protocol I of 1977, in which peoples are fighting against colonial domination and alien occupation and against racist regimes in the exercise of their right of self-determination, as enshrined in the Charter of the United Nations and the Declaration on Principles of International Law concerning Friendly Relations and Co-operation among States in accordance with the Charter of the United Nations.

## Commentary

The criminal offense of taking of hostages is derived from the International Convention against the Taking of Hostages. For a discussion of the drafting of this protocol and its substantive content, reference should be made to the *Legislative Guide to the Universal Anti-Terrorism Conventions and Protocols*, prepared by the United Nations Office on Drugs and Crime. The ratification and implementation of the convention is an international obligation under Security Council Resolution 1373 (2001), discussed above.

The wording of Article 153.1(1) is taken from Article 1(1) of the convention. In addition to the criminal acts listed above in Article 153, Article 1(2) requires that attempts to commit any of the acts mentioned in Article 1, or being an accomplice to any of these acts, also be criminalized in domestic legislation. While these grounds of liability are not specifically ennumerated in Article 153, attempt is covered under Article 27 of the MCC and accomplice liability is covered under Article 31. Article 5 of the convention further requires that jurisdiction over taking of hostages be asserted where the act is committed in the territory of the state or on board an aircraft or ship registered in that state; where the act is committed by nationals of the state or by a stateless person who has habitual residence in the territory of the state (where the state considers it appropriate); where the hostage is a national of the state (where the state considers it appropriate); and when the act of hostage taking is done to compel the state to do or abstain from doing any act. These grounds of jurisdiction, except for the final ground, are covered in Article 4 ("Territorial Jurisdiction") and Article 5 ("Extraterritorial Jurisdiction") of the MCC. The convention also contains provisions on investigation (Article 6), prosecution (Article 8), extradition (Articles 9 and 10), and mutual assistance (Article 11), and these should be looked at when domestically implementing the provisions of the convention. Reference should be made to Chapter 14, Parts 1 and 2, of the MCCP, on mutual legal assistance and extradition.

Paragraph 2: The Convention against the Taking of Hostages, as articulated in Article 12, does not apply to activities of armed forces during an armed conflict. When an act of hostage taking occurs during an armed conflict, the act is covered under Article 88 of the MCC on war crimes.

## *Article 153.2: Penalty*

The applicable penalty range for the criminal offense of taking of hostages is five to twenty years' imprisonment.

# Article 154: Offenses Related to Nuclear Material

## *Article 154.1: Definition of Offense*

1. A person commits a criminal offense related to nuclear material when he or she unlawfully:
   (a) receives, possesses, uses, transfers, alters, disposes of, or disperses, without lawful authority, nuclear material that causes or is likely to cause death or serious injury to any person or substantial damage to property;
   (b) commits a theft or robbery of nuclear material;
   (c) embezzles or obtains nuclear material through fraud;
   (d) demands nuclear material by threat, use of force, or any other form of intimidation;
   (e) threatens to use nuclear material to cause death or serious injury to any person or to cause substantial property damage; or
   (f) threatens to commit a theft or robbery of nuclear material in order to compel a natural or legal person, international organization, or state to do or refrain from doing any act.
2. For the purposes of Article 154:
   (a) *nuclear material* means:
      (i) plutonium, except that with isotopic concentration exceeding 80 percent in plutonium-238;
      (ii) uranium-233;
      (iii) uranium enriched in the isotope 235 or 233;
      (iv) uranium containing the mixture of isotopes as occurring in nature other than in the form of ore or ore residue; or
      (v) any material containing one or more of the foregoing.
   (b) *uranium enriched in the isotope 235 or 233* means uranium containing isotope 235 or 233 or both in an amount such that the abundance ratio of the sum of these isotopes to the isotope 238 is greater than the ratio of the isotope 235 to the isotope 238 occurring in nature.

## Commentary

The offenses related to nuclear material are derived from the Convention on the Physical Protection of Nuclear Material. For a discussion on the drafting of this convention and its substantive content, reference should be made to the *Legislative Guide to the Universal Anti-Terrorism Conventions and Protocols*, prepared by the United Nations Office on Drugs and Crime. The ratification and implementation of the convention is an international obligation under Security Council Resolution 1373 (2001), discussed above. The convention is mainly regulatory in nature, but it does contain one penal provision in Article 7.

In addition to the criminal acts listed above in Article 154, Articles 7(f) and 7(g) of the convention require that attempts to commit any of the acts mentioned in Article 7, or participation in any of these acts, should also be criminalized in domestic legislation. While these grounds of liability are not specifically enumerated in Article 154, attempt is covered under Article 27 of the MCC and participation is covered under Article 31. Article 8 of the convention further requires that jurisdiction over offenses related to nuclear materials be asserted where the act is committed in the territory of the state; against or on board a ship registered in that state; or by a national of that state. These grounds of jurisdiction are covered in Article 4 ("Territorial Jurisdiction") and Article 5 ("Extraterritorial Jurisdiction") of the MCC. The convention also contains provisions on fair treatment in the investigation of unlawful acts (Article 12), extradition (Articles 9–11), and mutual assistance (Article 13). These provisions should be looked at when domestically implementing the provisions of the convention. Reference should be made to Chapter 14, Parts 1 and 2, of the MCCP, on mutual legal assistance and extradition.

Paragraph 2: The definitions of nuclear material and uranium-enriched isotope 235 or 233 are taken from Articles 1(a) and 1(b) of the Convention on the Physical Protection of Nuclear Material.

## *Article 154.2: Penalty*

The applicable penalty range for offenses related to nuclear material is five to twenty years' imprisonment.

# Article 155: Unlawful Acts against the Safety of Maritime Navigation

## *Article 155.1: Definition of Offense*

1. A person commits the criminal offense of unlawful acts against the safety of maritime navigation when he or she unlawfully:
   (a) seizes or exercises control over a ship by force, threat of force, or any other form of intimidation;
   (b) performs an act of violence against a person on board a ship if that act is likely to endanger the safe navigation of that ship;
   (c) places or causes to be placed on a ship, by any means whatsoever, a device or substance that is likely to destroy or cause damage to that ship or its cargo or is likely to endanger the safe navigation of that ship;
   (d) destroys or seriously damages maritime navigational facilities or seriously interferes with their operation, if any such act is likely to endanger the safe navigation of the ship;
   (e) communicates information that the person knows to be false and thereby endangers the safe navigation of a ship;
   (f) threatens, with or without a condition, to commit an act described in Paragraphs (a) to (e), aimed at compelling a physical or juridical person to do or refrain from doing any act, if the threat is likely to endanger the safe navigation of the ship in question; or
   (g) injures or kills any person in connection with the commission of the offenses set out in Paragraphs (a) to (f).
2. For the purposes of Article 155, *ship* means a vessel of any type whatsoever, including dynamically supported craft, submersibles, or any other floating craft.

## Commentary

The criminal offense of unlawful acts against the safety of maritime navigation is derived from the Convention for the Suppression of Unlawful Acts Committed against the Safety of Maritime Navigation. For a discussion of the drafting of this convention and its substantive content, reference should be made to the *Legislative Guide to the Universal Anti-Terrorism Conventions and Protocols*, prepared by the United Nations

Office on Drugs and Crime. The ratification and implementation of the convention is an international obligation under Security Council Resolution 1373 (2001), discussed above.

The wording of Article 155 is taken from Article 2 of the convention. Articles 3(2)(a) and 3(2)(b) of the convention also require that attempts to commit any of the offenses mentioned in Article 3 of the convention, or abetting or being an accomplice to a person who commits such offenses, be criminalized in domestic legislation. While these grounds of liability are not specifically ennumerated in Article 155, attempt is covered under Article 27 of the MCC and abetting and accomplice liability are covered under Article 31. The convention further requires that jurisdiction over unlawful acts committed against the safety of maritime navigation be asserted where the act is committed in the territory of the state; against or on board a ship flying the flag of the state; or by a national of that state. These grounds of jurisdiction are covered in Article 4 ("Territorial Jurisdiction") and Article 5 ("Extraterritorial Jurisdiction") of the MCC. Article 6(2) of the convention further provides that a state may consider asserting jurisdiction over a stateless person whose habitual residence is in the state; where during commission of a criminal offense a national of that state is seized, threatened, injured, or killed; or where the criminal offense is committed in an attempt to compel that state to do or abstain from doing any act. The first two grounds of jurisdiction are covered in Article 5 ("Extraterritorial Jurisdiction") of the MCC. The third ground is not. The Convention for the Suppression of Unlawful Acts Committed against the Safety of Maritime Navigation also contains provisions on the investigation of unlawful acts (Articles 7 and 10), the delivery of an alleged perpetrator to the authorities of a state (Article 8), extradition (Article 11), and mutual legal assistance and international cooperation (Articles 12 and 13), and these should be looked at when domestically implementing the provisions of the convention. Reference should be made to Chapter 14, Parts 1 and 2, of the MCCP, on mutual legal assistance and extradition.

Paragraph 3: The definition of ship is taken from Article 1 of the Convention for the Suppression of Unlawful Acts Committed against the Safety of Maritime Navigation. Article 2 provides that warships, ships owned or operated by a state when being used as naval auxiliaries or for customs or police purposes, and ships that have been withdrawn from navigation or laid up do not fall under the scope of the convention.

## *Article 155.2: Penalty*

1. The applicable penalty range for the criminal offense of unlawful acts against the safety of maritime navigation is five to twenty years' imprisonment.
2. When unlawful acts against the safety of maritime navigation involve the killing of any person, the applicable penalty range is ten to thirty years' imprisonment.

## Commentary

Paragraph 2: In light of the fact that Article 155.1(1)(g) on unlawful acts against the safety of maritime navigation sets out killing as a potential element of this offense, which is liable to a higher penalty range under the MCC than the other acts mentioned in this article, it was decided to create a separate penalty range for unlawful acts against the safety of maritime navigation that involve the killing of a person.

# Article 156: Unlawful Acts against the Safety of Fixed Platforms

## *Article 156.1: Definition of Offense*

1. A person commits the criminal offense of unlawful acts against the safety of fixed platforms when he or she unlawfully:
   (a) seizes or exercises control over a fixed platform by force, threat of force, or any other form of intimidation;
   (b) performs an act of violence against a person on board a fixed platform if that act is likely to endanger its safety;
   (c) destroys a fixed platform or causes damage to it that is likely to endanger its safety;
   (d) places or causes to be placed on a fixed platform, by any means whatsoever, a device or substance that is likely to destroy that fixed platform or likely to endanger its safety;
   (e) threatens, with or without a condition, to commit an act described in Paragraphs (a) to (d), aimed at compelling a physical or juridical person to do or refrain from doing any act, if the threat is likely to endanger the safety of the fixed platform; or
   (f) injures or kills any person, in connection with the commission of the offenses set out in Paragraphs (a) to (e).
2. For the purposes of Article 156, *fixed platform* means an artificial island, installation, or structure permanently attached to the seabed for the purpose of exploration or exploitation of resources or for other economic purposes.

## Commentary

The criminal offense of unlawful acts against fixed platforms is derived from the Protocol for the Suppression of Unlawful Acts against the Safety of Fixed Platforms Located on the Continental Shelf (entry into force, March 1, 1992). For a discussion of the drafting of this protocol and its substantive content, reference should be made to the *Legislative Guide to the Universal Anti-Terrorism Conventions and Protocols*, prepared by the United Nations Office on Drugs and Crime. The legislative guide points out that it is in the interest of all states, even landlocked states, to ratify and implement this protocol for two reasons. First, the ratification and implementation is an international obligation under Security Council Resolution 1373 (2001). Second, a landlocked state, while it has no fixed platforms, may find itself in a position where a national has been killed or injured on board a fixed platform, and the landlocked state wishes to assert jurisdiction over the offense. Where the state has implemented offenses related to vessels and fixed platforms into its domestic law, and where it has incorporated the grounds of extraterritorial jurisdiction, under Article 3(2) of the protocol, it could prosecute a national for an offense committed on board a fixed platform.

The wording of Article 156.1 is taken from Article 1 of the Protocol for the Suppression of Unlawful Acts against the Safety of Fixed Platforms Located on the Continental Shelf. Articles 2(2)(a) and 2(2)(b) of the protocol also require that attempts to commit any of the offenses mentioned in Article 1, or abetting or being an accomplice to a person who commits such offenses, be criminalized in domestic legislation. While these grounds of liability are not specifically ennumerated in Article 156, attempt is covered under Article 27 of the MCC and abetting and accomplice liability are covered under Article 31.

Paragraph 2: The definition of fixed platform is taken from Article 1(3) of the Protocol for the Suppression of Unlawful Acts against the Safety of Fixed Platforms Located on the Continental Shelf.

# *Article 156.2: Penalty*

1. The applicable penalty range for the criminal offense of unlawful acts against the safety of fixed platforms is five to twenty years' imprisonment.
2. When the unlawful acts against the safety of fixed platforms involve the killing of any person, the applicable penalty range is ten to thirty years' imprisonment.

## Commentary

Paragraph 2: In light of the fact that Article 156.1(1)(f) on unlawful acts against the safety of fixed platforms sets out killing as a potential element of this offense, which is liable to a higher penalty range under the MCC than the other acts mentioned in this article, it was decided to create a separate penalty range for unlawful acts against the safety of fixed platforms that involve the killing of a person.

# Article 157: Piracy

## *Article 157.1: Definition of Offense*

1. A person commits the criminal offense of piracy when he or she commits any of the following acts:
   (a) any illegal acts of violence or detention or any other acts of deprivation committed for private ends by the crew or passengers of a private ship or a private aircraft and directed:
      (i) on the high seas against another ship or aircraft, or against persons or property on board such ship or aircraft; or
      (ii) against a ship, aircraft, persons, or property in a place outside the jurisdiction of any state; or
   (b) any act of voluntary participation in the operation of a ship or aircraft with knowledge or facts making it a pirate ship or aircraft.
2. The acts of piracy as defined, committed by a warship, government ship, or government aircraft whose crew has mutinied and taken control of the ship or aircraft, are assimilated to acts committed by a private ship.

### Commentary

Piracy was recognized as an international crime long before genocide, crimes against humanity, and war crimes were. Piracy, as a criminal offense, is no longer as prevalent around the world as it used to be. But there are certain regions of the world, including several post-conflict states, where piracy still represents a significant threat. The Convention on the Law of the Sea (1982) (the Montego Bay Convention) provides a definition of piracy in Article 101. This definition has been used in the MCC. Piracy is a criminal offense for which universal jurisdiction is claimed under Article 6 of the MCC.

When a state is dealing with outbreaks of piracy, investigating piracy, or seeking to implement legislation on piracy, reference should be made to the International Maritime Organization (IMO), a specialized United Nations agency whose purpose is to assist states in taking measures to improve the safety and security of international shipping. The IMO also operates an extensive technical cooperation program that focuses on improving the ability of developing states to combat piracy. Reference should be made to the IMO Recommendation to Governments for Preventing and Suppressing Piracy and the IMO Recommendation on Armed Robbery against Ships, Guidance to Ship-owners and Ship Operators, Shipmasters and Crew on Preventing and Suppressing Acts of Piracy and Armed Robbery. In addition, reference should be made to the Code of Practice for the Investigation of the Crimes of Piracy and Armed Robbery against Ships (Resolution A.922[22]) and Measures to Prevent the Registration of Phantom Ships (Resolution A.923[22]), both of which were adopted by the IMO assembly. Also of relevance is the International Maritime Bureau (IMB), a specialized division of the International Chamber of Commerce associated with the IMO. The IMB Piracy Reporting Centre maintains round-the-clock watch on the world's shipping lanes, reports pirate attacks to local policing agencies, and issues warnings about piracy hot spots to shipping, both throughout the year and in its annual reports.

## *Article 157.2: Penalty*

The applicable penalty range for the criminal offense of piracy is five to twenty years' imprisonment.

# Article 158: Bombing

## *Article 158.1: Definition of Offense*

1. A person commits the criminal offense of bombing when he or she unlawfully delivers, places, discharges, or detonates an explosive or incendiary weapon or device.
2. For the purposes of Article 158, *explosive or incendiary weapon or device* has the same meaning as in Article 148.1(2)(a).

### Commentary

**Paragraph 1:** The wording of Article 158.1 is identical to the wording contained in Article 148.1 on terrorist bombing, minus two elements of the latter crime: the defined target of the bombing (i.e., a place of public use, a state or governmental facility, a public transportation system, or an infrastructure facility) and the requisite intention under Article 148.1(1)(d). Therefore, a person who bombs, for example, another person's house or place of business could be convicted of bombing. The only intention element required is the intention to deliver, place, discharge, or detonate the explosive incendiary or other lethal device. The criminal offense of bombing has been common in some post-conflict states, particularly in states emerging from an ethnically charged conflict, such as Kosovo.

Paragraph 2: Reference should be made to Article 148 and its accompanying commentary.

## *Article 158.2: Penalty*

The applicable penalty range for the criminal offense of bombing is three to fifteen years' imprisonment.

# Article 159: Disruption of Supply of Public Installations

## *Article 159.1: Definition of Offense*

A person commits the criminal offense of disruption of supply of public installations when he or she, in the knowledge that his or her action may result in a disturbance to the supply of services to the population or the economy, destroys, damages, or removes public installations or equipment such as water, sewerage, energy, fuel, or communications.

### Commentary

The offense aims to prosecute those who seek to destroy, damage, remove, or disrupt public installations vital to the functioning of the state and the well-being of its population. The public installations referred to in Article 159 are illustrative and not exhaustive. Public installations could also include dams, pipelines, and underwater cables, and electricity, gas, and heating installations. This offense has been included in the MCC in response to the requests of experts working in post-conflict states, such as the Democratic Republic of the Congo, where such acts occur frequently but cannot be prosecuted due to a lack of legislative basis. The destruction of public installations has also been widely perpetrated in Iraq, where oil pipelines have been targeted, and was a common occurrence in Albania, where electrical lines were cut and other public installations interfered with during the nation's transition from the communist era. In some post-conflict states, such as Iraq, public installations have been targeted by criminal elements, often with the intention to intimidate the local population or to compel a government to act or refrain from acting.

A variety of means may be used to disrupt the supply of public installations, including the use of bombs. Where a bomb is used to disturb the supply of public installations, there may be an overlap between the criminal offense of disruption of supply of public installations and that of terrorist bombing under Article 148. This article refers to the destruction of an infrastructure facility, as defined in Article 148.1(2)(e), which could include a facility for the supply of water, energy, or fuel to the population. To convict a person of terrorist bombing, he or she needs to have the intention to destroy the infrastructure facility, as opposed to simple knowledge that his or her actions may result in disturbance to the supply of services to the population or the economy. Reference should be made to Article 148 and its accompanying commentary.

## *Article 159.2: Penalty*

The applicable penalty range for the criminal offense of disruption of supply of public installations is two to ten years' imprisonment.

# Article 160: Destruction or Unauthorized Removal of Cultural Property

## *Article 160.1: Definition of Offense*

1. A person commits the criminal offense of destruction or unauthorized removal of cultural property when he or she:
   (a) damages or destroys cultural property; or
   (b) unlawfully removes cultural property from the state.
2. For the purposes of Article 160, *cultural property* means property that, on religious or secular grounds, is of importance for archaeology, prehistory, history, literature, art, or science and that belongs to one of the following categories:
   (a) rare collections and specimens of fauna, flora, minerals, and anatomy, and objects of paleontological interest;
   (b) property relating to history, including the history of science and technology and military and social history; to the life of national leaders, thinkers, scientists, and artists; or to events of national importance;

(c) products of archaeological excavations (including regular and clandestine) or archaeological discoveries;

(d) elements of artistic or historical monuments or archaeological sites that have been dismembered;

(e) antiquities more than one hundred years old, such as inscriptions, coins, and engraved seals;

(f) objects of ethnological interest;

(g) property of artistic interest, such as:

  (i) pictures, paintings, and drawings produced entirely by hand on any support and in any material, excluding industrial designs and any manufactured articles decorated by hand;

  (ii) original works of statuary art and sculpture in any material;

  (iii) original engravings, prints, and lithographs;

  (iv) original artistic assemblages and montages in any material;

(h) rare manuscripts and incunabula or old books, documents, and publications of special interest (historical, artistic, scientific, literary, and so on), singly or in collections;

(i) postage, revenue, and similar stamps, singly or in collections;

(j) archives, including sound, photographic, and cinematographic archives; and

(k) articles of furniture more than one hundred years old and old musical instruments.

## Commentary

Paragraph 1: Organized criminal groups are routinely involved in trafficking cultural property, particularly in post-conflict states where weak criminal justice systems are unable to fully enforce the law. A number of international conventions focus on cultural property. These include the Hague Convention for the Protection of Cultural Property (1954); the Convention on the International Trade in Endangered Species of Wild Flora and Fauna (1963); and the Convention on the Means of Prohibiting and Preventing the Illicit Import, Export and Transfer of Ownership of Cultural Property (1970). Another international instrument, the Convention on Stolen or Illegally Exported Cultural Objects, addresses the problem of trafficking in cultural property from a private law perspective. The 1954 Hague convention focuses on the protection of cultural property in wartime only. The 1963 convention aims to ensure that the international trade in specimens of wild animals and plants does not threaten their survival. Finally, the 1970 convention sets out certain obligations upon states parties to protect cultural property through the regulation of the import, export, and transfer of ownership. It requires that a state party establish a national service for the protection of cultural property that would, among other things, create a national inventory of protected property (Article 5). Furthermore, the convention requires that a certification process for the exportation of cultural property be established. This process is a reciprocal one among states parties.

Article 3 of the convention says that the import, export, or transfer of ownership of cultural property in violation of the certification procedure should be deemed illicit, although it does not specify that penal provisions need to be introduced into domestic legislation. Article 8 of the convention provides, in relation to some obligations contained in it, that "penalties or administrative sanctions" must be imposed for their breach. A post-conflict state should consider implementing the provisions of the convention. The convention provides that technical assistance in doing so can be obtained from the United Nations Education, Scientific and Cultural Organization (UNESCO).

Although the convention contains no express requirements with regard to substantive criminal law, it was considered imperative to include criminal law provisions on cultural property in the MCC. The destruction of cultural property has been evidenced in post-conflict states, as has its removal, particularly at the hands of organized criminal gangs. There are two elements to Article 160. First, Article 160 focuses on the destruction of cultural property, as defined in Paragraph 2. Second, Article 160 focuses on the removal of cultural property from the state. Paragraph 1(b) refers specifically to the fact that the removal of cultural property must be "unlawful." In certain circumstances, its removal may be lawful and therefore not subject to criminal jurisdiction—for example, where it is permissible under a cultural-property licensing and regulation system established under the Convention on the Means of Prohibiting and Preventing the Illicit Import, Export and Transfer of Ownership of Cultural Property (1970).

Paragraph 2: The definition of cultural property in this paragraph is taken from Article 1 of the Convention on the Means of Prohibiting and Preventing the Illicit Import, Export and Transfer of Ownership of Cultural Property (1970). When a state has compiled an inventory of national cultural property, reference could be made to this list in the definition, either as a replacement for the provisions there or to supplement them.

## *Article 160.2: Penalty*

The applicable penalty range for the criminal offense of destruction or unauthorized removal of cultural property is two to ten years' imprisonment.

# Article 161: Incitement to Crime on Account of Hatred

## *Article 161.1: Definition of Offense*

A person commits the criminal offense of incitement to crime on account of hatred when he or she:

(a) directly and publicly incites another;

(b) to commit a criminal offense;

(c) on account of hatred for a national, ethnic, racial, religious, or similarly identifiable group;

(d) in circumstances in which there is a substantial likelihood of imminently causing the commission of such an offense.

## Commentary

The right to freedom of expression is guaranteed in the constitutions of most states. In addition, it is protected under international law in instruments such as the Universal Declaration of Human Rights (Article 19), the International Covenant on Civil and Political Rights (Article 19), the African Charter on Human and People's Rights (Article 9), the European Convention on Human Rights and Fundamental Freedoms (Article 10), the American Convention on Human Rights (Article 13), the Convention on the Rights of the Child (Article 12), and the African Charter on the Rights and Welfare of the Child (Article 7). A person's right to freedom of expression is not an absolute right, however, and may be limited in certain circumstances. According to Article 19 of the International Covenant on Civil and Political Rights, restrictions on freedom of expression must be "provided by law" and "necessary for respect of the rights and reputations of others" or "for the protection of national security or of public order, or of public health or morals." Other conventions provide for similar restrictions on this right. In particular, Article 20 of the International Covenant on Civil and Political Rights includes a positive obligation to restrict freedom of expression in the case of "advocacy of national, racial or religious hatred that constitutes incitement to discrimination, hostility or violence." Article 20(2) provides that such advocacy "shall be prohibited by law." Similar obligations are contained in Article 13(5) of the American Convention on Human Rights and Article 4(a) of the International Convention on the Elimination of All Forms of Racial Discrimination.

Incitement to crime on account of hatred, described in the conventions and in the MCC, is distinct from what is colloquially known as hate speech. Hate-speech legislation in many jurisdictions involves the criminalization of the spreading of or inciting racial, religious, or ethnic hatred. In contrast, the MCC requires actual incitement to a criminal offense (e.g., through encouragement, suggestion, request, persuasion, threats, or pressuring of another person) that is both direct and public and where there is a likelihood of the incitement provoking imminent commission of the offense. The international conventions do not specifically say whether or not incitement must be accompanied by the actual commission of a criminal offense. Some states have chosen to criminalize incitement without the need for the commission of a criminal offense. In other states, legislation requires a nexus between an act of incitement and the commission of a criminal offense. Under the MCC, incitement to commit a criminal offense is already criminalized under Article 30. Reference should be made to Article 30 and its accompanying commentary. Article 161, as it relates specifically to incitement based on hatred, is a hybrid of the two positions mentioned previously. There is no requirement that a criminal offense actually be committed, although it is necessary that there be a substantial likelihood of the imminent commission of a criminal offense.

Some argue that, particularly in a post-conflict state where different and adverse ethnic groups are spreading hatred through public proclamations, newspapers, or the radio, hate speech—as opposed to incitement to crime on account of hatred in Article 161—should be criminalized to address the problem. In contrast, others argue that this provision would impinge too much upon a person's right to freedom of expression, going well beyond what is permissible. The drafters of the MCC, and the experts consulted in its vetting process, many of whom had witnessed firsthand the spreading of ethnic or religious hatred in post-conflict states, sided with the latter view. Many experts believed it could be dangerous to introduce hate-speech legislation into a fragile post-conflict state where the criminal justice system may not be fully functional and may not have adequate controls. Another relevant factor is that such legislation may have been used during a conflict or under a prior regime as a tool of political and popular suppression of antigovernment sentiments, as was the case in South Africa during the apartheid era. The United Nations Mission in Kosovo Regulation 2000/4 on the Prohibition against Incitement to National, Racial, Religious or Ethnic Hatred, Discord or Intolerance introduced two offenses. The first was similar to that described in Article 161. The second offense was the spreading of "hatred, discord or intolerance between national, racial, religious, ethnic or other groups." The regulation was gravely criticized by the nongovernmental organization Article 19, which deals specifically with issues surrounding the right to freedom of expression. The criticisms are not unique to Kosovo but apply to any post-conflict state considering the introduction of similar legislation. In addition to criticizing the regulation on the grounds of violation of freedom of expression mentioned above, Article 19 stated that the "longer term solution [to ethnic hatred] lies in fundamental social processes—including conflict resolution and the building of tolerance and acceptance—which are only possible in an atmosphere of open debate. The simple expedient of banning speech may satisfy external demands for action, but will not advance social processes which could bring about a lasting solution to the problem." Significantly, the group went on to state that "imprisoning someone for breach of this regulation is more likely to generate a backlash than bring the various communities together or to prevent violent clashes."

### *Article 161.2: Penalty*

The applicable penalty range for the criminal offense of incitement to crime on account of hatred is two to ten years' imprisonment.

## Article 162: Unauthorized Border or Boundary Crossing

### *Article 162.1: Definition of Offense*

A person commits the criminal offense of unauthorized border or boundary crossing when he or she crosses a border or boundary of the state at any location other than an authorized border or boundary crossing.

#### Commentary

In many post-conflict states, there are too few policing officials, troops, or border-control agents to control the flow of persons into and out of the state. The regulation of the border region of a state may be a momentous task depending on the size of the state. In a peace operation, international military forces may initially be charged with border duty, a task that may then be handed over to national forces or border-control police. Without an effective border-control mechanism, a post-conflict state could receive an influx of people, potentially including criminals, rebel fighters, or terrorists, further destabilizing the state.

The United Nations Mission in Kosovo promulgated Regulation 2001/10 on the Prohibition of Unauthorized Border/Boundary Crossings to address the issue of border control. It provided for the designation of authorized border and boundary crossing points (section 2) and created a number of related criminal offenses (section 3). Article 162 draws inspiration from Regulation 2001/10. Further, measures additional to criminal legislation will be necessary to deal with border-related issues. Significant reforms will be required both in border control and in refugee or migration laws.

### *Article 162.2: Penalty*

1. The applicable penalty range for the criminal offense of unauthorized border or boundary crossing is one to five years' imprisonment.
2. The court may impose a fine, as a principal penalty, upon a person convicted of unauthorized border or boundary crossing.

# Section 12: Offenses against United Nations and Associated Personnel

## Article 163: Endangering United Nations and Associated Personnel

### *Article 163.1: Definition of Offense*

1. A person commits the criminal offense of endangering United Nations and associated personnel when he or she:
   - (a) unlawfully kills any United Nations or associated personnel;
   - (b) kidnaps any United Nations or associated personnel;
   - (c) commits an attack on the person or liberty of any United Nations or associated personnel;
   - (d) engages in a violent attack upon the official premises, private accommodations, or means of transport of any United Nations or associated personnel, where such an attack is likely to endanger his or her person or liberty; or
   - (e) makes a serious threat to commit the offenses set out in subparagraphs (a) to (d).
2. For the purposes of Article 163:
   - (a) *United Nations personnel* means:
     - (i) persons engaged or deployed by the secretary-general of the United Nations as members of the military, police, or civilian components of a United Nations operation; or

(ii) other officials and experts on missions of the United Nations, its specialized agencies, or the International Atomic Energy Agency who are present in an official capacity in the area where a United Nations operation is being conducted.

(b) *Associated personnel* means:

(i) persons assigned by a government or an international organization with the agreement of the competent organ of the United Nations;

(ii) persons engaged by the secretary-general of the United Nations, a specialized agency of the United Nations, or the International Atomic Energy Agency; or

(iii) persons deployed by a humanitarian, nongovernmental organization or agency, under an agreement with the secretary-general of the United Nations, a specialized agency of the United Nations, or the International Atomic Energy Agency, to carry out activities in support of the fulfillment of the mandate of the United Nations operation.

(c) *United Nations operation* means an operation established by the competent organ of the United Nations in accordance with the Charter of the United Nations and conducted under United Nations authority and control:

(i) where the operation is for the purpose of maintaining or restoring international peace and security; or

(ii) where the Security Council or the General Assembly has declared, for the purpose of the Convention on the Safety of United Nations and Associated Personnel of December 9, 1994, that there exists an exceptional risk to the safety of the personnel participating in the operation.

## Commentary

Paragraph 1: The criminal offense of endangering United Nations and associated personnel is taken from the Convention on the Safety of United Nations and Associated Personnel (1994). The drafting of this convention was prompted by "the growing number of deaths and injuries resulting from deliberate attacks against United Nations and associated personnel" (preamble, paragraph 1) in United Nations operations. This problem is evident in many past and current peace operations. In fact, such attacks have increased greatly in recent years. The convention covers both military and civilian United Nations and associated personnel. As existing measures of protection for these personnel were deemed inadequate (preamble, paragraph 6), Article 9 of the convention requires all states parties to the convention to introduce the acts set out in Article (9)(1) (reproduced above in Article 163.1[1]) into domestic criminal legislation.

Articles 9(1)(d) and 9(1)(e) of the convention further provide that attempts to commit the prescribed offenses, participating in them, or organizing or ordering such acts should also be penalized. All these grounds of criminal responsibility are covered in the General Part of the MCC under Section 10, "Criminal Attempt" (Article 27), and Section 11, "Participation in a Criminal Offense" (Articles 28–33).

Article 10(1) of the convention requires that territorial jurisdiction and extraterritorial jurisdiction based on nationality be established over the offenses, which are covered in Article 163 of the MCC. This requirement is covered by Article 4 ("Territorial Jurisdiction") and Article 5 ("Extraterritorial Jurisdiction") of the MCC. The convention also provides other discretionary grounds of jurisdiction, namely, jurisdiction over stateless persons based on their habitual residence, Article 10(2)(a); jurisdiction based on the nationality of the victim, Article 10(2)(b); and jurisdiction based on "an attempt to compel that State to do or to abstain from doing any act," Article 10(2)(c). Jurisdiction under the MCC is established on the first two discretionary grounds. Reference should be made to Article 5 and its accompanying commentary.

The Convention on the Safety of United Nations and Associated Personnel (1994) also has provisions on prevention of crimes against United Nations and associated personnel (Article 11), communication of information to the United Nations (Article 12), the duty to prosecute alleged offenders (Article 14), extradition (Articles 13 and 15), mutual legal assistance (Article 16), and notification of outcome of proceedings (Article 18), which should be referred to by a state implementing its obligations under the convention.

Paragraph 1(a): In the original text of the convention, the term *murder* is used. In Paragraph 1(a), this term has been replaced by *unlawful kills*, consistent with the terminology used in the MCC. Reference should be made to Article 89 on unlawful killing.

Paragraph 1(b): Reference should be made to Article 106 for the definition of kidnapping.

Paragraph 2(a): The definition of United Nations personnel is taken from Article 1(a) of the Convention on the Safety of United Nations and Associated Personnel (1994).

Paragraph 2(b): The definition of associated personnel is taken from Article 1(b) of the Convention on the Safety of United Nations and Associated Personnel (1994).

Paragraph 2(c): The definition of United Nations operation is taken from Article 1(c) of the Convention on the Safety of United Nations and Associated Personnel (1994).

# *Article 163.2: Penalty*

1. The applicable penalty range for the criminal offense of endangering United Nations and associated personnel is five to twenty years' imprisonment.
2. When the criminal offense of endangering United Nations and associated personnel involves the unlawful killing of any United Nations or associated personnel, the applicable penalty range is ten to thirty years' imprisonment.

## Commentary

Paragraph 2: Article 163.1(1)(a) states that killing United Nations or associated personnel may form part of the element of the criminal offense of endangering United Nations and associated personnel. Killing is liable to a higher penalty range under the MCC than the other acts mentioned in it. Thus it was decided to create a separate penalty range when the offense involves the killing of a person.

# Section 13: Offenses Involving Firearms, Ammunition, Explosives, and Weapons

## General Commentary

During a conflict, trafficking in weapons, firearms, or explosives is typically widespread, often orchestrated by organized criminal gangs to feed the conflict. In a post-conflict state, dealing with the surplus of weapons or firearms in circulation is a top priority for both the domestic government and international actors. Often, former combatants are brought into disarmament, demobilization, and reintegration (DDR) programs. Disarmament involves the collection and disposal of weapons; demobilization involves the disbandment of armed groups for administrative processing and discharge orientation; and reintegration seeks to reintegrate former combatants into society through compensation, training programs, or employment.

Once this problem has been addressed, other measures need to be taken to regulate weapons production, the flow of weapons into and out of the state, and issues of who can possess a firearm. These measures are more proactive in nature than DDR programs and involve the establishment both of regulatory licensing systems for firearms, explosives, and weapons and of criminal offenses for unlawful possession. (In contrast, in a DDR program a person is not penalized for admitting that he or she possessed a weapon and for handing it over; instead, he or she is usually paid for the weapon.) The United Nations Transitional Administration in East Timor promulgated UNTAET Regulation 2001/5 on Firearms, Ammunition, Explosives and Other Offensive Weapons in East Timor. The United Nations Mission in Kosovo promulgated UNMIK Regulation 2001/7 on the Authorization of Possession of Weapons in Kosovo. In Iraq, the Coalition Provisional Authority promulgated CPA Order No. 3 on Weapons Control. The regulations focused primarily on the internal regulation of firearms, ammunition, and explosives by establishing a scheme of registration under which a person could legally possess firearms, weapons, or explosives. In some cases, such as in East Timor, the scheme also regulated the import and export of weapons. In each case the scope of the prohibition on weapons, firearms, and explosives was slightly different. In East Timor, for example, machetes were not prohibited weapons, because they were required for farming. In Kosovo, hunting weapons were permissible. In Iraq, firearms for personal use at home or in businesses were permissible subject to the licensing regulations. Defining what weapons will be subject to a domestic regulatory regime should therefore be considered anew in each post-conflict state.

The regulation of weapons is a matter not only of domestic concern but also of international concern. In 2001 the Protocol against the Illicit Manufacturing of and Trafficking in Firearms, Their Parts and Components and Ammunition, supplementing the United Nations Convention against Transnational Organized Crime, was drafted. The protocol provides for a comprehensive system to control the movement of firearms, their parts, and ammunition. It focuses on their import, export, and transit and establishes a reciprocal system between states to track the flow of firearms and ammunition. It also deals extensively with record keeping (Article 7) and the marking of firearms (Article 8)—necessary to track and trace individual firearms—and the deactivation of firearms (Article 9). Furthermore, and important with respect to the MCC, it contains provisions on certain firearms-related criminal offenses under Article 4 that states parties should introduce into domestic legislation. Reference should be made to the *Legislative Guide for the Implementation of the Protocol against the Illicit Manufacturing of and Trafficking in Firearms, Their Parts and Components and Ammunition, Supplementing the United Nations Convention against Transnational Organized Crime* for a discussion of the substantive provisions of the protocol, including the regulatory system established under it.

The criminal offenses contained in Section 13 are a mixture of criminal offenses required under the Protocol against Illicit Manufacturing of and Trafficking in Firearms, Their Parts and Components and Ammunition, supplementing the United Nations Convention against Transnational Organized Crime (which have both an international and a domestic dimension), and criminal offenses provided for in regulations drafted for post-conflict states such as Kosovo, East Timor, and Iraq.

Ideally, a state would draft a separate piece of legislation that establishes a regulatory and licensing mechanism for firearms, their parts and components, ammunition, explosives, and weapons (all of which are dealt with in Section 13), including both procedural dimensions and substantive criminal offenses for breach of the mechanism. Under the Protocol against Illicit Manufacturing of and Trafficking in Firearms, Their Parts and Components and Ammunition, supplementing the United Nations Convention against Transnational Organized Crime, it is also necessary to establish a system of record keeping and marking of firearms. Reforms are necessary to establish and regulate a licensing system and a system of record keeping. These reforms may also include the extension of criminal legislation on weapons/firearms/explosives regulation to include minor offenses linked to breaches of procedural provisions, such as failure to inform the weapons-licensing authority of a change of address or failure to report a licensed weapon missing or stolen.

Other legal provisions are required with respect to firearms offenses and their regulation. These include provisions on confiscation and seizure (as set out in Article 6 of the protocol); cooperation between states (Article 13); training and technical assistance (Article 14); and the regulation of brokering in firearms (Article 15). To adequately address the issue of firearms, these provisions should be looked at by states seeking to implement the convention into domestic law. The legislative guide to the convention provides useful guidance on these provisions. Because the protocol is supplementary to the United Nations Convention against Transnational Organized Crime, Article 1(2) of the protocol provides that the provisions of the convention are applicable also, with necessary modifications. Reference should be made to the commentary to Article 136 of the MCC, which discusses these obligations.

# Article 164: Illicit Manufacturing or Trafficking in Firearms or Ammunition

## *Article 164.1: Definition of Offense*

1. A person commits the criminal offense of illicit manufacturing or trafficking in firearms or ammunition when he or she:

   (a) illicitly manufactures firearms, their parts, components, or ammunition; or

   (b) illicitly traffics firearms, their parts, components, or ammunition.

2. For the purposes of Article 164:

   (a) *firearm* means any portable barreled weapon that expels, is designed to expel, or may be readily converted to expel a shot, bullet, or projectile by the action of an explosive, excluding antique firearms or their replicas;

   (b) *parts and components* means any element or replacement element specifically designed for a firearm and essential to its operation, including a barrel, frame or receiver, slide or cylinder, bolt or breech block, and any device designed or adapted to diminish the sound caused by firing a firearm;

   (c) *ammunition* means the complete round or its components, including cartridge cases, primers, propellant powder, bullets, or projectiles used in a firearm;

   (d) *illicit manufacturing* means the manufacturing or assembly of firearms, their parts and components, or ammunition:

      (i) from parts and components illicitly trafficked;

      (ii) without a license or authorization from the state;

      (iii) without marking the firearms at the time of manufacture; and

   (e) *illicit trafficking* means the unlawful import, export, acquisition, sale, delivery, movement, or transfer of firearms, their parts and components, and ammunition.

## Commentary

Paragraph 1: Articles 5(1)(a) and 5(1)(b) of the Protocol against the Illicit Manufacturing of and Trafficking in Firearms, Their Parts and Components and Ammunition, supplementing the United Nations Convention against Organized Crime requires that a state party establish the criminal offense set out in Article 164. The definitions of illicit manufacturing and illicit trafficking are contained in Articles 3(d) and 3(e) of the protocol. For further discussion on the core content of these offenses, reference should be made to the *Legislative Guide for the Implementation of the Protocol against the Illicit Manufacturing of and Trafficking in Firearms, Their Parts and Components and Ammunition, Supplementing the United Nations Convention against Transnational Organized Crime*, in particular paragraphs 166–218. The protocol requires that any attempt at, participation as an accomplice in, organizing, directing, aiding, abetting, facilitating, or counseling on the manufacturing or trafficking of firearms, their parts and components, or ammunition be included in domestic criminal legislation. These grounds of liability are covered in Sections 10 and 11 of the General Part of the MCC. Reference should be made to Articles 27–32. As mentioned previously, many of the provisions from the United Nations Convention against Transnational Organized Crime, such as jurisdiction, apply to the present criminal offense. Reference should be made to the commentary to Article 136 of the MCC, which discusses this issue in greater detail.

Whether or not the trafficking or manufacturing of firearms, their parts and components, and ammunition is illicit will depend on legislation outside the MCC that regulates licit, or legitimate, manufacture, import, export, sale, delivery, movement, and so on of firearms, their parts and components, and ammunition. This legislation would be part of the regulation and licensing system discussed in the general commentary at the beginning of this section. Reference should be made to this commentary. Obviously, the criminal offense set out in Article 164 could not be introduced without this legislation having already been introduced or being introduced simultaneously.

Paragraph 2(a): The wording of this paragraph comes from Article 3(a) of the protocol. Reference should be made to the *Legislative Guide for the Implementation of the Protocol against the Illicit Manufacturing of and Trafficking in Firearms, Their Parts and Components and Ammunition, Supplementing the United Nations Convention against Transnational Organized Crime*, in particular paragraphs 24–43, for a discussion of the meaning of Article 3(a).

Paragraph 2(b): The wording of this paragraph comes from Article 3(b) of the protocol. Reference should be made to the *Legislative Guide for the Implementation of the Protocol against the Illicit Manufacturing of and Trafficking in Firearms, Their Parts and Components and Ammunition, Supplementing the United Nations Convention against Transnational Organized Crime*, in particular paragraphs 44–51, for a discussion of the meaning of Article 3(b).

Paragraph 2(c): The wording of this paragraph comes from Article 3(c) of the protocol. Reference should be made to the *Legislative Guide for the Implementation of the*

*Protocol against the Illicit Manufacturing of and Trafficking in Firearms, Their Parts and Components and Ammunition, Supplementing the United Nations Convention against Transnational Organized Crime*, in particular paragraphs 52–58, for a discussion of the meaning of Article 3(c).

Paragraph 2(d): The wording of this paragraph comes from Article 3(d) of the protocol. Reference should be made to the *Legislative Guide for the Implementation of the Protocol against the Illicit Manufacturing of and Trafficking in Firearms, Their Parts and Components and Ammunition, Supplementing the United Nations Convention against Transnational Organized Crime*, in particular paragraphs 181–200, for a discussion of the meaning of Article 3(d).

Paragraph 2(e): The wording of this paragraph comes from Article 3(e) of the protocol. Reference should be made to the *Legislative Guide for the Implementation of the Protocol against the Illicit Manufacturing of and Trafficking in Firearms, Their Parts and Components and Ammunition, Supplementing the United Nations Convention against Transnational Organized Crime*, in particular paragraphs 201–218, for a discussion of the meaning of Article 3(e).

## *Article 164.2: Penalty*

The applicable penalty range for the criminal offense of illicit manufacturing or trafficking in firearms or ammunition is three to fifteen years' imprisonment.

# Article 165: Illicit Obliteration, Removal, or Altering of Markings on Firearms

## *Article 165.1: Definition of Offense*

1. A person commits the criminal offense of illicit obliteration, removal, or altering of markings on firearms when he or she illicitly obliterates, removes, or alters the markings on firearms.
2. For the purposes of Article 165, *firearm* has the same meaning as in Article 164.1(2)(a).

## Commentary

Paragraph 1: Article 5(1)(c) of the Protocol against Illicit Manufacturing of and Trafficking in Firearms, Their Parts and Components and Ammunition, supplementing the United Nations Convention against Transnational Organized Crime, requires that a state party establish the criminal offense set out in Article 165. Reference should be made to the *Legislative Guide for the Implementation of the Protocol against the Illicit Manufacturing of and Trafficking in Firearms, Their Parts and Components and Ammunition, Supplementing the United Nations Convention against Transnational Organized Crime*, in particular paragraphs 219–228, for a discussion of the core content of this offense. The protocol requires that any attempt at, participation as an accomplice in, organizing, directing, aiding, abetting, facilitating, or counseling on the obliteration, removal, or altering of markings on firearms be included in domestic criminal legislation. These grounds of liability are covered in Sections 10 and 11 of the General Part of the MCC. Reference should be made to Articles 27–32. As mentioned previously, many of the provisions from the United Nations Convention against Transnational Organized Crime, such as jurisdiction, apply to the present criminal offense. Reference should be made to the commentary to Article 136 of the MCC, which discusses this issue in greater detail.

Whether the obliteration, removing, or altering of markings on firearms is illicit or legitimate will depend on legislation outside the MCC that regulates marking. This would be part of the regulation and licensing system discussed in the general commentary at the beginning of this section. Reference should be made to this commentary. Obviously, the criminal offense set out in Article 165 could not be introduced without legislation on the licit marking of firearms being introduced earlier or at the same time.

Paragraph 2: Reference should be made to Article 164.1(2)(a) and its accompanying commentary.

## *Article 165.2: Penalty*

The applicable penalty range for the criminal offense of illicit obliteration, removal, or alteration of markings on firearms is one to five years' imprisonment.

# Article 166: Illicit Manufacturing or Trafficking in Explosives

## *Article 166.1: Definition of Offense*

1. A person commits the criminal offense of illicit manufacturing and trafficking in explosives when he or she:
   (a) illicitly manufactures explosives; or
   (b) illicitly traffics explosives.
2. For the purposes of Article 166:
   (a) *explosives* means any chemical compound, mixture, or device, the primary or common purpose of which is to function by explosion. Explosives include but are not limited to dynamite and other high explosives, detonators, safety fuses, squibs, detonating cord, igniter cord, and igniters;
   (b) *illicit manufacturing* means the manufacturing or assembly of explosives; and
   (c) *illicit trafficking* means the unlawful import, export, acquisition, sale, delivery, movement, or transfer of explosives.

## Commentary

Paragraph 1: The regulation of explosives does not fall within the ambit of the Protocol against the Illicit Manufacturing of and Trafficking in Firearms, Their Parts and Components and Ammunition, supplementing the United Nations Convention against Transnational Organized Crime. However, trafficking in explosives has been subject to criminalization in the legislation of a number of post-conflict states in recent years. Article 166 uses the criminal offense contained in Article 164, above, as its basis, but it substitutes *explosives* for the term *firearms, their parts, components, or ammunitions.*

Whether the trafficking or manufacturing of explosives is illicit will depend on legislation outside the MCC that regulates their licit manufacture, import, export, sale, delivery, movement, and so on. This legislation would be part of the regulation and licensing system discussed in the general commentary at the beginning of this section. Reference should be made to this commentary. The criminal offense set out in Article 166 could not be introduced without legislation on the licit manufacture, import, export, sale, delivery, and so on of explosives being introduced earlier or at the same time.

Paragraph 2(a): The definition of explosives was arrived at through a comparative survey of the definition of explosives from different jurisdictions, whereupon the suitable definition was found based on the advice of explosives experts sought by the drafters. It is important to point out use of the term *primary* or *common purpose* in the definition. Many seemingly innocuous substances, such as a common fertilizer used in farming, are explosive in nature. That said, the fact that their primary or common purpose is as fertilizer exempts them from the definition of explosive.

Paragraph 2(b): The definition contained in this paragraph is based on Article 3(d) of the protocol. Reference should be made to the commentary accompanying Article 164.1(2)(d).

Paragraph 2(c): The definition contained in this paragraph is based on Article 3(e) of the protocol. Reference should be made to the commentary accompanying Article 164.1(2)(e).

## *Article 166.2: Penalty*

The applicable penalty range for the criminal offense of illicit manufacturing or trafficking in explosives is three to fifteen years' imprisonment.

# Article 167: Unlawful Purchase of Firearms, Ammunition, Explosives, or Weapons

## *Article 167.1: Definition of Offense*

1. A person commits the criminal offense of unlawful purchase of firearms, ammunition, explosives, or weapons when he or she unlawfully purchases firearms, ammunition, explosives, or weapons.
2. For the purposes of Article 167:
   (a) *firearm* has the same meaning as in Article 164.1(2)(a);
   (b) *ammunition* has the same meaning as in Article 164.1(2)(c);
   (c) *explosives* has the same meaning as in Article 166.1(2)(a); and
   (d) *weapon* means an instrument designed or redesigned for inflicting bodily harm such as crossbows, bows and arrows, pepper spray, blank-firing

weapons, replica weapons, stun guns, tasers, and all categories of weapons prohibited under the applicable law.

## Commentary

Paragraph 1: The criminal offenses of trafficking in firearms, their parts and components, ammunition, and explosives, set out above in Articles 164 and 166, all focus on criminalizing the conduct of a person involved in their removal from or introduction into the state and their sale. In contrast, Article 167 focuses on the buyer of firearms, ammunition, explosives, and weapons. No such provision exists in the Protocol against the Illicit Manufacturing of and Trafficking in Firearms, Their Parts and Components and Ammunition, supplementing the United Nations Convention against Organized Crime, but it is a common feature of domestic legislation. In addition to bringing firearms, ammunition, and explosives under the ambit of the MCC, Article 167 also criminalizes the purchase of weapons. Obviously, whether the purchase of any of these items is lawful will depend on legislation outside the MCC that regulates when they can be lawfully purchased. This legislation would be part of the regulation and licensing system discussed in the general commentary at the beginning of this section. Reference should be made to this commentary. The criminal offense set out in Article 167 could not be introduced without legislation, introduced earlier or simultaneously, that informs individuals of lawful and unlawful behavior with regard to the purchase of firearms, ammunition, explosives, and weapons.

Paragraph 2(a): Reference should be made to Article 164.1(2)(a) and its accompanying commentary.

Paragraph 2(b): Reference should be made to Article 164.1(2)(c) and its accompanying commentary.

Paragraph 2(c): Reference should be made to Article 166.1(2)(a) and its accompanying commentary.

Paragraph 2(d): This paragraph contains a general definition and a nonexhaustive list of weapons. A state may wish to incorporate more weapons into the applicable law. As mentioned above, the exact scope of the prohibition on weapons is slightly different in the legislation of different post-conflict states.

## *Article 167.2: Penalty*

1. The applicable penalty range for the criminal offense of unlawful purchase of firearms, ammunition, explosives, or weapons is one to five years' imprisonment.

2. The applicable penalty range for the criminal offense of unlawful purchase of firearms, ammunition, explosives, or weapons is two to ten years' imprisonment where a trafficable quantity of firearms, ammunition, explosives, or weapons is purchased.
3. The court may impose a fine, as a principal penalty, upon a person convicted of unlawful possession of firearms, ammunition, explosives, or weapons where the applicable penalty range is one to five years' imprisonment.

# Article 168: Unlawful Possession, Control, or Ownership of Firearms, Ammunition, Explosives, or Weapons

## *Article 168.1: Definition of Offense*

1. A person commits the criminal offense of unlawful possession, control, or ownership of firearms, ammunition, explosives, or weapons when he or she unlawfully possesses, controls, or owns a firearm, ammunition, explosive, or weapon.
2. For the purposes of Article 168:
   (a) *firearm* has the same meaning as in Article 164.1(2)(a);
   (b) *ammunition* has the same meaning as in Article 164.1(2)(c);
   (c) *explosives* has the same meaning as in Article 166.1(2)(a); and
   (d) *weapon* has the same meaning as in Article 167.1(2)(d).

### Commentary

Paragraph 1: The criminal offenses of unlawful possession, control, or ownership of firearms, ammunition, explosives, or weapons is not contained in the Protocol against the Illicit Manufacturing of and Trafficking in Firearms, Their Parts and Components and Ammunition, supplementing the United Nations Convention against Organized Crime, but it is characteristic of the domestic legislation of many states. In addition to bringing firearms, ammunition, and explosives under the ambit of the MCC, Article 168 also criminalizes the unlawful possession, control, or ownership of weapons, as defined in Article 167.1(2)(d). It is considered particularly important in a post-conflict context to criminalize the possession of firearms, ammunition, explosives, and weapons in order to facilitate the state's return to peace and normalcy. As discussed in the commentary to Article 167.1(2)(d), the particular weapons that are prohibited may vary from state to state and should be decided upon on an individual basis. For example, it would be unwise to prohibit the possession of instruments used for farming, such as machetes in East Timor.

Whether the possession, control, or ownership of any of these items is lawful will depend on legislation outside the MCC that regulates when they can be lawfully possessed, controlled, or owned. This legislation would be part of the regulation and licensing system discussed in the general commentary at the beginning of this section. Reference should be made to this commentary. The criminal offense set out in Article 168 could not be introduced without the prior or simultaneous introduction of legislation that informs individuals of lawful and unlawful behavior with regard to the purchase of weapons.

Paragraph 2(a): Reference should be made to Article 164.1(2)(a) and its accompanying commentary.

Paragraph 2(b): Reference should be made to Article 164.1(2)(c) and its accompanying commentary.

Paragraph 2(c): Reference should be made to Article 166.1(2)(a) and its accompanying commentary.

Paragraph 2(d): Reference should be made to Article 167.1(2)(d) and its accompanying commentary.

## *Article 168.2: Penalty*

1. The applicable penalty range for the criminal offense of unlawful possession, control, or ownership of firearms, ammunition, explosives, or weapons is one to five years' imprisonment.
2. The applicable penalty range for the criminal offense of unlawful possession, control, or ownership of firearms, ammunition, explosives, or weapons is two to ten years' imprisonment where a person possesses a trafficable quantity of firearms, ammunition, explosives, or weapons.
3. The court may impose a fine, as a principal penalty, upon a person convicted of unlawful possession, control, or ownership of firearms, ammunition, explosives, or weapons.

## Commentary

Paragraph 2: Article 168 includes two distinct penalty ranges, the higher of which applies to a person who bought a "trafficable quantity" of firearms, ammunition, explosives, or weapons. This distinction is meant to penalize persons involved in trafficking firearms, ammunition, explosives, or weapons more heavily than those who purchase them for personal use. Ordinarily, legislation would set down the quantity of firearms, ammunition, explosives, or weapons that would be deemed to constitute a trafficable quantity. For the purposes of the MCC, this has not been done. However, it is advisable that a state implementing provisions on firearms offenses do this.

# Article 169: Unlawful Use of Firearms

## *Article 169.1: Definition of Offense*

1. A person commits the criminal offense of unlawful use of firearms when he or she uses or brandishes a firearm in a threatening, intimidating, or otherwise unauthorized manner or directs another person to do the same.
2. For the purposes of Article 169, *firearm* has the same meaning as in Article 164.1(2)(a).

## Commentary

Paragraph 1: The perpetration of the criminal offense of unlawful use of firearms is independent of whether a person is lawfully in possession of firearms. The offense may be perpetrated by a person in lawful possession or unlawful possession of a firearm. In the latter case, the person would then also be criminally responsible for the criminal offense of unlawful possession of a firearm under Article 168, above. The use of a firearm in the context of aggravated robbery under Article 120 or burglary under Article 122 is an element of both criminal offenses. The person could be prosecuted for the offense of unlawful use of firearms in addition to aggravated robbery or aggravated burglary. In the present article, there is no requirement that a criminal offense be committed with the firearm. The focus of this article is simply the use of firearms in a threatening or intimidating manner.

Paragraph 2(a): Reference should be made to Article 164.1(2)(a) and its accompanying commentary.

# *Article 169.2: Penalty*

1. The applicable penalty range for the criminal offense of unlawful use of firearms is one to five years' imprisonment.
2. The court may impose a fine, as a principal penalty, upon a person convicted of unlawful use of firearms.

# Section 14: Drug Offenses

## General Commentary

Drug-related criminal offenses are often prevalent in post-conflict states, whether the drugs are being cultivated there (e.g., Afghanistan) or trafficked through the state (e.g., East Timor). Often, a post-conflict state can be a safe haven for criminal elements involved in drug-related crime, particularly where borders are porous, with no customs control, or where the police force and the criminal justice system do not function effectively or are easily subject to corruption. The drug trade in post-conflict states is often closely linked to organized criminal activities. In some cases, drug trafficking is used as a means to finance terrorist elements. Its potential to destabilize a post-conflict state and to impede the return to peace and the rule of law is great. It also has the potential to cause regional destabilization and to facilitate transnational crime. Thus tackling the drug trade in post-conflict states is often very high on the agenda for both the government and international actors and donors.

In the first place, a state needs to introduce adequate legislation penalizing drug offenses and defining what drugs are illegal to possess, import, export, and so on without authorization from the state. This list of drugs should include at a minimum those prohibited narcotic drugs and psychotropic substances listed in the schedules to the United Nations conventions referenced in the provisions below. Novel drugs are constantly emerging. A state should ensure that its drug schedule is up-to-date. Recourse should be made to the work of the Commission on Narcotic Drugs. The powers of the commission, as derived from the international treaties on narcotic drugs and psychotropic substances discussed below, include the amendment of the schedules to the conventions (once the World Health Organization makes certain findings on a particular narcotic drug or psychotropic substance). Reference should also be made to the International Narcotics Control Board (INCB). Like the Commission on Narcotic Drugs, the INCB is a subsidiary body of the United Nations Economic and Social Council. Its role is to monitor the enforcement of restrictions on narcotic drugs and psychotropic substances and to decide which precursors (defined below in Article 174) should be regulated and deemed illegal. In terms of legislation on drug offenses, reference should be made to the United Nations International Drug Control Programme (UNDCP, the predecessor to the United Nations Office on Drugs and Crime) Model Drug Abuse Bill, 2000, and the United Nations Office on Drugs and Crime's Model Law on the Classification of Narcotic Drugs, Psychotropic Substances and Precursors and on the Regulation of the Licit Cultivation, Production, Manufacture and Trading of Drugs (2003).

In conjunction with the criminalization of persons who deal illegally with drugs, it is also necessary to establish a regulatory system for the import, export, supply, and use of drugs by legitimate sources, such as pharmacies or hospitals. This was done quite early on in the United Nations Mission in Kosovo under Regulation 2000/52 on the Import, Manufacture, Sale and Distribution of Pharmaceutical Products, Including Narcotic Drugs and Psychotropic Substances. The absence of such a system can prove detrimental to the local population. In one post-conflict state, unqualified persons are importing and selling many illegal, expired, and counterfeit drugs to the local population, at a great risk to buyers' health. On the other hand, a regulatory system is vital to ensure that certain priority drugs are legally imported into a post-conflict state. For example, drugs to treat post-traumatic stress disorder (a condition prevalent among populations who have lived through the ravages of conflict) may need to be imported.

It may also be important to consider whether there are sufficient legal provisions on money laundering, as often money derived from drug-related activities is taken out of the state and laundered through complex international financial transactions. This situation is referenced in the Convention against Illicit Traffic in Narcotic Drugs and Psychotropic Substances (1988), Article 3(b), discussed below. Reference should be made to Article 135, "Money Laundering." At Article 3(5), the convention also references the cross linkages between organized crime and drug offenses. While the convention does not require the criminalization of organized crime, it requires it to be taken into account in imposing a penalty upon a convicted person. Since 1988, when the convention was drafted, a definition of organized crime has been agreed upon under the United Nations Convention against Transnational Organized Crime. This definition has been integrated into the MCC in Article 136.

Establishing effective investigative techniques is also crucial to the effective investigation of drug offenses. Such techniques include witness protection measures (see Chapter 8, Part 4, Section 1, of the MCCP), covert measures of surveillance and provisions on controlled delivery (see Chapter 8, Part 3, Section 5 of the MCCP), confiscation of proceeds of crime and instrumentalities (see Articles 70–73 of the MCC and Chapter 13 of the MCCP), and international cooperation and extradition (see Chapter 14, Parts 1 and 2, of the MCCP). In post-conflict states, very practical issues have stood in the way of prosecuting persons for drug offenses. For example, the lack of field testing kits and the absence of laboratories to test drugs makes it difficult to successfully investigate and prosecute drug offenses. Such resource needs should be considered by international donors and the local authorities in a post-conflict state addressing the problem of narcotic drugs and psychotropic substances.

In addition to these legislative measures, some states choose to adopt a special mechanism for the prosecution of drug crimes, which makes it easier for judges and prosecutors to be specially trained to deal with these highly complex cases. In Afghanistan, for example, counternarcotics tribunals were established. For a full discussion of these tribunals, see *Combating Serious Crimes in Postconflict Societies: A Handbook for Policymakers and Practitioners*, edited by Colette Rausch and published by the United States Institute of Peace. In other countries, special "drug courts" have been established. They deal more with the problem of drug users committing criminal offenses than with drug cartels. Integral to a drug court is its alternative-sentencing procedures, which look to rehabilitate drug-dependent offenders. Useful reference can be made to the UNDCP's Model Drug Court (Treatment and Rehabilitation of Offenders) Bill.

In addition to setting up a special mechanism to combat drug crimes, it may also be necessary to establish a special counternarcotic unit within the domestic police force. Many post-conflict states have established such units to deal solely with drug-related offenses. This process is also discussed in *Combating Serious Crimes in Postconflict Societies*. To address the problem of border control, a border-control police unit may also need to be established. The personnel involved in these units will require specialist and intensive training in the effective investigation of serious drug offenses.

Other measures to address serious drug problems in a post-conflict state include the development of alternative-livelihood programs (including crop-substitution programs) and eradication of drug crops (in conjunction with an alternative-livelihood program). Useful reference can be made to the United Nations Office on Drugs and Crime's *Alternative Development: A Global Thematic Evaluation, Final Synthesis Report*.

Drug offenses are the subject of a number of international treaties drafted between 1961 and 1988. They are the Single Convention on Narcotic Drugs (1961) (as amended by the 1972 Protocol Amending the Single Convention on Narcotic Drugs), the Convention on Psychotropic Substances (1971), and the Convention against Illicit Traffic in Narcotic Drugs and Psychotropic Substances (1988). The 1961 convention is primarily concerned with the regulation of the production and manufacture of controlled substances, and it limits their use to medical and scientific purposes. The convention, based entirely on the voluntary cooperation of states, sets out a system of international control under the leadership of the Commission on Narcotic Drugs of the United Nations Economic and Social Council and the International Narcotics Control Board (Article 5). The convention leaves it to the discretion of a state party to domestically implement the system. The Single Convention on Narcotic Drugs regulates only narcotic drugs. There is no definition of narcotic drugs per se. Instead, reference is made to the schedules of the convention. In short, the convention regulates only naturally derived drugs—those related to opium, cannabis, and cocaine—rather than synthetically produced drugs. The penal provision of the convention (Article 36) is discussed below under the relevant articles. In terms of procedural requirements, the convention contains provisions on seizure and confiscation (Article 37).

The Convention on Psychotropic Substances extends the scope of international control to synthetic drugs, or psychotropic substances such amphetamine-type stimulants, sedative-hypnotics, tranquilizers, and hallucinogens such as LSD. There are numerous provisions that establish an extensive regulatory system for the control of drugs under the International Narcotics Control Board. The penal provision of the convention (Article 22) is discussed below in relation to the relevant articles. The convention also contains provisions on international cooperation (Article 27) and measures to be taken to counter drug abuse (Article 20).

The main focus of the Convention against Illicit Traffic in Narcotic Drugs and Psychotropic Substances is to harmonize the scope and definition of drug offenses, provide effective measures of international cooperation and coordination among national authorities of different states, and provide the legal means to interdict illicit trafficking. The convention also contains provisions on eradication of narcotic plants

(Article 14). Significantly, it brings precursors under the scope of the convention. Precursors are substances used in the conversion of morphine into heroine and in the illicit manufacture of psychotropic substances (listed in tables I and II annexed to the convention and discussed in Article 12). The convention also addresses materials and equipment used for the manufacture of narcotic drugs or psychotropic substances (Article 13). The penal provisions of the convention are discussed below in relation to the relevant articles, with the exception of money laundering, which is discussed in the commentary accompanying Article 135. A state wishing to implement its obligations under the convention should look at numerous procedural provisions, such as those on confiscation, Article 3(4)(a) and Article 5; extradition (Article 6); mutual legal assistance (Article 7); transfer of proceedings (Article 8); cooperation (Articles 9 and 10); and controlled delivery (Article 11).

The criminal offenses set out below seek to comply with the obligations contained in the conventions relating to the introduction of penal provisions into domestic legislation. As mentioned above, obligations relating to procedural law are dealt with in more detail in the relevant provisions of the MCCP. In implementing obligations under the conventions, reference should be made to the law enforcement section of the United Nations Office on Drugs and Crime (UNODC), the UNODC Alternative Development Programme, and the Global Assessment Programme.

# Article 170: Trafficking in Narcotic Drugs and Psychotropic Substances

## *Article 170.1: Definition of Offense*

1. A person commits the criminal offense of trafficking in narcotic drugs and psychotropic substances when he or she, unlawfully:
   (a) produces;
   (b) manufactures;
   (c) extracts;
   (d) prepares;
   (e) offers or offers for sale;
   (f) distributes;
   (g) sells;
   (h) delivers on any terms whatsoever;
   (i) brokers;

(j) dispatches or dispatches in transit;

(k) transports; or

(l) imports or exports any narcotic drug or any psychotropic substance.

2. For the purposes of Article 170:

(a) *narcotic drug* means any of the substances, natural or synthetic, in schedules I and II of the Single Convention on Narcotic Drugs, 1961, and the convention as amended by the 1972 Protocol Amending the Single Convention on Narcotic Drugs, 1961, or in the applicable law; and

(b) *psychotropic substance* means any substance, natural or synthetic, or any natural material in schedules I, II, III, and IV of the Convention on Psychotropic Substances, 1971, or in the applicable law.

## Commentary

Paragraph 1: The wording of this paragraph is derived from Article 3(1)(a)(i) of the Convention against Illicit Traffic in Narcotic Drugs and Psychotropic Substances. Many of the methods of trafficking are also referenced in Article 36 of the Single Convention on Narcotic Drugs, which also requires that states adopt measures to ensure that these methods are made punishable offenses in domestic law. In addition, the convention requires that the organization, management, or financing of trafficking be criminalized. This offense is dealt with in Article 172, below. The convention also requires, under Article 3(1)(c)(iii), that a person who publicly incites another to commit trafficking or induces another to commit trafficking be prosecuted. Furthermore, under Article 3(1)(c)(iv), a person who participates in, is associated with, or conspires to commit the criminal offense of trafficking, or who aids, abets, facilitates, or counsels the commission of this offense, is also be liable for criminal prosecution. These grounds of liability are covered under Articles 28–32 of the MCC.

The jurisdictional provision of the convention, Article 4, requires that states establish jurisdiction over drug trafficking when it is committed on the territory of the state, on board a vessel flying its flag, or on an aircraft registered under its laws at the time the offense is committed. It also provides that states may establish jurisdiction over persons who have habitual residence in the territory or who are nationals of the state, among others. All the grounds of jurisdiction just mentioned are contained in Article 4 ("Territorial Jurisdiction") and Article 5 ("Extraterritorial Jurisdiction") of the MCC. Reference should be made to these articles and their accompanying commentary.

Paragraph 2(a): The term *narcotic drug* does not have a self-standing definition but instead is defined in relation to the schedules to the Convention against Illicit Traffic in Narcotic Drugs and Psychotropic Substances. Reference should be made to the schedules. It is worth noting that the classification method employed in the convention is based on the medical use of the drugs. Consequently, substances that do not have a medical use are automatically classed as particularly dangerous. For example, cannabis is classified in the same category as heroin. Instead of relying on the schedules to classify narcotic drugs, for the purpose of domestic criminal legislation, many states create a separate list, or schedule, of prohibited or controlled drugs.

It may, therefore, be wise to rethink the method by which narcotic drugs are classified. It might be better not to use the schedules as the basis for grading the dangerous nature of a particular drug. If a state chooses to do so, it may wish to add to the list of drugs contained in the convention. Hence the phrase "or in the applicable law" is used in this paragraph. The drugs that are controlled may differ from state to state. For instance, the possession of cannabis is legal in some states while not in others. Many states classify not only the category of a drug or substance but also the amount that the perpetrator traffics. In one state, for example, legislation distinguishes between a "trafficable quantity," a "commercial quantity," and a "large commercial quantity."

Paragraph 2(b): The term *psychotropic substance* does not have a self-standing definition but instead is defined in relation to the schedules to the Convention on Psychotropic Substances. Reference should be made to the schedules. The criterion used to classify psychotropic substances in the schedules is their therapeutic value but in essence their classification is related to whether they belong to the following groups: hallucinogens, amphetamines, barbiturates, and tranquilizers. As with narcotic drugs, a state may wish to reclassify psychotropic substances or add substances to the list contained in the convention. Hence the phrase "or in the applicable law" is used in this paragraph.

## *Article 170.2: Penalty*

1. The applicable penalty range for the criminal offense of trafficking in narcotic drugs or psychotropic substances is two to ten years' imprisonment.
2. The applicable penalty range for the criminal offense of trafficking in narcotic drugs or psychotropic substances is three to fifteen years' imprisonment where a large quantity of narcotic drugs or psychotropic substances is trafficked.

## Commentary

Paragraph 2: As mentioned above, the legislation of most states on drug offenses includes schedules or tables that set out a list of narcotic drugs, psychotropic substances, and other substances that are prohibited. Often, these schedules also categorize drugs according to their quantity—for example, a schedule may distinguish between an amount deemed to be for personal use and a trafficable amount. The MCC does not have a schedule like the one just described, however, and it is advisable that a state implementing legislation on drug offenses create one in which reference is made to quantities of drugs. For the purposes of the MCC, two separate penalty ranges have been created based on whether the drugs or psychotropic substances are a *large quantity* or not. Thus, when a very large quantity of narcotic drugs or psychotropic substances has been trafficked, a court may apply a higher penalty range to a person convicted of this offense.

# Article 171: Possession or Purchase of Narcotic Drugs or Psychotropic Substances for the Purpose of Trafficking

## *Article 171.1: Definition of Offense*

1. A person commits the criminal offense of possession or purchase of narcotic drugs or psychotropic substances for the purpose of trafficking when he or she possesses or purchases narcotic drugs or psychotropic for the purpose of trafficking.
2. For the purposes of Article 171:
   (a) *narcotic drug* has the same meaning as in Article 170.1(2)(a); and
   (b) *psychotropic substance* has the same meaning as in Article 170.1(2)(b).

## Commentary

Paragraph 1: The wording of this paragraph is derived from Article 3(1)(a)(iii) of the Convention against Illicit Traffic in Narcotic Drugs and Psychotropic Substances. This offense is also contained in Article 36 of the Single Convention on Narcotic Drugs. Reference should be made to Article 170.1(1) of the MCC for the definition of *trafficking*, which is referred to in Paragraph 1. The issues relating to the grounds for criminal liability and jurisdiction, as discussed in the commentary to Article 170, above, also relate to Article 171. Reference should be made to the commentary to Article 170.

Paragraph 2(a): Reference should be made to the commentary accompanying Article 170.1(2)(a).

Paragraph 2(b): Reference should be made to the commentary accompanying Article 170.1(2)(b).

## *Article 171.2: Penalty*

1. The applicable penalty range for the criminal offense of possession or purchase of narcotic drugs or psychotropic substances for the purpose of trafficking is two to ten years' imprisonment.
2. The applicable penalty range for the criminal offense of possession or purchase of narcotic drugs or psychotropic substances for the purpose of trafficking is three to fifteen years' imprisonment where a person possesses or purchases a large quantity of narcotic drugs or psychotropic substances for the purpose of trafficking.

### Commentary

Paragraph 2: Reference should be made to the commentary to Article 170.2.

# Article 172: Organizing, Managing, or Financing Trafficking in Narcotic Drugs or Psychotropic Substances

## *Article 172.1: Definition of Offense*

1. A person commits the criminal offense of organizing, managing, or financing trafficking in narcotic drugs or psychotropic substances when he or she organizes, manages, or finances trafficking in narcotic drugs and psychotropic substances, as set out in Articles 170.1(l).
2. For the purposes of Article 172:

   (a) *narcotic drug* has the same meaning as in Article 170.1(2)(a); and

   (b) *psychotropic substance* has the same meaning as in Article 170.1(2)(b).

### Commentary

Paragraph 1: The wording of this paragraph is derived from Article 3(1)(a)(v) of the Convention against Illicit Traffic in Narcotic Drugs and Psychotropic Substances. The issues relating to the grounds for criminal liability and jurisdiction, as discussed under the commentary to Article 170, above, also relate to Article 172. Reference should be made to the commentary to Article 170.

Paragraph 2(a): Reference should be made to the commentary accompanying Article 170.1(2)(a).

Paragraph 2(b): Reference should be made to the commentary accompanying Article 170.1(2)(b).

## *Article 172.2: Penalty*

1. The applicable penalty range for the criminal offense of organizing, managing, or financing the trafficking of narcotic drugs or psychotropic substances is two to ten years' imprisonment.
2. The applicable penalty range for the criminal offense of organizing, managing, or financing the trafficking of narcotic drugs or psychotropic substances is three to fifteen years' imprisonment where a person organizes, manages, or finances the trafficking of a large quantity of narcotic drugs or psychotropic substances.

### Commentary

Paragraph 2: Reference should be made to the commentary to Article 170.2.

# Article 173: Cultivation of Opium Poppy, Coca Bush, or Cannabis Plant

## *Article 173.1: Definition of Offense*

1. A person commits the criminal offense of cultivation of opium poppy, coca bush, or cannabis plant when he or she cultivates opium poppy, coca bush, or cannabis plant for the purpose of producing narcotic drugs or psychotropic substances or for personal use.
2. For the purposes of Article 173:

   (a) *opium poppy* means the plant of the species *Papaver somniferum L.*;

   (b) *coca bush* means the plant of any species of the genus *Erythroxylon*;

(c) *cannabis plant* means any plant of the genus *Cannabis*;

(d) *narcotic drug* has the same meaning as in Article 170.1(2)(a); and

(e) *psychotropic substance* has the same meaning as in Article 170.1(2)(b).

## Commentary

Paragraph 1: The wording of this paragraph is derived from Articles 3(1)(a)(ii) and (3)(2) of the Convention against Illicit Traffic in Narcotic Drugs and Psychotropic Substances. Article 173 targets two classes of individuals: those who are cultivating opium poppy, coca bush, or cannabis plant for the purpose of producing narcotic drugs; and those who are engaging in cultivation for their personal use. The distinction is reflected in the penalty ranges set out in Article 173.2, where a higher penalty may be imposed upon a person who cultivates opium poppy, coca bush, or cannabis plant for the purpose of producing narcotic drugs (and an even more severe penalty is imposed where a large quantity of these substances has been cultivated) than on a person who cultivates these substances for personal use.

The issues relating to the grounds for criminal liability and jurisdiction, as discussed in the commentary to Article 170, above, also relate to Article 173. Reference should be made to the commentary to Article 173.

Paragraph 2(a): The definition of opium poppy comes from Article 1(q) of the Single Convention on Narcotic Drugs (as amended by the 1972 Protocol Amending the Single Convention on Narcotic Drugs, 1961).

Paragraph 2(b): The definition of coca bush comes from Article 1(e) of the Single Convention on Narcotic Drugs (as amended by the 1972 Protocol Amending the Single Convention on Narcotic Drugs, 1961).

Paragraph 2(c): The definition of cannabis plant comes from Article 1(c) of the Single Convention on Narcotic Drugs (as amended by the 1972 Protocol Amending the Single Convention on Narcotic Drugs, 1961).

Paragraph 2(d): Reference should be made to the commentary accompanying Article 170.1(2)(a).

Paragraph 2(e): Reference should be made to the commentary accompanying Article 170.1(2)(b).

# *Article 173.2: Penalty*

1. The applicable penalty range for the criminal offense of cultivation of opium poppy, coca bush, or cannabis plant for personal use is one to five years' imprisonment.
2. The court may impose a fine, as a principal penalty, upon a person convicted of cultivation of opium poppy, coca bush, or cannabis plant for personal use.
3. The applicable penalty range for the criminal offense of cultivation of opium poppy, coca bush, or cannabis plant for the production of narcotic drugs is two to ten years' imprisonment.
4. The applicable penalty range for the criminal offense of cultivation of opium poppy, coca bush, or cannabis plant for the production of narcotic drugs is three to fifteen years' imprisonment where a person cultivates a large quantity of opium poppy, coca bush, or cannabis plant.

## Commentary

Paragraph 2: As mentioned above, Article 173 deals with persons who cultivate opium poppy, coca bush, or cannabis plant for their own personal use or for the purposes of production. Consequently, it was necessary to create two distinct penalty ranges, the heavier penalty range being applied to a person involved in cultivation for the purpose of producing narcotic drugs and psychotropic substances, and the lesser range being applied to those cultivating for personal use.

Paragraph 4: Paragraph 4 makes a further breakdown in terms of the applicable penalty range for persons cultivating opium poppy, coca bush, or cannabis plant for the production of narcotic drugs and psychotropic substances and those cultivating "large quantities" of opium poppy, coca bush, or cannabis plant. As discussed above, the legislation of most states on drug offenses includes schedules or tables that set out a list of narcotic drugs, psychotropic substances, and other substances (such as opium poppy, coca bush, or cannabis plant) that are prohibited. Often, these schedules also distinguish between different quantities of the relevant substances and indicate, for example, what quantity of each represents an amount that would be deemed for personal use, or trafficable or a large quantity. The MCC does not have a schedule like the one just described, however, and it is advisable that a state implementing legislation on drug offenses create one in which reference is made to quantities. For the purposes of the MCC, two separate penalty ranges have been created based on whether the opium poppy, coca bush, or cannabis plant are a *large quantity* or not. This way, when a very large quantity of opium poppy, coca bush, or cannabis plant has been cultivated, a court may apply a higher penalty range to a person convicted of this offense.

# Article 174: Manufacture, Transport, or Distribution of Precursors

## *Article 174.1: Definition of Offense*

1. A person commits the criminal offense of manufacture, transport, or distribution of precursors when he or she manufactures, transports, or distributes precursors, knowing that they are to be used in or for the illicit cultivation, production, or manufacture of narcotic drugs or psychotropic substances.
2. For the purposes of Article 174, *precursor* means a substance frequently used in drug manufacture and listed in tables I and II of the United Nations Convention against Illicit Traffic in Narcotic Drugs and Psychotropic Substances (1988) or in the applicable law.

### Commentary

Paragraph 1: The wording of this paragraph is derived from Article 3(1)(a)(iv) of the Convention against Illicit Traffic in Narcotic Drugs and Psychotropic Substances, although the term *precursor* is not used in the text of the convention. As mentioned above, a precursor is a substance used in the conversion of morphine into heroine and in the illicit manufacture of psychotropic substances (listed in tables I and II annexed to the convention and discussed in Article 12). The issues relating to the grounds for criminal liability and jurisdiction, as discussed in the commentary to Article 170, above, also relate to Article 174. Reference should be made to the commentary to Article 170.

Paragraph 2: The term *precursor* is not used in the convention. Instead the convention uses the phrase "substances listed in Table I and Table II." Reference should be made to the tables accompanying the Convention against Illicit Traffic in Narcotic Drugs and Psychotropic Substances. A state may wish to add to the list of precursors. Hence the phrase "or in the applicable law" is used in the paragraph.

## *Article 174.2: Penalty*

1. The applicable penalty range for the criminal offense of manufacture, transport, or distribution of precursors is two to ten years' imprisonment.

2. The applicable penalty range for the criminal offense of manufacture, transport, or distribution of precursors is three to fifteen years' imprisonment where a person manufactures, transports, or distributes a large quantity of precursors.

## Commentary

Reference should be made to the commentary to Article 173(2)(4), which discusses the term *large quantity* in the context of drug offenses.

# Article 175: Manufacture, Transport, or Distribution of Equipment or Materials for Use in the Illicit Cultivation, Production, or Manufacture of Narcotic Drugs or Psychotropic Substances

## *Article 175.1: Definition of Offense*

1. A person commits the criminal offense of manufacture, transport, or distribution of equipment or materials for use in the illicit cultivation, production, or manufacture of narcotic drugs or psychotropic substances when he or she manufactures, transports, or distributes equipment or materials, knowing that they are to be used in or for the illicit cultivation, production, or manufacture of narcotic drugs or psychotropic substances.
2. For the purposes of Article 175:
   (a) *narcotic drug* has the same meaning as in Article 170.1(2)(a); and
   (b) *psychotropic substance* has the same meaning as in Article 170.1(2)(b).

## Commentary

Paragraph 1: The wording of this paragraph is derived from Article 3(1)(a)(iv) of the Convention against Illicit Traffic in Narcotic Drugs and Psychotropic Substances (1988). The terms *equipment* and *materials* are not defined in the convention. The issues relating to the grounds for criminal liability and jurisdiction, as discussed in the commentary to Article 170, above, also relate to Article 175. Reference should be made to the commentary to Article 170.

Paragraph 2(a): Reference should be made to the commentary accompanying Article 170.1(2)(a).

Paragraph 2(b): Reference should be made to the commentary accompanying Article 170.1(2)(b).

## *Article 175.2: Penalty*

The applicable penalty range for the criminal offense of manufacture, transport, or distribution of equipment or materials for use in the illicit cultivation, production, or manufacture of narcotic drugs or psychotropic substances is two to ten years' imprisonment.

# Article 176: Possession or Purchase of Narcotic Drugs or Psychotropic Substances for Personal Use

## *Article 176.1: Definition of Offense*

1. A person commits the criminal offense of possession or purchase of narcotic drugs or psychotropic substances for personal use when he or she possesses or purchases a quantity of narcotic drugs or psychotropic substances for his or her personal use.
2. For the purposes of Article 176:

   (a) *narcotic drug* has the same meaning as in Article 170.1(2)(a); and

   (b) *psychotropic substance* has the same meaning as in Article 170.1(2)(b).

## Commentary

Paragraph 1: Article 3(2) of the Convention against Illicit Traffic in Narcotic Drugs and Psychotropic Substances (1988) requires that states parties criminalize the possession and purchase of narcotic drugs and psychotropic substances for personal use. This requirement is in contrast to Article 171 of the MCC which criminalizes the possession and purchase of narcotic drugs and psychotropic substances for the purpose of trafficking. Those who purchase or possess narcotic drugs or psychotropic substances for the purpose of trafficking are dealt with more severely when it comes to the imposition of penalties; see Article 171.2(2). Ordinarily, domestic legislation on drug offenses contains a schedule or a table that sets out the amounts of narcotic drugs and psychotropic substances that are deemed to be quantities that could reasonably be for personal use. A cutoff point is established that distinguishes quantities of narcotic drugs and psychotropic substances that are deemed to be "trafficable." If a person purchases or possesses narcotic drugs or psychotropic substances in an amount equal to that set out as a trafficable quantity in domestic legislation, the person is deemed to purchase or possess this quantity for the purpose of trafficking. This person would be dealt with under Article 171, above, rather than under the current article. The drafters of the MCC originally considered creating a schedule that would set out the exact amount of each narcotic drug or psychotropic substance deemed to be for personal use or for trafficking. Instead it was decided that this should be completed by a post-conflict state when implementing legislation on drug offenses, in light of the particular narcotic drugs or psychotropic substances prohibited under its laws and the context of the country.

The question of whether to criminalize the possession of all types and amounts of narcotic drugs and psychotropic substances for personal use is a very sensitive one. It is an issue on which there is considerable divergence of opinion among states. Many experts consulted as part of the process of vetting the MCC supported the inclusion of a provision on possession of narcotic drugs and psychotropic substances of any amount or type. In contrast, others opposed the inclusion of such a provision, both generally and specifically in relation to post-conflict states. The latter group argued that given all the crime problems that need attention in a post-conflict state, it would be best not to include the offense of possession of all amounts and types of narcotic drugs and psychotropic substances for personal use. Instead, they proposed that the MCC focus on more serious drug offenses that relate to trafficking of drugs, typically carried out by organized criminal gangs. In this way, the resources of the domestic police force and the criminal justice system would not be used on minor drug offenses but would be channeled into combating the suppliers and dealers of drugs. It is also relevant to note, in favor of not including an offense relating to possession of narcotic drugs or psychotropic substances for personal use, that there has been international support for the decriminalization of certain genres of drugs and the replacement of a criminalization policy with other strategies that tackle the root causes of drug abuse.

In some states that prosecute persons for possession of narcotic drugs and psychotropic substances for personal use, special drug courts have been established to deal only with drug users. These sorts of drug courts should not be confused with drug courts established to address criminal offenses committed by drug dealers and suppliers, created in post-conflict states where these high-level crimes are widespread. Research on drug courts that deal with personal users of drugs has shown that they work very successfully in tackling the problem of drug abuse. Instead of receiving a penalty of imprisonment, a person convicted of possession or purchase of drugs for personal use undertakes a court-ordered drug treatment program. Whether or not a post-conflict state wishes to implement a provision on possession of narcotic drugs or psychotropic substances for personal use is really a question of national policy and should be decided upon by a state when it is considering the variety of drug-related offenses it wishes to incorporate into domestic criminal legislation. The state may also wish to consider implementing provisions on special drug courts to deal with those subject to prosecution for possession of narcotic drugs and psychotropic substances.

Paragraph 2(a): Reference should be made to the commentary accompanying Article 170.1(2)(a).

Paragraph 2(b): Reference should be made to the commentary accompanying Article 170.1(2)(b).

## *Article 176.2: Penalty*

The applicable penalty range for the criminal offense of possession of narcotic drugs or psychotropic substances for personal use is one to five years' imprisonment.

# Section 15: Election Offenses

## General Commentary

In most post-conflict states, in particular those emerging from internal armed conflict, a peace agreement will normally contain provisions on the establishment of a transitional governance arrangement, as well as provisions on the timing and manner of conducting free and fair elections. Preparation for elections involves a plethora of activities, including drafting of legislation on elections. The election law or election code may contain details on the timing of the vote, eligibility of voters and candidates, acceptable campaign practices, and so forth. In some states, this law or code may itself contain criminal offenses. In other states, these offenses are contained in the criminal code. The MCC contains a number of election-related offenses that focus on interference with a citizen's right to vote (including the right to vote confidentially), abuse of the right to vote, interference with the integrity of the voting process, and interference with election candidates. Two offenses, those laid out in Article 177 ("Preventing the Exercise of the Right to Vote") and Article 182 ("Election Fraud"), specifically target election officials, while the remainder of the offenses target all citizens.

## Article 177: Preventing the Exercise of the Right to Vote

### *Article 177.1: Definition of Offense*

A person commits the criminal offense of preventing the exercise of the right to vote when he or she:

(a) in the exercise of duties entrusted to him or her relating to elections;

(b) with the intent to prevent another person from exercising his or her right to vote:

  (i) fails to record such person in a voter registration list;

(ii) removes such person from the voter registration list; or

(iii) in another manner prevents a person from exercising his or her right to vote.

### *Article 177.2: Penalty*

1. The applicable penalty range for the criminal offense of preventing the exercise of the right to vote is one to five years' imprisonment.
2. The court may impose a fine, as a principal penalty, upon a person convicted of preventing the exercise of the right to vote.

## Article 178: Violating the Free Decision of Voters

### *Article 178.1: Definition of Offense*

A person commits the criminal offense of violating the free decision of voters when he or she:

(a) during elections, a recall vote, or a referendum;

(b) compels another person:

(i) to vote;

(ii) not to vote;

(iii) to cast a void vote; or

(iv) to vote in favor of or against a particular proposal or person;

(c) by means of force, serious threat, corruption, or deception, or in any other unlawful manner.

### Commentary

A recall vote is a vote to remove an elected official for poor performance or malfeasance, an issue that will be dealt with in the relevant election law or election code.

The term *corruption* is referred to in Article 178.1(c). For a description of the elements of the criminal acts involved in corruption, reference should be made to Article 138 ("Corruption Involving a Public Official").

## *Article 178.2: Penalty*

1. The applicable penalty range for the criminal offense of violating the free decision of voters is one to five years' imprisonment.
2. The court may impose a fine, as a principal penalty, upon a person convicted of violating the free decision of voters.

# Article 179: Abuse of the Right to Vote

## *Article 179.1: Definition of Offense*

A person commits the criminal offense of abuse of the right to vote when he or she, during an election, a recall vote, or a referendum:

(a) votes under the name of another person; or

(b) votes even though he or she has already voted.

### Commentary

A recall vote is a vote to remove an elected official for poor performance or malfeasance, an issue that will be dealt with in the relevant election law or election code.

For a description of the elements of the criminal acts involved in corruption, reference should be made to Article 138 ("Corruption Involving a Public Official").

## *Article 179.2: Penalty*

1. The applicable penalty range for the criminal offense of abuse of the right to vote is one to five years' imprisonment.
2. The court may impose a fine, as a principal penalty, upon a person convicted of abuse of the right to vote.

# Article 180: Violating Confidentiality in Voting

## *Article 180.1: Definition of Offense*

A person commits the criminal offense of violating confidentiality in voting when he or she:

(a) by use of force, serious threat, corruption, or deception, or in any other unlawful manner;

(b) demands a person to reveal how he or she voted.

### Commentary

The term *corruption* is referred to in Article 180.1(a). For a description of the elements of the criminal acts involved in corruption, reference should be made to Article 138 ("Corruption Involving a Public Official").

## *Article 180.2: Penalty*

1. The applicable penalty range for the criminal offense of violating confidentiality in voting is one to five years' imprisonment.
2. The court may impose a fine, as a principal penalty, upon a person convicted of violating confidentiality in voting.

# Article 181: Buying and Selling Votes

## *Article 181.1: Definition of Offense*

1. A person commits the criminal offense of buying votes when he or she:

(a) promises, offers, or gives to a person, directly or indirectly, an undue benefit, for the person or a third party or entity;

(b) in order that the person:

(i) vote;

(ii) refrain from voting;

(iii) cast a void vote; or

(iv) cast his or her vote in favor of or against a particular person or proposal.

2. A person commits the criminal offense of selling votes when he or she:

(a) solicits or accepts, directly or indirectly, an undue benefit, for himself or herself or a third party or entity;

(b) in order that the person:

(i) vote;

(ii) refrain from voting;

(iii) cast a void vote; or

(iv) cast his or her vote in favor of or against a particular person or proposal.

### *Article 181.2: Penalty*

1. The applicable penalty range for the criminal offense of buying or selling votes is one to five years' imprisonment.
2. The court may impose a fine, as a principal penalty, upon a person convicted of buying or selling votes.

## Article 182: Election Fraud

### *Article 182.1: Definition of Offense*

A person commits the criminal offense of election fraud when he or she:

(a) adds, subtracts, or deletes votes;

(b) publishes election results that do not correspond with the actual voting results; or

(c) in any other manner falsifies the results of an election.

### *Article 182.2: Penalty*

The applicable penalty range for the criminal offense of election fraud is two to ten years' imprisonment.

## Article 183: Threat to an Election Candidate

### *Article 183.1: Definition of Offense*

A person commits the criminal offense of threat to an election candidate when he or she:

(a) threatens or commits any other unlawful act against an election candidate;

(b) with the intention of forcing him or her to withdraw his or her candidacy or to prevent him or her from exercising any activity legally permitted during an election campaign.

### *Article 183.2: Penalty*

The applicable penalty range for the criminal offense of threat to an election candidate is two to ten years' imprisonment.

# Section 16: Cybercrime Offenses

## General Commentary

A growing number of states have introduced or are in the process of introducing new legislation on cybercrime offenses. In some post-conflict states, cybercrime offenses have gone unpunished due to the lack of substantive legal provisions criminalizing this conduct.

In 2001 the Council of Europe adopted the Convention on Cybercrime, aimed at deterring "action directed against the confidentiality, integrity and availability of computer systems, networks and computer data as well as the misuse of such systems, networks and data" (preamble). Increasingly sophisticated technology has brought with it increasingly sophisticated criminals who have used computer systems, networks, and computers for illegitimate ends. To combat such conduct, the convention requires states parties to criminalize certain forms of conduct and to introduce procedural measures for the investigation of cybercrime (chapter 2, section 2, "Procedural Law") and provisions on international cooperation in the investigation and prosecution of cybercrime offenses (chapter 3, "International Cooperation").

The Convention on Cybercrime contains nine criminal offenses in four different categories: (1) offenses against the confidentiality, integrity, and availability of computer data and systems; (2) computer-related offenses (e.g., computer-related forgery and computer-related fraud); (3) content-related offenses (e.g., offenses related to child pornography); and (4) offenses related to the infringement of copyright and related rights. The creation of common language for cybercrime offenses aims at "establishing a common minimum standard" (explanatory report to the Convention on Cybercrime, paragraph 33). Section 16 of the MCC contains offenses in the first category, namely, illegal access, illegal interception, data interference, system interference, and misuse of devices. Section 5 of the Special Part of the MCC on offenses against children, and specifically Article 117 ("Child Pornography") and Article 118 ("Possession of Child Pornography"), incorporates the third category of offenses.

Close attention should be paid to the explanatory report to the convention for a description of the rationale behind including cybercrime offenses in domestic criminal law and for a discussion on their substantive content. Because the report goes into detail about each of the individual offenses listed in Section 16, the MCC makes reference to the relevant parts of the report rather than duplicating its content. When a state plans to introduce legislation on cybercrime, it should take into account the complexities involved in training personnel to conduct investigations of these offenses and the inherent complexity in the actual investigation of these offenses. Both activities are very resource intensive and will require a substantial commitment of personnel, money, materials, and equipment, coupled with a comprehensive training agenda.

Articles 14–21 of the Convention on Cybercrime also require states to implement a number of tools to assist in the investigation of cybercrime offenses. Some of these tools have been integrated into the MCCP. Reference should be made to Chapter 8, Part 3, Sections 4 and 5, and their accompanying commentary.

Comprehensive background on and discussion of computer-related crime and national and international initiatives to tackle it is presented in the background paper to Workshop 6: Measures to Combat Computer-Related Crime, prepared for the Eleventh United Nations Congress on Crime Prevention and Criminal Justice. Useful reference may also be made to the Computer Crime Research Centre, a nonprofit, nongovernmental organization established to conduct research into legal, criminal, and criminological problems of cybercrime with the purpose of rendering scientific and methodical aid to states tackling cybercrime.

# Article 184: Illegal Access to a Computer System

## *Article 184.1: Definition of Offense*

1. A person commits the criminal offense of illegal access to a computer system when he or she accesses the whole or any part of a computer system without right.
2. For the purposes of Article 184, *computer system* means any device or group of interconnected or related devices, one or more of which, pursuant to a program, performs automatic processing of data.

### Commentary

Paragraph 1: The wording of this paragraph comes from Article 2 of the Convention on Cybercrime. For a discussion of the criminal offense of illegal access to a computer system, reference should be made to paragraphs 44–50 of the explanatory report to the Convention on Cybercrime. Paragraph 38 discusses the meaning of *without right.*

Paragraph 2: The wording of this paragraph comes from Article 1(a) of the Convention on Cybercrime. For a discussion of the meaning of *computer system*, reference should be made to paragraphs 23–24 of the explanatory report to the Convention on Cybercrime.

## *Article 184.2: Penalty*

The applicable penalty range for the criminal offense of illegal access to a computer system is two to ten years' imprisonment.

# Article 185: Illegal Interception of Computer Data

## *Article 185.1: Definition of Offense*

1. A person commits the criminal offense of illegal interception of computer data when he or she:
   (a) without right; and
   (b) by technical means;
   (c) intercepts nonpublic transmissions of computer data to, from, or within a computer system, including electromagnetic emissions from a computer system carrying such computer data.
2. For the purposes of Article 185:
   (a) *computer system* has the same meaning as in Article 184.1(2); and
   (b) *computer data* means any representation of facts, information, or concepts in a form suitable for processing in a computer system, including a program suitable to cause a computer system to perform a function.

### Commentary

Paragraph 1: The wording of this paragraph comes from Article 3 of the Council of Europe Convention on Cybercrime. For a discussion of the criminal offense of illegal interception of computer data, reference should be made to paragraphs 51–59 of the explanatory report to the Convention on Cybercrime. Paragraph 38 discusses the meaning of *without right.*

Paragraph 2(a): The wording of this paragraph comes from Article 1(a) of the Convention on Cybercrime. For a discussion of the meaning of *computer system*, reference should be made to paragraphs 23–24 of the explanatory report to the Convention on Cybercrime.

Paragraph 2(b): The wording of this paragraph comes from Article 1(b) of the Convention on Cybercrime. For a discussion of the meaning of *computer data*, reference should be made to Paragraph 25 of the explanatory report to the Convention on Cybercrime.

## *Article 185.2: Penalty*

The applicable penalty range for the criminal offense of illegal interception of computer data is two to ten years' imprisonment.

# Article 186: Interference with Computer Data

## *Article 186.1: Definition of Offense*

1. A person commits the criminal offense of interference with computer data when he or she damages, deletes, deteriorates, alters, or suppresses computer data without right.
2. For the purposes of Article 186, *computer data* has the same meaning as in Article 185.1(2)(b).

### Commentary

Paragraph 1: The wording of this paragraph comes from Article 4 of the Council of Europe Convention on Cybercrime. For a discussion of the criminal offense of data interference, reference should be made to paragraphs 60–64 of the explanatory report to the Convention on Cybercrime. Paragraph 38 discusses the meaning of the phrase *without right.*

Paragraph 2: The wording of this paragraph comes from Article 1(b) of the Convention on Cybercrime. For a discussion of the meaning of *computer data*, reference should be made to Paragraph 25 of the explanatory report to the Convention on Cybercrime.

### *Article 186.2: Penalty*

The applicable penalty range for the criminal offense of interference with computer data is two to ten years' imprisonment.

## Article 187: Interference with a Computer System

### *Article 187.1: Definition of Offense*

1. A person commits the criminal offense of interference with a computer system when he or she:
   (a) without right;
   (b) seriously hinders the functioning of a computer system;
   (c) by inputting, transmitting, damaging, deleting, deteriorating, altering, or suppressing computer data.
2. For the purposes of Article 187:
   (a) *computer system* has the same meaning as in Article 184.1(2); and
   (b) *computer data* has the same meaning as in Article 185.1(2)(b).

#### Commentary

Paragraph 1: The wording of this paragraph comes from Article 5 of the Convention on Cybercrime. For a discussion of the criminal offense of interference with a computer system, reference should be made to paragraphs 65–70 of the explanatory report to the Convention on Cybercrime. Paragraph 38 discusses the meaning of *without right.*

Paragraph 2(a): The wording of this paragraph comes from Article 1(a) of the Convention on Cybercrime. For a discussion of the meaning of *computer system*, reference should be made to paragraphs 23–24 of the explanatory report to the Convention on Cybercrime.

Paragraph 2(b): The wording of this paragraph comes from Article 1(b) of the Convention on Cybercrime. For a discussion of the meaning of *computer data*, reference should be made to Paragraph 25 of the explanatory report to the Convention on Cybercrime.

## *Article 187.2: Penalty*

The applicable penalty range for the criminal offense of interference with a computer system is two to ten years' imprisonment.

# Article 188: Misuse of Devices

## *Article 188.1: Definition of Offense*

1. A person commits the criminal offense of misuse of devices when he or she, without right and with the intent that a device be used for the purpose of committing the criminal offense of illegal access to a computer system (Article 184), illegal interception of computer data (Article 185), interference with computer data (Article 186), or interference with a computer system (Article 187):

   (a) produces, sells, procures for use, imports, distributes, or otherwise makes available:

      (i) a device, including a computer program, designed or adapted primarily for the purpose of committing the criminal offense of illegal access to a computer system (Article 184), illegal interception of computer data (Article 185), interference with computer data (Article 186), or interference with a computer system (Article 187); or

      (ii) a computer password, access code, or similar data by which the whole or any part of a computer system is capable of being accessed with the intent to use; or

   (b) possesses any of the devices, passwords, access codes, or similar data referred to in Paragraphs 1(a)(i) and 1(a)(ii), above.

2. For the purposes of Article 188, *computer system* has the same meaning as in Article 184.1(2).

## Commentary

Paragraph 1: For a discussion of the criminal offense of misuse of devices, reference should be made to paragraphs 71–78 of the explanatory report of the Convention on Cybercrime. Paragraph 38 discusses the meaning of the phrase *without right.*

Paragraph 2: For a discussion of the meaning of *computer system*, reference should be made to paragraphs 23–24 of the explanatory report of the Convention on Cybercrime.

## *Article 188.2: Penalty*

The applicable penalty range for the criminal offense of misuse of devices is two to ten years' imprisonment.

# Section 17: Offenses against the Administration of Justice

## General Commentary

Very often, the legislation of post-conflict states lacks adequate administration-of-justice offenses. This section is a relatively extensive collection of such offenses, inspired by various domestic penal codes around the world, including both newly drafted legislation of post-conflict states and legislation of non–post-conflict states. Inspiration has also been drawn from the list of administration-of-justice offenses prescribed under the Rome Statute of the International Criminal Court, the Rules of Procedure and Evidence of the International Criminal Tribunal for the former Yugoslavia, and the Rules of Procedure and Evidence of the International Criminal Tribunal for Rwanda. For the efficient and effective administration of justice, it is imperative that the legislation of post-conflict states contain a comprehensive set of administration-of-justice offenses.

## Article 189: Alteration or Destruction of Evidence

### *Article 189.1: Definition of Offense*

A person commits the criminal offense of alteration or destruction of evidence when he or she alters or destroys evidence introduced, or likely to be introduced, in judicial proceedings.

## Commentary

Judicial proceedings include not only trials of criminal offenses but also pretrial hearings before a judge. For the definition of evidence, reference should be made to Article 1(4) of the MCC.

### *Article 189.2: Penalty*

1. The applicable penalty range for the criminal offense of alteration or destruction of evidence is one to five years' imprisonment.
2. The court may impose a fine, as an alternative principal penalty, upon a person convicted of alteration or destruction of evidence.

# Article 190: Fabrication of Evidence

### *Article 190.1: Definition of Offense*

A person commits the criminal offense of fabrication of evidence when he or she, with intent to mislead, fabricates anything intending it to be used as evidence in existing or proposed judicial proceedings.

## Commentary

Judicial proceedings include not only trials of criminal offenses but also pretrial hearings before a judge. For the definition of evidence, reference should be made to Article 1(4) of the MCC.

### *Article 190.2: Penalty*

1. The applicable penalty range for the criminal offense of fabrication of evidence is one to five years' imprisonment.
2. The court may impose a fine, as an alternative principal penalty, upon a person convicted of fabrication of evidence.

# Article 191: Presentation of False or Forged Evidence

## *Article 191.1: Definition of Offense*

A person commits the criminal offense of presentation of false or forged evidence when he or she presents evidence in judicial proceedings knowing it to be false or forged.

### Commentary

Judicial proceedings include not only trials of criminal offenses but also pretrial hearings before a judge. For the definition of evidence, reference should be made to Article 1(4) of the MCC.

## *Article 191.2: Penalty*

1. The applicable penalty range for the criminal offense of presentation of false or forged evidence is one to five years' imprisonment.
2. The court may impose a fine, as an alternative principal penalty, upon a person convicted of presentation of false or forged evidence.

# Article 192: False Testimony

## *Article 192.1: Definition of Offense*

A person commits the criminal offense of false testimony when he or she gives false testimony in judicial proceedings, where he or she is under an obligation to tell the truth.

## Commentary

Judicial proceedings include not only trials of criminal offenses but also pretrial hearings before a judge. They also include noncriminal proceedings, such as administrative proceedings.

An accused person who is on trial is not liable for the offense of false testimony where he or she gives testimony without an oath. Reference should be made to Chapter 11, Part 2 on "Statement of the Accused," of the MCCP.

## *Article 192.2: Penalty*

1. The applicable penalty range for the criminal offense of false testimony is one to five years' imprisonment.
2. The court may impose a fine, as an alternative principal penalty, upon a person convicted of false testimony.

# Article 193: Obstruction of Justice of a Witness

## *Article 193.1: Definition of Offense*

A person commits the criminal offense of obstruction of justice of a witness when he or she:

(a) uses physical force, threats or intimidation, or promises, offers or gives an undue advantage;

(b) to induce false testimony or to interfere in the giving of testimony or the production of evidence in judicial proceedings.

## Commentary

Obstructing a witness in giving testimony or providing evidence before a court is a threat to the integrity of the criminal justice system and also greatly compromises the prosecution of perpetrators. In addition, this offense represents a grave threat to the safety and security of witnesses in judicial proceedings. The obstruction of witnesses has become a common phenomenon in serious crimes cases, such as those involving organized crime and corruption. In post-conflict states, where organized crime and corruption are often endemic, obstruction of witnesses has been an obstacle to the prosecution of these offenses. Its perpetration has resulted in the evasion of justice and thus the facilitation of organized crime and corruption. Consequently, Article 23 of the United Nations Convention against Transnational Organized Crime and Article 25 of the United Nations Convention against Corruption require states parties to introduce this offense into domestic criminal legislation, if they have not already done so. The wording of Article 193 has been taken from those conventions, which share identical wording. Reference should be made to the *Legislative Guides for the Implementation of the United Nations Convention against Transnational Organized Crime and the Protocols Thereto*, drafted by the United Nations Office on Drugs and Crime.

Article 193.1(a) covers both coercive and corrupt means of influencing a witness in an effort to induce false testimony or to interfere in the giving of testimony or the production of evidence. The legislative guide states that the phrase *judicial proceedings* "should be interpreted broadly" (page 92) and should include pretrial processes.

The criminalization of obstruction of witnesses is not the only means by which the Model Codes seek to protect witnesses in judicial proceedings, who may be in physical danger from the perpetrator of a criminal offense or from persons connected with him or her. Reference should be made to Chapter 8, Part 4, Sections 1 and 2, of the MCCP on witness protection measures and witness anonymity. Witness protection and witness anonymity measures are a more proactive approach to ensuring the safety of witnesses in judicial proceedings. These provisions seek to preempt the commission of criminal offenses against witnesses, specifically obstruction through the use of physical force, threat, or intimidation. Under the provisions of the MCCP, a witness who is under threat may be granted protective measures or witness anonymity, thereby protecting the person from any potential coercive conduct aimed at obstructing him or her.

## Article 193.2: Penalty

1. The applicable penalty range for the criminal offense of obstruction of justice of a witness is one to five years' imprisonment.
2. The court may impose a fine, as an alternative principal penalty, upon a person convicted of obstruction of justice of a witness.

# Article 194: Obstruction of Justice of a Justice or Policing Official

## *Article 194.1: Definition of Offense*

A person commits the criminal offense of obstruction of justice of a justice or policing official when he or she uses physical force, threats, or intimidation to interfere with the exercise of official duties by a justice or policing official.

### Commentary

Both the United Nations Convention against Transnational Organized Crime (Article 23) and the United Nations Convention against Corruption (Article 25) urge states parties to introduce the offense contained in Article 194 into domestic criminal legislation, if they have not already done so. Reference should be made to the *Legislative Guides for the Implementation of the United Nations Convention against Transnational Organized Crime and the Protocols Thereto*, drafted by the United Nations Office on Drugs and Crime.

Article 193 ("Obstruction of Justice of a Witness") penalizes obstruction through coercion and corruption. A definition of the latter is not contained in Article 194; it is covered by Article 138 ("Corruption Involving a Public Official"), because justice and policing officials are considered public officials within the meaning of Article 1(9).

## *Article 194.2: Penalty*

1. The applicable penalty range for the criminal offense of obstruction of justice of a justice or policing official is one to five years' imprisonment.
2. The court may impose a fine, as an alternative principal penalty, upon a person convicted of obstruction of justice of a justice or policing official.

# Article 195: Retaliation against a Witness

## *Article 195.1: Definition of Offense*

A person commits the criminal offense of retaliation against a witness when he or she retaliates against a witness for giving evidence in the investigation of a criminal offense or for testifying in judicial proceedings.

## *Article 195.2: Penalty*

The applicable penalty range for the criminal offense of retaliation against a witness is two to ten years' imprisonment.

# Article 196: Retaliation against a Justice or Policing Official

## *Article 196.1: Definition of Offense*

A person commits the criminal offense of retaliation against a justice or policing official when he or she retaliates against an official of the court or a policing official on account of duties performed by that or another official.

## *Article 196.2: Penalty*

The applicable penalty range for the criminal offense of retaliation against a justice or policing official is two to ten years' imprisonment.

# Article 197: Failure to Respect an Order of the Court

## *Article 197.1: Definition of Offense*

A person commits the criminal offense of failure to respect an order of the court when he or she, in the course of judicial proceedings:

(a) fails to respect an order of the court; or

(b) fails to comply with a commitment made to the court.

### Commentary

Judicial proceedings include not only trials of criminal offenses but also pretrial hearings before a judge. An order of the court may be given orally in court proceedings, or it may be pursuant to a summons to a witness, an expert witness, or the accused to appear in court. It may also take the form of an order that has been granted pursuant to a motion of the prosecutor or the defense or a warrant that has been granted pursuant to an application of the police or the prosecutor. Where any of these orders is not respected by a person, he or she is liable for prosecution under Article 197.

## *Article 197.2: Penalty*

1. The applicable penalty range for the criminal offense of failure to respect an order of the court is one to five years' imprisonment.
2. The court may impose a fine, as an alternative principal penalty, upon a person convicted of failure to respect an order of the court.

# Article 198: Providing Assistance to a Perpetrator after the Commission of a Criminal Offense

## *Article 198.1: Definition of Offense*

A person commits the criminal offense of providing assistance to a perpetrator after the commission of a criminal offense when he or she:

(a) harbors a suspect or an accused person for the purpose of evading justice;

(b) helps the perpetrator of a criminal offense elude discovery by concealing instruments or evidence or aids the perpetrator in any other way;

(c) harbors a convicted person; or

(d) takes steps toward frustrating the execution of a penalty imposed by a court.

### Commentary

This criminal offense is referred to as accessory after the fact liability in some jurisdictions. In other jurisdictions, it is viewed as a form of accomplice liability rather than a stand-alone substantive offense. In the MCC, it is treated as a stand-alone criminal offense. For the definition of suspect, accused person, and convicted person, reference should be made to Article 1.

## *Article 198.2: Penalty*

1. The applicable penalty range for the criminal offense of providing assistance to a perpetrator after the commission of a criminal offense is one to five years' imprisonment.
2. The court may impose a fine, as an alternative principal penalty, upon a person convicted of providing assistance to a perpetrator after the commission of a criminal offense.

# Article 199: False Statements of a Cooperative Witness

## *Article 199.1: Definition of Offense*

A person commits the criminal offense of false statements of a cooperative witness when he or she:

(a) having been declared a cooperative witness under the MCCP;

(b) gives testimony that is false, in any relevant part, or purposely omits to state the complete truth to the prosecutor, the police, or the court during the investigation of the offense or in judicial proceedings.

### Commentary

A cooperative witness is a person suspected or accused of a criminal offense who is granted immunity from prosecution through a formal legal process by reason of his or her agreement to testify against another accused person in another trial. The MCCP contains extensive provisions that set out the formal legal process for the granting and revocation of cooperative witness status. Reference should be made to Chapter 8, Part 4, Section 3, of the MCCP and the accompanying commentary, which discuss the legal provisions on cooperative witnesses in greater depth.

Where a person who has been declared a cooperative witness is found to have made a false statement, either prior to or during the trial at which the cooperative witness is giving testimony, he or she may be prosecuted under Article 199. This provision is broader than Article 192 on false testimony in two ways. It covers the investigation prior to trial and not just statements delivered under oath before the court. A cooperative witness who makes a false statement to a prosecutor or the police during pretrial investigations can thus be prosecuted under Article 199. Under the MCC, it is not possible to prosecute other persons for false statements made to a prosecutor or the police in the investigation stage of proceedings.

## *Article 199.2: Penalty*

1. The applicable penalty range for the criminal offense of false statements of a cooperative witness is one to five years' imprisonment.
2. The court may impose a fine, as an alternative principal penalty, upon a person convicted of false statements of a cooperative witness.

# Article 200: Revealing the Sealed Order for Protective Measures or Anonymity

## *Article 200.1: Definition of Offense*

A person commits the criminal offense of revealing the sealed order for protective measures or anonymity when he or she reveals the sealed order for protective measures granted under the MCCP or the sealed order for anonymity granted under the MCCP, including the petition, any documents, or any information contained in them.

### Commentary

The MCCP contains extensive provisions on witness protection measures and the granting of witness anonymity. Reference should be made to Chapter 8, Part 3, Section 4, of the MCCP and the accompanying commentary, which discuss witness protection measures and witness anonymity in greater detail. In brief, witness protection measures and witness-anonymity measures aim to protect witnesses whose personal security may be under threat because they have agreed to testify at a trial. Witness protection measures aim to protect the identity of a witness from the public and the press and include things such as expunging the name of the witness from the public record and closing court sessions to the public. Witness-anonymity measures aim to protect the identity of a witness from the public, the press, and the accused person.

It is of vital importance that once an order for witness protection measures or anonymity is granted, the name of the witness in question and any details about the witness are not revealed by those persons who are privy to documentation pertaining to the witness protection order or the order for witness anonymity. These persons may include, for example, court staff, staff of the office of the prosecutor, or defense lawyers (where witness protection measures or orders for witness anonymity have been granted in favor of the defense). Thus, the criminal offense of revealing the sealed order for witness protection or witness anonymity was included in the MCC. Not only is revealing the final order for witness protection or anonymity criminalized, but so is revealing the petition for either order made by the prosecution or the defense, any other documents or information contained in the petition, the order, or other documents.

## *Article 200.2: Penalty*

1. The applicable penalty range for the criminal offense of revealing the sealed order for protective measures or anonymity is one to five years' imprisonment.
2. The court may impose a fine, as an alternative principal penalty, upon a person revealing the sealed order for protective measures or anonymity.

# Annexes

## Annex 1: Assessing Criminal Responsibility under the MCC

This flow chart shows the steps to be taken and the questions to be asked in determining if a person is criminally responsible under the Model Criminal Code.

### STEP 1: Preliminary Determinations

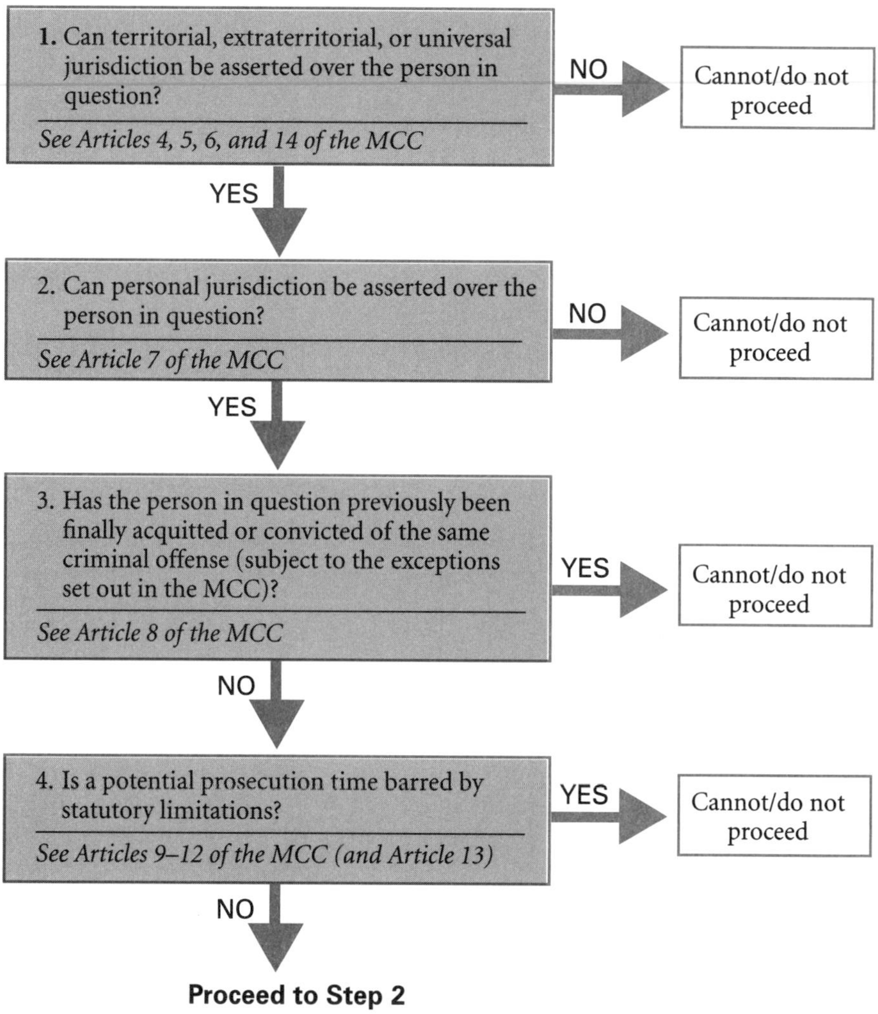

## STEP 2: Criminal Responsibility

5. Are the acts in question illegal (i.e., are they specified by law as a criminal offense)?

*See Article 15 of the MCC; also refer to the Special Part of the MCC*

NO → No criminal responsibility

YES ↓

6. Did the person in question commit the physical act of the criminal offense (i.e., the acts set out under the relevant offense):
   - voluntarily?
   - by act or by omission?

*See Articles 16 and 17 of the MCC; also refer to the criminal offense in question in the Special Part of the MCC*

NO → No criminal responsibility

YES ↓

7. Did the person in question commit the physical acts of the criminal offense:
   - through attempt?
   - personally?
   - through common purpose?
   - by ordering, soliciting, or inducing the criminal offense?
   - by incitement?
   - by facilitation?
   - through command responsibility?
   - as a legal person?

*See Articles 16, 17(3), 27 (attempt), 28 (common purpose), 29 (ordering, soliciting, or inducing), 30 (incitement), 31 (facilitation), 32 (command responsibility), and 19 (legal person) of the MCC*

NO → No criminal responsibility

YES ↓

## STEP 2: Criminal Responsibility (cont.)

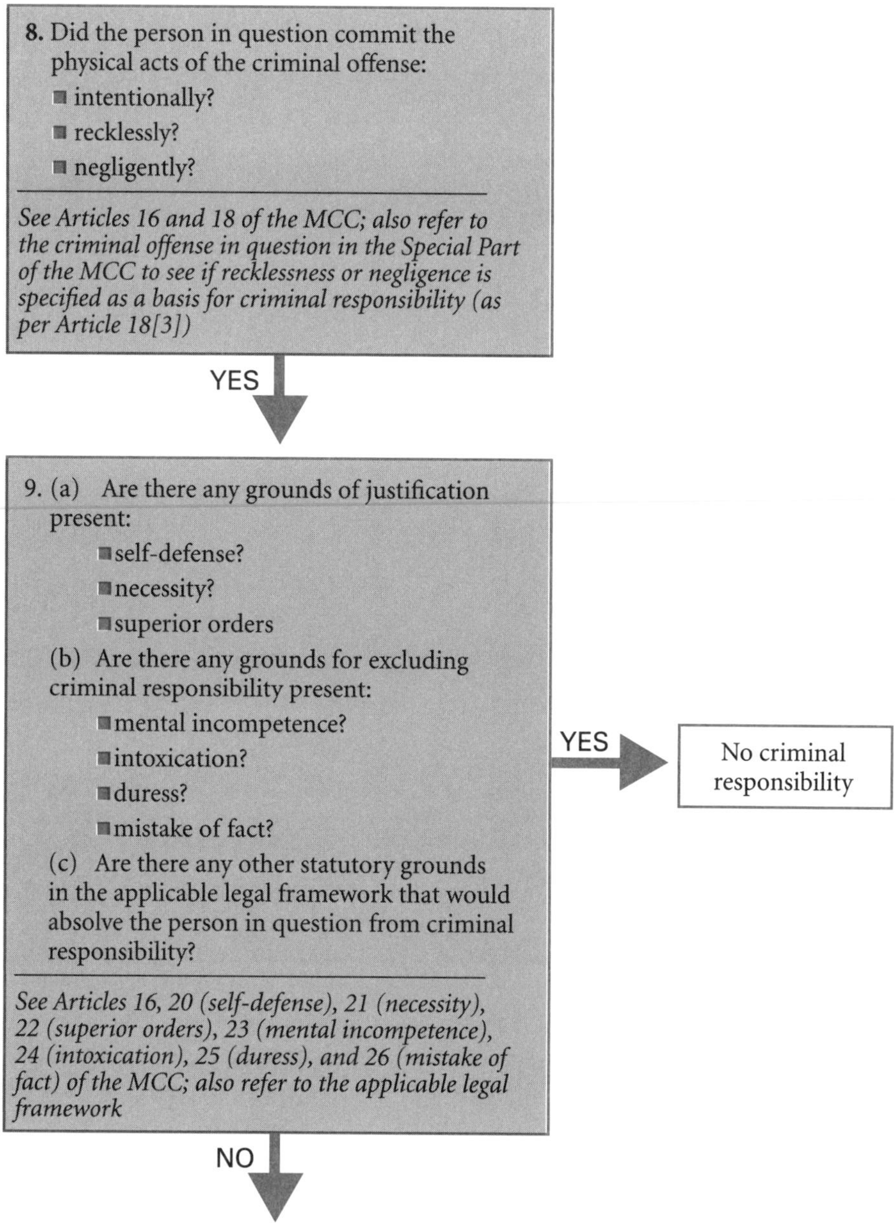


**RESULT:** The Person in Question is Criminally Responsible. Proceed to "Determination of Penalties" (see Annex 3)

# Annex 2: The Range of Penalties Provided for in the MCC

| Principal Penalties | Alternative Penalties | Additional Penalties |
|---|---|---|
| ■ Imprisonment<br>• 1–5 years<br>• 2–10 years<br>• 3–15 years<br>• 5–20 years<br>• 10–30 years<br>■ Life imprisonment<br>■ Fine<br><br>*See Articles 37, 38, 49 (life imprisonment), and 50 (fine) of the MCC; see also the Special Part of the MCC to determine the minimum and maximum period of imprisonment for a particular criminal offense and whether life imprisonment is provided as a maximum penalty or whether a fine is provided as an alternative principal penalty* | ■ Suspended sentence<br>■ Community service<br>■ Semiliberty<br><br>*See Articles 37, 39, 54, 55 (suspended sentence), 56 (community service), and 57 (semiliberty) of the MCC* | ■ Fine<br>■ Confiscation<br>■ Victim compensation<br>■ Deprivation of the right to be elected<br>■ Deprivation of the right to possess or carry firearms<br>■ Prohibition on holding a post as a public official<br>■ Prohibition on exercise of managerial or supervisory positions<br>■ Expulsion of a non-national<br><br>*See Articles 37, 40, 58, 59, 60 (fine), 61 (confiscation), 62 (compensation), 63 (right to be elected), 64 (right to possess or carry firearms), 65 (public officials), 66 (managerial and supervisory positions), and 67 (expulsion of a non-national) of the MCC* |

# Annex 3: Determination of Penalties under the MCC

This flow chart shows the steps to be taken and the questions to be asked in determining applicable penalties under the Model Criminal Code. It is important to note that at *all* stages of the process of determining penalties, the guiding principles (see Articles 34 and 36) and the fundamental principle (see Article 35) of the MCC apply.

## STEP 1: Determination of the Principal Penalty and the Applicable Penalty Range (in the Case of Imprisonment)

1. What is the minimum and maximum penalty range provided for the criminal offense in question?

*See Articles 41 and 42 of the MCC; refer to relevant criminal offense in the Special Part of the MCC; see also Articles 34–36*

↓

2. (a) Are there legal grounds and circumstances that allow for the augmentation of the applicable penalty range on the following grounds:
   - Individual aggravating factors attached to the particular criminal offense and set out in the Special Part of the MCC?
   - The criminal offense was committed as part of organized criminal activities?
   - The criminal offense was motivated by hatred?
   - The criminal offense was committed by a public official?

*(cont. next page)*

## STEP 1: Determination of the Principal Penalty and the Applicable Penalty Range (in the Case of Imprisonment) (cont.)

*(cont. from previous page)*

(b) Are there legal grounds and circumstances that allow for the reduction of the applicable penalty range on the following grounds:

- The criminal offense was motivated by hatred?
- The presence of particularly mitigating circumstances?
- The criminal offense was an attempted criminal offense?

*See Articles 41, 43 (individual aggravating factors), 44 (organized criminal activity), 45 (offense motivated by hatred), 45 (offense committed by a public official), 47 (particularly mitigating circumstances), and 48 (attempted offenses) of the MCC; see also Articles 34–36*

3. Should life imprisonment be imposed as the applicable principal penalty?

*See Articles 41 and 49 of the MCC; refer to the relevant criminal offense in the Special Part of the MCC to see if there is the possibility of life imprisonment as the maximum penalty; see also Articles 34–36*

YES → Go to Step 4

NO ↓

4. Should a fine be imposed as the applicable principal penalty?

*See Articles 41 and 50 of the MCC; refer to relevant criminal offense in the Special Part of the MCC to see if there is the possibility of a fine as the minimum penalty; see also Articles 34–36*

YES → Go to Step 4

NO ↓

**Proceed to Step 2**

## STEP 2: Determination of the Relevant Term of Imprisonment within the Specified Penalty Range

5. Within the penalty range determined, what should the applicable term of imprisonment be, taking into account:
   - aggravating factors?
   - mitigating factors?

*See Articles 41, 51(1) (aggravating factors), and 51(2) (mitigating factors) of the MCC; see also Articles 34–36*

**Proceed to Step 3**

## STEP 3: Replacement of the Principal Penalty of Imprisonment with an Alternative Penalty Where the Term of Imprisonment Decided upon is Less Than Three Years

6. Where the principal penalty assigned is less than three years, should it be converted into:
   - a suspended sentence?
   - community service?
   - semiliberty?

*See Articles 39, 41, 54, 55 (suspended sentence), 56 (community service), and 57 (semiliberty); see also Articles 34–36*

**Proceed to Step 4**

## STEP 4: Supplementation of a Principal or Alternative Penalty with an Additional Penalty

7. Should the principal or alternative penalty be supplemented by:
   - a fine?
   - confiscation?
   - victim compensation?
   - deprivation of the right to be elected?
   - deprivation of the right to possess or carry firearms?
   - prohibition on the exercise of public administration or service functions?
   - prohibition on the exercise of managerial or supervisory positions?
   - expulsion of a non-national?

*See Articles 37, 40, 41, 58, 59, 60 (fine), 61 (confiscation), 62 (compensation); 63 (right to be elected), 64 (right to possess or carry firearms), 65 (public administration or service functions), 66 (managerial or supervisory positions), and 67 (expulsion); see also Articles 34–36*

↓

**RESULT:** Final Determination of the Principal Penalty or Replacement Alternative Penalty (Where Appropriate) and any Additional Penalty

# Further Reading and Resources

## Legal Instruments

### International and Regional Human Rights Instruments Relevant to Criminal Law and Procedure

*International treaties that deal generally with fair trial and due process rights*

- United Nations International Covenant on Civil and Political Rights and its two additional protocols

*Regional treaties that deal generally with fair trial and due process rights*

- African Charter on Human and Peoples' Rights
- American Convention on Human Rights
- American Declaration on the Rights and Duties of Man
- Arab Charter on Human Rights
- European Charter of Fundamental Rights
- European Convention for the Protection of Human Rights and Fundamental Freedoms and its fourteen additional protocols

*International treaties that deal with specific rights and groups of persons*

- Optional Protocol to the Convention on the Rights of the Child on the Sale of Children, Child Prostitution and Child Pornography
- United Nations Convention against Torture and Other Cruel, Inhuman or Degrading Treatment or Punishment
- United Nations Convention on the Elimination of All Forms of Discrimination against Women
- United Nations Convention on the Rights of the Child
- United Nations International Convention on the Elimination of All Forms of Racial Discrimination

- United Nations International Convention on the Protection of All Persons from Enforced Disappearance

*Regional treaties that deal with specific rights and groups of persons*

- African Charter on the Rights and Welfare of the Child
- InterAmerican Convention on Forced Disappearance of Persons
- InterAmerican Convention to Prevent and Punish Torture
- Protocol to the African Charter on Human and Peoples' Rights on the Rights of Women in Africa

## International and Regional Instruments Relevant to Crime and Criminal Investigation

*Corruption*

- United Nations Convention against Corruption
- Council of Europe Criminal Law Convention on Corruption
- Council of Europe Civil Law Convention on Corruption
- European Union Convention on the Fight against Corruption Involving Officials of the European Communities or Officials of Member States of the European Union
- InterAmerican Convention against Corruption
- OECD Convention on Combating Bribery of Foreign Public Officials in International Business Transactions
- South African Development Community Protocol against Corruption

*Cybercrime*

- Council of Europe Convention on Cybercrime

*Drug trafficking and production*

- United Nations Single Convention on Narcotic Drugs
- United Nations Convention against Illicit Traffic in Narcotic Drugs and Psychotropic Substances
- United Nations Convention on Psychotropic Substances

*Extradition*

- Economic Community of West African States Convention on Extradition
- European Convention on Extradition and its additional protocols

- InterAmerican Convention on Extradition

### *Money laundering*

- Council of Europe Convention on Laundering, Search, Seizure and Confiscation of the Proceeds of Crime and on the Financing of Terrorism

### *Mutual legal assistance*

- Convention on Mutual Legal Assistance in Criminal Matters between Member States of the European Union
- European Convention on Mutual Legal Assistance in Criminal Matters and its additional protocols
- InterAmerican Convention on Mutual Legal Assistance in Criminal Matters and Optional Protocol Thereto

### *Organized crime*

- United Nations Convention against Transnational Organized Crime

### *Smuggling of migrants*

- Protocol against the Smuggling of Migrants by Land, Sea and Air, Supplementing the United Nations Convention against Transnational Organized Crime

### *Terrorist acts and terrorism*

- Arab Convention for the Suppression of Terrorism
- Council of Europe Convention on the Prevention of Terrorism
- Council of Europe Convention on Laundering, Search, Seizure and Confiscation of the Proceeds of Crime and on the Financing of Terrorism
- InterAmerican Convention against Terrorism
- OAU Convention on the Prevention and Combating of Terrorism
- United Nations Convention on the Marking of Plastic Explosives for the Purpose of Detection
- United Nations Convention on Offenses and Certain Other Acts Committed on Board Aircraft
- United Nations Convention on the Physical Protection of Nuclear Material
- United Nations Convention on the Prevention and Punishment of Crimes against Internationally Protected Persons
- United Nations Convention for the Suppression of Unlawful Acts against the Safety of Civil Aviation

- United Nations Convention for the Suppression of Unlawful Acts against the Safety of Maritime Navigation
- United Nations Convention for the Suppression of Unlawful Seizure of Aircraft
- United Nations International Convention against the Taking of Hostages
- United Nations International Convention for the Suppression of the Financing of Terrorism
- United Nations International Convention for the Suppression of Terrorist Bombings
- United Nations Protocol for the Suppression of Unlawful Acts against the Safety of Fixed Platforms Located on the Continental Shelf
- United Nations Protocol for the Suppression of Unlawful Acts of Violence at Airports Serving International Civil Aviation

*Trafficking in firearms*

- InterAmerican Convention againt the Illicit Manufacturing of and Trafficking in Firearms, Ammunition, Explosives and Other Related Materials
- United Nations Protocol against the Illicit Manufacturing of and Trafficking in Firearms, Their Parts and Components and Ammunition, Supplementing the United Nations Convention against Transnational Organized Crime

*Trafficking in persons*

- Council of Europe Convention on Action against Trafficking in Human Beings
- SAARC Convention on Preventing and Combating Trafficking in Women and Children for Prostitution
- United Nations Protocol to Prevent, Suppress and Punish Trafficking in Persons, Especially Women and Children, Supplementing the United Nations Convention against Transnational Organized Crime

## International Criminal Law Instruments

- Elements of Crimes to the Statute of the International Criminal Court
- Rome Statute of the International Criminal Court
- Rules of Procedure and Evidence of the International Criminal Court
- Rules of Procedure for the International Tribunal for the Prosecution of Persons Responsible for Serious Violations of International Humanitarian Law Committed on the Territory of the Former Yugoslavia since 1991

- Rules of Procedure and Evidence for the International Tribunal for the Prosecution of Persons Responsible for Serious Violations of International Humanitarian Law Committed on the Territory of Rwanda since 1991
- Statute of the International Criminal Tribunal for the former Yugoslavia
- Statute of the International Criminal Tribunal for Rwanda

## Nonbinding Human Rights Principles and Instruments

- United Nations Basic Principles on the Independence of the Judiciary
- United Nations Basic Principles on the Role of Lawyers
- United Nations Basic Principles on the Use of Force and Firearms by Law Enforcement Officials
- United Nations Body of Principles for the Protection of Persons under Any Form of Detention or Imprisonment
- United Nations Code of Conduct for Law Enforcement Officials
- United Nations Declaration on the Elimination of Violence against Women
- United Nations Declaration on the Protection of All Persons from Enforced Disappearance
- United Nations Declaration on the Rights of the Child
- United Nations Guidelines on the Role of Prosecutors
- United Nations Rules for the Protection of Juveniles Deprived of Their Liberty
- United Nations Standard Minimum Rules for the Administration of Juvenile Justice
- United Nations Standard Minimum Rules for Noncustodial Measures
- United Nations Standard Minimum Rules for the Treatment of Prisoners

# Further Reading Relevant to the General Part of the Model Criminal Code

## Jurisdiction

Amnesty International. *14 Principles on the Effective Exercise of Universal Jurisdiction.* AI Index: IOR 53/002/2001. 1 September 2001. http://web.amnesty.org/library/index/engIOR530011999.

> Amnesty International's "14 principles" aim to guide states in asserting universal jurisdiction over grave breaches of international law, namely, genocide, crimes against humanity, extrajudicial executions, enforced disappearances, and torture.

Amnesty International. *Legal Memorandum on Universal Jurisdiction.* AI Index: IOR53/001/1999. 1 May 1999. http://web.amnesty.org/pages/uj-memorandum-eng.

> Amnesty International's legal memorandum discusses the customary and conventional legal basis of universal jurisdiction over war crimes, crimes against humanity, genocide, torture, extrajudicial executions, and disappearances. This memorandum aims to assist ministries and legislatures in drafting or amending legislation providing for universal jurisdiction, as well as to assist prosecutors, judges, and ministries of justice and foreign affairs in effectively exercising universal jurisdiction.

Council of Europe, Select Committee of Experts on Extraterritorial Jurisdiction. *Report on Extraterritorial Criminal Jurisdiction.* 1988.

> This report provides a useful background on the topic of criminal jurisdiction. It makes a comparative study of the rules and principles of territorial and extraterritorial jurisdiction from both a domestic and an international law perspective, examines possible difficulties in establishing territorial and extraterritorial jurisdiction, and puts forward solutions to potential conflicts of jurisdiction between different states.

Princeton Project on Universal Jurisdiction, in cooperation with the Program in Law and Public Affairs, Woodrow Wilson School of Public and International Affairs, Princeton University, International Commission of Jurists, American Association for the International Commission of Jurists, Netherlands Institute of Human Rights, and Urban Morgan Institute for Human Rights. *Princeton Principles on Universal Jurisdiction.* http://www.princeton.edu/~lapa/unive_jur.pdf.

> The *Princeton Principles* provide a guide for state actors in the exercise of universal jurisdiction. They were drafted to advance the continued evolution of international law and the application of international law in national legal systems.

Zeid Ra'ad Zeid Al-Hussein, Prince. *A Comprehensive Strategy to Eliminate Future Sexual Exploitation and Abuse in United Nations Peacekeeping Operations.* 2005. UN Doc. A/59/710. 2006.

> Prince Zeid was appointed by the secretary-general of the United Nations to look into allegations of sexual exploitation of civilians by United Nations peacekeeping personnel working in peace operations. This report, the result of consultations with United Nations officials, police, and military personnel working in peace operations, contains recommendations on sexual exploitation and abuse by peacekeeping personnel. Except in extremely limited situations where immunity may be lifted, peacekeeping personnel generally possess immunity from criminal prosecution and therefore cannot be prosecuted in the post-conflict state. The report discusses in detail how such alleged criminal acts should be dealt with in light of the immunity issue.

## Juvenile Justice

Penal Reform International. *Ten Point Plan on Juvenile Justice: A Contribution to the Committee on the Rights of the Child Day of General Discussion on "State Violence against Children."* Geneva, 22 September 2000. http://www.crin.org/docs/resources/treaties/crc.25/penalref.pdf.

> Building on international instruments on juvenile justice, the *Ten Point Plan on Juvenile Justice* aims to reduce violence within justice systems through general education and social welfare. The *Plan* argues that parents, teachers, social workers, and psychologists are more likely to help young people in conflict become law-abiding adults than are police, courts, and prisons.

UNICEF International Child Development Centre. *Innocenti Digest: Juvenile Justice.* 1998. http://www.unicef-icdc.org/publications/pdf/digest3e.pdf.

> This resource focuses on young people under the age of eighteen who come into contact with the justice system. It addresses issues such as arrest and detention of juveniles and juvenile dispositions from the perspective of international human rights norms and standards.

## Liability of Legal Persons

Council of Europe, Committee of Ministers. Recommendation R (88)18 Concerning Liability of Enterprises Having Legal Personality for Offenses Committed in the Exercise of their Activities. 1990.

> In light of the increasing number of criminal offenses committed in the exercise of the activities of enterprises, the Council of Europe issued Recommendation R 88(18) to guide the law and practice of its member states. This recommendation contains ten core principles regarding liability and criminal sanctions relevant to legal persons.

## Penalties and Criminal Dispositions

Amnesty International. *Fair Trials Manual.* London: Amnesty International United Kingdom, 1998. http://www.amnesty.org/ailib/intcam/fairtrial/fairtria.htm.

This manual provides information regarding international and regional standards that protect the right to a fair trial. Its intended users are observers and others assessing the fairness of an individual case, as well as those evaluating whether a country's criminal justice system guarantees respect for international standards of fair trial. The manual covers pretrial rights, rights at trial, and during appeals, and special cases, which include death penalty trials, cases involving children, and fair trial rights during armed conflict.

Commission of the European Communities. *Green Paper on the Approximation, Mutual Recognition and Enforcement of Criminal Sanctions in the European Union.* COM (2004)334 final. April 2004. http://ec.europa.eu/justice_home/news/consulting_public/gp_sanctions/green_paper_en.pdf.

The *Green Paper* analyzes national differences regarding criminal penalties and the problems thus posed for judicial cooperation between member states in the European Union. The *Green Paper* provides a useful comparative discussion of a broad range of penalties and criminal dispositions.

Council of Europe, Committee of Ministers. Recommendation No. R(92) 17 of the Committee of Ministers to Member States on Consistency in Sentencing. 1992.

This recommendation sets out a body of principles applicable to the sentencing of convicted persons. The recommendations fall under a number of headings, including the rationale for sentencing; penalty structure; aggravating and mitigating factors; previous convictions; giving reasons for sentences; prohibition of *reformatio in pejus*; time spent in custody; the role of the prosecutor; sentencing studies and information; and statistics and research.

Council of Europe, Committee of Ministers. Resolution (76) 10 on Certain Alternative Penal Measures to Imprisonment. 1976.

This resolution urges governments to look to their criminal legislation and any obstacles to providing alternatives to imprisonment for persons convicted of criminal offenses. In doing so, this resolution discusses the merits and modalities of introducing alternatives to imprisonment into law.

Penal Reform International. *Draft Ten Point Plan to Reduce Imprisonment.* http://www.penalreform.org.

This ten-point plan provides practical recommendations that could serve as the basis of efforts to reduce the rate of imprisonment in a state.

Penal Reform International. *Good Practices in Reducing Pre-trial Detention.* December 2003. http://www.penalreform.org/download/Good%20practice%20paper.pdf.

Created with policymakers and stakeholders in criminal justice reform in mind, this draft index provides practical examples of good practices in reducing pretrial detention.

United Nations. *UN Basic Principles on the Use of Restorative Justice Programmes in Criminal Matters.* UN Doc. E/2000/INF/2/Add.2. 2000.

These principles were conceived in response to the international growth in the use of restorative justice programs, which often derive from indigenous or traditional forms of justice. This document defines the terms *restorative justice programme* and *restorative justice outcome,* and provides concrete and practicable principles on the use, operation, and further development of restorative justice programs.

United Nations Economic and Social Council, Commission on Crime Prevention. *Report of the Secretary-General on Restorative Justice.* April 2002. http://www.unodc.org/pdf/crime/commissions/11comm/5e.pdf.

This report focuses broadly on the issue of restorative justice. It summarizes comments from states, intergovernmental organizations, nongovernmental organizations, and the United Nations Crime Prevention and Criminal Justice Programme regarding the desirability and means of establishing common principles on the use of restorative justice programs in criminal matters. The report also describes a variety of restorative justice models from around the world.

United Nations Office on Drugs and Crime. *Handbook on Justice for Victims: On the Use and Application of the Declaration of Basic Principles of Justice for Victims of Crime and Abuse of Power.* 1999. http://www.uncjin.org/Standards/9857854.pdf.

This handbook was drafted to accompany the United Nations Basic Principles of Justice for Victims of Crime and Abuse of Power to assist states in giving effect to these principles in a domestic context. The handbook contains practical examples and illustrations on how to implement victim service programs; ensure victim-sensitive responses; and develop policies, procedures, and protocols for criminal justice agencies and others who come into contact with victims.

# Further Reading Relevant to the Special Part of the Model Criminal Code

## Corruption

Bolongaita, Emil. *Controlling Corruption in Post-Conflict Countries.* Kroc Institute Occasional Paper No. 26. Notre Dame, IN: Joan B. Kroc Institute for International Peace Studies, Notre Dame University, January 2005. http://kroc.nd.edu/ocpapers/op_26_2.pdf.

> This paper provides an analysis of corruption's corrosive effects on post-conflict agendas. Bolongaita argues that anticorruption efforts should be a component in any peace agreement and stresses the need for rigorous monitoring and evaluation mechanisms.

Center for Democracy and Governance. *A Handbook on Fighting Corruption.* 1999. http://www.usaid.gov/our_work/democracy_and_governance/publications/pdfs/pnace070.pdf.

> This handbook sets out a framework to assist in the development of strategic responses to public corruption. As part of the framework, it sets out the root causes of corruption, identifies a range of institutional and social reforms to address them, and introduces a methodology for selecting among these measures.

Council of Europe. *Criminal Law Convention on Corruption. Explanatory Report.* ETS No. 173. 1998. http://conventions.coe.int/Treaty/en/Reports/Html/173.htm.

> This report, an interpretative supplement to the Council of Europe Criminal Law Convention on Corruption, aims to facilitate a better understanding of the convention by explaining its various articles. It also presents a general discussion of corruption and the various legal and policy measures developed to combat it.

Council of Europe, Committee of Ministers. Resolution (97) 24 on the Twenty Guiding Principles for the Fight against Corruption. 1997.

> Aware that corruption represents a threat to democracy and the rule of law and constitutes a denial of human rights, Resolution 97 (24) of the Committee of Ministers elaborates twenty comprehensive and far-reaching guiding principles on the fight against corruption from both a legal and a policy perspective.

Council of Europe. *Model Code of Conduct for Public Officials.* Appendix to Council of Ministers Recommendation No. R (2000) 10. 2000.

> This resource, intended to help those drafting a code of conduct for public officials, addresses such topics as reporting, conflict of interests, political

and public activity of public officials, gifts, reactions to improper offers, information held by public authorities, and integrity checking.

Large, Daniel, ed. *Corruption in Postwar Reconstruction: Confronting the Vicious Circle.* Lebanese Transparency Association and UNDP. 2005. http://www.transparency-lebanon.org/Publications/Corruption%20in%20PWR.htm.

This is a collection of case study–oriented perspectives (including views from Lebanon, Bosnia and Herzegovina, and Sierra Leone) on the impact of corruption on postwar reconstruction and corruption's relationship to serious crimes.

Transparency International. *The Corruption Fighters' Toolkit.* 2001. http://www.transparency.org/tools/e_toolkit.

*The Corruption Fighters' Toolkit* is a compendium of practical civil society anticorruption experiences. It presents anticorruption tools developed and implemented by Transparency International's national chapters and other civil society organizations around the world. The publication highlights the potential of civil society to create mechanisms for monitoring public institutions and to demand and promote accountable and responsive public administration.

United Nations. *International Code of Conduct for Public Officials.* UN Doc. A/51/59. 1996.

In response to the growing problem of corruption, and in light of the link between corruption and the public sector, the United Nations developed a code of conduct for public officials. This code contains general principles regarding the role of public officials, as well as principles concerning conflict of interest and disqualification, disclosure of assets, acceptance of gifts and favors, confidential information, and political activity.

United Nations Office on Drugs and Crime. *Corruption: Compendium of International Legal Instruments on Corruption,* 2nd ed. New York: United Nations, 2005. http://www.unodc.org/pdf/crime/corruption/compendium_e.pdf.

The compendium includes both the summaries and the full texts of corruption-related international legal instruments from the United Nations, the African Union, the Council of Europe, the Organization of American States, the Organization of Economic Cooperation and Development, and the Council of the European Union.

United Nations Office on Drugs and Crime, Division for Treaty Affairs. *Legislative Guides for the Implementation of the United Nations Convention against Corruption.* New York: United Nations, 2006. http://www.unodc.org/pdf/corruption/CoC_LegislativeGuide.pdf.

This publication contains legislative guides for the Convention against Corruption. It provides states with practical guidance on how to implement the provisions of the convention into domestic law by identifying legislative requirements, issues arising from those requirements, and various options available to states as they develop and draft the necessary legislation.

United Nations Office on Drugs and Crime. *United Nations Anti-Corruption Toolkit*, 3rd ed. Vienna: United Nations, 2004. http://www.unodc.org/pdf/crime/corruption/toolkit/corruption_un_anti_corruption_toolkit_sep04.pdf.

Continually updated, the toolkit covers the following areas: assessments of corruption levels, institution building, social prevention, anticorruption legislation, monitoring and evaluation, international legal cooperation, and asset recovery and protection.

United Nations Office on Drugs and Crime. *United Nations Guide for Anti-Corruption Policies*. 2003. http://www.unodc.org/pdf/crime/corruption/UN_Guide.pdf.

This document, intended to be used by political officials, senior policymakers, and other actors, contains a general outline of the nature and scope of the problem of corruption and a description of major elements of anticorruption policies.

## Cybercrime

Council of Europe. *Convention on Cybercrime. Explanatory Report*. ETS No. 185. 2001.

This report, an interpretative supplement to the Council of Europe Convention on Cybercrime, aims to facilitate a better understanding of the convention by explaining its various articles. It also presents a general discussion of cybercrime and the various legal and policy measures developed to combat it.

## Domestic Violence and Sexual Violence

United Nations. *Women, Peace and Security: Report of the Secretary-General*. UN Doc. S/2002/1154. 2002.

This report is the result of a study carried out on the impact of armed conflict on women and girls, the role of women in peacebuilding, and the gender dimension of peace processes and conflict resolution. The report contains a series of recommendations and best-practice suggestions to enhance future efforts in post-conflict states, including efforts to tackle domestic violence.

United Nations Commission on Human Rights. *Report of the Special Rapporteur on Violence against Women, Its Causes and Consequences: A Framework for Model Legislation on Domestic Violence.* UN Doc. E/CN.4/1996/53/Add.2.

This resource, intended as a drafting guide for legislatures and advocates, outlines those elements that are integral to comprehensive legislation on domestic violence.

## Genocide, Crimes against Humanity, and War Crimes

Bassiouni, M. Cherif. *Crimes against Humanity in International Criminal Law.* Dordrecht, Boston, London: Martinus Nijhoff, 1992.

This book charts the evolution of crimes against humanity from the aftermath of World War II to their inclusion in the Statute of the International Criminal Court and includes both a historical and a legal analysis of crimes against humanity.

Dörman, Knut, with contributions from Robert Kolb and Louise Doswald-Beck. *Elements of War Crimes under the Rome Statute of the International Criminal Court: Sources and Commentary.* Cambridge: Cambridge University Press, 2003.

*Elements of War Crimes* is an interpretive aid to the crimes set forth in the Rome Statute of the International Criminal Court. The commentary provides insight into the negotiations of the Preparatory Committee and existing case law related to each war crime contained in the Statute of the International Criminal Court.

Human Rights Watch. *Genocide, War Crimes and Crimes against Humanity: Topical Digests of the Case Law of the International Criminal Tribunal for Rwanda and the International Criminal Tribunal for the Former Yugoslavia.* 2004. http://www.hrw.org/reports/2004/ij.

This resource focuses on the case law of the International Criminal Tribunal for Rwanda and the International Criminal Tribunal for the Former Yugoslavia regarding genocide, crimes against humanity, war crimes, individual responsibility, command responsibility, and sentencing. The digest provides summaries of and quotations from the tribunals' judgments, which are organized topically.

Schabas, William A. *Genocide in International Law.* Cambridge: Cambridge University Press, 2000.

In this work, Schabas analyzes the criminal offense of genocide, discussing the debates leading up to the 1948 Genocide Convention, the substance of the convention, and its subsequent judicial interpretation. Schabas also examines the growing body of case law from international and national courts on genocide.

## Money Laundering

Asian Development Bank. *Manual on Countering Money Laundering and the Financing of Terrorism.* 2003. http://www.adb.org/Documents/Manuals/Countering_Money_Laundering/default.asp.

> This manual brings together many of the various international conventions, principles, recommendations, guidelines, and model laws related to money laundering and financing of terrorism.

Commonwealth Organization. *Commonwealth Model Law for the Prohibition of Money Laundering and Supporting Documentation.* http://www.imolin.org/pdf/imolin/Comsecml.pdf.

> This resource provides a model anti–money laundering law that includes provisions on criminalization, freezing and forfeiture of assets, mutual legal assistance, and extradition.

United Nations Office on Drugs and Crime. *An Overview of the UN Conventions and the International Standards Concerning Anti-Money Laundering Legislation.* 2004. http://www.imolin.org/imolin/index.html.

> A collation of the various international conventions and standards on anti–money laundering legislation, this publication is subdivided into topics such as customer identification, record keeping, reporting, criminalization, international cooperation, and financial intelligence units.

United Nations Office on Drugs and Crime. *Model Anti-Money Laundering Legislation.* http://www.unodc.org/unodc/money_laundering_technical_assistance.html.

> This model law was developed for use in states whose fundamental legal systems are substantially based on the common law tradition. The law contains provisions on the criminalization of money laundering and the financing of terrorism, in addition to forfeiture and confiscation of property.

## Organized Crime

Austin, Alexander, Tobias von Gienanth, and Wibke Hansen. *Organized Crime as an Obstacle to Successful Peacebuilding: Lessons Learned from the Balkans, Afghanistan, and West Africa.* Berlin: Center for International Peace Operations, 2003. http://www.zif-berlin.org/Downloads/Berlin-Workshop_2004.pdf.

> This report summarizes the discussions at the Seventh International Berlin Workshop, which considered such topics as the effects of organized crime on successful peacebuilding, key organized crime actors and their methods, and the extent to which the fight against serious crime in peace operations is part of the overall international struggle against organized criminal activity.

CARDS Regional Police Project (CARPO). *Regional Strategy on Tools against Organised and Economic Crime with Project Area Specific Actions,* September 2005. http://www.stabilitypact.org/rt/Brijuni_Regional_strategy.pdf.

CARPO's high-level meeting of ministers and officials held in 2005 offered assessments of the progress in the fight against organized crime in southeastern Europe and examined common benchmarks and sectoral strategies on crime analysis and criminal intelligence, financial investigations and confiscation of criminal proceeds, special investigative means, witness protection, and cooperation in criminal matters that may be useful beyond the region.

Council of Europe. *Convention on Laundering, Search, Seizure, and Confiscation of the Proceeds from Crime and on Financing of Terrorism: Explanatory Report.* ETS No. 141. http://conventions.coe.int/Treaty/EN/Reports/Html/141.htm.

This report, an interpretative supplement to the Council of Europe Convention on Laundering, Search, Seizure, and Confiscation of the Proceeds from Crime and on Financing of Terrorism, explains the convention's various articles. It also presents a general discussion of money laundering and the financing of terrorism and the various legal and policy measures developed to combat these offenses.

Council of Europe, Octopus Program. *Combating Organized Crime: Best-Practice Surveys of the Council of Europe.* Strasbourg: Council of Europe Publishing, 2004.

A compilation of best-practice surveys of efforts to tackle organized crime, this publication offers information on a wide variety of measures, including witness protection, reversing the burden of proof in confiscating the proceeds of crime, intercepting communications, intrusive surveillance, crime analysis, cross-border cooperation, cooperation to combat human trafficking, and preventive legal measures against organized crime.

Financial Action Task Force on Money Laundering. *The Forty Recommendations of the Financial Action Task Force on Money Laundering.* 28 June 1996. http://www.fincen.gov/40rec.pdf.

The Financial Action Task Force on Money Laundering (FATF) is an intergovernmental body that promotes the development of policies to combat money laundering. The FATF aims to prevent criminal proceeds from financing other criminal activities and affecting legitimate economic activities. The *Forty Recommendations* sets out the basic framework for anti–money laundering efforts, focusing on the criminal justice system, law enforcement, the financial system and its regulation, and international cooperation.

United Nations, Eleventh United Nations Congress on Crime Prevention and Criminal Justice. *Effective Measures to Combat Transnational Organized Crime: Working Paper Prepared by the Secretariat.* UN Doc. A/CONF.2005/4.

> This working paper, produced in preparation for the Eleventh United Nations Congress on Crime Prevention and Criminal Justice held in Bangkok in April 2005, discusses both the phenomenon of organized crime and the kinds of international and national responses required to combat its various manifestations.

United Nations. *Interpretative Notes for the Official Records of the Negotiation of the United Nations Convention against Transnational Organized Crime and the Protocols Thereto.* http://www.uncjin.org/Documents/Conventions/dcatoc/final_documents/index.htm.

> These interpretive notes to the United Nations Convention against Transnational Organized Crime and the Protocols Thereto are taken from the negotiations of the Ad Hoc Committee on the Elaboration of a Convention against Transnational Organized Crime. They are helpful in deciphering the meaning of the final provisions included in the convention and its protocols.

United Nations Office on Drugs and Crime, Division for Treaty Affairs. *Legislative Guides for the Implementation of the United Nations Convention against Transnational Organized Crime and the Protocols Thereto.* New York: United Nations, 2004. http://www.unodc.org/unodc/organized_crime_convention_legislative_guides.html.

> This publication contains legislative guides for the Convention against Transnational Organized Crime; the Protocol to Prevent, Suppress and Punish Trafficking in Persons; the Protocol against the Smuggling of Migrants by Land, Sea and Air; and the Protocol against Illicit Manufacturing of and Trafficking in Firearms.

## Piracy

International Maritime Organization. *Code of Practice for the Investigation of the Crimes of Piracy and Armed Robbery against Ships.* 2001.

This resource provides guidance on the investigation of piracy and armed robbery against ships.

International Maritime Organization. *Guidance to Ship-Owners and Ship Operators, Shipmasters and Crew on Preventing and Suppressing Acts of Piracy and Armed Robbery against Ships.* 2002.

This document offers advice on measures that can be taken aboard ship to prevent attacks or, when attacks occur, to minimize the danger to the crew and the ship.

International Maritime Organization. *Measures to Prevent the Registration of Phantom Ships.* http://www.imo.org/newsroom/mainframe.asp?topic_id=144&doc_id=1973.

This document outlines various measures that states can take to prevent the registration of "phantom ships" (ships that are inaccurately registered and that are then sold by pirates with false documents).

International Maritime Organization. *IMO Recommendations to Governments for Preventing and Suppressing Piracy and Armed Robbery against Ships.* 1999. http://www.imo.org/includes/blast_bindoc.asp?doc_id=940&format=pdf.

This document presents possible countermeasures against piracy and armed robbery against ships. It includes a draft regional agreement on cooperation in the fight against piracy and armed robbery against ships.

## Terrorist Acts

Council of Europe. *Guidelines on Human Rights and the Fight against Terrorism.* 2002. http://www.coe.int/t/F/Droits_de_l'Homme/Guidelines.asp.

> The Council of Europe's guidelines on human rights and the fight against terrorism, adopted by the Committee of Ministers on July 11, 2002, affirm states' obligation to protect everyone against terrorism, and reiterate the need to avoid arbitrariness. They also stress that all measures taken by states to combat terrorism must be lawful, and that torture must be prohibited. The legal framework set out in the guidelines addresses, in particular, the collecting and processing of personal data, measures that interfere with privacy, arrest, police custody and pretrial detention, legal proceedings, extradition, and compensation of victims.

International Monetary Fund. *Suppressing the Financing of Terrorism: A Handbook for Legislative Drafting.* 2003. http://www.imf.org/external/pubs/nft/2003/SFTH/index.htm.

> This handbook is intended to assist states in preparing legislation to implement international obligations contained in a range of international norms and standards on the financing of terrorism.

United Nations Office of the High Commissioner for Human Rights. *Digest of the Jurisprudence of the United Nations and Regional Organizations on Protecting Human Rights while Countering Terrorism.* 2003. http://www.ohchr.org/english/about/publications/docs/digest.doc.

> This resource is a compilation of findings of judicial and quasi-judicial bodies of the United Nations and regional organizations regarding the protection of human rights in the struggle against terrorism. Its aim is to assist policymakers and other concerned parties in developing a vision of counterterrorism strategies that fully respect human rights.

United Nations Office on Drugs and Crime. *Guide for the Legislative Incorporation and Implementation of the Universal Instruments against Terrorism.* 2005. http://www.unodc.org/unodc/terrorism_tools.html.

> This guide is designed to assist lawmakers in the preparation of laws implementing the twelve international antiterrorism conventions. It contains a number of practical tips as well as model laws and provisions.

## Torture

African Commission on Human and Peoples' Rights. *Guidelines and Measures for the Prohibition and Prevention of Torture, Cruel, Inhuman or Degrading Treatment or Punishment in Africa* (the "Robben Island Guidelines"). 2002. www1.umn.edu/humanrts/achpr/tortguidelines.html.

These guidelines contain fifty separate sections on the prohibition and prevention of torture and cruel, inhuman, or degrading treatment or punishment.

Council of Europe. *The Prohibition of Torture: Human Rights Handbook No. 6*. http://www.coe.int/T/E/Human_rights/hrhb6.pdf.

This handbook, which offers guidance on the implementation of Article 3 of the European Convention on Human Rights and Fundamental Freedoms, explains the nature, scope, and meaning of "torture," "cruel, inhuman or degrading treatment," and "cruel, inhuman or degrading punishment" and outlines the measures that states should take to ensure that all persons are free from such practices. It also discusses the prohibition of torture with regard to arrest, detention, and conditions of detention and elaborates standards on forensics, the behavior of law enforcement forces, investigations, and prosecutions.

European Committee for the Prevention of Torture and Inhuman or Degrading Treatment or Punishment (CPT). *The CPT Standards: "Substantive" Sections of the CPT's General Reports*. CPT/Inf/E (2002) 1-Rev. 2006. http://www.cpt.coe.int/EN/docsstandards.htm.

This resource contains a set of standards developed by the CPT to guide national authorities on how persons deprived of their liberty ought to be treated and what treatment constitutes torture or cruel or inhuman treatment or punishment. The substantive sections address a range of issues, including police custody, imprisonment, training of law enforcement personnel, health care services in prisons, foreign nationals detained under aliens' legislation, involuntary placement in psychiatric establishments, and juveniles and women deprived of their liberty.

Foley, Conor. *Combating Torture: A Manual for Judges and Prosecutors*. Essex, UK: University of Essex, 2003. http://www.essex.ac.uk/combatingtorturehandbook/manual.

This manual provides guidance for judges and prosecutors on investigating acts of torture based on international human rights norms and standards. It contains checklists of good practice. The manual outlines the prohibition of torture in international law and safeguards that exist to guard against torture and other ill treatment of people deprived of their liberty. It describes the role of judges and prosecutors in ensuring that these standards are upheld and safeguards are in place. It also discusses the prosecution of those involved in torture or other forms of ill treatment, including the legal definition of torture and how to identify and prosecute those responsible for torture.

United Nations. *Manual on Effective Investigation and Documentation of Torture and Other Cruel, Inhuman or Degrading Treatment or Punishment* (the "Istanbul Protocol"). General Assembly Resolution 55/89. 4 December 2000. http://www.ohchr.org/english/law/investigation.htm.

The Istanbul Protocol developed by the United Nations is intended to serve as a set of international guidelines for the assessment of persons who allege torture and ill treatment, for investigating cases of alleged torture, and for reporting such findings to the judiciary and any other investigative body.

## Trafficking in Persons

American Bar Association and Central European and Eurasian Law Initiative (CEELI). *The Human Trafficking Assessment Tool.* Washington, D.C.: American Bar Association, 2005. http://www.abanet.org/ceeli/publications/htat/home.html.

CEELI's *Human Trafficking Assessment Tool* allows a state to measure its legal and practical compliance with the Protocol to Prevent, Suppress and Punish Trafficking in Persons, Especially Women and Children (United Nations Trafficking Protocol) that supplements the United Nations Convention against Transnational Organized Crime. This document also elaborates upon the obligations set forth in the protocol and its host convention and provides a sample analysis of national antitrafficking laws and government efforts to combat trafficking against the benchmark of these standards.

Global Rights. *Annotated Guide to the Complete UN Trafficking Protocol.* 2002. http://www.globalrights.org/site/DocServer/Annotated_Protocol.pdf?docID=2723.

This guide is designed to assist advocates in the development of an adequate legal and policy framework for combating trafficking in persons. It goes through the Protocol to Prevent, Suppress and Punish Trafficking in Persons, especially Women and Children provision by provision and deconstructs the obligations contained in each one, while providing examples of how states can comply with these obligations.

Oswald, Bruce, and Sarah Finnin. "Combating the Trafficking of Persons on Peace Operations." In *International Peacekeeping: The Yearbook of International Peace Operations,* vol. 10, ed. Harvey Langholtz, Boris Kondoch, and Alan Wells. Leiden and Boston: Martinus Nijhoff, 2006.

Inspired by the "Training Package on Human Rights for Military Personnel of Peace Operations," this article looks at the growing problem of trafficking of persons for the purposes of economic or sexual exploitation during peace operations.

United Nations Department of Peacekeeping Operations (DPKO), Best Practices Section. *Human Trafficking and United Nations Peacekeeping: DPKO Policy Paper.* March 2004. http://www.un.org/womenwatch/news/documents/DPKOHumanTrafficking Policy03-2004.pdf.

This DPKO policy paper examines the problem of human trafficking in the context of United Nations peacekeeping. Based on lessons from previous peacekeeping missions and consultations with partner organizations in the fight against trafficking, it proposes a comprehensive strategy for the DPKO to address human trafficking in post-conflict states.

United Nations Interim Administration in Kosovo (UNMIK). *Combating Human Trafficking in Kosovo: Strategy and Commitment.* May 2004. http://www.unmikonline.org/misc/UNMIK_Whit_paper_on_trafficking.pdf.

This UNMIK report defines the human trafficking problem in Kosovo, proposes strategies to combat it, and analyzes continuing problems in efforts to counter trafficking. It specifically addresses human trafficking in the overall fight against organized crime, zero tolerance enforcement against traffickers, protection and assistance for victims, and sustainability through local involvement in a multidimensional approach.

United Nations Office on Drugs and Crime, Division for Treaty Affairs. *Legislative Guides for the Implementation of the United Nations Convention against Transnational Organized Crime and the Protocols Thereto.* New York: United Nations, 2004. http://www.unodc.org/unodc/organized_crime_convention_legislative_guides.html.

This publication contains a legislative guide to the Protocol to Prevent, Suppress and Punish Trafficking in Persons.

# Criminal Law Reform Resources

## Assessment Tools

American Bar Association. *ICCPR Index.* 2003. http://www.abanet.org/ceeli/special_projects/iccpr/home.html.

The *ICCPR Index* is an assessment tool for measuring a state's legislative and programmatic compliance with the International Covenant on Civil and Political Rights.

Rausch, Colette, ed. *Combating Serious Crimes in Postconflict Environments. A Manual for Policymakers and Practitioners.* Washington, D.C.: United States Institute of Peace Press, 2006. http://www.usip.org/ruleoflaw/projects/serious_crimes.html#download.

Chapter 2 of this manual discusses the importance of undertaking a comprehensive and thorough criminal justice assessment. It also provides suggestions on how to conduct such an assessment, including recommendations on personnel, timing, and methodology. Chapter 3 discusses how to identify and assess the legal framework in a post-conflict state.

United Nations Office of the High Commissioner for Human Rights. *Rule-of-Law Tools for Post-Conflict States: Mapping the Justice Sector.* New York and Geneva: United Nations, 2006. http://www.ohchr.org/english/about/publications/docs/ruleoflaw-Mapping_en.pdf.

The result of two years of consultations with departments and agencies of the United Nations, civil society leaders, and national experts, OHCHR's report is based primarily on lessons learned in Kosovo, Sierra Leone, and East Timor. Topics addressed include assessing whether and how a country's justice system contributed to conflict; the prosecution of perpetrators of crimes such as genocide, crimes against humanity, and war crimes; the establishment of truth commissions; and the vetting and monitoring of legal systems established after the end of hostilities.

United Nations Office on Drugs and Crime (UNODC). *Criminal Justice Assessment Toolkit.* December 2006. http://www.unodc.org/unodc/criminal_justice_assessment_toolkit.html.

The UNODC *Criminal Justice Assessment Toolkit* is a standardized and cross-referenced set of tools designed to enable United Nations agencies, government officials engaged in criminal justice reform, and other organizations and individuals to conduct comprehensive assessments of criminal justice systems; to identify areas of technical assistance; to assist agencies in the design of interventions that integrate relevant United Nations standards and norms; and to assist in training on these issues. The toolkit contains sixteen separate assessment tools under the broad headings of policing (public safety and police service delivery; the integrity and accountability of the police; crime investigation; police information and intelligence systems), access to justice (the courts; the independence, impartiality, and integrity of the judiciary; the prosecution service; legal defense and legal aid), custodial and noncustodial measures (the prison system; detention prior to adjudication; alternatives to incarceration; social reintegration), and cross-cutting issues (criminal justice information; juvenile justice; victims and witnesses; and international cooperation).

## Comparative Criminal Law

Apple, Jamer, and Robert Deyling. *A Primer on the Civil Law.* 1995. http://www.fjc.gov/public/pdf.nsf/lookup/CivilLaw.pdf/$file/CivilLaw.pdf.

This publication charts the history and development of the civil law legal tradition and then compares it to the common law tradition. While the legal systems of the world today are often a mixture of different traditions and systems of law, this publication provides a useful background to the historical origins of many legal systems that lie in the civil law and common law traditions.

Fairchild, Erika, and Harry Dammer. *Comparative Criminal Justice Systems*. Belmont, Calif.: Wadsworth Thomson Learning, 2001.

The authors of this work compare crime and justice across national borders and use a historical-political approach to explain crime and criminal justice. This book outlines the different families of law and the legal systems of six model states. It also compares and contrasts the different legal actors, courts, sentencing procedures, law enforcement agencies, rules of criminal procedure, and modes of constitutional review in different legal systems around the world.

Glenn, Patrick. *Legal Traditions of the World*. Oxford: Oxford University Press, 2004.

This text provides a starting point on comparative criminal law. The author places national laws in the broader context of the major legal traditions of the world, including chthonic (or indigenous law), Talmudic law, civil law, Islamic law, common law, Hindu law, and Asian law, outlining the core characteristics of each tradition.

Merryman, John Henry. *The Civil Law Tradition. An Introduction to the Legal Systems of Western Europe and Latin America*. Stanford, Calif.: Stanford University Press, 1985.

This volume provides a history and analysis of the civil law tradition. Among other topics, it discusses the General Part of criminal law and criminal procedure.

## Customary/Traditional Systems of Justice

Chirayath, Leila, Caroline Sage, and Michael Woolcock. *Customary Law and Policy Reform: Engaging with the Plurality of Justice Systems*. 2005. http://siteresources.worldbank.org/INTWDR2006/Resources/477383-1118673432908/Customary_Law_and_Policy_Reform.pdf.

This work analyzes contemporary critiques of customary legal systems and argues that, despite the challenges such systems present, the success of a legal reform process depends on engaging with them. The authors draw lessons from experiences in Tanzania, Rwanda, and South Africa and present the implications for ongoing policy reform initiatives.

Penal Reform International. *Access to Justice in Sub-Saharan Africa: The Role of Traditional and Informal Justice Systems*. 2000. http://www.penalreform.org/interim/publications/manuals.

This work discusses the nature, scope, and relevance of traditional and informal justice systems in sub-Saharan Africa. It provides numerous examples drawn from not only Africa but also South Asia. It also offers guidance on the relationship that should exist between a state-run criminal justice system and traditional or informal justice systems and elaborates good practice guidelines for those working with traditional or informal justice systems.

United Kingdom Department for International Development (DFID). *Non-State Justice and Security Systems: A Guidance Note.* 2004. http://www.gsdrc.org/docs/open/SSAJ101.pdf.

Recognizing the importance of nonstate, or customary, systems of justice as complements to formal systems of justice, DFID drafted this note, which provides practical guidance on how to work with nonstate systems.

## Law Reform Agencies

Association of Law Reform Agencies in East and Southern Africa. *Best Practices in Law Reform.* 2005. http://www.doj.gov.za/alraesa/conferences/papers/s3B_sayers.pdf.

This paper looks at a number of topics and issues relating to law reform commissions, including consultants, legal research, consultation, policy papers, reports, and the need for publicity in the law reform process. The paper concludes with a chart showing the different stages in a law reform project.

Commonwealth Secretariat. *Law Reform Agencies: Their Role and Effectiveness.* 2005. http://www.calras.org/Other/future_commonwealth.htm.

This document presents an introductory overview of the variety of law reform agencies and provides basic information about such agencies.

Murphy, Gavin. *Law Reform Agencies.* 2005. http://www.justice.gc.ca/en/ps/inter/law_reform/index.html.

This guide examines the role, organization, and operation of reform agencies in the United Kingdom, Canada, and other Commonwealth countries for the purpose of outlining how a new law reform agency might be set up. The guide also presents a checklist of questions to be considered when establishing a law reform agency.

New South Wales Law Reform Commission. *The Law Reform Process: A Step by Step Guide.* 2006. http://www.lawlink.nsw.gov.au/lawlink/lrc/ll_lrc.nsf/pages/LRC_about1.

This guide includes discussion on the special features of law reform commissions and a step-by-step guide to the law reform process.

Opeskin, Brian, and David Weisbrot, eds. *The Promise of Law Reform.* Sydney, Australia: Federation Press, 2005.

This book, a collection of writings on law reform from around the world, is divided into seven parts and addresses numerous aspects of law reform and law reform commissions, including the history, purpose, and function of law reform commissions; their institutional design, methods, operations, outputs, and outcomes; and mutual assistance among different commissions. The book also provides practical examples of law reform in action around the world.

Robertson, Honorary Justice J. Bruce. *Law Reform: What Is Our Knitting? How Do We Stick To It?* 2005. http://www.lawcom.govt.nz/SpeechPaper.aspx.

The author, president of the New Zealand Law Commission, draws on the example of that body as he traces the history of law reform commissions. He also offers recommendations regarding the composition, mission, structural and operational framework, and workload of commissions.

## Law Reform Process

Berkowitz, Daniel, Katharina Pistor, and Jean-Francois Richard. *The Transplant Effect.* July 2006. http://www.sipa.columbia.edu/REGIONAL/HI/lawreview.pdf.

Drawing on extensive research and empirical data, the authors discuss the phenomenon of legal transplants and set out a methodology for employing external sources of law through a process of adaptation.

Bernstein, David S. "Process Drives Success: Key Lessons from a Decade of Legal Reform." In European Bank for Reconstruction and Development (EBRD), *Law in Transition.* Autumn 2002. http://www.ebrd.com/country/sector/law/articles/archive/index.htm.

This guide identifies lessons for institutions and agencies that provide legal reform assistance. It argues that a successful reform project is one that adapts internationally accepted principles and standards to the local legal environment, focuses time and resources on implementation and enforcement, and, most importantly, works through an open, transparent, and inclusive process.

Carlson, Scott. *Legal and Judicial Rule of Law in Multidimensional Peacekeeping Operations.* 2006. http://pbpu.unlb.org/pbpu/library/ROL%20Lessons%20Learned%20Report%20%20March%202006%20FINAL.pdf.

This report reflects on recent experience with judicial and legal reforms in United Nations peacekeeping operations, identifies a variety of lessons learned, and sets out recommendations for achieving future reforms.

Hammergren, Linn. *Code Reform and Law Revision.* Centre for Democracy and Governance, Bureau for Global Programs, Field Support, and Research, U.S. Agency for International Development. 1998. http://pdf.dec.org/pdf_docs/pnacd022.pdf#search=%22hammergren%2C%20code%20reform%20and%20revision%22.

This publication discusses the experience of the U.S. Agency for International Development in code reform and revision in Latin America. The author, reflecting on the mixed results of these reform efforts, outlines suggestions to improve future efforts and to avoid some of the mistakes that have been made in the past.

International Development Bank. *Resource Book on Participation.* 1996. http://www.iadb.org/aboutus/VI/resource_book/table_of_contents.cfm?language=english.

Based on decades of experience in the field of development, this report argues that participation can significantly enhance the effectiveness of law reform efforts. It elaborates upon the meaning and scope of participation and identifies who the stakeholders are, when participation should occur, how participation can be facilitated, and what challenges must be overcome to ensure a participatory approach.

Nelken, David, and Johannes Feest, eds. *Adapting Legal Cultures.* Portland, Ore.: Hart Publishing, 2001.

This book looks at the theory and practice of legal borrowing and adaptation around the world in the context of different legal cultures. The first part of the book examines what is meant by "legal transplantation," weighs arguments for and against it, and recounts successes and failures in legal transplantation. The second part sets out a number of case studies of legal adaptation.

## Legislative Drafting in Plain English

Australia Office of Parliamentary Counsel. *Plain English Manual.* 2003. http://www.opc.gov.au/about/docs/PEM.pdf.

The Plain English Movement promotes the drafting of legislation in language that is more accessible both to the legal community and to persons to whom the law applies. This manual provides guidance on how to draft in a plain English style, including how to plan a draft, aids to understanding legal provisions, good writing habits, and drafting phrases to avoid.

Turnbull, Ian. *Plain English and Drafting in General Principles.* 1993. http://www.opc.gov.au/plain/docs/plain_draftin_principles.rtf.

This paper discusses the various styles of drafting, including traditional drafting, drafting in plain English, and drafting in general principles. Examining the relative strengths and weaknesses of each style, the author argues in favor of the use of plain English drafting as a means of making law easier to understand without sacrificing high standards of precision.

## Legislative Drafting Manuals

Chabot, Elliot C. *List of Online Legislative Drafting Resources.* 2002. http://ili.org/ld/manuals.htm.

This document offers numerous samples of legislative drafting manuals that might be helpful when crafting new legislation.

# Useful Web Sites

## Council of Europe, Group of States against Corruption (GRECO)

http://www.coe.int/t/dg1/Greco/Default_en.asp

GRECO is a mechanism to monitor, through a process of mutual evaluation and peer pressure, the observance of the Guiding Principles in the Fight against Corruption and the implementation of international legal instruments adopted in pursuance of the Council of Europe's Programme of Action against Corruption. This Web site contains links to numerous web resources on anticorruption, as well as providing anticorruption-related documents and legal instruments.

## Council of Europe, Human Rights Handbooks Homepage

http://www.coe.int/t/e/human_rights/handbookse.asp

This Web site contains links to eight handbooks on various human rights, including the right to respect for family and private life (relevant to search, seizure, and covert surveillance in criminal investigations), the right to a fair trial, the right to liberty and security of the person, the prohibition of torture, and the right to life.

## Egmont Group

http://www.egmontgroup.org

The Egmont Group is an informal network of international financial intelligence units that cooperate and share information, training, and expertise. This Web site contains resources relevant to combating money laundering and financing of terrorism through the establishment of financial intelligence units.

## European Court of Human Rights (ECHR)

http://cmiskp.echr.coe.int/gentkpss/gen-recent-hejud.asp

This Web site provides access to the case law of the European Court of Human Rights.

## Financial Action Task Force on Money Laundering (FATF)

http://www.fatf-gafi.org

Created in 1989, FATF is an intergovernmental body whose purpose is the development and promotion of national and international policies to combat money laundering and terrorist financing.

## International Criminal Court (ICC)

http://www.icc-cpi.int/home.html&l=en

The ICC is an independent, permanent court that tries persons accused of serious international crimes, particularly genocide, crimes against humanity, and war crimes. This Web site includes the basic legal documents and jurisprudence of the ICC.

## International Criminal Tribunal for the former Yugoslavia (ICTY)

http://www.un.org/icty

The United Nations Security Council established the ICTY in 1993 to address the serious violations of international humanitarian law committed in the former Yugoslavia since 1991. This Web site includes the basic legal documents and jurisprudence of the ICTY on the crimes of genocide, crimes against humanity, and war crimes.

## International Criminal Tribunal for Rwanda (ICTR)

http://www.un.org/ictr

The United Nations Security Council established the ICTR in 1994 to prosecute persons responsible for genocide and other serious violations of international humanitarian law committed in the territory of Rwanda in 1994. This Web site includes the basic legal documents and jurisprudence of the ICTR on the crimes of genocide, crimes against humanity, and war crimes.

## International Maritime Organization (IMO)

http://www.imo.org

The IMO is a specialized agency of the United Nations whose purpose is to assist states in taking measures to improve the safety and security of international shipping. The IMO also operates an extensive technical cooperation program that focuses on improving the ability of developing states to combat piracy.

## International Maritime Piracy Reporting Centre

http://www.thedigitalship.com/webguide/imbpiracy.html

The International Maritime Bureau (IMB) is a specialized division of the International Chamber of Commerce that has been approved of by the International Maritime Organization. The IMB Piracy Reporting Centre maintains round-the-clock watch on the world's shipping lanes, reports pirate attacks to local policing agencies, and issues warnings about piracy hot spots to shipping, both throughout the year and in its annual reports.

## International Money Laundering Network

http://www.imolin.org/imolin/index.html

The International Money Laundering Network (IMoLIN) is an Internet-based network assisting governments, organizations, and individuals in the fight against money laundering. IMoLIN was developed with the cooperation of the world's leading anti–money laundering organizations. This Web site includes a database on money laundering legislation and regulations throughout the world, an electronic library, and a calendar of events in the anti–money laundering field.

## Organisation for Economic Co-operation and Development (OECD) Corruption Homepage

http://www.oecd.org/topic/0,2686,en_2649_37447_1_1_1_1_37447,00.html

The OECD Web site on corruption provides a range of anticorruption resources, including conventions and other resources on ethics in the public sector.

## Plain English Campaign

http://www.plainenglish.co.uk/drafting.htm

This site discusses and provides resources on the Plain English Movement, a movement that promotes the drafting of legal documents in easily comprehensible language.

## Privacy International (PI)

http://www.privacyinternational.org

PI is a human rights group formed in 1990 as a watchdog on surveillance and privacy invasions by governments and corporations. This Web site provides a wide range of materials on privacy-related matters, such as communication surveillance, data protection and privacy laws, financial surveillance, freedom of expression, and antiterrorism activities.

## Terrorism, Transnational Crime, and Corruption Center (TraCCC), American University

http://www.american.edu/traccc

TraCCC is devoted to teaching, research, training, and formulating policy advice in transnational crime, corruption, and terrorism. TraCCC's fundamental goal is to better understand the causes and scope of transnational crime and corruption and to propose well-grounded policy to reduce and eliminate these problems. This Web site contains numerous publications and online resources on terrorism, transnational crime, and corruption.

## Transparency International

http://www.transparency.org

Transparency International is a global civil society with the mission to create change toward a world free of corruption. This Web site provides numerous research briefs, tools, and other publications on combating corruption. It also contains region- and country-specific information on corruption.

## United Nations Counter-Terrorism Committee

http://www.un.org/sc/ctc/mandate.shtml

The Counter-Terrorism Committee derives its mandate from Security Council Resolution 1373, which imposes certain obligations on states in the area of counterterrorism, including the criminalization of terrorism-related activities and the provision of assistance to carry out those acts, the denial of funding and safe haven to terrorists, and the exchange of information on terrorist groups. This Web site includes relevant documents and statements on counterterrorism measures, as well as best practices and resources on human rights and counterterrorism.

## United Nations Office on Drugs and Crime (UNODC)

http://www.unodc.org

UNODC is a global leader in the fight against illicit drugs and international crime. Established in 1997, it is mandated to assist member states in their struggle against illicit drugs, crime, and terrorism.

## United Nations Office on Drugs and Crime, Anti-Corruption Resource Guide

http://www.unodc.org/unodc/event_2004-12-09_1_resource_guide.html

This Web site is an anticorruption Web resource with information on corruption and conflict, asset looting and the laundering of proceeds of corruption, corruption in international organizations, political corruption, corruption within the justice system, corruption in the private sector, corruption and organized crime, the United Nations Convention against Corruption, criminalization and enforcement, international cooperation and asset recovery, and technical assistance by UNODC in the field of corruption.

## United Nations Office on Drugs and Crime, Handbooks and Manuals on the United Nations Standards and Norms in Crime Prevention and Criminal Justice

http://www.unodc.org/unodc/crime_cicp_standards_manuals.html

This Web site collates the various handbooks and manuals on crime prevention and criminal justice produced by the United Nations. It includes resources on pretrial detention, prisons, criminal justice standards for peacekeeping police, juvenile justice, justice for victims and abuse of power, domestic violence, computer-related crime, extradition, and mutual legal assistance. It also contains links to the United Nations Special Rapporteur on Torture, the United Nations Committee against Torture, the Human Rights Committee, the Committee on the Rights of the Child, the Committee on the Elimination of All Forms of Discrimination, the United Nations Working Group on Contemporary forms of Slavery, the United Nations Special Rapporteur of the Commission on Human Rights on the Sale of Children, Child Prostitution and Child Pornography, and the United Nations Special Rapporteur on Violence against Women, Its Causes and Consequences.

## United Nations Office of the High Commissioner for Human Rights (OHCHR)

http://www.unhchr.ch

A department of the Secretariat of the United Nations, OHCHR is mandated to promote and protect the enjoyment and full realization of all rights established in the Charter of the United Nations and in international human rights laws and treaties. The home Web site includes links to such treaty bodies as the Committee on the Rights of the Child, the Human Rights Committee, and the Committee against Torture, and other special mechanisms such as the Special Rapporteur on Violence against Women and the Special Rapporteur on Torture. This Web site also contains the full text of the universal human rights instruments.

## University of Minnesota Human Rights Library

http://www1.umn.edu/humanrts/links/alphalinks.html

This site compiles various human rights documents, links, reports, and projects. Its list is alphabetized by topic.

## World Bank Anti-Money Laundering and Combating the Financing of Terrorism

http://www1.worldbank.org/finance/html/amlcft/

This Web site contains a variety of documents, resources, publications, and other resources on money laundering and the financing of terrorism.

## World Bank Anti-Corruption

http://www.worldbank.org/anticorruption

This Web site discusses various anticorruption strategies and provides information on tools, resources, and country and regional approaches to corruption.

# Index


Abandonment of attempt, 88
Abuse
  authority, violation of sexual autonomy by abuse of, 231–232
  functions, 317–318
  personal data, 258–259
  personal secrets, 259–260
  right to vote, 388
Accessories, 89, 134, 136
Accomplices, 89–90, 134, 136
Accused defined, 31
Active personality principle, 45
Acts of sexual nature with child below age of consent, 229–230
*Actus novus interviens,* 71
*Actus reus,* 92
Additional juvenile dispositions, 181–182
  *See also* Juvenile justice
Additional penalties, 146–157
  alternative penalties, supplementation of, 145–146
  confiscation of proceeds, 147–149
  elected, deprivation of right to be, 151–152
  expulsion of nonnationals, 156–157
  fines, 146–147
  firearms, deprivation of right to carry, 152–153
  overview, 114–115
  principal penalties, supplementation of, 146
  private sector, prohibition on exercise of managerial or supervisory positions in, 155–156
  public officials, prohibition on holding positions as, 154
  victims, compensation of, 149–150
Administration of justice, offenses against, 399–410. *See also specific offense*
Afghanistan, 4, 226, 369
African Charters
  Human and People's Rights, on, 38–39, 236, 240, 248, 349
  Rights and Welfare of the Child, on, 33, 174, 176, 254, 261, 349
Aggravated assault. *See* Assault
Aggravated bodily harm. *See* Assault
Aggravated burglary, 274
Aggravated criminal damage, 281
Aggravated robbery, 270–271
Aggravating factors
  augmentation of penalties for, 119, 122
  consideration required, 135–136
  term of imprisonment, determining in light of, 131–137
Aiding and abetting, 89–90, 134, 136
Aircraft, unlawful seizure of, 330–331
Airports serving international civil aviation, violence at, 333–334
Albania, 346
Alibi, 77
Alteration
  evidence, of, 399–400
  markings on firearms, of, 361–362
Alternative penalties, 139–146
  additional penalties, supplementation with, 146
  appropriateness of, 121
  community service, 142–144
  overview, 113–114
  principal penalties, replacement of, 138–140
  semiliberty, 144–145
  suspended sentence, 140–141
American Convention on Human Rights, 38–39, 51, 236, 254, 350
Ammunition, offenses involving, 357–369
  ammunition defined, 359
  manufacturing, illicit, 359–361
    definition of offense, 359–360
    discussion, 360
    penalty, 361
  possession, control, or ownership, unlawful, 366–368
    definition of offense, 366
    discussion, 366–367
    penalty, 367–368
  purchase, unlawful, 364–366
    definition of offense, 364–365
    discussion, 365
    penalty, 365–366
  trafficking in, 359–361
    definition of offense, 359–360
    discussion, 360

penalty, 361
training regarding, 357–368
Amnesty International, 46, 109–110
Angola, 4
Anonymity, revealing sealed order for, 409–410
Apartheid, crime of defined, 202
Arson, 282–283
Asian Development Bank, 288
Assault, 222
causing harm, 223
causing serious harm, 223–224
Associated personnel defined, 354
Attack directed against any civilian population defined, 201
Attempt, 87–88
abandonment of, 88
intention and, 87–88
reduction of penalties for, 119, 127
Augmentation of penalties, 122–126
aggravating factors, for, 119, 122
hatred, offenses motivated by, 124–125
organized criminal activity, for, 123–124
public officials, offenses committed by, 125–126
Australian Model Penal Code, 251–252
Automatism, 77
Autonomy, sexual
abuse of authority, violation by, 231–232
defenseless person, violation of, 231

Battery. *See* Assault
Beijing Rules, 33, 174–179, 191
"Belief principle," 67
Belongings, unauthorized search of, 253–254
"Best interests of the child" principle, 176
Bombing, 345–346
terrorist bombing (*See* Terrorism)
Border crossing, unauthorized, 352
Bosnia and Herzegovina, 239–240
Brahimi Report, 5–6
Bribery. *See* Corruption offenses
Bringing into state property obtained through crime, 274–275
Burglary, 273
Burning, reckless, 283–284
Buying votes, 389–391

Cambodia, 4–5, 226, 251
Cannabis plant, cultivation of, 378–380
cannabis plant defined, 379
definition of offense, 378–379
penalty, 380
trafficking and personal use distinguished, 379–380
Causation principle, 71
Central European and Eurasian Law Initiative, 241–242
Character evidence, 134
Charter of Fundamental Rights of the European Union, 54
Children
acts of sexual nature with child below age of consent, 229–230
defined, 31, 32–33
juvenile justice (*See* Juvenile justice)
life imprisonment for, 129
offenses against, 261–266 (*See also specific offense*)
offenses committed by (*See* Juvenile justice)
personal jurisdiction over, 47–49
pornography, 264–265
defined, 264, 266
possession, 266–267
prostitution, 263
defined, 263
sale of, 262–263
sexual intercourse with child below age of consent, 229–230
Civil aviation, unlawful acts against safety of, 331–333
definition of offense, 331–332
discussion, 332
penalty, 333
Coca bush, cultivation of, 378–380
coca bush defined, 378
definition of offense, 378–379
penalty, 380
trafficking and personal use distinguished, 379–380
Coercion, criminal, 253
Commanders and superiors, criminal responsibility of, 95–97
Commission on Narcotic Drugs, 370, 372
Common purpose, participation in, 90–92
Communications
defined, 257–258
privacy and confidentiality of, violating, 257–258
Community, role of in juvenile justice, 179, 181–182

Community service, 103–104, 142–144
Computer data
  defined, 394
  illegal interception of, 394–395
  interference with, 395–396
Computer systems
  defined, 264, 266, 393
  illegal access to, 393–394
  interference with, 396–397
  misuse of devices, 397–398
Concealment, 319–320
  stolen goods, 274–275
Conditional release, 109
Confidentiality
  communications, violating, 257–258
  voting, violating, 389
Confiscation of proceeds, 162–169
  additional penalties, as, 147–149
  burden of proof, 166
  civil proceedings, 166
  convicted persons, from, 166–168
  defined, 165
  definition of offenses, 165
  legal persons, from, 160
  overview, 162–164
  proceeds of crime defined, 165, 288
  retention of proceeds prohibited, 166
  third parties, from, 168–169
Congo, Democratic Republic of, 346
Conscious negligence, 69
Consular immunity, 49
Control of ammunition, explosives, firearms, or weapons, unlawful, 366–368
  definition of offense, 366
  discussion, 366–367
  penalty, 367–368
Controlled substances. *See* Drug offenses
Conventions
  Abolition of Slavery, the Slave Trade, and Institutions and Practices Similar to Slavery, Supplementary Convention to, 233
  American Convention on Human Rights, 38–39, 51, 236, 254, 350
  Corruption, against, 33, 57, 73, 148, 154–155, 162–165, 277, 304–313, 314–320, 403–404
  Council of Europe (*See* Council of Europe)
  Elimination of All Forms of Racial Discrimination, on, 350
  Elimination of Discrimination against Women, for, 248
  Enforced Disappearances, on, 81
  European Conventions (*See* European Conventions)
  Geneva Conventions, 206, 217
  Genocide Convention, 40, 196–199
  Illicit Traffic in Narcotic Drugs and Psychotropic Substances, against, 57, 109, 148–149, 162, 287, 371–377, 379, 381–384
  Inter-American Conventions (*See* Inter-American Conventions)
  International Trade in Endangered Species of Wild Flora and Fauna, on, 348–349
  Law of the Sea, on, 344
  Marking of Plastic Explosives for the Purpose of Detection, on, 321–322
  Means of Prohibiting and Preventing the Illicit Import, Export and Transfer of Ownership of Cultural Property, on, 348–349
  Non-Applicability of Statutory Limitations to War Crimes and Crimes against Humanity, on, 58–59
  Offenses and Certain Other Acts Committed on Board Aircraft, on, 321–322
  Physical Protection of Nuclear Material, on, 321, 339
  Prevention and Punishment of Offenses against Internationally Protected Persons, Including Diplomatic Agents, on, 321, 335
  Prohibitions or Restrictions on the Use of Certain Conventional Weapons Which May Be Deemed to Be Excessively Injurious or to Have Indiscriminate Effects, on, 218
  Protection of All Persons from Forced Disappearance, on, 135, 245
  Protection of Internationally Protected Persons, for, 46
  Psychotropic Substances, on, 109, 372
  Rights of the Child, on, 32–33, 48, 171, 174, 176, 191, 254, 261–263, 265–266, 350

Safety of United Nations and Associated Personnel, on, 354–355
Slavery Convention of 1926, 206, 243
Stolen or Illegally Exported Cultural Objects, on, 348–349
Suppression of Terrorist Bombing, for, 321, 328–330
Suppression of the Financing of Terrorism, for, 90, 162, 321, 324–325
Suppression of the Traffic in Persons and of the Exploitation of the Prostitution of Others, for, 244
Suppression of Unlawful Acts against the Safety of Civil Aviation, for, 45, 321, 332–335
Suppression of Unlawful Acts against the Safety of Maritime Navigation, for, 321, 340–341
Suppression of Unlawful Seizure of Aircraft, for, 45, 321, 330–331
Taking of Hostages, on, 321, 337
Torture Convention, 81, 209, 236–238
Transnational Organized Crime, against, 33, 57, 73, 93, 148, 162, 164–165, 167, 240–242, 271, 288–293, 295–297, 299–305, 358–359, 371, 403–404
Convicted persons
confiscation of proceeds from, 166–168
defined, 31
Cooperative witnesses, 135
false statements of, 408
Corporal punishment, 109–110
Corporations. See Legal persons
Corruption offenses, 304–320. *See also specific offense*
election offenses (*See* Election offenses)
foreign public officials, involving, 309–311
active corruption, 310–311
definition of offense, 309–310
passive corruption, 311
penalty, 311
further reading and resources, 422, 430–432
private sector, 311–313
active corruption, 312–313
definition of offense, 311–312
passive corruption, 313
penalty, 313
public international organizations, involving officials of, 309–311
active corruption, 310–311
definition of offense, 309–310
passive corruption, 311
penalty, 311
public officials, involving, 307–309
active corruption, 307–308
definition of offense, 307
passive corruption, 308–309
penalty, 309
training regarding, 305
Council of Europe
Civil Law Convention on Corruption, 304, 315
Convention on Laundering, Search, Seizure and Confiscation of the Proceeds of Crime and the Financing of Terrorism, 33, 73–74, 165, 288–292
Convention on the Prevention of Terrorism, 322–323
Criminal Law Convention on Corruption, 73, 304, 307–308, 310–313
Model Code of Conduct for Public Officials, 318
Octopus Programme, 295, 306
Select Committee of Experts on Extraterritorial Jurisdiction, 42
Counterfeiting of money, 286–287
defined, 286–287
Court orders
failure to respect, 406
revealing sealed order for protective measures or anonymity, 409–410
Crime Prevention and Criminal Justice Measures to Eliminate Violence against Women, 249
Crimes against humanity. *See* Humanity, crimes against
Criminal coercion, 253
Criminal damage, 284–285
aggravated criminal damage, 282
Criminal law reform resources, 441–446
Criminal offenses. *See also specific offense*
commission of, 65–66
defined, 63
omission, of, 65–66
participation in (*See* Participation in criminal offenses)

voluntariness, 65
Criminal responsibility
constructive liability, 70–71
exclusion of (*See* Exclusion of criminal responsibility)
generally, 63–65
intention, 66–71
direct intention, 67–70
eventual intention, 68–70
indirect intention, 67–70
oblique intention, 67–68
legal persons, of, 72–75
"directing mind principle," 74
double jeopardy and, 75
negligence and, 75
vicarious liability, 74
negligence, 66–71
conscious negligence, 69
legislative specificity, 70
unconscious negligence, 69
recklessness, 66–71
eventual intention and, 68–70
legislative specificity, 70
strict liability, 69
Culpability. *See* Criminal responsibility
Cultivation of opium poppy, coca bush, or cannabis plant, 378–380
definition of offense, 378–379
manufacture, transport, or distribution of equipment or materials for use in, 382–383
penalty, 380
trafficking and personal use distinguished, 379–380
Cultural property, unauthorized removal of, 347–349
cultural property defined, 347–348
definition of offense, 347–348
discussion, 348–349
penalty, 349
Customary humanitarian law, 216
Cybercrime offenses, 392–398. *See also specific offense*
further reading and resources, 422, 432
training regarding, 393

Damage, criminal, 284–285
Day fine system, 130
Declarations
Basic Principles of Justice for Victims of Crime and Abuse of Power, of, 34–35, 151
Protection of All Persons from Enforced Disappearance, on, 135, 245
Universal Declaration of Human Rights, 38, 195, 236, 350
Defenseless persons, violation of sexual autonomy of, 231
Defenses
automatism, 77
duress, 84–85
exclusion of criminal responsibility (*See* Exclusion of criminal responsibility)
infancy, 77
insanity, 83
intoxication, 83–84
justification (*See* Justification)
mental incompetence, 82–83
mistake of fact, 85–86
mistake of law, 86
necessity, 79–80
partial defenses (*See* Partial defenses)
self-defense, 78–79
superior orders, 80–81
Definitions, 31–35. *See also specific word or phrase*
Deportation
crime against humanity, as, 207
defined, 202
Deprivation of liberty, unlawful, 252
Destruction
cultural property, 347–349
evidence, 399–400
Deterrence as purpose of penalties, 102–103
Diminished responsibility, 76, 83, 134, 221
Diplomatic immunity, 49
Direct intention, 67–70
"Directing mind principle," 74
Disappearance, enforced, 244–246
crimes against humanity, as, 211
definition of offense, 244
penalty, 246
Disciplinary measures for juveniles, 188–189
Discretion in penalties, 98–100
Dispositions, juvenile. *See* Juvenile justice
Disruption of supply of public installations, 346–347
Distribution
drugs, equipment or materials for use in cultivation, production, or manufacture of, 382–383

precursors, 381–382
Diversion of property by public officials, 316–317
Domestic relationship defined, 247
Domestic violence, 246–250
definition of offense, 246–247
further reading and resources, 432
penalty, 250
separate offense, as, 247–250
training regarding, 249–250
Double jeopardy, 51–55
exceptions, 53–54
external applicability, 54–55
internal applicability, 51–54
legal persons, and criminal responsibility of, 75
offenses applicable to, 52
persons applicable to, 53
when applicability begins, 53
Draft Code of Crimes against the Peace and Security of Mankind, 197
Drug offenses, 370–385. *See also specific offense*
cultivation of opium poppy, coca bush, or cannabis plant, 378–380
definition of offense, 378–379
penalty, 380
trafficking and personal use distinguished, 379–380
further reading and resources, 422
manufacture, transport, or distribution of equipment or materials for use in illicit cultivation, production, or manufacture of, 382–383
personal use, possession or purchase for, 383–385
definition of offense, 383
penalty, 385
precursors, manufacture, transport, or distribution of, 381–382
trafficking in, 373–376
definition of offense, 373–374
discussion, 374–375
narcotic drug defined, 374–375
organizing, managing, or financing of, 377–378
penalty, 375–376
possession, 376–377
psychotropic substance defined, 375
training regarding, 372
Due process, further reading and resources, 421
Duress, 84–85
Dwellings, unauthorized search of, 254–255

East Timor
criminal law reform efforts, 4–5
domestic violence, 249–250
drug offenses, 370
evolution of Model Codes project, 7
firearms, offenses involving, 357–358, 367
genocide, 196–197
sexual offenses, 226
Economic offenses, 286–292. *See also specific offense*
Egmont Group, 289
Election offenses, 386–391. *See also specific offense*
abuse of right to vote, 388
buying votes, 389–390
confidentiality in voting, violating, 389
deprivation of right to be elected, 151–152
fraud, 390–391
free decision of voters, violating, 387–388
preventing exercise of right to vote, 386–387
selling votes, 389–390
threat to election candidate, 391
*Elements of Crimes. See* Rome Statute
Embezzlement
private persons, by, 277–278
public officials, by, 316–317
Enabling illegal residence, 301
Endangering United Nations and associated personnel, 353–356
definition of offense, 353–354
penalty, 356
Enforced disappearance, 244–246
crimes against humanity, as, 211
defined, 202
definition of offense, 244
penalty, 246
Enforced prostitution, 233–234
Enrichment, illicit, 318–319
Enslavement defined, 202
Establishing slavery, slavery-like conditions, and forced labor, 243–244
European Conventions
Cybercrime, on, 258, 265–266, 392–398

Fight against Corruption Involving Officials of the European Communities or Officials of Member States of the European Union, on, 304
Non-Applicability of Statutory Limitations to Crimes against Humanity and War Crimes, on, 58–59
Prevention of Torture and Inhuman or Degrading Treatment or Punishment, for, 238
Protection of Human Rights and Fundamental Freedoms, for, 38–39, 51, 254, 350
Eventual intention, 68–70
Evidence
alteration of, 399–400
defined, 31
destruction of, 399–400
fabrication of, 400
false evidence, presentation of, 401
forged evidence, presentation of, 401
penalties relating to, 400
Evolution of Model Codes Project, 6–7
Exclusion of criminal responsibility, 82–86
duress, 84–85
insanity, 83
intoxication, 83–84
mental incompetence, 82–83
mistake of fact, 85–86
mistake of law, 86
overview, 76–77, 133–134
Existing laws, revision of, 12
Explosives, offenses involving, 357–369
bombing, 345–346
explosive defined, 325, 361
illicit manufacturing, 363–364
possession, control, or ownership, unlawful, 366–368
definition of offense, 367
discussion, 366–367
penalty, 367–368
purchase, unlawful, 364–366
definition of offense, 364–365
discussion, 365
penalty, 365–366
reckless exploding, 283–284
terrorist bombing (*See* Terrorism)
trafficking in, 363–364
training regarding, 357–358
Expulsion of nonnationals, 156–157
Extermination
crime against humanity, as, 205–206
defined, 201
Extortion, 272–273
Extradition, further reading and resources, 419
Extraterritorial jurisdiction, 43–46
active personality principle, 45
"flag principle," 45
generally, 43–45
passive personality principle, 45–46

Fabrication of evidence, 400
Facilitation of criminal offenses, 94–95
Fact, mistake of, 85–86
Failure to respect order of court, 406
Fair trial, further reading and resources, 421
False evidence, presentation of, 401
False instruments
possession of, 281
use of, 280–281
False statements of cooperative witnesses, 408
False testimony, 401–402
Financial Action Task Force, 288
Financing
drug trafficking, 377–378
terrorism, 323–325
definition of offense, 323–324
discussion, 324–325
penalty, 325
Fines
additional penalties, as, 146–147
appropriateness of, 129–130
calculation of, 130
day fine system, 130
default on, 130
generally, 110–111
Firearms, offenses involving, 357–369
deprivation of right to carry, 152–153
firearm defined, 270, 359
further reading and resources, 424
imitation firearm defined, 270
manufacturing, illicit, 359–361
definition of offense, 359–360
discussion, 360
penalty, 361
obliteration, removal, or altering of markings, 361–362
parts and components defined, 359

possession, control, or ownership, unlawful, 366–368
definition of offense, 366
discussion, 366–367
penalty, 367–368
purchase, unlawful, 364–366
definition of offense, 364–365
discussion, 365
penalty, 365–366
trafficking in, 359–361
definition of offense, 359–360
discussion, 360
penalty, 361
training regarding, 357–358
use, unlawful, 368–369
Fixed platforms, unlawful acts against safety of, 340–342
definition of offense, 342
discussion, 343
fixed platform defined, 342
penalty, 343–344
"Flag principle," 45
Forced labor, establishing, 243–244
Forced pregnancy defined, 202
Forcible transfer of population defined, 202
Foreign public officials, corruption involving, 309–311
active corruption, 310–311
definition of offense, 309–310
foreign public official defined, 310
passive corruption, 311
penalty, 311
Forfeiture of proceeds. *See* Confiscation of proceeds
Forgery, 279–280
forged evidence, presentation of, 401
Fraud, 276–277
defined, 276
election fraud, 390–391
Fraudulent travel or identity documents
defined, 298, 302
procuring, providing, or possessing, 301
producing, 301
Free decision of voters, violating, 387–388
Functions, abuse of, 317–318
Fundamental principles, 36–41
legality, principle of (*See* Legality, principle of)
limits of criminal legislation, 36–37
purposes of criminal legislation, 36–37
Funds defined, 324

Geneva Conventions, 206, 217
Genocide, 196–200
definition of offense, 196
further reading and resources, 433–434
intention, 199
intentional killing as, 197
life imprisonment for, 119, 128
military commanders and superiors, responsibility of, 95–97
other methods of destruction as, 200
overview, 195–196
penalty, 200
principle of legality and, 40–41
serious bodily or mental harm as, 200
sexual offenses and, 226
sexual slavery and, 232
statutory limitations, inapplicability of, 58–59
torture as, 238
training regarding, 196
Genocide Convention, 40, 196–199
Grievous bodily harm. *See* Assault
Guidelines
Action on Children in the Criminal Justice System, for, 48–49
Prevention of Juvenile Delinquency, for, 33
Protection of Juveniles Deprived of Their Liberty, for, 33
Guiding principles for criminal law reform, 23–27
assessment of existing laws and systems, 23–24
breadth and inclusivity of process, 26
continuing nature of legal reform, 27
coordination by single independent body, 25–26
financial implications, 27
holistic nature of criminal law reform, 24–25
realistic time frames, 26
transplantation of legal models, 26
Guns. *See* Firearms, offenses involving

Habeas corpus, 245
Hague Convention for the Protection of Cultural Property, 348–349
Harm, 223
defined, 223

Hatred
augmentation of penalties for offenses motivated by, 124–125
incitement to crime on account of, 350–352
definition of offense, 350
hate speech distinguished, 350–351
penalty, 352
Homicide. *See* Killing
Hostages, taking of, 336–337
Human rights
further reading and resources, 421–422
use of Model Codes to comply with international standards of, 13
Human Rights Watch, 197, 203
Humanity, crimes against, 201–211
attack, 204
civilian population, 204
definition of offense, 201–202
deportation as, 207
enforced disappearance as, 211
extermination as, 205–206
further reading and resources, 433–434
imprisonment as, 207
life imprisonment for, 119–120, 128
military commanders and superiors, responsibility of, 95–97
murder as, 205
nexus element, 204
other inhumane acts as, 211
overview, 195–196
penalty, 211
persecution as, 209–210
principle of legality and, 40–41
rape as, 209
sexual offenses and, 226
sexual slavery and, 232
slavery as, 206–207
statutory limitations, inapplicability of, 58–59
torture as, 207–209, 238
training regarding, 196
widespread or systematic attack, 203

Illegal entry defined, 298
Illicit enrichment, 318–319
Illicit manufacture. *See* Manufacture
Illicit manufacturing defined, 359, 363
Illicit trafficking defined, 359, 363
Imitation firearm defined, 271
Immigration. *See* Migrants, offenses related to
Immovable property, 269
Immunity from prosecution, 49–50
consular immunity, 49
cooperative witnesses, 407
diplomatic immunity, 49
Imprisonment
aggravating factors, determining term in light of, 130–137
crimes against humanity, as, 207
generally, 110–112
juveniles, of, 190–192
avoidance of, 176–177
limited positive impact of, 179
life imprisonment (*See* Life imprisonment)
maximum terms, 111–112
minimum terms, 111–112
mitigating circumstances, determining term in light of, 130–137
procedures in imposing, 120
ranges, 111–112
semiliberty, 145–146
Improper influence and threat, 320
Incapacitation as purpose of penalties, 102–103
Incendiary weapon or device defined, 326
Inchoate offenses. *See* Attempt
Incitement of criminal offenses
hatred, on account of, 350–352
definition of offense, 350
hate speech distinguished, 350–351
penalty, 352
participation in criminal offenses, as, 94
Incomplete offenses. *See* Attempt
Indirect intention, 67–70
Inducement of criminal offenses, 93
Infancy as defense, 77
Influence
threat and improper influence, 320
trading in (*See* Trading in influence)
Infrastructure facility defined, 327
Insanity, 83
Institutional measures for juveniles, 189–190
Instrument defined, 279
Intangible property, 269
Intensive supervision of juveniles, 186–188
Intention, 66–71
attempt and, 87–88
direct intention, 67–70

eventual intention, 68–70
genocide, 199
indirect intention, 67–70
oblique intention, 67–68
transferred intention, 71
Inter-American Conventions
Corruption, against, 303
Forced Disappearance of Persons, on, 245
International Traffic in Minors, on, 240
Prevent and Punish Torture, to, 237
Prevention, Punishment and Eradication of Violence against Women, on, 248
Terrorism, against, 322–323
Interference
computer data, with, 395–396
computer systems, with, 396–397
International Centre for Criminal Law Reform and Criminal Justice Policy, 249
International Chamber of Commerce, 345
International Code of Conduct for Public Officials, 318
International Conventions. *See* Conventions
International Covenant on Civil and Political Rights, 38–40, 51, 54, 171, 174, 236, 254, 350
International Criminal Court. *See* Rome Statute
International Criminal Tribunal for Rwanda
administration of justice, offenses against, 399
crimes against humanity and, 203–211
genocide and, 197–200
military commanders and superiors, responsibility of, 97
mitigating circumstances, 133
rape and, 228–229
sexual offenses and, 226
superior orders defense, 81
war crimes and, 216
International Criminal Tribunal for the Former Yugoslavia
administration of justice, offenses against, 399
common purpose, participation in, 90–92
crimes against humanity and, 203–211
genocide and, 197–200
military commanders and superiors, responsibility of, 97
mitigating circumstances, 133
rape and, 228
sexual offenses and, 226
sexual slavery and, 233
superior orders defense, 81
war crimes and, 216
International Human Rights Law Group, 241
International humanitarian law, 216
International Labor Organization Forced Labor Convention, 243
International Law Commission, 197
International Maritime Bureau, 345
International Maritime Organization, 344–345
International Narcotics Control Board, 370, 372
Internationally protected persons, offenses against, 334–336
definition of offense, 334–335
discussion, 335–336
internationally protected person defined, 334–335
penalty, 336
Intoxication, 83–84
Iraq, 251, 357–358
Istanbul Protocol, 217, 238

Joint criminal enterprise, 90–92
Joint penalties, 136–137
juvenile justice, in, 184
subsequent offenses by convicted persons, 138
Judicial admonition, 109
juveniles, of, 185
Judicial restraint in penalties, 106–107
Jurisdiction, 42–50
extraterritorial jurisdiction (*See* Extraterritorial jurisdiction)
further reading and resources, 426–427
personal jurisdiction (*See* Personal jurisdiction)
territorial jurisdiction, 42
universal jurisdiction, 46
"Just desserts" principle, 120–121, 136
Justice or policing officials
obstruction of justice, 404
retaliation against, 405
Justification, 78–81
necessity, 79–80
overview, 76–77

self-defense, 78–79
superior orders, 80–81
Juvenile justice, 170–192
additional juvenile dispositions, 181–182
"best interests of the child" principle, 176
community, role of, 179, 181–182
disciplinary measures, 188–189
fundamental principle, 174–175
further reading and resources, 427
imprisonment, 190–192
avoidance of, 176–177
limited positive impact of, 179
individual circumstances, consideration of, 177
institutional measures, 189–190
intensive supervision, 186–188
international standards, incorporation of, 171
joint penalties, 184
judicial admonition, 185
juvenile defined, 31
minimal interference principle, 176
noncompliance with juvenile dispositions, 182
overview, 170–171
principal juvenile dispositions, 178–180, 185–192
principles applicable to juvenile dispositions, 175–177
proportionality requirement, 176
purposes of dispositions, 173–174
rehabilitation, 173–175, 179
reintegration into society, 173–175, 179
resources for, 180, 182
scope of application, 172
separate system for, 170
statutory limitations, 57–58
structure of juvenile dispositions, 18–182
training regarding, 180, 182
warnings, 185

Kadoma Declaration on Community Service, 144
Kidnapping, 251–252
Killing
crimes against humanity, as, 205
genocide, as, 199
threat of, 224–225
unlawful, 219–221
aggravating factors, 220
crimes against humanity, as, 205
definition of offense, 219
life imprisonment for, 120, 128
mitigating factors, 221
motives, 220
penalty, 221
premeditation, 220
special circumstances, 220
Knowingly. *See* Intention
Kosovo
alternative penalties, 114
criminal law reform efforts, 4–5
drug offenses, 371
evolution of Model Codes Project, 7
extortion, 271
firearms, offenses involving, 357–358
genocide, 196
hatred, incitement to crime on account of, 351–352
imprisonment of children, 191
juvenile justice, 180
sexual offenses, 226
state, offenses against, 322
trafficking in persons, 239–240
United Nations Interim Administration in Kosovo, 239, 294, 357

Larceny. *See* Theft
Laundering of money, 288–292
concealment or disguising, 290
conversion or transfer of money, 289–290
definition of offense, 288
further reading and resources, 423, 433
knowledge of crime, 290–291
penalty, 292
predicate offense defined, 291–292
proceeds of crime defined, 291
property defined, 291
recklessness or negligence, 291
training regarding, 289
Law, mistake of, 86
Legal persons
criminal responsibility of, 72–75
"directing mind principle," 74
double jeopardy and, 75
negligence and, 75
vicarious liability, 74
further reading and resources, 427
jurisdiction over, 47
penalties for, 158–161
confiscation of proceeds, 160
default on, 161

determining penalties, 159–161
types of penalties, 158–159
Legality, principle of, 37–41
analogy, use of, 41
crimes against humanity and, 40–41
generally, 38–39
genocide and, 40–41
international law and, 40–41
judicial interpretation and, 39
retroactivity and, 40–41
specificity, 39
strict construction, 41
war crimes and, 40–41
Liberia, 4, 7, 226, 239
Liberty, unlawful deprivation of, 252
Life and limb, offenses against, 219–225. *See also specific offenses*
Life imprisonment
appropriateness of, 119–120, 127–128
children, for, 128
crimes against humanity, for, 119–120, 128
genocide, for, 119, 128
procedures in imposing, 119–120
unlawful killing, for, 120, 128
war crimes, for, 120, 128
Limitations of actions. *See* Statutory limitations
Limits of criminal legislation, 36–37
London Charter, 40

Managing of drug trafficking, 377–378
Manslaughter. *See* Killing
Manufacture
ammunition, 359–361
definition of offense, 359–360
discussion, 360
penalty, 361
drugs, equipment or materials for use in cultivation, production, or manufacture of, 382–383
explosives, 363–364
firearms, 359–361
definition of offense, 359–360
discussion, 360
penalty, 361
illicit manufacturing defined, 359, 363
precursors, 381–382
Maritime navigation, unlawful acts against safety of, 340–342
definition of offense, 340
discussion, 340–341
penalty, 341–342
Markings on firearms, obliteration, removal, or altering of, 361–362
Maximum penalties
appraisal of, 121
imprisonment, 111–112
*Mens rea*, 66–67
Mental incompetence, 82–83
Migrants, offenses related to, 297–303
definition of offense, 297–298
enabling illegal residence, 301
fraudulent travel or identity documents
defined, 302
procuring, providing or possessing, 301
producing, 301
further reading and resources, 423
illegal entry defined, 302
liability of migrants, 302
penalty, 302–303
smuggling, 300–301
trafficking in persons distinguished, 300
Military commanders and superiors, criminal responsibility of, 95–97
Minimal interference principle, 176
Minimum penalties
appraisal of, 121
imprisonment, 111–112
Minors. *See* Children
Misappropriation of property by public officials, 316–317
Mistake of fact, 85–86
Mistake of law, 86
Misuse of computer devices, 397–398
Mitigating circumstances
consideration required, 133
reduction of penalties for, 119, 126–127
term of imprisonment, determining in light of, 131–137
Model Code of Criminal Procedure
aggravating factors, 135
child pornography, 264
children, offenses against, 262
confiscation of proceeds, 149
cooperative witnesses, 135, 408
corruption offenses, 305–306
crimes against humanity, 195
cybercrime offenses, 393
defined, 31
determining penalties and, 100

drug offenses, 371, 373
false testimony, 402
genocide, 195
habeas corpus, 245
juvenile justice and, 170
mitigating circumstances, 133
organized crime offenses, 295
parole, 109
persons, searches of, 254
potential uses of, 13, 15
premises, searches of, 255
pretrial detention, 137
privacy rights, 258
publication, 7
sexual offenses, consent in, 228
state, offenses against, 325–341
torture, 238
visual recordings, 256
war crimes, 195
witness and victim protection, 240, 403, 409
Model Codes for Post-Conflict Criminal Justice. *See specific code*
Model Criminal Code. *See also specific topic*
defined, 31
guiding principles (*See* Guiding principles for criminal law reform)
potential uses of (*See* Potential uses of Model Codes)
project overview, 3–8
publication, 7
synopsis, 17–21
tailoring to needs of postconflict states, 9–11
Model Detention Act
juvenile justice and, 170, 191–192
potential uses of, 16
publication, 7
Model Drug Abuse Bill, 370
Model Drug Court Bill, 372
Model Police Powers Act
persons, searches of, 254
premises, searches of, 255
publication, 7–8
Money
counterfeiting, 286–287
laundering (*See* Laundering of money)
Montego Bay Convention, 344
Moral purposes of penalties, 102–103
Movable property, 269
Multiple offenses. *See* Joint penalties
Murder. *See* Killing
Mutual legal assistance, further reading and resources, 423

Narcotic drug defined, 374. *See also* Drug offenses
*Ne bis in idem. See* Double jeopardy
Necessity defense, 79–80
Need for legal framework, 3–4
Negligence, 66–71
conscious negligence, 69
legal persons, criminal responsibility of, 75
legislative specificity, 70
military commanders and superiors, responsibility of, 97
unconscious negligence, 69
Nepal, 7, 251, 272
Noncompliance with juvenile dispositions, 182
Nonnationals, expulsion of, 156–157
Nuclear material, offenses related to, 338–339
*Nulla poena sine lege,* 38
*Nullum crimen sine lege,* 38
Nuremberg Tribunal, 202

Oblique intention, 67–68
Obliteration of markings on firearms, 361–362
Obstruction of justice
justice or policing officials, of, 404
witness, of, 402–403
Occupied structure defined, 282
Offensive weapon defined, 271
Office of the High Commissioner for Human Rights. *See* United Nations
Office on Drugs and Crime. *See* United Nations
Omission, criminal offenses of, 65–66
Opium poppy, cultivation of, 378–380
definition of offense, 378–379
opium poppy defined, 378
penalty, 380
trafficking and personal use distinguished, 379–380
Optional Protocols
Involvement of Children in Armed Conflict, on, 261
Sale of Children, Child Prostitution and

Child Pornography, on, 261–263, 265–266
Ordering criminal offenses, 93
Orders of court
  failure to respect, 406
  revealing sealed order for protective measures or anonymity, 409–410
Organization for Economic Cooperation and Development Convention on Combating Bribery of Foreign Public Officials in International Business Transactions, 34, 73, 304, 310, 315
Organization for Security and Cooperation in Europe, 5, 180
Organized crime offenses, 293–303. *See also specific offense*
  further reading and resources, 423, 434–436
  organized criminal group defined, 294
  participation in organized criminal group, 293–296
    augmentation of penalties for, 123–124
    definition of offense, 293–294
    penalty, 297
    underlying criminal activity, 294–297
Organizing of drug trafficking, 377–378
Ownership of ammunition, explosives, firearms, or weapons, unlawful, 367–368
  definition of offense, 366
  discussion, 366–367
  penalty, 367–368

Parole, 109
Partial defenses
  diminished responsibility, 76, 83, 134, 221
  provocation, 76–77, 131–134, 221
Participation in criminal offenses, 89–97
  accessories, 89
  accomplices, 89–90
  aiding and abetting, 89–90
  common purpose, 90–92
  crimes against humanity, 95–97
  facilitation, 94–95
  genocide, 95–97
  incitement, 94
  inducement, 93
  joint criminal enterprise, 90–92
  military commanders and superiors, responsibility of, 95–97
  ordering, 93
  organized criminal group, participation in (*See* Organized crime offenses)
  overview, 66
  perpetrators, responsibility of, 97
  solicitation, 93
  war crimes, 95–97
Passive personality principle, 45–46
Pathfinders, 99
Penal Reform International, 48, 192
Penalties, 98–161. *See also specific offense*
  additional penalties (*See* Additional penalties)
  adjustments, 118
  aggravating factors (*See* Aggravating factors)
  alternative penalties (*See* Alternative penalties)
  attempt, reduction for, 119, 127
  augmentation of (*See* Augmentation of penalties)
  community service, 103–104, 142–144
  conditional release, 109
  corporal punishment, 109–110
  deterrence as purpose, 102–103
  discretion in, 98–100
  fines (*See* Fines)
  fundamental principle, 104–105
  further reading and resources, 428–429
  imprisonment (*See* Imprisonment)
  incapacitation as purpose, 102–103
  individual circumstances, consideration of, 106
  joint penalties, 137–138
    juvenile justice, in, 184
    subsequent offenses by convicted persons, 138–139
  judicial admonition, 109
  judicial restraint, 106–107
  "just desserts" principle, consideration of, 120–121, 136
  juvenile justice (*See* Juvenile justice)
  legal persons, for, 158–161
    confiscation of proceeds, 160
    default on, 161
    determining penalties, 159–161
    types of penalties, 158–159
  less restrictive measures, use of, 107

life imprisonment (*See* Life imprisonment)
maximum penalty
appraisal of, 121
imprisonment, 111–112
minimum penalty
appraisal of, 121
imprisonment, 111–112
mitigating circumstances (*See* Mitigating circumstances)
moral purposes, 102–103
other principles relevant to determining, 105–107
overview, 98–100
parole, 109
principal penalties, 128–130 (*See also* Fines; Imprisonment)
additional penalties, supplementation with, 146
alternative penalties, replacement with, 139–140
life imprisonment as, appropriateness of, 128–129
overview, 110–112
procedure for determining, 116–157
generally, 117–121
overview, 116
proportionality principle, 104–105
purposes of, 101–104
reduction of (*See* Reduction of penalties)
rehabilitation as purpose, 102–103
reparations, 103
restitution, 103
restorative justice, 103–104
retribution as purpose, 102–103
safety measures, 109
security measures, 109
semiliberty, 145–146
sentencing guidelines, 98
seriousness of offense, consideration of, 106
structure of, 108–110
structured discretion, 99–100
subsequent offenses by convicted persons, 107, 121, 138–139
suspended sentence, 140–142
utilitarian purposes, 102–103
Periodic detention. *See* Semiliberty
Perpetrators
criminal responsibility of, 97
providing assistance to after commission of criminal offense, 407
Persecution
crime against humanity, as, 209–210
defined, 202
Personal data, abuse of, 258–259
Personal jurisdiction, 47–50
children, over, 47–49
immunity and, 49–50
legal persons, over, 47
Personal secrets, abuse of, 259–260
Persons
trafficking in, 238–242
children, 242
consent, 242
definition of offense, 238–239
discussion, 241
further reading and resources, 424, 440–441
penalty, 242
smuggling of migrants distinguished, 300
unauthorized search of, 253–254
Piracy, 344–345
further reading and resources, 436
Place of commission of offense, 61
Plea agreements, 135
Pornography, child, 264–265
defined, 264, 267
possession, 266–267
Possession
ammunition, explosives, firearms, or weapons, unlawful, 367–368
definition of offense, 366
discussion, 366–367
penalty, 367–368
child pornography, 266–267
drugs
personal use, for, 383–385
trafficking, for, 376–377
false instruments, 281
fraudulent travel or identity documents, 301
Potential uses of Model Codes, 11–16
existing laws, revision of, 12
international human rights standards, amending laws to comply with, 13
Rome Statute, amending laws to comply with, 15
special tribunals to address past abuses, 15–16
transitional laws, creating, 13–14

vulnerable groups, protection of, 14–15
Precursors, manufacture, transport, or distribution of, 381–382
Predicate offense defined, 288
Premises, unauthorized search of, 254–255
Presentation of false or forged evidence, 401
Pretrial detention, 136–137
Preventing exercise of right to vote, 386–387
Principal juvenile dispositions, 178–180, 185–192. *See also* Juvenile justice
Principal penalties, 128–130. *See also* Fines; Imprisonment
additional penalties, supplementation with, 146
alternative penalties, replacement with, 138–140
life imprisonment as, appropriateness of, 127
overview, 110–112
Principle of legality. *See* Legality, principle of
Principles on the Protection of All Persons from Enforced Disappearances, 81
Prior criminal law reform efforts, 4–5
Privacy of communications, violating, 257–258
Private sector
corruption in, 311–313
active corruption, 312–313
definition of offense, 311–312
passive corruption, 313
penalty, 313
prohibition on exercise of managerial or supervisory positions in, 155–156
Proceeds of crime defined, 165, 288
Procuring fraudulent travel or identity documents, 301
Production
drugs, manufacture, transport, or distribution of equipment or materials for use in, 382–382
fraudulent travel or identity documents, 301
Property offenses, 268–285. *See also* specific offense
cultural property, unauthorized removal of (*See* Cultural property, unauthorized removal of)
diversion by public officials, 316–317
embezzlement
private persons, by, 277–278
public officials, by, 316–317
misappropriation by public officials, 316–317
obtained through crime, bringing into state, 275–276
property defined, 31, 33, 268, 284
theft (*See* Theft)
Proportionality principle, 104–105
juvenile justice, in, 176
Prostitution
children, 263
defined, 263
enforced, 233–234
Protective measures, revealing sealed order for, 409–410
Protocols
Illicit Manufacturing of and Trafficking in Firearms, Their Parts and Components and Ammunition, against, 93, 148, 271, 293, 358–366
Involvement of Children in Armed Conflict, Optional Protocol on, 261
Prevent, Suppress and Punish Trafficking in Persons, Especially Women and Children, to, 240–242, 293
Sale of Children, Child Prostitution and Child Pornography, Optional Protocol on, 261–263, 266–267
Smuggling of Migrants by Land, Sea, and Air, against, 299–303
Suppression of Unlawful Acts against the Safety of Fixed Platforms Located on the Continental Shelf, for, 321, 343
Suppression of Unlawful Acts of Violence at Airports Serving International Civil Aviation, for, 321, 333–334
Providing
assistance to perpetrators after commission of criminal offense, 407
fraudulent travel or identity documents, 301
Provocation, 76–77, 131–134, 134, 221
Psychotropic substance defined, 374. *See also* Drug offenses
Public installations, disruption of supply of, 346–347
Public international organizations,

corruption involving officials of, 309–311
active corruption, 310–311
definition of offense, 309–310
official of a public international organization defined, 310
passive corruption, 311
penalty, 311
Public officials
augmentation of penalties for offenses committed by, 125–126
corruption involving, 307–309
active corruption, 307–308
definition of offense, 307
passive corruption, 308–309
penalty, 309
defined, 31, 33–34
diversion of property by, 316–317
misappropriation of property by, 316–317
prohibition against holding positions as, 154
Public transportation system defined, 327
Publication of Model Codes, 7–8
Purchase
ammunition, explosives, firearms, or weapons, unlawful, 364–366
definition of offense, 364–365
discussion, 365
penalty, 365–366
drugs, purchase for personal use, 383–385
definition of offense, 383
penalty, 385
Purposefully. *See* Intention
Purposes of criminal legislation, 36–37

Rape, 227–229
crimes against humanity, as, 209
definition of offense, 227
overview, 226–227
penalty, 229
rape kits, 227
statutory rape, 230
training regarding, 227
Receiving stolen goods, 274–275
Recidivism, 136
Recklessness, 66–71
burning, reckless, 282–283
eventual intention and, 68–70
exploding, reckless, 283–284
legislative specificity, 70
Reduction of penalties, 126–127
attempt, for, 119, 127
mitigating circumstances, for, 119, 126–127
Rehabilitation
juveniles, of, 173–175, 179
purpose of penalties, as, 102–103
Reintegration of juveniles into society, 173–175, 179
Removal
cultural property, unauthorized removal of (*See* Cultural property, unauthorized removal of)
firearms, markings on, 361–362
Reparations, 103
Resources for juvenile justice, 180, 182
Responsibility, criminal. *See* Criminal responsibility
Restitution, 103
Restorative justice, 103–104, 134
Retaliation
justice or policing officials, against, 405
witness, against, 405
Retention of proceeds prohibited, 165–166
Retribution as purpose of penalties, 102–103
Revealing sealed order for protective measures or anonymity, 409–410
Rights of persons, offenses against, 236–260. *See also specific offenses*
Riyadh Guidelines, 33
Robbery, 270–271
Rome Statute
administration of justice, offenses against, 399
attempt, 88
common purpose, participation in, 90–91
crimes against humanity and, 202–203
defenses under, 77
double jeopardy, 53–55
duress, 85
enforced prostitution, 234
extraterritorial jurisdiction, 45
facilitation of criminal offenses, 95
genocide and, 195, 197
intoxication, 84
legal persons, criminal responsibility of, 74
legality, principle of, 40
mental incompetence, 82
military commanders and superiors,

responsibility of, 97
mistake of fact, 85
necessity defense, 80
ordering, soliciting, or inducing criminal offenses, 93
participation in criminal offenses, 66, 90
rape, 209, 228–229
self-defense, 79
sexual slavery, 232
sexual violence, 235
statutory limitations, 58
superior orders defense, 81
use of Model Codes to comply with, 15
war crimes and, 216–218
Rules for the Protection of Juveniles Deprived of Their Liberty, 191–192
Running of statutory limitations, 59–60
Rwanda, 113, 226. *See also* International Criminal Tribunal for Rwanda

Safety, offenses against, 321–352. *See also* specific offense
civil aviation, 331–333
definition of offense, 331–332
discussion, 332
penalty, 333
fixed platforms, 342–344
definition of offense, 342
discussion, 343
penalty, 343
maritime navigation, 340–342
definition of offense, 340
discussion, 340–341
penalty, 341
Safety measures as penalties, 109
Sale of children, 262–263
Sanctions. *See* Penalties
Sealed order for protective measures or anonymity, revealing, 409–410
Searches, unauthorized
dwellings or premises, 254–255
persons and belongings, 253–254
Security, offenses against, 321–352. *See also specific offense*
Security measures as penalties, 109
Seizure of aircraft, unlawful, 330–331
Self-defense, 78–79
Selling votes, 389–390
Semiliberty, 144–145
Sentences. *See* Penalties
Separate system for juvenile justice, 170
Serious bodily or mental harm as genocide, 200
Serious harm, 224
threat to cause, 224–225
defined, 224
Sexual autonomy
abuse of authority, violation by, 231–232
defenseless person, violation of, 231
Sexual intercourse with child below age of consent, 229–230
Sexual offenses, 226–235. *See also specific offenses*
rape (See Rape)
Sexual slavery, 232–233
Sexual violence, 234–235
Ship defined, 340
Sierra Leone, 197, 239
Single Convention on Narcotic Drugs, 372, 376
Slavery
crimes against humanity, as, 206–207
establishing, 243–244
sexual slavery, 232–233
slavery-like conditions, establishing, 243–244
Slavery Convention of 1926, 206, 243
Smuggling of migrants, 300–301. *See also* Migrants, offenses related to
Solicitation of criminal offenses, 93
Sources of law. *See specific source*
South African Development Community Protocol against Corruption, 303
South Asian Association for Regional Cooperation Convention on Preventing and Combating Trafficking in Women and Children, 240
Special Rapporteurs, 238, 248, 250, 262
Special Trafficking Operations Programme (STOP), 240
Special tribunals to address past abuses, 15–16
Standard Minimum Rules
Administration of Juvenile Justice, for, 33, 48, 171, 174
Non-Custodial Measures, for, 113, 144
State, offenses against, 321–352. *See also specific offense*
state defined, 31, 34
training regarding, 322
State or governmental facility defined,

326–327
Statutory limitations, 56–60
crimes against humanity, inapplicability to, 58–59
criminal prosecutions, 56–57
genocide, inapplicability to, 58–59
juveniles, offenses committed by, 57–58
running of, 59–60
suspension of, 59–60
tolling of, 60
war crimes, inapplicability to, 58–59
Statutory rape, 230
Stolen goods, receiving and concealing, 274–275
Strict liability, 69
Structure of juvenile dispositions, 18–182
Structure of penalties, 108–110
Structured discretion in penalties, 99–100
Structured group defined, 294
Subsequent offenses by convicted persons, 107, 121, 138–139
Sudan, 7
Superior orders defense, 80–81
Supplementary Convention to the Abolition of Slavery, the Slave Trade, and Institutions and Practices Similar to Slavery, 233
Suspect defined, 32
Suspended sentence, 140–142
Suspension of statutory limitations, 59–60
Synopsis of Model Criminal Code, 17–21

Tailoring of Model Codes to needs of postconflict states, 9–11
Taking of hostages, 336–337
Tangible property, 269
Territorial jurisdiction, 42
Territory defined, 32, 34
Terrorism
bombing, 325–329
definition of offense, 325–327
explosive or incendiary weapon or device defined, 328–329
military force exception, 329
penalty, 329
financing, 323–325
definition of offense, 323–324
discussion, 324–325
penalty, 325
further reading and resources, 423–424, 438
Testimony, false, 401–402
Theft, 268–270
definition of offense, 268
embezzlement (*See* Embezzlement)
immovable property, 269
intangible property, 269
intention and, 268
misappropriation of property by public officials, 316–317
movable property, 269
penalty, 270
property defined for purposes of, 269
tangible property, 269
Third parties, confiscation of proceeds from, 168–169
Threat
cause serious harm, to, 224–225
election candidate, to, 391
and improper influence, 320
killing, of, 224–225
Time of commission of offense, 61
Tokyo Rules, 113, 144
Tolling of statutory limitations, 60
Torture, 236–238
crimes against humanity, as, 207–209
defined, 202, 236
further reading and resources, 438–440
penalty, 238
purposes of, 237
severe pain or suffering, 237
training regarding, 237
Torture Convention, 81, 209, 236–238
Trading in influence, 314–316
definition of offense, 314–315
penalty, 316
promise or offer, 315
solicitation or acceptance, 315–316
Trafficking
ammunition, 359–361
definition of offense, 359–360
discussion, 360
penalty, 361
drugs (*See* Drug offenses)
explosives, 363–364
firearms, 359–361
definition of offense, 359–360
discussion, 360
penalty, 361
illicit trafficking defined, 359, 363
persons (*See* Persons)

Training. *See specific topic*
Transferred intention, 71
Transitional laws, creating, 13–14
Transport
drugs, equipment or materials for use in cultivation, production, or manufacture of, 382–383
precursors, 381–382

Unconscious negligence, 69
United Nations. *See also* Conventions; Declarations; Guidelines; Protocols
associated personnel defined, 354
Office of the High Commissioner for Human Rights, 48–50, 242, 245, 255
Office on Drugs and Crime
corruption offenses, 305
drug offenses, 366–369
money laundering, 289
obstruction of justice, 403–404
state, offenses against, 321–343
personnel, endangering, 353–356
definition of offense, 353–354
penalty, 356
Special Rapporteurs, 238, 248, 250, 262
UNICEF, 47, 191
United Nations operation defined, 354
United Nations personnel defined, 353–354
Universal Declaration of Human Rights, 38, 195, 236, 350
Universal jurisdiction, 46
Unlawful killing. *See* Killing
Uranium enriched in the isotope 235 or 238 defined, 338
Using false instruments, 280–281
Utilitarian purposes of penalties, 102–103

Vicarious liability, 74, 97
Victims
compensation of, 149–150
defined, 32, 34–35
Visual recording, unauthorized, 255–256
Voters and voting. *See* Election offenses
Vulnerable groups, protection of, 14–15

War crimes, 211–218
customary humanitarian law, 216
definition of offense, 211–216
further reading and resources, 433–434
grave breaches, 217
international humanitarian law, 216
life imprisonment for, 120, 128
military commanders and superiors, responsibility of, 95–97
overview, 195–196
penalty, 218
principle of legality and, 40–41
prohibited weapons, 218
sexual offenses and, 226
sexual slavery and, 232
statutory limitations, inapplicability of, 58–59
torture as, 238
training regarding, 196, 217
Warnings to juveniles, 185
Weapons, offenses involving, 357–369
offensive weapon defined, 271
possession, control, or ownership, unlawful, 366–368
definition of offense, 366
discussion, 366–367
penalty, 367–368
purchase, unlawful, 364–366
definition of offense, 364–365
discussion, 365
penalty, 365–366
training regarding, 357–358
war crimes, prohibited weapons, 218
weapon defined, 364–365
Web sites, 446–451
Witnesses
cooperative witnesses, 135
false statements of, 408
defined, 32, 35
obstruction of justice, 402–403
retaliation against, 405
World Bank, 289, 305
World Health Organization, 370

Yugoslavia, former. *See* International Criminal Tribunal for the Former Yugoslavia

Zeid Report, 50, 427

## United States Institute of Peace

The United States Institute of Peace is an independent, non-partisan institution established and funded by Congress. Its goals are to help prevent and resolve violent conflicts, promote post-conflict peacebuilding, and increase conflict-management tools, capacity, and intellectual capital worldwide. The Institute does this by empowering others with knowledge, skills, and resources, as well as by its direct involvement in conflict zones around the globe.

## Model Codes for Post-Conflict Criminal Justice

This book is set in Minion; the display type is Zurich BT. Jeff Urbancic designed the book's cover and interior. Pages were made up by EEI Communications, which also proofread the text. The index was prepared by James Diggins. The book's editor was Nigel Quinney.